THE CEREMONIAL CITY

Iain Fenlon

THE Ceremonial City

HISTORY, MEMORY AND MYTH
IN RENAISSANCE VENICE

YALE UNIVERSITY PRESS * NEW HAVEN AND LONDON

PUBLISHED WITH THE ASSISTANCE OF
THE LILA ACHESON WALLACE – READER'S DIGEST PUBLICATIONS SUBSIDY
AT VILLA I TATTI

Designed by Emily Lees

Printed in China

Library of Congress Cataloging-in-Publication Data

Fenlon, Iain.
The ceremonial city / Iain Fenlon.
p. cm.
Includes bibliographical references and index.
ISBN 978-0-300-11937-4 (cl: alk. paper)
1. Venice (Italy)–History–1508-1797. 2. Rites and ceremonies–
Political aspects–Italy–Venice. 3. Venice (Italy)–
Religious life and customs. 4. City planning–Italy–Venice–History.
5. Architecture and society–Italy–Venice–History.
6. Christian art and symbolism–Italy–Venice. I. Title.
DG678.235.F46 2007
945'.31–dc22
2007025316

A catalogue record for this book is available from The British Library

ENDPAPERS: Paolo Veronese, *Allegory of the Holy League* (detail of pl. 142).
FRONTISPIECE: Domenico Tintoretto, *Venice, Queen of the Adriatic* (detail of pl. 23).
SECTION OPENINGS: Matteo Pagan, *Procession in St. Mark's Square* (details of pl. 82).

CONTENTS

ACKNOWLEDGEMENTS

The research and writing of this book have occupied, and at times dominated, my life for almost twenty years. In the process, I have incurred considerable debts of gratitude to the many friends and colleagues who, through discussion, exchanges of information and argument, have contributed to the shape and tone of the final result. Seminars, conferences and the comments of generations of students whom I have been fortunate enough to teach have also played their part. Among the many who have provided practical help, constructive criticism and moral support along the way I should like to mention Vicky Avery, Lorenzo Bianconi, Annaliese Bristot, David Bryant, Esperanca Camara, Donald Campbell, Salvatore Camporeale, Gian Mario Cao, Matteo Casini, Richard Charteris, Stanley Chojnacki, Frances Clarke, Sam Cohn, Michael and Dena Cowdy, Flora Dennis, Giuliano Di Bacco, Francesco Facchin, Patricia Fortini Brown, Richard Goldthwaite, Francis Haskell, John Henderson, Paul Hills, Andrew Hopkins, Deborah Howard, Caroline Humphrey, Metin Kunt, James Laidlaw, Robert Lindell, Tullia Magrini, Michael Mallett, Simona Mammana, Alexa Mason, Laura Moretti, Reinhold Mueller, Edward Muir, Giulio Ongaro, Mario Piana, Renata Pieragostini, Deborah Pincus, Elena Quaranta, Roger Rearick, Bette Talvacchia, Rob Wegman, and Bernard and Patricia Williams. Parts of the manuscript were read by Tracy Cooper, Sara Matthews Grieco, Rosamond McKitterick, Bronwen Wilson and Warren Woodfin, and all of it by the two anonymous readers appointed by Yale University Press; to all of them I am extremely indebted for their comments and suggestions.

My primary research in Italian archives and libraries was made possible through the generous financial support of the British Academy, the University of Cambridge and King's College, Cambridge. As the fortunate recipient of a

Detail of pl. 6.

Leverhulme Trust Research Readership in the years 1996–8, I was able to spend considerable periods of time working in Venice itself. Lengthy bouts of concentration on the material were also facilitated by two Visiting Fellowships in Oxford, one at All Souls College, the other at New College; I am grateful for the comradeship and lively interest in what I was doing that I experienced in both. Much of the writing was done in the impossibly beautiful and peaceful surroundings of the Villa I Tatti, the Harvard Center for Italian Renaissance Studies, where I had once held a Fellowship under the benevolent eye of the director, Craig Hugh Smyth; his successors Walter Kaiser and Joe Connors both did a great deal to make me feel welcome, and the enterprise benefitted enormously from the opportunity to discuss, with interested Fellows, the text as it emerged. Both the Villa (whose generous award of a publication grant from the Lila Wallace Fund has crucially aided the production of the book), and King's College, Cambridge, should be singled out for the consistent support that they have given me over the years. A special word of thanks is also due to my colleagues at the Fondazione Levi and the Fondazione Cini in Venice, and in particular to Giorgio Bussetto, Giulio Cattin and Giovanni Morelli, for their active support and encouragement over many years.

Professional assistance and advice from librarians in a number of crucial institutions has been critical. Prominent among them are the state archives in Mantua, Modena, Rome and Venice, the Biblioteca Apostolica Vaticana, the Bibliothèque Nationale in Paris, the Bodleian Library in Oxford, the Centre d'Etudes Supérieures de la Renaissance in Tours, the Fondazione Cini in Venice, the Herzog August Bibliothek in Wolfenbüttel, the Index for Christian Art at Princeton University, the Villa I Tatti in Settignano, and both the Warburg Institute and the Wellcome Institute in London. I have spent more instructive and enjoyable hours than I can count in the Biblioteca Nazionale Marciana and Biblioteca del Museo Correr in Venice, the British Library in London and the University Library in Cambridge.

This book would never have been completed without special encouragement from a number of close friends: *in primis* Christine Adams and Pete de Bolla, Allen Grieco and Sara Matthews Grieco, Nicoletta Guidobaldi, James Haar and John Nádas. Gillian Malpass has never faltered in her belief in the project, despite the length of time it has taken to complete it, and I count myself exceptionally fortunate to have had the benefit of her expert eye and editorial wisdom, as well as the thoughtful and creative attention of Emily Lees, who designed the book; Louise Glasson and Emily Wraith, who collected the pictures; and Emily Angus. My copy editor, Delia Gaze, has immeasurably improved the text. Any mistakes that remain, whether of fact, judgement or interpretation, are of course my own.

King's College, Cambridge
Vigil of the Feast of St Mark, 2007

INTRODUCTION

This book began life as a more modest project concerned with the cultural reactions to the battle of Lepanto in October 1571, when the Turkish fleet was decisively defeated by the forces of the Holy League. As the work progressed, it became clear that a wider range of contextual enquiry was needed. The result, some number of years later, is a text that falls into three distinct but closely related sections, each of which adopts a different approach and focuses on a different dimension of urban topography, ceremony and ritual, and cultural life. The first part examines Piazza San Marco from the point of view of the function of the buildings that frame it (while remaining organically and dynamically part of it) and the social and religious life that took place there. In the second section, the four major events that took place in the 1570s and critically shaped the history of late sixteenth-century Venice are considered both in themselves and in relation to their ceremonial and ritualistic consequences. The third part analyses the ways in which these events were metabolized in Venetian history, and in the process reconfigured in the realms of memory and myth. Although cast into these three sections, the argument constantly returns to two poles: Lepanto on the one hand and Piazza San Marco on the other.

Piazza San Marco is the most famous and instantly recognizable townscape in the West, if not the world. At its eastern end the square is dominated by the basilica dedicated to the evangelist Mark, begun in 1063 on the model of the church of the Holy Apostles in Constantinople and finally consecrated thirty years later. Embellishment with marble and mosaics both internally and externally continued long after this date. Many details of the external decoration, including sculptured panels, columns of marble and porphyry, and figured reliefs, came from the shiploads of loot conveyed to Venice during the Fourth Crusade. Most spectacular of all are the four bronze horses, displayed on eight short columns of white marble and four of porphyry, raised triumphantly on the loggia above the central portal, dramatically set against the dark central window. This prominent placing was the result of a political decision designed to emphasize not merely their beauty, but also their status as quite exceptional spoils of war, symbols of the Republic's imperial mission. Housing Mark's remains was the main purpose of the basilica, but its proximity to the Doge's Palace also gave it a distinct civic significance even in this, the earliest phase of the transformation of San Marco from private chapel to state church. During the centuries that followed, the bonds that tied San Marco to both doge and state were strengthened through the evolution of a calendrical sequence of liturgical and civic rituals. These were enacted mostly in the basilica, the Piazza and the Piazzetta, which for these purposes constituted a unified ceremonial area, and from where they could be transported in procession to other parts of the city.

From the very beginning, the basilica of San Marco and the ceremonial spaces that surrounded it were seen as the heart of the devotional and political geography of Venice, the centre of an intricate web of religious and civic conceptions, to be celebrated in a number of distinct processional forms, involving the highest officers of church and state, including the doge. In the absence of classical Roman origins, the legends that surrounded Mark's relation to Venice became the cornerstone of the foundation myth of the state itself. During the second half of the eleventh century, while the church was being built, the Piazza San Marco began to take on a more formal appearance, and one hundred years later the creation of a new civic square, the Piazzetta, was initiated by the Venetian government to order and embellish what had evolved as the main politico-ecclesiastical centre of the city. At this stage the main features of the area were the basilica, the Doge's Palace and the campanile, which served the practical function of summoning the members of the Great Council to business, announcing the death of the doge and the election of his successor, and articulating other ritual and official moments in the life of the Republic. Much altered over the centuries, the campanile has become almost a symbol for Venice itself.

The next major change to the appearance of Piazza San Marco took place in the sixteenth century following the appointment of Jacopo Sansovino as state architect. This placed him under the patronage of the wealthiest sponsors of new building work anywhere in the city, at a time when the political will to re-model the Piazza and its surrounding buildings was strong; the consequence was an ambitious *renovatio urbis*, inaugurated during the dogeship of Andrea Gritti, and carried out with his active encouragement. As it unfolded, Sansovino's task was to inaugurate the first phase of a grandiose plan to line the remaining sides of the Piazza and the Piazzetta together with the eastern end of the Molo with new structures in a classical style. Together with the earlier accretions, such as the *spolia* embedded in the walls of the basilica and the horses from Constantinople, these changes amplified and consolidated these interrelated spaces as a complex urban theatre that functioned as the principal arena (though not the only one) for the enactment of symbolic ritual. Images and objects accumulated in the area over time, from the so-called Pillars of Acre to the Pietra del Bando, from which official proclamations were made, both celebrated the Venetian past and instructed citizens and foreigners alike in the values of the city's history. Arranged as if on display, the different archaeological layers of that history were visible for all to see, a constant reminder to all who passed through the space of their own place in society, affirmed by the consoling continuities that shaped and informed daily life.

Sansovino's overall conception has been seen not only as a conscious attempt to evolve, in architectural terms, the Myth of Venice through the use of a distinctive classicizing language, but also as a courageous reinterpretation, on a monumental scale, of the typology of the ancient Roman forum as described by Vitruvius, superimposed upon the existing Byzantine elements in the square. A number of potent historical parallels were invoked in the process. In addition to being a new Jerusalem and, once again, a new Byzantium, Venice was also, for the first time, a second Rome. Completed only in the seventeenth century, Sansovino's scheme, with the basilica and Doge's Palace embedded within it, has survived intact except for its western flank, demolished to create a suitably imperial setting in the Neo-classical style for Venice's new master, Napoleon. At the same time, some of the city's treasures were removed, among them the four horses, originally plundered from Constantinople, which were now shipped to Paris, where they duly spawned their own progeny in the Tuilerie Gardens.

In common with the Roman forum as described by Vitruvius, Piazza San Marco was not only used for public meetings and gladiatorial contests, but was also a marketplace, where fish and meat were sold. Criminals were executed between the two columns in the Piazzetta, which runs down to the lagoon from the campanile and which functioned as a ceremonial entrance to the square itself, and charlatans and tooth-pullers plied their trades under the clock tower. Taverns operated in the square, pilgrims gathered to change money and arrange for travel to the Holy Land, and bread was baked in ovens. Some of these activities can still be seen in Canaletto's paintings, a gentle reminder that before Napoleon's arrival in 1797 the square was closer in spirit and function to an Arab souk than to the forecourt at Versailles. Yet while the everyday life of the square was not always consonant with the heroic solemnity of Jacopo Sansovino's architecture, which necessarily speaks in an elevated, classicizing tone of voice, it was rarely as moribund as the images of official ceremonies and processions suggest. News-sheets and popular prints were hawked in the Piazza by itinerant vendors around the basilica, and strolling players, the forebears of today's performers of Viennese salon music, stood on benches and improvised staging to entertain the crowds.

The second section of the book is essentially narrative history, argued from primary sources (manuscript chronicles, government records, printed commentaries and so forth) with, at the centre of attention, the victory at Lepanto, the visit of Henry III and, as a counterpoint, the plague of 1575–77. To contemporaries, the victory of the Holy League against the Turkish fleet in 1571 seemed to mark a momentous turning point in the fortunes of Christendom. In little more than two hundred years the Ottoman state had risen from obscure beginnings to become the terror of the Christian world. Now, finally, there were signs that this era of rapid conquest was coming to a close. As intelligence of the events of 7 October gradually spread throughout Europe, it brought with it waves of celebration, much of it hurriedly put together. Throughout the length and breadth of the Italian peninsula the good tidings from Lepanto were marked with public displays of collective joy and, sometimes, projects for more permanent memorials. But nowhere was the sense of relief and achievement more keenly felt than among the Venetians, and in the days after the news had reached the city the ceremonial machine was brought into immediate operation. After the official festivities promoted by the authorities, centred on San Marco and the surrounding spaces, had taken place, many of the professional organizations and guilds took up the challenge of competing to provide the most elaborate spectacles. From the presses of Venice, now at the sixteenth-century high point of their production, poured a torrent of pamphlets and broadsides giving accounts of the battle and prophesying the imminent destruction of the Turks, and even the repossession of the Holy Places. Although critics since Voltaire have contributed to an ironic chorus of amusement and disdain for a victory that led nowhere, it is through the 'popular' literature that the authentic period voice can be heard.

The end walls of Egnazio Danti's Gallery of Maps in the Vatican are frescoed with two scenes of enormous symbolic significance in the history, not only of Venice, but also of the contemporary Catholic world: the Siege of Malta in 1565, when the island was fiercely and successfully defended and the attacking Turkish forces repulsed, and Lepanto itself. While the years framed by these events were to be inscribed in the history of the Republic by its official historians, the reality of what followed must have been deeply disturbing for any intelligent Venetian. A separate peace with the Turks, contracted in 1573, may have re-established the trading links with the Ottoman empire that were vital to the Republic's economy, but it incurred the wrath of the other members of the League, who had been cynically suspicious of Venetian self-interested manoeuvres from the start. In addition, the price was high, and Cyprus was lost for ever. Isolated and exhausted as she was, Venice marked the visit of Henry III of France, who passed through the city on his way from Kraków to Lyons in the following year, with festivities of enormous elaboration (comparable in scale to the great Medici dynastic celebrations of the second half of the century), overseen by the authorities with great care and attention to detail.

Detail of pl. 142.

The truth of the matter is that Henry's visit was no ordinary entry, but provided the Venetians with a much-needed boost of confidence and visible public support.

But the euphoria did not last long. Beginning in the summer of 1575, the city was ravaged by a particularly severe outbreak of plague that lasted some two years and carried off one quarter of the population. In purely economic terms, the effects were grave, and the Republic was seriously hindered in its efforts to protect itself, in the wake of Lepanto, from the rapidly rearming Turkish navy. In terms of the collective consciousness of the Venetians, the visitation of the plague was widely and damagingly interpreted, according to traditional modes of interpretation, as clear evidence of divine anger for the sins of a wicked and corrupt city. As if in confirmation of this apocalyptic message, a few months later a sizeable part of the Doge's Palace was destroyed by a fire that symbolically burnt both a sequence of canvases showing important events from the Venetian past and the archives. These crucial events of the disquieting years that stretch from the War of Cyprus to the late 1570s allow observation of the historical 'machine' that produced the unique civic and cultural ethos of Venice in action, a process that provides insight into the conscious 'making' of history by Venetian government and society as seen through the eyes of contemporaries of different social rank, writing from a variety of viewpoints. Against the background of gradual decline, the ceremonial apparatus, ever more elaborate, served merely to deflect attention from the darker picture. Reading these events through the prism of the accounts of those who experienced them ultimately leads to a more complex interpretation of what it meant to be Venetian at the time than that offered by the standard 'Splendours of Venice' view of the Golden Age of Titian and Palladio.

Memorialization of these same events is the subject of the third and final part of the argument. In the years before the plague Venice was the most important city in Europe for the production of books, and despite the economic dislocation caused by the epidemic it continued to be a major centre. Accounts of current events were a significant aspect of local trade, and news of the formation of the Holy League, the battle of Lepanto and the visit of Henry III was disseminated in cheaply produced pamphlets, broadsides and prints. Further up the order of books, the major events and personalities of these years were commemorated and celebrated in less ephemeral formats. In addition to the press, memorialization was pursued through other means. Both the victory over the Turks and the delivery of the city from the plague led to the creation of new processions and rituals that, while being enmeshed with traditional forms, also partially redefined them. Palladio's church of the Redentore, the major Venetian monument commemorating the end of the plague, was designed as a structure capable of fulfilling the ceremonial and liturgical requirements of a spectacular procession that, having crossed the Giudecca Canal on temporary pontoons, constituted the congregation for the celebration of mass.

In this way the historical event itself was elided with the living memory and myth of Venice on a quite different level of abstraction from that offered by commemorative books, paintings or sculpture. The last two chapters of the book link such ritual transformations of inherited practice as well as paintings, sculpture and buildings, to the religious matrix that provides the ultimate key to understanding the civic ethos of the city in the final decades of the century.

Historical discussions of places and even of rituals and ceremonials are often silent. Throughout all three sections of the discussion, music of all kinds, from the enactment of the liturgy in the basilica to the songs of the *cantimpanchi* in the squares and the singing of litanies in the many processions that crossed the city every day, is constantly woven into the argument. The intention is to demonstrate that the soundscape of sixteenth-century Venice was rich and varied, and that music was a very real and functional dimension of urban life, not only in the rituals of civic and religious display. If the book does no more than convince others of this historical reality, then it will have served a purpose.

PROLOGUE

In the somewhat unexpected surroundings of the North Carolina Museum of Art hangs one of the last major works in the long tradition of Venetian history painting, Pompeo Batoni's large-scale canvas *The Triumph of Venice* (pl. 2). Originally commissioned by his patron Marco Foscarini, Venetian ambassador to the papal court, Batoni's picture was designed to hang in the Palazzo di Venezia, the ambassador's official residence in Rome. A member of one of the oldest Venetian patrician families, Foscarini was a traditionalist and a keen student of the history of the Serenissima, which he wrote about in his youthful *Discorso sulla perfezione della Repubblica*. This exercise in nostalgic antiquarianism, intensified no doubt by the sense of decline that marked the final decades of the Republic's existence, had brought him (just one year before his posting to Rome) the prized position of official state historian, as the latest (and as it was to turn out the last) in a distinguished line that had begun with Andrea Navagero (1483–1529), and in the sixteenth century had included both Pietro Bembo and Paolo Paruta. These features of Foscarini's career help to explain some of the unusual characteristics of Batoni's painting, also a youthful effort, painted in the late 1730s before the artist became established in Rome as a fashionable portrait painter much sought after by the British aristocaracy.[1] It is, in fact, only the fourth of Batoni's major commissions, and his first important nonreligious work. Its general theme, a celebration of Venetian prosperity and plenty as the fruits of good government, is immediately evident from its iconography, less so that a precise historical period is evoked as an instructive parallel. Francesco Benaglio, Batoni's biographer and Foscarini's secretary, wrote that the picture shows

1 Detail of pl. 2.

2 Pompeo Batoni, *The Triumph of Venice*, 1732. Raleigh, The North Carolina Museum of Art, Gift of the Samuel H. Kress Foundation.

the flourishing state of the Republic at the time when in the peace follow-ing the wars caused by the formation of the famous League of Cambrai, the fine arts were reborn, reinstated and fostered by Doge Lionardo Loredano of immortal memory . . . with the sea, the prospect of the city, architecture, dig-nified personages and spirits of all sexes and ages, symbols of literature and the fine arts.[2]

Although a no more precise literary programme has been identified for the painting, it seems likely that Foscarini himself was responsible for it. A keen collector of contemporary art, and a bibliophile in addition to being a histo-rian of note, he reportedly visited Batoni's studio daily to follow the progress of the work. The result is a mythological painting deeply inflected by the anti-quarian and historical interests of the patron.

Even by the standards of eighteenth-century Roman painting, which often relied on iconographical structures that assumed a high degree of general edu-cation, Batoni's canvas is complex. In addition to a knowledge of classical mythology and history, the equipped viewer would also have been aware of some of Batoni's visual models, and perhaps of a number of literary allusions that some have detected in the picture.[3] At the centre of the composition is the traditional female personification of Venice, seated on a shell-backed throne decorated with lions' heads, dolphins at her feet. 'The beautiful persona of the Queen of the Adriatic', as Venetia has been described, 'delighted the vision of foreign observers as a perpetual proof of divine intervention in the political affairs of men.'[4] As in Giacomo Franco's much earlier engraving showing the personification of the city set against a perspective view of the Piazzetta seen from the lagoon, Batoni's painting makes this connection explicit. Standing close to her and so intimately associated with her, can be seen Doge Leonardo Loredan, whose physiognomy is clearly derived from Giovanni Bellini's famous portrait, now in London (pl. 3). The choice of Loredan, who was doge during a period when the very existence of Venice and its dependent territories was under threat from the League of Cambrai, conjures up an analogy between the post-Cambrai world and the Republic of Foscarini's time, which many believed could be saved only by abandoning all claims to empire and concentrating on the conservation of the city and the *terraferma*.[5] At Neptune's feet a *putto* gestures towards a marble bust inscribed 'I.BRVTVS', perhaps an assertion of the successful harmony of an untroubled maritime republic. The central figure of Venetia, holding a sceptre, gestures towards Minerva to the left, who, holding an olive branch and supporting a lance, presents to her the arts, represented by the *putti* playfully scattered around her feet. In the foreground, images of Painting, Music (represented by the aulos of classical antiquity), Poetry (with lyre and sword), Theatre (with a mask), Sculpture and Architecture are all to be seen. Further still to the left, Neptune addresses Mars (or perhaps Aeneas), pointing out to him the entrance to the Piazzetta, framed by Jacopo Sansovino's Mint and Library buildings to one side, and the Doge's Palace and the Riva degli Schiavoni to the other. At the far right of the composition Ceres, whose hair is being combed, presented with an overflowing basket of fruit by yet another *putto* (in practice their presence knits the ensemble together), rests her elbow on a cornocopia. Accompanied by sheep and a model castle, this is suggestive of the ordered agricultural activity of the Republic. Above the scene, arranged on clouds, Fame is holding her traditional attribute of a trumpet, while the double-faced figure of History, symbolically looking both forwards and backwards, composes the official record, and Mercury presents an account of the Republic's achievements to six sages of classical antiquity, perhaps residents of Arcadia or the Groves of Academe, as it might be members of a Platonic Academy. Through these figures, a classical past is invoked, and the Myth of Venice relocated from Byzantium to Rome. The foremost figure, who is being presented with a history of the Venetian Republic, might well be a reference to Foscarini himself. It is here that the action of the painting takes place; the whole resembles a sort of floating opera set, dramatically side-lit from outside the frame.

In painting this rich cast of characters, Batoni quoted freely from well-known works of art, including not only Bellini's portrait (then in the Grimani collec-

3   Giovanni Bellini, *Portrait of Doge Leonardo Loredano*, 1501. London, National Gallery.

tion in Venice), but also Raphael's *Prudence* in the Stanza della Segnatura in the Vatican, which provided the prototype for Fame; a number of classical statues then in the Capitoline Museum in Rome; and Pietro da Cortona's fresco of the *Triumph of Ceres* in the Villa Sacchetti in Castelfusano, which inspired the central image of Venice in her chariot.[6] The result is one of a very small number of history paintings commissioned by Venetians that is exclusively directed towards the glorification of the state and makes no reference to the patron's family.[7] It is also notable for its complete reliance, with one exception, on an iconographical programme based on figures drawn from classical antiquity. The exception, significantly enough, is the evangelist Mark, present in the scene through the device of the team of winged lions that draw Venetia's chariot. This serves as a reminder of the absolute centrality of St Mark to any understanding of the linked themes of Venetian identity, mythology and history, as they evolved in tandem from the ninth century onwards, and as they came to be celebrated in ceremony, liturgy, music and the other arts during the early modern period. Mark is at the heart of the matter.

PART ONE

THE
CEREMONIAL
CITY

CHAPTER ONE

Constructing a Civic Religion

In the first chapters of his fourteenth-century *Chronicon venetum*, Doge Andrea Dandolo begins with an account of St Mark's evangelizing visit to Aquileia on the instructions of St Peter and the consecration of his disciple Hermagoras, who was to take control of the diocese after Mark's departure, as the first bishop of the province of Venetia and Istria.[1] Mark's reputed presence in Aquileia is not supported by either literary or archaeological evidence, and there is no sign that he was venerated there in the early Christian period. None of the early writers from the area mentions the episode of Mark's mission. It is shown neither in the early mosaics in the baptistery and cathedral in Aquileia, nor in the church of Santa Maria delle Grazie in Grado, all of which date from the sixth and seventh centuries. This absence is significant. In all probability, the legend of Mark's arrival in Aquileia was a piece of carefully fashioned mythology, crafted to suit the political and ecclesiastical circumstances in the aftermath of the schism of 606, when the original patriarchate of Aquileia was divided into two parts, one of which remained under the control of Aquileia, while the other, including the islands that were later to become Venice, passed to the jurisdiction of Grado.[2] As such, it is characteristic of a nexus of stories relating to Mark, an ingenious mixture of reality and legend, that evolved in response to jurisdictional disputes between Aquileia and Venice in the Carolingian period, and which were set into place as the foundation myths of both the patriarchate of Aquileia and, at a later stage, of the state of Venice itself.[3] The texts that transmit these stories, the buildings that articulate and celebrate them, the mosaics, fresco cycles and altarpieces that depict them, and the liturgies and ritual objects that articulate them, are not only things of beauty

4   Paris Bordon, *The Fisherman Delivering the Ring to the Doge* (detail), 1534. Venice, Gallerie dell'Accademia.

and historical fascination in themselves, but are also evidence of a sequence of politically constructed conflations of civic and religious ideas that provided the basis for local identities.[4] The legend of Mark's apostolic journey to Aquileia, which is the first phase of this history, is also the interpretational lever for the most powerful of all these interrelated myths, the story of the transferral (*translatio*) of Mark's relics from Alexandria to Venice in 828/9.

The early seventh-century schism created new jurisdictional domains that were at odds with each other, both culturally and politically. In its redrawn form, the patriarchate of Grado now extended along the Adriatic littoral, while Aquileia became the centre of an independent entity. Partly because of its original political connections to Constantinople, Grado remained in close contact with Byzantium and the Eastern empire, while, confined to the mainland, the new patriarchate of Aquileia retained its traditional historical links with the Western empire and the Lombards. Until the Frankish incursions into northern Italy, the two rivals coexisted in reasonable harmony, but with the arrival of imperial troops in Friuli in the early 780s the political equilibrium was disrupted. Recognizing the strategic importance of Aquileia, Charlemagne fully supported its claims to supremacy over Grado; based on the legend of Mark's mission to the area, which critically and effectively linked Peter, Mark and Hermagoras in a powerful foundation myth, this formulation conveniently satisfied Rome's insistence on Petrine validation for patriarchal titles.[5] The argument for the spiritual and temporal supremacy of Aquileia in the Upper Adriatic is powerfully presented in pictorial form for the first time in the frescos of the central apse of the Basilica Patriarcale in Aquileia. Created for the aggressively ambitious Patriarch Poppo (1019–44), some two hundred years after the Synod of Mantua had approved the Aquileian claim, they present a triumphal image of the early church, with Mark and Hermagoras placed in pride of place left and right of a central scene showing the *Virgin and Child in Majesty*, accompanied by a number of local saints including Fortunatus, the emperors Henry II, Conrad II and Henry III, and Poppo himself.[6] The distinctive nave capitals, also introduced as part of Poppo's reconstruction, are based upon antique Corinthian models, but with the classical acanthus leaves transformed into palmettes. This seemingly insignificant detail carried a political message of some importance; it was just one aspect of a sustained attempt to make an analogy between Aquileia and Rome by evoking a visual parallel between the building and the Constantinian basilica of St Peter's, a parallel that can be seen most clearly in the projection of the transept and the arrangement of arcades within it.[7] As such, it was part of a campaign to strengthen Aquileia's links with Rome, by stressing Aquileia's affinity with the Papacy, leaving Venice to pursue its traditional association with Byzantium.

The earliest written sources, which give a rather abbreviated version of Mark's mission, date from the eighth century. Paul the Deacon's *Liber de Episcopis Mettensibus* provides an account of Peter sending Mark to Aquileia to preach and convert, and also recounts the sequel of Mark's choice of Hermagoras as his disciple and successor; once again, the triumvirate is invoked to establish an apostolic succession, legitimate the Aquileian patriarchate and establish its supremacy over its rival.[8] It is hard to resist the impression that Paul, a native of Cividale writing in the 780s (but at that time based at Charlemagne's court in Francia), was participating in the early stages of an Aquileian bid for control that came to fruition at the Synod of Mantua in 827, when the legend was successfully deployed in support of the Aquileian case. Significantly, by the ninth century it had acquired a fresh amplification, in which Hermagoras, accompanied by Mark, journeyed to Rome and was consecrated as the first bishop of Aquileia by St Peter himself, a new detail that further strengthened the notion of apostolic succession by lending it the stamp of papal authority.[9] This is typical of the way that the legends surrounding Mark could be expanded for political reasons, and it is also characteristic that once this episode had been attached to the legend it remained in place. It is shown, for example, in the mosaics of the Cappella di San Pietro in the choir of San Marco, as well as in the Pala d'Oro, the large altarpiece made to decorate Mark's tomb, commissioned in 1102 and completed three years later.[10] By this time the power of Aquileia had diminished and the story of Mark's journey to the area and its various sequels had been astutely deployed by the Venetians as part of their justification for the removal of Mark's relics from Alexandria. As such, the mosaics marked the first stage in the Venetian elaboration of the myth of Mark's visit to the lagoon, which was to culminate in the mid-thirteenth-century addition of the *praedestinatio*.[11] This moment marks the transition from the first phase of the Marcian legends, which were concerned with the apostolic foundation of the early church in Aquileia-Grado, to a second period, characterized by the Venetian appropriation of Mark for political motives, expressed through ecclesiastical policy.

For the Carolingian bishops, meeting in Lombardy in 827, the dispute over ecclesiastical authority between the patriarchate of Aquileia, whose allegiances were to the empire and the Papacy, and that of Grado, whose links were mainly with the Greek churches of the Adriatic, including Venice, was more to do with political realities than with theological niceties or the status of competing claims.[12] Carolingian attempts to exercise influence in the area around the Venetian estuary had often taken the form of trying to gain ecclesiastical control, and it is not surprising that the Synod (meeting in Carolingian Mantua) declared in favour of Carolingian Aquileia. Had the decision received papal approval, it would have had the effect of unifying the two patriarchates, and relegating Grado (and with it Venice) to the status of a dependent *plebs*. This would plainly have been unacceptable to the Venetians. Their response nevertheless was to seek out the body of Mark in Alexandria. In this, they were following an established procedure in which apostolic relics were acquired for political or ecclesiastical reasons by churches that did not already possess them, a practice that had been common in northern Italy since the time of St Ambrose in the fourth century.[13] Although the outcome at Mantua was favourable to the Venetians, whose growing power and influence in the area it implicitly recognized, the matter did not end there. During the following centuries the two patriarchates continued to struggle against each other for sole possession of the patriarchal title and the authority that went with it, using every means to hand, including theological and historical evidence as well as occasional displays of armed force.

Whether the physical remains of Mark were actually transferred to Venice from Alexandria in 828/9 is not the issue, though the balance of opinion is now on the side of doubt.[14] By the tenth century the story of the *translatio* was sufficiently diffused for it to have travelled as far as the Benedictine abbey of Fleury on the Loire, where it was copied down together with the *Passio Sancti Marci*.[15] As a barometer of Venetian political concerns, the text of the *translatio* is of major interest irrespective of its historical authenticity: the possession of Mark's relics was the foundation stone of the Venetian state, based on a new configuration of civic and religious conceptions.[16] By choosing Mark as their principal patron, the Venetians moved decisively against Aquileia and its Carolingian supporters; the actual possession of the evangelist's body placed Venice in a quite different category from a patriarchate that was merely associated with him through his presence in the area while conducting an evangelizing mission.

At the same time, by replacing their existing patron saint, the Greek warrior Theodore of Heraclea (whose history was confusingly intertwined with that of St Theodore of Amasea), with a Roman saint who, according to legend, wrote his Gospel there, the Venetians provided a fitting agent for a new collective identity as they embarked upon the final phase of emancipation from Byzantine sovereignty and moved towards independence.[17] By the end of the eleventh century the palace chapel of San Teodoro, which had stood between the ducal palace and the first church of San Marco, had disappeared, perhaps symbolically subsumed into the reconstruction of the church by Doge Domenico Contarini, which had been begun only recently in the second half of the eleventh century. Although Theodore is only minimally represented in the mosaics and the liturgy of the basilica, he remained an important presence in the Venetian consciousness. His relics were brought to the city from Constantinople by Marco Dandolo and placed in the church of San Salvatore in 1267,[18] and his statue was raised in the Piazzetta; somewhat later, in 1329, the statue was replaced with a second, composite affair assembled from antique fragments.[19] A period of declining importance was followed by one of renewal. In 1450 the bishop of Venice, Lorenzo Giustiniani, ruled that his feast-day should be made into a solemnity of the first rank and, in a matching gesture, the Senate proclaimed shortly afterwards that 'in bygone times and ever thereafter St Theodore was the protector of this our city, together with St Mark the Evangelist'.[20] By this time, although the resonances of Theodore's Byzantine past were largely nostalgic rather than militant, his presence in the city, assured by his remains, guaranteed his status as a principal protector.[21] This role, symbolized by the strategic positioning of his statue, paired with the winged lion of St Mark,[22] on columns at the entrance to the Piazzetta from the lagoon, was still recognized at the end of the fifteenth century by Marin Sanudo.[23] Columns supporting statues of bronze, stone or even silver were common in antiquity and in the East, and in raising these two the Venetians were redeploying the tradition as a Christian symbol as well as civic insignia.[24] With their statues of the two main patron saints of the Republic, one Byzantine, the other Roman, the columns not only framed a ceremonial route from the water: passing between them processions would then enter San Marco from either the south atrium or through the main west door, and it was also there, watched over by these two holy protectors, that thieves, traitors and other criminals were dispatched.[25] This counterpoint of Eastern and Western saints, Theodore and Mark, Byzantium and Rome, has been taken to be typical of Venetian culture of the period, a constant interlacing of imperial models rather than, as is sometimes argued, a sequence of revivals.[26]

In the absence of classical origins for the city, the story of the *translatio* of the body of St Mark was more than a legend; it operated as an integral part of the ideological foundations of both church and state. By bringing Mark's body to Venice, the ruling elite was actively engaged in defining a new sacral geography. In its agglomeration of political and ecclesiastical ideologies for use in the construction of the community's collective memory, the story of Mark's *translatio* is characteristic of the genre. It is in turn just one stage of the traditional pattern established by medieval hagiographers for the authentication of relics. A tripartite process, this consisted of a martyrdom (*passio*), the discovery of relics (*inventio*) and their removal to a new site (*translatio*), to which a fourth element, involving the consecration of the building that housed them (*dedicatio*), could sometimes be added. In the case of Mark, both the *apparitio* (by which the relics miraculously revealed themselves in 1094 after having been lost following their supposed transfer to the city) and the *dedicatio* of the present basilica of San Marco a short time afterwards were associated with ducal action; like the *translatio* itself, they were politicized from an early date.[27] It has been argued that the four major Venetian feast-days associated with Mark were allegories for political or constitutional events.[28]

The essential narrative features of the *translatio* centre on the adventures of two merchants from the lagoon, Tribunus of Malamocco and Rusticus of Torcello. Their ship, together with nine others, was driven off course to Alexandria, an act of fate that justified their trade with the Saracens, which was otherwise forbidden. Hearing of the caliph's plans to desecrate Mark's tomb, they resolved to steal the body and take it to Venice. In an attempt to persuade the Greek custodians of the *martyrium* (the monk Stauracius and the priest Theodore) to collaborate in the scheme, Tribunus and Rusticus claimed that Mark had evangelized Aquileia and the surrounding area before arriving in

Alexandria; consequently, it was appropriate that his body should return to the lagoon where it belonged, and where it would be safe from Arab marauders. Under the weight of these arguments Stauracius and Theodore relented and agreed to the plan, substituting the body of St Claudia for that of Mark, which was then carefully removed from its silk shroud. Their scheme was nearly discovered when the wonderful fragrance given off by the relics aroused Muslim suspicions, but the seals were found to be in place and the body intact. This danger passed, the conspirators placed Mark's body in a basket and covered it with pork. The smell of the forbidden meat repelled the Muslim customs officers, who fled in disgust, allowing the body to be smuggled safely on board ship. After a trouble-free voyage, the sailors were roused from their sleep by Mark himself, whose warning that they were close to shore averted shipwreck. A second miracle soon followed, when, landing at Umago on the Istrian coast, a plague of devils was driven off. Once the party arrived in Venice it was greeted not, as had been feared, by reprimands, but by the gratitude of Bishop Ursus of Olivolo-Castello (the bishop of the city) and his clergy, who immediately accompanied the relics in a solemn procession to the palace of the doge, Giustiniano Partecipazio. Once the body arrived inside the palace, the cycle of miracles was completed through the agency of Mark's presence. The doge vowed to build a new *martyrium*, but died before his promise could be realized; it was carried out by his successor.

Most of the details in this colourful narrative are given in one of the earliest texts of the *translatio*, written around 1050.[29] Probably compiled from earlier manuscripts, perhaps dating from the time that the relics were transferred, it may well have been based on a straightforward account of the theft, which was then embellished by the addition of accounts of the obligatory miracles required for the tripartite authentication of relics. Further embellishments occur in some of the later sources. Regardless of its weak historical foundations, the *translatio* fulfilled its political purposes brilliantly. By simultaneously achieving Venetian superiority over, and independence from, both Byzantium and Aquileia, it secured Partecipazio's objective of uniting Venetian settlements and towns around a religious centre directly under the control of the doge.[30] It was also elaborated in other ways. The earliest liturgical sources of the episode, for example, come from the eleventh and twelfth centuries, when, perhaps significantly, Aquileia was entrenched in the final phase of its struggle for jurisdiction over not just its own diocese but Grado (which then included Venice) as well.[31] The story is repeated with some modifications by Martin da Canal in his chronicle, written between 1267 and 1275,[32] and became the basis for the many retellings of the episode in the Venetian chronicle tradition, from where it found its way into the popular printed histories that disseminated the outlines of the legend to a wider world in the age of print.[33] From the late middle ages onwards, the main outlines of the story provided artists from Venice and the Veneto with a rich fund of material (pl. 5).[34]

5 Jacopo Tintoretto, *The Rescue of the Body of St. Mark from Alessandria*,
1562–6. Venice, Gallerie dell'Accademia.

Martin da Canal is also the earliest source for an important modification
that was made to the Marcian legends through the addition of the *praedesti-*
natio or *vaticinatio*. This new episode, which is recounted in its fullest form in
Dandolo's *Chronicon*,[35] concerns Mark's journey to Rome with Hermagoras
before setting out for Alessandria. Surprised by a sudden storm in the lagoon,
Mark rowed their boat to a small island, which in later chronicles is identified
not only as the island of Rialto, but even more precisely as the place where the
church of San Marco was later to be built. The saint fell asleep, and in a dream
heard the voice of an angel announcing that this would be his final resting-

place: 'Pax tibi, Marce. Hic requiescat corpus tuum'.[36] Elaborated around the middle of the thirteenth century, a period of prolific growth in state-controlled mythologenesis (the legend of the *apparitio* dates from the same period), the *praedestinatio* appears at about the same time, both in a hymn inserted into the second part of Canal's chronicle[37] and in a marble sculpture placed above the central door of the west façade of the basilica, as well as in the atrium mosaics of the Cappella Zen.[38] Together with the ceremony of the 'marriage to the sea', which, grafted onto the existing ritual *benedictio* of the lagoon, was introduced at about the same time, it must be regarded as further evidence of Venetian thirteenth-century nationalistic self-confidence, the *Renovatio imperii* that followed the conquest of Constantinople in 1204 during the Fourth Crusade.[39] Through the device of the *praedestinatio*, both the acquisition of Mark's remains and the construction of a *martyrium* to house them were seen to be divinely preordained and therefore sanctioned; in the process the saint's bones were provided with a prehistory that both anticipated and justified the *translatio* itself.[40] The consolidation of the story of Mark's visit to the lagoon into the standard theological literature is clearly seen in the account presented in the *Legenda aurea*. Quoting Peter Damian, Jacobus de Voragine wrote that Mark's body 'was returned to Italy so that the land where it had been given him to write his gospel won the privilege of possessing his sacred remains'.[41]

From the arrival of Mark's body in the ninth century there flowed an identification with the saint as the special protector of the city, which in turn crucially determined the character of much Venetian ritual and of the spaces in which it was performed. This is a matter of both the structural organization of the Venetian liturgical calendar, as well as the detailed civic and religious practices that took place on individual feast-days. The most immediate and dramatic consequence of the *translatio* of Mark's relics was the planning and construction of a *martyrium* to house them, significantly enough not in Grado, the seat of episcopal power, but in Venice itself, where they had been deposited.[42] Construction of the first church of San Marco was begun shortly afterwards. According to the instructions of a fourteenth-century copy, the earliest to survive, of the will of Doge Giustiniano Partecipazio, who died in 829, a church in honour of Mark was to be constructed 'infra territorio Sancti Zachariae', that is, within the boundaries of the land belonging to the Benedictine convent and church of San Zaccaria.[43] In the gradual process of appropriation, in which Mark came to be associated not only with the Venetians but more specifically with the elected doge, the construction of a sufficiently imposing structure to contain the evangelist's body, which on its arrival had been temporarily placed 'ad ducis palatium', in an area now thought to have been subsumed into the basilica itself, became something of a priority. The construction of the church was not only a direct consequence of the *translatio*, but also the result of ducal initiative. It is entirely characteristic of the mixture of religious and civic elements that make up the foundation myth of

Venice that, from early in his career as the principal patron saint of the city, Mark was also presented as a specifically ducal one.

The site selected for the first church of San Marco had the merit of being close to the existing ducal palace, which had been transformed out of the ancient *castrum* by Doge Agnello Partecipazio, Giustiniano's immediate predecessor as doge, and the first of a long line of members of the family who occupied the office during the ninth and tenth centuries.[44] Little remains of this first building, which was severely damaged by the fire that ravaged Venice during the rebellion against Doge Pietro IV Candiano in 976, though this has not prevented considerable speculation about its dimensions, architectural type and even general appearance.[45] The consensus view is that the ground plan of Agnello Partecipazio's church was based on that of Justinian's rebuilt Apostoleion (church of the Holy Apostles) in Constantinople, where the relics of St Andrew, brother of St Peter and the alleged founder of the Constantinopolitan patriarchate, were preserved.[46] The idea of a Basilica Sanctorum Apostolorum was not in itself new; the earliest Italian example, the *basilica martyrium* founded by St Ambrose during his time in Milan, probably in 374 (the predecessor of the present medieval church of Sant'Ambrogio), had provided the model for others, including a number of sanctuaries in Ravenna, built to house the relics of Sts Stephen, John the Baptist, John the Evangelist, Peter, Paul and Andrew, a formidable collection brought back from Constantinople by Archbishop Maximian (546–56).[47] Since their foundation coincides with the attempts by the Emperor Justinian to make Ravenna the centre of the Italian church, superior to Rome itself, the architectural and decorative programmes of these churches provide clear examples of the politico-ecclesiastical significance of the possession of apostolic remains.[48] The Venetians may well have had these models in mind, as well as the competitive example of Aquileia, in formulating their own plans. Housing Mark's relics was the main purpose of the new building, but its proximity to the ducal palace also gave it a distinct civic significance even in this, the earliest phase of the transformation of San Marco from private chapel to state church. During the centuries that followed, the bonds that tied St Mark to both doge and state were strengthened through the evolution of a characteristically Venetian mixture of liturgical and civic rituals. These were enacted mostly in the basilica, the Piazza San Marco and the Piazzetta, which for these purposes constituted a unified ceremonial area, and from there they could be transported elsewhere in the city when the ducal procession (*andata*) visited sites of particular historical, religious or ritual significance. From the very beginning, San Marco, the Doge's Palace and the ceremonial spaces that surrounded them were seen as the heart of the devotional and political geography of the city. Taken together, they functioned as the centre of an intricate web of religious and civic conceptions, celebrated in a number of distinct processional rituals involving the highest officers of church and state, and above all the doge, that were enacted there.

A second church, built by Candiano's successors Pietro Orseolo I and II, lasted less than a century before it too was replaced by the present building, begun during the dogeship of Domenico Contarini in 1063, but not finally consecrated until 1094. For this the Venetians once again chose as their model Justinian's sixth-century church of the Holy Apostles in Constantinople. It was destroyed by Mehmed the Conqueror after the defeat of the city in 1453, but its general appearance can be reconstructed, principally on the basis of a description by the sixth-century historian Procopius.[49] This, taken together with his claim that the church of St John at Ephesus, the ruins of which do survive, was directly modelled upon it, suggests that Justinian's church, built to a cruciform plan with five domes (the central one slightly larger than the others), was quite exceptional for the period.[50] Onto the basic plan that the Apostoleion provided, the Venetians grafted elements from both Middle Byzantine architecture and Italian practice.[51] The parallels between the two churches imply ambitious motivations. Both housed relics connected with the earliest phase of the history of the church (an apostle and an evangelist), and in selecting an imperial model for the ducal basilica of San Marco, Contarini and his advisers were making a powerful advance in the continuing struggle with Aquileia for political and ecclesiastical supremacy in the Upper Adriatic. In this context, it has been suggested that the choice of a Byzantine model was a direct response to Patriarch Poppo's renovation of the Basilica Patriarcale in Aquileia, with its explicit parallels to St Peter's in Rome.[52]

In its original finished form, San Marco did not much resemble the splendid and ornate building that we are used to today, or even the late fifteenth-century church familiar from Gentile Bellini's *Procession in the Piazza San Marco* (pl. 6). Although most of the area occupied by the present building was originally part of the eleventh-century structure, some components were probably residues of earlier churches on the site, while others received their present shape only later. The Cappella di Sant'Isidoro, for example, did not acquire its present form until the fourteenth century, and the Cappella della Madonna dei Mascoli not until the fifteenth, while the entire north wing of the narthex is a thirteenth-century addition (see pl. 40).[53] The exterior has changed even more. Originally it was built of brick, and the marble cladding, friezes and sculptures that now decorate it were added later, much of the work carried out in the first half of the thirteenth century, when both the north and south atria were added. The west façade cycle, which acts as a preface to the building and serves as a reminder of the church's principal function as *martyrium*, was executed at about the same time, though decoration with marble and mosaics both internally and externally continued long after this date, and some of the work was not finally finished until the fourteenth century.[54] The craftsmen who carried it out were Italian, and the materials that they used were for the most part local. In this sense Contarini's church presents a strong contrast between the construction and ornamentation of the building as it was carried out from the late eleventh century onwards and its original Byzantine conception.[55]

6   Gentile Bellini, *Procession in the Piazza San Marco*, 1496. Venice, Gallerie dell'
Accademia.

Many details of the external decoration, including columns of marble and
porphyry, figured reliefs and the four horses placed above the main portico,
came from the shiploads of trophies brought to Venice after the capture of
Constantinople in 1204.[56] The removal of booty of all kinds, from precious
building materials to reliquaries, chalices and icons, continued until the collapse of the Latin kingdom in 1261; many of the most spectacular items in the
treasury also arrived as part of this traffic. Most of the capitals, columns and
marbles to be seen in the present façades also came in this way; the practice of
using *spolia* in architectural schemes was of long standing, and seems to have
originated in the Constantinian period.[57] The north side overlooking the
Piazzetta dei Leoncini contains a somewhat haphazard arrangement of elements,
randomly selected for their ornamental qualities rather than for their place in
any preconceived scheme. The balancing façade on the south side, and the area
immediately surrounding it, is differently organized, being rich in triumphal
motifs including the so-called Pillars of Acre, the famed porphyry *Tetrarchs* or
'Moors'[58] and the Pietra del Bando, from which official proclamations were
made and the heads of traitors displayed (pl. 7). The last was probably removed
by Lorenzo Tiepolo from Acre in 1258, where it had been used as a symbol of
Genoese authority, but the rest of these spoils came from Constantinople. The
Tetrarchs, long suspected to have Byzantine origins, were revealed as having
come from Istanbul when the missing foot was discovered there in 1985. Similarly, the Pillars of Acre, two free-standing piers incised with vine and pomegranate decoration, are now known to have come from the church of St

7   San Marco, south façade.

Polyeuktos in Constantinople, from which they were presumably removed shortly after 1204, together with capitals and other marbles.[59] The legend connecting them to Acre is recounted by Francesco Sansovino,[60] despite the presence of Greek monograms clearly indicating their place of origin. Together with the many precious chalices, book-covers, icons and other precious objects that fill the treasury and library of San Marco, the Pillars of Acre and the *Tetrarchs* are part of a rich haul of trophies brought from what had been the centre of power at the end of the first millennium, now redeployed as an index of Venice's new wealth and prestige.[61] Significantly, in view of their position, yet further captured trophies are set into the external wall of the treasury itself.

In terms of both language and style, the contrast between the north and south façades of San Marco is great, a reminder that the main entrance to the square throughout the middle ages was from the lagoon itself and that the south façade was the first part of the basilica to be seen, at least by honoured visitors and probably by many others as well. This also explains the counter-intuitive orientation of the original mosaics on the west façade, whose appearance can be recuperated from Bellini's painting; they read from right to left, which may reflect the direction from which Mark's relics arrived from the lagoon as the culmination of the *translatio*.[62] More importantly, this also underlines that before it was closed off by the construction of the Cappella Zen in 1504, the south door, framed by the Pillars of Acre, was the main entrance to the basilica from the Piazzetta. Close to the Doge's Palace, from where they are overlooked by a relief depicting the *Judgement of Solomon*, the Pillars have been read in a Solomonic context, as a columnar preface to a building that, after the addition of the atria, now measured 100 royal cubits in width, equivalent to both the width and length of St Polyeuktos, built in emulation of the Temple in Jerusalem by Princess Anicia Juliana.[63] By way of this Solomonic analogy, San Marco could be thought to assume the qualities of Constantinople itself, often regarded as a 'Second Jerusalem'.[64] Through the importation of Christian relics (and above all those of the Virgin), and the establishment of sanctuaries and monasteries where those 'in the habit of angels' maintained a round of ceaseless prayer, Constantinople had presented the image of a New Jerusalem founded upon the pagan imperial remains of the New Rome. Particularly after the Council of Ephesus (AD 432), this second identity (imposed upon the first) was increasingly reflected in the mirror of its own identity, now transposed to the Venetian lagoon.

On entering the atrium of San Marco from the south, the visitor is confronted with twelve mosaic panels showing scenes from the *Life of St Mark*, including the earliest full depiction of the *praedestinatio* in the vault; confined to the saint's exploits in Rome, Aquileia and Alexandria, this forms an iconographical counterpoint to the *translatio* mosaics on the west façade.[65] Probably executed in the third quarter of the thirteenth century, the cycle is based on a text by Martin da Canal, written in Alexandrines at the end of his chronicle. As such the scheme was also an important juncture in the ceremonial route followed on some important occasions from the Piazzetta, framed not only by the two columnar monuments at the entrance from the lagoon, but also by the Pillars of Acre.[66] It has been suggested that the Pillars recall the two piers known as Jachin and Boaz, wrought by Hiram of Tyre at the entrance of the Ark of the Covenant in the Temple in Jerusalem,[67] thus further reinforcing the Solomonic resonances of the western area of the basilica.

The main façade is the most coherently planned of all; here the iconography of the sculptural reliefs follows a carefully planned scheme. It serves not only as a visual preface to the interior, but also as a magisterial expression of dominion achieved through the display of trophies and the images of local saints, crucially punctuated by the sculptural programme of the *Last Judgement*. Although the widespread use of green and dark red porphyry may have been conditioned by what was available in the booty from Constantinople, it was also appropriate that both these types of stone, and in particular red porphyry, had carried strong imperial connotations since at least the time of Diocletian.[68] In something of a minor key, the incorporation of the *Virtues* in the main portal pro-

8   *Virgin Orans*, 13th century. San Marco, west façade.

vides a religious and ethical element, while the introduction of the *Labours of the Months* serves to emphasize the importance of civic duty.[69] The six plaques in the spandrels are a mixture of old and new. Three come from Constantinople, while the remaining three were carved as matching pieces in Venice. As a series they make constant reference to the origins of Venice, through images of the *Archangel Gabriel* and the *Virgin* (and so to the myth of the city's foundation on the feast of the Annunciation) (pl. 8), and to the two warrior-saints, George and Demetrius.[70] Among them is a late antique relief showing Hercules delivering the Ermanthian Boar to King Eurystheus, and a companion piece showing Hercules carrying the Cerynitian Hind while trampling the Hydra of Lerna underfoot. Since Eraclea, the earliest political centre in the lagoon and the seat of the first doge, had been named after him, this transformed a classical composition not merely into a Christian message, but into a specifically Venetian one.[71] It has been argued that this rich iconographical mixture of elements from both popular and learned traditions would have been understood, if only in part, by a wide audience.[72]

The most spectacular of all the trophies from Constantinople are the four bronze horses, displayed on eight short columns of white marble and four of porphyry, raised triumphantly on the loggia above the central portal, dramatically set against the dark central window. Originally they were gilded, and they appear as such in Bellini's painting, as well as in the reports of early travellers and local antiquarians (pl. 9). Pietro Giustinian's *Rerum venetarum ab urbe condita historia* (1560) is typical of these in its description of 'four unbridled horses glistening with gold', and also reports the belief, common in the sixteenth century, that they were made by the Greek sculptor Lysippus, and were taken to Rome before being sent to Byzantium by Constantine, prior to making their final journey to Venice.[73] Yet whatever was believed in the sixteenth century about the history of the quadriga, its location was the result of a political decision designed to emphasize not merely their beauty but also their status as quite exceptional spoils of war. In the early middle ages this was made even more explicit through a dramatic moment of state spectacle when, stand-

ing between the horses, the doge proclaimed his title of 'Lord of one quarter
and a half of the entire Roman Empire'
('Dominator quartae et dimidae parties
totius Romaniae').[74]

It has been suggested that the four horses
may have formed the culmination of a thematically integrated sculptural group consisting of the five reliefs of *Christ* and the
Evangelists now set into the north façade,
but originally placed in the second storey
above the present position of the quadriga.[75]
If this reconstruction of the tympanum is
correct, it encourages the association of the
four horses and the four evangelists with the
metaphor of the Quadriga Domini, charged
with spreading the Gospel throughout the
entire world.[76] In this context the church of
San Marco, as the repository of Mark's
remains, becomes the point of departure for
a historic mission, the centre not only of the
Venetian empire but also that of an evangelizing enterprise of universal significance,
directed from a favoured city inhabited by
a Chosen People. That ambitious and politically charged notion, destined to reverber-

9   Gentile Bellini, *Procession in the Piazza San
Marco* (detail), 1496. Venice, Gallerie dell'
Accademia.

ate throughout the following centuries, is also proclaimed by the overall scheme
of the west façade, which juxtaposes episodes from the *translatio* with scenes from
the New Testament, beginning with the marble reliefs of the *Virgin Mary* and
Gabriel and continuing with four Christological scenes in the mosaic lunettes of
the upper storey. The climax is reached with the central portal, which shows the
dead rising from their tombs while Christ, surrounded by angels, announces the
Second Coming.[77]

The determination of the Venetians to imitate Byzantium, and more precisely to rival the opulent interior of Justinian's Apostoleion, also influenced the
early mosaic decorations of San Marco; this is true both in general terms and
in details of the iconographical scheme and the arrangement of subject matter.[78]
This does not amount to a faithful copying of the originals, but rather to the
marriage of Middle Byzantine elements with Western features from a number
of traditions. In addition to these purely stylistic parameters, the results were
also conditioned by the political and ecclesiastical policies of the Venetian state
during the twelfth and thirteenth centuries, a time of consolidation and
mythologizing, when the Marcian legends were extensively deployed to elabo-

10   Pala d'Oro, 1105 with later revisions. San Marco.

rate the legend of its foundation in keeping with the exigencies of the time. Nowhere can this be more clearly appreciated than in the three pictorial narratives of the *Reception of Mark's Relics*, the final, climactic episode of the *translatio*, made during this same period.

The earliest of the three occurs in the lower section of the Pala d'Oro, commissioned in Constantinople by Doge Ordelaffo Falier in the early twelfth century (pl. 10).[79] Decorated with 187 enamel plaques and 1,927 gems arranged in a rectangular gilt frame, it replaced (and may even incorporate enamels from) an earlier altarpiece, also made in Constantinople, for Doge Pietro I Orseolo in 976. One of the most precious treasures of the basilica, the Pala d'Oro follows the general arrangement of a number of Italian Carolingian antependia in its incorporation of the individual figures of angels, saints, prophets, apostles and others arranged in horizontal bands around a central figure of Christ enthroned. In terms of sheer magnificence its only equal is the Golden Altar, built over the tomb of St Ambrose in Milan and commissioned by Archbishop Angilbert II (824–59), the sides of which are decorated with embossed sheets (gold for the front, silver, partly gilt, elsewhere). Through its exclusive use of precious metals, enamels and gems, the altar claims superiority over all others.[80] The Pala d'Oro, which stands over the tomb of St Mark, and in front of which was enacted a liturgy as specific to Venice as the Ambrosian rite was to Milan, makes a rival bid through similar means. Through such competitive strategies, equivalence was sought with a small number of famous shrines and altars in Constantinople, Jerusalem, Milan, Ravenna and Rome.

11   *The Reception of St. Mark's Relics, Pala d'Oro*, 1105. San Marco.

Although Falier's Pala d'Oro was subsequently enlarged on two occasions, its structure and scheme remain substantially unchanged. It is divided horizontally into two sections, with an upper storey that was probably added in 1209 when the Pala, which had been originally designed as an altar frontal, was converted into a retable.[81] Among the thirty-eight cloisonné enamels that make up the lower storey, a set of ten square panels showing episodes from the *Life of St Mark* is arranged along the vertical frames as a border. They are now disposed in two groups of five to be read in both cases from top to bottom, beginning at the top left-hand corner, but in terms of narrative action they divide into three groups, each tied to a different text. The first depicts Mark's foundation of the church at Aquileia, the second his mission to Alexandria and the third the translation of his relics to Venice.[82] It has been proposed that all ten scenes originally formed a single sequence running horizontally at the base of the antependium.[83] The climax of the sequence is the group of three panels showing the translation of Mark's relics to Venice. In the first of these, the body of the saint is being lifted from its tomb outside Alexandria by Bonus Tribunus and Rusticus. In the next, the two accompany Mark's relics on their voyage, while in the last scene the relics, now enclosed in a chest carried by the merchants, are being received by Bishop Ursus of Olivolo-Castello (bearded and carrying a double cross) and the Venetian clergy led by a deacon thurifer (pl. 11). Two bearers, presumably Tribunus and Rusticus, carry the *arca*, while a group of soldiers with lances follow behind. The single-domed church in the background may be a depiction of the first basilica of San Marco, which is described in the *Translatio Marci* as resembling the church of the Holy Sepulchre in Jerusalem.[84]

12   *The Reception of St. Mark's Relics*, mosaic, *c.*1150. San Marco, Cappella
S. Clemente.

Significantly, in view of later depictions of the scene in the mosaics of the basilica, the doge himself is neither shown in the enamel nor mentioned in the
inscription above, an accentuation upon the reception of Mark's body by the
ecclesiastical rather than the temporal authority that is in keeping with Byzantine tradition.[85] Although the Pala bears some resemblance to other early
Western altar frontals, notably the Golden Altar, its overall appearance for the
thirteenth-century viewer was unmistakably Byzantine and splendid, if not
imperial.[86]

The symbolic importance of the episode of the *Reception of Mark's Relics*,
and its central position in Venetian political theology, can be seen from the
way in which the incident is reported, with significant amplifications, in later
images of the *translatio*. In a mosaic in the Cappella di San Clemente, thought
to date from the middle of the twelfth century, an important alteration to the
traditional narrative is introduced.[87] This mosaic has often been noted for its
size, and particularly for its composition, designed to be read as a powerful
political statement (pl. 12).[88] Among the party of ecclesiastics frontally displayed
to receive Mark's relics, the central figure, more richly robed than the others
and wearing the archiepiscopal pallium, is not, as might be expected both from
the text of the *translatio* and from the panel in the Pala d'Oro, Bishop Ursus,
but rather the patriarch of Grado.[89] The remaining figures represent the dioceses of the lagoon that were under his jurisdiction, including the recently
attached archbishopric of Zara, and the bishopric of Olivolo-Castello, symbolized by the figure of Bishop Ursus, shown on the extreme left of the group
holding a processional cross. Read as an ensemble, these figures represent the
full authority of the Venetian patriarchate of Grado under the direction of its
metropolitan.

That is one half of the equation of power. The other is presented in a second, secular group centred on the doge, surrounded by an ensemble of five patricians together with a sword-bearer. It has been suggested that these are the members of the *consilium sapientium*, elected to represent the people of Venice, who, as the accompanying inscription maintains, were part of the reception party together with the bishops, the clergy and the doge.[90] In structure and vocabulary the mosaic is similar to a number of other ceremonial scenes, including those in the audience hall of Pope Calixtus II (1119–24) in the Lateran Palace and in the narthex of the church of San Clemente in Rome.[91] As a type, it also occurs in a number of scenes in the mosaics of San Vitale in Ravenna,[92] but ultimately the arrangement is derived from the official art of imperial Rome.[93] The adoption of this model in the *Reception of Mark's Relics* mosaic in the cycle in the Cappella di San Clemente transforms the conventional version of the *translatio* into a powerful affirmation of Venetian political and spiritual authority in the second half of the twelfth century. Through modification of the traditional narrative as handed down in the text of the *translatio*, it presents an image of the consolidation of Venetian institutions, both civic and ecclesiastical, under the patronage of Mark and the guidance of the doge. More precisely, it celebrates the moment between 1155 and 1157 when ecclesiastical power was redistributed through the transference of the patriarchal seat to Grado, then under Venetian control, a papal initiative that finally closed the centuries-old contest for supremacy between Venice and Aquileia.[94] In this context the San Clemente mosaic not only depicts the Venetian church and state in its totality, but also emphasizes the benefits and consequences of possession, and validates the transfer of authority from Aquileia to Venice. Mark was no longer the property of Aquileia or Grado as he had been previously, but of Venice itself. From this moment the identification of Mark with the state, at least in its official manifestations, entered a new phase.

The San Clemente mosaic marks the first stage of a lengthy historical process in which Mark became increasingly both more Venetian and more ducal. Once his relics had been appropriated by the doge and his officials of state, as well as by the ecclesiastical authorities, it was to be through ducal prayer and action, transmitted through the intercession of Mark, that Venice was to receive divine protection and favours. It is significant that, on its arrival in the city, Mark's body had been immediately placed in a specially constructed chapel 'in a secluded part of the palace' ('in palatii angulo'), or, to be more precise, 'in the upper room which is still visible today in the Doge's Palace' ('in cenaculi loco qui apud eius [ducis] palatium usque ad presens tempus monstratur'). Close physical proximity strengthened the bonds linking doge and evangelist, increasing the authority of the former in the process. It was only some eight years later, about 836, that Mark's relics were transferred to the first church of San Marco. Through this manoeuvre the episcopal seat of Grado was deprived of the possibility of acquiring a new and prestigious patron saint, and the Venet-

13   *The Reception of St. Mark's Relics*, mosaic, late 13th century. San Marco, Porta Sant'Alipio, west façade.

ian state, as represented by the doge, was the beneficiary. The importance of the doge in the early history of the Venetian cult of Mark is also underlined not only by the fact that Partecipazio had officially welcomed the relics, instead of condemning the two merchants for conspiring to despoil a Christian tomb, but also by the miracle that occurred almost immediately after the body had been carried into the Doge's Palace. As it was being taken up the staircase to the *piano nobile*, it miraculously became almost weightless, to the amazement of the bearers.[95] The association of Mark with the doge was expressed through ritual from an early date. From the time of Doge Domenico Selvo (1071–84), when the still unfinished church of San Marco replaced the cathedral of San Pietro di Castello as the home of ducal elections and coronations, the newly elected doge was invested with the *vexillum Sancti Marci* at the high altar of the ducal basilica. The custody of Mark's relics not only validated the transfer of ecclesiastical authority from Aquileia to the Venetian patriarchate of Grado, it also provided the basis for the doge's temporal power.[96]

The *translatio* is treated for the third time in the narrative decoration of the basilica in the thirteenth-century mosaics on the west façade, where the episode of the *Reception of Mark's Relics* occupies the lunette above the Porta Sant'Alipio, the only part of the scheme to survive (pl. 13). Some impression of how the façade looked at the end of the fifteenth century can be gained from Gentile Bellini's *Procession in the Piazza San Marco* of 1496 (see pl. 9),[97] and comparison of Bellini's depiction of the Porta Sant'Alipio lunette with the surviving mosaic shows a high degree of agreement, even if a certain amount of simplification has taken place.[98] Read from right to left, the various episodes that make up the *translatio*, including the most recent addition, the *praedestinatio*, have now been expanded from the seven scenes shown in the Cappella di San Clemente cycle to thirteen, a process in which the transferral of Mark's relics to Venice is given much greater prominence than in the earlier narratives. The content of the original cycle, as it can be deduced from Bellini's painting, is confirmed by the description of them in a later edition of Francesco Sansovino's *Venetia città nobilissima* (effectively the first guidebook to the city and its monuments), written by a canon of San Marco, Giovanni Stringa, when the originals were all still in place, and to a lesser extent by their present replacements, which were executed between the seventeenth and nineteenth centuries.[99] Immediately to the left of the central doorway, whose *sopraporta* is decorated with scenes of the *Last Judgement*, the next lunette in the sequence shows the relics being carried in solemn procession accompanied, as in the San Clemente mosaic of the *Reception of Mark's Relics*, by the patriarch of Grado and the bishops under his jurisdiction. Their point of arrival, a single-domed building shown on the left side of the vault in Bellini's painting, has been taken to be an image of the first church of San Marco,[100] which would make this scene in the lunette of the Porta Sant'Alipio the *collocatio* of 828–9.

It functions as the climax of the entire façade cycle. Here the richly dressed body of the saint, displayed in an open *arca*, is being carried through the main door of the church by the patriarch of Grado, identified by his *pallium*, and by another cleric who is conceivably the *primicerio* of San Marco. To the left a crowd of men, women and children acclaim the arrival of Mark's body, while to the right the doge, dressed in full regalia, joins in the welcome. Neither in terms of its action nor of its participants does this conform to traditional accounts of the *translatio*. On the contrary, the lunette mosaic above the Porta Sant'Alipio expands the reception of Mark's relics from a simple welcome to a formal ceremony, in which the principal representatives of church and state are present in a magisterial gathering of more than forty-six people, including state officials, clerics and people. In this sense it is obviously inspired by the *Reception of Mark's Relics* mosaic in the Cappella di San Clemente, whose formulation of the Venetian polity as 'Pontifices, clerus, populus, dux' it clearly echoes. Read in conjunction with the previous mosaic in the façade cycle, which, according to Bellini's *Procession*, originally showed the more traditional reception of Mark's body by a smaller gathering including the six bishops of Venetia (as in the San Clemente cycle), the Porta Sant'Alipio mosaic presents the arrival of Mark's body as a triumphal appropriation of his relics by the *commune veneciarum*. The basilica itself is shown in its thirteenth-century form, with its domes completed, marble cladding added and the four horses in position. It has been plausibly suggested that the occasion shown in the lunette of the Porta Sant'Alipio is not the ninth-century *collocatio*, as is often claimed, but the later one that took place during the dedication of the Contarini church in 1094.[101] As such, it provides a pendant to the third and final stage in the evolution of the Marcian legends.

The critical junctures in the development of the Venetian cult of Mark, when important episodes in the complex of legends surrounding him were elaborated, coincide with historically significant moments in the evolution and consolidation of the Venetian state. The story of the *translatio* itself is a clear example, and so too is the rediscovery of the saint's relics (the *apparitio*) that allegedly took place in 1094, and which has been aptly described as a 'state miracle'.[102] As has been recognized by historians for some time, both these important hagiographical moments inaugurate new historical phases in the evolution of the Republic.[103] The earliest literary sources of the *apparitio* date from the thirteenth century. One, Canal's chronicle, states that Doge Ranieri Zen 'renewed' the feast on 25 June, suggesting that it had existed earlier but had fallen into disuse. Canal, a Venetian who probably worked in the ducal curia, was an uncritical recorder whose work may even have been overseen; his view is the official one.[104] Since neither the anonymous monk who wrote the *Translatio Sancti Nicolai* (the earliest source of the *collocatio*) shortly after 1100[105] nor any of the twelfth-century chroniclers make any mention of the episode, the *apparitio* looks suspiciously like yet another late thirteenth-century fabrication along with the *praedestinatio*.[106] Its earliest appearances in the basilica's liturgical books are as early fourteenth-century (or slightly earlier) additions to a *Leggendario* and an antiphoner.[107]

The essential features of the legend itself are simple. In the confusion that followed the destruction of the second church by fire in 976, during the popular revolt against Doge Pietro Candiano iv, all traces of the saint's remains, which for reasons of safety were a closely guarded secret known to only a few, were lost. This detail of the legend may well reflect some kind of historical reality. The theft of sacred relics was widespread in the early middle ages, and it is likely that the precise location of Mark's body was transmitted from one doge to the next, perhaps through an intermediary such as the *primicerio* or one of the procurators. Notwithstanding the devastating loss of the saint's relics, the building of this third church continued and was well advanced by the dogeship of Vitale Falier, when it was finally completed.[108] After a number of searches to identify the place where Mark's remains had been preserved had failed, Falier ordered three days of fasting and prayer on the part of the entire city. As a direct consequence of this early example of the doge's role as official intercessor on behalf of Venice and its citizens, the saint's relics were miraculously disclosed when a pillar opened to reveal the sarcophagus where Mark's body had been placed. Following conventional practice, the *inventio* was turned into an *apparitio* by a sequence of miracles and signs. At the moment of rediscovery a rich perfume filled the air, while two later events in which a possessed woman was exorcized and a ship saved from certain shipwreck are also recorded.[109] Significantly, these episodes, necessary for the validation and authentication of the relics, are absent from the earliest version, suggesting that they were a later addition to the story as it evolved. These miraculous happenings took place during the five-month period that the body remained on display in the basilica following the *inventio*; their practical consequence was to close the tripartite cycle of *passio–translatio–inventio*. This structure articulated many of the later tellings of the story, through which Venetians of the sixteenth and seventeenth centuries became familiar with Mark and his miracles.[110] They also generated a rich iconographical harvest in the south transept, where two mosaic panels show communal prayers being led by the doge and the clergy, and the discovery of the body in the presence of the *commune veneciarum* (pl. 14). As an image of Venetian society in all its constituent parts – doge, clergy and people – the latter is a prototype of the same concept depicted in the mosaics of the Porta Sant'Alipio some twenty years

14   *The Miracle of the Apparitio*, mosaic, late 13th century. San Marco, south transept, west wall.

later.[111] As a pendant to the *translatio*, the *apparitio* also served to renew Mark's tomb as the site of civic authority as well as sacred power.[112]

It is typical of the process by which the memory of Mark was constantly rewritten by the Venetians to accommodate new political realities that the place where the *apparitio* took place became the focal point for liturgical practices. The right-hand pier of the choir, known as the 'pilastro del miracolo', marks the spot where it is said to have occurred; it has been described as the 'fulcrum' of the basilica, the symbolic 'omphalon' of the *commune veneciarum*.[113] Significantly, it also stands close to the *pulpitum magnum* from which every new doge was presented to the people, and marks an important juncture on the processional route from the Doge's Palace to the doge's throne via the Porta Media. This area of the basilica, where the doge sat and from where he could participate in religious rituals as the 'verus gubernator et patronus ecclesiae Sancti Marci' ('the governor and protector of the church of St Mark'), was common both to Mark (as the site of the *apparitio*) and to the sacral and intercessionary duties of the principal guardian of his relics, the doge.[114] Long after the saint's remains had been removed, this reliquary-column continued to be a focal point for rituals and even for miracles through which the Venetians continued to record and reinvent their relationship to their prime protector.[115] Of all the rituals that took place at the column, only one was interwoven into the basilica's liturgy; this took place during the *Visitatio Sepulchri* ceremonies on Good Friday, when the doge processed to a temporary sepulchre and symbolically sealed the Host within it. Although various locations have been proposed for this structure at different times in the long history of the ceremony, it seems most likely that in the early middle ages it was placed close to the 'pilastro del miracolo', a conclusion that is supported by the fragmentary mosaic, still attached to the pillar, that, together with a complementary panel now detached, forms a scene showing the *Deposition of Christ*.[116] Contrary to previous opinion, it has recently been shown that this mosaic is not a remnant of a Middle Byzantine cycle executed in the tenth century and later concealed from view, but rather a twelfth-century work. As such, it too was part of the extensive *renovatio* of the interior of San Marco that began shortly after the consecration of the building (which took place in the same year as the *apparitio*), in the course of which the walls were lined with marble. If the *translatio* was the determining moment in the delineation of the foundation myth of the Republic, the *apparitio* inaugurated a new phase of self-confidence.[117]

The final phase of the Marcian legends is, like the *translatio* and the *inventio* with its pendant *apparitio*, entirely Venetian in both setting and significance. Probably of fourteenth-century origin, this final instalment of the legends surrounding Mark functioned as a simple allegory of the continuing protection of the city by its holy patrons.[118] The story runs as follows. On 25 February 1341 a heavy storm caused the waters of the lagoon to rise dramatically, threatening to flood the entire city. A poor fisherman, who had taken refuge under the Ponte della Paglia with his boat and tackle, was unexpectedly hailed by a complete stranger who ordered him to row across to the island of San Giorgio Maggiore. Paying no attention to the fisherman's protests about the adverse conditions, the stranger insisted on making the crossing. There they were joined by a second mysterious passenger, and this time the fisherman was commanded to row even further out into the lagoon in the direction of the Lido, despite the poor weather. Once they had arrived at the island of San Nicolò a third stranger boarded, and all three gave instructions to head for the open sea. At the mouth of the lagoon they came across a ship full of demons, who were responsible for causing the storm. The three strangers, now revealed as Sts Mark, George and Nicholas (hence the articulation of the journey into three places, each of which was identified with one of the saints through the possession of relics), exorcized the ship, destroying both the demons and their vessel. With the waters now calmed, St Mark gave his ring to the fisherman as proof of the miracle, with instructions to present it to the doge during a meeting of the Council of Ten (the executive council for secret affairs and state security) on the following day.[119] Once this had been done, the ring was placed along with other ritual objects associated with the evangelist in the treasury of San Marco.[120] Its presence there completed the act of Venetian appropriation of the saint inaugurated by the *translatio*, and conferred upon the state a symbol of ecclesiastical jurisdiction. Communal identification with Mark was annually renewed on the feast-day of the *apparitio* on 25 June, when a second ring, allegedly removed from Mark's hand at the *apparitio* and acquired by the Scuola Grande di San Marco from the Dolfin family who had sold it to them for 100 ducats, was carried in procession.[121] Writing in the 1530s, the diarist and senator Marin Sanudo noted that the manuscript of the Gospels believed to have been written by Mark himself, another prized relic from the treasury, was also displayed on this occasion.[122]

The appearance of the military saint, George, and the patron saint of sailors, Nicholas, in the legend of the fisherman and the ring completes the traditional triumvirate of Venetian saintly protectors, fusing control of the seas with military might under the overall guidance and protection of Mark. Venetian devotion to St George, already evident from his presence in the thirteenth-century mosaics in San Marco, and as one of the trio of patron saints in the fourteenth-century legend of the fisherman and the ring, was further strengthened in the fifteenth century by the acquisition of the island of Aegina, and with it the legendary relic of St George's head. In 1462 this was retrieved and sent to Venice, where it was placed, appropriately enough, in the church of the Benedictine monastery dedicated to him, on the island of San Giorgio Maggiore. This added to an already considerable presence of his relics in the city, which included the Byzantine reliquary containing the saint's arm in the treasury of San Marco, one of the most prized relics in the collection, which had been brought back to Venice after the conquest of Constantinople.[123] (The treasury also contains a relic of the leg of St George, brought to Venice by Christian immigrants from Scutari at the end of the fifteenth century.)[124] It was during the late fifteenth century that the Scuola di San Giorgio degli Schiavoni was founded by some two hundred immigrants from Dalmatia, with Sts George and Tryphon (patron of the town of Cattaro) and later St Jerome as patron saints. Much involved with sponsoring naval expeditions against the Turks, the Scuola had become sufficiently wealthy by the early years of the sixteenth century to be able to build a new meeting-house in the *sestiere* of Castello. Among the nine (or perhaps eight, since the authorship of one is in doubt) canvases that Carpaccio painted for the new building, all of which are still in place, three show episodes from the *Life of St George* (pl. 15).[125]

Possession of the remains of St Nicholas was less easily secured, since their authenticity was fiercely contested between the citizens of Bari, who claimed to have removed them from Myrna in 1087, and the Venetians, who allegedly rescued them during a raid in the twelfth century. Venetian acquisition of the relics is commemorated in an inscription in the mosaics of the apse in San Marco. As the patron saint of mariners, Nicholas was of considerable importance for any seagoing community, and the competition between Bari and Venice for his relics has been interpreted as a battle over trade routes and shipping.[126] Even though San Marco did not then possess a relic of the saint, the new arrival was allocated to the existing Benedictine monastery of San Nicolò al Lido.[127] It is entirely typical of the literature generated by such disputes that

15   Vittore Carpaccio, *St. George Fighting the Dragon*, 1504–7. Scuola di San Giorgio degli Schiavoni.

one of the early accounts of these events, the *Historia de translatione sanctorum magni Nicolai*, is an attempt to belittle the claims of Bari and to assert the authenticity of the relics brought to Venice. Having achieved military and political hegemony in both the Adriatic and the Mediterranean, the Venetians were hardly likely to relinquish religious domination of those seas, symbolized through their possession of Nicholas's relics.[128] The considerable geo-political significance of their arrival partly explains the importance of San Nicolò al Lido as a site of official rituals in the middle ages and later.

Constructed in the eleventh century at the wish of Doge Domenico Contarini, the first church on the Lido was of considerable importance in the ceremonial life of the city.[129] It was there that ducal elections and investitures took place before they were transferred to San Marco, and there too that the annual *benedictio*, which later grew into the Ascension Day ritual of the marriage of the sea, was staged from the eleventh century onwards. The climax of this ceremony occurred when the doge married Venice to the Adriatic, as a sign of dominion, by casting a ring into the waters.[130] San Nicolò's role as a geographical marker, both symbolic and real, fixing the borders of Venice in a way analogous to the function of walls in a land-locked city, defined its public role in the later period.[131] Despite the church's diminished importance once the ceremonial and political centre of Venice had been transferred to San Marco, St Nicholas continued to be venerated by the Venetians as a major protector of the city and its empire. If Mark represented the foundation of Venice, Nicholas was the symbol of its maritime history, a duality that has been broadly compared to the roles of patriarch and doge, the highest-ranking figures in the ecclesiastical and political hierarchies.[132] It has been suggested that St Nicholas was so important to the Venetians that his cult rivalled even that of St Mark.[133]

Other ritual practices emphasize the importance of Nicholas as a patron saint of the state from at least the thirteenth century, when the tradition was established of celebrating mass in the chapel of San Nicolò in the Doge's Palace. Doge Pietro Ziani had built the chapel in fulfilment of a vow made by Enrico Dandolo, who had led the Venetian assault on Constantinople in 1204, but who had died before he could return to Venice. It was Ziani who also added the stipulation that mass should be celebrated annually on the saint's feast-day (5 December) in the presence of the doge and Signoria.[134] Decorated in the fourteenth century with a narrative cycle showing scenes from the *Story of Pope Alexander III*, the 'Ecclesia Sancti Nicolai de Palatio' was destroyed in 1525.[135] A second chapel dedicated to the saint on the second floor of the east wing of the Doge's Palace was used by the doge as a place of private prayer. Burnt down in the late fifteenth century, it was reconstructed between 1505 and 1523 with walls frescoed by Titian, and contained an altar incorporating a marble relief showing Andrea Gritti, during whose dogeship the work was completed.[136] It was presumably in this chapel that the annual mass in the doge's presence continued to be celebrated.[137] The strong connections between the office of doge and official devotion to St Nicholas emphasize the political aspects of his cult as protector and patron of Venetian sea power, a feature already present in Ziani's original chapel, which, significantly, also served to commemorate Dandolo as the hero of one of the greatest of all Venetian naval and military exploits.

The prominent position of George and Nicholas in the pantheon of Venetian saints was maintained in the sixteenth century through ceremony, ritual and liturgy. At an official level the feast of St George was celebrated as a major feast, which involved polyphony sung by the choir at both first and second vespers as well as at high mass; the doge was present and there was also a ducal procession, which transported the entire ceremonial machine across the lagoon to the island of San Giorgio, where mass with double-choir polyphony was sung in the Benedictine church of San Giorgio Maggiore.[138] The importance of San Giorgio in the ritual life of the city was further amplified on Christmas Day, which is also the Vigil of St Stephen, when the doge went to the church to hear vespers chanted by the monks, and participated by symbolically holding a lit candle during the singing of the Magnificat (pl. 16).[139] On the feast-day of St Stephen, whose relics were among the monastery's most treasured possessions, he returned with half of the musicians from the *cappella marciana* for a sung mass.[140] This degree of elaboration was comparatively rare and underlines the importance of the occasion; only nine other major feasts were treated in this way in the period.[141] Although there was no procession in the Piazza San Marco on the feast of St Nicholas, something quite distinctive occurred, since, while first and second vespers were celebrated with music in the basilica, the principal mass of the day took place at the church of San Nicolò al Lido, again with polyphony.[142] By the sixteenth century this short pilgrimage across the lagoon served to renew contact with the saint's remains, as well as evoking resonances of the feast of the Ascension, when mass was again celebrated in the church.

16 Giacomo Franco, *Andata* to S. Giorgio
Maggiore on Christmas Day, engraving. Venice,
Museo Civico Correr.

Although the legend of the fisherman
and the ring is not part of the *passio–translatio–inventio* sequence (which was effectively brought to a close with the *apparitio*),
but rather a late supplement to the corpus
of Marcian legends, it continued to have
considerable popular appeal during the late
fifteenth and sixteenth centuries. Both
Sanudo and the historian Marc'Antonio
Sabellico rehearse the main features of the
legend,[143] and when the Scuola Grande di
San Marco came to decorate the *albergo* of
their new premises in the Campo Santi
Giovanni e Paolo, two of the seven canvases
commissioned for the room took aspects of
the story as their subject matter. Constructed in the years immediately following
1485, after the previous building had been
destroyed by fire, the decoration of the
albergo was carried out over some decades
beginning in 1492, when Gentile and Giovanni Bellini proposed to carry out the
entire scheme.[144] Although the paintings
that decorated the *albergo* are now dispersed, their original disposition in the
room can be reconstructed, with pride of
place being given to two pictures by the Bellini on the long walls.[145] Of the two
canvases added later showing episodes from the story of the fisherman and the
ring, the first to be completed, *St Mark Saving Venice from the Ship of Demons*
(pl. 17), was begun by Palma il Vecchio and finished by Paris Bordone,[146] who
went on to paint the final picture in the sequence, *The Fisherman Delivering
the Ring* (see pl. 4). Set in a theatrical architectural fantasy, it shows the doge
seated on a dais surrounded by the Council of Ten, while the fisherman, half-
kneeling, stretches out his hand to offer the evangelist's ring. Some of the
bystanders are to be identified as members of the Scuola, while other anecdo-
tal references are to scenes from everyday life.[147]

This choice of subject matter is unusual in the context of a cycle of *istorie*,
which otherwise is iconographically entirely conventional in its presentation of
episodes from Mark's life. Beginning with *St Mark Preaching in Alexandria*
(Milan, Brera), begun by Gentile Bellini and finished by his brother Giovanni,
the sequence then continues with the latter's *Martyrdom of St Mark* (*in situ*),
and then three canvases by Giovanni Mansueti, who was then a member of the
Scuola. At this juncture the cycle would normally have been brought to a close.

17   Palma Il Vecchio and Paris Bordon, *Saint Mark saving Venice from the Ship of Demons*, 1527–8. Venice, Gallerie dell'Accademia.

It has been suggested that the insertion of Palma Il Vecchio's *St Mark Saving Venice* at this point in the cycle was planned about 1513 as an allegory of Venice's survival of the war of the League of Cambrai.[148] Certainly, the spectacular defeat of the Republic's forces at Agnadello in the summer of 1509 was traumatic, and its impact upon the self-esteem of the patrician class considerable,[149] but a more likely explanation of both Palma's painting, and of Bordone's pendant to it, is that they proudly reflect the Scuola's possession of one of the evangelist's rings, even if not the one that actually commemorated the event (such historical confusions seem not to have bothered sixteenth-century Venetians). The Dolfin ring had been acquired within recent memory, in 1509, just nine years after the *guardian grande* of the Scuola, accompanied by its *scrivan* and a notary, had copied out an account of the legend from chancery documents.[150] By commemorating the story in the final two paintings of the *albergo* cycle, the Scuola Grande di San Marco was actively competing with the Scuola Grande di San Giovanni Evangelista, whose possession of the relic of the True Cross is famously memorialized in Gentile Bellini's *Procession in the Piazza San Marco*.[151] Competition and a sense of rivalry between the confraternities was often the spur to new building projects and decorative schemes (as well as to the acquisition of relics), and Gentile Bellini's contract for *St Mark Preaching in Alexan-*

18   Giovanni Bellini, *St. Mark Preaching in Alexandria*, 1504–7. Milan, Pinacoteca di Brera.

dria (pl. 18) quite specifically mentions that it must be as admirable as his earlier painting for the Scuola Grande di San Giovanni Evangelista.[152] Similarities in the pictorial composition of the two canvases suggest that the *Procession* might well have served as Bellini's model, heightening the sense of competition between the *scuole*.[153]

Devotion to Mark was not uniquely or uniformly practised throughout Venetian society, and devotional allegiances were shaped as much by local loyalties of class, parish and occupation as by attachment to the patrician vision of the Republic that he came to represent. In this sense Mark may have been the official patron of doges and the government, but Nicholas had an equally strong following among those who worked at sea, and particularly among the inhabitants of the *sestiere* of San Nicolò, known as the *nicolotti*. Rivalry with the *arsenalotti*, who lived in the area around the Arsenal, and mostly worked in the dockyards and associated industries such as rope-making, was fierce. Famously, it found expression in the annual 'War of the Fists', when teams from the two districts, armed with pointed canes, fought for possession of the Ponte San Barnaba.[154] One consequence of this ritualized violence was to cement a sense of local identity, based on a complex of geographical, devotional and occupational elements, even more firmly into place.

St Mark was the patron saint of Venice, but he was not its only protector. Through her long-standing association with the foundation and early history of the city itself, the Virgin Mary also played an important role in Venetian state theology.[155] In the rhetoric of this central aspect of Venetian official historiography, the city was presented as a pure, uncorrupted virgin state, unwalled and yet unconquered for more than a thousand years, a city unviolated by outside forces.[156] In this way, Marian devotion and the designation of Venice as a special protectorate of the Virgin completed the notion of uniqueness and perfection that lies at the heart of the 'Myth of Venice', and which had been so eloquently delineated by Petrarch in his famous description of the city as 'the one home today of liberty, peace and justice, the one refuge of honourable men, the one port to which can repair the storm-tossed, tyrant-hounded craft of men who seek the good life'.[157] Since, according to legend, Venice had been founded on the feast of the Annunciation, the *Origo Venetiarum*, the city also assumed the attributes of the Virgin, in particular her purity and immortality. Combined with the historical reality that, unlike most other Italian states, Venice had not been invaded by foreigners, not even during the summer of 1513 when the whole of the *terraferma* was occupied and Mestre set on fire,[158] the association produced a visualization of the Pax Venetiana that relied upon the resonances of Marian iconography. It is in this guise that *Venetia* appears on the façade of the Doge's Palace, where, in the 1340s, work was begun on the Sala del Maggior Consiglio, the great council chamber of

19   Filippo Calendario (?), *Venecia*, c.1345. Ducal Palace, west façade.

the Venetian government in its reformed condition after the *serrata* (closure) of 1297, which had been intended to weld the patrician class into an effective and self-contained instrument of government. On the façade *Venetia* appears as a modified figure of Justice, holding scales and sword and seated upon a Solomonic throne of lions (pl. 19). The scroll in her left hand reads 'Fortis / Iusta / Trono / Furias / Mare / Sub Pede / Pono' ('Enthroned just and strong, I defeat the furies by sea'). By conflating the image of the Virgin enthroned with the common personification of Justice, a new civic image was created that made specific reference to Venetian domination of the seas.[159] The allegorical personification of Venice as a woman addresses the requirement of representing the Republic in the absence of sovereigns and dynasties; it also highlights a contradiction of the Venetian system in which women, in contrast to their position in contemporary court society, had no political role.

Devotion to the Virgin herself, previously present largely through Byzantine traditions, seems to have increased and taken on new forms at about the same time, as in the lunette of the tomb of Doge Francesco Dandolo (1329–39), in the Franciscan church of the Frari, which shows Mary as the Queen of Heaven.

It has been suggested that Franciscan devotion to the cult of the Virgin may have provided an important stimulus to this development, which also provided numerous progeny in which the figure of the Virgin Triumphant is identified as the protectress of Venice.[160] An early version of this theme occurs in Guariento's *Coronation of the Virgin*, the central moment of the *Paradise* fresco that originally decorated the tribune wall of the Sala del Maggior Consiglio. The political message of the scene, painted for the principal debating hall of the Republic, is made explicit through the large number of attendant figures, while the presence of the Virgin together with the Archangel Gabriel recall once again the legend of the foundation of the city on 25 March 421.[161] Commissioned by Doge Marco Cornaro and painted shortly after 1365, Guariento's *Coronation* was severely damaged in the fire that devastated the Doge's Palace in 1577. The task of replacing it was originally assigned to Paolo Veronese, but work was never begun, and after the artist's death the commission was given to Tintoretto, whose vast *Paradise* canvas was executed between the years 1588 and 1592.[162]

Once established, the twin images of Venetia / Justice, with its thinly disguised evocation of the Virgin, became a prominent feature of Venetian state iconography. Having made an early appearance, holding a sword but without scales in the mid-fourteenth-century roundel on the façade of the Doge's Palace, the visualization of this central concept produced a series of offspring. In the guise of a crowned female figure holding sword and scales and seated upon a throne of lions, it reappears in a number of later official commissions, including the central panel of Jacobello del Fiore's triptych *Justice with the Archangels Michael and Gabriel*, painted for the Magistrato del Proprio in 1421 (pl. 21), and the statue, sculpted by the Bon workshop, placed on top of the Porta della Carta twenty years later (pl. 20).[163] Sixteenth-century examples of the official use of the image culminate in the new ceiling of the Sala del Maggior Consiglio commissioned after the fire of 1577 with, as its climax, Veronese's *Apotheosis of Venice (Pax Veneta)*. This overtly political image of Venetia could be merged quite conveniently with another, iconographically more immediate one, that of Venice as

20 Bartolomeo Bon the elder, *Justice*, 1441. Ducal Palace, Porta della Carta.

21   Jacobello del Fiore, *Justice with the Archangels Michael and Gabriel*, *c*.1421. Venice, Gallerie dell'Accademia.

Queen of the Adriatic. A number of painted versions of this subject also survive, of which the best known, a collaboration between Jacopo and Domenico Tintoretto, occurs in the central compartment of the ceiling of the Sala del Senato, divided into three registers (pl. 22).[164] At the centre of the first is a crowned female personification of Venice seated on a circle of clouds surrounded by a number of gods including Apollo, Mercury, Saturn, Jupiter and Hercules. The middle zone shows a group of ten men; said to be the codifiers of the law,[165] they could well constitute a symbolic reference to the Council of Ten. At the bottom of the scene, grouped around the figures of Neptune and Mars, Nereids and Tritons bring the fruits of wise, judicial administration. Iconographically less complicated, but similarly related to the theme of the Pax Venetiana, is Domenico Tintoretto's canvas in which a female personification of Venice, Queen of the Adriatic, regally and vividly dressed in yellow, gold and red, bestows a crown of olive leaves (to represent peace) upon the Lion of St Mark. In the background can be seen the lagoon (pl. 23). At a more personal level, the image of Venice, seated on a lion, holding the scales in one hand and a cornucopia in the other, with galleys to the left and arms to the right, appears on a medal by Andrea Spinelli issued to mark the election of Doge Pietro Lando in 1539 (pl. 24).[166] The reverse bears the label ADRIACI REGINA-MARIS (a similar design with the simple label VENET[IA] appears on an earlier medal for Doge Andrea Gritti), the obverse the legend CONCORDIA PARVAE RES CRESCVNT: Justice, peace and prosperity are secured by Venetian dominion in the Adriatic.[167]

Venice was hardly the only Italian state devoted to the Virgin (the case of Siena, 'City of the Virgin', immediately comes to mind),[168] but there Marian veneration was distinguished by a particularly complex and distinctive mixture of sacred and civic conceptions. In the background was the example of Constantinople in its guise of the New Jerusalem, the tabernacle of God, whose

22 Jacopo and Domenico Tintoretto, *The Triumph of Venice as Queen of the Seas*, 1588–90. Ducal Palace, Sala del Senato.

mistress was the Queen of Heaven.[169] The centrality of the Virgin in the iconography of Constantinople after the Council of Ephesus of 431, as reflected in icons, relics and sanctuaries, is mirrored in Venetian experience, particularly after the Fourth Crusade, when sacred objects such as the icon of the *Madonna Nicopeia* were removed to Venice. Sixteenth-century *madonnieri*, the small icons of the Virgin painted in the Byzantine style that were commonly found in Venetian houses, are a reminder of this historical continuity of function and meaning. By the sixteenth century, the doge attended mass at San Marco on all the major feast-days of the Virgin, and the Venetians celebrated both the Annunciation and the Assumption as great civic celebrations of the Republic. In all, a third of the major Marian feasts in the Venetian calendar had by then acquired civic connotations.

By this time the annual blessing of the Adriatic on the feast of the Ascension had grown into a complex ritual in which Venice was symbolically remarried to the sea through a fixed ritual of considerable elaboration.[170] This too carried Marian overtones through the proximity of the images of Venice herself, Venice as Queen of the Adriatic (and its more ambitious variant, Venice, Queen of the Seas) and the Virgin. Comparison of these three common figures as they appear on coins and in

23 Domenico Tintoretto, *Venice, Queen of the Adriatic*, late 16th century. Dublin, National Gallery of Ireland.

paintings emphasizes the point. A *benedictio* of the Adriatic probably dates from about 1000, when the bishop of Olivolo, accompanied by the doge, annually blessed the waters of the lagoon in thanksgiving for Doge Pietro II Orseolo's successful expedition to subjugate the Slavs. By 1267, when the ceremony was

24 Andrea Spinelli, medal to celebrate the election of Doge Pietro Lando, 1539.

25 Bartolomeo Bon the elder, *Madonna della Misericordia*, *c.*1460. London, Victoria and Albert Museum.

described by Canal, a *desponsatio* had been added to the ceremony, to create a ritual that is recognizable as the prototype of the *sensa* (or marriage of the sea) as it is described in later sources.[171] The central feature of the sixteenth-century version was the blessing of the doge with an olive branch by the patriarch, followed by the marriage ceremony itself, in which the doge dropped a ring overboard with the words 'We marry thee as a sign of true and perpetual dominion.'[172] By this date the choir of San Marco was usually present and a motet was sung.[173] While on the one hand the message of the *sensa* was political and imperial, proclaiming Venetian dominion over the seas, on the other it invoked a complex of images centred on the Virgin-Venetia motif, and in the process 'deprived the sea of its frightening demeanor by feminizing it'.[174]

In addition to being constantly reminded of the local resonances of the cult of the Virgin through the annual liturgical cycle, the inhabitants of the city were everywhere confronted by Marian images (pl. 25). On the façade of San Marco itself, that most politically charged of all Venetian churches, thirteenth century Veneto–Byzantine reliefs of the *Virgin* and the *Archangel Gabriel* are accompanied by other protectors of the city, including not only *St George* and *St Demetrius*, but also *Hercules*, the mythical tribal hero of the Venetii, who is represented twice. At Rialto, the other pole of official Venice and the alleged site of the first settlement, the *Annunciation* appears on the façade of the stone bridge across the Grand Canal, built by Antonio da Ponte in 1588–92 to replace the previous wooden bridge (pl. 26).[175] At a more general level, the figure of the Virgin as protectress occurs in dozens of canvases executed for Venetian churches and other buildings in the course of the Renaissance. Venerated in shrines in *calle* and *campo*, and commemorated as protectress in stone reliefs and statues, the Virgin was a constant presence. At the Arsenal, the shrine of the Beata Madonna dell'Arsenale, built in the early sixteenth century to contain a miraculous image of the Virgin, was the shipyard's spiritual centre, and a focal point for the devotional lives of the many *arsenalotti* who habitually prayed there.[176] Much further north, in the Campo San Tomà, the tympanum of the meeting-hall of the Scuola dei Calegheri (the shoemakers' guild) is decorated with a relief showing *St Mark*

26 Agostino Rubini, *Archangel Gabriel* and *Virgin Annunciate*, late 16th century. Rialto Bridge.

Healing Anianus, Mark's first convert in Alexandria, who was himself a cobbler,[177] while higher up the façade is a much larger relief of the *Madonna della Misericordia* (pl. 27), and a similar scene is depicted on another sculptured tablet set into the wall of the nearby church. It was through such means that the presence of heavenly protectors was intertwined with the daily activities of ordinary Venetians as they went about their business in the workplace, the street and the guildhall. For citizens of all social classes, the comforting image of the Virgin carried a precise political and civic message that was intimately connected to the origins, evolution and future of the Republic, placed under the protection of Mark, and guided with wisdom by his representative on earth. This duality is neatly expressed in the text of the motet 'O Rex gloriae qui beatum Marcum', set to music by the Venetian composer Giovanni Bassano, who worked in San Marco.[178] Here the opening words are a modification of the *Oratio di San Marco*, 'Deus qui beatum Marcum', frequently set by composers connected with the basilica, and sung on a number of liturgico-civic occasions, including the votive service that followed the election of a doge or procurator, and the installation of a new captain-general of the Venetian armed forces. Thereafter, Bassano's motet takes up the liturgy for Ascension Day:

> O king of glory, who honoured
> your evangelist blessed Mark
> thanks to his preaching of the gospel.
> Alleluia.
> Bring it about that we to whom he appeared on earth
> deserve to see him in heaven, rejoicing.
> Alleluia.

By the sixteenth century, a number of separate legends had been developed by the Venetians to explain the origins of their city.[179] According to one, elegantly articulated in the fifteenth century by Sabellico, the original settlers of the

27 Scuola dei Calegheri, façade.

lagoon had come from Gaul. An alternative theory, widely disseminated in the Renaissance despite being equally without historical foundation, claimed that the first inhabitants of *rivum altum* were Trojans, who had escaped to Italy after the destruction of Troy. The first serious attempt to write an account of the earliest phase of Venetian history, Bernardo Giustiniani's *De origine urbis Venetiarum*,[180] published posthumously in 1493, opens with a discussion of the question of Venetian origins that ingeniously attempts to unite both versions: 'And indeed, both opinions are supported by great authors . . . I do not see what prohibits both from being combined into one.' While the Gallic explanation encouraged Venetian friendship with the French, the Trojan story was also attractive since it prefigured the notion of Venetian *libertas* through the image of a people that famously had never been servile, had never paid tribute.[181] In the late thirteenth-century chronicle of Martin da Canal, it is stated that the Trojans built a number of cities in the upper Adriatic, including both Aquileia and Venice;[182] in practice, this was an extension of the claim in the *Aeneid* that Padua was a Trojan foundation. This led in turn to the popular myth that Venice had been settled by refugees from Attila the Hun, including a contingent of aristocrats from Padua. Jacopo Dondi, a fourteenth-century Paduan physician, elaborates in his chronicle the further gloss (already present in Martin da Canal's account) that this contingent arrived at about noon on 25 March 421, thus conveniently conflating the foundation of the city with the established Venetian practice of marking the start of the year on the feast of the Annunciation. Later historians and chroniclers, including Sabellico, Sanudo and Sansovino, all accepted the date as official.[183]

So too did Bernardo Giustiniani, who, sometime after completing his history, added three brief pieces dealing with the life of St Mark, explaining the connection in the following terms:

> When I had determined to write about the origin of the city of Venice, I remember that I mentioned in the beginning of the work that nothing had happened in the founding of Venice which was usual in the establishment of other cities; neither walls, nor gates, nor even fortresses were constructed. Then it occurred to me that a few years after the transference of the Doge-

ship, the most holy Mark, the Evangelist, was carried off by Venetian merchants from the city of Alexandria, where he had lain for nearly eight hundred years, and he was brought to Venice. Therefore I considered it neither irrelevant to our subject nor beside the point to add also this to those matters which I have so far set forth. I decided to record in what way he, almost as a founder, and certainly as a noble protector, came to this new city, by whose vigilance and patronage it was finally rendered unconquerable and impregnable.[184]

While clearly separating the political and religious strands in his account of the foundation of Venice, Giustiniani treats much of the Marcian mythology as historical truth. In the second work of his trilogy dealing with the evangelist, Bernardo returns to the story of the *translatio*, and to its sequel, the construction of the basilica of San Marco. In the final essay, 'On the Place of Burial', the proofs are assembled for the presence of the saint's remains inside the building, ending with the hope that no one could be so impervious to truth as to doubt the veracity of what he had written. All this is prefaced by a brief life of Mark, which isolates the principal biographical elements: his composition of a holy Gospel, his foundation of the church in Aquileia and Alexandria, his invention of the monastic life, and finally his martyrdom.[185] It was this story that was transmitted to Venice itself, the home of his relics, where it formed the cornerstone of its greatness, its unbroken traditions of liberty and its sacred laws, all of which were embodied in evolving rituals of church and state, which connected the changing history of the Republic from its foundation onwards to the realities of sixteenth-century ceremonial.

CHAPTER TWO

Praesentia and Identity

During the middle ages and beyond, the tombs of saints were regarded as sites of sacred power, bestowed through *praesentia*, the notion that, although in heaven, the saint was in some powerful and effective sense 'present'.[1] Such environments were never simple physical constructs, no matter how sparsely decorated, but rather the focal points of sacral authority. It was here that intercession took place and pardon was received; here that good reigned and evil was exorcized. Since the benefits of possession were great, no effort was spared to obtain relics. Initially, the church was opposed to the removal of whole bodies, let alone parts of them, but from the eighth century onwards attitudes changed under the weight of practical pressure. Thereafter, competition among Italian rulers and churchmen to acquire the most prestigious examples available, often by unscrupulous means, was intense. To obtain them monks raided churches, merchants plundered tombs and relic-hunters scoured the catacombs. Far from being considered a crime, the thefts necessary to create the extensive and lucrative market in religious relics were sanctioned by all parties to the transaction, from the pope down to the individuals and institutions that received them.[2]

Since many of the more important saints had originally been interred in Asia Minor, their transfer to European sites inaugurated a process of transferral and authentication that began with a *translatio*. The fact that this process had been completed was taken as a sign of divine benevolence, a confirmation that the community at the point of arrival had been judged fit to accommodate relics, and to become a suitable place for the saint's *praesentia* to reside. From the moment when Mark's body was received in the city, the Venetians began to deploy every resource of art, architecture, ceremony, literature and liturgy to

28. San Marco, main apse looking east.

dignify his tomb and celebrate his presence. Initially, this was a matter of advertising possession, but in the wake of the *apparitio* the range of reference was expanded to elaborate a civic myth located within universal history, and to claim a privileged role for the Venetians as the Chosen People.[3] In addition to being a site of power, conferred through intercession, the saint's tomb was also a site of memory, a place where the sacred past could be recalled and re-engaged to validate current practice. One consequence of this dynamic between past and present was that the legends that accumulated around the memory of a saint were constantly being revised to meet fresh political circumstances.[4] In the case of Venice, what had begun as an ecclesiastical matter, though hardly one shorn of political implications, gradually assumed more significant temporal dimensions. By the eleventh century, with the subjugation of Aquileia well advanced, the Venetian future was inextricably, definitively and primarily (though not exclusively) bound to Mark's patronage.

Among the ways that this special relationship was emphasized was through ceremonies such as the ducal investiture, when, in the 'presence' of the saint, immediately above his tomb, every doge (at least from the time of Sebastiano Ziani [1172–8] until the end of the Republic) received the *vexillum* and swore an oath of loyalty. More than a simple proclamation of intent, this ritual action, the central moment of the investiture ceremony, confirmed the doge's position as both a spiritual and a secular leader.[5] Within a few decades of Ziani's investiture this critical juncture in the ceremony began to appear on Venetian coins in a way that marked a radical departure from the imagery of earlier types.[6] On the obverse of the silver *grosso* issued for the first time during the dogeship of Enrico Dandolo (1192–1205), St Mark is shown presenting the standard to a standing doge, while the reverse shows Christ enthroned; this design is thought to be Byzantine in inspiration (pl. 29).[7] More specifically, the obverse follows the model of Venetian ducal seals, which are themselves derived from Byzantine prototypes, in which the doge stands next to the seated figure of St Mark.[8] Beginning in March 1285, when Giovanni Dandolo was doge, the first Venetian gold ducats were minted, competitively valued as the equivalent of the Florentine florin. This commercially combative development, of sufficient importance to merit a commemorative plaque on the external wall of the Mint, was accompanied by a new design whose basic iconography is derived from the earlier silver *grosso*. The reverse of this type presents the figure of Christ ascending, closed within a mandorla against a background of stars. The surrounding legend reads SIT.T.XRE.DAT.Q TV REGIS.ISTE.DVCAT, which expands to 'Sit tibi Christe datus Quem tu Regis iste ducatus'

29   Silver grosso of Doge Enrico Dandolo (1192–1205), obverse. London, British Museum.

('May this duchy which thou rulest be given to thee, O Christ').[9] Dandolo himself appears on the obverse, named and captioned, kneeling before St Mark (who is identified as S. M[ARCVS]. VENETI) to receive the *vexillum*. This iconography dramatically sets up a transmission of power from Christ to the doge through the agency of Mark;[10] exchanged in international trade as well as locally, the ducat explicitly proclaimed Christ as the ruler of Venice, and conveyed this message abroad (pl. 30). Incorporated into the design of such everyday objects, this potent image became the most familiar expression of the conception of divinely sanctioned authority, embodied in the person of the doge as the cornerstone of the Venetian state. It was retained on Venetian coins, virtually unchanged, until the end of the Republic.[11]

Underpinned by Mark's *praesentia*, the expression of this central idea is one of two considerations that shaped the arrangement and decoration of the central sacral area of the choir and apse of the basilica of San Marco. The needs of liturgical choreography, the more prosaic consideration of how ceremonies of all kinds were to be performed within the space, was the other. The positioning of the altar is just one of a number of significant differences between the Contarini church and its model in Constantinople. In the Apostoleion, a true centralized church with projecting arms of almost equal length (the nave is slightly longer than the other arms), the altar stood in the central square; Nicholas Mesarites' description of the church on the eve of the Fourth Crusade confirms that the sanctuary still occu-

30 Gold ducat of Doge Giovanni Dandolo, 1284. Mark hands the vexillum to the doge (obverse); Christ enthroned (reverse). London, British Museum.

pied the centre, with a free-standing semicircular stepped apse, or synthronon, behind the altar for the seats of the clergy.[12] At San Marco, on the other hand, the east end was built with a semicircular apse rather than a flat terminal wall with galleries. Together with two apsidal side chapels, this encloses the central area, the high altar being placed under the most eastern of the five domes.[13] The altar, with the crypt below that housed Mark's body, constitutes the spiritual core of this inner sanctum, whose western boundary is delineated by the iconostasis (see pl. 10). Its central significance is clearly signalled by the apse mosaics. Although some of them were restored in the early sixteenth century, it is usually assumed that the image of the *Enthroned Pantocrator* that was then put into place replaced an earlier and similar one that had been in the same position. Beneath, on the semi-cyclindrical apse wall, stand four imposing

31. San Marco, main apse looking east.

figures of saints, all of whose relics had arrived in the city by 1100: *Peter* and *Mark* in the middle, *Nicholas* and *Hermagoras* to the sides (pl. 31). Connected by gesture and pose, Peter, Mark and Hermagoras portray the political idea of the apostolic succession as the cornerstone of the foundation myth of Venice. In this context the apse mosaics are a simple affirmation of Mark's position as the apostolic founder of the Venetian church, and a visual symbol of his *praesentia*;[14] standing slightly apart, in an attitude of benediction, Nicholas takes his place as both patron of the state and of Venetian sea power.[15] The presence of these four saints, all of whose relics were prized in the Western church, proclaims the official ducal character of the sanctuary beyond its primary importance as Mark's tomb. As such, it ingeniously combines a set of religious and political ideas that form the basis of Venetian state mythology in its earliest phases. Protected by these formidable guardians, Mark's tomb lies further to the east under an elaborately carved ciborium; sometimes dated to the fifth and sixth centuries, but more generally thought to be from the eleventh, it is supported by four richly carved Corinthian columns decorated with acanthus leaves.[16] This was not the tomb's original position. Following the *translatio* the saint's body was entombed prior to being moved shortly afterwards to the new basilica built in his honour before finally being transferred to the Contarini church in 1094. The Cappella di San Clemente to the south, and its matching chapel on the north side, the Cappella di San Pietro, are iconographically related through their mosaic decoration. This is most obviously true of the two major narrative cycles showing the *Life of St Mark* and the *Translatio of Mark's Relics*, which are thematically and stylistically homogeneous.[17]

Above Mark's tomb stands the Pala d'Oro (see pl. 10). On the occasion of its second enlargement, during the years 1343–5, the enamel plaques from Doge Ordelaffo Falier's early twelfth-century altar frontal were reset, and an elaborate Gothic frame, embellished with gilded arcades and decorated with pearls and precious stones, was constructed to house the enamels, which were then remounted, presumably in their original order. It was at this juncture that seven new plaques were added to the ensemble: five small discs showing images of *Matthew*, *Mark*, *Luke*, *John* and *Christ* respectively, and two rectangular panels bearing inscriptions. One of these records the commissioning of the Pala. The other, which was inserted in place of an enamel showing the Emperor Alexius II Comnenos, states that Doge Andrea Dandolo was responsible for

52

32   Paolo Veneziano, *St. Mark Appears on the Ship
Transporting his Body*, from the *Pala feriale*, 1345. San Marco.

commissioning the new work, and that the procurators Marco Loredan and
Francesco Querini were also involved.[18] The *Pala feriale*, a painted altarpiece
that covered the Pala d'Oro when it was not exposed, and which is dated April
1345, was completed at about the same time, probably as part of the same
project, by Paolo Veneziano and his sons. Its upper registers, each of seven
panels, show the *Dead Christ* together with the *Virgin* accompanied by five
saints: *Mark, Theodore, Nicholas of Bari, John the Baptist* and *Peter*.[19] Beneath
are five scenes from the *Life of St Mark*, together with an episode from the
translatio, in which the saint appears on deck during the voyage to Venice in
order to prevent a shipwreck (pl. 32), and the *apparitio*, whose text was being
elaborated in precisely these years.[20]

   Contemporary chronicles confirm that Andrea Dandolo was the architect of
this final *renovatio* of the Pala d'Oro.[21] Since 1328, when he was elected procurator, he had played a prominent role in the running of the basilica, and when
he achieved ducal office in 1342, at the unusually young age of 36, he embarked

on an extensive remodelling of the central ritual area of the church. Historian, lawyer, author of both the *Summula* (a manual of Venetian law) and a major chronicle of Venice from its origins until 1280 (the *Chronica per extensum descripta*, written after he had been elected doge), Dandolo is best known as a friend of Petrarch, who described him as 'famous for his high office no less than for his studies of the liberal arts'.[22] An educated man, he gathered around him a small nucleus of humanists employed by the government, of whom Benintendi Ravagnani, who was Grand Chancellor during Dandolo's dogeship, was the most important.[23]

Dandolo also showed a keen interest in a number of artistic initiatives, of which the enlargement and embellishment of the Pala d'Oro and the commission for the *Pala feriale* were the most important, all of which aimed at enriching the high altar and the rituals that took place there. Along with the Pala d'Oro and many of the *spolia* that decorate the exterior of San Marco, three-quarters of the objects of Byzantine origin in the treasury had originally arrived in Venice between 1204 and 1261, during the period of French–Venetian domination of Constantinople. Since the nineteenth century moralistic historians have regarded them as ill-gotten gains, and the Venetians as ruthless and insensitive in their adaptation or reuse of ritual objects revered in the East for political purposes in the West.[24] This is to misunderstand not only medieval conceptions of legitimate war booty, but also the activities of the French and Flemish during the Fourth Crusade.[25] More to the point, it undervalues the religious as well as political significance that these objects held for the Venetians themselves once they had been placed in their new setting. Prominent among them was a set of three Byzantine book-covers, which had been reused to enclose liturgical books for the basilica that needed to be recopied because of the addition of the *apparitio*, and possibly other changes to the liturgy, such as the alteration of the text of the *translatio* to accommodate the *praedestinatio*.[26] Although these manuscripts (a Sacramentary, an Evangeliary and an Epistolary) had been prepared as a single group, each is of a different size so that they could be fitted into the covers, which, decorated with enamels and pearls, had also probably been acquired in the wake of the Fourth Crusade; certainly they were in the treasury of San Marco by 1325, when they were inventoried. As with the Pala d'Oro itself, these books were now subject to a process of renewal rather than replacement; their covers were retained, much as Falier's enamels were reused, so that their distinct historical and political resonances were not lost.[27] Together with chalices, patens and reliquaries, many of which were also from Byzantium, these refashioned liturgical books constituted a central group of precious ritual objects that were used regularly at mass and vespers. Along with draperies and cloths, the richly carved columns of the ciborium, the coloured marbles of the pavement woven into intricate geometrical designs, and the reliquaries ornamented with precious enamels, these objects proclaimed the character of the sanctuary through visual splendour. The distinction between red and green porphyry used on the exterior of the basilica is also continued inside the building, where it is used to discriminate between ecclesiastical and ducal authority, the former to the south, the latter to the north. There is also conceivably an echo here of the five bands of green marble inserted into the floor of the nave of Hagia Sophia in Istanbul.[28] Since these bear no relation to any architectural feature of the building, they relate, as do the uses of green and red in San Marco, to some other organizational principle; it has been suggested that they were choreographic markers, perhaps indicating the stoping points of processions.[29] A halo of candlelight, reflected and amplified by the mosaics in the cupola, illuminated the whole.[30]

The role of Andrea Dandolo in these commissions for the high altar was part of a more extensive patronage that reveals his dual, interlinked concerns for the authority of the dogeship and for the centrality of San Marco in the devotional life of Venice, or at least in that of its ruling caste. These preoccupations were allied to literary activity through the writing of two chronicles, the first of which, the *Chronica brevis*, finishes with the death of his predecessor.[31] It is in the second, the *Chronica per extensum descripta*, that the figure of the doge is transformed from an abstract idea into a distinct personality, the agent through whom the objectives of the state were realized.[32] This represents a considerable amplification of ducal presence and, in consequence, of his power, and it has been claimed that Dandolo's achievement in writing the *Chronica* eventually led to the establishment of the post of official historiographer to the republic. Dandolo's literary activities have also been seen as a somewhat intellectual response to, or perhaps an avoidance of, the troubles of the times, including the conflict with Genoa and the plague of 1348, major catastrophes that led Sanudo to characterize his dogeship as a grim time of almost unceasing war, disease and famine.[33]

The most extensive of all Dandolo's projects in the basilica was the construction and decoration of the Cappella di Sant'Isidoro. Originally, Isidore's body had been brought to Venice from Chios during the dogeship of Domenico Michiel (1118–30). Lost sometime afterwards, it was rediscovered (according to the chronicle of Raphaynus de Caresinis) by Dandolo himself. This fortuitous *inventio*, which inevitably recalls the *apparitio* of 1094, added the intercessionary powers of yet another Byzantine saint to San Marco's formidable armoury of relics, and further strengthened the doge's role as mediator.[34] Dandolo's identification with Isidore was strong, and when he subsequently promoted a scheme to replace a cycle of fresco decorations in the baptistery of San Marco with a programme of mosaics, Isidore was one of the saints depicted, significantly enough, close to the position eventually chosen for Dandolo's own tomb.[35] Given his concern with the sacred aura of office, it is not surprising that Dandolo made careful plans for his own final resting-place, specifying in his will not only that he should be buried in San Marco, something that no

33 Tomb of Doge Andrea Dandolo, *c.*1354. San Marco.

previous doge had done, but also designating the chapel of San Giovanni Evangelista, which is prominently located in the north transept, as his preferred site. The final choice he left to the procurators, who instead opted for the baptistery, in the southern section of the narthex, where Doge Giovanni Soranzo's somewhat austere tomb had been installed some twenty years earlier. By comparison, Dandolo's tomb chest is iconographically much richer and sculpturally more exuberant, with a twelve-line inscription recording his virtues and achievements running below. Isidore appears once more among the saints shown, as does the doge's patron saint, Andrew. Dandolo himself is presented in effigy on top of the chest, laid out in full ceremonial attire, the first instance of such a scheme in the Venetian repertory of doges' tombs (pl. 33).[36]

The choice of the baptistery as the site of Soranzo's tomb marked a dramatic break with previous general practice. It is, in fact, the earliest Western example of the use of a baptistery for the burial of a ruler rather than, as was conventional, a high-ranking cleric, usually a bishop. It also inaugurated a return to the practice of using San Marco as a ducal burial space after an interval of some seventy-five years.[37] Placing Soranzo's tomb on the north wall of the baptistery, directly in front of the main entrance from the Piazzetta, invoked a series of interrelated civic and religious messages, and lent heightened emphasis to the ducal presence in the church.[38] By causing it to be erected in the baptistery, the procurators consolidated the notion of this location as the site of ducal burial. The decision was also iconographically appropriate since the mosaic cycle that had been executed in the baptistery during Dandolo's dogeship contains a remarkable depiction of Dandolo himself, kneeling at the foot of the cross, in the *Crucifixion* scene that fills the lunette above the altar. Here he is accompanied by two other members of the Venetian government: on the left Ravagnani, who as Grand Chancellor was the senior representative of the *cittadino* class, and on the right an unidentified young patrician (pl. 34).[39]

Dandolo's *renovatio* of the central ritual area of San Marco, the most extensive remodelling to take place between the twelfth century and the work of Jacopo Sansovino in the sixteenth, also gave the Pala d'Oro a more central role in the liturgy, particularly at mass and vespers. On ferial days and minor feasts the Pala was covered by the *Pala feriale*, but on major occasions Veneziano's altarpiece was removed by an elaborate system of wheels and pulleys, which was operated from two serpentine columns behind the altar.[40] The arrangement remained in operation in the sixteenth and seventeenth centuries (it is described by both Sansovino and Stringa),[41] and it can still be seen in an eighteenth-century engraving by Antonio Visentini. While the procedure was primarily functional (it allowed the Pala d'Oro to be revealed on major feast-days), the columns themselves accommodated statues of the *Virgin* and the *Archangel Gabriel*,[42] thus making a clear reference to the story that the city was established at *Rivum altum* in the lagoon by a group of Paduans on 25 March 421.[43] The story appears in Martin da Canal's *Les escritoires de Venise*, and recurs three-quarters of a century later in Dandolo's *Chronica per extensum descripta*,[44] from where it passed into the mainstream fourteenth- and fifteenth-century chronicle tradition and beyond.

34   Crucixion mosaic, *c*.1350. San Marco, Baptistery.

35 Detail of the tomb of Doge Bartolomeo Gradenigo, *c.*1342. San Marco.

During the fourteenth century the Venetians began to make much greater use of *Annunciation* imagery. The tomb of Doge Bartolomeo Gradenigo (1339–42) in the narthex of San Marco makes extensive use of Marian themes in the three reliefs that decorate the plain rectangular tomb chest: a central one showing the *Virgin and Child* (a miniscule figure of the doge kneeling at her feet) enthroned between *St Bartholomew* and *St Mark* (pl. 35), and two end panels depicting the *Archangel Gabriel* and the *Annunciate Virgin*. This arrangement may have been influenced by the tomb of Marsilio da Carrara, lord of Padua, who died in 1338 (while Dondi's chronicle was being written), which shows Carrara kneeling in adoration of the *Virgin and Child* in the centre of the chest, and displays the two figures of the *Annunciation* at its corners.[45] Alternatively, it could have been an adaptation of the Byzantine practice of depicting the *Annunciation* flanking the sanctuary arch or on the doors of the iconostasis. A further amplification of this tradition occurs in Poreč Cathedral, where the boldly decorated apse contains a marble synthronon and a ciborium (a later copy, dated 1277, of that in San Marco), decorated with mosaics showing the *Annunciation*;[46] interestingly, this work was carried out by the craftsmen who were then engaged at San Marco itself.[47] The use of *Annunciation* iconography on the Gradenigo tomb in the basilica was in turn part of a longer process in which, shorn of its Paduan references, the episode became a symbol for the origins of Venice itself.[48]

The moment when the significance of the Annunciation began to be developed in official Venetian historiography coincided exactly with Dandolo's realization of its potential. As procurator he may have played a role in establishing the location and the iconography of the Gradenigo tomb, and the Annunciation myth entered the chronicle tradition with his own *Chronica per extensum descripta*, being absent from both the *Chronica brevis*, written before he became doge, and from Canal's account of the foundation of the city.[49] The placing of the *Annunciation* statues on columns behind the Pala d'Oro, as part of the mechanism for moving the *Pala feriale*, was part of Dandolo's renovation of the altar and its ritual objects, notably liturgical manuscripts; it also strengthened the significance of the altar itself as a politically charged site. Through these projects at San Marco, Dandolo enhanced his personal reputation while also

36 Jacopo Sansovino, *Pergolo*, 1536–7. San Marco.

consolidating the bonds linking the doge to St Mark, a particularly useful asset in a period of war and famine. In a more general sense, his achievement was to implant firmly the idea of the doge as animator and embodiment of the Venetian polity through the force of his own persona, 'the sacred aura that could irradiate the increasingly complex structures of government'.[50]

As the site of the evangelist's *praesentia*, and of the foundation myth of the city itself, this focal point of civic pride and sacral power became the object of a second *renovatio* carried out in the 1530s by Sansovino, who as *proto* (architect) spent much of his time supervising routine maintenance in San Marco. Ultimately, it was the question of liturgical performance, as much as the urge to modernize, that guided his *renovatio* of the area, in a scheme that not only lent a classical touch to its essentially Byzantine character, but also heightened its already considerable sense of theatricality.[51] Sansovino began with a major overhaul of the *coro maggiore*, which stretched from the iconostasis to the steps leading to the presbytery, and was reserved for the doge and the most important officials of state. Here he provided a new ducal throne, stalls and tapestries to decorate them, and two tribunes (*pergoli*), decorated with bronze reliefs showing scenes from the *Life of Mark*, attached to the north and south walls (pl. 36).[52] The use of bronze was new to Sansovino's Venetian sculpture, and the tribune reliefs heralded his deployment of the same medium elsewhere in the choir. As work on the two tribunes was drawing to a close, Sansovino turned his attention to the *coro minore*, which, approached by two steps leading up to the presbytery, served as the canons' choir ranged round the high altar, and included the throne of the *primicerio*. Among the new work here were two important sculptural projects: bronze figures of the *Four Evangelists* and a spectacular bronze door leading to the sacristy. The evangelists, originally designed to stand on a low balustrade running in front of the high altar, oversaw the liturgical and other ceremonies enacted at Mark's tomb, and in particular the investiture of the doge, when they were invoked as witnesses (pl. 37).[53] In a final phase Sansovino also designed a new bronze door for the tabernacle of the altar of the sacrament, and the door to the sacristy; the latter, 'the great masterpiece of Venetian bronze-relief casting of the High Renaissance', and one of the few sixteenth-century bronze doors to be made, carries obvious reso-

nances of Ghiberti's 'Doors of Paradise' in Florence, just as the two tribunes recall the *cantorie* designed there by Donatello and Luca della Robbia.[54] Taken as a whole, these commissions imposed a new degree of coherence and artistic unity on the central liturgical space of the basilica by recasting it in a mid-sixteenth-century idiom. It would seem that the procurators were as keen to transform the area around the high altar, visited by every procession that passed through the basilica, as they had been to transform the square outside.[55]

The overall effect of Sansovino's scheme is now substantially lost because of nineteenth-century mutilations, mostly carried out when San Marco became the seat of the patriarch, but from an early seventeenth-century description, the only near-contemporary source, the sixteenth-century appearance of the choir can be reconstructed.[56] Except for the Epistle and Gospel during mass, which were both read or chanted from the *pulpitum novum* in the north side of the transept, the daily liturgy was performed entirely within this space. On entering the *coro maggiore* through the central opening of the iconostasis, the doge's throne originally

37   Jacopo Sansovino, *St. Mark*, 1550–52. San Marco.

stood to the right. Next to it, running the length of the inside of the iconostasis, were seven stalls that were occupied by the papal nuncio and the foreign ambassadors who attended the doge on grand ceremonial occasions. A second set of stalls, attached to the south wall of the choir, was reserved for the magistrates of the *sestieri* of the city, where they were appropriately overlooked by panels inlaid with the figures of *Faith*, *Fortitude* and *Charity*. The equivalent stalls on the north side of the choir, guarded by the remaining virtues of *Temperance*, *Prudence* and *Hope*, were reserved for the procurators, the knights of the Republic, and any male members of the ducal family. On the occasions when both the doge and Signoria were present, the stalls were decorated with tapestries showing episodes from the *Life of St Mark*, woven in the recently established Medici workshops in Florence in 1551.[57] In the space in between sat the most important state officials together with the sixty senators who were required to attend when the doge was present. In its final configuration the choir was closed off by the iconostasis to the west, consisting of eight marble columns supporting fourteen statues (pl. 38). Constructed by the Dalle Masegne

38   San Marco, looking east.

brothers in the 1390s (the central section is dated 1394), this replaces an earlier structure (traces of which remain), four of whose *plutei* are now in Santa Maria Assunta in Torcello.[58] Some idea of the arrangement can be seen in a number of later images, including an anonymous late seventeenth-century painting showing the presentation of the sword to Doge Francesco Morosini by Pope Alexander VIII (pl. 39),[59] and an eighteenth-century ground plan (pl. 40).

As with all local cults, Venetian devotion revolved around sacred places and holy protectors. In the 'presence' of the saint at Mark's tomb, the most important site of Venetian collective memory, vows were sworn and pacts made to guard against disaster. Memory was in turn reinforced through a busy cycle of annual observances, a sacred calendar articulated by supernatural interventions and the feast-days of important patron saints. Throughout Catholic Europe, liturgical usages gave particular prominence to saints with a local significance, while still retaining the basic outline of the standard festal year that was observed throughout the Western church. As elsewhere, the Venetian calendar was one in which the specifically Venetian was mixed with elements of universal observance, for reasons that were simultaneously both devotional and political. The calendar was flexible, and could be changed to take account of fresh events of historical importance to the Venetians; it was thus organic, in a way that is characteristic of the Republic's attitudes towards its past.

39 Anonymous, *Consignment of the Sword to Doge Francesco
Morosini by Pope Alexander VII in St. Mark's in 1690*, c.1690.
Venice, Museo Civico Correr.

The earliest historical traces of a specifically Venetian calendar date only
from the eleventh century, but, by the fourteenth, local influences were becoming increasingly prominent. This evolution can be traced not only in the few
relevant liturgical manuscripts to have survived, but also through the decisions
of provincial synods, such as those taken at Grado in 1296, when it was decreed
that the feast-days of Sts Hermagoras, Fortunatus and Mark (who were associated with Grado, Aquilia and Venice respectively) should be commemorated
throughout the diocese.[60] Flexibility allied to continuity, the ability of the
Venetian calendar to change emphases according to circumstance, remained
one of its features throughout its long history. In addition to military victories, new saints could also be accommodated, as in the case of St Lorenzo
Giustiniani, the first bishop of Venice to bear the title of patriarch, whose
feast-day was added to the calendar in 1524 as a result of a concession made
by Clement VII. This was in turn merely one step in the early phase of Venetian agitation for Giustiniani's canonization, a lengthy process that finally
reached fruition in 1727 after more than two centuries of political campaign-
ing.[61] Even during his own lifetime Giustiniani had been regarded as a saint,
and he became the object of increased devotion in the years immediately after
his death in 1456, partly because of his role as a protector against the plague.
There were three principal protagonists in the seemingly endless process to
secure Giustiniani's canonization: the canons of the congregation of San
Giorgio in Alga (of which he was the co-founder), the patriarch of Venice and
the government of the Republic. A formal request was made to Sixtus IV in

1472, but initial progress was slow. In the devotional climate of post-Tridentine Italy, with relations between the Republic and the Holy See initially somewhat eased, Venetian efforts finally bore fruit in 1598, when Giustiniani was raised to the ranks of the blessed, and his body was transferred to the cathedral of San Pietro di Castello. In common with other Italian states, Venice was not slow to appropriate images of conformity with the ideals and objectives of the Catholic Reformation for immediate gains in terms of influence and status, and the case for Giustiniani's elevation also benefitted from the post-Tridentine accentuation upon the cult of saints.[62] The case for canonization was supported by Paul v, who moved matters on by giving the canons of San Giorgio permission to celebrate mass in Giustiniani's honour once a week, and his stock rose higher during the plague of 1630–31 when his feast-day was marked for the first time by a ducal procession to his tomb, and his relics were carried through Castello, the

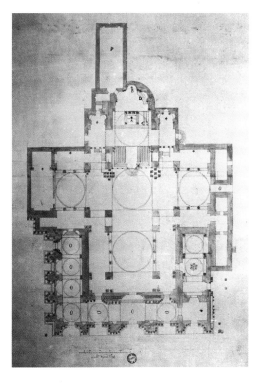

40   San Marco, ground plan *c*.1761. Venice, Biblioteca Nazionale Marciana.

northernmost *sestiere* of the city. This had been done on the orders of the patriarch, Giovanni Tiepolo, an inveterate hunter of relics, whose verbose treatise, *Dell'ira di Dio*, advocates their use as objects of veneration during times of pestilence. It was also a deliberate evocation of Giustiniani's own behaviour during the plague of 1447, when he organized processions and communal prayer, and obtained indulgences from Nicholas v for those who helped the sick and the dying.[63] The flamboyant high altar in San Pietro, based on a design by Baldassare Longhena, culminates in an urn, supported by two angels, that contains the saint's remains; the surrounding marble statues are of *Peter*, *Paul*, *Mark* and *John the Baptist*, and the ensemble is completed by Josse de Corte's statue of Giustiniani himself (pl. 41). Together with the paintings and frescoes that decorate the apse and the lateral walls, this ensemble constitutes a politically charged shrine to the saint's memory, and an important site of intercession, particularly during moments of crisis. In common with many of the saints who lend the Venetian calendar its distinctive shape and colouring, Giustiniani thus had a precise local association, and the extended struggle to ensure his elevation to sainthood is in itself an indication of the political ramifications of his cult.

41 Baldassare Longhena, high altar, 1649. San Pietro di
Castello.

The role of San Marco's own liturgy, the *rito patriarchino*, was central in
lending a peculiarly Venetian emphasis to the various official civic and liturgical
occasions that filled the festal calendar. As a genre, any *patriarchino* consists of
a body of regional or local uses, normally tied to Latin liturgical texts. The
melodies themselves sometimes differ from established chant traditions (though
some exchange can also take place), and 'primitive' harmonization in two or
three vocal parts sometimes occurs. In many parts of northern Italy, in the area
delineated by the Istrian coast to the east, Lombardy to the west and Venice to
the north, *patriarchino* dialects have been practised within living memory. Until
recently, the plainchant of the liturgy celebrated in San Marco was largely
unknown, except for what could be recuperated from relatively late manuscript
sources. This is obviously a potentially hazardous method, since changes to both
texts and melodies could be introduced over time, though, as it has emerged,
the *patriarchino* remained comparatively stable.[64] A complete repertoire of manuscripts that allows detailed reconstruction of the liturgy to take place properly
begins with a thirteenth-century Venetian antiphoner containing chants for the
period between Holy Saturday and Advent.[65] Comparison with a late copy of
the San Marco orational, and with a fourteenth-century antiphoner, confirms
that this richly illuminated manuscript is the earliest source of the chants of the
patriarchino to have survived (pl. 42). Further study of the orational also reveals
that a homiliary and the oldest passionals, some parts of which date from the
end of the twelfth century, were still in use in the sixteenth. Because of these
historical continuities, the absence of a complete range of early sources becomes
less of a hindrance to a reconstruction of the office than had been previously

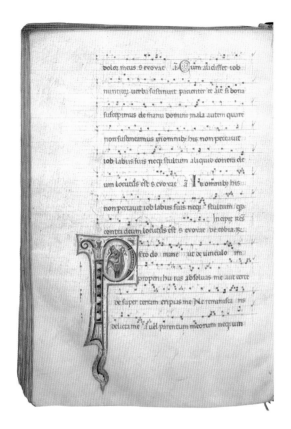

42   Venetian antiphoner for San Marco, 13th
century. Italy, private collection.

thought. Other liturgical books have also been identified. Through comparison
with another late source (four graduals, which together cover the whole year),
an early gradual in Berlin, long believed to be from Aquileia, has been shown
to be from San Marco, which makes it possible to reconstruct not only the
liturgy of the office but also that of the mass.[66] The Berlin gradual is of interest too because of the presence of a number of tropes and sequences, indicating
musical practices that could not have been deduced from other sources.
Although some parts of the liturgy, including a notated hymnal, a processional
and a complete missal, are still missing, scholarship from the known tally of
sources has been able to reconstruct a substantial part of the San Marco liturgy
as it was practised from the thirteenth century onwards. In some manuscripts
the evolution of the liturgy is evident from sections that have been re-copied to
insert the *apparitio*, or to accommodate the *praedestinatio* within the *translatio*.[67]

From the middle of the sixteenth century, both the textual details of the rite
and its ceremonial specifications are much more fully documented. After 1456
the *patriarchino*, which was under the control of the patriarch and which orig-

inally had been used throughout the diocese of Venice, was confined to the basilica itself; the rest of the diocese, including all the parish churches of the city, now followed the use of Rome. From this date the principal function of the chants of the *patriarchino* was to decorate a liturgy that could be performed there and nowhere else; this only intensified its political accentuation. As a result of a campaign of recopying in the 1560s, finely illuminated manuscripts of the gradual and Kyriale were produced.[68] From the liturgical books of the basilica a detailed picture emerges of a usage that differs from standard Roman practice in important ways. The psalms, for example, were drawn from a textual tradition that lay outside the Vulgate, and their arrangement throughout the year differed from Roman arrangements.

The special character of the *patriarchino* is often made explicit in its rituals, most obviously in ceremonies accompanying the investiture and the burial of the doge himself. On other occasions the priestly nature of the dogeship[69] is made clear through his involvement in liturgical functions, as in the ceremonies that took place on the four days of the San Marco cycle, which required the doge to participate at mass in the basilica by reciting the ordinary together with four chaplains.[70] It was also on such major feast-days in the Venetian calendar that a strong sense of history and identity was present in parts of the office. This is particularly true for the service of second vespers, which became, on these occasions, a powerful and theatrical evocation of the past glories of the Republic. This was partly liturgically defined, since it was on these days that the sequences of psalms prescribed by the *patriarchino* took on a distinctive form. On these occasions the choir was required to be present, and the Pala d'Oro was opened. Then, according to the Ceremony Book of 1564 compiled by the master of ceremonies Bartolomeo Bonifacio, 'the singers must sing Vespers in two choirs with psalms set for eight voices'.[71] The polyphonic elements of this requirement were then recent, but the central feature of the alternatim performance of the psalms can be traced back earlier, and undoubtedly has an even longer history that reaches back, beyond the written sources, to the early days of the Contarini church. Encapsulated in this ritual, with its musical embellishments, are many of the essential peculiarities that made the Venetian official liturgy, a form that was at once both sacred and civic, so particular.

While on the one hand the *patriarchino* was fiercely defended as a symbol of Venetian independence and ducal authority, on the other it embodied flexible ritual forms that could be altered according to political circumstance. A great deal of liturgical elasticity, allowing for the addition, subtraction, promotion or demotion of individual feasts according to considerations that were essentially political, is a distinct feature of the *patriarchino* and of its ceremonial extensions through processions, particularly the ducal procession or *andata*. During the sixteenth century the Venetian rite found itself increasingly embattled, particularly in the decades immediately after the Council of Trent, when local uses in much of the surrounding area were gradually abandoned.[72] Tridentine reform was suspiciously and characteristically viewed in Venice as yet further evidence of papal attempts to broaden its secular power, but benefitting from a clause in the papal bull that made adoption of Pius v's *Breviarium romanum* mandatory except for liturgies more than two hundred years old, San Marco was able to continue to follow its ancient practices. This favoured treatment was largely because of Carlo Borromeo's energetic lobbying on behalf of the Ambrosian rite, which was exempt from abolition because of the same provision. As a symbol of Venetian independence and ducal authority, interventions to preserve the *patriarchino* from Roman liturgical innovation were frequently stressed, often at the highest level. In June 1628, for example, Doge Giovanni Contarini ordered the *maestro di coro* at the basilica to ensure that the mass and office be celebrated 'according to the rite, form and ancient use of this Church, without the slightest innovation'.[73] While the structure and detail of the *patriarchino* remained fixed in its inherited, historical form as a liturgy that was ultimately under the control of the doge, the possibility of amplification remained.

In addition to the use of Rome, other liturgical traditions were also to be heard: the Albanians, the Dalmatians and the Greeks all maintained their own churches and charitable institutions. Of these the Greek community was the largest, and it has been estimated that, by the end of the sixteenth century, there were 4,000 Greeks in Venice; certainly, there were enough to sustain a printing and publishing trade, some of whose products were bought locally.[74] The Venetian liturgical soundscape, which filled the meeting-halls of the foreign 'nations' as well as parish churches, convents and monasteries, was both complex and cosmopolitan, and in these circumstances traditions mingled. During the last third of the fifteenth century, Ioannes Plousiadenos, the spiritual director of a small Greek colony in Venice, and later bishop of Methone, spent some twenty years in the city copying manuscripts. His experiences there may be reflected in his own compositions, which consist of one (possibly two) communion verses in primitive two-voice polyphony, probably an adaptation of *cantus planus binatim*, the simple improvised style (occasionally it was written down) that was the polyphonic *lingua franca* of the confraternities and parish churches of the city.[75] Other examples of the type, including a doxology and two settings of the Creed (sung in the Western church but not the Eastern), composed in the early fifteenth century for the ruler of the island of Lefkas by Manuel Gazes, have survived; his compositions also circulated elsewhere, at least to the islands of Lesbos and Crete.[76] Another Byzantine composer and copyist, the Cypriot Hieronymus Tragodistes (Geronimo Cantore), who studied for three years with Gioseffo Zarlino, then *maestro di cappella* at San Marco, wrote a four-voice setting of the final troparion of the Easter canon; this survives in a manuscript that probably belonged to Cardinal Alvise Cornaro, a member of a Venetian patrician family with strong connections with Cyprus.[77] Such merging of cultures, on the borders of written and oral practices, which must have been far more common than indicated by notated records, would have been further facilitated by the experiences of Roman clergy returning from service in the Venetian colonies. Heard in *campi* and *calle*, as well as in private and public enclosed spaces, these 'other' musics added a further dimension to the rich texture of urban devotional practice and experience. Nonetheless, the official centre of devotional life in the city was the basilica of San Marco, where a unique and particular liturgy was enacted on a daily basis. Varied though this was, the activities of San Marco stood at the centre of official musical life as it was experienced by those Venetians and foreigners who gathered in the Piazza San Marco, the basilica and the other major churches and squares of the city.

It is within the framework of the *patriarchino* that the activities of the *cappella marciana* and the performance of polyphony in San Marco took place. The history of the choir of the basilica, and of the music that it performed, is in this sense intimately related to the changing vision that those responsible for overseeing the ceremonial life of San Marco had in the articulation and elaboration of the rite.[78] In this context two officials were of particular importance: the master of ceremonies and the *primicerio*. In Roman times, the latter title was held by senior administrative officials who, in an ecclesiastical context, were often charged with regulating the common life of the clergy in collegiate and cathedral churches. As the senior ecclesiastic at San Marco, and the only one to be appointed by the doge rather than by the procurators, the holder of the post had authority over the clergy of the basilica, together with ultimate responsibility for the day-to-day operation of the liturgy within it, functions that parallel those of the *primicerio* of the papal court in the early middle ages.[79] But when, in 1251, Pope Innocent IV granted the *primicerio* of San Marco the right to wear mitre and ring and to carry the pastoral staff, an ambiguity was created that was to cause considerable difficulty in later centuries.[80] Astonishingly, following this ruling the *primicerio* of San Marco could now appear in public dressed as a high-ranking ecclesiastic, with all the powers and authority of a bishop, while in legal terms these same papal privileges provided immunity from episcopal supervision. Although Innocent's decision is clear enough in its detail, in practice it was not always easy to convince the bishop of Castello (who during the pontificate of Nicholas V was raised to the status of patriarch, with Lorenzo Giustiniani as the first incumbent) of the validity of this separation of power. In an age in which questions of precedence between representatives of the various Italian states assumed a high degree of symbolic importance, conflicts between the patriarch (as the representative of Rome) and the doge were often caused by disagreements over jurisdiction.[81] An early example occurred in 1347, when Bishop Francesco Foscari ordered the *primicerio* and the canons of San Marco to appear before him. Quite naturally, this provocative action, regarded as a challenge to the doge's absolute jurisdiction over the chapel and its officials, produced a brisk reply that hung on three main arguments. First, the church of San Marco had been a ducal chapel for more than five hundred years, from the moment when the *translatio* had taken place and the first church had been built. Second, the canons of San Marco (as Foscari insisted on calling them) were in reality the chaplains of the doge, while their superior, the *primicerio*, had always been a ducal rather than a patriarchal appointment. Lastly, the celebrated visit of Alexander III to Venice in 1177 for his historic meeting with the Emperor Frederick Barbarossa was invoked, and it was claimed that among the many privileges conceded to the doge on that occasion for his support of the papal position was that of absolute control over San Marco and its clergy.[82]

During the fifteenth century, a period of grave crisis for the Holy See, which also coincided with one of self-confident expansion for the Republic, as it imposed its rule on Padua, Verona, Vicenza and the other cities of the *terraferma*, the privileges granted to the *primicerio* by Innocent IV were consolidated and enlarged, notably by the 'antipope' John XXIII, who authorized the incumbent to give blessings without bearing the pontifical insignia of mitre, ring and staff. In 1493 the process was taken one step further when Pope Alexander VI removed the church of San Giovanni Elemosinario from patriarchal jurisdiction and assigned it instead to San Marco. The ease with which Doge Andrea Gritti, a few decades later, was able to secure the papal concession of the *ius patronatus* of San Giacomo di Rialto, a concession that Alexander VI had declined to grant, is symptomatic of the new atmosphere of cooperation that characterized relations between the Papacy and the Republic during the middle decades of the sixteenth century. In effect, the process begun by Alexander created a diocese that included not only the parish churches of San Basso and San Geminiano, both within the confines of the Piazza San Marco, but also the church of San Giorgio Maggiore in the lagoon, and the devotional heart of the other official pole of the twin axis of Venetian civic administration at Rialto. Authority over these subservient churches, exercised by the doge through the *primicerio*, was ritually consolidated on the occasion of the annual *andata* to each church, in which the doge himself participated. Through such processional forms and liturgical ceremonies ducal authority was asserted.

Control of daily liturgical operations within San Marco was largely in the hands of the master of ceremonies and the chapel master.[83] What this meant in terms of musical practice, allied to liturgical action and processional forms, begins to become clear only from the middle decades of the sixteenth century. Bonifacio's *Ceremoniale* of 1564 is essentially the earliest significant ceremony book from San Marco to have survived,[84] while the arrival of the Flemish composer Adrian Willaert as *maestro di cappella* in 1527 marks the beginning of the tradition of the performance of polyphony, not only for occasions of special significance, but also for everyday decoration of the liturgy. Some traces of earlier polyphonic musical activity survive, but they add up to very little in terms of what is known about repertory. An organist is documented at San Marco for the first time at the beginning of the fourteenth century, and others are subsequently recorded in the post with some regularity. This continual tradition was expanded by the addition of a second organist in 1490, and one year later Pietro de Fossis is noted as *maestro di cappella*;[85] his immediate predecessor, the Frenchman Albert Pichion, is named on the earliest known list of singers, which dates from 1486.[86] Although at this stage in its history the choir was largely recruited from Venice and its dependent territories, and from nearby towns and cities such as Ferrara and Bologna, it also contained a small number of Frenchmen and Flemings, who were often members of the clergy, if only in name.[87] This sort of proportion remained fairly stable throughout Willaert's period as *maestro* making the choir relatively provincial in character for such a prominent institution in comparison with the court chapels established in Ferrara and Milan in the last decades of the fifteenth century. Singers for Venice were sometimes recruited through the personal initiatives of high-ranking officials, and often (as was common elsewhere) through the diplomatic system; they were rewarded (at least from the early sixteenth century) with sinecures and benefices as well as salaries, and seem to have been reasonably provided for with incomes equivalent to those of skilled artisans and minor government officials.[88] Salaries from San Marco were often supplemented by payments for work done outside, which typically involved singing for other churches in the city, or for the *scuole grandi*, on an occasional basis.[89] As early as the 1520s, the singers from San Marco began to organize themselves into two companies designed to facilitate the distribution of outside work for the benefit of their members, who paid a fee to belong to what was effectively a form of trade union, and to receive a due share of the income from engagements. Despite the formation of a single company of singers

43   Leone Leoni, medal of Jacob Buus, 1544. London, British Museum.

in 1553, with its own bye-laws and proper disciplinary procedures to enforce them, rivalry between factions continued to be intense, so much so that in 1579 Doge Nicolò da Ponte decreed that the two should be amalgamated into a single body.[90] Beginning with the Fleming Jacob Buus, evidently a man of some substance or at least well connected, to judge by Leoni's elegant medal and his capacity to bear the cost of publishing his own works (pl. 43),[91] who was appointed as second organist by the procurators in 1541, a succession of distinguished organist-composers, including Andrea and Giovanni Gabrieli, Claudio Merulo and Annibale Padovano, occupied the organ lofts of the basilica.

In addition to the adult singers there were also the choristers (*zaghi*), local boys who were taught the rudiments of music and trained to sing in the choir school, which had been in operation at San Marco since at least the early fifteenth century.[92] The composer Antonius Romanus was employed there from about 1420 and possibly earlier; his three surviving motets, which probably form part of a larger repertory of large-scale occasional music, all celebrate Venetian events and personalities – Doge Tommaso Mocenigo (1414–23), the visit of Giovanni Francesco Gonzaga to Venice in 1432, and Doge Francesco Foscari who became doge in 1423.[93] By the sixteenth century the overall size of the choir was similar to that of comparable institutions elsewhere, such as the cathedrals in Florence and Milan, with an average membership of fourteen adults and twelve boys.[94] It remained at this sort of size until the later decades of the sixteenth century, when a certain amount of expansion took place, the post of third organist was created, and the vocal forces were supplemented by a group of instrumentalists.[95] In contrast to the singers in the choir, who were recruited from outside Venice and sometimes from beyond the Alps, the instrumentalists, who were first employed on a regular basis in 1568, were local men.[96]

The paucity of information about the choir in the fifteenth century is paralleled by the almost complete lack of written polyphonic music from the same period that can be definitively associated with San Marco, or indeed with any other institution in the city. According to the received view, there was no significant composer of polyphony active in Venice, or working for Venetian institutions, between the death of Ciconia (in 1412) and the arrival of Adrian Willaert (in 1527), a gap that becomes even greater if Ciconia's connections with Venice are placed in doubt. Ciconia was in Padua from 1401, initially as the holder of a benefice and a chaplaincy probably obtained with the help of Francesco Zabarella, archpriest of Padua Cathedral, legal scholar, humanist and a powerful local patron, and later as the official *cantor et custos* at the cathedral. His double-texted piece 'Venecie mundi splendor / Michael qui Stena domus', written in honour of both Venice and Doge Michele Steno (1400–26), is sometimes claimed as another investiture motet (as are a number of pre-Ciconia pieces of this kind), but it is more likely to be an expression of Paduan obeisance to its Venetian rulers, who conquered the city from the Carrara family in November 1405.[97] Conceivably, it was performed during the embassy to Venice (the second of three), made early the next year by a contingent of sixteen Paduan representatives under the leadership of Zabarella, sent to negotiate the terms of the surrender on behalf of the commune.[98] If 'Venecie mundi splendor' is deprived of a Venetian patron (though not of a Venetian performance), this brings to nine the number of Ciconia's eleven motets (including two addressed to Zabarella himself) that were Paduan commissions. This is not surprising, given Ciconia's firm grounding in Paduan society and his connections to both his patron and the city. It also reflects Padua's importance as a centre of humanistic learning (the bishopric of Padua was occupied throughout the fifteenth century by distinguished intellectuals), an importance perhaps greater than that of Venice itself in this period, at least until the influx of Greek scholars such as Bessarion into Venice after the Fall of Constantinople in 1453.[99] Although the fourteenth-century tradition of motet composition was centred on the Veneto, it was Padua rather than Venice that lay at the heart of the phenomenon, and the earliest motets composed in honour of the doge were probably composed there.[100] The Paduan fragments from Santa Giustina, an important centre of manuscript production, include one motet in honour of St Anthony of Padua and another in praise of the abbot of Santa Giustina, Andrea Carrara.[101] Such remains are probably the fragile remnants of a now lost but originally rich tradition.

Even so, it is likely that there would have been a late fifteenth-century Venetian tradition of polyphonic composition and performance, given the wealth, political importance and imperial style of Venice at mid-century, following the *terraferma* expansion during the dogeship of Francesco Foscari (1423–57). Apart from Johannis de Quadris, who held an appointment at San Marco as 'musicus et cantor' from at least 1436 until about 1457,[102] it seems that there were no musicians of any consequence at all working at the basilica between the generation of Antonius Romanus, Hugo de Lantins and Cristoforo de Monte (all of whom wrote large-scale celebratory motets for Foscari) and the 1480s, when the documentation improves.[103] It is conceivable that the fourteenth-century tradition of civic motets (including eight in honour of six of the of the fourteen Venetian doges installed between 1329 and 1423) effectively came to an end with Foscari's long dogeship,[104] a period of some thirty-four years, which may either have caused the death of the practice through lack of continuity and the absence of a strong collective memory or, more probably, was the consequence of the discernible move to diminish the outward trappings of personal ducal authority that followed Foscari's death.

The more general picture of a sizeable gap in compositional activity surely reflects the scarcity of sources rather than the reality of fifteenth-century practice. A number of pieces by de Quadris have survived in manuscripts that can be connected if not unambiguously to Venice, at least to the Veneto. First, there is a group of works in a manuscript in Oxford, one of which, a four-voice Magnificat setting, is dated '1436, in the month of May in Venice';[105] this, the most elaborate of his surviving compositions, is indebted to the music of Ciconia.[106] Two further pieces, a short three-voice hymn, 'Iste confessor', and a cycle of two-voice pieces for Good Friday processions, occur in manuscripts copied in Verona and Padua respectively towards the end of the century.[107] Finally, the complete cycle of de Quadris's two-voice Lamentations, known from other manuscripts and printed sources, is preserved in a separate fascicle inserted into a manuscript in Vicenza,[108] which originally belonged to Bartolomeo Rossi da Carpi, a canon at the cathedral there, and chaplain to Pietro Emiliani, humanist, collector of Greek manuscripts and bishop of the diocese from 1409 to 1433.[109] Like other high-ranking ecclesiastics at the cathedrals of Padua and Vicenza, Emiliani is known to have had musical interests. Feragut's motet 'Excelsa civitas Vincencia', composed for his enthronement, survives uniquely in a manuscript now in Bologna, the largest compilation of international repertory from the early decades of the fifteenth century to have survived.[110] This anthology was written in Padua and Vicenza, and almost certainly reflects the tastes of the circles in which Emiliani moved. It seems that music, in the sense of written rather than improvised polyphony, was cultivated by humanists and churchmen in the major urban centres of the Veneto to a much greater extent than has been generally recognized.[111] In part, that impression is caused by the scarcity of sources.

Printed by Ottaviano Petrucci in Venice in 1506 together with other settings,[112] the de Quadris Lamentations remained current long after they had been composed. It seems that at San Marco they continued to be performed throughout the sixteenth century, until they were joined by Giovanni Croce's settings early in the seventeenth, which may have replaced them in the basilica's repertory.[113] Interestingly, two of de Quadris's Good Friday pieces also appear in editions of Alberto da Castello's *Liber sacerdotalis*, first published in 1523 and often reprinted,[114] which probably means that they were among the most frequently circulated pieces of sacred polyphony in sixteenth-century Italy. For much of his adult life Alberto lived and worked at Santi Giovanni e Paolo, where for a period he had a cell next to Pietro da Castello, the editor of Petrucci's first publication, the *Odhecaton A*.[115] Pietro may well have provided Alberto with the text of de Quadris's compositions, and was conceivably involved in editing them for publication.[116]

The importance that has traditionally been assigned to composed polyphony does not fully reflect the realities of fifteenth- and sixteenth-century performance. Until the early sixteenth century, the kind of polyphony most frequently encountered in most Italian churches was likely to have been what the contemporary Paduan theorist Prosdocimus described as *cantus planus binatim*, plainchant sung in note-against-note style. The result, inevitably simple (it is sometimes referred to misleadingly as 'primitive polyphony'), is essentially the outcome of traditions of improvised singing rather than written composition, and since it was a largely oral tradition there are few written survivals. Most of those known are Italian, and represent a geographical spread from east to west along the Alps, and from the north to the south of the Po valley. Although many can be connected to the religious orders (one fifteenth-century source has been linked to a Dominican friary in Venice itself), some can be associated with the secular clergy in the cathedrals of small towns.[117] A number of liturgical manuscripts that were copied for the collegiate church of Santa Maria Assunta in Cividale del Friuli contain substantial passages of *cantus planus binatim*;[118] their survival alongside compositions in the style of high-art music is a reminder that the two traditions coexisted in performance.[119] In practice, the polyphonic pieces that are to be found scattered throughout the Cividale liturgical books are written in a range of styles (stretching from note-against-note style to comparatively elaborate counterpoint), showing a variety of complexity that is disguised by the anachronistic description 'primitive'. This repertory, reflecting practice in a single important institution, includes settings of the ordinary, parts of the liturgy for Christmas Day and Easter Day, and tropes to 'Benedicamus Domino' to be sung in procession on a number of other major feast-days. It is highly likely that polyphony of this kind would have been performed at San Marco in the fourteenth and fifteenth centuries; it is clear from passages written into eighteenth-century chant manuscripts from the basilica that the practice of *cantus planus binatim* was still current at this late date alongside the performance of contemporary polyphonic repertories.

A second category of sacred music that is both relatively simple and was often improvised is *falsobordone*, a type of chordal recitation based on the melody of a Gregorian psalm tone. Often in four parts, this style of writing occurs in a great variety of music, both sacred and profane, spanning some three centuries.[120] The earliest examples, which come from the end of the fifteenth century, are to be found in manuscripts written in Portugal, Spain and Italy, including one copied in Verona.[121] For obvious reasons, *falsobordone* is most frequently encountered during dominical or festal vespers, the major occasions for public performance of the office, which is structured around a sequence of five sung psalms. It is in this context that the technique is described being used at San Marco in a travel diary written by Arendt Willemsz, a barber-surgeon from Delft, who, together with a number of companions, stayed in the city for some weeks in 1525 on his way to the Holy Land (pl. 44).[122] Willemsz, who by profession must be counted a reasonably educated and literate man (at one point he cites Isidore), gives as his reason for writing down such a detailed account of his journey the 'instruction and devotion of other pilgrims so that everyone can learn of the places where Christ carried out miracles'. As such, and in common with many such accounts, the main weight of his diary falls on his description of the Holy Land itself, and of the places associated with the life of Christ. From his writing it is clear that Willemsz was observant about human nature but was also inclined to be factual and to proceed cautiously, all of which makes him a witness of some reliability. Among his fellow travellers was a priest, Jan Goverts van Gorcum, who has also left an account of the pilgrimage. This is textually so close to Willemsz's diary that both manuscripts must have been made from a common exemplar, perhaps notes that they made together on the journey, which were then used as the basis for professional copies made after their return.[123]

It may well have been Jan van Gorcum's knowledge of the liturgy, and of north European musical practices, that makes their accounts of the performance of music and liturgy inside San Marco so valuable. Certainly their description of hearing mass and vespers in the basilica is unusually detailed and musically well informed for the period. It notes that the Pala d'Oro was on display, thus establishing the occasion as a major feast-day, and describes in some detail the

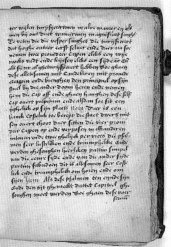

44 Diary of Arendt Willemsz, 1525. Amsterdam, University Library.

elaborate procession from the sacristy to the high altar that took place before mass began. This included a processional cross incorporating a relic of the True Cross,[124] and a precious missal 'decorated with an image of St Mark'; the latter is probably a reference to one of the Byzantine book covers, showing an image of the saint, that enclosed the most prized liturgical manuscripts. Both these ritual objects played a significant part in the celebration of mass itself. At both the Epistle and the Gospel, the missal was solemnly carried behind the cross to what Willemsz describes as a 'high chair' (presumably the *pulpitum novum*) from which the celebrant intoned. As for music:

> The canons of St Mark's perform beautiful song, year in, year out. Outside the sanctuary there is a beautiful, round, big, high pew, decorated and draped with red velvet cloth of gold, in which the discanters stand and sing. And those who palmodize, sitting on both sides of the choir, one side *simpelsanck*, the other *contrapunt* or *fabridoen*, whichever term you understand best. These three each wait for their time to sing, up to the end of the mass.[125]

This can be supplemented by his description of vespers, which began with the customary initial intonation of 'Deus in adjutorium nostrum' and the incensing of the ritual space. For the central musical part of the liturgy, the sequence of five vespers psalms, the celebrant and other officiating clergy took their seats. Then, in Willemsz's words:

> There is a bench, preciously made, which is placed squarely in the middle of the choir. Here the precentors are sitting, and they alternate with one another, two together alternately intoning the psalms, very pleasantly and

magnificently. And they sing splendidly, partly simple [i.e., *simpelsanck*], and partly *fabridoen* on the other side. This is altogether very beautiful and magnificent to hear and to see.[126]

Here, too, as in the Dutchman's account of attending mass, the essential feature is the alternation of plainsong (*simpelsanck*) and improvised polyphony (*fabridoen*), sung from within the sanctuary. This practice is enshrined in embryo psalm settings that alternate chant with composed polyphony, one of the three stylistic categories present in Willaert's psalms of 1550.[127] Taken together, these two passages provide remarkably precise descriptions of the positions and musical functions of the canons of San Marco, 'those who psalmodize', during the celebration of mass and vespers; at this date they were evidently disposed on both sides of the sanctuary, one group singing chant (*simpelsanck*) and the other *contrapunt* (i.e., *cantus figuralis*, not necessarily counterpoint) or *fabridoen*. The professional singers (the 'discanters'), who performed only during mass, were accommodated in the 'beautiful, round, big, high pew', which must be the hexagonal *pulpitum magnum cantorum*, more popularly known as the *bigonzo* or 'tub' (see pl. 38). It was from here that notated polyphony, most probably a motet at the offertory, was performed. In view of the many Byzantine influences present in the decorative and liturgical arrangements within the sanctuary of San Marco, it may be that there is a historical echo here of the way in which the ambo functioned in the nave of Hagia Sophia. This consisted of a raised platform, supported by eight columns and approached by stairs, leaving space underneath to accommodate a group of professional singers.[128]

Assembled from elements of different origins, the *pulpitum magnum*, together with the *pulpitum novum lectionum*, a two-tier structure surmounted by a ciborium, had been installed in the first half of the thirteenth century. Composed of slabs of *verde antico* raised on columns, the lower platform of the *pulpitum novum* was used for singing the Epistle on solemn feasts, and for preaching in the presence of the doge on five major feasts of the year. The upper section contains a lectern and was used for singing the Gospel.[129] On the other hand, the principal purpose of the *pulpitum magnum*, which was constructed of red porphyry sections supported on columns, was to accommodate the doge. It was from here that the doge listened to mass and was presented to the people after his election. Documents of various kinds, ranging from Martin da Canal's chronicle to Sanudo's diary via early fourteenth-century liturgical and ceremonial specifications, all locate the doge in the *bigonzo*. It has been argued that, in recognition of the doge's status, this practice equated the doge with the Byzantine emperor, who heard mass from a throne situated in the southern exedra of Hagia Sophia, beyond the iconostasis. There were exceptions though, such as the solemn feast-days when processions passed before the doge or the doge participated in the liturgy; on these occasions he was placed in the Cappella di San Clemente, close to the high altar.[130]

Sometime in the 1530s, during the dogeship of Andrea Gritti, it was decided (presumably by Gritti himself) to accommodate the doge and the members of the government who accompanied him in the chancel, where previously the *primicerio* and the canons of San Marco had sat, and to move the clergy. In 1535 Sansovino's new ducal throne, constructed of walnut, was installed together with the seating for the Signoria and other government officials. In the following year work began on the first of Sansovino's tribunes, which was erected on top of a pre-existent medieval structure of similar size and dimensions. At this stage there is no indication that a second tribune was intended, but in 1541 payments were made for work on this second structure, which continued until 1544.[131] That it was not originally planned is suggested by the iconographic scheme of the reliefs; while those of the first tribune show familiar scenes from the *Life of St Mark*, those on the second illustrate three posthumous miracles that are comparatively obscure and that do not occur elsewhere in the decoration of the basilica.[132]

The motives for this sequence of changes are unclear. It has been suggested that the decision to move the doge from the *bigonzo* might have been due to Gritti's immobility, caused, according to his early biographers, by gluttony; famously, the doge is reported to have died from an excess of lampreys, prepared for the Christmas vigil.[133] It seems more likely that the *renovatio* was an attempt to impose a classicizing style on the central sacral area of the basilica that was in keeping with Sansovino's scheme for the Piazza. It may also have been prompted by Willaert's double-choir psalm-settings, some of which were undoubtedly composed long before they were published in 1550. This might also account for the interval between the construction of Sansovino's first and second *pergoli*, since pieces in the first section of *I salmi appertinenti alli vesperi . . . a uno et a duoi chori*, the first printed monument to Venetian practice, are written for one polyphonic choir singing alternatim with chanted verses. In practice, this could have been done by a small choir of polyphonists standing in the first *pergolo*, which in any case was merely a replacement for an existing structure. On the other hand, the addition of the second *pergolo* a few years later might have been prompted by the performance problems posed by the more compli-cated pieces in the second and third sections of the collection, both of which require two four-voice choirs. It is the psalm-settings in this last category, which are exclusively by Willaert, that the printer Antonio Gardano calls *salmi spez-zadi*.[134] The spatial separation of the two choirs is mentioned by Willaert's pupil Zarlino as the preferred method of performance for double-choir pieces written in harmonically self-sufficient, that is, independent sections.[135]

However suitable Zarlino (and perhaps Willaert) considered the arrangement to be, it did not survive the composer's death in 1562. In his *Delle cose nota-bili*, published in the previous year, Francesco Sansovino noted that the tri-bunes were new, and that they were used for singing the Epistle and Gospel as needed.[136] Two years later, Bartolomeo Bonifacio wrote in the new version of the *Ceremoniale*:

Formerly, on all solemn feasts, the psalms were sung by the small choir, and by the singers who normally sing from practice [*ex pratica cantant*, that is, from memory], if they were available; in which case they were appointed to sing *more georgiano* [simple two-part polyphony].[137] Today this practice has fallen into disuse, and the singers of the greater choir sing all the psalms and whatever remains. And they sing the psalms divided into two choirs, namely four singers in one choir and all the rest in the other, since the small choir no longer exists.[138]

Thereafter the continued use of the *bigonzo* as the principal location for the *cappella marciana* throughout the latter part of the sixteenth century and beyond is well documented. Writing in the early seventeenth century, Stringa described the arrangement as follows:

> Opposite the two pulpits just described [the *pulpitum novum*], in which as I said the Gospel and Epistle are sung, is found the musicians' pergola. This is an octagonal form and it is supported by seven columns of the finest stone; two lower [ones] against the wall also help to support it. In this the musicians sing High Mass and the Divine Office of Vespers on almost all the ferial days and especially on those solemn feasts when the Signoria comes to church[139]

This arrangement was noted by the English traveller Thomas Coryate on his visit to Venice in 1608, and is repeated by Stringa in his *Vita di San Marco*.[140] Later in the century it is described in Giovanni Pace's new *Ceremoniale* for San Marco, which was first drawn up in 1678, and in a number of drawings and paintings by Canaletto showing the interior of the basilica, the best known of which is a drawing inscribed in the artist's hand; it is, in fact, his last known dated work (pl. 45).[141] In addition to music for mass and vespers performed close to the high altar, other areas of the basilica were also sometimes used. The balcony, which gives onto the Piazza at the west end of the church, was used by the choir on occasion, and for the grandest polychoral works temporary staging was put up.

For some time it has been clear that Willaert did not 'invent' the genre of *salmi spezzati* as often used to be claimed, but rather contributed to a practice that had already emerged in the works of native Italians working in the Veneto, possibly as early as the 1520s.[142] In the early years of that decade vespers for two choirs were sung at the annual commemoration of defunct members of the Confraternità del Santissimo Sacramento in Treviso, one of a number of confraternities connected to the cathedral and baptistery, by the choir of the cathedral under the direction of Francesco Santacroce; the music itself is presumably to be identified with Santacroce's double-choir psalms that partially survive in a later manuscript preserved in the cathedral archive.[143] In addition to Santacroce's psalms, the earliest sources of the repertory also include *salmi*

45   Giovanni Antonio Canal, *Musicians Singing in San Marco*, pen-and-ink drawing, 1766. Hamburg, Kunsthalle.

spezzati by Fra Ruffino Bartolucci d'Assisi, who was active in Padua after 1510 both at the Santo and at the cathedral, where Santacroce sang under his direction before leaving for Treviso. These two composers are generally credited with having written the earliest double-choir pieces to have survived.[144] Ruffino was in turn succeeded there by Giordano Passetto, whose settings of vesper psalms survive in a manuscript probably copied in the city in the mid-1530s. To the names of Treviso and Padua as places where the style was cultivated should be added that of Bergamo. In a letter to Giovanni del Lago written on 13 March 1536, the theorist Pietro Aron describes the music that he had heard there the previous day when he had taken the habit of the Crutched Friars:

> Messer Gasparo [Alberti], choirmaster here, and twenty-two singers attended. They sang Vespers for double choir very beautifully, with *salmi spezzati*, a Magnificat for two choirs, and all the antiphons in counterpoint – something I should never have believed, and even worthy of Venice.[145]

46 Giovanni Falier, medal of Andrea Gritti, procurator of San Marco, *c.*1517–23. Venice, Museo Civico Correr.

The principal interest of this passage is that it describes the practice of *salmi spezzati* in Bergamo some years before the date of the earliest surviving sources (three manuscripts from Santa Maria Maggiore, two of which are dated 1541–2),[146] and confirms the importance of Gasparo Alberti, who worked at the basilica of Santa Maria Maggiore, in the early history of double-choir compositional technique. Significantly, it also implies that the practice was well established in Venice, presumably at San Marco, by the mid-1530s, some fifteen years before the appearance of *I salmi appertinenti.*[147] In other words, this small group of interrelated manuscripts relays a distinct corpus of double-choir music, mostly vesper psalms, written by a group of composers, all of whom were working in the cities of the Veneto.[148] While two of these, Padua and Treviso, lie geographically close to Venice itself, it is also worth recalling that Andrea Gritti, responsible for so many cultural initiatives during his period as doge, had gained extensive knowledge of the principal towns of the *terraferma* during his career in the army before being captured by the French after the siege of Brescia in 1512; following his release he returned to his command.[149] He had been famously present at the retaking of Padua in 1509, was made *provveditor generale* of the army in 1516, and led the Venetian troops at the battles for the liberation of Bergamo, Brescia and Verona; a medal issued as public recognition of his valour was probably issued between this last event (in 1517) and his election as doge. It shows, on the reverse, Gritti in classical dress arriving on horseback at speed in front of the gate of a city (pl. 46). Gritti was still in post, with responsibility for maintaining territorial defences, when he was nominated for the dogeship in May 1523.[150] It may well be that the idea of introducing the polychoral style at San Marco was his, and that it was based on his having heard music composed in this style, and above all vespers psalms, performed in the towns and cities of the Veneto. Of these, the most important was undoubtedly Treviso, which, as the only foothold on the *terraferma* to remain in Venetian hands immediately after Agnadello, was mythologized as a model city. More practically, it was to Treviso that patricians were sent to restore morale and captain the garrison.[151] As part of such an experience, Gritti's exposure to the double-choir repertory of Santacroce and his contemporaries may have been critical for later developments in Venice itself.

In the absence of surviving polyphonic sources from San Marco, the descriptions of musical practice in the diaries of Arendt Willemsz and Jan van Gorcum are precious. From them a clear picture emerges of a range of musical practices at the basilica before Willaert's arrival there. The most basic form of musical provision, provided by the canons, involved an alternatim style in which some chanted and the remainder sang simple improvised polyphony; this was done from within the area of the choir. To this music, provided by what the documents describe as the small choir (*cappella parva*), could be added extra polyphony sung by the musicians in the *pulpitum magnum*. Presumably this would occur only on major feast-days, and is evidently what the two Dutchmen heard when they attended mass on a day of sufficient importance for the Pala d'Oro to be open. By the time that Bonifacio came to compile this section of his *Ceremoniale* the small choir had been discontinued,[152] and responsibility for polyphonic music had passed to a single choir, the *cantores maioris capellae*, who could perform from a number of places, but on major feasts sang from the *bigonzo*. It was for this group, which was divided into two choirs with 'four singers in one choir and all the rest in the other, since the small choir no longer exists', as Bonifacio puts it, that *cori spezzati* settings were written.

The origins of the Venetian polychoral style clearly lie in the simple alternation of chant and improvised polyphony that Willemsz and Van Gorcum describe and Bonifacio terms 'more georgiano'.[153] That the *mos georgianus* was simply *falso bordone* under another name current in north-east Italy is further supported by Willemsz in his diary, who in providing a clear and technically competent description of the practice refers to it as *contrapunt* or *fabridoen*. In other words, a common and perhaps the most frequently heard polyphony at San Marco during the fifteenth and early sixteenth centuries was a form of improvised polyphony executed by the *cappella parva* from memory. It was during this period that Willaert was first employed, presumably with the intention of extending the general policy of enhancement to the functions of the *cappella marciana* and the repertory that they performed, as a musical expression of the glories of the Republic and its new-found confidence after the war of the League of Cambrai; it was this, rather than Gritti's determination to act against the procurators' wishes, that was the main motor of change.[154] Nonetheless, Gritti did have a role in the transformation of the choir, as the person responsible for engaging Willaert as *maestro di cappella*.[155] In relation to vespers in particular, Willaert's development of the *cori spezzati* style was based on the existing alternatim tradition in which the music of the liturgy was provided by the canons, some chanting and the remainder singing simple improvised polyphony. The result, monumentalized in Willaert's contribution to *I salmi appertinenti alli vesperi . . . a uno et a duoi chori*,[156] may be thought of as a classicizing of ancient tradition, an equivalent in music to Sansovino's architecture. A very particular arrangement, with the vespers psalms possibly being sung from Sansovino's tribunes, which may well have been designed in response to existing musical practice, seems to have been in operation only during Andrea Gritti's dogeship, but the organizational principles of the Venetian *cori spezzati* style, as formulated by Willaert on the basis of the existing musical practices of the basilica, in turn provided the stylistic starting point for the monumental polychoral manner of Andrea Gabrieli, who, beginning in the 1560s, wrote music for two and more choirs. A critical feature of this further expansion of the style was the decision, taken in the same decade, to add instruments to the ducal chapel. The traditional style of polychoral music persisted well into the seventeenth century (by which time it had, of course, been joined by others, including eight-voice concertato settings), and it can still be identified in pieces by Giovanni Gabrieli, Claudio Monteverdi, Rovetta, Grandi and Cavalli. By this time the organ lofts were also being used by the choir.[157] In addition to polychoral works, some of which were composed to non-liturgical texts for performance on important civic occasions, the composers associated with San Marco also contributed more modest works with a distinctive Venetian stamp. Gioseffo Zarlino's setting of 'Beatissimus Marcus', and Claudio Merulo's of 'Cum beatissimus Marcus' both written for five voices, form part of a substantial repertory of smaller-scale liturgical motets in honour of St Mark.[158]

While on the one hand the basilica's exclusive use of the *patriarchino* after 1456 only strengthened the social and political functions of the rite, on the other it made it less accessible. This may in turn have been another element that encouraged the increase in public occasions, above all processions, when a wider public was able to participate. For all that San Marco was the private chapel of the doge, it is clear that its congregation, the 'audience' for this elaborate liturgical ritual so richly spiced with prominent civic overtones, was drawn from Venetian society at large. The development of a close relationship between music, liturgy, ceremonial and architectural design that occurred within the chancel during the first six decades of the sixteenth century created a unique theatre, based on a keen sense of tradition and history, for the expression of Venice's own self-image. But who constructed it and for whom was it intended? Venetians, who could often see the doge surrounded by officials and clergy, accompanied by symbolic objects, in impressive processions in the Piazza San Marco and elsewhere in the city, were also present inside the basilica on liturgical occasions, including the investiture of the doge.[159] The magnificence of these occasions, with doge, officials and clergy splendidly dressed as prescribed, would have contributed to a sense of awe, and the choreography of the spectacle, the chanting of the liturgy and the performance of music must all have created an overall effect of magisterial splendour. Nonetheless, it is not clear that either the processions in the Piazza or the ceremonies inside the basilica led to feelings of great warmth and affection towards the doge, or that the *popolani* identified as strongly with the Lion of St Mark as did the patriciate. In the sixteenth century, popular unrest largely took the form of heresy or religious dispute,[160] and the people generally caused little trouble. Popular violence and excess were catered for by rituals such as Carnival, or the factional battles for possession of the city's bridges,[161] which were sanctioned by the authorities, who were often involved either structurally (as in the case of Giovedì Grasso, when the presence of the doge and other officials was essential) or as casual spectators. These democratic rituals, when citizens of all classes were involved, as well as those centred on the Doge's Palace and San Marco when ordinary Venetians were present as observers, functioned as a method of social control as much as stimulating wonder or providing entertainment. The more important audience was to be found elsewhere, among the patricians who took part and who constituted the governing class of the Venetian empire. It was from among their number that the doge, who was at the heart of official ceremony, was selected. In this sense the rituals themselves, and the music that accompanied them, functioned primarily as visual and aural codifications of the hierarchy of power. Their evolution from the twelfth century onwards is paralleled by the expansion and embellishment of the two principal official spaces of the city and the buildings that framed them, as they were developed into theatrical arenas suitable for the enactment of such spectacular rituals.

CHAPTER THREE

Theatre of the World

During the period of the communes, between the eleventh century and the fourteenth, many Italian cities were expanded and their features remodelled as both their economic importance and their populations increased. The new building that accompanied this development usually involved modification of existing urban structures, the streets, squares and monuments inherited from the classical past. Venice, a later settlement standing on wooden piles driven into the mud of the lagoon, was obviously not conditioned in this way. Although it was unique among the great cities of Italy in that it had no Roman roots, no ancient grid plan or classical monuments to determine the essential outline of its urban landscape, in common with other urban centres Venice grew in size during this period of general expansion. Initially this took place around the two focal points of ecclesiastical and political life in the emergent city. The first of these, on the island of Olivolo, had become the seat of the bishop by the end of the eighth century; its role as the administrative centre of the local church continued after Venice had become a patriarchate and the cathedral of San Pietro had been constructed. The second was the area around San Marco.[1]

During the second half of the eleventh century, while Contarini's church was being built on the site, the Piazza San Marco began to take on a more formal appearance. By this date the area immediately surrounding the church included a tower, originally built as a fortification but subsequently transformed into a campanile (bell-tower), a hospice for pilgrims and the ducal palace itself. Originally this terrain consisted of two islands facing the Bacino di San Marco, separated by a canal. The Doge's Palace and the church of San Marco occupied the eastern end, and the free-standing bell-tower stood among the shops,

47   Detail of pl. 74.

houses and other buildings that ringed the area. In front of the church was an L-shaped open field that extended towards the lagoon in one direction and away from San Marco in the other. Owned by the nuns of San Zaccaria, this space had been traditionally used as a meeting-place where important matters of state were discussed. It was probably during the dogeship of Sebastiano Ziani (1172–8) that this area was radically transformed in ways that imposed a more official dimension and brought it closer in configuration to what later became the Piazza and the Piazzetta. The space itself was enlarged, and a continuous series of houses of the same height, with shops on the ground floor, was constructed around its northern, western and southern boundaries. All of the shops and some of the houses could be rented, which not only provided valuable income for the procurators, whose offices and residences occupied the southern edge of the complex, but also gave the square a distinctive mixed character that it was to retain in subsequent remodellings.[2] These changes were characteristic of a more general approach to the urban fabric in late twelfth-century Venice, when, as the authority of the commune increased, the state began to take over responsibilities that previously had been in the hands of individuals. The creation of a new civic square was one of three major projects initiated by the Venetian government in the late twelfth century, the others being the construction of the naval complex at the Arsenal and the development of the area around the Rialto bridge.[3] Taken together, they represent a sustained attempt by the authorities to order and embellish the military, commercial and politico-ecclesiastical centres of the city with suitable structures.

As part of the first of these schemes the Doge's Palace was enlarged, and the two granite columns, later to be surmounted by figures of the *Lion of St Mark* and *St Theodore*, were placed at the edge of the water. The practice, ultimately derived from imperial example, of displaying statues on columns as a way of emphasizing authority was widespread.[4] In the Venetian case the figures of these two patron saints combined references to both spiritual and temporal rule. Later a number of other free-standing columns, including the Pillars of Acre (pl. 48) and the Pietra del Bando, were also placed in the Piazzetta. Originally, the Pillars flanked the main southern entrance to San Marco where, in addition to functioning as markers of the main ceremonial route through the Piazzetta from the lagoon, they also played a significant role in the symbolic transformation of the basilica. This, achieved through analogy with the Temple of Solomon, whose porch, as described in the Bible, was similarly framed by two large columns,[5] is also expressed through decorative detail. Both the columns of the Temple and the Pillars bear pomegranate motifs, while a stone relief showing the *Judgement of Solomon* is incorporated into the façade of the Doge's Palace at the corner closest to the south door of San Marco.[6] Both the basilica and the Doge's Palace are presented, in terms of decorative detail and function, as Solomonic, appropriate structures for the role of Venice as a new Jerusalem.[7] The concept itself is clearly modelled on the precedent of Constantinople.[8]

48   Pillars of Acre. Piazza San Marco.

In addition to the structure and decoration of San Marco and its immediate surroundings, the concept of Venice as a new Jerusalem was incorporated
into ritual action. During the Easter morning ceremonies in the basilica, the
doge processed to the Easter Sepulchre, where the 'Quem queritis' dialogue was
sung according to a local practice, determined by the participation of the doge
as principal witness to the Resurrection, and by the role of San Marco as both
private chapel and state church.[9] In the Piazza San Marco itself, parallels
between Venice and Jerusalem were also strongly evoked on the feast of Corpus
Christi, when, following mass in the basilica, some of the pilgrims gathered in
the city to make the trip to the Holy Land participated in a procession around
the square, each accompanied by one of the senators.[10] Two fifteenth-century
pilgrims, Pietro Casola and Sir Richard Guylforde, recorded this experience, the
latter noting that the pilgrims processed 'with lyghte in our hands of wexe, of
the freshest formynge, geven unto us by the mynysters of the sayde procession'.[11] These candles were then preserved and carried to Jerusalem, where they

were lit and placed in front of the Holy Sepulchre. In later centuries, when the pilgrimage trade had effectively become a thing of the past,[12] each senator accompanied a member of the Venetian poor, who was presented on the occasion with clothing, money and a candle, the last a remnant of the previous practice.[13] The process is characteristic of much ritual of the Republic, transforming the universally Christian into the specifically Venetian, by appropriating a common festal act celebrated throughout Catholic Europe and investing it with local significance.[14] In this process the city became a psychological and symbolic extension of the sacred space of Jerusalem itself, and the ceremonies in the Piazza and the basilica, carried out in the presence of the doge, an official benediction of a great spiritual enterprise. This imaginative and characteristic exercise in appropriation was assisted by the presence, close by, in the convent of Santo Sepolcro on the Riva degli Schiavoni, of a local version of the Holy Sepulchre, which consisted of a marble monument, executed by Tullio Lombardo, decorated with the inscription HIC INTVS EST CORPVS IESV CHRISTI.[15] Venice had become Jerusalem.

By filling in a narrow canal that originally ran across the middle of the present Piazza San Marco, and demolishing the church of San Geminiano, the procurators brought a new sense of spaciousness and order to the area to the west of the church and palace during the late twelfth century.[16] With these changes, San Marco became, for the first time, the focal point of what was now a genuine square, which functioned as an imposing forecourt, and the two were both visually and ceremonially connected. The total area, which has been calculated at 12,000 square metres, made the Piazza and Piazzetta together larger than any of the squares of mainland Italy, including those of Bologna, Florence and Siena.[17] Finally paved in 1266, the new ensemble was now complete. Although its shape and area had been determined by the available open space acquired from the nuns of San Zaccaria, its mid-thirteenth-century form and function were also the product of a coherent plan, almost certainly devised by the procurators. This made its development quite different from the Piazza del Campo in Siena, for example, where the variety of building heights and fenestration patterns reflects the fact that many of the properties bordering the square remained in private hands. Something similar is to be seen throughout northern Italy, where early medieval arcaded street fronts and continuous porticoes are commonly found in civic squares, but the buildings themselves are often of different heights and periods, reflecting a heterogeneous pattern of ownership. In its mid-thirteenth-century configuration the Piazza San Marco had more in common with the imperial *fora* of the Byzantine empire, some examples of which were visible and had been in continuous use since late antiquity, rather than with these developments elsewhere in Italy. As with the basilica itself, the prime source of inspiration was Constantinople, where a sequence of *fora* and forum-like squares was strung out along the city's principal thoroughfare, the Mese.[18] Surrounded by meeting-halls, public baths, shops, churches and palaces all linked by porticoes, many of these spaces still remained in use after the Venetians began to frequent Constantinople; it is not surprising that some of these features reappear in the Piazza and Piazzetta.[19] Just as the appropriation of the Apostoleion gave the Venetians an architectural archetype that provided them with the opportunity to assert the status of San Marco as an apostolic foundation, so too the modelling of the Piazza, following the example of Constantinople, and the embellishment of both it and the Piazzetta with *spolia* from the Fourth Crusade supplied an imperial metaphor. Initially, during the dogeship of Sebastiano Ziani, the intention had been to dignify the official image and functions of the *commune veneciarum*, and it was only later, under Ziani's son Doge Pietro, that the scheme took on a more ambitious inflection. Later changes not only amplified the Piazza and enlarged its frame of imperial references, but also made it more scenographic, with the basilica now located more centrally along the eastern side of the square and the Campanile more obviously a free-standing structure. The symbolic location of buildings and monuments within the square defines the purposes and meanings of its extended confines (the buildings do not merely frame the space but are also contained within it), while the addition of symbolic objects such as clocks, *spolia* and statues combine to augment these purposes and meanings. Until the end of the Republic the Piazza and Piazzetta served as the main arena for religious and civic ritual in Venice, for the processions and ceremonies that filled the annual calendar, as well as those that marked military and naval victories, alliances and peace treaties, the election of the doge, and other public events.

The heightened theatricality with which state processions could be enacted in this expanded space was almost immediately realized as a consequence of the decision to demolish the medieval church of San Geminiano on the western flank of the Piazza. According to Francesco Sansovino, admittedly a somewhat distant witness, the destruction of the church, which served one of a number of parishes that abutted onto the area around San Marco, aroused papal displeasure, which was finally assuaged only by expressions of repentance and a series of compensatory measures. These included Ziani's undertaking that an annual *andata* was to be made in perpetuity to a new church of San Geminiano, which was to be rebuilt further to the west. Giovanni Stringa, a canon of San Marco, recounting the details of the occasion in its early seventeenth-century form, implies that this procession was elaborate and involved not only the doge, but also the apostolic legate and other dignitaries together with the Signoria. Once it had reached the church of San Geminiano, mass was celebrated with music sung by the choir of San Marco. On its return, the procession stopped at the site of the earlier, demolished church, where the officiating priest recalled the historical origins of the *andata* and issued an invitation to the doge to renew the procession the following year.[20] Whether or not Sansovino's anecdote is to be believed (it is otherwise found in only one of the sixteenth-century chroniclers),[21] there can be no doubt that state ceremonial life

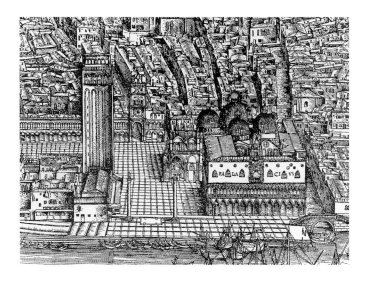

49   Jacopo de' Barbari, *View of Venice* (detail), woodcut, 1500.
Venice, Museo Civico Correr.

must have taken on a new dimension as a result of Ziani's creation of the Piazza.
Ziani gave it a form that remained more or less unchanged until the early sixteenth century. It is possible to recover some impression of how it then looked
from two famous views of about the same date: Gentile Bellini's painting of
1496 showing a procession in the square, one of a cycle of scenes commissioned
by the Scuola Grande di San Giovanni for their *albergo* depicting miracles associated with the True Cross,[22] and Jacopo de' Barbari's detailed bird's-eye view
of the city published in 1500 (pl. 49). In scale similar to a mural, the map, the
largest and most detailed plan of Venice before modern times, is of exceptional
quality.[23] It is made up of six large sheets, which together present a view of the
city seen from the south-west, with the islands of the lagoon visible in the distance and the Alps on the horizon. Compared with the illustrations in printed
books, which are the only views of the city to precede it, its monumentality is
breathtaking.[24] It is often praised for its accuracy, but despite its naturalism and
a high level of detail, the real subject of the map is not so much the physical
city as the commonwealth of Venice, the hub of trade between East and West,
the home of the most powerful European maritime nation.[25] It is, in other
words, the earliest cartographical expression of the Myth of Venice, an equivalent on paper to Carpaccio's *Lion of St Mark* (pl. 50), which stands in dominion over land and sea, with the galleys that ensured its economic prosperity in
the background to the right, and the Doge's Palace, the home of justice and
good government, to the left. In practice the map contains more omissions and
distortions than are usually recognized,[26] while the value of Bellini's painting,
traditionally regarded as an almost archaeological record of how the square

50 Vittore Carpaccio, *Lion of St. Mark*, 1516. Ducal Palace.

looked at the end of the fifteenth century, is compromised by extensive nine-teenth-century restoration. Both of them show, on both the north and south sides of the Piazza, a mixture of buildings of different periods and styles – Gothic, Romanesque and fifteenth century – united by the porticoes that had been such a feature of the area since the space had been enlarged in the twelfth century (pl. 51). The map in particular gives a good impression of the size of the square itself, which, before Jacopo Sanso-vino's intervention, corresponded in length to its present dimensions but was much narrower in width, since the southern side of the square was aligned with the bell-tower. In locating the Library to the south of the tower, Sansovino also established the boundary of the Procuratie Nuove, which, having been continued under Vincenzo Scamozzi's direction in the late six-teenth century, was finally completed, though in altered form, by Baldassare Longhena in the seventeenth.[27] It was only with the demolition of the Ospizio Orseolo, clearly shown at the foot of the bell-tower in Bellini's painting, that the west façade of San Marco was fully revealed on the eastern flank of the Piazza. One consequence was that the Campanile itself became even more independent and monumental, a characteristic that Sansovino's decorative Loggetta emphasized further.[28]

With one exception, both painting and map record how the square looked before work on Sansovino's scheme began in the

51 Gentile Bellini, *Procession in the Piazza San Marco* (detail), 1496. Venice, Gallerie dell'Accademia.

52 Torre dell' Orologio, 1496–9. Piazza San Marco.

1530s. The exception is significant, though, since the Procuratie Vecchie, built by 'maistro Bon' (now thought to be Pietro rather than Bartolomeo, to whom the overseeing of the work, though not necessarily the design, has been traditionally assigned), was not put up until later.[29] Its construction, prompted by the destruction by fire of some Veneto-Byzantine houses, was just one of a number of contributions, including the completion of Mauro Codussi's Torre dell'Orologio on the north side of the square at the entrance to the Merceria (pl. 52), that Bon made to the appearance of the square in the second decade of the sixteenth century. Bon's building, sometimes thought to be eclectic and even anachronistic, deliberately enforces a sense of continuity with Venetian traditions and institutions,[30] largely through the repetitive arcading, which recalls the previous arrangement of this side of the square (pl. 53).

Sansovino's vision was different. His appointment as *proto magister* to the procurators in 1529, two years after arriving in Venice en route for France as a refugee from the Sack of Rome, placed him in charge of the construction of all new building in the Piazza and the Piazzetta, including San Marco, except for the Doge's Palace. His duties, which included the day-to-day maintenance of all properties, both there and elsewhere, owned and administered by the procurators, placed Sansovino under the patronage of the wealthiest sponsors of new building work anywhere in the city, at a time when the political will to remodel the Piazza and its surrounding buildings was strong. The consequence was what has been described as an ambitious *renovatio urbis*, inaugurated during the dogeship of Andrea Gritti (1523–38) and carried out with his active encouragement.[31] Following the disaster of Agnadello, and the loss of Venetian prestige that followed, it was Gritti's intention to restore the city's image as a great cosmopolitan entrepôt, founded on the twin pillars of commerce and culture, flourishing once again under a benign republican regime administered with justice and wisdom. Physical expression of this concept was to be secured through a radical architectural renewal of the central civic spaces at San Marco and the Rialto, so as to lend them a sense of splendour, magnificence and *auctoritas*.[32] Venetian interest in Roman architectural style, often associated with the diaspora that followed the Sack, was promoted by Gritti from shortly after his election.[33] Sansovino, whose second period in Rome lasted from 1518 to 1527, except for a brief spell when he was in Florence and possibly Venice, was the instrument that made its realization possible. Although Gritti was undoubtedly the moving force behind the overall scheme, the overseers of the work on a daily basis were the procurators who lived on the square (as did Sansovino himself), and whose decisions are recorded. In practice, the support of important procurators was essential for the successful launching of the project.

53 Procuratie Vecchie. Piazza San Marco.

One of the most ancient offices in the Venetian constitution, the post of procurator was conferred for life, and as such it carried a status and prestige that was second only to the dogeship itself. The position may have existed as early as the ninth century, since, according to legend, it was the construction and decoration of the ducal church as a repository for the sacred relics of St Mark that had originally led to its establishment, but the earliest documentation comes from the twelfth century.[34] Originally the procurator had been the doge's nominee, but during the first half of the thirteenth century the holder was made responsible to the Great Council, which also assumed the power of election. This important change in the constitutional arrangements is a clear indication of the changing nature of the procuratorship, which, largely because of bequests, had grown into the most important financial authority of the state; it has also been taken to mark the moment when San Marco began to evolve from the private chapel of the doge to the state church of Venice.[35] Responsibilities now included those of maintaining a depository for the specie of both the commune and of individual citizens, of administering estates and perpetual trusts, and of running a lending bank, which as early as 1198 had been called upon by the state itself. In keeping with the increase in power and responsibility that this transformation of the office brought in its wake, the number of procurators was gradually increased, a second post being added in the first half of the thirteenth century and two more in the course of it.[36]

This arrangement did not last long. By the early fourteenth century it had become apparent that the burden of work had increased enormously and that the office was under great strain. In 1318 the Great Council appointed a committee to present a written consideration of the situation. Its report, adopted the following year, added two more procurators to the original four, and further refined the division of labour along topographical lines. San Marco would continue to be supervised by two procurators *de supra*; two more would handle property and estates on the San Marco side of the canal (*de citra canale*); and the remaining two were to administer those on the opposite bank (*de ultra Rivoaltum sive ultra canale*).[37] This important reform established a structure that was to remain essentially intact until the fall of the Republic. In 1443, as work levels increased and special duties multiplied, three more procurators were added to the existing six, one in each of the three divisions. During the second half of the fifteenth century an earlier provision that forbade the procurators to hold other offices gradually broke down, and by 1523 it was made possible for two procurators in each division to sit and vote in the *savi* or in the *zonta* of the Council of Ten. This official benediction of a political voice for the procurators was the culmination of a long evolution. Already in 1454 they had been automatically made *ex officio* members of the Senate, and subsequently the procurators accumulated the rights to be nominated as ambassadors and to hold command in the navy or with the Venetian forces on the *terraferma*. From the moment in the thirteenth century when the procurators had first been made responsible to the Great Council, the potential had existed for curtailing ducal jurisdiction over the affairs of San Marco, of which the doge was both *patronus et gubernator*. Henceforward it was not the ecclesiastical authorities that were to provide the ultimate check in the affairs of San Marco, but a civic magistracy, which had gradually evolved into one of the most powerful offices of all. To be elected as a procurator was to arrive close to the pinnacle of political power and public recognition. This stage of advancement invariably occurred in what contemporaries would have regarded as old age, when the necessary qualities of *gravitas* and wisdom had been acquired; as has often been observed, the upper reaches of the patrician hierarchy was a gerontocracy.[38] The ethos of Venetian public service placed a strong emphasis upon seniority and continuity. Age was preferred over youth, and wisdom over imagination. Despite the large number of offices in Venice and throughout the empire to which any male noble could be elected, in real terms power was concentrated in the hands of just thirty-seven men who served on the more important bodies. In practice, the system encouraged a handful of patricians from a small number of prestigious families to move from one important office to another, in a *cursus honorem* that often culminated in the most coveted offices of all, those of procurator or doge. When, in 1482, Piero Priuli was elected a procurator, it was the culmination of a political career stretching over three decades, in the course of which he had served as one of the three *avogadori di comun* and, at the precocious age of 29, had been elected to the Forty, the highest court of the Republic,[39] a progression that was typical of someone of his class and formation. The sometimes manipulative behaviour of the rich and powerful, keen to be elected into a procuratorship, reflects the prestige and political importance of the post itself. As a decree from the Council of Ten noted in 1503, dubious electoral practices to secure nominations and block the progress of rival candidates were common, contrary to the conventions of voting according to personal knowledge and conscience.[40] In this, as in many other things, the Venetian patriciate often used government office for its own advancement.[41]

During the first half of the sixteenth century, the post of procurator underwent a yet further transformation as it became increasingly honorific, a prestigious reward, usually given late in life to those patricians who had served the state with distinction. Beginning with the crisis of the League of Cambrai, it was not unknown for election to the post to be facilitated by a financial contribution to the state.[42] Later still it could be bought outright. At times of uncertainty and crisis this policy was often extended, as it was during the War of Cyprus in the mid-sixteenth century, when several new procurators were elected from among those who were able to support their candidacy with 20,000 ducats. Alongside these developments went a corresponding increase in pomp and ceremony. When Zorzi Emo was elected procurator in 1516, a celebratory mass was said in San Marco, after which Emo, accompanied by a large number of patricians, presented himself in the Collegio, where he thanked the

54   Jacopo Tintoretto, *Portrait of Procurator Antonio Cappello*, c.1565. Venice, Gallerie dell' Accademia.

Signoria for the honour bestowed on him and undertook to devote himself to the service of the Republic as his predecessors had done. The following month the election of Alvise Loredano, son of the doge, was celebrated with even more elaborate festivities that lasted for more than a day. Once again the new procurator attended mass in San Marco and subsequently made an appearance in the Collegio to express his gratitude.[43] Significantly, the ritual forms used on this occasion paralleled those that followed the ones enacted for the installation of a doge. Both these men had paid substantial sums for their offices. Of particular interest here is the mixture of sacred and civic elements in the official proceedings in San Marco and in the Doge's Palace, and the use of these particular buildings (both of which were laden with historic and symbolic resonances) to enact the official confirmation of the election of a member of the patrician class to one of the most prestigious posts in the service of the Republic. Together with the unofficial festivities held in the family palace, these demonstrations of authority, usually carried out in front of highly placed relations (spectacularly so in the case of Loredano), were also visible celebrations of an elite power structure.

The prestige attached to the position, its often honorific nature and the pomp and circumstance that surrounded the procurators are reflected in the iconographically distinct genre of procuratorial portraits, in which the sitters are usually presented in their official robes and are often identified through initials and armorial devices. Although small-scale portraits of doges occur among the earliest examples of panel painting in Venice, those of procurators are rare before 1500. Titian's *Portrait of a Procurator*, of about 1510, has been identified as the first in a tradition of official independent portraits, a genre that reached something of a crescendo in the second half of the sixteenth century, by which time Jacopo Tintoretto's workshop seems to have gained a virtual monopoly of this aspect of the trade (pl. 54).[44] This earned Tintoretto the sobriquet of 'official portraitist to the Venetian gerontocracy', a role that he evidently found congenial;[45] it has been calculated that altogether the artist and his associates painted the portraits of four doges, thirty-six senators and dozens of procurators. Later, when the artist began to abandon civic portraits, the commissions passed to the studios of Leandro Bassano and Palma il Giovane.[46] As with civic ceremony itself, the height of production of official portraits of procurators coincided with a moment when self-promotion through displays of wealth was at a high point among the patrician governing elite, but this should not obscure either the political importance of the procuratorship or its function as a launching-pad for the ultimate prize. Two of the early sixteenth-century procurators most involved in building on and around the Piazza San Marco, Antonio Grimani and Andrea Gritti, later became doges. In the sixteenth century procurators could, and did, wield considerable political power.

From the beginning of their history the procurators had made decisions of artistic importance. It was the procurators who chose the *proto*, the procurators who supervised the mosaic decorations of the interior of San Marco, and the procurators who chose most of the officials who administered the liturgy within it, including not only the canons of San Marco, but also the organists and the *maestro di cappella*. The early development of the procuratorship from its original dual function of doge's deputy and guardian of San Marco into a more prominent role is paralleled by the gradual transformation over the centuries of the church itself from the private chapel of the doge to that of the state church of Venice. This transformation, which inevitably shaped artistic decisions of all kinds, is reflected in the character and iconography of the mosaics as they were executed from the late twelfth century onwards, in the architectural developments in the Piazza and the Piazzetta during the fifteenth and sixteenth centuries, and in the ceremonial and ritual arrangements that were evolved for use both inside and outside the basilica during the same period. In this sense the evolution of music and ritual, as it gradually passed from the private liturgical sphere to the public one, was just one element in a lengthy process of civic self-fashioning that can be charted in detail from the thirteenth century onwards, and in which the procurators were the main agents. In practice, not all the procurators were equally interested in these matters, and not all were equally diligent in attending meetings. Francesco Sansovino credits Vettore Grimani and Antonio Cappello, two of the younger and more forceful procurators of their time, with fostering and supporting the projects for the Library and Loggetta.[47]

Andrea Gritti's *Renovatio urbis* was clearly dependent upon the support of the procurators, who, in a practical everyday sense, were Sansovino's patrons. As it unfolded, the architect's task was not merely to complete Bon's building, but rather to inaugurate the first phase of a grandiose plan to line the remaining sides of the Piazza and the Piazzetta, together with the eastern end of the Molo, with new structures in the classical style.[48] According to Francesco Sansovino, his father had realized that the Piazza was the most noble public space of any Italian city, and had resolved that it should be dignified with buildings that, following ancient practice, were to be adorned with Doric and Ionian orders 'full of columns, friezes and cornices'.[49] The effect was to superimpose an evocation of ancient Rome upon the existing Byzantine elements of the square, whose presence had been strengthened by the neo-Byzantine revival of the late fifteenth and early sixteenth centuries. Then, encouraged by the unity of the Eastern and Western churches after the Council of Florence, the fall of Constantinople, the peace with the sultan in 1479, and the conflict between Venice and the papacy, Venetian architectural alignment with its Byzantine past was once again briefly encouraged in its search for a distinct and independent voice.[50]

By the time of his death Sansovino had completed the Loggetta at the foot of the bell-tower, sixteen bays of the Library facing the Doge's Palace, and the Zecca (Mint). His overall conception has been seen not only as a conscious attempt to evolve, in architectural terms, the Myth of Venice through the use of a distinctive classicizing language, but also as a courageous reinterpretation, on a monumental scale, of the typology of the ancient Roman forum as described by Vitruvius. This analogy is made explicit in Daniele Barbaro's commentaries on the *Dieci libri dell'architettura* (1556), where each of Vitruvius' building types is matched to Venetian examples in general and to Sansovino's work in the Piazza in particular.[51] A new sense of Venetian self-confidence is apparent in this campaign of renewal, a desire to impress the world with its *splendor civitatis* in the atmosphere that followed the identity crisis provoked by the trauma of Agnadello. A number of potent historical parallels were invoked in the process. In addition to being a new Jerusalem and, once again, a new Byzantium, Venice was also, for the first time, a second Rome.

Although the three buildings that Sansovino designed for the Piazza and Piazzetta were planned at more or less the same time, in appearance they are quite different. The Venetian Mint or Zecca had been located close to the Doge's Palace, at the heart of political power, from at least the end of the thirteenth century, when, at full capacity, about a hundred workmen were employed under the supervision of a master.[52] Two centuries later it consisted of a large three-storey building on the Molo, and a smaller one-storey structure facing the Piazzetta, which seems to have functioned as an entrance to the whole complex.[53] Sansovino's new building probably provided much the same facilities, since production was maintained during the rebuilding. Most of the work was done in individual 'shops', with silver being minted on the ground floor and gold on the floor above. Inside was a large inner courtyard; the workshops were ranged around it, and the furnaces were in the front part of the building.[54] The new Mint not only replaced the cramped and dangerous conditions of the previous building with a more efficient and secure version, it also provided the Republic with a suitably imposing symbol of its own economic power (pl. 55).[55] Conceived in the years following the Peace of Bologna in December 1529, as Venice shifted its stance from militant expansion to a more politically realistic appreciation of its role, now reduced in importance by the weight of the Habsburg presence in Italy,[56] Sansovino's building nonetheless

55 The Mint. Piazza San Marco.

speaks in imperial tones. Faced in white Istrian stone attached to a brick structure, both the façade and the internal courtyard beyond were originally articulated by different orders, with rustic columns on the ground floor, and a Doric
entablature above Tuscan columns on the *piano nobile*. This adventurous mix
of the Doric with rustication, famously characterized by Pietro Aretino in a
letter of 1537 praising Sansovino's work in the city,[57] was also admired by other
contemporaries. Giorgio Vasari, who was familiar with the architect and his
work, described it as 'entirely in the most beautiful rusticated order which,
never having been seen in the city before, considerably amazed the inhabitants'.[58] Justification for the juxtaposition of the two styles is also provided by
Sebastiano Serlio, another of Sansovino's close contacts, who in Book IV of his
treatise on architecture, first published in Venice (also in 1537), pointed out that
the rustic order had been mixed with Doric, Ionic and Corinthian in ancient
Rome. The result, he continued, 'is very attractive to look at, and represents
great strength. Thus I would consider it more suitable for a fortress than for
anything else.'[59] Similar sentiments are expressed in sources even closer to the
architect, the two guidebooks to Venice published by his son. In *Delle cose notabili che sono in Venetia* (1556), which takes the form of a conversation between

a Venetian and a visitor to the city, Francesco Sansovino describes the Mint as looking 'like a fortress in its outer entrance', and praised it as a 'worthy prison for most precious gold'.[60] Sanctioned both by classical precedent and architectural authority, Sansovino's ingenious combination of the orders proclaims the purpose of the Mint as a place of manufacture and storage, while visually defining the building's symbolic role as an emblem of the resources of the state.[61]

The Library, the second of Sansovino's buildings on the site, runs along the west side of the Piazza facing the Doge's Palace (pl. 56). Its stone façade incorporates a Doric order on the ground floor, with an Ionic *piano nobile* above, surmounted by a balustrade carrying a sequence of statues. The procurators had originally commissioned a three-storey building, but in his letter of 1537 Aretino describes it as a two-tier elevation.[62] By this time it had also been decided that Cardinal Bessarion's collection of books and manuscripts, bequeathed to the Republic in 1468, should be housed in the new building, a decision that finally resolved what had become an embarrassing dilemma. Bessarion's donation, which included one of the most important collections of Greek manuscripts ever assembled, had been made with the provision that the procurators should provide adequate accommodation for the library somewhere close to San Marco, and that the books should be available for consultation, but in practice the collection had been moved from one temporary home to another, with some books being damaged and others lost in the process.[63] The proposal to build a permanent and suitably distinguished library for the collection had been

56   The Library. Piazza San Marco.

57 Jost Amman, *The Piazzetta*, engraving, *c*.1565. Venice, Museo Civico Correr.

urged since the early 1530s, first by Vettor Grimani, and then by Pietro Bembo, who had been appointed librarian by the Council of Ten in 1530. Sansovino's design was accepted in 1535, but building progressed only slowly. Demolition of the existing buildings on the site, which included five inns and a number of shops, proceeded piecemeal in order to minimize the loss of revenue, and by 1540 only a small section of the scheme had been completed.[64] Ten years later the first seven bays, which incorporated the reading-room of the Library on the *piano nobile*, had been constructed; the curious appearance of the Piazzetta at mid-century, with the building half-finished and shops and taverns still occupying the corner site between the Library and the Mint, can be seen in a number of contemporary paintings and engravings (pl. 57). The buoyant economic conditions in the 1530s had by now been superseded by inflationary times, but the unfinished condition of the building, in such a prominent and symbolically significant position, was an embarrassment to the procurators. Keenly aware that their predecessors had spared no expense in embellishing the city, they determined to press on with the work 'for the honour and dignity of the Republic and for the benefit of the church',[65] and although the Venetian economy had continued to worsen, extra funds were allocated and building proceeded. During the later 1550s the reading-room, whose ceiling incorporates twenty-one roundels by seven artists including Titian and Veronese, was decorated, and it was probably shortly afterwards that Bessarion's books were finally moved into their new home, almost a century after his original bequest had been made.[66] Decoration of both the reading-room and the vestibule, which separates it from the staircase, continued throughout the 1560s, and although the library proper was already in use by the time of Sansovino's death in 1570, the scheme was only finally completed by Vincenzo Scamozzi, who became involved in the project during the 1580s, when the rest of the site was cleared and the remaining bays added.[67] In this final form the façade consisted of twenty-one two-storey openings flanked by columns.[68] Although Scamozzi's proposal to add an extra storey to the Library was rejected after considerable debate,[69] he did build to that height in the Procuratie Nuove, which continued the scheme along the south side of the Piazza, and so finally realized Sansovino's objective of a unified plan, achieved by a continuous and stylistically coherent façade running from the Library building at the Molo to the Torre dell'Orologio.[70]

Housing Bessarion's books and making them available for study had always been the primary motivation behind the planning and construction of Sansovino's Library, but at the end of the 1550s the Accademia Venetiana della Fama was also briefly given a home there. Founded in 1557 by Federigo Badoer, a successful diplomat and man-of-letters, the Accademia was an ambitious and even megalomaniac undertaking. In pursuit of its aims the Venetiana established two main activities: public lectures on the one hand and an ambitious publishing programme of more than three hundred titles, of which only forty or so ever appeared, on the other. This close connection between its intellectual enterprises and the press is clearly indebted to the example of its predecessor, the Aldine Academy, founded by Aldo Manuzio. Meetings of the Accademia Venetiana were initially held daily at Badoer's residence. As a semi-public arrangement with lecture rooms and library, the academy united and promoted distinctly Venetian ideas about education and public service in the formation of the Republic's ruling elite. Luca Contile, who joined this group of what he describes as the 'primi intelletti' of Venice in 1558, reports in a letter to Marc'Antonio Piccolomini that he attended for one-and-a-half hours every day. According to the *Instrumento di Deputatione*, a published manifesto setting out the financial, administrative and intellectual structure of the academy, by 1560 the Venetiana had a membership of about one hundred, which included nearly all the most prominent intellectuals of the city, many of whom were also active in its political life.[71]

A strong sense of the responsibilities of the academy, of its function as the engine of civic virtue, was common throughout Italy. In his treatise on the subject, Scipione Bargagli recommends the academies as 'contributing to the glory of cities and to the education of young nobles in the government of the state'.[72] In Venice this formulation took the particular form of a direct equation between the academy and the Republic, in which the one could be expressed as a metaphor of the other. From its very inception, Badoer's academy was seen not merely as an intellectual undertaking, but as the embodiment of the Venetian ideal of learning and religion allied in the service of the Republic. As such it was to be both decorative and useful, the ultimate instrument for achieving a powerful fusion of the *vita attiva* and the *vita contemplativa* undertaken in the context of the 'true and divine Christian religion', an orientation made explicit in the Venetiana's device, which shows the figure of *Fame* accompanied by the legend IO VOLO AL CIEL PER RIPOSARMI IN DIO ('I fly to heaven to rest with God') (pl. 58). This was not merely a simple statement of religious sentiment, but a calculated stance with precise political consequences.[73] Within the academy's rather short life this ambitious project was ostensibly realized. Many of its members, including Badoer himself, were active in politics, and for a while the Venetiana became the official publisher to the Venetian state, with the exclusive right to publish its decrees and other legislation.[74] With the transference of its seat from Badoer's palace to the *antisala* of the Library in 1560, the links between the Venetiana and the Republic were even more strongly symbolized (pl. 59). Beyond metaphor, Badoer's intention was to increase the audience for the public lectures given there, and to assist the librarian with the arrangement of Bessarion's collection in its new home. Notions of civic responsibility were to be translated into action. The installation of the Venetiana in the vestibule of Sansovino's Library emphasized that the new building, constructed directly opposite the Doge's Palace and within sight of the basilica, symbolized the values of the new republic, erected on the foundations of knowledge, civic duty and Christian ideals. When, in 1586, the Senate accepted Giovanni Grimani's gift of his famous collection of antiquities, Vincenzo Scamozzi was given the task of transforming the *antisala* into a museum under the supervision of one of the procurators *de supra*, Federico Contarini (1538–1613).[75] Work began in 1591, and notwithstanding disputes with Giovanni Grimani's heirs, who refused to allow a number of antique marbles fixed to the walls to be brought from the family palace at Santa Maria Formosa, the transfer of the collection was finally completed by January 1595. Contarini was himself a keen collector of medals, books, epigraphs, cameos and paintings, and at his death he left a group of seventeen classical marbles to join Grimani's collection, which now, thanks to Contarini's zeal, had been inventoried and placed on public view.[76] There, overseen by the presiding spirit of Titian's *Sapienza* (pl. 60), the collection was displayed as an appropriate frontispiece to the Library itself, lending to this temple of Renaissance learning a sense of antiquity that the Venetian past could not provide.[77] The Marciana had been both library and academy, and was now a museum.

58   Device of the Accademia Veneziana. Cambridge, University Library.

59   Antisala, Libreria di San Marco. Piazza San Marco.

At the other end of the Piazzetta, at the point where it joins on to the square proper, stands Sansovino's Loggetta, the third of his buildings on the Piazza San Marco (pl. 61).[78] This replaced a wooden and stone building used as a meeting place by members of the nobility who came to the Piazza on government business. There had been a structure there for this purpose at least since the thirteenth century, and its later appearance and function are shown in the background of a painting usually attributed to Lorenzo Bastiani (pl. 62). This main function of the loggia as a patrician meeting-place was also carried over to Sansovino's Loggetta, shown in a later engraving by Giacomo Franco being used in precisely this way (pl. 63). In addition, the Loggetta was regularly used by the procurators for transacting business relating to the nearby shops and markets that lay under their jurisdiction. With its unmistakable rhetorical invocation of the classical triumphal arch, and rich sculptural programme executed in coloured marbles, the Loggetta provided a more dignified setting for such activities. Situated at the focal point around which official pageantry and processions revolved, it was also planned as a sort of permanent *apparato* for the display of the four bronze figures that inhabit the niches.

Perhaps the most decorous of all of Sansovino's Venetian buildings, executed in his best Roman manner (it has been suggested that its model was Bramante's Santa Casa in Loreto),[79] the Loggetta emphatically proclaimed patrician control of the square and of the surrounding buildings, which housed the major offices of state, while also underlining the authority of the procurators themselves. At the same time, Sansovino's building celebrated Venetian state ideology through an elaborate scheme

60 Titian, *Sapienza*, c.1564. Piazza San Marco, Library.

of statues and bas-reliefs of historical and allegorical scenes. The meaning of its iconography is described for the first time by Francesco Sansovino in a treatise on rhetoric, *L'arte oratoria secondo i modi della lingua volgare* (1546), published when he was only 25 years old; this formed the basis for Sansovino's interpretations in *Tutte le cose notabili e belle che sono in Venetia* of ten years later, which,

61 The Loggetta. Piazza San Marco.

62 Lorenzo Bastiani, *Piazzetta* (detail), c.1487. Venice, Museo Civico Correr.

together with its later version, flows directly into his description of the Loggetta in the first edition of *Venetia, città nobilissima* (1581).[80] In the main panels of the attic, *Jupiter on Cyprus* (pl. 64) and *Venus on Crete* (pl. 65) are shown disposed on either side of a female personification of Venice, an allusion to the origins of the Venetian state, its imperial dimensions and its ability to resist its enemies successfully. Echoing the common trope of Venetia/Justice, and more particularly the figure of *Justice* on the nearby façade of the Doge's Palace, the image of *Venice* is, in Francesco Sansovino's words, 'una santissima giustitia' (pl. 66).[81] Beneath the attic the four bronze statues, which were placed in their niches on the façade in 1545, constitute an allegory of Venetian government. As explained by Sansovino, of the three gods in the sequence *Pallas* represents preparedness, secured through the wisdom of the Venetian Senate, *Mercury* stands for eloquence, and *Apollo* for the harmoniousness produced by good government. The cycle is rounded off by the allegorical figure of *Peace*, whose special relationship to Venice is expressed in the words of Christ to the apostolic protector of the city: 'Pax tibi, Marce Evan-

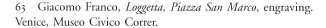

63 Giacomo Franco, *Loggetta, Piazza San Marco*, engraving. Venice, Museo Civico Correr.

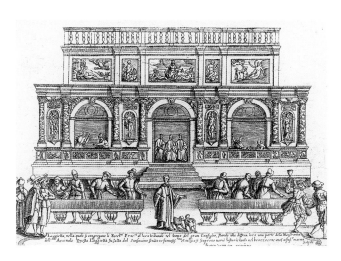

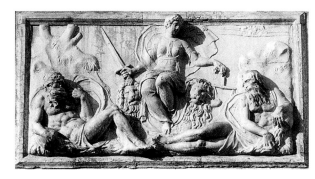

TOP 64 Jacopo Sansovino, *Jupiter on Cyprus*, c.1546. Piazza San Marco, Loggetta.

MIDDLE 65 Jacopo Sansovino, *Venus on Crete*, c.1546. Piazza San Marco, Loggetta.

BOTTOM 66 Jacopo Sansovino, *Venice/Justice*, c.1546. Piazza San Marco, Loggetta.

gelista meus' (pl. 67).[82] Of the remaining bronze panels decorating the base of the façade, not all can be identified; those that can allude to various maritime gods, in continuation of the theme presented in the attic reliefs.[83] With its relentless emphasis upon the imperial theme and the virtues of the Republic, the Loggetta, the first public monument to be constructed after the Peace of Bologna, takes up and amplifies some of the motifs of the bronze standard bases designed and executed for the Piazza by Alessandro Leopardi between 1501 and 1505, as Francesco Sansovino recognized.[84] These supported flagpoles from which the standard of St Mark, with the Lion picked out in gold against a crimson background, was flown on major feast-days. The central pedestal, the first to be put in place and iconographically the most complex, presents an alle-

67 Jacopo Sansovino, *Peace*, c.1546. Piazza San Marco, Loggetta.

68 Alessandro Leopardi, *Astrea*, standard base, 1505–6. Piazza San Marco.

gory of Venetian power and prosperity expressed through a sequence of marine creatures and goddesses holding attributes, among them *Minerva* (peace), *Ceres* (abundance) and *Astrea* (justice) (pl. 68).[85] The Loggetta has been called 'the most complete surviving visual representation of the Myth of Venice' – that is, the Venetian view of their own state as the perfect republic.[86] Its overall message is that the Venetian empire, supported by the virtues represented by the bronze statues in the niches below, is governed above all by justice, whose image had now become indissoluble from that of Venice itself.

The accrued political meanings of the Loggetta and its sculptural programme were developed in part because of its location in the Piazza San Marco, itself the principal site for official constructions and representations of the state.[87] During the seventeenth century, the roof of the Loggetta, transformed into a terrace through the addition of a balustrade, absent in Francisco de Holanda's drawing in his sketchbook in the Escorial but present in Franco's engraving,[88] provided a vantage-point from which patricians could watch the processions in the square beneath. In practice, this was just one of a number of places from which to view them, with some of the procurator's offices providing a reserved space from which patrician women could observe the spectacle below (they are shown doing so in Matteo Pagan's *Procession in St Mark's Square* (see pl. 82)), while ordinary citizens gathered in the square. These arrangements should not obscure the fact that the true ceremonial entrance to San Marco, and more particularly to the Doge's Palace, was not so much from the Piazza and the streets leading into it but rather from the lagoon and the Piazzetta. This was the route normally followed not only by the doge on ceremonial occasions, but also by visitors, who would arrive by boat and disembark

69   Bonifacio de' Pitati, *God the Father Blessing Venice*, c.1540.
Venice, Gallerie dell'Accademia.

at the Molo. The function of the Piazzetta as a ceremonial gateway to the square
and the official buildings that surround it is immediately proclaimed by the
two granite columns that stand at its southern edge. Further dignity is leant to
the arrangement by the Torre dell'Orologio in the background, which marks
the entrance from the Piazza to the Merceria. By emphasizing the importance
of the view into the Piazzetta and beyond, contemporary woodcuts and paintings stress its identity as the principal entrance to the city (pl. 69). Given its
function as a symbol of the city itself, it is not surprising that Sansovino should
have chosen the view from the Molo as a means of orientation; it is only from
there that his three buildings are visible as a coherent ensemble.[89]

The conception is essentially theatrical. As is often pointed out, the architect's varied use of the orders on the façades of his three buildings (rusticated
on the Mint, Doric and Ionic on the Library, Composite on the Loggetta) is
closely analogous to Serlio's design for a Tragic scene. In this sense the design

70   Giacomo Torelli, set for the prologue of
Bellerofonte (detail), engraving, 1642.

of the Piazzetta carried political meaning
not only through the function of the
Loggetta as a meeting place for aristocratic
politicians, but also as an appropriate backdrop for the virtuous actions of the patrician class.[90] The notion of the Piazzetta as
an essentially theatrical space is made even
more explicit in the engraving of Giacomo
Torelli's stage set for the prologue to his
opera *Bellerofonte*, given for the first time
in the Teatro Novissimo in 1642, with
music by Francesco Sacrati, which presents
a perspective view of that most common
of all images of the city, the Piazzetta seen
from the water (pl. 70).[91]

The Piazzetta (and the Piazza) also accommodated shops and taverns, as well
as being the sites of spectacles both dignified and otherwise. This too resonates
with the echoes of the Roman forum which, as described by Vitruvius, was used
for public meetings and gladiatorial contests in addition to being a marketplace.
Characteristic of the popular public rituals that took place there were the events
of Giovedì Grasso, the Thursday of the last week of Carnival, when twelve pigs
and a bull were released into the Piazzetta where they were chased, captured
and decapitated, before the meat was cut up and distributed.[92] This bloodthirsty
performance, which took place before the doge, foreign ambassadors and
members of the Signoria as well as a large public, followed a mock trial in which
the animals were condemned to death by the *magistrato del proprio*, one of the
senior law officers of the state, before being entrusted to members of the black-
smiths' and butchers' guilds to be slaughtered. The origins of this bizarre ritual
lay in the twelfth century, when, in the course of a dispute over ecclesiastical
jurisdiction between Aquileia and Venice, the patriarch of Aquileia was taken
prisoner, to be released only on condition that an annual tribute was sent to
Venice to arrive in time for Giovedì Grasso. It was specified that this gesture of
submission should consist of twelve loaves of bread, one bull and twelve pigs,
and that the animals were to be killed in public as a symbolic recollection of
the defeat of the patriarch and of the twelve Friulian lords who had supported
his cause. Just as the original 'trial' had taken place *in camera* before an elite
audience, so too did the final stage of the proceedings, when the doge and other
dignitaries, dressed in ceremonial scarlet (which was otherwise worn only on
Palm Sunday and Christmas Day), retired to the Doge's Palace, where they
smashed small wooden models of the Friulian castles destroyed after the
Venetian victory. Although Aquileia ceased to exist as a territorial entity in 1420,
the Venetian government felt obliged to continue what had become a popular
and integral part of the Carnival season long after its political significance had

faded from the collective memory. During the sixteenth century there were attempts to abolish the tradition. In 1525 the Council of Ten, as part of a general overhaul of popular festivities thought by some to be degrading, attempted to limit the slaughter, but despite an official decree the reform did not take hold. Sanudo reports the killing of animals in the Piazzetta in the following year,[93] and it is clear from legislation to supervise it that it was still continuing in the second half of the century. An engraving by Giacomo Franco shows this gruesome spectacle taking place before a large audience, including patricians seated on temporary raked seating, while other spectators look on from the windows of the Doge's Palace and the Library (pl. 71). This spatial arrangement effectively creates a theatrical stage and auditorium complete with 'boxes' out of the Piazzetta and its surrounding buildings.[94]

71 Giacomo Franco, *Giovedì Grasso in the Piazzetta*, engraving. Venice, Museo Civico Correr.

According to Francesco Sansovino's later account of the matter, Andrea Gritti had been the moving spirit behind the attempts to reduce the embarrassment of the occasion by reducing the number of animals to be slaughtered to one; but as the decree admitted, the event was popular, and could not be entirely abolished.[95] This was just one attempt among many to move the Venetian Carnival into a higher artistic sphere for a combination of moral, aesthetic and political reasons. The results often involved introducing classicizing elements in keeping with the surrounding area, which was itself taking on an increasingly Roman appearance as Sansovino's works progressed. On Giovedì Grasso in 1532 an allegorical procession was staged in the Piazza as an introduction to a mock-battle in which the Virtues triumphed over the Vices, the Temple of Peace was symbolically opened, and the victors celebrated with a concluding triumphal dance.[96] The distancing from more popular traditions that Gritti and his supporters began has been seen as symptomatic of a more general trend towards the cultural separation of social classes that characterizes the last two-thirds of the century. In this process, concern for a more noble lifestyle was culturally transmitted through an insistence on classical vocabulary in much official art and architecture, and in the increased extravagance of state pageantry and spectacle.[97] Both were to be seen at their most developed in the processions and rituals, both religious and civic, that took place in both the Piazza and the Piazzetta in the late sixteenth century. In practice, there was a sense of functional separation between these two spaces, with the Piazzetta being used for more politically inflected occasions, such as the reception of distinguished foreign visitors, while the Piazza was deployed for ceremonial of all kinds that usually contained a religious element. While the square served as a frontispiece to the basilica and was used as an extension of it, particularly through processional forms, the Piazzetta was both the forecourt of the Doge's Palace and the entrance to the square itself, a symbolically charged area connecting the principal site of Venetian authority to the lagoon.

Emphasis upon Jacopo Sansovino's transformation of both the Piazza and the Piazzetta, and of the political ideology that shaped them, should not disguise the mixture of ordinary functions that frequently took place there. Ultimately it is the Venetian citizenry that renders meaning to the square; the Piazza was not only a space for sacred and political spectacles, but also the principal theatre of the city in a broader sense. In tandem with the development of the area as the focal point of the Venetian church and state, it had also evolved since the early middle ages as a home for trade of all kinds. Fruit-selling is one of the few activities identifiable in the earliest view of the Piazzetta, and is also shown in some of the first woodcuts of the city.[98] Sabellico's description of the square mentions shops, taverns and markets along the Molo (they are clearly visible in Jacopo de' Barbari's bird's-eye view), while in front of the basilica stood meat and vegetable stalls. Bread was baked in nearby shacks. Many of the shops in the area were owned by the procurators. In 1531 the five on the Ponte della Pescaria were being rented to a glazier, a cheesemonger, a fruiterer and two poulterers,[99] the successors to the sequence of cheese and salami stalls shown on the bridge and along the waterside facade of the old Mint in Jacopo de' Barbari's view of the area;[100] they are still there, together with the fish market, in eighteenth-century views.[101] Next to them stood the principal granaries of the Republic.[102] Constructed according to a traditional typography found throughout the towns and cities of the *terraferma* (as well as at the Rialto), the meat market was in the most seaward section of the row of buildings opposite the Doge's Palace in the Piazzetta, where it was to remain until the 1580s,[103] while close by were the butchers' shops that it served. Other goods were also on offer. As early as 1394 sellers of jewellery and trinkets had been granted the right to sell in the Piazza San Marco on market days, and despite periodic opposition from the guilds, this was upheld and they continued to trade.[104]

The frequency with which the procurators proposed to remove shops and taverns from the area, some of them clustered at the base of the Campanile, or to rebuild them, suggests that they were a considerable presence.[105] In May 1531 the Great Council passed a resolution to remove unsightly obstructions from the Piazza, adding that this was a 'cosa laudabile et di gran ornamento de la città nostra'.[106] But in the battle between decorum and income, the latter was often triumphant.[107] The stalls, crowded around Leopardi's standard bases in front of the basilica, and in the north-east corner of the Piazza, are still visible in Canaletto's views and drawings (pl. 72).[108] The Piazzetta was also the site of

72   Giovanni Antonio Canal, *Piazza San Marco*. London, Sir John Soane's Museum.

more sombre proceedings. The criminals executed between the two columns at the edge of the lagoon, on a temporary platform built to give the crowds a good view, were accompanied by a priest and members of the Scuola di San Fantin, dressed in black robes and hooded, who rattled their chains to announce the event (pl. 73).[109] This was the climax of a longer procedure in which the convict was taken back to the scene of the crime to be mutilated, most frequently by having his right hand cut off and then hung round his neck, before being taken to San Marco. In serious cases a horse was used to drag the victim from one part of the city to another. This drawn-out spectacle, which inevitably drew large crowds, also reinforced the subliminal message that in Renaissance Venice violence was controlled; crime would be punished and the city purged of evil.[110] The theme of the Piazza as the *locus* of justice was continued in the Doge's Palace; here errant patricians were sometimes hanged between the two red marble columns where the doge occasionally appeared, and sometimes at the Pietra del Bando, where the heads of traitors were also displayed. All this took place under the watchful eye of the allegorical figures of *Justice* on top of the Porta della Carta[111] and on the façade of the Doge's Palace. The use of columnar forms, and of the porphyry from which they are made, is important in this configuration; together with the arrangement of orders on the façade of the Library, they helped to consolidate the notion of

73 Cesare Vercelli, costume of the members of the Scuola di San Fantin, from *Degli habiti antichi et moderne*, 1590.

the Doge's Palace as the Palace of Justice, strategically located opposite the Palace of Wisdom.[112]

To an even greater extent than today, both the Piazza and the Piazzetta were important gathering points for tourists, not only in the sense that St Mark's shrine could be visited and the wonders of the basilica admired, but also because facilities for foreigners were provided there. The proximity of the Mint encouraged money-changers to trade from the foot of the Campanile; small operations often run by no more than a couple of partners, they could nevertheless be in the hands of nobles, as were most of the larger and more structured banking activities at the Rialto.[113] Although non-Venetians were forbidden to export specie overseas, an exception was made in the case of pilgrims.[114] By the sixteenth century most of those travelling to the Holy Land embarked at Venice, where galleys licensed by the Republic left for Jaffa every year on the spring tides and returned in the autumn.[115] In the early middle ages, other important ports including Genoa, Pisa, Ancona, Marseilles and Montpellier had all maintained a share of the trade, but by the fifteenth century only the Venetians could provide a reasonably secure passage, with the ports of the *terra da mar* providing safe havens for much of the distance, and government regulation ensuring standards of safety and commercial morality that were uncommon in other places.[116] Venice was the starting point not only for other Italians, but also for most English, French, Dutch and German pilgrims. Once they had arrived in the city, many stayed for some weeks, making the necessary arrangements for the voyage – changing money, laying in provisions for the trip and reaching agreement with the ship's master offering berths to the Holy Land, many of whom operated from booths in the Piazzetta.[117]

The everyday activities in the square were not always consonant with the heroic solemnity of Sansovino's architecture, and they were rarely as silent as the images of official ceremonies and processions suggest. In the Piazza itself news-sheets and popular prints were hawked by itinerant vendors around the basilica, and strolling players (*cantastorie* and *cantimpanchi*), standing on benches and improvised staging, entertained the crowds. These popular entertainers, usually professional buffoons and comic actors, played for a mixed audience in open urban spaces all over the city, particularly during the Carnival season. Described at length by the English visitor Thomas Coryate, among others, they too are shown in engravings (pl. 75).[118] Often written by amateurs,

74 Giovanni Domenico Tiepolo, *The Storyteller*, mid-1770s. Austin, Texas, Jack S.
Blanton Museum of Art, Suida-Manning Collection.

the texts that they performed were sometimes
published in modest pamphlets of a few
pages, to be sold to members of the audience;
Sanudo records that one actor hawked the
words of his monologues in the Piazza San
Marco immediately after his performance.[119]
Cantastorie are known often to have commissioned cheap copies of the texts that they sang
from jobbing printers, and there is even the
case of the Florentine Paolo Danza, who not
only wrote and sang his own verses, but also
printed and sold them as well.[120] Both in the
Piazza, and in the larger squares of Venice,
these raconteurs performed daily on improvised stages as late as the end of the eighteenth century. A painting by Giovanni
Domenico Tiepolo from the 1750s shows one
of them, armed with a guitar, entertaining a
small and attentive audience drawn from a
wide range of Venetian society (pl. 74).

75 Anonymous, *Mascherate*, engraving.
Venice, Museo Civico Correr.

In practice, there was a often little difference between the *cantimpanchi* and the charlatans and mountebanks who used music as part of their pitch to attract business; these are overlapping rather than discrete categories. An element of performance was also used by itinerant healers, often from the country, including the *pauliani*, who, claiming to have inherited immunity to snake poison from St Paul, offered to cure bites. By the time of Tommaso Garzoni's description of them their theatrical handling of snakes and other poisonous reptiles was often accompanied by music.[121] Coryate speaks of the wide availability of 'Apothecary drugs, and a Commonweale of other trifles and trinkets', all part of 'a world of new-fangled trumperies . . . drugs and confections . . . many of them . . . very counterfeit and false . . . oyles, soveraigne waters, amorous songs printed'.[122] The generic term 'charlatan' covers a wide variety of occupations, ranging from pedlars to properly qualified physicians and experienced tooth-pullers who combined healing and entertainment in the form of a public, social drama with its own long-standing rituals.[123] As a category it also spans a wide social as well as occupational range. At the upper end of the spectrum was someone like Leone Tartiglino, appointed to oversee the charlatans in Venice by the *provveditori alla sanità* in 1563. Tartiglino was an educated man who published a treatise on sleep, together with 'alchuni bellissimi et utilissimi secreti medicinali'. After his death in 1576, an apothecary was given the right to sell Tartiglino's remedy for intestinal worms, provided that he distributed it to Venetian hospitals without charge, a clear recognition of his professional standing.[124]

It is clear that charlatans and mountebanks were operating in the Piazza and Piazzetta at least from the early sixteenth century and probably earlier, much as they were elsewhere in Europe, and by the middle of the sixteenth century their performances had become sufficiently intrusive to require regulation. Yet despite occasional official restrictions, usually of a minor kind, the charlatans and mountebanks, exhorting, cajoling, swindling and entertaining, continued to populate the Piazza until the end of the Republic. As genre paintings such as the anonymous seventeenth-century picture of *Mountebanks Performing in Piazza San Marco* remind us, they were a permanent presence, an accepted and prominent component of the boisterous character of the square, a defining element of its soundscape (pl. 76). A later work, Gabriel Bella's *I ciarlatani in Piazzetta*, shows two troupes of quacksalvers to the left and right of the painting (there is also a tooth-drawer in the middleground), accompanied by two female singers to attract the crowds (pl. 77). Music used in this way, usually by comedians and musicians, seems to have been common in many parts of Europe, at least by the sixteenth century; in addition to attracting attention, it was also thought to bring solace and relief to the afflicted, and so to assist in the healing process.

During the sixteenth century the functions of public square, religious centre and market coexisted at San Marco, despite the long campaign conducted by

ABOVE 76   Anonymous, *Mountebanks Performing in Piazza San Marco*, 17th century. Venice, Casa Goldoni.

BELOW 77   Gabriele Bella, *I ciarlatani in piazzetta*, *c*.1790. Venice, Palazzo Querini-Stampalia.

the authorities to eliminate at least some of the less decorous forms of trading from the area. For the procurators this was partly a matter of decorum, a way of ennobling the religious and civic centre in tandem with its architectural redevelopment, and as such it was a symptom of the magistrature's desire to order the city. At the same time it was part of a process in which the Piazza San Marco and the market area around the Rialto bridge came to acquire distinct identities as a result of the government's attitude to urban renewal. By the end of the century these two areas, on different sides of the Grand Canal but linked by both the bridge and the Merceria, had acquired a much clearer functional separation, the one as the representative centre of civic and religious power, the

78   Palazzo dei Camerlenghi.

other as a market and trading centre that served both local and foreign needs. This was a matter of accentuation rather than a clear-cut distinction. Although the character of the Rialto as a thriving market attached to an international port became more pronounced, administrative offices had been located there since an early date, and the gradual growth of the market was accompanied by the installation of regulatory bodies and the building of offices to accommodate them. Jurisdictional control was symbolized by a second Pietra del Bando outside the church of San Giacomo di Rialto; identical in form and materials to the one in the Piazza San Marco, it too was used for public announcements of government decrees.[125] The clock-tower of San Giovanni Elemosinario nearby articulated the temporal divisions of the mercantile day,[126] much as did the clock-tower in the Piazza San Marco; both established these public spaces as places of work and commerce. In addition to the handling of imports and exports, the Rialto was also the centre of a thriving bullion market, thanks to proper regulation and a reputation for fair competition, which had stimulated the reputation of Venice as a centre for demand equal to Milan and Bologna.[127] Over time, and in addition to the more informal activities of money-changers at San Marco, the Rialto became the centre of local banking.[128]

The process of developing the Rialto as a second focal point of government and trade was accelerated with the rebuilding of the area after the disastrous fire of 10 January 1514, vividly described by Sanudo, which devastated a large area around the bridge.[129] One of the most imposing consequences of that renewal is the addition, completed in 1525, of the new section of the Palazzo dei Camerlenghi of 1488, the offices of the public treasurers of the Republic (a group originally of two and, after 1527, three patricians appointed for the purpose), one of the few buildings in the immediate area to escape the conflagration (pl. 78).[130] The presence of such institutions emphasized the political framework within which trade operated, dignifying it as a critical element within the evolving Myth of Venice. The interior of the Camerlenghi's three-storey building was decorated in the course of the sixteenth century with almost two hundred canvases, about half of which have survived, many of them by Tintoretto and his workshop.[131] One of the standard iconographical schemes in this repertory shows the treasurers, usually identified by their coats of arms, protected by one of the patron saints of the city or by the Virgin. Such images, commissioned by the state, unite God and Mammon in the projection of a common ethos (pl. 79).

As one of the earliest areas of the city to be settled, the Rialto was also a ritual and sacred space that contained two ancient churches: San Giovanni Elemosinario and San Giacomo di Rialto. Following its destruction in the fire, San Giovanni was rebuilt as part of Andrea Gritti's rebuilding of this part of the city, yet a further consequence of his far-reaching *renovatio urbis*. Constructed to a neo-Byzantine plan, the new church was visited each Ash Wednesday by an official *andata* consisting of doge, Senate and Signoria accompanied by the ducal insignia.[132] Shortly afterwards, another church in the area, San Giacomo di Rialto, also came under ducal jurisdiction as a result of a direct appeal by Gritti to Pope Clement VII. According to tradition, San Giacomo was the oldest church in Venice, and its incorporation into Gritti's *renovatio* lent the area around the Rialto bridge further accentuations of antiquity and authority, in part derived from its own long history and in part from its proximity to the Pietra del Bando. San Giacomo di Rialto was also made the subject of a full annual procession that took place on Holy Thursday, and which conferred a plenary indulgence upon the participants.[133] As these examples suggest, in func-

79   Jacopo Tintoretto, *Madonna and Child with Saints Sebastian, Mark, and Theodore with Three Treasurers of the Republic and their Secretaries*, 1566–7. Venice, Gallerie dell' Accademia.

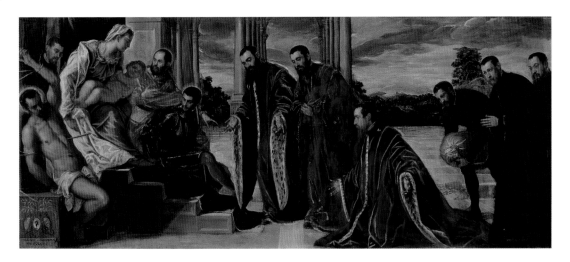

tional terms the area around the Rialto and the Piazza San Marco continued to constitute the twin poles of the city's official presence in the sixteenth century, much as they had done so since the twelfth. Linked by the main commercial thoroughfare of the city, they combined the requirements of religion, government and trade, as regulated activities and potent symbols of the life and foundation principles of the state itself.

During the sixteenth century, and particularly during Andrea Gritti's dogeship, both these areas were part of an extensive process of urban renewal that culminated in Sansovino's project, which was accompanied by and was perhaps a response to the increasingly elaborate official rituals that took place in the square. Of these the most frequent was the *andata*, described for the first time by Martin da Canal, whose account of the procession in the Piazza on Easter morning clearly prefigures later versions.[134] Beginning with the eight standards bearing the Lion of St Mark, Canal notes the presence of *trionfi* including the faldstool, and the six silver trumpets accompanied by two men playing silver cymbals. Dressed in cloth of gold and wearing the distinctive ceremonial cap (*corno*) decorated with precious stones, the doge walked at the centre of the procession preceded by the sword-bearer. The *primicerio*, dressed in episcopal vestments, is given a certain prominence in Canal's account, as are three acolytes; one carried a gold and silver processional cross, the second a copy of the Old Testament and the third a silver censer. Behind them walked the canons of San Marco, who sang as they went. The second half of the procession, which followed the doge, included members of the patriciate and 'molti autorevoli popolani'.[135] Elsewhere, Canal describes the ducal insignia, which were carried in the *andata*.[136] One significant omission from the list, familiar from later accounts, is the sceptre (*baculus*), the use of which was probably suppressed during the period of the *commune veneciarum* (1146–78) when legislative power was removed from the doge.[137] The remaining *trionfi* were given to Doge Sebastiano Ziani by Pope Alexander III, during his visit to Venice to seek reconciliation with Frederick Barbarossa (who had refused to respect the Concordat of Worms) in 1177, an event of sufficient importance to be commemorated in Spinelli Aretino's biographical fresco cycle in Siena (pl. 80). Unable to sustain his opposition to the pope, the meeting culminated with the emperor prostrating himself at Alexander's feet outside San Marco. Ziani's determination on this occasion to protect the pope and to mediate in the dispute was rewarded by the Alexandrine Donation of these symbolic objects, each of which came to be interpreted as the symbol of a distinct ducal privilege. These gifts, which, as Sansovino recognized,[138] empowered the doge as a princely equal of popes and emperors, were carried in the ducal procession on all the major occasions in the ceremonial year as both historical relics and emblems of status and authority.[139] The continuing significance of the Alexandrine Donation in the evolution of the office of doge is commemorated in a set of four canvases painted for the Sala del Maggior Consiglio at the end of

80   Spinello Aretino, *Pope Alexander III with Emperor Frederick I and Doge Sebastiano Ziani*, 1406–15. Siena, Palazzo Pubblico.

the sixteenth century; they each show the presentation of a single *trionfo* – candle, sword, umbrella and ring (pl. 81).[140]

Sansovino's casual mention of imperial and papal models for the *andata* carries an element of truth; parallels with the papal procession are particularly close, and extend to details such as the position of the members of the *famiglia* (immediately in front of the principal actor in both cases) and the place of the

81   Leandro Bassano, *Pope Alexander III Presents the White Candle to Doge Sebastiano Ziani in San Marco*, 1604–5. Ducal Palace, Sala del Maggior Consiglio.

ABOVE AND BELOW: 82   Matteo Pagan, *Procession in St. Mark's Square*, woodcut, *c.*1550. Venice, Museo Civico Correr.

electors, cardinals in the Roman example and senators in the Venetian one, immediately behind. The other significant detail of Canal's account is his mention of the *Laudes regiae*,[141] an acclamation of the doge, derived from both Byzantine tradition and Gallo-Frankish liturgy, chanted in his honour by the canons of San Marco. In Venice the singing of *Laudes* at the investiture of the doge is recorded as early as 1071, but how long the tradition persisted is not known; it is unlikely to have survived the gradual diminution in ducal power and pomp that followed the dogeship of Francesco Foscari. Matters were different in the Venetian colonies, where the singing of *Laudes* to the doge was used as an instrument of dominion, a liturgical reminder of St Mark's sovereignty over a subject people.[142] In Dalmatia and Istria the practice continued as late as the seventeenth century.[143]

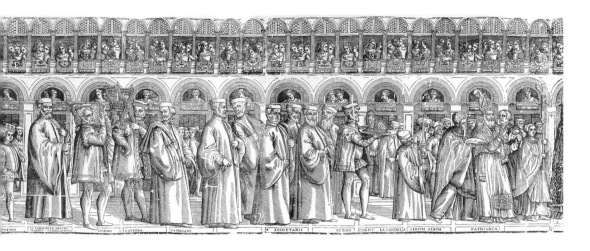

By the sixteenth century the *andata*, which in its most elaborate version
included all the principal office-holders together with some minor officials, the
ambassadors of foreign states, the canons of San Marco, the patriarch and, at
the physical core of the procession, the doge himself, had become the most
elaborate processional form in Venice. As such it became an image of the city
itself, through vignettes on maps and engravings of scenes from Venetian life,
presumably produced for pilgrims, tourists and bibliophiles rather than for
Venetians. The most detailed of these is Matteo Pagan's monumental series of
eight folio woodcuts (pl. 82), which when placed in sequence present a continuous image some four metres long.[144] Strictly speaking, this is not a straightforward visual account of how the ducal procession looked since it includes the
patriarch of Venice, who, according to Sansovino's description of the *andata*,
was not customarily present.[145] Nonetheless, it achieves its primary purpose of
fixing the relative positions of the participants, something that concerned the
chroniclers and others responsible for codifying ceremonial detail.[146] While the

hierarchical ordering of the procession was fixed, the personnel were constantly changing; all the individuals who walked did so as the temporary holders of official positions. It has been suggested that, with its three clearly differentiated segments, each of which were organized in order of precedence, it is possible to see the ducal procession as a detailed presentation of the hierarchical conception of the Republic.[147] As an interpretation this is probably too schematic, and contemporary observers would have been more likely to have recognized the principal participants in the procession rather than some overarching constitutional principle. The canons of San Marco also walked in the *andata*, and it was through their participation that the *patriarchino*, the rite peculiar to San Marco, could be transposed from one place to another.[148] In consequence, when mass was celebrated as part of the ducal procession to a particular church or convent, it was done so according to a liturgy that was exclusively associated with the basilica. In this symbolic practice the use of the *patriarchino*, sometimes elaborated by the *cappella marciana*, served to emphasize the doge's authority over the clergy of the city.

Although the *andata* was both exclusive and hierarchical,[149] its basic arrangement was supplemented on occasion by the addition of other social groupings, such as the *scuole grandi*, the *scuole piccole* (both lay religious associations), the trade guilds, or even a particular parish. All the *scuole* (of which the six *scuole grandi* represented the elite among their numbers) cut across neighbourhood loyalties by drawing their membership from across the city. The effect, which broadened participation, was presumably intended to underline the allegedly harmonious corporate organization of the city, one of the basic underpinnings of the Myth of Venice. In sixteenth-century Venice the meaningful focus of identity was not the *sestiere*, which was merely an administrative unit, but the parish; more than any other form of association, it was this that generated a sense of local loyalty and identity.[150] Similarly, while the *scuole* represented the notion of communal devotion and charity, the guilds symbolized the complementary idea of commerce as the foundation of civic concord.[151] In addition to a changing cast-list of social components, the *andata* and its various ritual amplifications often expanded its frame of reference by including various additional musical and religious elements. On many of the more important feasts in the Venetian calendar, the choir of the basilica walked in the *andata*, as did the singers employed by some of the wealthier *scuole*, as their participation in the public ceremonial of the city became even more pronounced in the course of the sixteenth century.[152] In Bellini's painting showing the Scuola Grande di San Giovanni carrying their prized relic of the True Cross in the procession on 25 April, the feast-day of St Mark, a group of five singers are shown accompanied by an instrumental ensemble (pl. 83).[153] In expanded form, these processions amplified the liturgy outside San Marco by making use not only of the central civic space of the city, but other areas as well. In this way, civic and liturgical acts that were usually associated with ducal authority were able to broaden their audience, which could participate not only passively (by observing), but also actively by walking in the procession, chanting litanies and singing *laude*. At the same time, the wide geographical dispersal of the *andata* knitted together *sestieri*, parishes, *scuole* and guilds in a closely woven fabric of religious and civic observance.

Venetian ceremonies were also able to incorporate an even wider audience, such as the visitors for whom the city itself was a place of pilgrimage, as well as the principal European staging-post on the journey to and from the Holy Land. The Venetian celebration of Corpus Christi is perhaps

83 Gentile Bellini, *Procession in St. Mark's Square* (detail), 1496. Venice, Gallerie dell' Accademia.

the most spectacular example of state appropriation, for a mixture of economic, political and devotional motives, of an event of universal spiritual significance.[154] The Senate decree of 1407, which established the procession, specified that the Host be carried, under a baldachin, by four patricians, 'in reverence of Our Lord, Jesus Christ, and in honour of the Fatherland'.[155] The Corpus Christi procession, in which both Venetians and foreign pilgrims walked, is a reminder that while the motivations for Venetian civic and religious rituals were complex and interlocking, the audience for them was certainly not uniform, but expanded and contracted for different occasions. On this one, as a number of pilgrims noticed, groups of about thirty children carrying flowers walked between the various *tableaux vivants* mounted by the *scuole grandi* (the Englishman Richard Guylforde calls them 'pagentis of ye olde lawe, and the newe').[156] The diaries of Willemsz and van Gorcum make a number of references to music in the procession, ranging from the general observation that it proceeded 'with beautiful, lovely and splendid music' to more precise descriptions of the groups from the *scuole grandi*, each of which 'remained kneeling before the holy sacrament, singing discant or *simpelsanck* for a while ... "Tantum ergo sacramentum" or similar'.[157] Ottaviano Petrucci's *Laude libro secondo*, published in 1508, contains a single anonymous setting of 'Tantum ergo', the text specifically mentioned by Willemsz.

By 'discant' Willemsz evidently means polyphony, such as the fairly uncomplicated pieces in the *Laude libro primo*, a collection also printed by Petrucci in 1508, and the only true Venetian collection of *laude* to survive from the early sixteenth century. It contains sixty-six pieces, mostly for four voices, all written by Innocenzio Dammonis, a priest intermittently in the service of the church of San Salvatore, which was the home of the Scuola di San Teodoro, which had been founded as a *scuola piccola* in the thirteenth century but became a *scuola grande* in 1552. Among the obligations of San Salvatore to the Scuola was

84 Giacomo Franco, *Corpus Christi Procession in Piazza San Marco*, engraving. Venice, Museo Civico Correr.

one to provide music for its celebrations, which included processions.[158] The simpler hymns of the church were known to all and would have encouraged 'congregational' participation; a seventeenth-century ceremony book mentions the singing of 'Pange lingua gloriosi', the eucharistic office hymn traditionally associated with the feast of Corpus Christi in Roman usage.[159]

Clearly the *andata* was not a silent affair. As one of the prized *trionfi*, the six silver trumpets were carried in the procession primarily for symbolic reasons, but they could also be played, even if technically they could do little more than sound triads. In bureaucratic terms, the trumpets and shawm players, clearly visible in Pagan's engraving, were members of the doge's *famiglia* rather than employees of the basilica. They participated frequently in the procession, and would have been capable of playing polyphonic pieces. The canons of San Marco, one of the fixed elements of the *andata* are sometimes described as chanting simple hymns and liturgies as the procession moved forward, and on other occasions the singers of the basilica also participated. When the purpose of the *andata* was to visit a church or monastery in another part of the city, as was often the case, the principal function of the choir was to sing during the ritual that was usually celebrated on arrival. At the same time it would sometimes also sing along the route, if only simpler repertory suitable for outdoor performance. On occasions when contingents from the *scuole grandi* walked in the *andata*, they also brought with them their own musicians, usually small groups of singers and instrumentalists; their presence, well documented in the archives and by the remarks of pilgrims, is also confirmed both by Bellini's painting and an engraving by Giacomo Franco (pl. 84).[160] The procession moved at a sedate and solemn pace. As it passed, the crowds that lined the streets, bridges and squares of the city would have been treated to a sequence of different sights and sounds as the various elements of this colourful spectacle gradually unfolded in front of them. To the already variegated soundscape provided by singers and instrumentalists should be added the shouts of the onlookers and the ferocious interjections of the *trombe squarciate*, primitive instruments often mentioned in descriptions. The overall impression of the *andata*, frozen in unnatural solemnity in woodcuts, engravings and paintings, must often have been somewhat disorderly, for all of its visual impact and fine apparatus. Despite its official character, the peripatetic nature of the procession must have helped the cause of common identity by bringing a ritual act that included the head of the Venetian state and the traditional symbols of his authority to areas and communities comparatively remote from the seat of power. The *andata*, sometimes described as yet another display of splendour, tied together the complexities of Venetian society, whose components were defined and socially organized by class, occupation and *sestieri*, into a web of topographically separate sites of historical consciousness and collective memory. Notions of a common identity, shaped by shared histories and recorded through ceremonial continuities, also structured the rituals that surrounded the doge himself, irrespective of the gradual diminution in the political weight of his office that took place in the early modern period. They are perhaps most in evidence in the details of the ceremonies that inaugurated and terminated his period of authority: his investiture as doge and the rites that surrounded his passing. It was at such critical junctures, when jurisdiction changes hands, that any political system is put to the test.

CHAPTER FOUR

The Sacral Prince

On the morning of 21 November 1505, a lampoon was discovered stuck to the façade of the church of San Giacomo di Rialto, significantly, in the circumstances, one of the parish churches under the *ius patronatus* of the doge. According to the diarist Girolamo Priuli, it showed the Virgin, St Mark and Doge Leonardo Loredan (then just entering the fourth year of his dogeship) grouped around an image of the city of Venice. While the Virgin complains to Mark about the doge's style of government, Loredan complacently makes his famous remark: 'I don't care so long as I grow fat, I and my son Lorenzo.' The next day a placard was found on the wall of the Doge's Palace predicting that Loredan would meet the same fate as Doge Marino Falier, beheaded in 1355 for treachery.[1] A few days later a similar incident occurred. Although suspicion initially fell upon Alberto di Padova, a bookbinder living in the parish of San Zulian, the perpetrator seems not to have been discovered.[2] Commenting on the incident, Priuli writes:

> It is commonly said that a Venetian prince is a mere tavern sign and that he cannot do anything without the agreement of his councillors, the Collegio, or the councils. But I want to emphasize that a Venetian prince may do as he wants. Everyone seeks his goodwill and tries to be agreeable to him, and if occasionally there is a councillor or someone else who wants to oppose him, it is best to proceed with caution, otherwise he will meet a severe rebuff and embarrassment. It is true that if a doge does anything against the Republic he won't be tolerated, but in everything else, even in small matters, he does as he pleases so long as he doesn't offend the honour and dignity of the state.[3]

85   Giovanni Antonio Canal, *Interior of St. Mark's at Night* (detail), *c.*1730. Windsor, Collection of Her Majesty Queen Elizabeth II.

Priuli's remarks contrast quite sharply with the view of the dogeship held by most other sixteenth-century Venetian writers.[4] Donato Giannotti, for example, believed that

> the insignia of the Venetian empire are invested in the person of the doge, since in the Republic only he has the appearance of a lord. But though he alone possesses such a dignity, he is not given complete power in anything, since not only is he unable to make decisions however insignificant, but also he cannot do anything without his councillors.[5]

A Florentine republican opposed to the Medici, Giannotti was inevitably drawn to Machiavelli, as well as to what he regarded as the best features of the Venetian governmental system. In his book *De magistratibus*, which rivalled Giannotti's *Libro de la republica* in popularity, Gasparo Contarini implies something similar: 'Nevertheless, so is this authoritie of his by lawes retracted, that alone hee may not doe any thing, neither being joined to the other magistrats hath he any farther power then every other president in his office.'[6]

The notion that by the sixteenth century the doge's role had been reduced to a largely administrative and ceremonial function is in keeping with the way in which the nature of the office gradually changed. Indicative of this process is the history of the Venetian use of the *Laudes regiae*, not only during the ducal investiture, but also as an acclamation during the Easter morning ceremonies and on other occasions.[7] Although the origins of the *Laudes regiae* go back to classical times, it was in the Gallo-Frankish church that they took on their distinctive form, appearing for the first time in an eighth-century psalter from Soissons.[8] The earliest texts form part of the Litany of the Saints, but already by the ninth century the *Laudes regiae* had become established as a separate liturgical form. Addressed to the triumphant Christ, through the opening and usually repeated tricolon 'Christus vincit, Christus regnat, Christus imperat', they then proceed to call for divine aid for the powerful of the world. The formulation made its appearance on Sicilian coins in the early twelfth century, and later still on those of France.[9] Beginning in the twelfth century, textually simplified versions of this arrangement, the *Laudes imperiales* and *Laudes papales*, evolved; these did not open with the tricolon, but instead concentrated on the titles of either pope or emperor. Normally they were intoned between the Gloria and the collect at mass on the major church festivals, and particularly at Easter, for which their texts celebrating Christ Triumphant are particularly appropriate.[10]

During the eleventh century the coronation of the doge was marked by the presentation of a sceptre during his enthronement and by the singing of some form of the *Laudes regiae*, whose original function in classical antiquity had nothing to do with the church, and was intended to recognize and legitimize a ruler.[11] As with so many features of the rituals surrounding the doge, the acclamations were a prominent characteristic of Byzantine ceremonies both secular and ecclesiastical; in this context their prime purpose was to increase the pomp of the emperor and his court.[12] The gradual diminution of the imperial elements in the Venetian investiture ceremony in later centuries parallels the tendency both to restrict the scope for ducal action and to spread the power base, rather than allowing power to accumulate in the hands of a single individual. At the election of Pietro Polani in 1130 the sceptre was replaced by the banner of St Mark, symbol of the *commune veneciarum*. More significantly, it was also on this occasion that the *promissione ducale*, an oath of office that limited ducal power, was first administered. At the investiture of Lorenzo Tiepolo in 1268 these two symbolic changes were still in place, but so too was the practice of singing the *Laudes regiae*.[13]

Interestingly, Martin da Canal notes that the *Laudes regiae* were intoned by the 'chapelains de Monsignor Saint Marc' (the canons of San Marco) on Easter Sunday, and on the feast of the *translatio*, as well as during the ducal investiture. Although there is no earlier written record of the Venetian *Laudes*, it seems likely that their specific form was devised during the dogeship of Pietro Ziani (1205–29), when, following the Fourth Crusade, the doges added the title 'quarte partis et dimidiae partis tocius imperij Romaniae dominator' to their existing titles of dukes of Dalmatia and Croatia.[14] In Venetian hands the ducal *Laudes* were sung not only on festal occasions in Venice itself, but also as an assertion of dominion in the colonies.[15] In Dalmatia in 1000, Zara in 1204 and Crete in 1211, all of which had recently been conquered by the Venetians, it was decreed that *Laudes* should be offered to the doge.[16] The practice continued in Dalmatia and Istria at least as late as the seventeenth century.[17] In Venice itself the tradition of singing the *Laudes* continued at least until the first half of the fifteenth century, when the text was set to music by the Franco-Flemish composer Hugo de Lantins. This is comparatively late.[18] Outside Rome, the singing of the *Laudes* had never been much practised in Italy, and even at the papal court the custom had fallen into disuse by the fifteenth century.[19] Hugo's composition has survived uniquely in a contemporary manuscript copied in Bergamo.[20] Its literary text corresponds almost exactly to the French version of the Venetian *Laudes* transmitted by Martin da Canal well over a hundred years earlier,[21] opening with the tricolon and then proceeding to a simple acclamation of the doge, Francesco Foscari, through a listing of his titles according to the traditional formula: 'Christus vincit, Christus regnat, Christus imperat. Domino nostro Francisco Foscari, Dei gracia inclito duci Venecie, Dalmacie atque Croacie et dominatur quarte partis et dimidie totius imperii Romanie, salus, honor, vita et victoria. Amen.'

Hugo de Lantins' setting of the *Laudes regiae* is one of eight polyphonic motets from the fourteenth and fifteenth centuries written in praise of Venetian doges, three of which were composed in honour of Foscari.[22] His dogeship, the longest in the history of the Republic, was famously controversial for the way in which the office was amplified and its powers extended at a time when Venice

86   Porta della Carta. Ducal Palace.

had come to occupy an increasingly prominent role in European affairs, and the conquest of the *terraferma* was completed. It was Foscari who commissioned the Porta della Carta, decorated with a sculpture of Foscari himself kneeling in front of the Lion of St Mark; surmounted by the figure of *Venetia/Justice*, it marks the official route linking the Doge's Palace to the basilica (pl. 86). This is just one of a number of grandiose projects that he inaugurated, including the lower part of the Arco Foscari, both of whose façades were also originally decorated with sculptures of *Foscari* and the *Lion*,[23] the façade of the Doge's Palace facing the Piazzetta, and the construction of Ca' Foscari on the Grand Canal, the most imposing private *palazzo* to be constructed there since the Ca d'Oro, with which it invites comparison.[24] All of these projects deploy the architectural language of

Venetian Gothic on a grandiloquent scale designed to memorialize Foscari and his achievements. It may well have been the self-aggrandizing tendencies of Foscari's dogeship that caused a further reduction in ducal power, underlining the theoretical legal position in which the doge was nothing more than *primus inter pares*.[25] The diminution in personality cults that the three motets for Foscari embody seems to bring the tradition of such pieces to an end, in functional terms as well as stylistic ones. It is not coincidental that Foscari's death in 1457 also marked the end of a period in which seven doges had been assassinated, one had been sentenced to death and had been beheaded, twelve had abdicated, two had been deposed, and nine had been blinded and exiled. After that date the Venetians feared the doge no longer.[26] Nor did they honour him in music.

Whatever the realities of power in the sixteenth century, election to the dogeship continued to be regarded as the pinnacle of patrician achievement. Typically, this most sought-after of prizes was attained at an advanced age, after a career of service in the most important executive committees of the state. The wisdom and experience conferred by longevity continued to be prerequisites for election. The average age of a doge of the period was more than 72 years old at the time of election; he ruled for just seven years, at a time when the average life expectancy was less than 40.[27] In the Venetian system, government was in the hands of a select group of old men drawn from the hereditary patrician caste, while the highest offices of state were normally closed to the young. Often elected from among the procurators, the doge was simply the ultimate representative of a gerontocracy whose continued existence has been judged responsible, at least in part, for the persistence of the Myth of Venice and the successful survival of history's most long-lived republic.[28] In these circumstances ducal funerals and investitures, relatively common as they were, provide a good vantage point from which to view the multi-faceted character of the dogeship, and in particular the tensions between the individual and the office as they shifted over time.[29] In terms of the latter, at least as practised from the thirteenth century, Venetian political theology assigned to the elected head of the Venetian polity a role that was analogous to that of the pope in Rome. Ceremonies that surrounded the doge, and in which he participated, emphasized his position as an intermediary, a function that became particularly crucial at moments of crisis. It was then that the doge was placed in the role of prime agent of intercession, the true representative of St Mark on earth. Beyond such moments there were four major liturgical feasts of the year when the doge's political position was underlined through his participation in ritual and ceremony: Good Friday, Holy Saturday, Easter Morning and Ascension Day, all four of which are shown in the Christological cycle in the upper-storey mosaics of the west façade of San Marco. These, which were executed in the early seventeenth century, replace earlier scenes on the same themes that can be clearly seen in Gentile Bellini's *Procession* of 1496 (see pl. 6).[30] This underlines the general principle that the public rituals that involved the doge were invariably religious before they were political.

The contrast between the semi-sacral character of the office, as it had evolved by the sixteenth century, and the nature of the individual who had been elected to the post became particularly marked during the funeral rites that followed the death of a doge.[31] As with all momentous events in the city, this was announced by the ringing of bells. This was essentially a practical matter that not only announced the death to the population, who in most cases must have been expecting it from the rumours emerging from the Doge's Palace, but also warned the members of the Great Council, the sovereign assembly of the Republic made up of all patricians over the age of 25, that the election of a successor was about to begin. It also had a symbolic aspect, since the number and types of changes rung located the event itself within a hierarchy determined by social status. On the death of a doge, nine peals of doubles sounded from the bell-tower in the Piazza, and the same pattern was then taken up by all the *scuole* and churches of the city.[32] The number nine, which recurred during the ceremonies on the day of the doge's interment, probably refers to the nine congregations of the Venetian clergy.[33] At this moment three contingents from the Arsenal, each of fifty men, were sent to guard the Doge's Palace. This may have been a remnant of an early medieval practice (until 1328 the *popolani* had been allowed to ransack the ducal apartments following the death of a doge), but even in the sixteenth century popular unrest was not unknown, and in 1538 a detachment of *arsenalotti* actually lived in the Doge's Palace during the election of Andrea Gritti's successor.[34] During the conclave of 1559, which finally elected Girolamo Priuli, the crowd, having heard that there was a strong body of opinion in favour of the much-disliked Girolamo Grimani, beat on the doors chanting: 'If you elect Grimani we will throw him to the dogs!'[35] At Alvise Mocenigo's election in 1570 it was forbidden to carry arms in the Piazza, since violence was feared from the large numbers of footloose soldiers in the city, recruited for the war against the Turks.[36] These glimpses of a more disordered world provide a corrective to the official image of a harmonious republic moving seamlessly from one elected head of state to the next.

Once the Great Council had assembled, the doors were locked, and they were to remain so (except for the funeral itself and the necessary meetings of the Great Council) until a new doge had been elected.[37] This was a lengthy and complicated business, originally evolved in the twelfth century, that took at least five days and often longer to come to a conclusion. The process began with the selection by lot of thirty members of the Great Council, excluding those under the age of 30. These then retired to a separate room and reduced themselves, again by lot, to a group of nine, who then drew up a list of forty nominees (all of whom were required to have at least seven votes), for approval by the Great Council. This process (Henry Wotton called it 'one of the most intricate and curious forms in the world') continued through several more phases until the eleven elected the forty-one who then elected the doge, who had to have a majority of at least twenty-five votes. At first glance it might seem that this involved method eliminated the possibility that mere ambition could triumph, but in practice it ensured that access to the dogeship remained in the hands of an inner elite, since it was expected that the nine selected by lot from the thirty members of the Great Council would nominate notables only in their list of forty, and that once elected these would in turn select kindred spirits in the later stages of the election. In effect, the result was a compromise between direct election by the Great Council and one restricted to 'the most experienced, worthy and important of the city' (to use Contarini's description of the forty-one), who made the final choice.[38] In its ideal form the success of the electoral process depended upon confidentiality, but in practice news of the separate ballots leaked out, often with the help of inducements offered to servants attending the electors. Bribery was not uncommon. The dogeship was a matter of great public interest, not just among the professional classes whose livelihoods might be affected by the outcome, but also among the *popolani*, who tended to favour candidates according to their reputation for generosity, a quality that was put immediately to the test during the investiture ceremonies. Both the election and its ritual confirmation moved between public and private actions, to secure widespread approval of the outcome through a sense of popular participation.

The intrigues and antics of electioneering, often less dignified than might be imagined from the bland mythologizing of Contarini and other sixteenth-century political writers, stand in stark contrast to the solemn rituals that were being enacted elsewhere in the Doge's Palace. One of the first of these was the destruction of three selected symbols of the deceased doge. First his gold ring, engraved with his family escutcheon, the Lion of St Mark and the words 'Voluntas Ducis', was removed and handed to one of the secretaries of the Council of Ten, who smashed it to pieces. Similarly, the matrix of the doge's seal was then shattered.[39] Two silver vessels sent from the salt works in Chioggia were next to receive attention. The larger of the two, decorated with a design showing the doge in full coronation robes and holding the banner of St Mark, together with the inscription 'Sigillum salis domini venetiarum', was destroyed, while the smaller one was preserved to be presented to the new doge by the senior of the six councillors.[40] This carried the words 'bulleta salis', and was engraved with the name of the new doge after his election. These actions all emphasized the ending of the doge's personal authority and the continuity of republican government through the patriciate.

On the same day that these rituals were executed, the body of the deceased doge, dressed in a golden robe and *corno* (ducal cap), was carried in solemn procession from the doge's private apartments, where it had been placed on a catafalque covered with rugs, to the Sala dei Pioveghi. As was usual for persons of rank, the corpse, borne on a ceremonial bier by sailors from the Arsenal and escorted by the commanders carrying lighted torches, remained visible, as is still the case at papal funerals. Escorting it were the *scarlatti*, usually a group of some twenty patricians dressed in scarlet and with purple stoles over their shoulders, whose presence, as well as the festive colours of their dress, was intended 'as a sign', as Sanudo put it, 'that the Signoria still lives though the doge is dead'.[41] They were accompanied by the canons of the basilica, the Grand Chancellor and other officials, members of the family, and the Signoria, preceded by a processional cross.[42]

In the Sala dei Pioveghi the corpse was now placed on another catafalque, this time covered with a cloth of gold, while the *corno* was placed on the faldstool that accompanied the doge on official occasions. The gold ceremonial sword, also carried in the ducal procession, was arranged with its hilt pointing downwards, an inversion of its normal position when worn, while reversed spurs were attached to the feet and a shield bearing the arms of the deceased was set up facing towards the body. All took their places, leaving the doge's throne empty. Prayers were said and a psalm recited by the canons of San Marco, before they withdrew together with the Signoria. While the canons went to officiate at a solemn requiem mass in the basilica, together with the *primicerio*, the Signoria heard mass in the chapel of San Nicolò in the Doge's Palace. These solemn requiems were repeated on each of the three days and nights that the corpse lay in state, attended by a rota of the *scarlatti*.

On the day of the funeral itself the ceremonies began with the chanting of the Office of the Dead around the catafalque by the canons, usually in the presence of the papal legate and the ambassadors. Then, having accompanied the corpse to the head of the Scala dei Giganti – that is, to the very spot where the deceased doge had taken his oath and been crowned – the Signoria retired into the Doge's Palace to continue the election; their absence from both the requiems in the basilica and the funeral procession that followed was intended as a further symbolic underlining of Sanudo's sentiment.[43] This moment also marked the passing of the funeral rites from the domain of religious and government elites into a more public sphere. It is characteristic that the most important ceremonies marking a change of doge – funerals and coronations – were also public occasions.[44] Although predominantly religious in form and content, both contained distinctive civic elements, and were centred on San Marco, the Doge's Palace and the surrounding ceremonial spaces.

The long procession that now escorted the body around the Piazza San Marco included all the *scuole piccole*, the monastic and religious orders, the nine clerical congregations of the city and members of the doge's family and other important mourners who had usually gathered at the *primicerio*'s palace.[45] On the death of a doge, all the nuns, monks and clergy of the city were ordered to pray for the soul of the deceased and to attend his funeral, as were the members of the *scuole*.[46] All of the *scuole grandi* also walked in their usual positions in the procession except one, usually that of which the doge had been a member, which walked behind the body protected by a baldachin and carried by a contingent of sailors from the Arsenal. During the procession that escorted

Antonio Grimani's body in 1523, parts of the office and various *laude* were sung,[47] probably a standard practice. In front of the basilica the procession stopped and the corpse was raised on its stretcher nine times, while the members of the members of the *scuola grande* accompanying the body cried out for divine mercy, 'Iddio habbia misericordia!', and the bells rang out nine doubles.[48] Conceivably, this referred to the nine congregations of clergy that were not only physically present in the Piazza, but that were also in this way symbolically united in a general call for clemency for the soul of the deceased through a formula that evoked the ninefold invocation of the Kyrie. The procession then continued through the narrow streets to the church where the burial was to take place, which in the sixteenth century was usually one of the two great mendicant churches of the city: the Frari and Santi Giovanni e Paolo. There the stretcher was raised on a catafalque covered with black velvet worked with the doge's family escutcheon and the Lion of St Mark, and a Latin oration was given. Following some final prayers and a blessing by the patriarch, the body was interred.

From the accession of Domenico Selvo in 1071 until the death of Ordelaffo Falier in 1118, all the doges had been buried in San Marco. So too were a number of their successors: Marino Morosini (d. 1253), Giovanni Soranzo (d. 1328), Bartolomeo Gradenigo (d. 1342) and Andrea Dandolo (d. 1354), after which the practice stopped. It may be that by making San Marco the final resting-place of this particular series of doges the Venetians were again taking as their model the Apostoleion in Constantinople, which, connected to the Mausoleum of Constantine the Great, had been for some time the favourite burial place of the Byzantine emperors. It seems more likely, though, that these particular doges of the late eleventh and early twelfth centuries were buried in San Marco in recognition of their contributions to the building and embellishment of the Contarini church.[49] Whatever the reason, Dandolo's tomb in the baptistery, which in terms of style and location would have turned San Marco into a ducal mausoleum had it been followed by his successors, put a stop to the practice. The author of the *Chronaca magno* reports that no further ducal burials in San Marco were allowed after Dandolo's death, which, if true, probably was as much a result of the enhanced sense of ducal presence that Dandolo's alterations to the interior had introduced as an aesthetic reaction to the tomb itself.[50]

After this date all ducal burials took place elsewhere. During the late middle ages the *cappella maggiore* of the Dominican church of Santi Giovanni e Paolo became a major site for ducal tombs and funerary monuments,[51] while the Franciscan church of the Frari also provided a home for the final remains of a number of doges, including Francesco Dandolo and, spectacularly, Nicolò Tron (d. 1473). Until well into the fourteenth century the tombs of the doges had been mostly simple affairs, usually sculpted in the form of antique or Early Christian sarcophagi attached to the wall and accompanied by Latin inscrip-

tions. Andrea Dandolo's tomb in San Marco introduced a new element by including an effigy of the deceased, and later examples continued the trend towards increasingly elaborate and grandiose structures.[52] Something of a landmark in this general development was reached with Tron's tomb, which, in addition to showing the doge himself (he appears twice), includes Latin inscriptions, classically inspired medallion heads and twenty-seven free-standing sculptures as part of an iconographical scheme that presents the doge as the ideal ruler, the central agent in the harmonious operations of the Republic.[53] Facing Tron's tomb is that of Francesco Foscari. Designed as a wall-tomb decorated with a canopy suspended from the relief architecture of the wall behind, it is generally regarded as the first Renaissance ducal tomb in the church (pl. 87).[54] Foscari's tomb also marks a boundary in a political as well as a stylistic sense, as the last monument to an age of troubled dogeships often marked by power struggles between families and factions. In the decades that followed, the

87 Attributed to Antonio and Paolo Bregno, tomb of Doge Francesco Foscari, c.1457. Santa Maria Gloriosa dei Frari.

rituals that marked the transition from one dogeship to the next might be enacted with due solemnity, but the power of the doge remained in check.

The investiture of a new doge, an event that was both public and symbolic, transformed the individual from an ordinary member of the patrician class into an office-holder with sacral powers. The electoral procedures that led up to it, which in practice were also semi-public, were also designed to demonstrate the virtues of Venice, its ruling patrician class and the constitution of the Republic. Once the forty-one had reached a decision and the news of the election had been made, the bells of San Marco were rung to announce to the city that a new doge had been elected. Members of the Signoria were the first to offer their congratulations, followed by others, and the councillors then presented the *ballotino* to the doge-elect.[55] This post was filled afresh before each ducal election, by the simple expedient of one of the heads of the Quarantia al Criminale (the Court of the Forty), the supreme appeals court for criminal cases, walking through the basilica and selecting the first boy under fifteen years of age that he encountered on emerging from the west door. After the election was over, the *ballotino*'s main responsibility was to draw lots and count ballot papers at meetings of the Great Council, but he also walked in the ducal procession as a permanent reminder of the supposed impartiality of the election procedure.[56] Orders were now given for the bells to be rung three times, and the main doors of the palace, which had mostly been kept locked since the vote began, were thrown open to allow in members of the public. It is reported that after the election of Sebastiano Venier in 1577, a popular hero on account of his leadership of the Venetian forces at Lepanto, a great crowd of both patricians and *popolani*, including a good number of Armenians and Turks, pressed forward to kiss his hands.[57] In the Doge's Palace the doge was received by a group of office-holders, including all the members of the forty-one who had elected him, together with the six ducal councillors. These men, elected by the Great Council to serve for eight months, were each chosen from a different *sestiere* of the city. In practice, the doge needed the agreement of at least four councillors before making any decision, and at least the same number had to be present at all meetings of the Council of Ten. The withdrawal of the councillors at the precise moment when the funeral cortège of a doge moved from the Doge's Palace to the Piazza San Marco neatly completed a cycle inaugurated by this initial encounter, after which the new doge was unable to leave the palace without them.

The investiture ceremonies that followed, while presenting the doge in an almost monarchical light, also emphasized his obligation to follow the duties and restrictions on his power laid down by a republican patriciate.[58] Entering San Marco by the south door leading from the palace, the doge-elect mounted the *pulpitum magnum*, and from there was presented to the crowds massed below in the nave by the senior elector of the forty-one. The formula used, which varied only insignificantly in the course of the centuries, stresses the role of both Signoria and Senate in the election of the new doge, 'the virtues and worthy condition of whom are such that, through divine grace, he will fervently strive for the good and conservation of the state, and every public as well as private interest'.[59] After the doge had made a brief statement promising justice, plenty, peace and the protection of the Venetian empire, again according to a standard formula, he descended from the pulpit and, having walked the short distance to the high altar where he was embraced by the *primicerio*, kissed it. This simple gesture, normally made by all celebrants at both the beginning and the end of mass, is a reminder of the priestly aspects of the dogeship, and is reminiscent of the prerogatives of the Byzantine emperor. In the brief period between his election by the forty-one and the beginning of the investiture ceremonies, the doge-elect had already received minor ecclesiastical orders in the basilica, mainly so that he could administer benediction. More broadly, it also enabled his participation, albeit in a minor capacity, on a number of religious and liturgical occasions. Here too there is an analogy with Eastern practice. By the Late Byzantine period, the emperor's quasi-sacerdotal status had been tamed by treating him as a *depotatos*, a cleric in minor orders ranking somewhere between fortieth and fiftieth in the hierarchy of the Great

Church (Hagia Sophia), but still retaining the traditional rights to cense the altar.[60] The sacral aspects of the dogeship became of paramount importance at moments of crisis such as war and plague, when his function as an intercessor on behalf of Venice and its inhabitants became urgent. On such occasions the analogy between pope and doge, explicit in the Marcian legends (and above all in the *apparitio*), reached one of its clearest practical expressions.

Facing the *primicerio*, and placing his hand on a copy of the Gospels,[61] the doge-elect now swore an oath to protect the honour and patrimony of San Marco 'bona fide et sine fraude', a direct reference not only to the basilica's substantial holdings of land, property and trusts, but also to the doge's funda-mental and traditional role as the principal guardian of the saint's relics.[62] Then, as his final act in the investiture, the *primicerio* took one of the eight red cer-emonial banners bearing the image of the Lion of St Mark from the admiral of the Arsenal, and presented it to the doge-elect, saying: 'We consign to your Serenity the banner of St Mark as a sign of true and perpetual dogeship', to which the reply came, 'I accept', before the standard was passed back. The banner of St Mark was a familiar part of the ceremonial apparatus, since all eight of them, usually kept in the Arsenal, were carried at the head of the ducal *andata*. Venetians would also have been familiar with it from coins, where the banner is shown being handed to the doge by the Lion of St Mark. This was obviously intended to represent both the role of the individual doge and his historic position in a continuous process of descending authority, in a design that symbolically evoked one of the most solemn moments of the investiture ceremony itself.[63] It was immediately after the consignment of the *vexillum* that the 'Oration di San Marco' was sung by the choir:

> O Lord who has exalted your Evangelist, blessed Mark, because of his preach-ing of the gospel, we implore you, grant that we may always be assisted by his teaching and protected by his prayers. Alleluia.[64]

The importance of this moment is reflected in the number of large-scale set-tings of the text written by composers associated with San Marco that survive, including two by Andrea Gabrieli, one by his nephew Giovanni, and one by Giovanni Bassano.[65] In functional terms the text was appropriate for perfor-mance not only at the votive service that followed the election of a doge or procurator (or on the anniversary of such an election), but also at the ceremony that installed a new captain-general of the Venetian armed forces in office (in the Tridentine rite the text served as a collect for the feast of St Mark).[66] All these compositions, which can be thought of as musical equivalents of the omnipresent emblem of the Winged Lion, could also be performed on major civic and religious occasions. The same is true of obvious derivations from the *Oratio*, such as Giovanni Bassano's five-voice motet 'O rex gloriae, qui beatum Marcum Evangelistam', whose opening line parallels the *Oratio* but which then continues with part of the liturgy for the feast of the Ascension, and was presumably performed on this day.[67] These texts underline Mark's fundamental significance in Venetian civic liturgy as a personification of the Republic that prospered under his protection and guidance; through such means the constitution and government of Venice were celebrated and sanctified. This widely understood conception, communicated in much Venetian visual art of the period, is vividly expressed in the words of Gabriele Fiamma, a fifteenth-century canon regular of San Marco: 'I was born a Venetian and live in this happy homeland, protected by the prayers and guardianship of St Mark, from whom that Most Serene Republic acknowledges its greatness, its victories and all its good fortune.'[68] Musical settings of these texts, and of others celebrating the principal Venetian protectors, lent further rhetorical emphasis to this familiar notion.

The mood of the proceedings now changed as the new doge was presented to the people. At the entrance to the choir, he stepped into a portable wooden pulpit with low wooden sides together with two male members of his family and the admiral of the Arsenal, who was still holding the ceremonial standard of St Mark. Carried aloft by a squad of sailors from the Arsenal, they moved through the square throwing coins to the crowd. To judge by Franco's engraving, this could be something of an unruly occasion (pl. 88). The final phase of the investiture ceremonies was the coronation itself, which took place at the top of the Scala dei Giganti, traditionally used as a grand balcony and entrance to the Doge's Palace, a place where Venetian patricians could be greeted and foreign ambassadors received by the doge (pl. 89).[69] Sansovino's giant marble statues of *Mars* and *Neptune*, symbols of Venetian territorial and maritime power, commissioned in 1554 but not installed until 1567,[70] lent it an additional political dimension (pls 90, 91). First the *promissione ducale* was handed to the oldest councillor by the Grand Chancellor, and the doge-elect publicly swore to obey its provisions. To the sound of church bells (they were rung continuously for three days and nights), drums and the noise of the crowds, the white cloth skull-cap was placed on his head by the youngest ducal councillor, and the doge was then crowned with the *corno* by the senior councillor, with the words 'accept the ducal crown of Venice'.[71] According to Bernardo Giustiniani, the unusual form of this distinctive piece of headgear was intended to parallel the papal mitre.[72] To the

88   Giacomo Franco, *The Doge Presented to the People*, engraving. Venice, Museo Civico Correr.

89 Scala dei Giganti. Ducal Palace.

applause of the onlookers the doge then moved to the third arch of the loggia of the palace, where, having called for silence, he repeated the promises that he had made earlier in the basilica. Still accompanied by the banner of St Mark, he then went to the Sala dei Pioveghi to take his place for the first time on the ducal throne. To the assembled company he repeated his election promises for the third time.[73] Many of the significant ritualistic components of the investiture ceremony in its fully fledged sixteenth-century form were inherited from

LEFT 90   Jacopo Sansovino, *Mars*, 1554–66. Ducal Palace, Scala dei Giganti.

RIGHT 91   Jacopo Sansovino, *Neptune*, 1554–66. Ducal Palace, Scala dei Giganti.

tradition. The earliest reasonably detailed description of a ducal investiture, that of Doge Domenico Selvo, which dates from the end of the eleventh century, was written by an eyewitness, the priest Domenico Tino.[74] In its description of ritual, Tino's account is quite different from the few lines in John the Deacon's chronicle describing the short ceremony that marked Doge Pietro Candiano I's formal acceptance of the dogeship after his election by popular assembly in 887. The chronicler's brief note of that occasion, 'After summoning [him] to the palace, he presented him with the sword, the baton, and the faldstool' ('ad palatium convocans spatam fustemque ac sellam ei contradidit'), gives the impression of a simple, almost private affair, apparently devoid of religious content, held in the Doge's Palace. Its most significant feature is the presentation of the *fustis*, presumably to be identified with the *baculus* mentioned in later medieval accounts of the ducal investiture, a baton or sceptre whose exchange symbolized the transfer of power.[75]

By the time of Selvo's election, held at Olivolo, the practice was for the bishops of the area, together with other members of the clergy, to retire to the newly consecrated church at the monastery at San Nicolò al Lido; there they prayed for divine guidance for the electors and a felicitous outcome of their deliberations. Selvo's election itself was still by popular acclaim, as Candiano's had been, but according to a precise formula, 'Dominicum Silvum volumus et laudamus', after which he was carried on the shoulders of enthusiastic supporters to San Nicolò, and from there he was taken to Venice by boat. During the short voyage the Te Deum and the Kyrie Eleison were sung, together with 'ceterasque laudes'. On his arrival at San Marco, then still under construction, Selvo, having been welcomed by the priests of the basilica and other ecclesiastical dignitaries, entered the church barefoot, having performed the ritual *spogliazione* that was universally practised in the middle ages on the assumption of a new religious or political role of elevated rank. He then prostrated himself on the ground and gave thanks to God for his election. The presence of a large rectangular slab of porphyry, which carried imperial resonances, in the pavement of San Marco directly in front of the High Altar, may mark the spot where the act of prostration took place. After this he was formally invested with the functions of doge through the symbolic presentation, at the high altar, of the *baculus* with the words 'As a [sign of] the conferment of ducal power, he received the sceptre at the altar of the most holy saint Mark' ('ob investituram ducatus baculum ab altari sanctissimi Marci suscepit'). The ceremonies came to a close with the procession of the new doge to the Doge's Palace, where the people swore an oath of allegiance and gifts were distributed to the crowd. A number of these elements were clearly related to Byzantine precedent, notably the formula that had been used to greet the election of a new emperor since at least the sixth century, the *spogliazione*, and the carrying of the doge-elect on the shoulders of the crowd and the distribution of gifts. These last features, present in the early medieval ceremony as described by Tino, were eventually amalgamated into the final form of the investiture ceremony as it became established by the end of the fifteenth century.[76]

The *baculus*, the most important of the three insignia conferred during the earliest recorded investiture ceremonies, was still in use at the time of Selvo's dogeship, but was later replaced with the *vexillum*. By the time of Doge Sebastiano Ziani's investiture, a hundred years later, the new doge received the banner of St Mark directly from the *primicerio*.[77] A second important change was that the doge was now required to swear on the Gospels, in front of the high altar, an oath according to a formula that was then incorporated into later versions of the *promissione ducale*.[78] That these changes remained in place in a ceremony that then changed little before the end of the fifteenth century is clear from two late thirteenth-century investitures described by Martino da Canal. Both are in agreement about the main phases of the ritual, which began with the announcement of the result of the election and the approval of the people. There followed the entry into San Marco, the presentation of the doge-elect to the congregation by the electors, his short address, his symbolic *spogliazione* and his progress to the high altar, where he publicly made the oath to protect the interests of the basilica, and was finally presented with the standard of St Mark.[79] The final ceremonies were conducted on the steps of the Doge's Palace, where the procession from the basilica came to a halt and the doge, still holding the banner of St Mark, turned to face the crowd. It was at this juncture that the *laudes* were sung by the canons of the basilica, after which the oath made earlier in San Marco was repeated. This last detail was an important modification of the earlier practice, described by Tino, in which the people swore their loyalty to the new doge.

The rituals that marked both the investiture and the funeral of the doge, and the way that they changed over time, reveal a great deal about the fluid conception of the dogeship. In broad terms, the power of the doge declined over the centuries, but even within this overall pattern there was another feature at work in which strong doges such as Francesco Foscari or Agostino Barbarigo in the fifteenth century, or Andrea Gritti in the sixteenth, provoked a reaction in the patriciate that led to a reduction of authority, which was sometimes accompanied by a diminution in the ceremonial trappings of office. A further insight into the nature of the dogeship, and in particular into its semi-sacral character, is suggested by the way in which the doge participated in the liturgy on major feasts. It seems likely that the historical model for this was again Byzantium, where the emperor played a significant role in Hagia Sophia on more than a dozen occasions in the church year, including Christmas Day, Epiphany, Palm Sunday, Easter and Ascension Day. According to the *Book of the Ceremonies* of Constantine VII Porphyrogenitos (913–59), which dates from the tenth century, the Eastern emperor was commemorated by name in the liturgy, and occasionally lit candles and placed offerings on the altar. Similarly, the doge assisted at mass at least from the thirteenth century, and was incensed and received the kiss of peace from the *primicerio*. Together with six canons he recited parts of the ordinary, and his name was also introduced into both the canon of the mass and other liturgical formulas. On occasion the doge chanted the 'Pater noster' standing at the high altar. Both emperor and doge were involved in special rituals involving processional forms on the feast of the Annunciation and Palm Sunday.[80] The sacral aspects of the doge's function became visually more explicit in the final decades of the sixteenth century, as in a number of paintings by Palma il Giovane, including the canvas in San Fantin showing the mass of thanksgiving for the victory at Lepanto (see pl. 99), and the cycle in the oratory of the Crociferi depicting Pasquale Cicogna participating in a number of devotional contexts. In these images the doge is presented as mediator between the Venetians and the Almighty.

During Holy Week the doge was at the centre of a symbolic re-enactment of the events in Jerusalem in a sequence of rituals and ceremonies grounded in liturgical ceremony supplemented by civic ritual.[81] Comparison between its thirteenth-century form and the version in use at the end of the sixteenth century again reveals a considerable amount of continuity. As is often the case with Venetian ritual, the earlier version changed slowly over time; it was not discarded, but merely reinflected to take account of new realities. In the case of the Holy Week ceremonies as a whole, the principal alteration concerns the Mandatum during the Evangelium at mass on Maundy Thursday, when, in a ritual recalling Christ's service to the apostles as recounted by St John, the doge washed the feet of twelve hand-picked members of the congregation. In Byzantium, the washing of the feet, which had long been a monastic ritual in the Middle Byzantine period, occured in the fourteenth century as an imperial ceremony for Maundy Thursday, with the emperor acting in the place of Christ.[82] In their incorporation of the Mandatum (which at some later date was dropped from the ceremony), as in many other details, the Holy Week rituals at San Marco were distinctive and unique to the basilica.[83]

The complete ritual sequence began on the morning of Palm Sunday with the blessing and distribution of palms, followed by a procession in which the doge, the *primicerio* and other dignitaries each carried an artificial palm decorated with silver and gold leaves.[84] Turning back towards the basilica, the procession came to a halt at the west door, and the choir, positioned above in front of the four gilded bronze horses, sang the hymn 'Gloria, laus et honor', to which the clergy standing in the Piazza below supplied the chorus. Birds were now released from the roof by the sacristans, their legs weighted down with paper crowns so that they could be caught by the spectators, killed and finally eaten as a festive delicacy on Easter Sunday. This ritual, which was repeated twice, recalled the applause that greeted Christ on his entry into Jerusalem.[85] The procession then re-entered the basilica and both mass and the Passion were sung. After the 'Asperges me' had been chanted, the celebrant offered a palm branch to the doge; following this, 'Pueri hebraeorum' was sung, conceivably in polyphony, and a general distribution of palms took place. Matters were brought to a close with vespers and then compline.[86]

The doge, present throughout the day, reappeared in San Marco for compline, matins and lauds (the latter two transposed) on Wednesday, the first day of the *triduum sacrum*. On Thursday, Friday and Saturday he again attended for the complete office, as well as for mass and vespers. This was not merely a question of ceremonial presence but of active participation,[87] a pattern of involvement that continued and increased in intensity as Easter approached. The survival of all nine lessons of the Lamentations in two-voice settings by Johannis de Quadris, together with polyphony for the Good Friday procession and a number of other Holy Week texts by the same composer, strongly suggests that this music was performed in San Marco. Not only is Quadris known to have worked at the basilica, but many of the manuscript and printed sources that contain this repertory are connected either with Venice or the Veneto.[88]

Early in the morning of Good Friday, before the Sacrament had been removed from its tabernacle where it had been placed the previous evening, the doge went to the sacristy, where he was joined by the Signoria. There he removed some of the most potent symbols of his authority and, dressed as a simple penitent, knelt and kissed the cross that contained the precious relic of the True Cross. The patriciate then followed his example. In the afternoon the Host was removed from the sacristy and carried round the Piazza in a bier covered with black velvet by four canons dressed in black dalmatics accompanied by incense and candles. The procession, which was led by the *scuole grandi* also carrying candles, included the clergy of San Marco and the *cappella cantorum* divided into two groups. On arrival at the door of the sacristy one of them sang the invitatory 'Venite et ploremus' while all knelt, then the second group responded with the opening of the Improperia 'Popule meus' as all rose again and the procession continued on its way. This was repeated in front of the church of San Basso (which was under the ducal *ius patronatus*) and in other nearby locations.

The procession now re-entered the basilica and went to the sepulchre, a temporary structure set up in the nave of the church to recall (symbolically rather than physically) the Holy Sepulchre in Jerusalem. Its precise location changed from time to time. In the early middle ages it was placed close to the 'pilastro di miracolo', so-called because it was believed that there the *apparitio* had taken place.[89] Before 1527, according to Sanudo, it was placed in the middle of the church, covered with cloth of gold and decorated with tapestries showing scenes from the *Life of Christ*. Later the sepulchre was placed 'in capo' of the church, that is, presumably further towards the iconostasis.[90] This was a particularly appropriate location in view of the Resurrection/Ascension iconography of the central dome above, which would thus tie in the Easter ritual to that most fundamental of Venetian myths, the *sensa*. Bonifacio's *Ceremoniale* of 1564 specifies that the sepulchre was then put up in the north transept, which may well have been its position in the mid-eighteenth century, since some sort of funerary monument, clearly temporary, is shown in a number of Canaletto's drawings and paintings (see pl. 85).[91] Having arrived at the sepulchre, the celebrant took the Host and placed it inside, and the entrance was sealed with wax by the Grand Chancellor using the doge's ring, while the choir intoned 'Sepulto Domino signatum est monumentum ad ostium monumenti'. All the candles were then extinguished.[92] The day finished with a nocturnal candlelit procession of the *scuole grandi* in the Piazza, while throughout the city the *scuole piccole* also processed with torches, and in the Mercerie the shops, hung with black drapes, were illuminated. Windows of private houses were similarly lit as a mark of devotion.[93]

The climax of the Holy Week ceremonies in San Marco occurred on Easter morning.[94] Inside the basilica the Pala d'Oro was opened and precious ritual objects from the treasury were placed on the high altar as a sign of the importance of the occasion. A procession, formed to collect the doge from his private apartments, left the Doge's Palace by the Porta della Carta, and moved around the Piazza to arrive at the west door of the basilica. The basic form of the procession was that of the ducal *andata* with, at its core, the doge, the celebrant and the senior procurator, all of whom carried large candles, two pounds in weight, which had been lit and presented to them by the clergy in the palace. This ritual detail recalls the earlier practice of visiting the church of San Geminiano as described by Canal, when candles were also carried. Bonifacio's *Ceremoniale* insists upon the splendour of the occasion, with the canons wearing precious copes according to rank.

If that is one aspect that distinguishes the arrangements at San Marco from practice elsewhere, the other is the precise form of the 'Quem queritis' dialogue itself, and of the subsequent *Visitatio Sepulchri* ceremony.[95] At the main door of San Marco the celebrant knocked three times, using the bronze ring that hangs from the inner door, an action that is unknown in the liturgy outside the ceremony for the consecration of a church. The dialogue then began with the singers inside singing 'Quem queritis', to which those outside responded 'Iesum nazarenum', to which the reply from within the basilica was 'Non est hic'. Then, at the sung invitation from within, 'Venite et videte', the doors were flung open and all moved inside and processed to the sepulchre. There the last part of the 'Quem queritis' ceremony was performed. Early in the morning the consecrated Host had been moved from the sepulchre, where it had been deposited on Good Friday, to its normal altar. The absence of the usual *Elevatio* ceremony stands in contrast to the proceedings on Good Friday, when the Deposition was the culmination of a magnificent evening procession involving the doge, the clergy, the foreign ambassadors and members of the *scuole*. It has been suggested that the Easter morning ceremonies were constructed, or had evolved, so that the emphasis was upon the role of the doge. Finding the sepulchre empty, the celebrant turned to the congregation and announced 'Surrexit Christus', the Latin translation of the Greek Easter greeting 'Christos aneste', to which the choir responded 'Deo Gratias'. Approaching the doge and the senior procurator, the celebrant kissed them both before saying 'Surrexit Christus', to which they too replied 'Deo Gratias'. The same was then repeated with all the clergy present, in order of seniority. The use of a Greek greeting, ritualized as the conclusion of the ceremony, places an emphasis upon the doge's position both as equivalent to that of a Byzantine emperor and as the principal and first witness to the Resurrection.

As expressions of political power sanctioned by ecclesiastical authority, Venetian official ceremonial experienced its most severe test at moments of crisis. On a small scale this can be seen in many aspects of the rituals that accompanied the transfer of power from one doge to another. It also became evident during the middle decades of the sixteenth century, a period of uncertainty despite the apparent triumph of the victory of Lepanto and the confident expressions of Venetian strength and perfection to be read in the paintings of Titian, Tintoretto and Veronese. For the citizens of the Republic who lived through a decade of war, plague, famine and a sequence of devastating fires, which threatened the Arsenal and destroyed a large part of the Doge's Palace, the experience of these years could be read only in a dark and ominous register. It was precisely in these years that the ceremonial rituals of state, with their unique mixture of religious and civic elements, were brought into play on an unprecedented scale.

PART TWO

A
DISQUIETING
DECADE

CHAPTER FIVE

A Holy Crusade

O Massa and Sorrento, mourn your misfortunes
Deplore, all Christendom, our misery
Death would have been a better fate for us.

. . .

We call on all Christian princes to unite,
And rescue us from this evil . . .[1]

In the summer of 1558 the Turkish fleet, openly encouraged by the French as part of their traditional anti-Spanish designs, unexpectedly appeared in the Bay of Naples. Men were landed and the towns of Sorrento and Massa were sacked, churches were destroyed and the more elderly citizens savagely executed.[2] As the anonymous author of *Il gran lamento* recognized, the Turkish threat would never be removed as long as the Christian powers continued to squabble among themselves instead of uniting to repel the Infidel. Venice, Genoa, the dukes of Florence, Ferrara and Urbino, and the kings of Hungary, Portugal and Bohemia were all begged to support the cause. Not just the French and the Spanish, but all the princes of Italy needed to pool their efforts against the common foe, in what was, effectively, a call for a new crusade.

This appeal, to be reiterated with increasing frequency over the following ten years as the Turkish threat increased in intensity, was hardly new. Turkish incursions into Italian waters, and reprisals against the towns and villages of the Kingdom of Naples, had been common for generations. Worst of all had been the siege of Otranto in 1480, when the Turks had landed on the Salentine peninsula, invaded the city, despoiled its churches and monasteries, and slaughtered 800 of its inhabitants.[3] This was an event of tragic proportions, whose details were endlessly repeated and elaborated in the following decades. More recently, the appearances of the Ottoman fleet had become if not an annual fixture at least disturbingly frequent. In 1535 the Turks invaded Capri, and in 1543 Massa. The following year they tried to land and were beaten off by a storm, but in 1552 and 1554 they were back again.[4] The apogee of Turkish sea power in the Mediterranean was reached in 1560, when the Spanish stronghold on the island of Djerba was taken, and the victorious Turkish fleet returned home by way of Gozo, Sicily and the Abruzzi, where villages were plundered and torched.[5] The Christian world, unaware of the fundamental concept of a holy war conducted to defend the faith and extend the boundaries of Islam, regarded such incidents as isolated if worrying indications of Turkish power. In practice, the Ottoman state was in a permanent condition of war with Christian Europe from the fall of Constantinople in 1453 until the Treaty of Zsitva-Torok in 1606.[6] Within this arc of two-and-a-half centuries, the final years of Suleiman I (1520–66) and the first ones of his successor, Selim, mark the moment when territorial ambition extended the limits of the Ottoman empire to their greatest extent. From the siege of Malta in 1565 until the separate Venetian peace treaty of 1573, the Turks dominated the external politics of the Republic, the Papacy and, to a lesser extent, the Holy Roman Empire. During these years the general climate of apprehension grew in intensity as each spring posed afresh the question of whether or not the Ottoman fleet would reappear in the Adriatic.

The pleas of the Sorrentines fell upon deaf ears, not least in Venice, where Turkish adventures of this kind had never been regarded as a serious threat to the Treaty of Constantinople, which in 1540 had brought to an end the war between the Holy League and the Ottoman empire. The intervening years of peace had brought some stability and a certain degree of prosperity to the Republic's affairs, justifying the position of those Venetians who pressed for accommodation with the Turks at all costs. Many never doubted that peaceful coexistence, beneficial to both sides, was seriously at risk, not even after the spring of 1565, when Turkish troops had landed on Malta, fiercely and successfully defended by the combined forces of the Knights of Malta and a contingent of Spanish soldiers.[7] Six months later, in a show of determination, the city of Valletta was founded. A number of medals were issued to commemorate the event, all carrying a portrait of Jean de la Vallette, Grand Master of the Order of Malta, on the obverse, and different legends on the reverse, including the optimistic DEI PROPVGNATORIS ('Of God, the champion of the victory to follow') and the celebratory MELITA RENASCENS ('Malta reborn'). These were reputedly buried in the foundations and under the walls of the new city, which was conceived as a symbol of resistance to the Turkish threat (pl. 93).[8] Nevertheless, the optimists increasingly found their position undermined in the years after the Maltese episode, as the frequency of Turkish attacks increased. At the time it was believed that the Turkish fleet, berthed at Valona on the Albanian coast, consisted of some 200 vessels and had the ability to land 25,000 men,[9] and while the Venetians continued to hope for the best, foreign observers noted Turkish preparations with alarm. Writing to William Cecil early in 1566, William Phayre reported that 'the Turk makes the wonderfullest haste in setting forth his armada, increasing his galleys to the number of a hundred more than he had last year', and added that all the trees around Constantinople had been cut down to make ships.[10] There was vague talk in Madrid of some form of alliance, but the Venetians, whose galleys were essential to such a scheme, dismissed the proposal out of hand, only too aware of the potential damage to both trade and treasury.[11] For the time being at least, there was to be no accommodation with the king of Spain.

In the summer of 1566 the Turks began a limited campaign of attacks upon the coastal towns and villages of the Adriatic. The armada, though not as large as the force that had landed on Malta in the previous year, was still impressive: 140 sail, of which 120 were galleys, galliots or foists. On 13 July the *bailò* (the Venetian governor, with responsibilities for commerce and diplomacy) of Corfu informed the Venetians that the Turkish fleet had been sighted off Zante,[12] and just over a fortnight later some 6,000 men landed near Francavilla and, finding the town deserted, razed it to the ground. From here the fleet moved on to Ortona, which

93 Federico Cocciola, medal of Jean de Vallette, 1565/6. London, British Museum.

also proved to be abandoned by its terrified inhabitants; it too was put to the torch, together with a number of small hamlets along the coast. On 5 August the Turks made a bold strike against Serra Capriola 8 miles inland, but meeting with unexpectedly stiff resistance they were forced to retreat in some disorder. On the evening of the next day eighty Turkish galleys made a brief appearance off Vasto, further north, but by morning they had gone. A few days later four Turkish ships were driven onto the shore near Fortore; their crews fled in panic, but all the artillery and rigging were recovered before orders were given to set fire to the hulls. Shortly afterwards the Turks turned for home, and it was later reported that their crews were in poor condition, much reduced by sickness. It was, then, somewhat against expectations that the Turkish fleet made one more short foray in September, sailing up the Albanian coast as far as Valona before finally returning to its home port for the winter. For the time being the threat had passed.[13]

The impact of these Turkish manoeuvres in the Adriatic had been widely reported, and on hearing of them the viceroy in Naples arranged for the evacuation of all undefended towns and villages along the coastline. This policy successfully limited the amount of damage that the enemy could cause; the summer campaign of 1566 could not be equated even with the assault on the Sorrentino in 1558, let alone to the legendary massacre at Otranto. On previous strikes of this kind the Turks had usually taken some thousands of prisoners to provide manpower for the galleys, but on this occasion they had made off with just three. No fortified town of any importance had been attacked, and the single Turkish galley and its two accompanying sloops that had ventured close to the fortifications at Pescara had been firmly dispatched with a few rounds of cannon fire from the ramparts. The Venetians reacted by preparing thirty galleys for war, commissioning another twenty, and dispatching 2,000 infantrymen to Dalmatia.[14] Comparatively slight though the real damage had been, the news from the Abruzzi sent ripples of alarm throughout Italy and beyond, as the French ambassador to Spain reported.[15] The reappearance of the Turkish fleet in the Adriatic was a clear signal that the relief of Malta by the Spanish fleet, in September 1565, had neither diminished the size of the Turkish threat nor altered the scope of Ottoman plans. Christian optimism, on hearing that the island had been saved from the fate that had befallen Rhodes in 1522, was now replaced with the fear that Malta had merely been a minor reversal in the triumphant progress of the Porte's imperial ambitions. With Philip II's attention diverted to the Netherlands, where both popular unrest and aristocratic opposition to Spanish authority had grown to disturbing proportions, Venice found itself facing isolation in the Mediterranean.

The newly elected pope, Pius V, chose this moment to propose a league against the Turk, in effect a revival of Pius II's scheme of a union of Christian princes dedicated to fighting Islam. Those with long memories would have recalled the heady moment in late 1537 when Paul II had succeeded where ten of his predecessors had failed, and had persuaded the Venetians to enter an alliance against the Ottomans.[16] This too had been undertaken in a historical spirit, exemplified by the reprinting of Bessarion's famous letter, issued after the fall of Negroponte in 1470, exhorting the princes of Italy to form a defensive league.[17] The formation of the Holy League with Charles V, finally ratified in 1538, and the *cruzada* that had ensued, provided a practical model that fired Pius V's determination to revive the crusading spirit in defence of Christendom. A Dominican of humble origins, committed to leading an exemplary austere and pious life (one ambassador described him as an ascetic who was nothing but skin and bone),[18] Pius had been elected in 1566 more because of his virtue than as a consequence of the usual Vatican intrigues, though the support of Carlo Borromeo had been critical. The very opposite of a Renaissance pontiff on the model of Leo X or Julius II, more of a medieval pope or an Old Testament patriarch, Pius brought to the chair of St Peter the passion, rigour, intransigence and vision that made him a legend in his own lifetime, and caused contemporaries to regard him as a saint. Cardinal Granvelle, a skilled and careful diplomat, wrote that 'the pope appears to me every day more holy', while the Spanish envoy in Rome, Luis de Requesens, was of the opinion that there had not been a better pope for three hundred years.[19] His determination to deal with infidels and heretics, a policy pursued with stiff resolve through the agency of the Inquisition, now showed itself in the international political arena. Despite the force of his personality, the pope's initial attempt to interest Philip II in the idea of a Holy League only brought the response that it would be 'useless, for such enterprises can only be undertaken when the princes involved have a full complement of reliable forces, and when they have confidence one in another; whereas at the present time those forces are divided, diminished, and set at odds by mutual suspicions'.[20] This was a pragmatic and, as it turned out, prophetic reply. Meanwhile, there was a growing sense of general apprehension. In May 1566 the French ambassador in Madrid heard from a courier, recently arrived from Seville, that the Turks were planning a fresh assault upon Malta, and in the following month he reported their capture of 28 Spanish ships and 800 men.[21] Such reports were obviously alarming, but for the time being, with open war now taking place in the Netherlands, the Mediterranean had become a secondary theatre of Spanish interests.[22]

In the spring of 1567 the viceroy of Naples, believing that the Turkish fleet would reappear yet again in Italian waters, set into motion his successful strategy of the previous year. A prominent naval presence was built up in Sicily, and strongholds elsewhere in the kingdom were strengthened.[23] At the same time, the Venetians voted 50,000 ducats to reinforce the fortifications at Famagusta, Nicosia and Kyrenia in Cyprus, against the recommendations of Ascanio Savorgnan's much-diffused official report of five years earlier. Savorgnan had recommended both the destruction of Kyrenia, as being of little strategic importance and difficult to defend, and the improved fortification of Famagusta. Nicosia, wrote Savorgnan, should be left undefended.[24] On the island itself an equivalent sum of money was raised to bolster its defences,[25] but the Turks, perhaps preoccupied with the severe food shortages of that year, did not send their galleys into the Adriatic, and Venetian hopes were raised again when their peace treaty with the sultan was renewed.[26] The news from elsewhere was less reassuring. In the autumn it was reported that extensive fortifications were being constructed at Karamania opposite Cyprus, in preparation (it was assumed) for an attack upon the island itself. In Madrid it was rumoured that 160 galleys were ready at Constantinople, waiting for the first signs of temperate spring weather, a story that re-emerged at the end of the year.[27] A purely routine inspection brought the Turkish fleet as far as Valona in the summer of 1568, but even this was sufficient to put the eastern coast of Italy on full alert.[28] In August it was reported that a Turkish fleet of seventy-seven galleys and thirteen foists had been sighted off Zante and Corfu, bound, it was believed, for

Apulia and Calabria. But at the end of the season it simply returned to Constantinople, allegedly in poor condition and with some of the crews infected by plague.[29]

Tension now increased as wars began to break out all over Europe: in the Netherlands, where Spain was now deeply engaged; in France, where a fresh spate of religious conflict had begun; and in two separate zones along the borders of the Turkish empire.[30] It was probably the last, more than anything else, that explains the absence of Turkish galleys from the Mediterranean arena in 1569, but any euphoria that might have been felt was quickly dispelled by the latest intelligence from Constantinople in the second half of the year. There, the inaction that had characterized the years since the retreat from Malta, intensified no doubt by the death of Suleiman the Magnificent in September 1566, and the transfer of power to the new sultan Selim, was now dramatically replaced by massive preparations for an expedition, presumed to be against Cyprus. The island, which had been under Venetian control for eighty years, was prized for its strategic trading position as well as for its produce.[31] It was well known that Selim had long coveted it, the last Christian outpost in the Muslim East. That an offensive of some sort was in the air had been apparent since reports describing the constructions at Karamania had begun to circulate towards the end of 1566; now it seemed that the Turks were busily rearming, perhaps for the great military victory that convention demanded of a new sovereign.[32] When Marcantonio Bragadin, the newly appointed military commander of Cyprus, arrived on the island in the autumn of 1569, he quickly became aware of the intensity of Turkish preparations. Even if their ultimate objective still remained unclear, it was generally acknowledged that their military might would be ultimately directed against Venetian possessions, and that the great armada, once assembled, would make for La Goletta, Malta, or, most probably, Cyprus itself.

Yet despite the frenzied activity in the arsenal at Constantinople, the moment for engagement had not yet arrived. Although Philip II was now considerably distracted by the added burden of the War of Granada, Turkey itself was still preoccupied with the border conflicts on the Russian front and along the Red Sea. During the winter of 1569–70 speculation about Turkish intentions intensified, and when a serious fire took hold in the Arsenal, completely destroying the nearby monastery of the Celestia, many in Venice feared that some kind of treachery had taken place.[33] Some believed the explosion to be the work of Turkish agents, while others spoke of a plot against the Republic organized by the sultan and the Jews, and many took it to be a portent of worse things to come.[34] There were even signs of popular discontent, because some blamed the disaster on patrician tyranny.[35] It was for Cyprus that the Venetians feared most, despite the common opinion that Turkish efforts were to be directed against the Spanish rather than themselves. In December, 1,000 men were dispatched to strengthen the garrisons on the island,[36] and instructions were given to intensify work on the fortifications at Famagusta. By the middle of January 1570, the *bailò* in Constantinople, Marcantonio Barbaro, who had been in post since September 1568,[37] was firmly of the view that the Turks were preparing for a spring offensive, with either Cyprus or Crete as the main objective.[38] From this moment, the Senate became increasingly involved in orders about troop movements, fortifications, ships and supplies.

Venetian preparations for war, described in deliberately exaggerated terms to their ambassadors in Rome, must have highlighted the poor condition of the Republic's forces. Technically, Venice had been at peace for thirty largely prosperous years, but one consequence had been to induce a false sense of security.[39] This had been accompanied by a new sense of collective identity, in which the earlier notion of Venice as a powerful, militant, republic had been gradually replaced with the more tranquil image of the city as the home of the *Pax Venetiana*.[40] The magnificent series of Venetian fortifications, formidably effective in the past, had in some cases been woefully neglected, while the army that manned them was disorganized and chaotic.[41] When Astorre Baglione arrived as governor of Nicosia in March 1569, determined to improve the island's defences, he was obstructed both by the military incompetence of the lieutenant-general, Nicolò Dandolo, and by the hostility of the local population, weary of the financial burdens of Venetian rule.[42] Worst of all, the Venetian fleet had gradually been reduced in its effectiveness.[43] Characteristic of official thinking since the end of the previous conflict with the Turks in 1540 had been the notion that the Republic's relationship with the Porte, based on mutually beneficial trading arrangements, would never succumb to direct aggression, irrespective of the pose that had to be adopted on the diplomatic stage.

From the Venetian point of view, the critical moment of revelation and disillusion seems to have been late January 1570, when the first reports of a spate of shipbuilding in the Bosphorus arrived in Venice. Preparations now got under way in earnest. The Republic already had about forty-five galleys at sea, some manned by convicts; to these were added reserves from the Arsenal, to make up a fleet of more than 150 ships, assembled at 'the greatest cost that we have ever incurred'.[44] These efforts were in turn sustained by fresh reports from abroad: of Turkish troop movements in Dalmatia and Albania, of the unusually provocative treatment of Venetian merchants in the Morea and the sequestering of two Venetian galleys, and of Turkish raids and mobilizations.[45] Matters took a more serious turn when, in February, the Turks began a series of systematic attacks upon Venetian outposts along the Dalmatian coast, at a time when Venice itself was badly affected by famine.[46] According to traditional wisdom, the shortage of food and basic supplies, and the deaths that followed, were yet further signs of divine displeasure. Certainly the situation was grave. One observer recounts that groups of the poor, driven wild by hunger, roamed the city in search of food, and that bread had to be brought in from as far away as Lonigo, south-west of Vicenza, only to be sold at inflated prices.[47] It was against this disturbing background that the papal nuncio was able to report a certain degree of enthusiasm in Venice for the idea of a Holy League.[48] That is not surprising. In contemporary thought divine displeasure demanded palliative action.

Shortly afterwards, towards the end of March, news of the official Turkish claims over Cyprus reached Venice, brought by Kubad Cha'ush, an official state messenger who had first visited the city two years earlier, in a letter from the sultan. These, public knowledge in Constantinople for more than a month, stipulated that, for historic reasons, the island was part of the Turkish domains and should be surrendered unconditionally. In Venice these demands met a brisk reception. Outside the Doge's Palace a large crowd had gathered, and the Cha'ush, who had not been accorded the usual diplomatic niceties, would undoubtedly have been stoned to death if the captains of the Council of Ten had not intervened.[49] Meanwhile, the Turkish demands were summarily dismissed by the Senate.[50] It was at this juncture that the doge, Pietro Loredan, died, to be replaced after a comparatively speedy election by Alvise Mocenigo (pl. 94). Loredan's dogeship had witnessed fires, hunger and now war, and despite his integrity and strong moral commitment he was remembered with little affection by the Venetians.[51] On the day of his funeral it rained heavily, fortunately it was said, otherwise 400 *popolani* would have stoned the bier with loaves of millet,[52] the lowest form of grain, usually fed only to animals.

By now it was clear that the crisis had turned into war, and the pace of Venetian preparations intensified. From the cities of the *terraferma* came offers of men and money. Brescia decided to pay for 1,000 infantry and Padua for 200, while Treviso undertook to support 400 infantry for six months, and Verona agreed to finance 500 troops for as long as the war should last.[53] In Vicenza the town council agreed to supply either men or money in a number of separate tranches; in order to meet this obligation all public works were halted, including the construction of Andrea Palladio's basilica, already well advanced. Work was not resumed until February 1584.[54] At the end of March, Hieronimo Zane was made admiral of the fleet, and presented with the baton of office in the traditional ceremony in San Marco. Zane had taken command of the fleet on two previous occasions (in 1566 and 1568), but on neither had it engaged with the enemy. These earlier commissions, and a successful public career culminating in a procuratorship, had earned him a reputation for reliability and achievement; the crowds that lined the Piazza and the Riva degli Schiavoni to witness the traditional procession following the ceremony in the basilica clearly believed that his authoritative presence would guarantee the preservation of peace.[55] In the Arsenal galleys were refitted for action, several thousand troops were dispatched to Dalmatia, and an expeditionary force arrived on Cyprus unopposed. On the diplomatic front, an ambassador was sent to Philip II, while the Spaniards, for their part, strengthened their positions in Naples, Sicily and North Africa, despite being heavily engaged both in

94   Jacopo Tintoretto, *Portrait of Doge Alvise Mocenigo*, *c.*1570. Venice, Gallerie dell'Accademia.

the Netherlands with the rebels and at home with the Moors in Granada. In order to defray the expenses of the war preparations, substantial imposts were levied upon the cities of the *terraferma*. In Padua individual families each armed a galley; Riviera del Garda offered men and money; and the Veronese provided five ships equipped with soldiers recruited both in the city and in Mantua.[56] Strenuous diplomatic attempts were made to gather support from outside Italy, and ambassadors were sent to the imperial court, and even to the king of Persia, the traditional enemy of the Turks.[57] The Ottoman forces (estimated at some 76,000 men) finally landed on the island in July, and by early September they had taken the capital, Nicosia. In the face of these developments Pius V, thwarted on the subject in 1566, rekindled his cherished dream of a Holy League. Persuading the Spaniards to take up arms was not easy, but the papal envoy, Luis de Torres, was effective in presenting the financial and political arguments to Philip.[58] Encouraged also by the Venetians, whose special representative urged rapid action, Spain finally agreed to participate in an attempt to relieve Cyprus.[59]

Seizing the initiative, Pius appointed Marcantonio Colonna, a Roman aristocrat and soldier with little experience of naval affairs, as commander-in-chief of the Christian forces.[60] The choice was surprising, and one that was much criticized at the time. The papal fleet was hastily assembled at Otranto, where it was joined by fifty-two galleys from Genoa with Gian Andrea Doria in charge; the Venetian galleys, some sixty of them, had been sent to Zara under Zane's command at the end of March. By June the fleet was at Corfu, and by the end of July it had been reinforced by a detachment of twenty-two galleys from Crete, which brought the news that 300 Turkish sail had been sighted off Rhodes. Meanwhile, the Spanish fleet, no better equipped or manned than those of the other allies, had gathered at Messina. All this was put in hand, even though the negotiations to establish a formally constituted Holy League were still far from being concluded. After an unsuccessful rendezvous off the northern coast of Crete in September, where disputes between Colonna, Zane and Doria became daily more acrimonious and the necessary fresh supplies failed to materialize, the entire force set sail for Rhodes. It was an impressive fleet of more than 190 galleys and galleases, 1,300 cannon and 16,000 troops. Nevertheless, on hearing the news that the Turks were now in control of the whole of Cyprus except for Famagusta, which was bravely holding out, the commanders, realizing the impossibility of wintering their enormous forces without adequate provisions, decided to retreat to the safety of Italian waters, leaving behind a small contingent of Venetian ships to guard Crete.[61] In a masterpiece of understatement, the pope expressed his displeasure that the armada had not made the progress that had been hoped for at the start of the campaign.[62] The return journey was not easy. On the way back the Venetians lost perhaps a third of their squadrons in severe storms, while Colonna returned in November with only three of the galleys that he had started out with. Only Doria, the most experienced of the three, managed to arrive in Messina with a reasonable complement of ships, having landed 2,000 infantry at Lecce. Following these failures in the winter of 1570, the future of the League, which had still not been agreed formally, was severely compromised.

By now Famagusta, which had been besieged by Turkish troops for eleven months before capitulating, had fallen to the enemy.[63] Its heroic defence by a garrison inspired by the leadership of Bragadin who, together with Astorre Baglione, was determined to resist until the end, became legendary. At first Bragadin had intended to hold out until Famagusta could be relieved by a counter-offensive led by the Venetian fleet and its allies, but with the passing of the months these reasonable if ill-founded hopes gradually faded. The Turks, who had been camped around the city since September of the previous year, kept up a continuous attack, aimed at slowly demoralizing the Venetians as their supplies dwindled and their defensive walls began to give way. Hardly a day passed without some minor offensive action until June, when a large enemy mine exploded under the walls and the Turks were able to make their first general assault. A week later there followed a second. In the face of the inevitable, the bishop of Limassol appealed to Bragadin to accept defeat rather than risk the massacre of the inhabitants. Sustained by a firm sense of duty and family pride, allied to a strong belief in the mission of a Christian crusade, Bragadin continued to resist throughout July, until, with supplies of food and munitions virtually exhausted, the garrison was effectively reduced to a few hundred men. With the walls of the city now seriously breached, he was finally forced to accept the advice of Baglione and other officers, and agreed to capitulate. A treaty signed the next day allowed for the safe conduct of all the defending forces and civilians to Crete.[64]

The fate of Bragadin and his officers was to be different. Seizing a pretext to break the terms of the agreement, the Turkish commander, Mustafà Pascià, proceeded to exact vengeance on those who, for almost a year, had inflicted considerable losses on the Turkish forces holed up under the city walls. After being forced to witness the summary execution of his officers, including Baglione, Bragadin was briefly imprisoned before his own long torture and execution began. Already seriously wounded (the Turks had cut off his ears and infection had followed), he was forced to carry two heavy baskets of earth along the enemy trenches to the jeers and shouts of the enemy soldiers. Following this he was lashed to the mast of one of the galleys anchored in the harbour, and then left for some time suspended above the deck. Finally dragged to the main square of the city and tied to a column, he was subjected to the final torture. It is recorded that the skin had been stripped from both his chest and arms before Bragadin, who had never stopped reciting the *Miserere* and calling upon Christ for aid, expired. His body was then quartered and his skin, stuffed with straw and cotton and dressed in his uniform, paraded around the streets of Famagusta before being taken to Constantinople, together with the heads of the other Venetian officers, as a war trophy.[65] Witnessed by Nestore Martinengo, a Venetian military engineer who managed to escape execution, the grim details of Bragadin's fate were reported to a shocked public in a short pamphlet that rapidly went through a large number of editions.[66]

Public opinion in Venice was so unprepared for such a disastrous outcome to the joint expedition of 1570 that jubilant crowds were waiting to greet the first galley to return, believing it to be bringing news of victory.[67] Faced with a good deal of popular discontent, sustained by reports of the mass desertion of Venetian troops and oarsmen in Crete due to poor leadership and maltreatment at the hands of their commanders, the Council of Ten instigated inquiries. Two galley commanders, Girolamo Gritti and Carlo Querini, were permanently banished from Venetian territory for misconduct.[68] Placed under arrest and detained in a room in the Doge's Palace, Zane was put on trial for mishandling the Republic's funds and maintaining poor discipline, the causes, it was alleged, of the disease and the shipwrecks that had undermined the fleet and had led to its undignified retreat. Zane's trial, which lasted until January 1572, had still to reach a conclusion when he died in October of that year.[69] Elsewhere, reactions to the defeat only confirmed Philip II's doubts over the solidity of the alliance. In Rome, blame for the debacle was laid firmly at the door of Doria, while the Spanish retorted by questioning the abilities of Marcantonio Colonna, who had been placed in overall command of the expedition, much to Doria's displeasure. Doubts about Colonna's leadership and experience were widespread. Cardinal Granvelle, one of the three Spanish commissioners, who spent most of his life in a sedentary position, trenchantly remarked that 'Colonna knows no more about the sea than I do', and the technical inadequacies of both the papal commander and the unfortunate Zane run like leitmotifs through contemporary comments.[70] On one thing all were agreed: the performance of the Christian armada could only be judged a failure. Faced with its first serious challenge, the allied fleet had been forced to return to port in disharmony and disarray.

It was against this sombre background that talks were reopened in Rome in yet a further attempt to agree the articles of the League.[71] At an earlier session, in July 1570, the papal representatives had suggested that the text of the treaty, which had been signed in February 1538 between the Papacy, Spain and Venice, should be used as a basis for discussion, and on these terms some progress had been made. By the end of the month an outline agreement was already in circulation.[72] In general, it was proposed that the League should operate for an initial period of twelve years, and that its primary purpose should be to mount a campaign against both Turkey and Turkish interests in North Africa. The armada was to be commanded by Don Juan of Austria, while the financial burden of all joint actions was to be divided into six parts, of which three would be borne by Spain, two by Venice and one by the Papacy. This formula exactly repeats the terms of the accord of 1538. Lastly, and significantly in view of subsequent events, all parties to the agreement were to undertake not to pursue separate peace treaties with the Turks. At this juncture, negotiations had been suspended for two months to allow for consultations with individual governments to take place, but when they reopened in October the atmosphere was decidedly tense. The Venetians in particular seemed to be in an obstructive mood, challenging the smallest points of detail and seizing every conceivable opportunity to delay agreement. Suspected by their allies of holding out for a separate and not-too-disadvantageous peace, they effectively brought the discussions to breaking point. Just before Christmas, the papal nuncio in Venice, Giovanni Antonio Facchinetti, reported his suspicion that, since the Council of Ten was meeting so frequently, the Venetians must have been drawing up their own treaty.[73] To the bitter disappointment of the pope, and the distinct annoyance of Cardinal Granvelle, the discussions finally collapsed in discord in December. As 1570 drew to a close, the future of the League, agreed in principle but never formally ratified, seemed to be in serious doubt. Coming, as it did, on the heels of the failure to relieve Cyprus, the stalemate over the League brought morale among the allies to a very low ebb.

In February of the following year, the commissioners reassembled in Rome and tried again, and by the following month a new draft had been produced. Although the spring tides now approached, and with them the annual spectre of the threat from the Turkish fleet, all their discussions continued to run into difficulties, while in Venice refitting the fleet proceeded slowly. In Rome, the negotiations dragged on endlessly. Representatives of the other Italian states, picking up such scraps of information as were available on the diplomatic circuit, became increasingly despondent about the chances of a successful conclusion of the discussions. At the end of March, Claudio Ariosti, the Ferrarese ambassador in Venice, wrote that 'all were still waiting for either the conclusion or otherwise' of the League.[74] Once again, it seems that the Venetian delegation was largely responsible for this fresh crisis, and in April Colonna arrived in person to try and expedite matters by more direct appeals to the Venetian government. Despite his efforts, some members of the Senate, while expressing enthusiasm for the League in general terms, continued to obstruct final agreement on almost any pretext.[75] As discussions continued, it became clear to Facchinetti that the Venetians were playing for time, in the hope that the negotiations in Constantinople to secure a separate peace might bear fruit.[76] By early May, as Ariosti reported, the papal commander was claiming that the League had been 'finally agreed and established',[77] but then the whole circus began again, and even as late as the middle of the month the matter still seemed in doubt. Against this background of dissension and procrastination, it is small wonder that when the ratification of the articles of the League was finally announced a few days later in Rome, it was followed by a week of public celebrations and processions. For almost a year it had proved impossible for Pius v's dream of a holy crusade to become reality, with all that this implied for the more secular hopes of the leaders of the Christian alliance to provide an effective counter to Turkish military actions. Now, at last, it seemed that the dream had been realized. It is not surprising that the predominant theme in papal presentations of the history of the League was that of the triumph of divinely inspired papal wisdom, allied to the courage and skills of Colonna.

The Venetians, however, had nurtured quite serious motives for producing delay, motives that were not as hidden from the eyes of the rest of the world as they liked to believe. Ambiguity had long characterized Venetian relations with the Porte, dependent as they were both upon trade with the Turks and some freedom of action in Eastern markets. Frances de Álava was simply expressing a widespread view when he wrote in the summer of 1570:

The French hope that no agreement will be reached. The Venetians, they say, are complete fools if they sign that treaty and do not retain their freedom to treat with their great enemy the Turk. Here in France, everyone is doing his utmost to prevent the League from taking shape and to encourage an entente between Venice and the Sultan.[78]

French animosity towards the Habsburgs obviously lay behind these moves, but their ambassador in Venice displayed endless ingenuity in setting out the case for Venetian non-involvement in the League.[79] Scepticism about Venetian behaviour in general, and about the possibility of double-dealing in particular, was common. When the negotiations over the League were still inconclusive at the end of March 1571, the Mantuan ambassador in Venice wryly reported that there were few who believed they would come to anything, and some even held that Venice had already contracted a separate peace.[80] His informants were almost right. Since January of that year, after talks between the allies had broken down largely as a result of Venetian intransigence, the Republic had indeed been attempting to arrive at a secret peace settlement in Constantinople, where contacts between the Turks and the Venetian *bailò* had been preserved. This was more or less common knowledge among the foreign ambassadors in Venice. It was only when it had become completely clear that there was no hope of any agreement at all that the Venetians finally consented to sign the articles of the League, and to become participating members of the alliance. Hence the long delays during March and April when Colonna was pursuing matters in Venice, and hence too the frequent changes of diplomatic direction as the League was first reported to be agreed, only to be declared in doubt a few days later. In the end Venetian minds may well have been concentrated by the arrival of the great Turkish armada at Cyprus in the middle of May, which effectively put an end to any hope of further Venetian intransigence.

Finally signed on 20 May 1571, then formally ratified at a Consistory in St Peter's a few days later, the articles that established the Holy League as a *foedus perpetuum* against the Turks were proclaimed at the end of May.[81] For many observers this was a somewhat unexpected outcome of the months of tortuous negotiation and frequent disagreement, months that had been characterized more by suspicions and denunciations than by expressions of Christian fraternity. The agreement, more modest in scope than the original papal proposal of a year earlier, allowed for a three-year military and naval alliance that had as its first duty the provision of a grand armada of some 200 galleys and 100 roundships, manned by 50,000 infantry and 4,500 light horse. Although this fleet was primarily to be launched against Turkey itself, action against dependent territories in North Africa was also envisaged; in this way Spanish interests, above all in relation to Tunis, were taken into account. As for expenses, it was agreed that Spain and Venice would divide the costs between them in the ratio of three to two if the Papacy were to default on its obligations. This clause was evidently of some public interest, sufficiently at least to be set out in cheaply produced pamphlets aimed at a wide audience.[82] The embargo on separately negotiated treaties, of particular concern to Spain and the Holy See, both ever-suspicious of Venetian duplicity, was also written into the final version of the treaty.[83]

In Venice, the clauses of the agreement arrived on Ascension Day, shortly before Mocenigo was due to entertain the foreign ambassadors at the traditional public banquet that concluded the official ceremonies of the *sensa*. Declaring himself to be well pleased with the final outcome of the negotiations, the doge expressed two fervent hopes for the immediate future: one that Don Juan should arrive from Spain with complete authority to prosecute the war successfully, the other that the emperor would join the confederation, thus putting pressure on the French to do likewise.[84] Yet despite this warm reception, the Venetians insisted on further modifications to the agreement, and it was not until more than a month later that its details were finally made public in the Piazza San Marco in the course of a carefully managed piece of state ceremonial. Previous events of a similar kind, such as the procession organized to celebrate the peace of Bologna in 1530,[85] may have provided precedents. Described in contemporary pamphlets and illustrated in an engraving by Giacomo Franco, the Venetian celebrations for the League were typical of Venetian public ceremonial in their carefully balanced fusion of civic and religious elements cast in a fairly traditional mould; it is here that we gain a first glimpse of some of the principal components of the celebratory rhetoric that followed Lepanto itself. Solemn high mass, celebrated by the Spanish ambassador, Diego Guzmán de Silva (archbishop of Toledo), at San Marco in the presence of the doge and Signoria, was followed by a procession of all the clergy and the *scuole grandi* accompanied by the Spanish, Neapolitan, Genoese and Milanese 'nations' in the Piazza. The square had been decorated for the occasion, with tapestries hung from the windows, and the arms of the Papacy, Spain and Venice prominently displayed. The basilica's prized relic of the True Cross was solemnly carried in procession by Guzmán, and after the details of the League had been proclaimed from the Pietra del Bando, Venice erupted into the clamorous din of celebration. Church bells were rung, the noise of drums and the *trombe squarciate* resonated through the narrow *calli*, and, as it grew dark, torches were carried from the Arsenal to illuminate the bell-towers of the city. The celebrations went on for three whole days, while, according to one account, the junketings at Guzmán's palace continued for eight.[86] To contemporary Venetians, the formation of the League, finally agreed after months of speculation and disappointment, represented if not the last, at least the best possible hope in the increasingly desperate struggle to turn back the Turk.

A detailed impression of the Venetian procession for the Holy League can be pieced together from published pamphlets, manuscript chronicles and the reports of visiting ambassadors,[87] while Franco's print is designed to capture the moment when the clauses of the League were publicly proclaimed. As an accurate record it does not inspire total confidence. The Doge's Palace, for example, is inaccurately drawn, and the bell-tower of San Marco has been obligingly moved some distance to the south to accommodate the crowd.[88] But in its depiction of the elaborate series of platforms (*tribunali*), sponsored by the Scuola Grande di San Rocco and shown in the foreground, there is a high degree of agreement between the engraving and the various manuscript and printed descriptions of the event. In this first section of the procession, the purpose of the League was simply and effectively explained to the crowd through a series of dumb-shows. At its head a crucifix was carried, followed by the floats of the *scuole*. The first group showed the Great Turk as a ferocious dragon emerging from a cave, easily identified by a pyramid surmounted by a crescent moon. In front, three richly dressed youths attacked the dragon with swords; they symbolized Peter, James and Mark, the patron saints of the Papacy, Spain and Venice, their respective allegiances made plain by the designs on their shields. Next came boys dressed to represent Faith, Justice and Fortitude, virtues equated with the three principal signatories of the League. Here the pope, chalice in hand, was presented as Faith, the doge as Fortitude and the king of Spain as Justice. God the Father appeared in the next show; seated in the clouds, he was seen blessing the pope, doge and emperor kneeling below, a clear presentation of the League as a divinely protected crusade. The following floats showed further virtues associated with the principal commanding officers of the armed forces of the League: Colonna (Charity), Don Juan of Austria (Prudence) and Sebastiano Venier (Hope). The next display had as its principal image Christ in Majesty, with the three generals kneeling in adoration and St Roch standing nearby,[89] while towards the end of this section of the procession Charon's boat was shown transporting the Turk to Hades (in the engraving the order of the floats has been altered so that this episode is placed in the centre of the foreground). Further displays followed, then various *scuole* carrying banners, and finally the doge and Signoria accompanied by the Spanish ambassador. The atmosphere was enlivened, and a bellicose note inserted, by the improvised music of groups of the drummers and trumpet players that punctuated the procession. Seen from the vantage point of a bird's-eye view, Franco's engraving invites participation in this parade, just as the event itself co-opted those present in the square.[90]

The ceremonies to celebrate the formation of the League are a convenient place to consider the simple iconographical language that the Venetians elaborated in the years 1570–71, and which was to be brought into full operation in the wake of Lepanto. Some of the visual codes came out of stock: the tradition of identifying individual states with their patron saints was one of long standing, and so too was that of associating the government of the Republic with the Virtues. A typical expression of this last commonplace is found in the writings of the fifteenth-century Venetian physician and humanist Giovanni

Caldiera, who claimed that the Cardinal Virtues underscored the republican ones, thus metaphorically equating obedience to God and obedience to the state. This transference of values is vividly present in Caldiera's treatment, in his *De politia*, of the three Theological Virtues, where Faith is equated with the Republic itself, Charity is expressed in the activities of the *scuole* (charitable institutions were of general importance in Italy, but of unique significance in Venetian life), while Venice itself inspires Hope because of its social and governmental system, which rewards men on their merits.[91] The personification of the members of the League through images of pope, emperor and doge, ubiquitous in Lepanto iconography, reappears in many of the paintings executed after the victory, and at a less elevated level was caricatured in the pamphlets that were now issued prophesying success for Venice and its allies. In the flurry of advice and admonition that had been filling the Venetian bookstalls since the notion of a crusading league had first begun to seem plausible, the crude visual symbols representing Venice, the Empire and the Papacy, as well as their common enemy, had become familiar through cheap pamphlets and popular woodcuts. Venetians had come to know the Lion, the Lamb and the Eagle, united against their common foe (see pl. 119). In its use of these images, the procession for the League relied on a combination of well-tried and familiar ritual elements both civic and religious, while at the same time helping to cement into the popular consciousness a series of striking images and visual metaphors, based on tradition, which were to recur with renewed force in much of the art, music and literature that appeared in the post-Lepanto euphoria. Nonetheless, it is clear that the intention of the organizers was to amuse the crowds as well as to instruct them, an objective that was widely appreciated, though not by everyone: Vito di Dornberg, the imperial ambassador, who walked in the procession together with the Spanish ambassador and the papal nuncio, found the displays 'assai ridicolose, et male intese'. The entirely traditional procession that had celebrated the conclusion of the Holy League in 1526 had consisted of the *scuole*, the religious orders, the chapter of San Pietro di Castello and, finally, the doge, members of the Senate and other officials dressed in scarlet robes.[92] In other words, it had been no more than a slightly amplified version of the ducal *andata*. By comparison, the procession for the League in 1571 was a much more grandiose affair. As such, it served as a model for the next great official procession in the Piazza San Marco to celebrate the peace of 1598.[93]

In Rome, the sense of relief that greeted the successful conclusion of the negotiations was considerable. Sitting beneath Raphael's frescos in the Sala di Constantino at the Consistory that had ratified the articles of the League, the pope offered thanks to the Almighty for having finally brought together the Catholic princes to campaign against the common enemy.[94] For Pius, firm as ever in his simple convictions, the final agreement owed more to divine intervention, secured through the agency of papal intercession, than it did to any human actions. When

95   Giovanni Antonio Rossi, medal for the formation of the Holy League, 1570. London, British Museum.

the official announcement of the articles of the League had been made, it was accompanied by mass concelebrated by the cardinal of Augsburg and the pope, in the presence of the ambassadors of the three signatories. An oration was then given by the cardinal of Aragon, a Te Deum was sung, and the proceedings were brought to a close with a papal benediction given to the enthusiastic crowds gathered below. In the following days Pius participated in a sequence of three public processions clearly designed to strengthen the religious orientation of this Holy and Apostolic League, the first to Santo Spirito, the second to San Giacomo degli Spagnuoli (the church of the Spanish 'nation') and the last to San Marco, the church of the Venetians in Rome.[95] A medal by Giovanni Antonio Rossi, issued to mark the occasion, shows on its obverse a portrait bust of the pope wearing a cope, his hands joined in prayer, and on the reverse personifications of Spain, Venice and the Papacy with, inscribed around the border, the legend FOEDERIS IN TVRCAS SANCTIO ('Ratification of the alliance against the Turk') (pl. 95).[96] Rossi's medal also transmits the idea that the formation of the League had been achieved through papal wisdom and leadership, a conception that was later to be incorporated into a more general official Roman interpretation of Lepanto itself. As such it was to form part of a specific version of the victory as a divinely inspired and protected consequence of inspired papal action, which had begun with the diplomatic struggle to persuade the Spanish and Venetians to join the Holy League.

Despite the impression of fraternity conveyed by the celebrations in Rome and Venice, suspicion among the allies was rife. No sooner had the details of the League been made public than fresh rumours began to circulate. The Spaniards believed that the Venetians, fearful for their trade with the East, would make peace with the Turks as soon as possible, a view that found some adherents in the Vatican. This, after all, was what had happened in 1540, when the Republic had negotiated a humiliating treaty, which required it to pay a substantial indemnity of 300,000 ducats and to cede territories in the Morea and the Aegean in order to exit from Paul III's Holy League, whose war was damaging its commercial interests and depleting its coffers.[97] In Venice it was said that Spain was preparing for war against the Italian states, first Genoa, then Tuscany, and finally

Venice itself, in a last effort to conquer the entire peninsula. This gave a new twist to the 'black legend' of Spanish tyranny, the common belief that 'where the Spaniard sets his foot no grass grows'. With it came the fear that the brutality with which the Spaniards had imposed their presence on the New World would eventually be experienced by the Old, and particularly by the inhabitants of the peninsula that they had come increasingly to dominate. In this configuration Spanish power was simply a mechanism for facilitating papal policy.[98] The ratification of the League had done little to dispel well-established prejudices, which had only been intensified by the chaotic and demeaning performance over the relief of Cyprus.

Doubts notwithstanding, the Spaniards and the pope had promised the Venetians, in a separate agreement, that the various squadrons would combine at Otranto before the end of May. Since the news that the League had been agreed did not reach Spain until 6 June, this was an impossibly optimistic undertaking. After a series of delays, the fleet was finally assembled under the command of Venier, who had replaced the disgraced Zane, to the satisfaction of the Venetians, who reportedly prayed that his appointment would bring good luck to the campaign.[99] Having put to sea on 18 July, the fleet reached Naples on 9 August and Messina on the 24th. There it joined Colonna's ships, which had arrived on 20 July, and Don Juan

96 Giovanni Melon, medal of Antoine Perrenot de Granvelle, 1571. London, British Museum.

of Austria's contingent, which had arrived in the middle of August. Meanwhile, the Turkish fleet, some 300 sail between galleys and foists, had been at sea since April. In June it had attacked the port of Chania in Crete, and it had also briefly occupied Rethymnon before sailing westwards to Zante and Cefalonia. At the end of July a number of Dalmatian islands fell into Turkish hands, Curzola was besieged, Zara raided and Corfu attacked.[100] Having flexed their muscles, the Turks then decided to drop anchor off Modon and monitor events.

They did not have long to wait. In August Cardinal Granvelle presented a consecrated standard showing the Crucifixion to Don Juan in Naples; the ceremony is shown in a medal that carries the legend IN HOC VINCES ('In this sign you will conquer') (pl. 96).[101] His contingent then set sail. At the end of the month the Venetian fleet in Crete, some sixty galleys in all under the command of Agostino Barbarigo, set sail to join the rest of the allied forces assembled at Messina. It was

97   Andrea Vicentino, *The Battle of Lepanto*, 1595–1605. Venice, Doge's Palace.

from there that it finally put out to sea on 16 September, having been detained longer than planned because of adverse weather conditions. According to one of Granvelle's informants, the Venetians were confident of Don Juan's leadership, and the Spanish fleet had never looked in better shape.[102] Initially, the armada headed for Corfu, where it was learnt that the Turks had established themselves in the Gulf of Lepanto. On 7 October, at sunrise, the two fleets found themselves facing each other in the narrow entrance to the bay. Numbers were more or less evenly matched, with 208 Christian warships against 230 on the Turkish side.[103]

Lepanto has been described as 'the last great confrontation of floating armies, rowed methodically into formation, firing artillery as the distance between them narrowed but relying in most cases on closing to board infantry for the coup de grace' (pl. 97).[104] As for the causes of the allied victory, opinions differed, some praising the determination of the troops, others the superiority of the arquebuses over the bows used in quantity by the Turks, yet others the firepower of the galliases. The east wind that had faced the Christians before the battle suddenly turned into a favourable westerly, 'per l'opera del Signor Dio', as many accounts

put it, just as the forces began to engage.[105] This benefitted the Venetian oarsmen, who were more easily able to take up arms as they came closer to the enemy. Inevitably, all three members of the League claimed that their own contribution, whether the heroism of Don Juan, the firepower of the Venetian cannon or the skill of the Spanish infantry, had been decisive. These are technical and ultimately unquantifiable arguments. The culturally significant fact is that, no matter what the judgement of later writers, the victory of the Holy League at Lepanto was seen by contemporaries to have been decisive, an event that, although it did not end the war, determined a victorious out-come. Psychologically it marked the end of a period of uncertainty and even a sense of inferiority in the face of Turkish supremacy. Giampietro Contarini was merely expressing a common view when he wrote in his *Historia* 'that this has been the greatest and most famous naval battle which has occurred from the time of Caesar Augustus until now'.[106] Christians everywhere considered the victory as nothing less than a miracle, a sure sign of divine favour, a gift received 'from the hands of God', as the popular pamphlets endlessly repeated. They were to celebrate it accordingly.

CHAPTER SIX

Victory at Lepanto

In the years immediately following Lepanto, the victory of the Holy League was permanently inscribed in the calendar of Christian celebration as one of the most momentous events in the seemingly endless struggle against the Infidel. By way of contrast, many writers since Voltaire have contributed to an almost unanimous ironic chorus describing it as an empty achievement, a great spectacle that led nowhere.[1] Whatever the judgements of history, the authentic period voice should not be forgotten. For contemporaries, the victory marked a decisive turning point in the fortunes of Christendom, a critical moment of enormous psychological importance in a historic struggle that, in recent years, the Christian West had seemed destined to lose. No matter what occurred in the following years, as the Venetians reached a separately negoti-ated peace treaty with the Turks, to the disgust of Spain and the Papacy, com-pared with what had gone before, the victory at Lepanto marked the end of a genuine crisis of confidence. Among the countries of Christian Europe it seemed to signal the beginning of the end of Ottoman supremacy, after a period of some three hundred years in which the Turks had risen from obscure origins to become the terror of the Christian world. Now it finally seemed that their power was on the wane, that the threat had been exorcized.[2] It was the sheer enormity of the achievement of Lepanto, as it was perceived at the time, together with its great symbolic importance, that helps to explain the extraor-dinary round of celebrations that greeted the news of the victory. Everywhere there were celebratory processions, plays and orations, as the towns and cities of Europe manoeuvred all the traditional components of festal rhetoric into place. As intelligence of the events of 7 October gradually spread throughout the continent, disseminated by couriers from Venice and the dispatches of agents and ambassadors, it brought with it waves of public celebration, some of it spontaneous, much of it hurriedly prepared. By 25 October the news had reached Lyons; 'grandissime allegrezze' were reported as it arrived in Brussels five days later; and there were processions and prayers in Madrid shortly afterwards.[3] This was a general pattern.

Since, for all Italians, the Turkish question had become one of perennial interest, news of the outcome of the battle reverberated throughout the whole of the peninsula, particularly in cities such as Genoa, Rome and the major towns of the Veneto, which had supplied men, money and galleys. But nowhere in the whole of Italy was the sense of relief and achievement more keenly felt than in Venice, and here too the celebratory rhetoric took on a distinctly local character.[4] The immediate celebrations lasted only a few weeks, but in that short time the victory at Lepanto was powerfully etched into the Venetian consciousness through characteristic transformations of local traditions of civic and religious display. For the Republic, Lepanto was no ordinary victory; it marked a crucial moment in its history equal in significance to the legendary defeat of Frederick Barbarossa, a comparison that contemporaries were quick to invoke.[5] At the time it seemed to be the first military triumph for decades in which Venice could take pride; its effect on Venetian morale at all levels of society was great.

Victory had been widely predicted in the city, and as late as the morning of the battle a Carmelite saying mass suddenly turned to his congregation and said: 'Brothers, I have good news to give you. The fleets have engaged, and the Christians have won. Be joyful, give honour and glory to God and continue to live in fear of Him.' Notwithstanding the friar's conviction, the Signoria awaited more concrete intelligence, while the Venetians continued to live in the hope that the hand of God had guided their ships to success.[6] News of the outcome finally arrived in the city twelve days after the battle, brought by the Venetian galley *Angelo Gabrieli*, captained by Onofrio Giustiniani and piled high with Turkish spoils, captured banners and a riotously jubilant crew dressed as Turks.[7] This piece of cultural cross-dressing played upon established practice; travellers to the Levant often dressed in Ottoman costume for protection, and the *bailò* and his entourage appeared in public in similar attire before their departure for Constantinople.[8] Rocco Benedetti, a notary and pamphleteer who published extensively in these years, thought it was a sign of divine favour that the news of the victory should have been brought to Venice, a city dedicated to the Virgin, by a galley named after the Angel Gabriel.[9] Benedetti was a member of the *cittadino* class, from a family that had provided the Republic with generations of churchmen, soldiers and a handful of grand chancellors.[10] His published account of the Lepanto festivities, sympathetic to the official view of the significance of the victory, and eloquent in its praise of the local arrangements to celebrate it, was widely distributed.[11]

Initially, the appearance of the *Angelo Gabrieli* caused alarm, but the sight of the Turkish banners being trailed through the water and the discharge of cannon confirmed that Giustiniani brought good news. Such trophies, together with genuine Turkish prisoners of war, were later to form a distinct element in popular celebrations in both Rome and Venice, booty both human and material to be displayed as validation of the victory.[12] At the Lido the galley was greeted with artillery and improvised music of drums and trumpets, and from there it moved on to Venice. At this time of the day, about 11 o'clock in the morning, there were few people around, but those that were, realizing the significance of Giustiniani's appearance, began running about wildly shouting 'Vittoria! Vittoria!' and embracing each other. As news of the victory at Lepanto spread through the city, the streets filled with people shouting 'like madmen', embracing each other, weeping and raising their hands to heaven in gratitude.[13] Such details indicate the strength of popular feeling, the extent to which ordinary Venetians had come to identify with the War of Cyprus.

Almost immediately, a great crowd gathered in the Piazza San Marco, Giustiniani's ship docked, and Venier's official account of the action was presented to the doge in the Collegio. Church bells were rung, the parishes of the city taking their cue from the bells of San Marco, and then the doge and those members of the Signoria that could be assembled hurriedly processed to the basilica, where they were joined by the papal legate, the patriarch Giovanni Grimani and other ambassadors. According to one observer, the body of the basilica was packed with both patricians and *cittadini*, weeping for joy and embracing each other.[14] Another claimed that, in the heat of the moment, sworn enemies buried their differences, and that all passions and rancour were forgotten.[15] When the solemn moment came for the Te Deum to be sung it was intoned by the doge in person; mass was then celebrated by 'a foreign priest', evidently the only one that could be found at short notice.[16] It is this occasion that is recalled in Palma il Giovane's votive picture of 1596 (the date comes from a preparatory drawing for one of the figures in the composition), now in the church of San Fantin, where it was seen by Stringa, who described it in his additions to Sansovino's *Venetia città nobilissima*. According to Stringa, the painting depicts the moment when, having heard the news of the victory, Doge Alvise Mocenigo and the Signoria convened in San Marco (pl. 99).[17] On the right of Palma's painting, the doge and Signoria give thanks to the Virgin, who is shown above with St Mark and St Justina, on whose feast-day the victory took place. The lively group on the left of the picture refers to the widespread popular enthusiasm that greeted the news, while the severe figure of a mature woman dressed in mourning in the foreground symbolizes the Venetian dead.[18] In its emphases on popular involvement in the victory, and the special relationship between Venice and the Virgin, Palma's painting is a typical example of Lepanto celebratory art. It is also characteristic of the artist's interest, seen at its most developed in the Cicogna cycle in the oratory of the

99　Jacomo Palma Il Giovane, *Doge Alvise Mocenigo Gives Thanks to the Virgin for the Victory at Lepanto*, 1596. Venice, Church of San Fantin.

Ospedaletto dei Crociferi, painted in the same decade, in the details of ordinary, everyday existence and in the lives of the marginalized.[19] From Venice official confirmation of the victory was immediately dispatched by courier to the princes of Italy and beyond.[20] Among the letters that were submitted to the Senate for its approval was one to Emperor Maximilian II, urging that the victory be considered not as an end but the beginning of a concerted campaign to 'bring down this haughty and natural common enemy'. Charles IX of France was also urged to join the anti-Turkish League in much the same terms. If the resources of France could be added to those of the existing alliance, success, it was felt, would be assured. Although Pius V added his voice to these pleas a few days later, it had no effect. Both rulers preferred peace with the Turk to war.[21]

　In the following days and weeks, a whole succession of celebrations took place in Venice. There had been little time to prepare for these, and reading the accounts gives a striking impression of the rich variety of ceremonial resources to hand, and the speed with which they could be mustered. In his oration before the doge and Senate, Luigi Groto singled out the music that could be heard everywhere, as the sounds of voices and instruments mingled with the general festive hubbub.[22] In the face of these Christian rejoicings, the Jewish and Turkish communities withdrew to their own houses, particularly the Turks who lived in Cannaregio in the palace of Marcantonio Barbaro, *bailò* in Constantinople. Fearful of being stoned in the streets by gangs of youths, they locked themselves away for four days.[23] Hostility towards the Turkish residents had grown in intensity since the landings in Cyprus, and many of the shop-keepers who now closed their businesses put up the simple explanation: 'For the death of the Turks', in ironic parody of the practice normally followed by bereaved families.[24] At an official level the state reacted by giving orders for public prayers and processions, while alms and food were distributed to the poor. Less officially, inmates at the two state prisons at San Marco and the Rialto were liberated by a jubilant mob.[25]

For three days the church bells were rung and fireworks discharged. In a society that had assiduously cultivated the image of its special relationship with the Almighty, religious and devotional practices naturally formed the most important element of the official arrangements. As an immediate response the doge and Signoria led the way by voting alms to monasteries, convents and charitable foundations in the city.[26] On the first Sunday after news of the victory had arrived in Venice, high mass was sung in San Marco by the Spanish ambassador in the presence of the doge and Signoria, festally dressed for the occasion. This was accompanied by music, described by Benedetti as 'concerti divinissimi', in which the two organs of the basilica played together with voices and instruments, an unambiguous reference to the Venetian tradition of music for *cori spezzati*.[27] Although the 'concerti' that he describes cannot be identi-fied with certainty, a number of pieces by Andrea Gabrieli with texts appro-priate for the occasion have survived in the Venetian repertory. Some of these, such as 'O salutaris hostia' and 'Isti sunt triumphatores', were fully liturgical and generally appropriate for the sentiments of the moment; it is impossible to say whether they were specially composed in honour of the victory.[28] Another of Andrea Gabrieli's large-scale polychoral compositions, 'Benedictus Dominus Deus Saboath', is a composite text whose references to battle, and use of Old Testament themes, preceded by the opening words of the Santus-Benedictus section of the ordinary of the mass, seems to constitute an explicit reference to both the battle and to the special status of the Venetians. It too might well have been written in celebration of Lepanto:

> Blessed be the Lord of Hosts. Blessed be those who fight in the name of the Lord. His powerful and inexorable hand fights for them. The hand of the Lord defends them. Samson has fought, Gideon has fought. Samson has won, Gidenon has won. Our armies have fought in the name of the Lord. God has sustained us in battle and won over His enemies. Let us exult and rejoice and sing his praise.[29]

The twin references to Samson and Gideon, both of whom are portrayed in the book of Judges as hero-liberators who protected the Israelites from extinction at the hands of the Philistines, place Gabrieli's piece among a number of late sixteenth-century motets written in the Lepanto years on Old Testament texts written by composers working in Venice and the Veneto. The notion that the Venetian constitution was based on Judaic law was frequently asserted by writers and public orators, who claimed that the Venetians were a 'Chosen People', and that the doge, whose wisdom was comparable to that of Moses and Solomon, was divinely sanctioned.[30] The city itself was often extolled as a New Jerusalem and as a Promised Land. Another work in this group of Old Testament motets, Giovanni Croce's setting of 'Benedictus Dominus Deus Saboath', perhaps influenced by Andrea Gabrieli's example, was published in his book of double-choir motets of 1594. There it appears alongside an eight-voice motet 'Percussit Saul', whose text is taken from the words of the Israelite women following David's execution of Goliath:

> Saul has slain his thousands, and David his ten thousands, because the hand of the Lord was with him. He killed the Philistine and removed disgrace from Israel. Is this not David, the one they made songs about in their dances, saying, Saul has slain his thousands, and David ten thousand?[31]

There was already a history of association between this text and the War of Cyprus by the time that Croce wrote his piece. A medal by Federico Cocciola showing the Grand Master of Malta, Jean de la Vallette, different from the type reputedly buried under the walls of Valletta,[32] makes a reference on its reverse to the defence of Malta in 1565. This shows David, holding a sabre in both hands, standing over a recumbent Goliath, against the background of the sea with galleys. The legend around the border reads VNVS X MILLIA, a clear adaptation of the phrase 'Percussit Saul mille, et David decem millia' ('Saul has slain a thousand, and David ten thousand').[33] Croce went on to make the text of his own composition the basis for his *Missa Percussit Saul*, the first of three masses published in 1596 with a dedication to Lorenzo Priuli, patriarch of Venice, where it is immediately and significantly followed by a *Missa sopra la battaglia*.[34] Croce rose to prominence at San Marco during the 1590s, becoming vice-master of the chapel under Donato,[35] and these grandiloquent works (the title-page specifies performance by both instruments and voices) reflect the resources now at his disposal. Equivalents in sound to the large-scale battle-pieces painted by Tintoretto and others, they also perhaps evoke the troubled nature of the post-Lepanto world. It is even possible that, together with Palma il Giovane's painting in San Fantin,[36] they are the products of a wave of nostalgic commemoration precisely a quarter of a century after the battle.

On this first Sunday after news of the victory had reached Venice, the celebratory mass in the basilica was followed by a procession around the square in which all the clergy of the city participated, and the basilica's prized processional cross was carried by the doge himself as a clear sign of gratitude for divine benevolence.[37] Some days later the official requiem mass for the Venetian dead was sung in San Marco, again in the presence of the doge and Senate; and the public orator, Giovanni Battista Rasario, delivered a Latin address in praise of all those who had fought for the glory of God and the 'universal liberty of the Christian Republic'.[38] The final event in this cycle of official religious events took place on the following Sunday, when mass was again solemnly celebrated by the Spanish ambassador, who personally administered communion, not only to the doge but also to all the members of the Senate, a rare honour that was again intended both to underline the special circumstances of the occasion and to sanctify symbolically and strengthen the ties that had united the members of the Holy League in their hour of victory.

The passage from official ceremonies to public celebration was accompanied by a change from liturgical and civic rituals to popular ones, which incorporated different orders of visual and musical experience. A small group of cheap pamphlets, presumably intended for those who had witnessed the celebrations, describes some of them with varying degrees of accuracy and clarity. The first event was put on by the German merchants, who had been quick to present themselves in the Collegio to receive a licence that allowed them to organize public festivities. Since the religious ceremonies were now over this was granted, and they quickly decorated their *fondaco* (warehouse) with tapestries, and then for three successive nights mounted spectacular firework displays, accompanied by music, which lasted well into the night.[39] Every evening the illuminated courtyard echoed to the raucous sound of drums, fifes and trumpets, while more decorous ensembles played in temporary pergolas.

Following the German example, different parts of the community competed to produce the most impressive celebrations. Somewhat provocatively, one noisy spectacle was presented in Cannaregio, under the gaze of the resident Turks. Another three-day affair, this time organized by the drapers' guild, was concentrated in the area around the Rialto bridge and the square in front of San Giacomo di Rialto, which was decorated with scarlet hangings and banners bearing the arms of the League. Here too different kinds of music were played, ranging from the 'celestial harmony' of sedate ensembles, to the din of drums, shawms and *trombe squarciate*. According to one account, these were intended to evoke the sounds of battle,[40] but in reality they had long been part of the Venetian soundscape on occasions of public celebration. (Sanudo notes them in his description of the festivities held in Campo di San Polo to mark the election of Pope Leo X, and again four years later when the peace concluded with the empire was officially announced.)[41] Many of the drapers' shops displayed weapons and captured Turkish trophies,[42] while with the help of tapestries, canopies and lanterns, the surrounding streets were also transformed with, as a centrepiece, a display of paintings. Works by Giovanni Bellini, Giorgione, Raphael, Pordenone, Sebastiano del Piombo, Titian and Bassano (which one is not specified), among others, were on show.[43] The listing of these artists, most of them Venetian, suggests that their work had already become canonic; evidently their pictures were displayed because of their status as treasures and luxury items.[44] Although, in the absence of significant detail, they cannot be identified with known works, in some cases their subject matter is specified: pastoral scenes were noted by one writer, and there were also pictures of sea-gods, appropriate symbols of naval victory, hung against a background of red cloth.[45] Turkish themes were particularly prominent.

In addition to what may have been effectively one of the first documented public exhibitions of fine paintings, there were also others to be seen, executed in *grisaille*, the traditional medium for temporary decorations. On one side of the bridge there was a picture of Karakosh, a renegade who, since he had fought on the Turkish side, was a subject of great popular hatred.[46] Here he was shown being received into hell by Charon, a fate that had been prophesied the previous summer in the procession for the League. On the other side of the bridge could be seen the Turkish commander Ouloudji Ali. His name had been corrupted by the Venetians to 'Occhiali', and he was often caricatured, as here, with staring eyes and spectacles. These satirical images were counterbalanced by more conventional ones showing Christ and a figure symbolizing Venice, while a central painting presented the traditional allegory of Venice as Queen of the Seas. This further variation on the familiar theme of the female personification of Venice deliberately plays upon the conflation of the political representation of Venice with traditional images of the Virgin, so successfully that Thomas Coryate mistook the former for the latter in his reading of Veronese's canvas in the ceiling of the Sala del Maggior Consiglio.[47] The painting displayed on the Rialto bridge was presumably iconographically more straightforward, perhaps similar in content to Domenico Tintoretto's painting, now in Dublin, showing Venice, Queen of the Adriatic, crowning the Lion of St Mark with a laurel wreath against the lagoon in the background (see pl. 23).[48]

While substantially devoted to trade, the area around the Rialto bridge also functioned as a secondary area of government. A number of state offices were located there, and two of the churches close to the market came under the *ius patronatus* of the doge and were the subjects of ducal processions.[49] One, San Giacomo, had come under the doge's jurisdiction as a result of a direct appeal by Andrea Gritti to Pope Clement VII; its status lent authority to the square in front of the church, in part derived from its own long history as the oldest church in Venice, and in part from its proximity to the Pietra del Bando from which official decrees were made. During the celebrations organized around the Rialto bridge by the drapers' guild, each day began with a high mass celebrated 'with fine music' on temporary staging in front of the church. Later in the day, the clergy, singers and members of the guild walked in procession accompanied by drums, shawms and *trombe squarciate*, and in the evening vespers were sung, accompanied by wind instruments.[50] There could hardly be a more explicit demonstration of the Venetian belief in the unity of commerce and religion in the affairs of the perfect Christian republic.

At dusk the area took on an almost magical appearance. To illuminate the scene candles were placed everywhere, on the bridge and along the sides of the square, on balustrades and in windows, on the benches in front of shops, and under the porticoes. Circulating among the crowds, masked revellers strummed lutes and sang. From under the arches other music could be heard, played so well, said Benedetti with his customary classicizing touch, that it was possible to believe that one had been listening to the Muses.[51] Elsewhere in the crowded lanes around the bridge, groups put on classical 'triumphs' in imitation of Scipio Africano or the Roman emperors who, returning victorious, made a solemn entry through the Forum to the Capitol. According to Benedetti's rhapsodic account, it seemed as if all the inhabitants of the city were there, even the halt and the lame, united in harmonious celebration. Wives were not threatened by their husbands, he continues, or children by their parents, and even thieves, who would have normally regarded such an occasion as a considerable professional opportunity, suspended operations. The sky was clear, the stars shone, and all was peace, harmony and tranquillity.[52] The example of the drapers was followed by the jewellers and the goldsmiths, and then by the Tuscan merchants and other trade guilds.[53] The Tuscans, who specialized in importing silk into the city, were particularly keen to rival the drapers. They too decorated the whole of the area around the Rialto bridge with silk hangings, velvet drapes, tapestries and displays of paintings, including portraits of Venier and Agostino Barbarigo.[54]

Venetian public celebration of Lepanto revived in the spring of 1572, when an elaborate costumed procession (*mascherata*) with music of various kinds, some traditional and some specially composed, was presented on Carnival Sunday. According to the undated and crudely printed anonymous pamphlet that provides all that is known about the occasion, 340 people took part, including a large number of musicians and many dressed as Turkish slaves;[55] one spectator thought it the most beautiful event of its kind that had ever been organized, a testimony, in this city of processions, to its visual and perhaps also musical qualities.[56] Eighty large torches were carried, and thirteen triumphant displays were mounted. Beginning from the church of the Madonna dell'Orto in the north of the city, this vast procession gradually wound its way through the narrow streets and along the Merceria to the Piazza San Marco (which was then encircled in the traditional fashion), before moving on through the Campo Santo Stefano to finish at San Samuele. It may well be that the *mascherata* was devised by the Scuola di San Cristoforo, the *scuola piccola* of the Venetian merchants, whose new meeting hall in the square in front of the church of the Madonna dell'Orto, to designs by Palladio, had recently been finished.[57] Since 1570, the Scuola had formed an association with the nearby Scuola della Misericordia,[58] one of the *scuole grandi*, whose ambitious new building designed by

Jacopo Sansovino to fill an enormous site still remained incomplete.[59] This unusual alliance between a *scuola grande* and a *scuola piccola* is probably to be explained by economic necessity on the one hand, and the need for social advancement on the other; while the Misericordia was perpetually short of funds in the second half of the sixteenth century (its grand building was never finished), the merchants were distinctly wealthy.[60] Between the two sites there would have been plenty of space to assemble the participants and paraphernalia of the *mascherata* before the procession began.

Despite the superficial semblance of unity provided by the regular insertion of groups of chained Turkish prisoners, whose presence recalls classical Roman triumphs, the *mascherata* fell into two quite distinct segments. The first, clearly didactic in purpose, presented in striking terms a simple political allegory. At the head of the procession, preceded by two young men representing Hope and Charity, was the figure of Faith trampling on the Turkish serpent. This is a piece of standard rhetoric, a visual display of the orthodox humanist assumption that the virtues singled out by the moralists of antiquity, and without which no one can be accounted a man of true *virtus*, will only be in vain unless stiffened and supported by fundamental Christian qualities. Of these the most important was Faith, which, as the political theorist Francesco Patrizi had put it, 'gives forth such splendour that all the other virtues of kings and princes become obscure without it'.[61] By implication, it was precisely the possession of these virtues, and above all Faith, by the members of the Holy League that had secured victory. There followed the figures of the four Cardinal Virtues and then, in an amplification of this theme, allegories of Rome, Spain and finally Venice. Rome was represented by three plaster images of the city (shown as Romulus and Remus being suckled by a wolf); Spain (symbolized as an eagle) was also evoked by images of the Rock of Gibraltar and the Pyrenees, while the Venetian chariot, covered with carpets and brocades and decorated with pearls, gems and gold chains, all symbols of the luxury goods for which the city was famous, was adorned with symbolic images. The fifth and final display in this first sequence of floats presented Victory, a woman dressed in red velvet, riding in a chariot, carrying a palm branch in her left hand and three laurel wreaths in her right. Under her feet was a Turkish slave, while the design of the chariot itself incorporated the symbolic image of the Turkish serpent cut in half. Following on immediately were three groups of four singers, each representing a continent; the first dressed in the Turkish fashion to represent Asia, the second 'alla Moresca' to suggest Africa, and the last in contemporary Italian dress to personify Europe. The topos of the continents was familiar enough to Venetians through atlases, travel literature and other books published in the city.[62] Each group performed a four-part madrigal in praise of the victory, before all twelve singers joined together in an exuberant demonstration of universal joy, in which the ubiquitous theme of Lepanto as Christ's victory made its reappearance:

Cantiam dunque cantiamo; e in ogni parte
Gratie si renda al sommo Re del Cielo.
Et sol a lui si dia con puro zelo
Lode, e Gloria de ben che a noi comparte.[63]

The music for the three continents, but not for the final peroration, was published almost twenty years later in Andrea Gabrieli's *Madrigali et ricercari a quattro voci*.[64] There it occurs alongside a mixed bag of genuine madrigals, instrumental pieces and simple choruses from plays written over a period of many years. The collection, which appeared without dedication or preface, was probably assembled by Andrea's nephew Giovanni, as part of a project to publish a good deal of his uncle's music that had not reached print by the time of Andrea's death in 1586. These three short pieces for the *mascherata* are not advertised as such (by the time of their publication the event had long passed from memory), but their texts are in agreement with those published in the anonymous description of the procession. In musical terms all three are cast in a simple homophonic language occasionally enlivened by madrigalian touches, yet within the obvious constraints of a style clearly designed for outside performance, the composer has sought to characterize each continent by the use of different clef combinations and arrangements of vocal range. In practice, the contrasts between the three continents are not so great as their similarities, but it is clear that, taken together with its missing final section for twelve voices, Gabrieli's music constitutes a modified form of dialogue madrigal in which each group is differentiated before all the voices join together to deliver some generalized statement.

Following Gabrieli's musicians, the character of the *mascherata* moved away from this serious if crude exposition of simple political themes to Carnival traditions spiced with a whiff of victory. During the Carnival season, which stretched from the feast of St Stephen to the first day of Lent, a sequence of popular entertainments took place.[65] Characteristic of these celebrations, in which role reversal was fundamental, was a mingling of the popular and carnivalesque with official ritual. This was seen most clearly on an annual basis on the morning of Giovedì Grasso itself, when the doge and other dignitaries participated in a procession in the Piazzetta, which finished with the slaughter of twelve pigs, in commemoration of a twelfth-century Venetian victory over the patriarch of Aquileia and twelve Friulian lords who had come to his aid. After the meat had been distributed to the crowd, the ducal party withdrew to the Doge's Palace, where a group of senators, festally dressed in red for the occasion and armed with clubs, destroyed model wooden castles, constructed to recall the Friulian strongholds destroyed in the conflict.[66] Not only did the presence of the doge and other officials lend a political dimension to what was otherwise a popular blood-sport, but the procession itself, in effect a simplified version of the ducal *andata* (in which, however, the *trionfi* were not carried), legitimized this gruesome spectacle through the incorporation of a common Venetian ritual practice familiar from other more formal ceremonial contexts, many of which were associated with the same urban space. This fusion of the traditional and the official is entirely typical of the Venetian Carnival of the second half of the sixteenth century, in which it was common for chivalric conceits and neo-classical iconography to be mixed with popular themes. Critical to its development were the attempts made during Andrea Gritti's dogeship to dignify the proceedings, at least in the Piazza San Marco, by removing some of the coarser carnivalesque elements, and introducing classicizing ones, thought to be more in keeping with the solemn overtones of the square, still in the process of being embellished by Sansovino's architectural scheme.

The *mascherata* of 1572 is characteristic of the phenomenon, in which popular and learned traditions intersected, in its clear formal separation into two halves. While the first part was a *mascherata* in the prime sense of the word in that it presented pantomimed action involving allegory and music requiring a basic degree of knowledge (sufficient to recognize the Virtues, for example), in order to be understood fully, the remaining sequences of the procession were more miscellaneous and traditionally 'popular' in character. Most were connected with annual Venetian feasts and customs, and were related to Carnival traditions in which more widely familiar music such as villanellas were sung by masked performers dressed in costumes. A number of these displays involved groups of musicians, though the music that they sang was decidedly different in style from Gabrieli's music for the continents. Onto these spontaneous traditional elements political messages of the moment, associated with Lepanto, had been grafted; the personification of Carnival itself, for example, appeared sitting over a winged animal holding the head of a Turk in its clutches. Another display portrayed Lent as an emaciated elderly woman dressed in black, and a third showed Easter complete with cows and dairymaids, while behind these followed four rustics singing 'Ceccon, cantemo frello', a specially composed dialect text in praise of Venier. There followed a scene devoted to the familiar ritual marriage of Venice to the Adriatic on the feast of the Ascension. With its intimate connection to the foundation myths of the Republic, by following the route taken by the fishermen who rowed Sts Mark, George and Nicholas to the confines of the lagoon, the recall of this annual affirmation of Venetian dominion of the sea was clearly appropriate to the celebration of a great naval victory. Then came the feast of 1 August, a popular celebration that involved exchanging gifts of melons and wine, represented by Bacchus seated under a pergola together with 'five Germans' (often parodied for their drinking habits), clutching flasks of Malvasia and, glasses in hand, singing 'viva viva Bacco, Bacco'. Following the figure of Carnival itself came three groups of musicians, including four 'villani' singing *villotte* to the accompaniment of a lira da braccio and an instrumental ensemble and, finally, a quartet of 'magnifici' singing 'Se ben semo cosi quattro vechietti', which recalled the *commedia dell'arte*. A number of these songs are in dialect, while the performers were dressed as familiar caricatures from Venetian life and customs (pl. 100). Particularly characteristic was the penultimate scene, which consisted of four children who sang a simple song to the accompaniment of small drums, an evocation of the specifically Venetian custom that took place on the feast of San Martino, when children dressed in white and with candles in their hands noisily celebrated in the streets. The words of this song were presumably the same or at least similar to the *Canzon de San Martino*, which has survived as a broadside.[67] Although it is likely that some of these songs came out of unwritten popular traditions, a number of them can be recuperated from elite written forms, since fragments of melodies from such orally transmitted musical practices were extensively drawn upon by a number of composers in their collections of *giustiniani*, *mascherate* and

100   Giacomo Franco, *Masked Figures in Piazza Santo Stefano During Carnival*, engraving. Venice, Museo Civico Correr.

similar pieces that portray Venetian customs and traditions. In Venice this tradition goes back at least as far as Willaert, whose settings of Ruzante's 'canzone' make use of popularesque melodies attributed to him, and also includes pieces by Andrea Gabrieli and Giovanni Croce.[68] At the end of the Lepanto *mascherata* came a display showing the figure of Time, and a Triumph of Death, 'to demonstrate that it had also triumphed in this victory', thus fusing popular themes with a Petrarchan motif.

In common with the other public processions and the celebrations organized by the merchant communities, the Lepanto *mascherata* was widely propagandistic. Much of its effect was achieved by drawing upon a simple and traditional series of images accompanied by rousing and unsophisticated music. At the same time some of the more dignified elements operated on a different level, as with the initial group of five allegorical floats with which Andrea Gabrieli's music was associated. In fact, with its rather obvious structural division into two parts, made explicit in the printed description, the *mascherata* of 1572 is a perfect example of the differentiated modes of celebration that were characteristic of Venetian public ritual. Like Carnival itself, the *mascherata* did not have single purpose, but a variety of meanings according to the differing expectations of a socially varied audience. It seems that while certain motifs seen in temporary decorations and ephemeral literature were easily absorbed into the symbolic language of more permanent media, others were not. There was some exchange, as with scenes showing the disposition of the opposing fleets at Lepanto or the moment of their engagement, which appeared in cheap broadsides as well as in oil paintings (a good number of which have survived), but in other areas the genres were clearly differentiated.[69] The 'high art' that celebrates the battle often exploits an iconography that largely excludes the satirical caricatures of the popular woodcuts and verses. The significant fact is that the results, however different both stylistically and iconographically, reached all areas of society. Similar differentiations exist between the different genres of music that were performed in the *mascherata*, from the specially composed madrigals in a learned manner by Andrea Gabrieli, to popular songs with dialect texts. In common with the other Venetian processions that filled the annual calendar, the *mascherata* was not only a form of public entertainment, but also an instrument of social order, which it attempted to achieve by creating the impression of social cohesion. In the light of Venetian official policy towards the future of the League, and the apparent duplicity with which Barbaro's negotiations with the Turks was carried out, the *mascherata* may well have served a politically precise and useful function at a difficult moment for the Republic's relations with its citizens.

Publicly at least, it was generally accepted that the war would continue. Just three days after news of the victory had arrived in Venice, the doge and Senate ordered Sebastiano Venier to put the Venetian fleet in order as soon as possible so that the military advantage might be pressed home. For his part, Venier was keen to pursue further offensive action, and to spend the winter months in Turkish waters, pillaging and raiding to keep up the pressure on the enemy. New oarsmen, many of them captured Turkish slaves, were recruited, and by December a Venetian fleet of some sixty-four galleys had been assembled to pursue the campaign. The other members of the League had been equally assiduous in renovating their forces, and early in the new year plans were being laid to assemble an even larger fleet of 100 galleys at Corfu to make a pre-emptive strike against the Turks in the following spring. Popular opinion was evidently in favour of pressing on with the war, and popular pamphlets appeared from the Venetian presses urging the government to action, invoking the traditional dream of recapturing the Holy Places and pushing the Turks back to their own lands, 'as Xerxes had done with the Athenians, and Hannibal with The Romans'.[70] Details of a concerted plan were finally agreed in February 1572, when the undertakings that bound the members of the League were renewed in the Vatican Palace. Everything seemed set for a spring offensive.

Alongside the League's joint declarations of intent, the Venetians had been pursuing a parallel policy aimed at securing a separate and advantageous peace, exactly as their allies had prophesied from the outset. The cost of the war was crippling, and the resumption of traditional bilateral trading arrangements with the Turks was vital to the Venetian economy. It was widely perceived in official Venetian circles that, in the long run, peaceful coexistence with the Ottoman empire was to be preferred to continuing the conflict alongside Spain and the Papacy. While in public Venetian participation in the Holy League's project to safeguard the future of Christendom was assured, and its success at Lepanto continued to be celebrated, in practice (and for the time being in secret) the Republic's main concern was self-protection rather than the promotion of worthy crusades. This attitude, something of a Venetian tradition, had brought accusations of treachery ever since Pius ii's failed crusade of 1464; memories of the separate Venetian–Turkish treaty of 1540, which had brought with it the collapse of the previous three-way alliance, had made a decisive impact on the framing of the articles of the League in May 1571. Throughout 1572, and into the spring of the following year, this dual Venetian policy of preparing for war while negotiating for peace continued, though the discussions were known just to a few, and remained hidden not only from the pope and Philip ii, but even from the Venetian commanders at sea.

Keen and sceptical observers of the scene had never doubted that, right from the beginning of the War of Cyprus, important elements within the Venetian oligarchy had been advocating a separate treaty. These suspicions had been strengthened only by the obstructive behaviour of the Venetian contingent at the discussions, convened by Pius v to advance the formation of the Holy League, in the summer of 1570. In terms of political realities, the pursuit of a dual policy reflected a division between the Senate on the one hand, where the consensus was for a sustained effort to recapture Cyprus, and the Council of Ten and the Zonta on the other, where the balance of opinion was in favour of accommodation. It is entirely characteristic of this situation that, at the beginning of March 1571, when the details of the League were still being earnestly debated in Rome, the Council of Ten and the Zonta (a group of sixty men elected to the Senate every September) had been independently attempting to secure a secret agreement with the sultan through Marcantonio Barbaro in Constantinople, who had been authorized to cede Cyprus, if essential, in order to secure terms. Of necessity, Barbaro's negotiations were carried out without the knowledge of Leonardo Donà (a future doge) and Lorenzo Priuli, the two Venetian ambassadors in Madrid, who had become increasingly frustrated at the lethargic pace of Spanish preparations for a new campaign. Following Philip's return to Madrid after Easter, the two sought an audience, partly to assure the king of the Republic's determination to continue the war in conformity with the original articles of the League, unlike Spain, which, they had learnt from officials, had decided to reduce its quota of galleys. Donà and Priuli departed from their audience in disappointment, but the situation was soon turned on its head with the news, brought by a courier from Venice, that peace between Venice and the Turks had been agreed. Their next meeting with Philip was uncomfortable. The king, having heard their account of the Republic's decision, replied with an imperceptible and ironic movement of the mouth, and the words: 'You have replied exactly as they told me you would.'[71] The Venetians had behaved precisely according to type.

As for the Turks, they had struck a highly advantageous bargain. Within the following three years they were to receive a total payment of 300,000 ducats as indemnity, together with an increased annual payment for their continued use of Zante. As for territory, the borders of Dalmatia and Albania were to return to their pre-war status, while Cyprus was to remain in Turkish hands. In return, Venice was able to secure the restitution of the previous trading agreements that guaranteed access to markets in the Levant, while all impounded merchant vessels on both sides were to be repatriated. These clauses, finally agreed in Constantinople in March 1573, and then forwarded to the Heads of the Ten by Barbaro, were formally presented to the Senate for ratification in the spring. The standard explanation for the separate treaty, as recounted by the chroniclers, was that the terms of the League had been effectively broken by the Spanish and that this, together with the frightening speed with which the Turks had rearmed, had left the Venetians with no choice but to negotiate.[72] In this there may have been an element of truth. Within two years of Lepanto the Turkish navy had been rebuilt to its old level, while the Holy League had collapsed. Such realities were unwelcome. When Marcantonio Barbaro claimed that the Ottoman empire was 'in large part weak, uninhabited and ruined', and its soldiers exhausted from an 'odious and spoiled life', he was giving substance to a common piece of optimism.[73] The inability of the Christians to push home their advantage is underlined by the events of 1574, when the sultan's forces began by taking the Spanish fortress of La Goletta near Tunis, and finished by razing to the ground the Spanish bastions guarding the straits between Sicily and North Africa.[74]

In Venice, the announcement of the terms of the treaty, reported in the Sala dei Pregadi in the Doge's Palace, caused surprise if not astonishment. The general public was unprepared for such a dramatic turn of events, and the displeasure of the Spanish ambassadors and, in particular, of the papal nuncio, quickly became widely known.[75] Public disappointment at this seemingly sudden reversal of official policy, which had thrown into reverse the brave plans for a final resolution of the Turkish question forged in the post-Lepanto euphoria, was widespread both in Venice and in the cities of the *terraferma* that had contributed so much to the war effort. According to the papal nuncio, many patricians regarded it as an arrangement made for the benefit of a handful of the powerful, whose wealth was derived from trade with the Levant, against the wishes of the majority. This too is an indication of the extent to which widespread support for continuing the war had been generated. Matters were not helped by the fact that the terms themselves were widely perceived to be disadvantageous. Among Venetian ambassadors abroad there was considerable disquiet. Donà made his position clear: the treaty with the Turks he believed to be a serious mistake and would last only a short time until the enemy, refreshed and rearmed, would once again launch an attack. Ruy Gómez de Silva, one of Philip II's most trusted councillors, expressed a common sentiment when he met Donà and Priuli on the day after their audience with the king. Offence had been caused not so much by the treaty itself, which in the face of insuperable Ottoman power was even comprehensible, but by the total secrecy that had surrounded the Venetian negotiations. Although it had been laid down in the articles of the League that the pope would be the arbiter in the case of disagreements between the allies, neither Spain nor the Papacy had been consulted.[76] Such details took time to achieve circulation; at the beginning of May the Florentine representative in Venice had still not gained any impression of Spanish reactions.[77] In Vienna, Giovanni Correr heard nothing but condemnations and threats against Venice and its citizens.[78] In contrast to the formation of the League just two years earlier, the conclusion of peace passed without celebration. More than a year was to go by before the Venetians felt that the times were right for festivity.

HENRICO III FRANCIÆ ATQ
POLONIA REI CHRISTINÆ
RELIGIONIS ACERRIMO PROPV
NATORI ADVENIENTI ÆTERVM
RESP DVLTERIS BENVOLEN
TIÆ ATQ OBSERVANTIÆ
DECLARATIONEM

CHAPTER SEVEN

His Most Christian Majesty

On Sunday, 18 July 1574, at about midday, a richly decorated galley anchored in front of the Doge's Palace. From the main mast hung a standard of vermilion silk bearing the official emblem of the Lion of St Mark worked in gold thread. The sides of the ship were hung with thirty flags of various colours, all decorated with the same emblem together with the coat of arms of the Soranzo family worked in silver and gold. Thirty-four pieces of cannon were carried aboard, and the ship was rowed by no fewer than 354 Dalmatian oarsmen, all identically dressed in dark blue and yellow jackets, and caps decorated with the fleur-de-lis. The galley's commander, Giacomo Soranzo, and the other officers wore uniforms in the same colours. As soon as the doge, Alvise Mocenigo, had embarked, this magnificently decorated and stately vessel set out for Murano accompanied by a small flotilla of fourteen galleys and innumerable smaller boats. At Sant'Elena the procession was joined by 200 brigantines manned by the trade guilds, together with other craft belonging to Venetian patricians.[1]

This brief trip across the lagoon inaugurated an occasion that the Venetians came to think of for many decades afterwards, and to describe and celebrate in words, music and painting, as the most significant ceremonial occasion of the entire sixteenth century: the visit of His Most Christian Majesty, King Henry III of France, who passed through the city on his way from Cracow to Lyons.[2] At Murano Soranzo docked, and Mocenigo disembarked and entered the main door of the Palazzo Cappello, the summer palace of Bianca Cappello's family. It was there, at the foot of the main staircase, that the doge of Venice and the king of France met for the first time. The usual diplomatic rituals were observed and compliments exchanged. Mocenigo insisted upon Venetian devotion to the French monarchy, and thanked Henry for the confidence he had demonstrated by his decision to visit the city, words that carried a particular resonance in the aftermath of Lepanto. French policy had always predicted and had been in support of a separate Venetian treaty with the Turks, and French support was a significant counterbalance to Spanish and papal attitudes. The Venetians, reviled by their former allies, were now desperate to receive support and recognition. For his part, the king spoke at considerable length in French, thanking the Venetians for their courtesy and cordiality, and expressing gratitude for the treatment he had received since first arriving on Venetian soil. These pleasantries concluded, king and doge, together with the dukes of Ferrara and Nevers, the cardinal of San Sisto (the pope's nephew) and other dignitaries, went on board Soranzo's galley. Escorted by his entourage of forty patricians, and accompanied by dozens of other vessels brightly decked-out for the occasion, Soranzo set out for the Lido. It was from here that Henry formally made his entry into the city.

This procedure was unusual. Generally, though not invariably, distinguished visitors to Venice were received by the doge and Signoria at the Lido, where a ceremony of welcome took place in the church of San Nicolò. Among the exceptions was the important precedent of Duke Alfonso II d'Este's entry in 1562, probably the most important model for Henry's reception. On that occasion the duke, who had embarked at Chioggia, was formally received at the church of Sant'Antonio di Castello, which, like San Nicolò, was a monastic foundation and hence comparatively neutral territory.[3] It was this ceremonial template that the Venetians now chose to adopt from Henry's entry, though not without considerable debate. On 14 July, just three days before the king was due to make his entry, Vincenzo Mocenigo, speaking in the Senate, put to the vote the motion that he be received not at the Lido but at Murano. This failed, as did the counter-proposal that the conventions be respected. These disagreements have been interpreted as an early example of conflict between the *giovani* and the *vecchi*,[4] two opposing factions whose confrontational politics were to characterize the final decades of the sixteenth century. The elaborate compromise solution that was finally adopted retained the principle of neutrality, and when Henry first arrived at Marghera, the effective boundary of the *terraferma*, he was met by a large crowd of Venetians and a party of senators who escorted him across the lagoon to Murano. There he was lodged for the night. Although geographically close to Venice, Murano was governed with a degree of self-autonomy, as were the towns and cities of the *terraferma*. In purely ceremonial terms Murano's function on this occasion was similar to that of the Medici villa at Poggio a Caiano outside Florence, or the Villa Madama near Rome, as the place outside the city from which official entries were symbolically launched.

Political difficulties also surrounded some of the other arrangements. News of Henry's intention to visit Venice had reached the government only on 30 June, barely a fortnight before the king arrived in person, and almost immediately the

Senate was convened to discuss matters of protocol.[5] It was comparatively simple to issue papers giving Henry free passage through Venetian territory, but things became more complicated when it came to deciding where the king was to be lodged. One proposal, that Palazzo Cornaro at San Maurizio should be used, was overturned by the strongly supported alternative to commandeer Ca' Foscari, together with its adjoining palaces, at the bend of the Grand Canal.[6] This was indeed a prominent and luxurious palace, which not only lay midway between San Marco and the Rialto, but also stood immediately opposite Doge Alvise Mocenigo's family palace on the other side of the canal.[7]

When it came to artistic arrangements for the visit discussions seem to have progressed less rancorously. Time was short, and as late as 7 July the Florentine ambassador reported that work was much behind, particularly at the Lido, where the temporary constructions for Henry's entry were unfinished.[8] A few days later the Senate was advised of the king's wish to see a performance by the renowned Gelosi company of actors, then in Milan, one of its frequent ports of call.[9] This was arranged at short notice through the efforts of the Venetian Resident in the city, and it was agreed that a specially commissioned play by Cornelio Frangipane, with the simple title *Tragedia*, would be staged.

Henry's visit to Venice was the high point of his triumphal return to France from Warsaw, where he had been crowned king of Poland in the previous year, an event that had been widely reported in the Venetian press, always keen to be abreast of French affairs. The matter was also of genuine political interest to the Venetians, and an anonymous four-page pamphlet describing the coronation itself reveals that, together with Ferrara (whose connections with France were equally strong), the Republic was the only Italian state to send an ambassador to Cracow.[10] Following the death of his elder brother, Charles IX, on 30 May 1574, Henry had been urgently recalled to France to take the throne by his mother, Catherine de Médicis, thus preventing his younger brother François, duke of Alençon, from doing so in his absence. Although the Poles had always regarded Henry as untrustworthy, they were opposed to his return, and he was forced to leave surreptitiously under cover of darkness. Following Catherine's advice he went first to Vienna, where he was given hospitality by the emperor. On 29 June Henry left the imperial capital to begin his journey south, and on 11 July he arrived at Venzon near the borders of Friuli. At Pontebba he was met by 500 gentlemen on horseback, accompanied by halberdiers and 800 infantry; since sixteenth-century Friuli was a desolate and dangerous place, despite the collapse after the Cambrai war of the factional politics and the traditions of vendetta that had previously united Friulians of all classes in a shared culture of violence,[11] provision of such a large armed escort was more than a mere ceremonial detail. It was also at Pontebba that the four specially appointed Venetian ambassadors (Andrea Badoer, Giovanni Soranzo, Giovanni Michiel and Giacomo Foscarini), who had been designated to accompany the king from the confines of the Venetian state to the city itself, presented their credentials. The Republic had provided a ceremonial carriage for Henry drawn by four horses, and after a brief speech of welcome by Badoer and other courtesies, the entire company set out for Venice.[12] In the course of the journey the entourage was joined first by the duke of Nevers and later, at Spilimbergo, by the duke of Ferrara, Alfonso II d'Este. The former was related to the Gonzaga of Mantua, while the latter, the son of Ercole II and Renée of France, was almost more French than Italian, having spent much of the 1550s at the French court. Famously present at the tournament at which Henry II was mortally wounded (he is reported to have held the king's head as he lay dying), Alfonso would certainly have been known to his son.[13] These carefully calculated appearances of the two most senior Italian princes with strong French family connections were political before they were social.

At Feltre, Belluno and other small towns along the route, Henry was welcomed by large crowds, and at Conegliano he made a triumphal entry through the main gate of the city, which had been decorated with the arms of France and statues of St Mark. The inevitable salvoes of artillery were discharged, and in one of the main streets two large pyramids had been constructed and painted with the arms of Poland, France and Anjou with inscriptions. It was also at Conegliano that Carlo Pascale delivered a Latin oration in praise of Henry, the first of many such compositions that marked the king's triumphal progress through northern Italy. At Lavadina, near Treviso, Henry and his entourage crossed a specially constructed bridge decorated with the royal arms and mottoes. As Tommaso Porcacchi, always the most erudite and antiquarian of the chroniclers remarks, earlier bridges had been built here for the visits of both Emperor Charles V and Queen Bona of Poland earlier in the century.[14] Outside Treviso, where Henry arrived on 15 July, he was met by the *podestà*, Bartolomeo Lippomano, and a large number of city notables and gentlemen-at-arms with their companies of soldiers. He was then escorted to the city gate, where he was greeted by the bishop, Giorgio Cornaro, together with the clergy. From here the ceremonial procession made its way to the cathedral, where speeches were made, prayers said and Henry received the kiss of peace. It then continued, to the sound of trumpets and drums, to the main square along a route punctuated by three arches. These were decorated with royal coats of arms, mottoes, and painted scenes showing Henry's victories over rebels and heretics, as well as images of Venice and of the River Sile that passes through the city.[15] These unambiguous references to the recent religious disturbances in France, and to Henry's role as 'Defender of the Faith', was to become one of the most common leitmotifs of his visit through northern Italy in general, and in Venice in particular. All the temporary triumphal arches erected in Henry's honour in the towns and cities along his route projected moral and political messages through images and inscriptions: celebrations of Henry's achievements in the fight against Protestantism, and good auguries for the future. The use of Latin, and the adoption of the classical Roman arch as the vehicle of such messages was hardly new, but it displayed learning, erudition and skill of a kind that was not only appropriately decorous but must have appealed to Henry, whose taste for such things is clear from his visit to Giovanni Grimani's collection of antiquuities during his stay in Venice.[16]

From Treviso quick progress was made to Mestre, and then on to Marghera, where a large crowd of some 30,000 people was waiting, together with an official deputation of seventy senators dressed in their sumptuous vermilion robes, led by Giovanni Correr, who delivered a short address.[17] Each gondola was fitted out with a festive awning made of silk or velvet, while the gondoliers were dressed in livery.[18] To the sound of cannon-fire and instrumental music, Henry and his immediate company, which still included the dukes of Ferrara and Nevers, embarked in three gondolas. Accompanied by 2,000 smaller craft, many flying the colours of their patrician owners, they now made their way across the lagoon, to shouts of welcome and the accompaniment of music. As the flotilla passed the smaller islands of San Giuliano and San Secondo, artillery was discharged and church bells rung. At the island of San Luigi, Henry was met by a squadron of forty gondolas arranged in a half-moon formation; these contained the forty young patricians whom the Senate had assigned to the king's service for the duration of his visit.[19] Beyond the island of San Cristoforo the boats were joined by the *podestà* of Murano, accompanied by 500 gondolas. At Murano itself, Henry disembarked, to be welcomed by 'most excellent musicians with instruments of all kinds'.[20] Preceded by the forty young patricians walking in pairs, and passing between lines of halberdiers ceremonially dressed in armour from the treasury of the Doge's Palace,[21] Henry entered Palazzo Cappello. From the balcony he presented himself three times to the crowds gathered below, before officially receiving the cardinal of San Sisto and the imperial ambassador, Vito di Dornberg. Later in the evening Henry made an unscheduled visit to Venice by gondola in the company of the duke of Ferrara, before returning to Murano, where music for voices and instruments was performed outside the palace. This probably consisted of large-scale compositions of the kind that were to be played outside Ca' Foscari on subsequent evenings.[22] Alfonso d'Este's role in this was much criticized by some Venetians, who accused him of deliberately attempting to blunt the effect of the following day's *entrata* by removing the element of surprise.

A second phase of the entry delineated the moment of arrival at the Lido, which was both the actual and symbolic boundary of Venice, an island that protected the city both from its enemies and the sea. It was for these strategic and symbolic reasons that the edge of the lagoon, close to the island, was the site of the doge's annual marriage of Venice to the sea on the feast of the Ascension. In this context, the church of San Nicolò al Lido, and the area immediately in front of it, functioned as a metaphorical extension of the Piazza San Marco and the basilica. At San Nicolò, the principal functionaries of church and state, together with some of the main components of the Venetian cere-

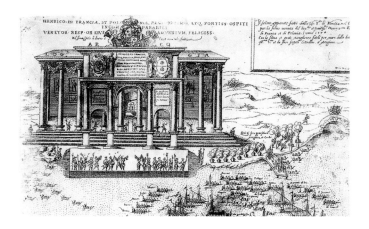

102 Domenico Zenoi, *The Reception of Henry III at the Lido*, engraving. Venice, Museo Civico Correr.

monial machine, welcomed the visitor onto Venetian soil, and so into the Venetian *civitas*. The commercial foundations of the Republic were represented by a flotilla of decorated brigantines, manned by the guilds. The ceremonies conducted at the Lido provided the Republic with the opportunity both to honour its distinguished guest and his achievements, and to instruct those present in the virtues and power of the state, through a spectacle of unusual beauty, theatrically enacted at the boundary of land and sea.

For Henry's visit two temporary structures said to have been designed by Andrea Palladio had been put up at San Nicolò (pl. 102).[23] The first was a triumphal arch consciously modelled, according to most commentators, on that of Septimus Severus in Rome. Palladio was hardly a newcomer to the genre; in Vicenza he had been called upon at least twice to design temporary structures of this kind, first in 1543 and again in 1565. Made of wood simulated to resemble marble, the arch at the Lido was decorated with a sequence of statues, inscriptions and paintings; although there are discrepancies between the sources about the number of paintings displayed,[24] there is agreement about their subject matter. The main iconographical themes were those of Venice as the dispenser of peace and justice, and Henry, 'Rex Christianissimus Francorum', as Defender of the Faith. Having disembarked, together with the doge and the cardinal legate surrounded by other dignitaries, Henry was received by the Signoria and then accompanied towards the arch under a baldachin of cloth of gold carried by the six procurators of San Marco. Among them were Sebastiano Venier, soon to be elected doge in gratitude for his gallant leadership at Lepanto, and another future doge, Nicolò da Ponte. The three main openings of the arch were framed by four Corinthian columns on each façade, which in turn supported a cornice. On top of the entire structure, the royal arms of France were displayed supported by two angels, while in the attic, between statues of *Victory* and *Peace*, ran the inscription 'To Henry III King of France and Poland, and Most Christian King and most fervent defender of Christianity [offered by] the Republic of Venice as a sign of long-standing benevolence and deference.'[25]

On either side of the arch the arms of France and Venice were shown, while above the three arcades paintings by Veronese and Jacopo Tintoretto (according to one account) had been mounted.[26] Those above the side openings showed Henry's great triumphs over his Huguenot enemies at Jarnac and Moncontour, while, over the central passageway, further historical scenes showed his election as king of Poland and the reception of the Polish ambassadors in Paris, where they had come to offer the crown of their country to Henry in the summer of 1573.[27] The high point of the festivities on this occasion, commemorated in one of the Valois Tapestries now in Florence, was an elaborate danced spectacle, an early example of the French *ballet de cour* tradition.[28] Having passed under the arch, the first of the two temporary structures, the procession now mounted the steps to the second temporary structure, a loggia, where Henry was received by the patriarch of Venice, Giovanni Trevisan, accompanied by the clergy. From a typological point of view, Palladio's structure (if indeed it was his design) was altogether less conventional as a piece of *ingresso* furniture than the triumphal arch. As it came into view, it was revealed as a tall and airy construction, also painted to imitate marble. The front façade was made up of ten Corinthian columns joined by garlands, while each of the side walls was pierced by an arcade, and the rear wall was articulated by columns to form compartments, each of which contained a statue of one of the Virtues, placed beneath a painting. In the central compartment, which lay directly in front of the main arcade of the arch, stood an altar placed in a circular niche, while a painting on the ceiling above presented four figures of Victory, their arms raised in the act of coronation with laurel wreaths. The evident reference here was to the four great battles that Henry had won against his enemies, battles that had already been seen in the paintings of the preceding arch, while the Virtues were clearly intended to be those of the king himself. Above the altar had been placed a picture of *Christ the Redeemer* by Jacopo Tintoretto.[29] The iconography is that of a site designed for a Christian apotheosis.

This was a remarkable and, for Venice, an unprecedented decorative scheme. Temporary arches had been put up before to welcome distinguished guests to the city, as in the case of Duke Alfonso II of Ferrara in 1562,[30] but the sheer scale of the operation in 1574 was not only a novelty, but also an impressive testimony to the Venetians' ability to call upon experience and tradition in mounting such displays at short notice. Although it is reported that the ceiling of the loggia remained unfinished, the three principal artists involved in the arrangements – Palladio, Tintoretto and Veronese – were probably chosen for their skill at fast collaboration, as well as for the quality of their work.[31] Porcacchi, normally meticulous in his antiquarian researches, was so over-whelmed by the splendour of the arrangements that he incorrectly claimed that nothing of the kind had been done before in Venice, not even for the visit of Emperor Frederick III in 1452.[32] In general outline, the loggia, with its classical motifs, continued the theme already established by Palladio's arch, that of Venice as the New Rome, which was not only equivalent to the ancient capital, but was superior to it, since the triumph of Catholicism, repeatedly referred to in the paintings of both arch and loggia, raised this new civilization to a higher level than that of pagan antiquity. The focal point for the ritual that confirmed this message was the altar, standing in the centre of this loggia-temple, where Henry now knelt surrounded by the *Victories*. The traditional Te Deum and other pieces of music, which cannot be identified, were now sung by the choir of San Marco,[33] and the patriarch then gave his blessing. This solemn moment would have been heard by few since the choir competed with the 'strepito di trombe e di tamburi'[34] and the noise of artillery described in the accounts and shown in Domenico Zenoi's engraving. The sacred ceremonies finished, the procession descended the steps of the loggia, and once more passed under the arch to the sound of artillery.[35] As it did so, it was confronted with another inscription of welcome, again clearly visible in Zenoi's engraving, this time framed by the complementary statues of *Faith* and *Justice*: 'To Henry III, most superior and strong king of France and Poland, incomparable guest of the Venetian Republic, on the happy occasion of his entry [into the city].'[36]

The paintings on this side of the arch showed Henry's official reception in Poland (a parallel to the entry then being enacted on the Lido), together with the moment of his coronation, mirrored a few moments earlier in the ceremony in the loggia. Further canvases showed an expectant France eagerly awaiting the king's return, and the event itself,[37] which was yet to take place. This ingenious intertwining of historical events with present ceremonial critically relies upon the invocation of ritual parallels, in which the king's coronation in Poland was symbolically re-enacted at the Lido. Retracing his steps to the quay, with the cardinal legate to his right and the doge to his left, Henry then boarded the Bucintoro (the state barge used by the doge). It was at this juncture that a piece of music, composed by Gioseffo Zarlino, *maestro di cappella* at San Marco, was performed by the choir. As it did so all the church bells of the city were rung.[38] The text, which is cast in the form of a dialogue in elegiac distichs, had been written for the occasion by Cornelio Frangipane.[39] The extent to which it, or indeed Zarlino's music, could be heard in the din of artillery fire and the noise of the crowds must be doubted, but such practical matters were probably of secondary concern to the choreographers of the occasion; it was more impor-tant that a sense of decorum was satisfied, through the performance of a piece in Latin (the language of the educated elite), appropriately cast in a form derived from classical literature. In other words, Zarlino's piece (the music itself has not survived) was a decorous response to the resonances of the ancient world evoked by Palladio's temporary structures, the full significance of which may also not have been fully understood by some of the onlookers. One eyewitness, for example, described them as 'a most beautiful theatre with steps', which led to 'a most beautiful distinguished place', characterizations that fail to grasp their allusive power.[40] This is not surprising. Sixteenth-century entries, characteristically constructed upon erudite programmes, were rarely understood by those present. The objective of those responsible for devising such events was to meet the requirements of a theory of decorum.

At first glance, the arrangements at the Lido would simply appear to be a local Venetian adaptation of a common celebratory topos, in which both the distinguished visitor and the state that welcomed him were to be equated with momentous parallels taken from the history of ancient Rome. Throughout the Renaissance, the recuperation of the lost festival forms of the ancient world had always been an important element in the more general revival of the classical past; as in other fields, the influence of humanist learning had been critical in transforming the late medieval entry into a latter-day *trionfo*. From the middle of the fifteenth century onwards, classical arches had gradually become the principal feature of the architectural vocabulary deployed to articulate imperial themes in entries and triumphs throughout the length and breadth of Italy. In cities with medieval walls and gates, these were usually temporary structures made out of painted and gilded wood, decorated with Latin inscriptions and paintings in praise of the honoured guest, be it foreign dignitary, newly arrived bride or conquering hero. By the sixteenth century, it had become common practice for a series of such arches to be constructed along the ceremonial route of an *entrata*, often presenting a series of interlocking dynastic and historical themes through a coherent iconographical programme. Those devised by Vincenzo Borghini and constructed by Vasari and his assistants as part of the *apparato* of 1565 celebrating the wedding in Florence of Duke Cosimo de' Medici's son Francesco to Joanna of Austria incorporated celebrations of the city's republican past (brought to a sharp conclusion with the ill-fated rule of Cosimo's immediate predecessor, Alessandro), as well as those of the Medici family and the current regime.[41]

By this period, the use of such temporary structures had become quite common in the cities of the *terraferma*. The reasons are perhaps obvious. In the first place, and in contrast to Venice itself, the cities of the mainland had Roman histories, together with often substantial archaeological remains to prove it. In these places, the erection of temporary arches to welcome notable visitors, as happened at Chioggia, when Duke Alfonso II d'Este passed through the city en route for Venice in 1562, was more usual.[42] A few years earlier, when Bona Sforza, queen of Poland, made an entry into Padua, the design of Michele Sanmicheli's triumphal arch was said to have been based on the Roman arch near the Castelvecchio in his home town of Verona.[43] Sanmicheli was particularly admired for his gateway designs, which gave many of the towns in the Veneto a dignified entrance, and his most magnificent and elaborate structure of this kind, the Porta Palio in Verona, is said to have been based on the walls of the Roman theatre in the city.[44] Here, as in other instances, gate architecture and

103 Andrea Vicentino, *The Reception of Dogaressa Grimani in the Piazzetta*, 1593. Venice, Museo Civico Correr.

temporary structures share a common vocabulary. In Venice itself, probably for topographical and political reasons more than anything else, the use of the temporary classical arch was not an established feature of official state rituals of welcome. The physical characteristics of an unwalled and gateless island, without any approaches by land that could be conceived of as constituting a ceremonial route, made the more conventional Italian *ingresso* nothing more than the most distant of models. At the same time, the general policy of the government was strongly opposed to any self-glorification of individual doges that was conveyed, in the case of princes, by the apparatus of the traditional *entrata*. The few sixteenth-century exceptions were made, suggestively enough, not for doges but for their wives. In 1557 'portoni', based on the temporary arch constructed for the visit of Bona Sforza in the previous year, were erected in the Piazzetta for the entry of Dogaressa Zilia Dandolo Priuli,[45] and forty years later Morosina Grimani was accorded an official *trionfo* on the wishes of her husband made public at the time of his election two years earlier. The decorations on this occasion included a triumphal arch in the Piazzetta, which features prominently in a number of paintings recording the event (pl. 103).[46]

The second temporary structure constructed at the Lido for Henry was the freely designed loggia. The significance of the choice of this architectural type, made by a group of patrician advisers, would not have been lost on the more alert members of the largely Venetian population that watched the spectacle from sea and land.[47] In the public realm, such structures were often used as ceremonial spaces, sometimes as places of debate and public discussion, occasionally even with a juridical function. Palladio had used the motif of the loggia on other occasions, but in quite different contexts, notably in his two related schemes for the Rialto bridge, which have been compared to Sansovino's Loggetta in the

Piazza San Marco.[48] A more recent, and perhaps more relevant experience of a free-standing loggia inserted into a civic complex, was Palladio's Loggia del Capitaniato in Vicenza, but Sansovino's Loggetta, an aristocratic forum reserved specifically for members of the ruling class, was the example most familiar to Venetians. With its triumphal iconography (it has been described by one architectural historian as 'the most complete visual representation of the Venetians' view of their own state as the perfect republic'),[49] and a changing cast of state officials, it functioned as a permanent reminder of the rich benefits of Venetian government and of the Republic's dominion over the Adriatic. Palladio's temporary loggia at San Nicolò also served as a 'ritrovo della nobiltà', a 'loggia fabricata all'incontro', as one observer described it,[50] a reserved space where the king of France, accompanied by doge and papal legate, was to be received by the official representative of the church in Venice, before an exclusively elite audience. At the same time, Palladio's structure functioned as the arena for a very particular and highly suggestive piece of ritual, which placed a strong emphasis upon Henry's role and title of 'Most Christian Majesty'.[51]

Zarlino's music marked the end of the official rituals, performed by the highest officers of church and state, through cultural forms that were visual, literary, musical and ceremonial, and dense with symbolic meanings. Now began what was, for most of those crowded into the hundreds of vessels moored in front of the Lido, the true entry of Henry III. These, maintained at the expense of the trade and craft guilds of the city, were to be the principal escorts as Henry now made his triumphal entry into the city. The air resounded to the traditional sounds of trumpet calls, shawms, drums and the ringing of church bells.[52] From the Lido, the Bucintoro accompanied the king past the Riva degli Schiavoni and the Piazzetta, to the Grand Canal and Ca' Foscari, where he and his retainers were to stay for the next ten days. The chroniclers, unanimous in their expressions of wonder at the splendour of the scene, are equally united in the difficulty of setting down in words some sense of the heady mixture of sounds and colours, as music, artillery rounds and the shouts and cheers of the crowd collided. At the centre of attention was the Bucintoro itself, freshly gilded for the occasion, the great standard of the Republic at its main mast. Flanked by the doge and the cardinal of San Sisto, Henry sat in the poop protected from the summer sun by a baldachin. Behind sailed ten other ships carrying the Signoria and other officers of state. Prominent in the flotilla that swarmed around the Bucintoro and the other official vessels, as they made their stately progress across the lagoon, were the brigantines of the guilds.[53] Aboard most of them groups of musicians played and sang (the demand for professional players had been so great that they had been able to raise their rates for the occasion).[54] All these craft were colourfully decked out, and competition between them to achieve the most eye-catching results had been strong. One of the most elegant of all was that of the silk merchants, a picture of Christ at its prow, its sides draped with expensive figured silks and rich velvets, the oarsmen dressed in livery, and the bridge lined with halberdiers in gilt armour.[55] Porcacchi was particularly struck by the brigantine of the mirror-gilders, which was hung with examples of their work to catch the reflections of the sun.[56] For their brigantine the goldsmiths had chosen to play on the colours white, yellow, gold and silver. Even the main mast had been silvered, while from a large container placed at its summit fireworks rained down. In case there should have been any doubt of the authorship of this extravagant floating spectacle, a silver lantern had been hung from a gold chain strung above the bridge together with the tag 'Corona artium'.[57]

The escort of decorated craft manned by the guilds was a traditional part of the official welcome given to important guests, as well as a feature of the *sensa*, an event on which Henry's entry drew for a number of its prominent features. When Emperor Frederick III made his triumphant entry into Venice, having been crowned in Rome by Pope Nicholas V, he was met by a similar flotilla, which escorted him to San Clemente, where he was officially greeted by the doge and Senate,[58] and the same procedure had been followed when Alfonso II d'Este made his entry into the city.[59] The *mariegola* of the grocers' guild gives an interesting account of how this flotilla was put together in 1574. It was on the doge's orders that all the trade guilds were required to decorate and man an armed vessel to accompany Henry, and on 6 July their representatives had been called before the treasurer of the *giustizia vecchia* in order to receive detailed instructions. These included the specification that the oarsmen were to be dressed in livery decorated with blue and yellow fleurs-de-lis, and that there were to be twelve halberdiers on each vessel. Failure to meet the total cost would result in a fine of 100 ducats.[60] Zenoi's engraving of the Lido shows the flotilla of brigantines drawn up in front of Palladio's temporary structures, most of the participants identified with a caption.[61]

As this dazzling armada arrived in front of the Riva degli Schiavoni, salvoes of artillery were discharged, while, taking their cue from the bell-tower in the Piazza, all the church bells of the city began to ring. An unimaginable celebratory soundscape erupted, as music from the ships, the report of the cannon and the pealing of bells, all fused together with the shouts and applause of the crowds massed into the Piazza San Marco and lining the *riva*, or crammed into the hundreds of gondolas that vied for the best view.[62] According to one eyewitness, the din was so great and oppressive that it seemed as if the whole city was inebriated.[63] Having passed in front of the Doge's Palace, the Bucintoro now eased gently into the mouth of the Grand Canal. At Ca' Foscari a wooden landing-stage had been built, capable, it was rumoured, of berthing 100 gondolas. The king, accompanied by the doge and Signoria, was escorted to the sumptuously decorated quarters that he and his extensive entourage were to occupy for the duration of his visit, after which his hosts returned to the Piazzetta in the Bucintoro and Henry was left to the crowds. From the balcony a large swathe of cloth of gold had been draped; here he now appeared as the brigantines, which had been temporarily anchored off the island of San Giorgio

Maggiore, once more made their appearance, passing beneath in review. Now it was the turn of the private gondolas, many with musicians aboard, who passed up and down the Grand Canal from the Dogana to the Rialto bridge. Strategically and theatrically positioned at the bend of the canal, with clear views in both directions, Ca' Foscari provided the best conceivable vantage-point from which to experience this display, as well as being symbolically located directly opposite the palace of Doge Alvise Mocenigo, on the other side of the Grand Canal.[64] Most of the gondolas had been elaborately, and in some cases even bizarrely, decorated. One of the most noticeable, that of Giacomo Pisani, had been covered with painted canvases and gilded stucco-work. At its prow were two rearing horses, and at the poop a seated figure of *Neptune* brandished a triton. Pisani's four gondoliers were dressed as gods with long white beards to represent the four principal rivers of the Veneto – Adige, Brenta, Piave and Po – while under a baldachin supported by columns sat Pisani and his guests.

Another change of scene took place at dusk. As if choreographed to be performed as a single action, lamps and brightly coloured paper decorations in the shape of crowns, pyramids and fleurs-de-lis now appeared in the windows and along the balustrades overlooking the Grand Canal. Even the smaller palaces put out thirty or forty lamps, the larger ones as many as five hundred, so that the canal was illuminated for its entire length, from the Piazza San Marco to the church of Santa Lucia.[65] As the spectacle moved towards its climax, hundreds of fireworks were let off from gondolas, lighting up the night sky and then cascading into the water, their reflections glittering on the surface of the waves. Elaborate firework displays were something of a ceremonial speciality in Venice, and one imitating the eruption of Mount Etna was put on for Henry later in the week.[66] It was the sound of lutes and singing that now dominated as, from other gondolas passing in front of Ca' Foscari, the sound of music gently drifted upwards.

Singing and playing music on the canals, and particularly the Grand Canal, during the summer months was an established Venetian pastime.[67] From inventories of the houses of Venetians from a wide range of social class and occupational type, including clockmakers, merchants, cloth dyers and engravers, it emerges that the possession of musical instruments was widespread, and that among patricians it was very high indeed.[68] One curiosity of sixteenth-century inventories of Venetian palaces is the frequency with which musical instruments, together with furniture, pictures and mirrors, are recorded in the *androne*, the hallway that usually linked the main entrance from the water to the inner courtyard in larger houses and palaces, and one of the coolest areas of the house in the summer months. A second curiosity is that the musical instruments most frequently recorded there were keyboard instruments, sometimes a harpsichord but often a clavichord. Both, but especially the clavichord, were portable. Their presence in the *androne* relates to a particular Venetian social practice described by a number of late sixteenth-century writers, and illus-

*i questa Maniera la Stade ne' gran Caldi si va ai freschi per li canali della Citta la sera fino a meza notte con musiche di voci,
e diuersi istrumenti, con grandissimo diletto, con le signore Cortegiane, e spesso anco si Cena in barca con i mirabil piacere*

104 Giacomo Franco, *Music-making on the Grand Canal in Summer*,
engraving. Venice, Museo Civico Correr.

trated in an engraving by Giacomo Franco (pl. 104). Cesare Vecellio's costume
book *De gli habiti antichi e moderni* contains a section with the title 'Concerning the Dress of Boatmen and the Commodiousness of Boats', which
describes the various 'sweet pastimes' that can be enjoyed in a gondola. During
the summer when the weather is hot, says Vecellio,[69] it is possible to picnic at
various islands and monasteries of the lagoon, taking along not only food but
also musical instruments. Franco's engraving shows Venetians enjoying themselves in much the same way on the Grand Canal, while his caption explains
that 'signore cortigiane' were among the participants. Most of the passengers
shown by Franco are indeed women, and presumably not all of them courtesans. It seems to have been common practice among women from elite families, wealthy enough to maintain a gondola and its boatman, to take to the
canal in the evening during the hot summer months, where they could take
the air and make music. Portable keyboard instruments could be brought from
the *androne* and carried aboard for this purpose. In this way, the space of the
gondola, protected by a male liveried servant, became an extension of the house
itself. In general terms, gondola travel helped both to preserve and celebrate
the honour of male elites by publicly displaying their wives, mothers and
daughters, while at the same time protecting them from the dangers of foot
travel. But as well as being associated with the sexual honour of elite women,
gondolas were also associated with courtesans, as a number of writers relate,
and as Franco shows. His engraving depicts both these segments of Venetian
society evidently coexisting in the same space (though not in the same boats);
they did so to the sound of music. It was this tradition that was called on to
provide a musical backdrop to Henry's stay in Ca' Foscari.

206

During the king's time there, the stretch of the Grand Canal in front of the palace was also transformed into an arena for the performance of various spectacles and entertainments. On one evening a furnace supported on rafts was moored in front of the palace, so that the king could watch while craftsmen fashioned glass, crystal vases and other objects, a skill that then as now was a speciality of Murano.[70] But above all it was music that was produced outside Ca' Foscari to entertain Henry. Running like a thread through the various manuscript and printed accounts of his visit are frequent references to music of all kinds, from the trumpets and drums that accompanied him throughout the city and announced his presence to the crowds, to the vocal and instrumental performances that had been organized by his hosts. Once Henry and his entourage had settled in Ca' Foscari and the neighbouring Palazzo Giustinian, united for the occasion into a single complex luxuriously furnished and decorated,[71] music was provided on an elaborate scale. On the instructions of the Signoria, a platoon of boats had been lashed together outside Ca' Foscari to support a temporary loggia covered with an awning decorated with swags.[72] Here, on more than one occasion, groups of professional singers and instrumentalists performed music, some of which, specially commissioned for the occasion, set texts in praise of the king and his virtues.

Two of these pieces were published some years later in a lavish set of partbooks whose contents were put together by Giovanni Gabrieli, then organist at San Marco.[73] Both were written by Gabrieli's uncle, Andrea, who had also served the basilica as organist until his death in the previous year. The text of the first, 'Ecco Vinegia bella', scored for twelve voices arranged in two six-voice choirs, evokes the clamorous din of Henry's entry, and although rather general in its eulogistic rhetoric, is quite specific in its reference to the king's ceremonial visit.[74] Following introductory flourishes by drums and trumpets, the piece was performed by the two choirs accompanied by large instrumental forces. The text relates that Hercules, now grown old and tired of his labours, has come to relax in the embrace of his sister, Vinegia. She, at the apogee of her fame and content with the presence of her brother, is encouraged to welcome 'il glorioso Henrico' and to rejoice in his ascent to his father's throne. The two choirs, whose music is written in alternating blocks of sound, compete with each other before uniting for the final section in praise of Henry.

A second work, 'Hor che nel suo bel seno', for eight voices arranged in two choirs, with its specific references to Henry's military enterprises (and so implicitly to his battle against Protestantism, and the victories at Jarnac and Moncontour), is an analogue in music to the exploits depicted in the celebratory canvases of the arch at the Lido. It is a comparatively short piece, composed in the classic Venetian manner, with motifs exchanged between the choirs until the entire ensemble comes together for a highly characteristic triple-time conclusion.

A third piece, 'Questo Re glorioso' by Vincenzo Bell'haver (or Bellavere), organist of the Scuola Grande di San Rocco from 1568, was also probably written for this occasion or for a similar one during Henry's visit. Composed in the sonorous style of the Venetian grand manner, and scored for twelve voices arranged in three choirs, its text makes reference to the prophecies of Proteus, one of the themes of Frangipane's *Tragedia*, and it may even be that Frangipane was the author of the text; the music was published ten years after the event.

An official programme of events had been planned for the remainder of Henry's visit. On his second day at Ca' Foscari he was visited by the doge and Senate, and then by the duke of Savoy, who had come specially to Venice and had taken up residence in the nearby Ca' Mocenigo in order to meet him.[75] Other visitors who came to Venice specifically to greet the king included the duke of Mantua and the Grand Prior of France, Henry's natural brother.[76] These private receptions of important guests, whether for familial or political reasons, took place in the days immediately following the entry itself, in accordance with contemporary notions of decorum.[77]

On his first important official occasion Henry was collected by the doge and Senate in the Bucintoro, and taken to the landing stage close to the Ponte della Paglia. Winding its way through the Piazzetta to the west door of San Marco, a scarlet awning had been erected, supported on columns swathed in silks of the royal colours. As soon as the Bucintoro came into view, the bells of the basilica began to ring, and welcoming rounds of artillery fire were discharged from the lines of galleys that had been drawn up in front of the island of San Giorgio Maggiore. After disembarking, Henry processed to the basilica, accompanied by the cardinal legate and the doge, under a baldachin carried by six procurators, led by the ubiquitous halberdiers, trumpeters and drummers and preceded by the dukes of Nevers and Savoy. Having being welcomed at the west door by the canons, together with the *primicerio* and the patriarch, the entire assembly moved inside; Henry knelt in front of the high altar, and a sequence of music, now impossible to identify with specific pieces, was performed by the choir.[78] Following this, prayers calling for divine protection of the king were read by the patriarch.[79] Once this ceremony had finished, a banquet for 3,000 guests was held in the Doge's Palace,[80] followed by the performance of Frangipane's *Tragedia*.[81] In common with Henry's entry at the Lido, this sequence of events achieved its effect through a discrete combination of religious and civic elements.

After the banquet in the Sala del Maggior Consiglio, during which 'musiche e concenti divini dai più eccellenti musici d'Europa' brought to Venice specially for the occasion was heard,[82] the evening's entertainment began. One of the booklets published to commemorate Henry's visit describes an introductory dumb-show, in which Jove, Juno and Venus, together with Amphion and Orpheus, offered gifts to Henry and then recited verses in his honour.[83] Frangipane's play then opened with an instrumental prelude for fifteen trumpets and five percussion players (most probably drummers), after which Proteus, 'pastor del mare', took to the stage and began to sing to the accompaniment of a lute:[84]

> Have set out from Neptune's realm,
> Where I abandoned my marine shoals;
> And I have come to these shores
> To watch such glorious spectacles . . .

There can hardly be any question, at this early date, that this forty-line prologue was set to composed monody of the kind introduced into the early Florentine operas of some twenty-five years later. It is more probable that Proteus embellished a set of formulaic melodies of the kind familiar from sung performances of extracts from Ariosto's *Orlando furioso* and other epics.[85] This may have been lifted out of stock or, alternatively, might have been composed by Claudio Merulo, first organist at San Marco since 1557, and an experienced composer who already had some experience of working in the theatre; he it was who had been responsible for the music for Lodovico Dolce's play *Le Troiane*, given in Venice in 1566 with Antonio Molino as the principal actor. This is just one indication of Merulo's connections with the musicians and writers who gathered around Molino in the 1560s,[86] which must have given the composer both contacts and experience that would have been useful when he came to write music for the *Tragedia*. It should be emphasized that while this play is short, and must be properly thought of as a kind of detached theatre-piece rather than a fully fledged sung drama, the presence of passages for one and two voices is a significant departure from standard procedure, while the opening song for Proteus, designed to present the general theme of the entertainment, prefigures what was to become standard practice in early opera.

Frangipane's play itself consists of a sequence of speeches, choruses and instrumental interludes stitched together in a continuous musical fabric; that it was sung throughout is evident both from rubrics in the libretto, indicating that some passages were for solo voice and at least one for two, and from the explicit statement printed at the end of the text. In other words, his model was that of Greek tragedy, sung throughout.[87] The idea was not without precedent, but it was still rather new in Venice, its immediate forebears being two *rappresentazioni* by Celio Magno, including his *Trionfo di Christo* of 1571, written to celebrate the victory at Lepanto. In this sense, the Venetian tradition of plays sung throughout is an important foreshadowing of the prehistory of opera itself, usually presented as an essentially Florentine phenomenon, ballasted by the antiquarian researches of Girolomo Mei and others.[88] Clearly indebted to the *intermedio* tradition, both in terms of its length as well as in its instrumental resources, which was such a feature of that tradition,[89] the piece is nonetheless notable for being sung throughout, a procedure that the author justifies through reference to ancient practice.[90]

In the following days Henry was accorded various honours that emphasized his rank and status, the most prestigious of which was his participation in a specially convoked session of the Great Council, at which he personally nominated Jacopo Contarini as a senator of the Consiglio de' Pregadi. This had been prepared for during the previous day, when both Henry and the duke of Savoy were made members of the Venetian nobility by the Council of Ten,[91] so that they were legally qualified to participate in the election. During a visit to the Arsenal, the king was shown the armoury together with captured war trophies, including the most recent ones brought back from Lepanto. Accompanied by members of the nobility, and the four ambassadors who had originally welcomed him on his arrival in Friuli, Henry was also treated to a display in which a group of workers outfitted (or constructed *ex novo* according to some accounts) a galley for war in less than the time it took for the king to be given a banquet lunch.[92] Henry was also offered refreshment in the form of sugar sculptures, designed by the artist Niccolò di Pigna in the shape of gods, goddesses and exotic animals; a similar display was presented during the ball given in the Doge's Palace a few days later, when 300 figures were provided for the admiration and delectation of the guests. The next morning the king heard a sung mass at which polyphony was performed,[93] before returning to Ca' Foscari, where Luigi Groto delivered an oration in his honour.

Later the same day Henry was again collected in the Bucintoro and taken to the Doge's Palace where a ball, attended by some two hundred of the most beautiful aristocratic women of the city (it is reported), was held in the Sala del Gran Consiglio, richly adorned for the occasion with coloured fabrics, flowers and Turkish rugs. The event had been organized by one of the *compagnie della calza*, the associations of unmarried young patricians who organized festivities in the city, and who were particularly active during Carnival. Their curious name derived from their habit of wearing brightly coloured hose. An important arena for male sociability, the *compagnie* stage-managed a wide range of entertainments both public and private, from banquets to firework displays and momaria (allegorical pantomimes often acted on boats), to performances of comedies by Plautus and Terence. These socially beneficial functions usefully harnessed youthful energies to projects that required skill and organizational ability.[94] As was usual during the visits of foreign princes, the Venetian sumptuary laws had been suspended for the entire period of Henry's stay. Common throughout Italy, these regulations had been developed in a particularly elaborate way in Venice, to produce an intricate and detailed system of sartorial control. Due to its importance as a centre of both trade and commerce, the city boasted an extensive trade in luxury goods. Drawn up for a mixture of moral, economic and socio-political motives, the sumptuary laws were intended to control public displays of wealth by private individuals; applied with vigour, and frequently revised to take account of fresh developments, they were primarily designed to encourage abstemiousness in the midst of plenty.[95] Henry's visit, regarded as a social high point even in this most cosmopolitan and ceremonial of cities, provided a rare opportunity for display.[96] The patrician women who gathered in the Sala del Gran Consiglio were uniformly dressed in white, and wore the finest jewels (pl. 105). Their purpose was to dance.

As to how the dancing started and what exactly took place, the sources differ, some saying that forty gentlemen, some French and others Italian, passed in front of the king as they each danced with two ladies. This arrangement *à trois* is unusual; it seems more likely that this first dance, which was a *pavana*, was performed by couples as described by Rocco Benedetti. At the end two more expert couples danced the *gagliarda* 'molto bene'.[97] Although Henry was enthusiastic about dancing, he did not participate but sat under a baldachin to watch the proceedings. It seems that the experience made a deep impression on the king and other members of his entourage, and that after his return to France it reinforced his taste for such

105   Giacomo Franco, *Ball in the Ducal Palace in Honour of a Visiting Prince*, engraving. Venice, Museo Civico Correr.

things. All the French depictions of formal dancing, whether social or specially choreographed (as in the well-known case of the *Ballet comique*), can be associated with Henry and his court (pl. 106).[98]

In sharp contrast to the elegance of this event was the traditional battle between opposing factions, which the king witnessed on the following day. This traditional ritual was fixed around the Castellani (who took their name from the *sestiere* of Castello at the north-eastern extremity of the island) and the Nicolotti (from the parish of San Nicolò), who fought for possession of the bridge at the Carmini.[99] Traditionally, the Nicolotti were mostly fisherman, the Castellani workers in the Arsenal (*arsenalotti*). By the time of Henry's visit, these two factions effectively divided the city between them, with the boundary dividing the city more or less in half. Excluded were the 'official' areas at the Rialto and the Piazza San Marco, neutral sites of commercial and government activity, as well as the Merceria that joins them. This partition naturally gave certain bridges prominence as the focal points for the *battagliole*, brawls fought with sharpened sticks or canes from the lagoon known as *canne d'India*,[100] which usually coincided with some of the major festivals of the Venetian year – includ-

106   Anonymous, *A Ball at the Valois Court*, late 16th century. Kent, Penshurst Place.

ing All Saints, Santa Giustina and Christmas – when the fleet was idle, the *arse-nalotti* were not at work, and many (including the authorities) were drawn to the Piazza San Marco to witness the official ceremonies (pl. 107). Whilst the procession in the square, with the doge at its centre, represented decorum, power and order, the *battagliola*, staged in a more peripheral area of the city, expressed the contrary. These occasions constituted an exercise in plebeian chaos that inverted the solemnity of the patrician rituals enacted elsewhere (for instance in the *andata*) in a way that parallels the 'world turned upside-down' spirit of Carnival, and in particular the excesses of Giovedì Grasso.[101] In this context, the decision to stage this bloody and dangerous spectacle, in which each faction was said to be 300 strong, to entertain the visiting monarch (something similar had been organized for Alfonso II's visit to the city twelve years earlier)[102] was an appropriation, on the part of the ruling elite, of a disruptive and even subversive element of popular culture; this had the effect, if only on this occasion, of neutralizing its power.

It also sanitized it. The use of the traditional pointed canes, soaked with boiling oil to make them more effective, was forbidden, and the hundreds of spectators who crowded the balconies, windows and roofs of the surrounding buildings were prevented from showering the combatants with stones and other missiles.[103] In effect, the *battagliola* had been reduced to a mere fistfight. For Henry's visit the bridge of the Carmini had been selected as the battleground, rather than the Ponte dei Pugni at San Barnaba, which, by the late sixteenth century, had become the most popular venue for the contest; this was so that Henry, accompanied by the duke of Nevers and other high-ranking members of his entourage, could watch from the balcony of Palazzo Foscarini, the property of one of the four ambassadors who had escorted him from Verzon, which lies directly opposite the bridge.[104] During the morning the crowds arrived both on foot to line the *fondamente* and in gondolas to secure a good view. The spectacle began with a contest involving the principal pugilist from each faction, both of whom had fought with distinction at

107   Giacomo Franco, *War of the Fists*, engraving. Venice, Museo Civico Correr.

Lepanto;[105] thereafter it degenerated into a more general brawl fought with sticks by the two 'armies', each dressed in uniforms of blue and white.[106] This was a seriously bloodthirsty business; as an encouragement to make it so Zuane Cocalini, the commander of the Nicolotti, had reminded his men in his pre-battle oration that in 1555 more than thirty Castellani had been beaten to death or drowned. Originally, it had been planned that there should be twelve one-on-one duels at intervals, but in the event only five could be staged before the two factions rushed to the bridge and fought violently. After almost two hours of fighting, Henry made a sign that the battle should stop. Despite attempts to dignify the proceedings in the printed accounts (one pamphleteer compared this institutionalized violence to the gladiatorial battles of the ancient Romans),[107] the effects of the brutality were evident: some contestants fell into the water (where a number, including a woman disguised as a man, drowned); many fell to the ground and were trampled underfoot; and others were seriously wounded. According to one report, the king wryly remarked that if the event was intended as a joke it was too much, and if serious really too little.[108]

Quite apart from these public and official occasions, Henry also found time for more private amusements: a visit to the shops in the Merceria, another to the Fondaco dei Tedeschi, lunch with the French ambassador and another with the patriarch, some time with Veronica Franco (the most celebrated of the Venetian courtesans) and a private viewing of the famous collection of antiquities at the Palazzo Grimani at Santa Maria Formosa.[109] During his few days in Venice Henry satisfied his princely tastes with purchases of glass, jewels and paintings, visited Titian's studio and bought a painting from Tintoretto.[110]

On his final day in Venice, Henry was once more accompanied by the doge and Signoria to the Doge's Palace, where mass was heard in a private chapel. To the cheers of the assembled crowds, a flotilla of brightly decorated gondolas steered by oarsmen in livery then accompanied both doge and king to Fusina. There, after the parting compliments had been exchanged, and Henry had presented Mocenigo with a diamond ring, said by some to have been valued at 10,000 ducats, in gratitude for the many favours and courtesies that he had received during his visit,[111] the royal party took to the Brenta canal in a gilded barge. Along the route to Padua it stopped first at the Villa Foscari and later at Federico Contarini's villa at Mira. As in Venice itself, these arrangements bestowed honour and status upon the more powerful patrician families who had been involved in the arrangements for the king's visit.

Of a number of different themes that can be detected in the arrangements made to celebrate Henry III's visit to Venice and the Veneto, the most persistent relates to the king's title of 'His Most Christian Majesty'. Henry's worthiness to inherit this title from Charles IX had been transformed into necessary action through the suppression of the Protestants, a policy that reached a climax with the infamous massacre of 24 August 1572, the details of which were reported to the Senate by the two Venetian ambassadors to the court of France, Giovanni Michiel and Alvise Contarini.[112] In common with the papal court, the Venetians viewed the events of St Bartholomew's Day as essential to the salvation of France and, more generally, as serving the interests of the Catholic world; it was widely known that the Huguenot party had made common cause with Elizabeth I of England, the German Protestants and the Dutch Calvinists in the hope of mobilizing France against the Spanish presence in Flanders.[113] Read in the context of the mutual suspicion and hostility between Venice and Spain that worsened during 1572, as the allies failed to galvanize the Holy League into further action against the Turks, and only deepened further after the Venetian–Turkish peace of the following year, the warmth with which Henry's visit was greeted becomes comprehensible.

Understandably enough, in the light of Venetian strivings to establish a more effective alliance with the French, the Christian motif was uppermost in the arrangements that were made to welcome Henry onto Venetian soil. At Treviso Henry had been met by the bishop, Giorgio Cornaro, together with the clergy of the city, who are said to have received him with 'solemn sacred ceremonies'. Dismounting from his horse, the king genuflected in front of a cross, prayers were said and the kiss of peace and the bishop's blessing were given. The procession then made its way to the cathedral, where further religious ceremonies took place. It was only after this that the proceedings took on a more civic character, as Henry was escorted to the main square of the city along a route decorated with triumphal arches. Even here, for all the classical allusions that were made through inscriptions and statuary, the central theme was essentially Catholic, with the king presented as the true defender of the faith and the heroic oppressor of rebels and heretics.[114] Something similar happened at Padua, where Henry was greeted at one of the city gates by a great assembly of the clergy carrying relics and other sacred objects. Although the king stayed in Padua only overnight, he heard mass and, at his own request, visited the Santo.[115] In Venice itself, Henry's role, as an indefatigable defender of Catholicism against all kinds of heresy, inevitably coloured the official ceremonies in San Marco.[116] There he knelt in front of the high altar, on which the most precious relics of the basilica had been displayed. This was a traditional feature of the arrangements made for distinguished visitors; when Bona Sforza visited San Marco, she was shown the relics of the True Cross, one of the nails with which Christ had been crucified, a fragment of the column at which he had been whipped, and the relic of the Precious Blood normally displayed to the Venetians only on Holy Saturday.[117] After Henry had taken communion, music for two organs was played by Andrea Gabrieli and Claudio Merulo, after which the choir under Zarlino's direction sang some short responses, followed by a polychoral setting of the Te Deum, while the king remained kneeling. The proceedings closed with prayers said by the patriarch, calling upon God to show divine favour to His Most Christian Majesty.

If this was one important message, another was the persistent portrayal of Venice as a New Rome, superior to that of the ancient world by virtue of its Christianity. The most obvious visual expression of this idea was the construction of Palladio's temporary structures at the Lido in a style that evoked parallels with Sansovino's grand scheme in the Piazza. There were musical analogies as well, notably Zarlino's Latin dialogue performed at San Nicolò and Cornelio Frangipane's *Tragedia* with Merulo's music. In this sense, Henry's visit seems to have provoked an official response in which some of the most important local artists, architects and musicians collaborated in the production of ceremonial and theatrical spectacles united by the classicizing theme. The enthusiasm and splendour with which Henry was received in Venice, reported in printed accounts published not only in Venice but also in Paris and Lyons, could only have strengthened his image at home. For the Venetians themselves, the visit of His Most Christian Majesty was seen not only as an opportune moment to strengthen an important alliance with one of the two great European powers, but also a sign, much needed in the aftermath of their peace treaty with the Turks, of the continuing special status of the Venetians in the eyes of the Almighty. It was an impression that was to be short-lived.

CHAPTER EIGHT

The Hand of God

In the summer of 1575, Matteo Farcinatore and Lucia Cadorino, recently arrived in Venice from their home in the Val Sugana near Trent, took lodgings together with their children in the house of Vincenzo Franceschi in the parish of San Marziale. Within a few days all the members of the family fell ill and died. Their clothes, sold to pay for the funeral expenses, found their way into other hands, and soon more deaths occurred.[1] The officials of the health board, the *provveditori alla sanità*, took possession of the house, and having arranged for the bodies to be medically examined, declared that all had died from the plague. The terrible epidemic that was to rage in Venice for the best part of two years, destroying more than a quarter of the population in the process, had begun.

This simple version of events, endlessly repeated and elaborated by contemporary observers of the Venetian scene, from the anonymous authors of popular pamphlets to cultivated commentators such as Rocco Benedetti, Alessandro Canobbio and the papal nuncio Giambattista Castagna, includes a number of characteristic features.[2] The search for a single individual as the author of the crime is typical, as is the charge that the city had been infected by an outsider, in this case by a foreigner who came from beyond the Venetian dominions.[3] Nor is the story necessarily without some foundation. Outbreaks of plague had occurred in Trent in 1574 and again in the following year, and the city was an important commercial crossroads, occupying a significant position in the web of trade routes across the Alps. Well connected to important trading centres on both sides of the mountains, it was also the place where merchants from both north and south gathered once a year for St John's Fair. In the eyes of at least one chronicler, Trent was indeed the source of the epidemic, while according to another it had merely arrived

108 Anonymous, the Madonna Nicopeia, early 12th century. San Marco.

there from Hungary, having been spread easily along the Danube and the Adige and from Trent to Verona, Mantua and finally Venice itself.[4] Another opinion, quite commonly held, was that the infection had arrived in some mysterious and imprecise way from the Muslim world.[5] Although sixteenth-century science was unaware of the aetiology of the plague, the Venetians knew from long experience that merchandise from the East and serious epidemics often travelled together.

By the autumn of 1575 it was already clear beyond any shadow of doubt that the disease had taken root in the city. The *provveditori* had moved quickly to put a number of traditional measures in place, including the removal and subsequent burning of the possessions of the afflicted, and the purgation of their houses. The Florentine representative in Venice, under no doubt that he was witnessing 'true' plague, noted the daily publication of the numbers of dead and the frequent transports of 'white boats' to the plague hospitals in the lagoon.[6] The bodies were buried in deep trenches at the Lazzaretto Vecchio, which also accommodated hopeless cases, while those thought to be capable of recovery were sent to the Lazzaretto Nuovo to be cured. As the epidemic took hold temporary wooden shacks were erected, 500 alone on the island of Le Vignole.[7] Most of these procedures were carried out during the hours of darkness so as not to cause public alarm.[8]

In following them, the health board was to some extent drawing upon accumulated experience. The Lazzaretto Vecchio, built on a small island in the lagoon about two miles from the city, had been founded by Senate decree as early as 1423, and in 1490 the health board had been established, initially with responsibility for the city, but later with jurisdiction over the *terraferma* as well. By the early years of the sixteenth century, largely because of their status and their ability to organize remedial measures effectively, its officials had transformed their position into one of considerable political leverage. Following the epidemic of 1527–9, when the *provveditori* began to control policy during outbreaks of plague on the *terraferma*, the administrative structure of the board, now centralized and increased in size and strength, adopted a more coherent policy. After 1530 Venice suffered from outbreaks of the plague on only a few occasions in comparison with other large cities. As the events of 1575 demonstrated only too clearly, this lack of recent experience, combined with conflicting advice from the medical profession, could undermine the board's efforts to tackle the disease.[9] The previous outbreak, in 1556, had been minor, and the terrible effects of the Black Death of 1348 had long vanished from the collective memory, though the plague tracts continued to mention them.[10] The epidemic of 1575–7 caught the authorities unawares.

At the same time as the health board was putting legislation into place in the last months of 1575, the Venetians were strenuously denying to the outside world that there was any cause for alarm. In this the authorities were encouraged by some physicians, who argued that as long as only a few cases had been reported, the disease could not be considered as 'true' plague, since the same air was common to all.[11] The papal nuncio, Castagna, noted with surprise the authorities' determination that life should continue as normal, despite the increased risks of contamination that were the inevitable consequence of travel, trade and commerce. Worse, he encountered a stubborn refusal among government officials to acknowledge that any serious problem existed. In November Castagna reported to Pope Gregory XIII his view that the plague was genuine, while the Venetian Senate, for its part, sought to convince the nuncio that, even if there had been some sort of disease in the city, the outbreak was now virtually over and there was no longer any danger. The nuncio remained unimpressed. 'Anyone who says that there is no plague in Venice at the moment', he observed drily, 'is simply telling an enormous lie.'[12]

It is not hard to imagine some of the political motivations that lay behind the official attitude, and Castagna, an acute and critical observer of Venetian affairs, must have been aware of them too. At the heart of Venetian policy lay the continuing question-mark that hung over the Republic's relationship with the Turks. Lepanto had done a great deal for Venetian morale, but it had achieved little else either economically or politically, and it was now more than two years since the separate peace treaty had been signed. Publicly presented as an honourable agreement, in practice the terms were far from good from a Venetian perspective. Peace had certainly been purchased and continuing trade with the eastern Mediterranean assured, but at the cost of considerable financial sacrifice, and with a noticeable loss of face. Cyprus, the original cause of the conflict, had been permanently lost. The heavy expenses incurred by the war itself were now compounded by the longer-term effects upon Venice's finances, industry and trade of a three-year struggle that had brought the Republic little practical benefit. Obliged by the treaty to limit their fleet to just sixty galleys, the Venetians feared a rapid Turkish rearmament with the objective of adding Corfu and Crete to the growing list of conquered Adriatic outposts. In the end, internal politics, fears of a new Holy League and perhaps the rumours circulated by the *bailò* that, despite everything, the Venetians remained at a high level of military readiness, combined to dissuade the Turks from embarking upon fresh anti-Venetian manoeuvres. In the meantime, the thought that a new conflict in the East might be added to the already paralysing effects of the plague conditioned the thinking of the Venetian patriciate in matters of both foreign affairs and public health. It is no surprise to find Venetian diplomats abroad systematically painting a reassuring picture of conditions in the city and insisting upon the effectiveness of the measures being taken by the authorities, while at the same time dramatically underestimating the mortality rate. The ploy was so successful that the pamphleteer Alessandro Canobbio, writing from no further away than Padua, was able to claim that the health board had successfully eliminated the first phase of the epidemic at an early stage.[13]

This policy of counter-intelligence and misinformation was followed not only in the autumn and winter of 1575, when the number of victims was comparatively low, but even during the terrible summer months of 1576, when the plague was at its height, and its pitiful consequences dramatically evident. By then, according to one observer, the daily death-toll had risen to 700,[14] but even so, the Venetian Resident in Milan was calmly claiming that whether or not the epidemic was really the plague still remained a matter of dispute among the medical authorities, and that it was only the lower orders ('la gente bassa') who had been affected.[15] This was a common argument, even among doctors, many of whom adopted the view that if the number of deaths was low, and was concentrated among the poor, then the disease could not be the plague.[16] This traditional definition, contested by other authorities, was politically convenient, and it is not surprising that the doge and the officials of the board were convinced by it. 'If', the official historian Andrea Morosini wrote, 'it were noised abroad that the city was in the grip of a pestilential disease, terror would arise in every estate, customs revenue would be diminished, the traders of Europe and Asia would recoil from the city, and enemies of the Republic would be incited to revolt.'[17] Nonetheless, as the Florentine Resident noted, deaths among the patriciate occurred with some frequency.[18] Morosini's view was entirely characteristic of the official stance. The Republic's ability to trade with outsiders, and in particular to build up its contacts with the East, substantially damaged during the War of Cyprus and only partially recovered as a result of the peace, was paramount. Also important was the public image of Venice as a powerful state capable of dealing effectively with both internal division and external aggression. In order to preserve these traditional components of Venetian mythology, the patriciate colluded in suppressing the gravity of the situation. The claim that there was a connection between poor living conditions and the spread of the epidemic was accepted by the government, even though it ran counter to the position of the health board. A number of counter-measures were discussed. One of the most ambitious, a scheme to evacuate the poor to wooden shacks in the countryside, remained only a proposal for the time being, but it served as a reminder that the state was capable of hesitation in the face of that most drastic of measures, the imposition of a general quarantine. On the surface, matters were under control.

The truth was somewhat different. On the basis of the health board's records, it has been calculated that, from 1 July 1575 until February 1576, 3,446 people died of the plague in Venice, while from 1 March 1576 until 28 February 1577, 43,025 perished. To this awesome total should be added another three or four thousand who died in the final months of the disease, before it finally abated in July 1577. Certainly, the true scale of the epidemic was known to some of the chroniclers, who report mortality rates that are reasonably close to the figures recorded by the health board; it seems likely that the true scale of the tragedy was generally known.[19] Since the total population of the city stood at about 180,000 in the autumn of 1575, it would seem that about 26 per cent of the total Venetian population lost their lives in the outbreak of the disease. Although this is not as high as the figure for the ferocious plague of 1630–31, for which an estimated 32 per cent of the city's inhabitants perished, it is nevertheless very considerable in comparison with other contemporary outbreaks of the plague.[20]

Behind the impersonality of the statistics lies the horror of a collective traumatic experience that was truly frightening in its dimensions. Initially hopes ran high, when two distinguished lecturers in physic from Padua, Girolamo Mercuriale and Girolamo Capodivacca, were invited to give their opinions on the nature of the epidemic, which by then had been afflicting the city for several months. At first they were welcomed as saviours, and flattering comparisons with Sts Cosmas and Damian, the patrons of their profession, were made. Every morning, they went out to visit the sick in gondolas, together with a Jesuit who heard confessions. On arrival, they threw open the windows and fumigated each room, but praise for their courage (they did not hesitate to touch the afflicted) rapidly turned to delusion and ridicule as the disease continued unabated, and the mortality rate increased despite their ministrations.[21] Nevertheless, the visit of the Paduan doctors, short-lived and ineffective though it was, did bring some benefits.

The sheer desperation felt by the Venetians, as the death-toll mounted, made them particularly susceptible to all kinds of alleged remedies – medical, pseudo-medical and superstitious. Francesco Rodoano, one of the many doctors, quacks and charlatans to apply to the government with offers of miraculous cures, was given permission to experiment on the sick with his 'secret antidotes'. Another, Ascanio Olivieri, a doctor at the Lazzaretto Vecchio, was paid by the health board for the recipe of his miraculous remedy, which was then made freely available. The existence of the cure was publicly advertised at both the Rialto and San Marco, and thirteen pharmacists (*speziali*) were officially licensed to make up the preparation.[22] A Flemish merchant, Antonio Valtemo (Gualtiero), promised to free the city from the disease in eight days if his prescription, which involved the infected drinking a concoction that included three drops of their urine, was followed.[23] Since both official and unofficial measures failed, sacrificial victims were sought. Even cultivated commentators questioned whether the unfortunate Farcinatore had deliberately introduced the plague to Venice out of malice. Others blamed the *picegamorti* (the band of vagabonds, refugees from the galleys and other unfortunates who had been employed to remove corpses), allegedly keen to profit from the thefts that their grim trade made possible. In the seemingly endless task of removing the bodies as quickly as possible, even criminals had been brought in from the prisons and promised liberty in return for transporting the dead.[24] Other sections of public opinion attributed the disease to the *untori* (anointers), who roamed the street by night, spreading the blood of the infected on the doors of the healthy; if discovered, these malefactors were publicly tortured and executed.[25] After much debate, it was finally decided to build 1,200 wooden shelters, 200 for each *sestiere*, on the Lido at public expense; these were assigned to the healthy poor, so that they could escape the city and take fresh air and recreation in order to avoid infection.[26] In addition, the Lazzaretto Nuovo was enlarged

109 Government publication of a
papal indulgence for the plague.
Venice, MS Donà delle Rose MS.
181/14.

by a fleet of some three thousand boats anchored around it, making it possible to accommodate approximately ten thousand patients.[27] The islands of San Lazzaro, San Clemente, Sant'Erasmo, Sant'Elena and Mazzorbo, as well as parts of the Lido, were all pressed into service, but despite the amount of available space, the conditions still remained intolerable. According to one account, there were between seven and eight thousand patients at the Lazzaretto Vecchio when the plague was at its height in the summer of 1576. Beds were in short supply, staff hard to find, and the stench and sufferings of the sick appalling.[28]

By July 1576 the habit of posting lists of the dead at the Pietra del Bando in the Piazza was abandoned, since the numbers had become so great that the effect on public morale was thought to be damaging. In the same month, a papal indulgence was granted to all those suffering from the 'mal contagioso', together with those who attended them, or were working in other ways to eliminate the disease (pl. 109).[29] Foreign merchants and diplomats had long ago returned home. Lawyers and other professionals had also stopped work, and had left for the countryside, and nearly all the shops in the city were closed.[30] Even the narrow street where the prostitutes operated at Rialto was shut down, and the girls packed off to work in the Lazzaretto Vecchio.[31] No sounds of enjoyment were to be heard in this half-abandoned city, just the anguished cries of the suffering.[32] According to one eyewitness, the city had become so totally abandoned that it was possible to walk from the Rialto to San Marco without encountering a soul. Grass had begun to grow between the cobblestones, and by July the depopulation of the city had become so grave that the Senate was forced to introduce punishments for patricians who abandoned their official duties.[33] Perhaps inevitably, Savonarolan figures emerged from the shadows, cursing the wickedness of the city and promising salvation through repentance. On three successive evenings an unknown man appeared, crucifix in hand, to lead a crowd chanting litanies to the church of San Rocco, after which he disappeared as quickly as he had arrived.[34] In October the order was given that the inhabitants of the three most affected *sestieri* (Castello, Cannaregio and San Marco) should be confined to their houses for fifteen days. The experiment was not continued beyond that period, since the death-rate had now dropped to thirty or forty a day, perhaps, wrote one commentator, because winter had set in.[35] A census taken at the time revealed that the population then stood at more than 40,000 less than two months previously.[36] With memories of the recent war fresh in their minds, the authorities made special arrangements to ensure that work in the Arsenal continued.[37] At the beginning of November new methods of disinfecting 'suspected' linen and textiles taken from plague houses were used, apparently for the first time.[38] During earlier epidemics the Venetian government had adopted legislation to destroy the possessions of the plague dead, and to prohibit the trade in used goods (particularly second-hand clothing and stuffs).[39] The burning of goods was now halted, and in its place a new procedure was adopted in which textiles were boiled, while merchandise continued to be aired. Incense placed over burning charcoal for a day and a night was advocated as a disinfectant to be used indoors.[40] Books and documents, thought to be particularly dangerous as carriers of the disease, were to be fumigated.[41]

Some idea of the sense of complete hopelessness felt by the Venetians in the face of a rampaging disease that struck quickly and mercilessly, without respect for class, age or sex, comes through poignantly in the apocalyptic and desperate tones in which some of the contemporary chroniclers described daily life in these months of terror. None is as eloquent as Benedetti:

> The plague continued, killing more people with every hour that passed, and every day inspiring greater terror and deeper compassion for its poor infected victims. Onlookers wept, as these people were carried down to their doors by their sons, fathers and mothers, and there in the public eye their bodies were stripped naked and shown to the doctors to be assessed. The same had to be done for the dead, and I myself had to carry down three whom I had lost: my mother, my brother and a nephew. Neither in life nor in death had they shown any symptom of plague, but they were assessed by the parish doctor as 'of concern', and, since there was an order that [two] cases 'of concern' were equivalent to one 'of suspicion', I was compelled to spend forty days confined at home.
>
> The fate of those who lived alone was wretched, for, if they happened to fall ill, there was no one to lend them any assistance, and they died in misery. And, when two or three days had passed without their appearing and giving an account of themselves, their deaths were suspected. And then the corpse-bearers, entering the houses by breaking down the doors or climbing through the windows, found them dead in their beds or on the floors or in other places to which the frenzy of the disease had carried them.
>
> It was a frightful sight to see the thousands of houses around the city crossed with wooden planks as a sign of plague. But even more horrifying was the spectacle of so many boats plying continuously back and forth: some being towed by other boats to quarantine at the Lazzaretto Nuovo; some heading out to certain appointed places, loaded up with the mortal remains of the wretched and luckless victims; some returning to the city laden with poor unfortunate widows and orphans who had completed their quarantine. Thinking it a miracle that they had been restored to life, they did not cease to offer up to heaven praise and thanks to the Lord God. All these things represented a sad and sorrowful triumph of death. . . .

But, to leave the city and turn to the pesthouses, I say truly that on the one hand the Lazzaretto Vecchio seemed like Hell itself. From every side came foul odours, indeed a stench that none could endure; groans and sighs were heard without ceasing; and at all hours clouds of smoke from the burning of corpses were seen to rise far into the air. Some who miraculously returned from that place alive reported, among other things, that at the height of that great influx of infected people, there were three or four of them to a bed. Since a great number of servants had died, and there was no one to take care of them, they had to get themselves up to take food and attend to other things. Nobody did anything but lift the dead from the beds and throw them into the pits. It often happened that those who were close to death or senseless, without speech or movement, were lifted up by the corpse-bearers as though they had expired, and thrown onto the heap of bodies. Should one of them be seen to move hand or foot, or signal for help, it was truly good fortune if some corpse-bearer, moved to pity, took the trouble to go and rescue him. And many, driven to frenzy by the disease, especially at night, leapt from their beds, and, shouting with the fearful voices of damned souls, went here and there, colliding with one another, and suddenly falling to the ground dead. Some who rushed in frenzy out of the wards threw themselves into the water, or ran madly through the gardens, and were found dead among the thornbushes, all covered with blood . . .

To sum it all up, in maintaining so many people and bearing such expense, the doge spent a huge sum of money. Administration became chaotic, so that all the *Savi* were bewildered, not seeing how to provide for so great a need, nor which course to take to protect us from such a hail of arrows, showered down in all directions by the plague.[42]

During these years the Venetians prayed a great deal, both in private and in public, to be released from the horrors of the plague. Whatever the physicians might say (which in any case was often contradictory and confusing), the people were less convinced by medical theories than by traditional belief. In particular, there was a widespread attachment to the notion, derived from Hebrew tradition, that all pestilence was visited upon a sinful nation as divine retribution, as with the plagues of Egypt or the epidemic that broke out among the Philistines after their capture of the Ark. When God's anger was expressed against states, recourse to prayer and repentance was essential. Processions and the worship of relics were fundamental weapons. Amulets, charms and written prayers worn on the body protected the individual.[43]

Undeterred by the ineffectiveness of their appeals, the Venetians continued to pray. An important aspect of contemporary spiritual thought was that serious transgression could be redeemed only through great effort. The extent of God's anger, visible to all in the mounds of corpses heaped on the barges of the *piaceg-amorti*, inevitably required urgent and persistent intercession through prayer, charitable works and communal spiritual exercises. A strong sense of the *respublica Christiana*, an integrated state of mind in which a strong sense of religion and a deep attachment to the state overlapped to the point of indissolubility, had long been present in the Venetian mentality, and the idea of collective guilt, of the need for atonement for the city's sins, was expressed strongly and frequently during the plague years, though not always with official approval. When the printer Pietro de Faris, who had a workshop near the Greek church and sold his broadsheets near the Piazza San Marco, printed a sequence of prayers promising immunity from the plague to all who recited them three times, making the sign of the cross on each occasion, the Holy Office took a hand.[44]

In terms of action, the emphasis on prayer, piety and penitence induced an intense atmosphere of collective devotion strongly framed by Tridentine thinking. Sermons, processions and fasting were the most common expressions of collective atonement, and 'good works' the principal means of expiation. Every evening at the Lazzaretto Nuovo as the Ave Maria sounded, the voices of the afflicted could be heard singing psalms and litanies, 'una harmonia mirabile di diversi voci' says Sansovino.[45] Both the civic and ecclesiastical authorities actively encouraged popular involvement in the common responsibility of repentance. In August 1576 the government called on all Venetians to continue to pray and fast, and a few days later the patriarch laid down a precise set of instructions for the faithful to follow, which included prayers at home, work and in the street, supplemented by acts of mortification. Although ordinary Venetians responded best to these exhortations, among patricians the call to religion was also taken seriously. When, on 14 August 1576 (the feast of San Rocco), a large crowd gathered in front of the church dedicated to the saint, every parish of Venice was represented by a delegation made up not only of *cittadini* and ordinary parishioners, but also patricians. Led by the local priest carrying a cross, these groups formed a procession of atonement; as they walked, prayers were recited and litanies chanted.

Contrary to some medical thinking, which was doubtful about allowing free public association, believed only to encourage the spread of the disease, public expiation through prayer and procession was one of the church's main strategies to combat the epidemic. Here, as in other areas (such as trade with the outside world), official opinion was often divided about how to react. At a popular level it was strongly believed that both scriptural authority and previous experience dictated that divine anger could be placated only through public displays of humility and devotion.[46] On the other hand, the health board, believing that crowds only encouraged the disease to spread, was in favour of preventing church services and processions. That the plague was contagious had been claimed by chroniclers and historians at least since the Black Death of 1348; it was believed at the time that the disease spread when crowds gathered, and that it could be transmitted by smell, touch, breath and even sight. By the end of the fourteenth century no one doubted that the plague was contagious, and by the fifteenth most authorities agreed that contagion was a sign of the presence of 'true' plague rather than any other epidemic. Plague legislation limiting both trade and travel was put in place during outbreaks in a number of north Italian towns and cities (including Venice) as early as the 1420s, and medical tracts from the same period speak of the danger of mixing in groups, an extension of the simple diagnostic observation that once one member of a family or religious community had contracted the disease, the rest were likely to follow.[47] For much of the fifteenth century, the religious interpretation had triumphed over the contagionist one, which gave an entirely secular account of the plague and its causes. In this context, any action that limited the opportunities for cult activities would lead only to an increase rather than a diminution of the epidemic. During the plague of 1575–7, these conflicting arguments became subservient to Counter-Reformation doctrines, which gave fresh impetus to the old idea of pestilence as God's punishment, and encouraged the Venetians to respond with the traditional means of prayer, fasting, good works and processions. The last, to be held on three successive days, (Thursday, Friday and Saturday), were strongly advocated by the patriarch, who urged that prayers be said and litanies sung 'per impetrar più facilmente la misericordia divina'. Shops were to close while these communal acts of contrition took place.[48]

In practice, these processions, which were semi-liturgical, recited a precise sequence of prayers 'in tempore pestis et mortalitatis', as printed in one of the most popular of contemporary manuals, Alberto da Castello's *Liber sacerdotalis*, as well as in a number of liturgical books which give the San Marco usage.[49] Beginning with the antiphon 'Exaudi nos Domine, quoniam benigna est', sung as the procession was formed at the church of departure, the participants then moved onto the Litany of the Saints. This was then followed by Psalm 102 and the antiphon 'Recordare Domine testamenti tui', a common prayer in times of plague. The theme of divine mercy was then taken up in a set of concluding prayers. At the church of arrival, mass was celebrated according to the form established by Pope Clement VI, with a 250-day indulgence for all those present who worshipped on their knees with a lighted candle in their hands.[50]

As the crisis mounted, public processions were given official sanction through ducal example. In September 1576, after a fierce summer that had seen the plague at its worst, the Senate decided that the doge, accompanied by the magistrates and all the other members of the Council, should process around the Piazza and hear mass in San Marco on three successive days. On the first day the Blessed Sacrament was carried, on the second a large crucifix, and on the last the icon of the *Madonna Nicopeia*. Double-choir litanies were sung by the choir of San Marco as these dignitaries made their stately progress around the square. This was a more elaborate version of the procession in the Piazza ordered by the Senate during the plague of 1474, when the participants included all the clergy and religious of the city, the *scuole grandi* and finally the flagellant confraternities, who chanted:

Alto re della Gloria,
Cazzé via sta moria,
Per la vostra Passion
Habiene misericordia.[51]

The arrangement of the ducal procession in time of plague was distinct from its usual festal form. One of its main features was the presence of the *Madonna Nicopeia*, carried under a white baldachin accompanied by lighted candles (see pl. 108). This precious piece of Byzantine art was one of a large number of religious images and sculptures brought to Venice from the Middle East during the middle ages, much of it booty captured during the Fourth Crusade.[52] Previously it had been kept in the upper sacristy of the basilica, where it is recorded for the first time in 1559.[53] It was believed that the *Nicopeia*, which consists of a central image of the Virgin framed by sixteen small enamels, had brought good fortune to those who had carried it in battle in Asia Minor, and the Venetians venerated it in the hope that it would bring similar blessings upon the Republic. According to Sanudo, during the celebrations of the victory at Marignano in 1515, the *Nicopeia* was placed in front of the basilica and psalms were sung to instrumental accompaniment.[54] Throughout the centuries, it was the *Nicopeia* that was publicly carried in procession to ask for deliverance from the plague, and it was her image that graced the title-pages of the various reprints of the Litany of the Blessed Virgin Mary, to be recited 'in time of war', published during the seventeenth century, by which time her cult had been through a process of renewal.[55] A close functional parallel to the Venetian procession with the *Madonna Nicopeia* is to be found in Milan, where Carlo Borromeo's procession of the Holy Nail, originally enacted in October 1576 as an expiatory ritual, became permanently enshrined after the saint's death through altarpieces, 'popular' engravings, ritual action and liturgy.

Having wound its way around the Piazza, following the traditional route to the Piazzetta dei Leoncini, the procession then returned to the west front and entered San Marco by the main door. As in the Roman rite, the chanting began with the penitential antiphon 'Exaudi nos Domine', followed by the Marian litany, Psalm 102, and the medieval antiphon 'Media vita in morte sumus'. Following various prayers, including one addressed to St Mark, the sequence finished with the 'Salve Regina', which Gregory the Great had allegedly sung in Rome during the plague of 590.[56] In this way, a para-liturgical processional form, which is common throughout the Catholic world, was given local identity through the insertion of prayers to Mark and the Virgin, and the presence of the treasured icon of the *Madonna Nicopeia*. Through the prayers and chants of the ducal procession 'in tempore pestis', the intercession was sought not only of the Communion of Saints, but also of two of the major protectors of the city, through the agency of the doge, Mark's representative on earth.

In September 1576, as the climax of this campaign of public prayer and atonement, the doge publicly announced the Senate's vote to construct a votive church dedicated to Christ the Redeemer,[57] and in March of the following year he laid the foundation stone of the new building. It was to be one of his last important ceremonial appearances. Three months later Alvise Mocenigo died, having lived through one of the most troubled dogeships of the century.[58] In an address in San Marco, Mocenigo compared the Senate's motivation to the Israelites' decision to build a new altar in appeasement for the three-day plague that had followed David's census. This rhetoric, if not very original, is at least indicative; comparisons between the plague and the afflictions suffered by the Israelites during their exile in the desert, are a common literary topos as are Old Testament themes in the Lepanto literature. On 6 and 7 September, the doge and Signoria attended low mass in San Marco; the choir was present, and double-choir litanies were sung. On the following day, when the vote was officially announced, a high mass was celebrated and prayers were offered for the liberation of the city.[59] According to the *patriarchino*, this day was celebrated as the feast of the Birth of the Virgin, and among Andrea Gabrieli's motets is a large-scale seven-voice setting of the Antiphon to the Magnificat to be sung at first vespers on that day:

> 'Your nativity, O Virgin, Mother of God, has proclaimed joy to the whole universe. The Sun of Righteousness, Christ our God, has shone from you. By breaking the curse, He blessed us; by defeating death He granted us eternal life.'[60]

At first vespers on this feast-day, the *Madonna Nicopeia* was carried in procession from the upper sacristy while the hymns 'Maria mater gratie' and 'Gloria tibi Domine' were sung by the choir. On arrival, the icon was placed on the high altar surrounded by candles. This added piece of ritual, which intensified the act of supplication, must have been even more appropriate during the plague years, particularly since it was the *Nicopeia* that had been carried in procession during the previous days. It seems likely that Gabrieli's motet was performed, if not actually composed, for the quite special circumstances in which the feast of the Birth of the Virgin was celebrated in September 1576.[61]

In a speech made in 1576, Alvise Mocenigo admitted that the famine of 1569–70, the War of Cyprus and the fire of 1574, which destroyed part of the Doge's Palace, had all been portents of divine wrath.[62] Even more pointedly, this last disaster had occurred on 11 May, the fourth anniversary of Mocenigo's election.[63] The conflagration began in the chimney of an upstairs kitchen, during the traditional banquet given by the doge to mark that anniversary. Fanned by the wind, the flames spread rapidly into the roof space of the palace, destroyed six rooms including the Collegio and the Senate, and penetrated as far as one of the cupolas of San Marco. The loss of the gilded ceilings and paintings was much regretted by contemporary writers, who also noted that only through the efficiency of a contingent from the Arsenal was the fire prevented from causing even greater damage. So great was the heat and the danger that Mocenigo was forced to find lodgings with one of the procurators who lived in the Ospedaletto in the Piazza San Marco, while the treasury of the basilica was hurriedly transferred to the Mint for safety. This was on 11 May. Shortly after this disaster a second fire, which began in a shop, destroyed all the stalls that had been set out for the Ascension Day fair, burnt alive a boy who had been placed on guard, and spread perilously close to Sansovino's Library. The fair, which had brought crowds of outsiders into the city, was deferred, 'in the interests of public order', until the feast of Corpus Christi.[64] Work, in which Andrea Palladio was involved, to replace the destroyed paintings and woodwork in the Doge's Palace took three years to complete,[65] but no sooner had this happened than a further, even more disastrous fire broke out on 20 December 1577. This time it began in the Sala del Scrutinio, where the whole of the ceiling was burnt, and from there it spread to a sequence of smaller rooms, and then finally to the Sala del Maggior Consiglio, which was also badly affected. Pictures by Bellini, Vivarini, Carpaccio, Titian, Veronese and Tintoretto were all lost, and Guariento's great *Paradise* fresco was also severely damaged. In addition to the havoc that it wrought in the rooms of the *piano nobile*, and above all in the Sala del Maggior Consiglio itself, the fire also destroyed the rooms on the floor beneath that housed official documents and records.[66] The destruction of both the seat of government and the documentary history of the Republic was not taken lightly, and reactions were dramatic. It was reported that a monk had quelled the wind, and so reduced the extent of the fire, by dropping to his knees in front of the door of the Sala del Maggior Consiglio and, clasping a relic in his hands, calling upon God's mercy.[67] Another writer associated the fire with the recent appearance of a comet, trailing a tail of fire, which many took to be a portent.[68] Rumours abounded. One commentator believed the fire to be the work of arsonists.[69] The more common view was that it, like the plague itself, was an Act of God.

To many, the decade of the 1570s must have seemed a time of divine reckoning. The victory at Lepanto and the visit of Henry III could be celebrated as signs of God's favour towards a Chosen People, but these moments of triumph and glory, celebrated with all the resources of the state ceremonial apparatus, were framed by disasters. In this, the latest episode in the long history of Venetian mythologenesis, the more comforting aspects of recent history were fabricated into a further chapter. In the process the press, liturgy, ceremony and the arts were all engaged in a way that is highly revealing of Venetian sensibilities and political processes in these troubled years. Music, liturgy and ceremony, literature, architecture, painting and the press, were all brought into service as the Venetian ruling class attempted to inscribe the events of the post-Lepanto years into a heroic narrative that effectively underplayed its political realities. In this process the power of print was fundamental.

PART THREE

HISTORY, MEMORY AND MYTH

CHAPTER NINE

Republic of Letters, City of Books

In time-honoured custom, the calamitous events that separated the siege of Malta from the end of the plague were described by the chroniclers, while the ceremonies that celebrated the victory at Lepanto and the visit of Henry III were carefully entered into the ceremony books of the Republic. Such traditional forms of record were essentially compiled by the ruling elites for their own purposes. At a more general level, and to a greater extent than ever before, the medium of print provided the main conduit through which Venetians were informed of events as they occurred, and it was partly through print that they were memorialized and mythologized for posterity.

By the middle of the sixteenth century, the use of the press for the construction of local identity and allegiance was hardly a new cultural phenomenon, and in Venice in particular it had a long and impressive history, tied to the city's position as a major producer of printed material of all kinds. Although the first Venetian book was not published until 1469, almost twenty years after Gutenberg's invention, by the end of the fifteenth century the city's book trade had grown so quickly that it had come to be of international significance.[1] This can partly be attributed to the stability of the Venetian economy during the critical period stretching from the 1470s until the beginning of the second decade of the sixteenth century. In common with the other major European centres of the publishing trade, all of which were north of the Alps, Venice had long maintained an important position in international commerce, and the coincidence of the development of the press with the power of the Venetian economy ensured publishers a network for the distribution of their books, as well as a ready source of capital investment.

110   Detail of pl. 113.

The success of the Venetian system is reflected in the high percentage of incunabula, most of which were imported in the fifteenth and sixteenth centuries, that still survive in countries outside the central European heartland, while its cosmopolitanism is indicated by the wide range of dioceses whose local liturgies it catered for, from York to Seville, and Antwerp to Zaragoza.[2] Together with the security provided by government regulation, and a ready supply of locally manufactured paper, these factors were decisive in establishing Venice as one of the most important cities in Europe for the making of books. It has been estimated that about 4,500 editions were printed there before 1500, almost one-eighth of all fifteenth-century titles known to have been produced.[3] As the hub of a trading empire whose products had been dispersed and exchanged along well-established trade routes, the city had an obvious competitive edge over Rome and Florence, the other two important Italian centres of the book business, both of which, despite their political and artistic importance, were geographically unsuited for major commercial activity.

For certain kinds of material Venice was unrivalled. Liturgical books had been a great local speciality from the start, while Aldo Manuzio had led the diffusion of humanistic scholarship with editions of the Latin classics, and Greek literary and philosophical texts. Other Venetian printers followed his example, as did some northern ones, notably Froben in Basle.[4] The cosmopolitan nature of the Venetian population, and the variety of cultural practices that could be found there, is reflected in book production. The Greek community was the largest of these immigrant groups, and Greek printers such as Zacharias Callierges (who in collaboration with his fellow Cretan Nicola Vlastò founded the first Greek press in Venice) contributed to the development of the city as the major centre for the production of Greek texts of all kinds, including liturgical books.[5]

Fewer titles were brought out in the first twenty-five years of the sixteenth century, partly because of the economic disruption caused by the war of the League of Cambrai, but from the fourth decade onwards there was a noticeable expansion in Venetian book production, which then continued to grow steadily until the outbreak of plague in 1575.[6] The image of Venice as a safe haven in the midst of general Italian turmoil at the end of the 1520s – as the last republic collapsed in Florence and a half-savage Lutheran soldiery brutally sacked Rome – has been exaggerated, for these were also troubled times for Venice itself. Faced by Charles v's claims to southern Italy and the Milanese state, which would have reduced the Republic to a minor role in a peninsula under Habsburg domination, the Venetian government committed troops and ships to the campaigns in Lombardy and Apulia. Two years of war also coincided with an outbreak of plague, which, though not as severe as that of 1575–7 or 1630–31, certainly took its toll. The same years witnessed a sustained bout of famine.[7] It was not until the Treaty of Bologna of 1529, when pope and emperor settled the future of Italy, that a new vision of Venice's international role was shaped. In what has been described as 'a remarkable paradigm shift on the part of the Venetian ruling elite', the Venetians rapidly replaced the previous image of a militant, self-confident republic with that of Venice as the haven of peace and the home of the Pax Veneziana.[8] In these new circumstances conditions in Venice stood in some contrast to the political and economic dislocation evident elsewhere in Italy, particularly in Rome and Florence, and printing benefitted, as did other aspects of Venetian life, from the skills and enterprise of a new wave of immigrants, many of them refugees. Among the major producers at mid-century, both Paolo Manuzio and Girolamo Scotto were Venetian, but Giolito was born at Trino near Vercelli, and Antonio Gardano was French. Most if not all of the first generation of the Bindoni family came from the Lago Maggiore area, Vincenzo Valgrisi was Lyonese, Michele Tramezzino arrived from Rome in the wake of the Sack, and Marcolini came from Forlì. As the Venetian book trade gathered pace and expanded the pattern continued: Nicolò Bevilacqua, Giovanni Battista Ciotti and Francesco Ziletti were all 'foreigners'.[9]

It was largely through the application of Manuzio's principles to the editing of vernacular texts that the growth of the market was further stimulated. After the publication, in 1525, of Bembo's *Prose della volgar lingua*, which argues for the preference of Italian over Latin, using the language of Petrarch and Boccaccio as a model, writers on a wide range of subjects turned to the vernacular. Further impetus was provided by the publication of a number of influential classic texts in Italian, including Ariosto's *Orlando furioso* (1516) and Baldassare Castiglione's *Il libro del cortegiano* (1528). From the end of the 1530s, when Marcolini and Giolito began to print, the tempo increased. Their commercial strategies were similar. Both brought out editions of Petrarch's *Rime* and Boccaccio's *Decameron* with some regularity, together with a number of devotional works in Italian; the *Sette psalmi penetenziali* was one of Marcolini's stocks-in-trade, and Giolito brought out Domenico Cavalca's much-reprinted classic *Lo specchio de la croce*. But there the similarities end. Giolito, with a certain amount of capital to hand, made an early decision to use italic type, originally introduced by Aldo Manuzio at the beginning of the sixteenth century, but still resisted by some printers.[10] This gave his books an elegant feel that, together with his adoption of small formats, also made them highly distinctive and immediately recognizable in the trade, at least until others began to copy the formula. It also reduced costs. In addition to the *Decameron* and the *Canzoniere*, Giolito also relied on frequent editions of the *Orlando furioso*; between 1542 and 1560 he published twenty-two editions of Petrarch's *Rime*, twenty-eight of the *Orlando* and nine of the *Decameron*.[11] Frequent reprintings of these three popular classics provided a regular income and a high degree of financial security that allowed Giolito to encourage literary buccaneers such as Ortensio Landi and Niccolò Franco, as well as Pietro Aretino and Anton Francesco Doni, to send him their work, and to pay other *poligrafi* as collaborators. The deci-

111   Jacopo de' Barbari, *View of Venice* (detail), woodcut, 1500. Venice, Museo Civico Correr.

sion to satisfy the new vogue for vernacular texts was to set the tone of Giolito's list for the next thirty-five years.[12] At about the same time, music printing, previously a sporadic and uncertain feature of the book trade, finally became established in Venice through the activities of two printers, Antonio Gardano and Girolamo Scotto, who independently began producing books using the new technology of single-impression printing.[13]

Most of the print workshops, some of which also doubled as retail outlets, were to be found in the centre of the city, with important concentrations in and around the Campo Sant'Angelo, the church and *piazza* of Santa Maria Formosa, and Santi Apostoli. Both the Merceria, stretching from the Torre dell' Orologio to the Campo San Bartolomeo, and the Frezzeria that runs parallel to it from San Moisè to San Fantin, were lined with bookshops. Engravers, printers and print dealers were concentrated in the same area: Nello Nelli was at the Rialto itself, Giovanni Francesco Camoccio was at San Lio, while Matteo Pagan operated from a shop in the Frezzeria (pl. 111). A little later Giacomo Franco also had his base in the Frezzeria, as did Cesare Vecellio before his move to the Merceria. The presence of all these associated crafts and trades in the same area of the city encouraged a high degree of collaboration and cooperation.[14] Outside this central conglomeration the trade was more scattered, but there was hardly an area of the city where books were not available either from shops or outdoor stands (a feature of the streets around the Rialto bridge), or from itinerant sellers who hawked broadsheets as well as other less expensive printed matter in the larger squares and around the major churches, including San Marco.

By the beginning of the War of Cyprus there were somewhere between thirty and fifty publishers working in Venice. Among these a number of the larger workshops were issuing an average of ten titles a year, while Giolito, one of the most productive of the bookmen, brought out about 900 editions between 1541 and 1578, an average of about two books per month. At the other end of the scale there were dozens of small enterprises, some no more than one-man operations, that printed a couple of books or broadsheets before disappearing into obscurity. In between these extremes there were many medium-sized operations, often with short lifespans, such as that of Melchiore Sessa and Pietro di Ravani, who burst into print with eleven editions in their first years of business, rapidly dropped to two titles just two years later, and then stabilized at five or six books a year until the firm was wound up after nine years of activity.[15] Altogether, the names of about five hundred publishers appear on the title-pages and colophons of sixteenth-century Venetian books,[16] and behind them lay an army of printers, pressman, binders, booksellers, tradesmen, apprentices and other print workers. At the peak of the phenomenon, just after the middle of the century, the Venetian presses probably employed somewhere between five and six hundred workers, while related activities such as bookbinding must have accounted for several hundred more.[17]

Taking the century as a whole, the Venetian presses published some 15,000 editions, an average of 150 new or reprinted books every year, or about half of all the books produced in Italy.[18] In practice, there was considerable variation in the rate of production over the period. More than two-thirds of the books printed in Italy during the third quarter of the sixteenth century came from Venice, and in 1600 the figure still stood at 50 per cent.[19] Despite the Republic's declining international significance in the last decades of the century, Venice itself was represented in print to a much greater extent than before. As Francesco Sansovino put it, the city 'can be called the theatre of the world, and the eye of Italy'. One of the functions of the Venetian press was to satisfy the needs not only of the local population, but also those of the thousands of visitors who passed through every year.[20] Religious literature, both doctrinal and devotional (traditionally one of the largest fields of interest that the press sought to satisfy),[21] was produced in greater quantity from the 1560s onwards, as the arguments of the Reformers, crystallized in the publications of the Council of Trent and in the stream of decrees and legislation that followed, touched the reading habits of the average clerical or lay believer.[22] Spiritual treatises, sermons, meditations and hagiography, usually in the vernacular, were now produced in greater number than ever before; such books accounted for most of the religious books produced, while scriptural commentaries, patristic literature, manuals, catechisms, liturgies and guides, usually in Latin and intended (in the main) for a professional audience, made up the rest. Among the imprimaturs issued for new publications, the percentage of religious titles rose steadily from the middle of the century (when it accounted for only about 15 per cent of the total number of books printed), to about 25 percent during the 1560s and '70s, before climbing to 33 percent, where it remained for the rest of the century. This doubling of production was partly at the expense of secular vernacular literature, the largest category of new titles at mid-century, but only a fifth of the total in the decades after Trent.

The example of Giolito is indicative. In 1557 he published Aretino, previously one of the mainstays of his list, for the last time, and in the following years, as the attitude of the Holy Office hardened and the *Index librorum prohibitorum* (Index of Forbidden Books) was finally issued in definitive form, new and reprinted religious works came to occupy an increasingly important place in his catalogue.[23] By the 1570s religious books represented more than two-thirds of the firm's output. The Venetian trade, supported by a patriciate as suspicious as ever of papal motives, had resisted censorship for decades, but in the years after Trent, with the Republic's embrace of the *Index*, it seemed that the tide had turned, at least for the time being. This enabled the shrewder publishers to capitalize on the new circumstances to meet the demand for religious books, particularly those of a functional and practical kind such as catechisms. The dominant trend in the vernacular realm was now towards texts concerned with prayer and behaviour and, to a lesser extent, popular history.[24]

Symptomatic of these new trends, and of the general character of Venetian book production in these decades scarred by war and plague, is the career of Francesco Sansovino. At the beginning of 1560 he opened his own press 'at the sign of the crescent moon', which, following common practice, also functioned as an element of his printer's mark,[25] but he continued to write and edit for other bookmen as well. Over the course of a long career in the trade, Sansovino produced some eighty titles, including orations, treatises, the first guidebook to Venice (*Delle cose notabili che sono in Venetia*, later to become *Venetia città nobilissima*) and many works of popular history.[26] The growth of interest in accessible historical writing, which could take the form of epitomes or translations of established texts, as well as the commissioning of new ones, was a product of the convergence of the preference for works in the vernacular on the one hand, and the expansion of the Venetian trade on the other. Sansovino's best-known histories were his popularized versions of the histories of Francesco Guicciardini and Paolo Giovio, publications that are as characteristic of the second half of the century, with its growing interest in popular history, as the scurrilous, satirical, and at times licentious works by Aretino and Doni are of the 1530s and '40s. In common with Giolito, Marcolini and other printers before him, Sansovino was responsible for shaping this new intellectual fashion as well as responding to it; his histories were on the shelves of a wide section of the reading public.[27] The character of his output, and the physical appearance of his books, places Sansovino among the more earnest *poligrafi*, authors who, in close association with the Venetian vernacular trade, wrote works in Italian with a serious purpose, aimed at a broad audience. Another favourite theme was genealogy, while the perennial Italian interest in all matters Turkish, particularly strong in Venice where it was later sharpened by the loss of Cyprus, produced a series of historical works beginning with the frequently reprinted *Historia universale dell'origine et imperio de Turchi* of 1560.[28] Sansovino himself was the author of a number of these texts. Published in inexpensive editions and sometimes illustrated, often in the smaller and more portable formats, these books were the backbone of an important sector of the book trade that had successfully developed the market for affordable Italian texts. Many other writers and publishers of Sansovino's generation went on to reap yet further benefits from this productive alliance of low cost and topicality, most obviously in the production of maps and pamphlets describing and commenting on the major events of the late 1560s and '70s: the struggle against the Turks, the loss of Cyprus, the victory at Lepanto and the spectacular reception in the city of Henry III.

Although most of the larger and medium-sized publishers spread their risks by putting out a wide variety of literature, including stock favourites that could be guaranteed a steady sale, there was also a tendency to specialize. In practice, most printers aimed at creating a distinctive niche in an increasingly crowded market. Continuing the tradition established by its founder, the Aldine press carried on publishing editions of the classics and humanist commentaries upon them, and in the hands of Paolo Manuzio and Aldo the Younger the tradition carried on almost until the end of the sixteenth century.[29] Following another long-standing tradition, the Giunti relied heavily upon liturgical books, a speciality of their shop since the fifteenth century; during the 1560s and '70s these accounted for between one-third and a half of their output.[30] Giolito published a significant range of vernacular works, from devotional books to histories, plays and treatises, but largely avoided Latin titles, philosophy, science and mathematics. One of his mainstays was the *Orlando furioso*, which by mid-century was being republished more frequently than Petrarch's *Canzoniere*. Between 1542 and 1560 Giolito produced some twenty-seven editions of the poem, an average production rate of one every nine months, and other publishers such as Valgrisi and Valvassori also relied heavily upon this, now the most canonical of sixteenth-century Italian lyrics.[31]

In a similar fashion, Tramezzino's shop placed a considerable emphasis upon vernacular texts in a number of fields, and also issued maps, but conspicuously avoided contemporary literature and science. The thirteen separately produced books of the works of Amadis de Gaul, many of which Tramezzino reprinted, account for almost one-sixth of the total number of books that he produced, and were published at regular intervals during the forty years that the firm remained in business, suggesting a steady reliance upon this one title alone. It is indicative that when the Tramezzino brothers divided their stock in 1562, there were 849 copies of this title on the premises.[32] Marcolini, on the other hand, took on precisely the kind of material that Tramezzino avoided, specializing in local authors including Pietro Aretino, who assigned to him exclusive rights to all his books published in the period 1535–45.[33] Along with these often controversial titles (his editions of Aretino, which were still being sold ten years after the publisher's death in 1559, earned him an entry in the Index) Marcolini also published the first editions of two of Sebastiano Serlio's books on architecture and, in the late 1530s, a small amount of music, including a book of lute tablature and a volume of five masses by Willaert. A scheme to bring out a separate volume of motets, madrigals and further masses as a sort of *opera omnia* of the *maestro di cappella* of San Marco, announced in the preface to the mass volume, seems not to have been realized.[34] Taken together, these initiatives show Marcolini's commitment to local city culture in a number of different areas.

At about the same time as Marcolini produced his few music editions, Gardano and Scotto, the two printers who were to dominate the Venetian market for printed music during the middle decades of the century, began work. From the early 1540s Gardano settled into a rhythm of production that allowed him to issue an average of fifteen or so new editions per year, produced in print runs of five hundred or so copies. One of his first music books, an edition of the music composed for the wedding of Cosimo de' Medici, duke of Florence, and Eleonora of Toledo in 1539, was a very prestigious early commission, and the earliest example in the history of music printing of a 'vanity press' publication designed to be owned, and conceivably read, but not used for performance.[35] The whole nature of what rapidly became a successful business venture was based upon the rapid turnover of short print runs of new music interspersed with reprints of well-tried and successful editions. As a strategy this approach seems to have worked well almost from the start, and for the first time in the history of the trade, music printing was not only financially secure, but was much more responsive to the work that composers were currently producing. Unlike Gardano, Scotto printed other titles in a wide variety of subjects, particularly the classics and commentaries upon them, alongside his editions of music. In this way, with interests in a number of different areas of the trade, he was able to distribute to a more differentiated public, and so to minimize the risks of his financial outlay. Nevertheless, the production of music represented an important component of Scotto's business, and beginning in 1539 he managed to maintain a steady annual output of some dozen or so titles for the next thirty-three years. Both printers were aiming at an international market from the start, and as early as the 1540s music printed by Gardano and Scotto had made its way abroad in considerable quantities.[36]

The physical appearance of a book – its size, format, layout, the quality of the paper and the elegance or otherwise of the typographical materials used – is an indicator of its intended audience.[37] Books produced by printers such as Tramezzino, Giolito, Gardano, Scotto and Marcolini were largely aimed at the professional classes – merchants, doctors, lawyers, teachers and the clergy – though some were also bought by (or came into the possession of) small traders and artisans. Their social destination is proclaimed through conformity to certain norms of design and typography. In this repertory of books a number of structural features are common. One is the presence of a title-page, which nearly always carried the printer's name and the place and date of publication, together with more optional information such as the printer's mark (which also often hung outside his shop as a painted sign) and, though more rarely, his address. Another is the presence of prefatory matter, or at least a prose dedication addressed to a socially prominent person; of the various explanations of how this aspect of the publishing operation functioned, the most likely is that it was a strategy to attract financial reward either before or after the title appeared. These kinds of books, carefully designed on the page, with each new chapter or section inaugurated with decorative initials selected from a single font, and often completed with an index or a table of contents (or both), occupy the middleground of the world of books, situated between the more expensive folio volumes and those in the lowest category of all.

Chapbooks were at the bottom of the ladder of book production. Usually of small format (octavo or quarto) containing two, four or at most eight leaves, often poorly produced on cheap paper using worn and antiquated type, these were often published without indications of place, date or even printer (pl. 112). As a whole they belong to a genre that has been traditionally described as 'popular' literature, in the sense that in terms of both production and price they represent the lowest common denominator in the hierarchy of printed books. In terms of content the range of this literature is comparatively narrow, and its emphases somewhat expected, with religious and devotional texts, including prayers, *laude* and the lives of the saints, prominent. Ancient histories, legends from

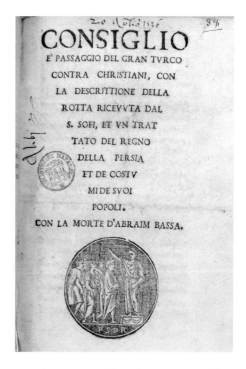

112 Anonymous, *Consiglio e passaggio del Gran Turco*, title page, Venice, 1535. Paris, Bibliothèque de l'Arsenal.

classical antiquity, such as the frequently reprinted *Historia di Orpheo*, and chivalric tales were another staple. It was from these that the ordinary Venetian might learn of the most important moments in the history of the Republic, or of the legendary benefits of its constitution, through the *Historia di Papa Alessandro et Federico Barbarossa imperadore* or the *Capitolo in laude di Venetia*. Among literary pieces short extracts from Ariosto's *Orlando furioso* – often in dialect and frequently illustrated – form sub-categories of their own. Laments, some satirical or bawdy, others relating to recent events and bemoaning the fate of individuals or cities, form another distinct genre.

It would be wrong to assume that chapbooks were aimed only at the lowest social and educational categories; prognostications, astrological booklets and pamphlets describing entries and other public rituals often required learning and a considerable knowledge of other literature to be read. There is also plenty of evidence that 'popular' pamphlets and engravings, even in cases where their content did not require specialized knowledge in order to be understood, were bought and read by the professional classes. The notion that some sort of matrix of class structure, however arrived at, can be directly and straightforwardly mapped onto book production, with the upper reaches of society owning only the more elegant formats, and the lowest order of books being acquired exclusively by the less well-off, is an artificial construction.

Many of the single-sheet broadsides, engravings and pamphlets that kept the Venetians in touch with the progress of the War of Cyprus, and which celebrated the victory at Lepanto or the visit of Henry III to the city, fall into the category of the 'popular'. Often the texts themselves are either anonymous or are falsely attributed to lend them authority and status. These features principally reflect both the character of the readership of these print pieces and the place of such goods within the economy of the market. By stripping out inessential information from the text, and focusing attention on the titles, those who put them together were aiming to attract the curious and to increase sales. Extravagant titles, boldly picked out in type and often accompanied by a woodcut illustration, also functioned as an advertisement for the contents. These booklets were often sold by pedlars and local street sellers who operated in the squares and the main thoroughfares of the city, but they could also be bought in shops as well as in markets, in squares and in front of churches.[38] In a seventeenth-century Bolognese engraving by Giuseppe Maria Mitelli, one of the most prolific of Italian seventeenth-century printmakers, who worked much in the manner of Jacques Callot and Stefano della Bella, a pedlar, his baskets overflowing with broadsides and prints, offers a map of Buda and a portrait of the Turk, shouting 'Let him who wants buy news of war, maps of war, cheap at two bolognini each!', while his onlookers protest and take to their heels at the announcement of yet more news on offer (pl. 113).[39] Some decades earlier Pietro Aretino gave a colourful sketch of one street vendor, who had on offer:

> Pretty tales, tales, tales, the Turkish war in Hungary, Father Martin's sermons, the Council, tales, tales, the facts of England, the festivities of the Pope and the Emperor, the circumcision of the Voivoda, the Sack of Rome, the Siege of Florence, the battle at Marseilles and its conclusion, tales, tales . . .[40]

During the Lepanto years similar figures roamed the area around the Merceria offering views of the relief of Malta, or hawking the latest news from Cyprus under the arcades at the Piazza San Marco or around the Rialto bridge. In addition to ephemera, the lower echelons of the trade also dealt in literary classics. Presented in new guises that completely changed the way in which the text had originally been presented, divided into sections and illustrated, verses from works such as the *Orlando furioso* could now reach a wider, less learned audience than the one that the author had intended, and his first readers constructed. By the second half of the sixteenth century Ariosto's poem was available in a greater variety of formats and typographical arrangements than ever before, from luxury quarto editions with an engraved illustration at the beginning of each canto, to the 'popular' editions in octavo or even smaller format that were initially printed in Gothic or semi-Gothic type (later in roman

113   G. M. Mitelli, *Per Bologna arti per via*, engraving, 1688. London, British Museum.

or even italic), with the text disposed in two columns. Francesco Caburacci, in the course of his defence of the *Orlando furioso* published in 1580, claims that he had seen the poem 'handled by the old, read by the old, read by the young, cherished by men, valued by women, prized by the learned, sung by the ignorant, possessed by all in the cities, and taken with them to the country'.[41] Some at least of these readers must have come to the work through these inexpensive formats. Cheaper still were the pamphlets that contained a single canto, often in dialect.

Distinctions between the production of books on the one hand, and that of other kinds of printed material such as maps and prints on the other, are artificial and misleading. Some print shops were dependent upon the book trade, and some bookmen also issued prints. In addition, a number of 'books' of prints turn out to be collections made by individual buyers rather than editions produced by the bookmen for the market. This is true of Giacomo Franco's *Habiti*, where no two copies are the same, a characteristic that has been implausibly attributed to the imperfect nature of the surviving examples.[42] Usually dated 1610 on the basis of the separate title-page that occurs in some copies, in practice every version is distinct and different from every other, being made up of engravings bought singly and drawn from a series showing Venetian scenes and customs produced by Franco over a forty-year period.

A good example of a versatile bookman is Tramezzino, who began to publish books in the 1530s, but once established he also started to issue maps and archaeological prints, some of which, though engraved in Rome, were granted a Venetian privilege and were presumably printed and sold there.[43] Nearly half of the thirty or so shops that are known to have produced prints in the second half of the century spent most of their time and energy publishing and selling books.[44] Among the engravers, there were artisans who were often also entrepreneurs and published prints; Donato, Ferdinando and Luca Bertelli all produced books as well as single sheets, and Giovan Francesco Camoccio, though not an engraver himself, owned a workshop for producing prints as well as a bookshop. Among those who worked for him was Martino Rota, who engraved important works of art by Michelangelo and others,[45] as well as political allegories, such as the *Wheel of Fortune*, where armed Venetians and Turks rise and fall with every turn of the wheel. Camoccio's best-known work is the *Isole famose*, a collection of small-format maps that could be made up into a book and supplied with a title-page according to choices made by the customer. Nicolò Nelli, who also worked for Camoccio, was the most prolific and versatile of this group, but produced only one book of his own, a treatise on the horse, which he illustrated and published in 1569.[46] Nonetheless, he did work extensively for other publishers, including Francesco Sansovino, whose *L'historia di Casa Orsini* he illustrated with a title-page and a number of portraits,[47] and for whom he also engraved a single-sheet folio genealogical tree hung with portrait medallions of the Turkish sultans surrounded by potted biographies, part of the growing fashion for portraits of the Ottomans.[48] There was a great deal of collaboration and exchange between these different sectors of work. The world of books was not as differentiated as might be thought, distinctions between genres or classes of printed material being more to do with later nineteenth-century curatorial orderings and notions of artistic worth than with the realities of sixteenth-century working practices.

Venice was at the centre of the trade in 'popular' prints, whose inferior craftsmanship and cheap paper distinguishes them from the higher reaches of the production of engravings and other images on paper, much as the 'popular' pamphlet is visibly recognizable as belonging to the lowest level of the order of books. Often given over to social comment, or to aspects of spiritual, political or religious life, these are a long way from the 'top' of the print market.[49] Modest in artistic scope in comparison with the grand tradition, they often reach into areas of Venetian popular attitudes and activities that are absent from the mainstream. As with pamphlets, their production was a distinct area of the trade and the range of material was considerable. Nelli, a man of relatively modest means, and one of the most productive and eccentric of these publisher-engravers, produced a steady stream of satires, proverbs, allegories, maps, portraits, title-pages and illustrations to printed books, all executed with considerable skill and technical assurance. As well as working the plates, he also probably supervised the business.[50] Among his book illustrations are five monogrammed engravings for Alessandro Caravia's third and last published poem, *Naspo bizaro*.[51] This has as its central focus the amorous adventures of Naspo, a swaggering, self-assured, low-life character accompanied by his servant Zan Polo, in pursuit of Cate Bionda Biriota, whose name shows her to be from the Contrada Biri, a workers' area of Venice well known as a haunt of tramps and prostitutes. Although loosely related to the stock figures of Zanni and Pantalone from the *commedia dell'arte*, Caravia's characters and Nelli's images of them are firmly grounded in local observation and the experience of Venetian life.[52] Rich in references to games and sports, recipes and remedies, courtship rituals, marriage ceremonies and funerals, *Naspo bizaro* is a richly textured account of popular customs, aimed at a largely local audience (pl. 114).[53]

114 Nicolò Nelli, engraving from *Naspo bizaro* by Alessandro Caravia, Venice, 1565.

The rapid technique of etching facilitated the quick production that the businesses of Nelli and others depended on for their economic success. The results, if not of the highest degree of technical finish, were produced in large numbers and were widely diffused. Here too the 'industrialization' of the trade encouraged expansion in the latter decades of the century, partly in response to the new religious preoccupations of post-Tridentine Italy.[54] The same is true for single maps, which were thought of as prints,[55] and were often engraved by the same artists, printed in the same workshops and sold in the same way.[56] By the sixteenth century, both maps and prints were familiar objects, part of everyday life. They could be bound into books to make personalized geographical or historical reference works, but they were just as likely to be used to decorate rooms, attached to walls or doors. Poor man's paintings, they were produced in thousands of copies. Franco's *Rosario*, commissioned by the Scuola del Santissimo Rosario for its members, is an example of one commercial facet of the trade that was quite common, and which brought images into humble homes.[57] The *Miracoli della Croce Santissima*, printed for the Scuola Grande di San Giovanni Evangelista to explain the history of its precious relic of the True Cross, the object of Gentile Bellini's famous painting showing it being carried in the Piazza San Marco, is another example.[58]

To speak in any meaningful way of 'mass' publication in Venice during the Lepanto years is to speak of a group of printers and publishers that dominated

115 Nicolò Nelli, *Il porto dell'Isola di Malta*, state 1, 1565. Milan,
Civica Raccolta di Stampe Bertarelli.

the 'popular' market, and it was largely through their production of prints,
pamphlets and small-format single-sheet maps that a wide spectrum of the
Venetian public was kept abreast of events. The same is true of maps, which
helped to create visual contexts for momentous events taking place in distant
lands, and to provide some sort of physical reality for a geography that otherwise could be only vaguely imagined through hearsay and travellers' tales.
Engravings of military or naval victories fixed such events for posterity,[59] and
could even provide a running commentary on manoeuvres and counter-
manoeuvres as they unfolded. A particularly striking example of this function
of the press is Nicolò Nelli's series of maps charting the progress of the siege
of Malta in 1565. The first in the series, dated 8 July, shows the early stages of
the assault, including the loss of the fortress of Saint Elmo (pl. 115). Subsequent
stages of the action are shown in later maps in the sequence, until, in a final
version produced by Nelli in October, the Turks are shown rapidly retreating
to their galleys and sailing away (pl. 116). It took only six days for news from
Malta to reach Italy, and the speed with which Nelli could translate the information as it arrived into visual images is testimony to the power and efficacy
of the broadsheet at this early stage in its development.[60]

While some of the images that appeared in books spoke immediately and
clearly, many relied upon theological, classical or philosophical knowledge to
be interpreted properly. Sanudo pasted all kinds of ephemeral material into his
diary, including pamphlets, broadsheets and prints. Symptomatic of his thirst
for news, these insertions are also a valuable record of what was available in

116 Nicolò Nelli, *Il porto dell'Isola di Malta*, state 6, 1565. San
Marino, California, Huntington Library.

Venice at the time, and they equip his already extraordinary diary with a supporting archive of printed ephemera.[61] They also demonstrate the social mobil-
ity of the material. Topical items in particular were bought throughout the
century by professional classes, as well as by artisans and unskilled workers,
who, if they came into contact with the written word, did so largely through
broadsheets and pamphlets. The same could be said for prints and maps, which
were cheaper than the average book. Venetian inventories of the household
goods of all social classes living in all the *sestieri* of the city make frequent references to prints displayed in interiors.[62] Singly, or in groups, they were often
coloured and used as decorations, cheap substitutes for paintings. This is a continuation of the uses to which the early woodcut was often put. Pasted onto
ceilings and doors, or inside deed boxes and travelling trunks, woodcuts
had served a variety of functions, from ornaments to objects of devotion and
amulets for personal safety.[63] Interestingly, these same inventories reveal that
few images of either Venice or St Mark[64] were owned by Venetians irrespective
of social class, suggesting that the vast production of such prints was directed
at different audiences, such as pilgrims and foreign visitors.

Ideas about the ownership of books, and the reading habits of those who
bought them, come from a variety of sources, including the books themselves,
inventories and information about the purchasing power of different occupational groups in relation to book prices. It has been calculated that some 33 per
cent of adult males and 13 percent of adult females in sixteenth-century Venice
were literate. As might be expected, most of these were from the upper reaches

of society – the nobility, merchants, lawyers, doctors and the clergy – but some craftsmen and small shopkeepers could also read.[65] Both inventories (usually made *post mortem*) and the records of the Inquisition support the idea of a broad social range of local Venetian readers, at least for the cheaper classes of material. A schoolmaster from Cremona, Francesco Scudieri, described himself to the Inquisitors as a 'man of letters who teaches music and the Italian language to Germans and other northerners'. It was these social contacts that had aroused suspicion, and as part of its enquiries the Holy Office made a list of Scudieri's library. Apart from a good deal of music, it also included medical treatises, Bembo's *Prose della volgar lingua*, a number of works by Erasmus, Demosthenes in Greek and Cicero, Hesiod, Homer, Quintilian, Terence and Virgil in Latin. In a red trunk they discovered a copy of Luther. Scudieri was found guilty, and despite having publicly recanted in the pulpit of Padua Cathedral was imprisoned for three years, and his goods (including his books) were confiscated and sold.[66] The Inquisitors might be assiduous, but they were not always knowledgeable. In the case of Fra Adriano da Fiandra they were baffled by titles 'in German or Flemish', but nonetheless spotted a copy of Raymund Lull.[67] Another suspect, Giovanni Zonca, was a wealthy mercer (he had premises in the Merceria and a villa at Mogiano) whose business interests took him abroad. His letters from Antwerp, where he stayed for four years, reveal a taste for high living (oysters and girls were particular favourites) and a passion for books. In 1582, when he was brought before the Inquisition in Venice, his collection was listed: it included Livy, Ovid's *Metamorphoses*, Caesar, Apuleius, Plautus, Petrarch, Boccaccio, a number of songbooks ('libri da cantar'), two histories of Venice (Bembo and Scalzi), Aretino and, unfortunately for Zonca, Erasmus.[68]

While tastes for these kinds of literature are not particularly surprising among members of the educated and moneyed classes, more interesting are the glimpses that the records provide of reading habits and book ownership lower down the social scale. Inventories reveal some surprising instances of book ownership among the artisan class. One of the most unusual is that of Andrea Faentino, an 'intagliatore in legno', who lived in the Campo San Vidal and owned a small collection of architectural treatises in folio, Serlio among them. It seems that it was largely the upper reaches of society that owned atlases, which were expensive.[69] More commonly found in the lower stratum of society were religious books. Amongst those who admitted to possession of the Gospels *in volgare* to the Inquisitors were a clockmaker, Lorenzo Vex, and a carpenter, Serafin de Magri. Francesco di Rado, a silk-worker, was reported with the apparently dubious information that 'he reads all the time', while another suspect, the swordsmith Lunardo de' Gabardi, 'stays up all night reading'. From these and other instances in the records of the Inquisition, a sample that has obvious limitations and peculiar features, it seems that literacy among artisans was higher than might be thought, and book ownership relatively common.[70] It also supports the view that religious heresy was widespread among the city's artisans. This was a cultural milieu in which reading, even if regarded as potentially subversive, was normal.[71] A weaver recites a Petrarchan sonnet that he has overheard, and a cobbler quotes in Latin, while the swordsmith's apprentice reads Ariosto and a cook has a collection of 'war stories and plays'.[72] Some of these experiences shade into oral tradition, but others are clearly reliant upon the possession, however temporary, of printed texts. Transformed into public performances through reading out loud, recitation or even song, such texts could reach a wider audience. Only one member of a group gathered round a workbench or sitting in the local square needed to be literate in order for texts to travel further.

This brings us into the world of the strolling players, the *cantastorie* and *cantimpanchi*, who, standing on benches and improvised staging, entertained the crowds gathered outdoors.[73] The wide range of names used for these performers betrays a great diversity of careers, from those who specialized in epic verse to itinerant street singers. Even so, the category of 'singer' had untidy boundaries, since in practice there was a rather thin professional dividing line between these performers, and the charlatans and mountebanks who used music as part of their pitch. The portmanteau term 'charlatan' itself covers a wide variety of activities and competences, ranging from pedlars of dubious elixirs to properly qualified physicians and experienced tooth-pullers, who combined healing and entertainment in the form of a public, social drama with its own long-standing rituals.[74] Two characteristics united these often overlapping medical activities: the practitioners were itinerant, operating from temporary staging in the square, and their performances were essentially theatrical.[75] The texts that were performed by the *cantastorie*, usually anonymous, were sometimes published in modest pamphlets of a few pages to be sold to members of the audience. This could sometimes lead to legal difficulties. In 1545 the *Esecutori contra la bestemmia* (a civil tribunal that dealt with accusations of blasphemy, moral wrongdoings and infractions of press legislation) prosecuted and fined two printers and one Francesco Faencino, 'canta in banco', for having sold copies of a work with the title 'Il dio Priapo' and others without licence.[76] The details of the case emphasize the close professional contacts between small-scale printers of this kind and outdoor entertainers.

Many 'popular' printed poems cast in *ottava rima* were intended to be sung.[77] In its blend of direct expression and lack of pretension, as well as its deployment of an initial rhetorical gesture revealing the presence of an audience, the following is typical of the genre:

> Per dar diletto et infinito piacere
> A tutti quelli che stanno [per] aspettare
> Ma prima voglio fare el mio dovere
> Inanzi ch'io voglia cominciare . . .[78]

And so on for a grand total of 115 verses, which in performance would have been sung to simple melodic formulas, embellished and modified in response to changes of mood. In the Piazza San Marco, the Piazzetta and the larger squares of Venice these raconteurs performed daily on improvised stages up until the end of the republic. In the sixteenth century, when the *cantimpanchi* were engraved by Franco (pl. 117) and described by Garzoni, there was a thin line between the professionals in the square and the amateurs in the *calle*, such as Caravia's swashbuckling hero, Naspo Bizaro:

> Per confortar la mia malenconia,
> Che'l cuor me strenze, e l'anema me strazza
> Canterò per passar mia fantasia
> Quel che no suol cantar chi canta in piazza:
> Che sempre dise calche gran busia
>
> . . .
>
> Zaratan mi no son da dar balote
> Ni anche ortolan da venderve carote
> Impresteme Zan Polo el vostro agiuto,
> Che impiantar possa d'amor versi in rima,
> In mezzo al cuor sonando mio lauto.[79]

The repertories that the *cantastorie* sang can be divided into various subgenres, but they are unified by being mostly written in *ottava rima*, the rhyme scheme that since the time of Boccaccio had been established as the principal narrative metre of Italian poetry; its continuing success is evident from the rapidity with which it was taken up by street singers.[80] Although it cannot be assumed that all *ottave* were always sung (some may have been read, perhaps silently), most were, particularly those that recount heroic deeds or tales of war, and which characteristically begin with an invitation to the audience:

> Almi signori io vi voglio pregare,
> Che tutti quanti mi state ad ascoltare,
> Che una gran battaglia son venuto per narrare,
> La più famoso certo che mai sia stata in mare . . .[81]

The tradition of printed texts recounting the events of famous wars and battles began with the fall of Constantinople in 1453, and was already well established by the time of Lepanto.[82] It is not surprising to find that many of the cheaply produced pamphlets that recount the most important moments from the fall of Famagusta to the victory itself were designed to be sung to the stock formulas of tradition, either publicly by the *cantastorie* or even more privately before smaller groups of listeners. Other Lepanto pieces that are also cast in *ottava rima* readily fit into various subgenres such as that of the lament, an obvious example being the *Lamento de Selin* and its many relatives.[83] These too were to be sung, as were pieces in other poetic metres such as the 'Barzelletta contra Mustafà Bassa', written by Manoli Blessi (in reality the actor-poet Antonio Molino) and cast in the classic form of a six-line stanza and a four-line refrain.[84] Their texts, usually of a few pages, crudely produced by jobbing printers and often adorned with simple woodcuts to attract the curious, could have been bought by all but the most economically hard-pressed.

What is known about both the affordability and the availability of middle-range books also supports the idea of a wide social range of owners and readers, especially for less expensive titles. In all areas of the trade, the economics of production were critically dependent upon accurate judgements about the market. Although the standard press run in late sixteenth-century Venice was about 1,000 copies, popular or established texts were printed in much larger numbers.[85] This had been true at least from the beginning of the century. The first edition of Ariosto's *Orlando furioso* was printed in about 1,300 copies, but by the time of the third edition sixteen years later the popularity of the poem had led the printer to double the print run.[86] This is an exceptional case. From the first

117   Giacomo Franco, *Charlatans in Piazza San Marco*, engraving. Venice, Museo Civico Correr.

edition of Castiglione's *Il cortegiano* to new works by Girolamo Ruscelli,[87] 1,000 copies seem to have been more the norm in Venice (and elsewhere in Italy), suggesting that an edition of this size responded best to the economics of book production. Smaller print runs could be profitable only if fixed costs remained low in relation to variable ones such as ink and presswork, and there was also a convention that privileges would be granted to editions only with a projected print run of more than 400.[88] One area of the Venetian trade where edition sizes were usually below 1,000 copies was music, where the standard press run, according to the few contracts that have survived, was 500 copies of each part-book.[89] These smaller runs were presumably based upon an empirical notion of market size. The figure would have been doubled or even trebled for those books of Latin masses and motets that had a large and secure international market. It could also, in exceptional cases, drop to a few hundred copies.

The price of a book obviously varied according to size and length (the cost of paper remained the single most important element of production costs), but with the average price standing between one and two *lira* for much of the century, it is clear that standard editions (that is, without illustrations, and not in the more expensive folio format) could be purchased by readers from a reasonably wide economic spectrum of society. In 1554 one *lira* would buy the vernacular translation of Cicero's *De oratore* in duodecimo, while later in the century it could even purchase an illustrated edition of Tasso's *Aminta* in quarto. At the lower end of the price range, a short book in duodecimo or octavo could be bought from Giolito for as little as 4, 6 or 8 *soldi*,[90] and broadsides and other single-sheet print pieces must have cost even less. These prices were for new books. There must also have been a developed trade in second-hand copies, as there was for clothes, furniture and other items. Used goods were actively sought by all social classes, and were not regarded as being tainted by previous ownership.[91] Demand was partly met not only by second-hand dealers, but also by public auction, a quick and effective way of realizing personal effects.[92]

Despite its specialized audience and shorter print runs, music was not more expensive on average than other kinds of literature. From the earliest account-books of the Accademia Filarmonica we learn that the four part-books of Gardano's *Motteti del frutto* of 1539 then cost 1 *lira* 4 *soldi*, while six Gardano sets containing an average of four part-books each were bought for a total of 6 *lira* 11 *soldi*. Other groups of part-books were purchased for about 1 *lira* each, a price that seems to have remained constant throughout the middle decades of the century.[93] When Scotto printed 500 copies of Paolo Ferrarese's *Passiones* for the Benedictines of San Giorgio Maggiore in 1565, he charged 550 *lire* for a run of 500 copies of a set of five part-books.[94]

In practice, these figures mean that some members of the lower economic strata with an interest in reading could afford to buy less expensive books, and with something of an effort could even acquire folio editions. Between 1551 and 1565, a period of stability when daily rates of pay did not change, a master mason or carpenter working at the Scuola Grande di San Rocco earned about 30 *soldi* per day, a rate that had risen to 35 *soldi* by 1574, while the figures for a semi-skilled journeyman in the same period are 20 *soldi* rising to 24 *soldi*.[95] Towards the lowest end of the economic spectrum, unskilled casual labourers working in the Arsenal received between 8 and 10 *soldi* per day,[96] while the base pay of the *galeotti* was about the same at 10 *lire* a month.[97] By the second half of the sixteenth century, the idea that the press was an instrument for the democratization of knowledge was commonplace. In *La piazza universale di tutte le professioni del mondo*, Tommaso Garzoni wrote that printing preserved knowledge, had awoken spirits that were previously ignorant, and had reduced the previously high cost of books.[98]

Both Lepanto and the visit of Henry III occurred when the Venetian presses were at their historic peak of production, after which there was a steep falling off in the number of books printed there. The reasons for decline were various. A substantial slice of the lucrative trade in liturgical books – a significant element of the Venetian market since the fifteenth century – was undoubtedly lost as a result of Philip II's granting of an exclusive patent to the Antwerp printer Plantin, but otherwise the argument that there was a real connection between the reduced productivity of the Venetian industry and the Council of Trent cannot be sustained.[99] The high mortality rate among Venetians, the flight from the city by the wealthier citizens and the measures that the government was finally forced to introduce in the face of the plague of 1575–7 all drastically affected the economy of the entire city. Many forms of business were affected by this paralysis, the press included.[100] The case of the Giolito shop is typical. In the early 1570s it was producing an average of thirteen titles per year, but fifteen years later this had dropped to eight.[101] A similar pattern, measured according to the numbers of printing plates known to have survived, can be observed for maps. A high point in their production was reached in the 1560s; there was then a gradual falling off, but the plague reduced activity to almost nothing, after which the Venetians were unable to compete with engravers and cartographers in the Low Countries.[102] A similar history characterizes print production.[103] Throughout the decade that followed the outbreak of the epidemic, the average number of book imprimaturs issued fell by half, and although there was a recovery in the trade in the late 1580s, further depression was caused by the famine of 1590–91.[104] Recovery this time was slower and incomplete. Never again were the Venetian presses to be as active as they had been during the years before the plague.[105]

The exchanges between authors and publishers that took place in the new world of the 'industrialized' book are suggestive of an atmosphere, characterized by a common sense of purpose, where ideas moved freely. Perhaps a little too freely for the Inquisition, which, with increasing conviction, suspected the role played by the Venetian press in the printing and distribution of heretical works. For a mixture of political, religious and shared moral reasons, both the civil authorities and the church had a vested interest in controlling the press, and during the middle decades of the century they did so through concerted action. Protestant books had been first imported into Venice in large numbers during the 1520s, but the government of the time made little effort to prevent their circulation beyond making the existing system of pre-publication censorship more effective. In theory, authors and publishers were expected to apply to the state for a privilege for a new work, and the Council of Ten then appointed readers to ensure that it was free of offensive material before issuing the imprimatur. In practice, the system was not backed up by sanctions of any kind, and most books continued to be published without authority. It was only in the 1540s that matters began to change.[106] Prompted by increased demands for stricter control of the press from the Council of Ten, the Republic established a new body, the Tre savii sopra eresia, charged with supporting the Venetian Inquisition. Its members were chosen for their known opposition to heresy and for holding views sympathetic to the aims of the Counter-Reformation church, but this is not to say that they were all in thrall to Rome. On the contrary, supporters of papal politics and patrician relatives of high-ranking ecclesiastics are noticeably absent from the ranks of those appointed, though some defenders of the interests of the church, such as Federico Contarini, did serve.[107] Above all, the Tre Savii was a genuinely powerful instrument of social control, and no fewer than three future doges were among its members in the 1560s and '70s. Later, as relations between Venice and Rome began to deteriorate, men who were more opposed to papal policies began to be elected.[108]

As majority opinion among the patriciate slowly shifted in favour of Counter-Reformation policies, the first book-burnings took place in the Piazza San Marco and at the Rialto bridge, and a number of bookmen were prosecuted. The most celebrated case was that of the writer Antonio Brucioli, who, together with his two brothers and a collaborator, set up his printing business in 1540 and in the space of four years produced a series of books including his own translation of the Bible. These were denounced to the Inquisition for their allegedly Lutheran tone. Worse was to follow. Three months later Brucioli was discovered to own three bales of heretical books, including works by Luther; in addition to ordering that these be burnt, the authorities fined him and sent him into exile for two years.[109] At about the same time the Council of Ten ordered that the first Venetian list of banned titles should be drawn up and printed. Although this was subsequently withdrawn, the idea that the Venetian authorities should seriously consider embracing restrictions of a kind that had not been adopted in Rome itself is indicative of a new mentality, which can be seen at work in the case of Alessandro Caravia.

Caravia was a goldsmith, a keen member of his guild and the author of a satirical poem, *Il sogno di Caravia*, published in 1541. This savagely attacked the *scuole grandi* for their excessive expenditure on buildings and display, leaving those in need to suffer. Such ostentation, Caravia argued, was a betrayal of their foundation principles, based on the works of corporal mercy:

> For they do not offer shelter to the poor
> So numerous are they in Venice,
> Hungry and naked, united in their need . . .
>
> If they were to think on death,
> Pondering on that as good brethren,
> They would help the poor
> Through their love for each other . . .
>
> They were founded to good purpose these *scuole*
> And they originally governed their affairs properly . . .
> Each loved his fellow as good brothers,
> While now what one is against is promoted by another
> They didn't need to spend their money
> On architects and gilded objects,
> They clothed the naked and looked after prisoners.[110]

Despite its strong criticism of a powerful interest group, *Il sogno* did not land Caravia in immediate trouble, but in his second published poem, *La vera* [i.e., *guerra*] *dei Nicoloti e Castellani* of 1550, the Holy Office detected traces of Protestantism. The action is based on the famous 'battles', in practice hearty and sometimes violent scrimmages using fists and canes, that took place between the two working-class factions of the city, the Castellani and the Nicolotti, who fought for possession of one of a number of the city's bridges.[111] Caravia's poem is just one of a number of works, mostly of a popular character, provoked by this bloodthirsty spectacle over the centuries. As well as providing an account of the battle that, being cast in *ottava rima*, was intended to be sung by ordinary Venetians, it also reflects the spiritual crisis of the time, and in this sense is an effective example of how a burlesque text could be a vehicle for the transmission of serious arguments, in this case religious.[112] This becomes explicit in the last section, where the deaths of the two champions, Gnagni and Giurgo, reveal their different attitudes towards the church and various articles of faith. Gnagni opts for an entirely orthodox departure, professing his faith, confessing his sins and expressing his wishes for an elaborate funeral. As he dies, Giurgo confides only in God. It was these details, which resonate with the ideas of the *spirituali* and the *Beneficio di Cristo*, that attracted the suspicions of the Holy Office. Caravia's trial began in 1556 and lasted three years, and although in the end he escaped imprisonment or worse, he did not abandon his religious convictions. In a neat demonstration of life imitating art, the arrangements for his funeral were a mixture of the wishes of Gnagni and Giurgo.[113]

Throughout the 1550s, the Venetian book trade had successfully resisted repeated attempts by the Papacy to impose a new Index of Forbidden Books. Vincenzo Valgrisi, who led the opposition to the Pauline version of 1559, was tried and given the mild sentence of doing good works by visiting the hospital of the Incurabili every Friday for two months, and undertaking to hear mass, recite the rosary and to confess and communicate frequently.[114] Toleration still characterized Venetian attitudes towards offenders, but the atmosphere was now definitively changing in favour of a more positive Counter-Reformation stance, as the generation of Aretino, Doni and Marcolini died or stopped work. Printers, always keenly attuned to shifts in intellectual fashion, detected the change and sought to satisfy it by bringing out more devotional titles at the expense of literature and poetry. Collaboration between church and state helped to tighten legislation, and the number of imprimaturs started to rise. During the period, the average number of imprimaturs issued annually was fifty-five; by the years 1565–9 it had risen to almost double that figure.[115] The siege of Malta, which finally brought home to many Venetians the precariousness of the Republic's position and its need of allies, inaugurated a period of much closer cooperation with the Papacy. The Tridentine Index had already been accepted by the Venetian government without protest in 1564, but it was ignored by the trade, and five years later legislation was passed that facilitated its enforcement.

Some proprietors (Francesco Ziletti was one) put up resistance and denied the Inquisitors access to their premises, but most complied. Shops and warehouses were visited by officials in search of prohibited titles, and inventories were made of stock and other effects. A number of those reported were fined after trial, and a large number of books were confiscated and burnt. Some suspect publications were discovered in the warehouse of Luc'Antonio Giunta, hidden behind bales of more innocent material, but the main offender was Valgrisi. Twenty-two books, including the complete works of Erasmus, were eventually removed from his warehouse, and a lengthy trial ensued.[116]

This situation was new, the fruits of enhanced levels of cooperation between Venice and Rome apparently on better terms than ever before. They were to remain so until jurisdictional disagreements over comparatively minor matters boiled over into the Interdict crisis of 1605–7. This, though, was some decades away. For the moment relations between the two were conducted in a new, cooperative spirit, as the *giovani*, a recently arrived pressure group in the patriciate, took up the cause of a reformed and renewed Venetian church, and appealed for direct, tolerant faith to be placed in the service of the state. It was in this changed climate, characteristic of the decades after the closure of Trent, that the Venetian bookmen now operated, and it was the tastes of the times that they sought to satisfy. Only later, when the renewal that the *giovani* had inaugurated in the mid-1570s was transformed into resistance to both the dogmatism of the Counter Reformation and the hegemonic ambitions of Spain, did the atmosphere change once more.[117]

In addition to the Inquisition, the *Esecutori contra la bestemmia* also went into action, searching warehouses, observing the activities of those suspected of transgression and reporting to the Holy See. The foundation, in February 1537, of the *Esecutori* is an indication of the authorities' growing determination to control the press; it was followed, eight years later, by the introduction of the *Riformatori dello Studio di Padova*, attached to the university, charged with the scrutiny of all material, including both books and prints, submitted to it for approval.[118] Then, in 1568, the gaze of the *Esecutori* fell on those involved in the printing and selling of Hebrew books, most of whom were Jews living and working in the ghetto. Official authorization for a Jewish community continuously resident in Venice since 1382 dates only from the second decade of the sixteenth century, when the Ghetto Nuovo was established; the first synagogue was built in 1532, and the area was extended by the addition of the Ghetto Vecchio in 1541 (the story that the island of Spinalunga became known as Giudecca because of the presence of Jews there as early as the twelfth century is apocryphal).[119] While on the one hand the inhabitants of the ghetto could be viewed as a separate entity subsumed into a harmonious urban complex, on the other the Jews were always regarded as a danger to the state, an attitude that increased in intensity with the arrival of Jews and Muslims, many of them Moriscos and Marranos, from the Iberian peninsula after the savage expulsions of 1492.[120] By the late sixteenth century, when the life of the ghetto, and in particular its religious ceremonies, were described by travellers (many of them English),[121] there were between two and three thousand Jews in Venice, from a variety of ethnic backgrounds.[122] Although the Venetian government was generally tolerant of the community, more so than many other Italian states, there were moments of tension, of which this was one.

It was also an example of history repeating itself. The first edition of the Babylonian Talmud was brought out in Venice during the years 1520–23, only shortly after the ghetto had been founded, by the publisher Daniel Bomberg, a Christian from Antwerp, assisted by a team of editors and typesetters, many of whom were Jewish. Of prime importance for Jewish culture and devotional practice, Bomberg's Talmud, an ambitious undertaking in fifteen volumes, established the format and pagination for virtually all subsequent editions. Then, in the early 1550s, prompted by Julius III's recent prohibition of

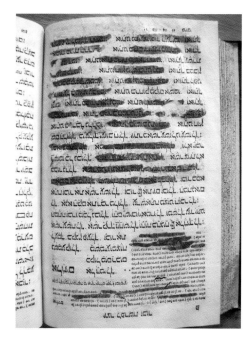

118   Censored page from *Hahzor mi-kol ha shanah*, Venice, 1567. London, Valmadonna Trust Library.

the book in the Papal States, the *Esecutori* were ordered by the Collegio to examine the Talmud and declared it to be blasphemous. This opened the way for a purge. The ghetto was combed and houses searched for books for the pyre (the 'good fire' as the papal nuncio described it), on which thousands of copies were burnt, in the Piazza San Marco. Since the condition now imposed that the Talmud could circulate only in expurgated form was unacceptable to the leaders of the Jewish community, the Hebrew trade simply moved elsewhere until the dust had settled.[123] In 1563, ten years after this first burning of the Talmud, the ban on Hebrew printing was lifted, and five independent Christian workshops began to print Hebrew books in competition with each other. Nonetheless, conditions remained difficult, and the censors sometimes intervened to efface individual copies, often selecting uncontroversial passages, apparently in ignorance of their true meaning (pl. 118).

The revival was to be short-lived. During the years between the siege of Malta and the battle of Lepanto, Venetian printers of Jewish books fell once more under suspicion. In common with their attitudes towards the Turks,[124] the Venetians had always regarded the Jews with a mixture of wariness and toleration born of expediency, though conscious of their importance for Venetian trade and vitality, they had usually left them in peace. But with the growing

Ottoman threat to Turkish possessions in the Mediterranean, official attitudes towards the Jews began to harden. The catalyst was provided by the activities of Don Joseph Nasi, a Marrano merchant from Portugal, who, having taken refuge at the Turkish court, had devoted his considerable wealth to the development of an extensive commercial empire. Stretching from Antwerp to Palestine, this threatened the profits of Venetian merchants since it bypassed Venetian ports in the Mediterranean and around the Adriatic. In Constantinople Nasi had become a valued adviser to the sultan, providing finances and raising taxes, for which he was rewarded with the title of duke of Naxos. Estimations of his influence over Ottoman policy were undoubtedly exaggerated by nineteenth-century historians, but Venetian hostility to the Jews certainly became more vocal as a result of the rumours of Nasi's complicity, and he rapidly became a figure of popular suspicion and hatred.[125] When fire broke out in the Arsenal in September 1569, causing extensive damage to both the shipyard and the surrounding area, where the convent of the Celestina was severely affected, it was put about that Nasi's agents were responsible. Anti-Jewish sentiment became even more intense with the Turkish invasion of Cyprus,[126] since it had been rumoured for some time that Nasi's ultimate ambition was to become king of Cyprus, and that he had played a major role in urging the sultan to attack. This common belief informs Antonio Molino's popular pamphlet *Dialogo de Selin con Giosuf ebreo*, published after Lepanto, in which Sultan Selim I complains that the Cyprus adventure, which 'Joseph the Jew' had encouraged him to undertake, had in the end turned out to be too expensive, to which Joseph replies that the outcome had been thoroughly worthwhile.[127]

The Nasi episode was the most significant in a series of incidents that increased Venetian hostility towards the Jews in the late 1560s, and helped to convince the local population that they were actively working on behalf of the Turks to bring down the Republic from within. It was at the height of public anger at what was thought of as Jewish treachery and ingratitude that the *Esecutori* once again took action. In 1568 thousands of copies of Hebrew titles were destroyed on the grounds that they had been published unexpurgated, and heavy fines were levied on those believed to be responsible. This was the second time in just fifteen years that Hebrew books, many of which were essential to the daily life of the community, had been consigned to the flames. From the government's point of view, it was more important to improve relations with the Papacy than to protect the press, and although Hebrew books were printed and published again in some number after 1568, and Venice gradually regained its position in the trade, this took place in an increasingly threatening atmosphere. In 1570 Marc'Antonio Giustiniani, accused of clandestinely importing Hebrew texts that had been printed on the island of Cefalonia, was brought before the Inquisition and subjected to a gruelling trial.[128] The peak of anti-Jewish feeling was reached a few months later, after the loss of Cyprus, when the Senate voted to expel the community. Although the decision was reversed shortly afterwards, it was not until after 1573 that relations returned to some sort of normality. In the chequered history of Venetian relations with its Jewish subjects, the years after the siege of Malta mark a low point, as the ruling elite, for political reasons, abandoned tolerance in favour of repression.[129]

Official attitudes also have a wider significance for what they reveal of the state of the book trade, and the fears of those who worked in it, on the eve of Lepanto. The Jews suffered most from the government's campaign of censorship, but they were not the only part of the business to be affected. Some Christian printers, such as Nicolò Bevilacqua and Giovanni Griffio, who had produced Hebrew titles for Jewish publishers, had their books confiscated and were fined. In more general terms, the years following the introduction of the Index were not easy ones for the Venetian trade. Censorship, previously a rather distant and vague legislative possibility, which rarely touched the lives of most of those working in the business, had now become a reality. No one was immune from the attentions of the Holy Office, not even the larger publishing operations like that of Valgrisi. A further turn of the screw took place in June 1569, when the pre-publication licence system was extended by the Council of Ten to include all books printed abroad, including those produced in the towns and cities of the *terraferma*, and the Inquisition was given authority to make inspections at the customs.[130]

Relations between the Venetian government and the Holy Office were at their most cordial and collaborative at precisely the moment when the rumours that had been circulating for years about Turkish designs on Cyprus were finally translated into action. In view of the severity of the censorship regime that by then had been put into place, the almost unanimous and monothematic reaction to Lepanto itself can obviously be read in more than one register. The traditional picture of universal Christian rejoicing over the defeat of the Turks must be tempered by the fact that, with control of the press by an alliance of church and state at its most developed, there was little room for voices of caution, let alone dissent.

The buoyancy of the Venetian book trade during the years 1560–74 is dramatically reflected in its reaction to the major political events of these years, beginning with the War of Cyprus itself. The siege of Nicosia, and the fall of the island, was quite widely reported in the Venetian press. Typical is Altomira's account, a short quarto booklet, which finishes its historical narrative with the Turks advancing on Famagusta, and concludes with lists of Italian combatants both alive and dead. As with all wars, this one generated prophecies. Both before and after the victory at Lepanto, this distinct and characteristic Renaissance genre, which sits astride both written and oral traditions as well as learned and popular ones, came back into its own. Among the pamphlets that appeared prophesying the destruction of the Turks, Giovan Battista Nazari's *Discorso della futura et sperata vittoria contro il Turco* stands out for the range of its references to biblical, astrological and historical texts,[131] as well as for being widely diffused. Its Brescian author, best known as an accomplished alchemist,[132] was also interested in ancient history, and had made prognostications on previous occasions; the *Discorso*, apparently available to any visitor to the Piazza San Marco,[133] went through a number of editions.

Nazari's learned text is divided into seven sections, each of which deals with a particular group of past prophecies concerning the Turkish question. Towards the central section, Nazari comes closer to current events, and to the notion that the Ottoman empire would end during the reign of the fifteenth sultan, Selim II.[134] This was taken up by other writers, notably Sansovino, and re-entered circulation in the pamphlets celebrating Lepanto. Towards the end of the *Discorso*, Nazari describes two prodigious phenomena that had appeared in the sky over Caffa, a Crimean port on the Black Sea, then under Turkish control. In January 1567 three suns appeared framed by two arches, one white, the other multi-coloured, and stayed there for three hours. This display of parhelion (or in this case triple parhelia) was usually interpreted as an inauspicious portent, a 'fearful sign', though exceptionally it could also precede good news. In 1531 the appearance of three suns at Modena had been interpreted as an omen of universal peace 'as in the time of the Emperor Octavian', a reference, evidently understood by the crowds that gathered in the square, to the three suns that had appeared after the death of Julius Caesar to foretell the Augustan age as a necessary prelude to the birth of Christ.[135] The Caffa triple parhelia were also to be read as an optimistic sign, as Nazari goes on to relate, prophesying the end of Turkish power. Two days later, above the same city, a second portent appeared in the sky. This time a cross was seen, topped by a star with a crescent moon beneath it, a clear sign of a forthcoming Christian victory over the Turk. After dealing with astrological predictions of victory for the Holy League, Nazari ends by exhorting all good Christians to pray for success.

The *Discorso* is illustrated with a number of woodcuts, some showing the two portents, others the destruction of the Turks by the members of the League. One of these designs, showing the Turkish dragon being savaged (pl. 119), also makes an appearance in an anonymous pamphlet exhorting action and prophesying victory, following an interpretation of the prophecies of the Eritrean Sibyl, to predict the defeat of the Turkish empire (the dragon) and the reconquest of Constantinople, by the combined efforts of the bear (Spain) and the lion (Venice).[136] The connection between the triple parhelia and the victory at Lepanto is also made explicit on the title-page of Bartolomeo Meduna's four-page *Dialogo* published more than a year later.[137] Meduna, a Franciscan from Friuli, was best known to readers for his short life of the Virgin, a popular devotional text characteristic of the Venetian press in the post-Trent period: Giolito produced a number of editions of the book.[138] In the *Dialogo*, a woodcut of the three suns from Nazari's *Discorso* makes a further reappearance in the place traditionally occupied by a printer's mark on the title-page. Cast as a dialogue between two speakers, Alessandro and Stefano, the text praises both Pius v and Philip ii, before going on to make the prediction that the League would finally drive the Turks out of the Holy Places. A description of the battle itself finishes with a rhetorical flourish, claiming that not even Hannibal or Scipio had won such a decisive victory. The main theme of the *Dialogo*, announced in its title, is the common trope of the victory as the work of God and a sign of divine favour.

Some sense of the general Italian anxiety about the Turkish threat, an anxiety that was renewed annually each spring as the first news of naval preparations and fleet movements filtered through diplomatic channels, comes through strongly in an anonymous poem that was often set to music by contemporary Italian composers. One of the first to do so was Pietro Vinci, a Sicilian by birth who had been *maestro di cappella* at the basilica of Santa Maria Maggiore in Bergamo since 1568. During the twelve years that Vinci stayed in this post, he forged strong links with Antonio Londonio, a high-ranking official in the Spanish administra-

119 Giovan Battista Nazari, *Discorso della futura et sperata vittoria contra il Turco*, Venice, 1572. Venice, Museo Civico Correr.

tion in Milan, and an enthusiast for music who maintained an informal academy (*ridotto*) in his residence there. No fewer than four of Vinci's publications are dedicated to him, and it is in one of these, the third book of five-voice madrigals, that the following piece appears:

> Le strane voci i dolorosi accenti
> Ch' empion l'aere di pianti & di querele
> Sono di quel ribello empio e crudele
> Al suo Re contra Dio con le sue genti,
> Santo Pastor, et de domati e spenti
> Seco i più rei per man del tuo fidele
> Popolo eletto il divo Michaele
> Moss' a pietà de tuoi giusti lamenti

> Hor ben dovrebb'al par de gl'aurei gigli
> Roma mostrar di vero gaudio segno
> Lieti cantando i suoi più chiari figli

> Come non forza di terren ingegno
> L'ha libertà da tanti perigli
> Ma'l valor certo del superno regno.[139]

This text, at times technically incompetent and in places obscure in meaning, is nevertheless clear in the general thrust of its message. It calls upon the pope, the Holy Shepherd of tradition, to counter the Turkish threat personified by the sultan and his followers. The transformation of Pius v into the Archangel Michael, made possible through play on the pope's own Christian name, was a common topos, as in the following anonymous canzone, published separately in pamphlet form:

> Ma poi ch'ingiuria vide
> Farsi alla Croce, & danno alla sua legge,
> Il pianto udì del gregge,
> Mandò l'Angelo suo Michele in Terra,
> Con le veci di Pietro a far lor guerra . . .[140]

The words of 'Le strane voci', which could have been written at any time after the beginning of the War of Cyprus, continued to be set to music and published during the following decade by a number of composers living and working in different parts of Italy. Its sentiments are relevant to the generally unsettled atmosphere that continued to obtain in Italy as a whole both before and after Lepanto. The same is true of the small corpus of Venetian battle-pieces, designed to imitate in sound the noise of war, that dates from about the same time. In itself the idea was not new; vocal music of this kind had begun to appear in both French and Italian song repertories in the late fifteenth century, and by the sixteenth they constituted a continuous tradition. In part this was due to the enormous popularity of one piece, Clément Jannequin's chanson 'La guerre, ou la bataille', thought to have been composed in celebration of the battle of Marignano in 1515;[141] it is just one among a number of long programmatic works, including other battle-pieces, that he wrote. In its use of stock figures, such as triadic motifs and rapidly repeated single pitches to evoke trumpet calls, military signals, drum rolls and the sounds of war, Jannequin's chanson gave rise to both arrangements (particularly for lute) and imitations. Resonances of 'La guerre' are strongly present in Andrea Gabrieli's vividly martial madrigal cast in two unusually long sections, 'Sento, sent'un rumor', labelled in the part-books that are its only source 'Battaglia'.[142] In essence this is a reworking of Jannequin's piece, with similar musical responses prompted by similar texts, larded with onomatopoeic imitations of combat.

The transfer of this musical concept to the medium of instrumental ensemble is implicit in the text of Jannequin's chanson (and Gabrieli's derivative madrigal), and the result, Andrea Gabrieli's eight-voice 'Aria di battaglia', is one of the earliest examples of the genre. It is described on the title-page of the printed collection of *Dialoghi musicali* in which it first appears as suitable for performance by an ensemble of *cornetti* and trombones.[143] There it is paired with another instrumental battle-piece, by Annibale Padovano, which is probably to be identified with the work performed in Munich during the celebrations that accompanied the Bavarian wedding of Duke Wilhelm V and Renée of Lorraine, in 1568. Padovano, who was employed at San Marco from 1552 to 1565, had by then moved to Graz, and Massimo Troiano's reference to 'Una battaglia ad otto, di Messere Aniballe Organista, con tromboni, e cornetti alti' is fairly conclusive, given the particularity of the genre.[144] Although it has been suggested that Andrea Gabrieli's 'Aria di Battaglia' may have been stimulated by the victory at Lepanto,[145] neither it nor 'Sento, sent'un rumor' can be precisely dated, though the decade or so after the composer's return from Munich in 1562 must be, on stylistic grounds, the most likely period of composition. Both are to be thought of as evocative historical traces of the War of Cyprus and its aftermath.

The general climate of anxiety in 1571 was such that, when victory came, the response of the Venetian press was unprecedented. A population that had been kept in touch with the progress of the war through broadsheets, and which so strongly identified with it, now celebrated the news in print.[146] From the presses of Venice poured a torrent of poetic anthologies, paraphrases of the psalms, accounts of the action and prints showing the battle at its height or the disposition of the opposing fleets before it began, creating a form of visual reportage that implicitly claimed the authority of an eyewitness account (pl. 120),[147] united in a collective response that in quantitative terms is without parallel in sixteenth-century literature. According to one estimate, more than three hundred poets contributed to the phenomenon.[148] Quality is another matter. Benedetti wrote, perhaps a little too enthusiastically, in view of the low standard of much Lepanto verse, that latter-day equivalents of Apollo and Orpheus could be heard on all sides.[149] The single-sheet print and the short pamphlet, which had become established viaducts of communication during the siege of Malta, now came into their own, with the brothers Domenico and Giovan Battista Guerra (from Valvasone in Friuli, an area particularly susceptible to Turkish incursions) coming to the fore as the most prolific printers of such material. In 1571 they published fourteen titles relating to Lepanto (all of a popular nature and in Italian), to which a further eleven, five in Latin and the rest in the vernacular, were added the following year.[150] No other event of this calamitous century, not even the Sack of Rome, seems to have moved the hearts and minds of writers and composers, printers and publishers to the same extent.[151] Every conceivable ingenuity was deployed to attract the buying public. Acrostics, Latin epigrams, parodies of popular devotional texts and trivial stanzas based on simple word-play ('Selin, es nil, nil es, Selin') fill the popular anthologies.

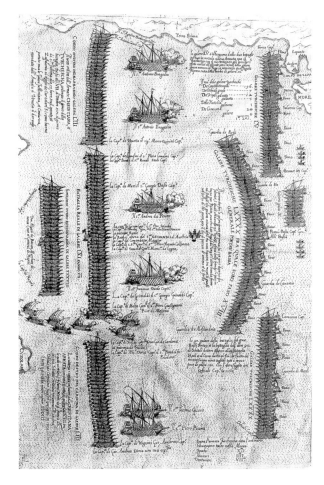

120   Anonymous, *The Battle of Lepanto*, engraving, 1571.
Venice, Museo Civico Correr.

The most successful of all the Lepanto anthologies was Luigi Groto's *Trofeo
della vittoria sacra*. Best known as a playwright, Groto became prominent in
Venetian public life during the 1570s with the publication of his orations,
including a number composed for the coronations of doges. Printed individu-
ally at the time, they were then gathered together in a collective volume both
as a testimony to Groto's abilities in this somewhat stereotyped classicizing
rhetorical genre and as a model for others.[152] His engagement with the Lepanto
literature begins with an oration in celebration of the victory,[153] continues with
a poem in praise of Agostino Barbarigo,[154] Venier's second-in-command who
died from his injuries two days after the battle, and reaches a climax with the
Trofeo, a miscellany that contains dialect verses, Latin poetry, a plan of the battle
and an engraving of the standard of the Turkish fleet with its Kufic inscriptions,

which elaborated the theme of 'There is no other God but God [Allah], and Mahomet is his prophet', explained.[155] This trophy, which had been among those brought back to Venice from Alì Bassa's galley, had become something of a cult object and had changed hands rapidly, first being sold to a jeweller who in turn sold it to the Signoria, who then placed it in the armoury of the Council of Ten (pl. 121).[156] The *Trofeo* is not only the most substantial of the Lepanto anthologies, but also one of the most informative about the motives guiding the process of editorial selection, and in consequence about its intended audience. Presented to the public as a selection of *rime* and *carmi*, it is in reality mostly devoted to the former, since the Latin verses occupy only the last few pages, an imbalance that is typical of collections containing a mixture of Latin and Italian verse. What is more indicative is the strong presence, alongside pieces in these two languages, of dialect poetry. This feature, hinted at on the title-page of the *Trofeo*, which advertises its contents as being written 'by the

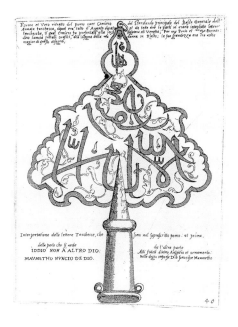

121 Anonymous, engraving of the finial of the Turkish standard, from *Trofeo della vittoria sacra* by Luigi Groto, Venice, 1572. Venice, Museo Civico Correr.

most learned spirits of our time in the most famous languages of Italy', becomes a matter for explanation in the preface. Here Groto, who had evidently been taken to task for having included poetry that was in neither Tuscan nor Latin, replied that God could be praised in all languages, and an idea as successfully expressed in the Bergamasque or Friulian dialect as in Italian or Latin. In addition to poetry in the accepted 'literary' language, a parallel body of dialect work had developed; the catalyst of Lepanto was all that was needed to bring the two tendencies together within one set of covers.[157] In other words, Groto's *Trofeo* was directed at a wide audience, including the communities of dialect speakers and readers who constituted such a considerable portion of the local readership of the Lepanto celebratory literature.[158]

Emboldened by success, some writers now prophesied the complete destruction of the Turkish empire, and the return of the Holy Sepulchre into Christian hands.[159] Orazio Toscanella's *Essortatione ai Cristiani*, whose title recalls Bessarion's famous pamphlet (reprinted in the Lepanto years as it had been during the Holy League's crusade in the late 1530s), emphasizes the Christian duty to reclaim the Holy Land, the birthplace of both Christ and Adam, from the ever-growing threat of Islam.[160] The allies should overcome their differences, urges Toscanella, no doubt with the troubled history of the League in mind, and should drive the Turks back to their own lands, as Alexander the Great had done with Darius, the Athenians with Xerxes, and Hannibal with the Romans.[161] Prominent among the various categories into which this flood of indifferent verses can be subdivided are poems in praise of the architects of victory – pope, doge or emperor – or the military commanders of the various contingents. Another distinct genre among these often trivial outpourings is the lament in which, typically, the sultan blames Muhammad for his defeat, and is either exhorted to become a Christian or spontaneously converts.

Often issued as separate pamphlets of just a few pages, laments were an adaptation of an established genre of the popular press. Cheaply produced, and sold in the squares and streets of the city by ballad-mongers, they were usually topical, prompted by recent political events or natural disasters. Lepanto gave fresh impetus to the tradition, encouraging not only anonymous rhymesters, but also established poets such as Molino, to contribute to the corpus of laments for the loss of the Turkish fleet.[162] Another wave of such verses was directed against the family of Karakosh, the renegade who had fought on the Turkish side.[163] The language of many of these short pieces, some no longer than a couple of stanzas, presents a colourful picture of the passions, rancour and hostility that the Venetians evidently felt for the Turks. The following short piece in the dialect of the Veneto, interesting for what it reveals of popular attitudes, makes play with Selim I's reputed fondness for wine, despite the dictates of his religion:

> Canzon va da Selim
> Pregalo ch'el no beva tanto vin
> Ma che'l cognossa Christo per suo Dio,
> Giusto clemente, e pio
> Che lui solo e quel, che'l puol salvar
> In ste ruine da terra, e da mar.[164]

This draws upon a common topos of the period, which relies upon the notion, enshrined in the insult that someone 'swears, drinks and smokes like a Turk', that Islamic strictures against wine, gambling and other social practices were rarely adhered to. Selim was the embodiment of the stereotype.[165] Another typical and frequently reprinted piece in this vein is 'Quae pars est', a spirited denunciation of the sultan composed in Bergamasque dialect, which was set as a polyphonic *villanella* by Giovanni Ferretti, then living and working in Ancona on the Adriatic coast of the Papal States (and so vulnerable to Turkish attack), in his first book of six-voiced *Canzoni alla napolitana* of 1573:[166]

> Quae pars est, o selim[167] salamelech
> De l'Uniu del Hic, & Hec, & Hoc?[168]
> Sessanta mille de quei to Tarloc
> Co tresent Galer son stag a stech.

E g'anime t'aspetta ilo a Lamech
D'Ali,[169] Piali,[170] Caracossa,[171] e Siroc,[172]
Perque in Bisanz, ne in Algier, o Maroc
Te si segur da sti gran Scanderbech.[173]

Pensavet fors havi a fa co merlot,
con Zent co ti e ti usag al bif?[174]
Despresiador del Santo Sabaot.[175]

L'Aquila[176] co'l Lio[177] col'l bech, e i grif,
Te Squarzara ol cur fo del magot;
Sta mo a senti el tof, el taf, e'l tif?[178]

A similar process of musical adaptation of pre-existent verse is at work in the seven-sectioned 'Canzon nella gran vittoria' that appears in Ippolito Baccusi's second book of six-voiced madrigals of 1572, though here the text is excerpted from Celio Magno's long poem *Fuor fuori o Muse*, one of the more elevated contributions to the Lepanto literature.[179] Baccusi, a Mantuan by birth but then working for the lords of Spilimbergo in Friuli, also published in the same year another seven-sectioned cycle in praise of Lepanto in his second book of five-voiced madrigals. Once again the text, 'Ai più gravi accenti' by Vincenzo Giusto of Udine, had been widely circulated in popular anthologies, and Baccusi must have used some version of it as a source.[180] Both of these large-scale cycles contain sections composed by a local musician, Giovanni Battista Falcidio, thus strengthening the already strong Friulian associations of these two publications. Victory mattered greatly in this wild and somewhat remote area under Venetian control, where the Turks could easily arrive. *Fuor, fuori o Muse* become so well known that other verses were published in its praise. Thus the celebrators became celebrated themselves in the midst of this tide of patriotic sentiment.[181]

After the avalanche of literature of all kinds that followed Lepanto, the next great editorial boom of the 1570s was that which accompanied the visit of Henry III. Some dozen accounts in Italian describing Henry III's progress through the *terraferma*, his reception at the Lido and the subsequent entry into Venice were published in the city, as well as a Latin translation of the main account in French, aimed at the international learned market. In addition, there were collections of celebratory poetry (Pindaric odes were a favoured medium), collections of lyrics put out in short eight-page booklets, orations and Cornelio Frangipane's *Tragedia,* specially written for the king, which was brought out in a number of editions.[182] There was to be nothing quite like it again during the rest of the sixteenth century until a group of Japanese princes visited Venice in 1585 in the course of a triumphal progress that had begun in Portugal, continued in Spain and was to finish in Rome.

The most popular of all the printed descriptions of Henry's visit was written by Rocco Benedetti. His authorized version of the text was published by the bookshop at the Sign of the Star, for which it was anonymously printed in at least two editions, one of ten pages and another of twelve in a larger format. Evidently it sold well, since a few months later the shop issued a further edition, advertised on its title-page as containing additional details not found in the first.[183] Certainly, the wording is somewhat different in places, but the real motivation may have been to combat the cheaper editions that had been appearing in both Venice and Verona, rather than to offer a significantly different account. The most modest edition of all is the pamphlet version, printed anonymously for Vincenzo and Bernardo Viani, a small firm that produced only a small number of books in the 1570s before disappearing from view. By using a small font of almost illegible size and making cuts to the text, the printer was able to reduce Benedetti's original to just four pages.[184] Interestingly, the same setting of this text is found with at least one other printer's mark on the title-page in place of Viani's, suggesting that a consortium of bookmen had been established to share the printing costs and divide the print run between them.[185]

In Viani's shortened version the reader's attention is concentrated on the major events that took place in Venice itself: Henry's official entry into the city under Palladio's triumphal arch at the Lido; the ceremonies in the temporary loggia erected there in front of the church of San Nicolò; the ceremonial progress to the Grand Canal and Ca' Foscari; and the public festivities in the days that followed. By focusing on events in which many Venetians had participated, Viani was shaping his pirated material to an audience that to a considerable extent was local, and eager to purchase an inexpensive memorial to a great historical event that it had witnessed. Aimed at a different market were the descriptive accounts and other literature in Latin, designed to appeal to an educated, professional audience. The main protagonist in this market was not Benedetti's text, which never emerged from the vernacular, but the translation of the principal French account of Henry's progress through Italy, Charles Dorron's *Discours des choses mémorables*, first published in Lyons.[186] The Venetian edition of Dorron's text, issued sometime after September 1574 by Vincenzo Valgrisi, demonstrates the essentially commemorative character of this literature, produced in this case some months after the sights and sounds of the event itself had begun to fade from the collective memory. Quite different in style from the immediacy of Benedetti's text, Dorron's *Narratio rerum memorabilium* was offered to its public as a short instalment of history or chronicle.[187] This sort of approach is even more evident in Nicolò Lucangeli's *I successi del viaggio d'Henrico III*, published in Venice by Giolito, but clearly aimed at a public with an interest in the historical and political background to the celebrations.[188]

One of the longer accounts of Henry's sojourn, Porcacchi's *Le attioni d'Arrigo terzo re di Francia*, is cast in the form of a dialogue between two fictional characters, Ottaviano Manini and Giovanni Gherardeo.[189] Porcacchi is a characteristic example of the new Venetian *poligrafo*, an educated man with antiquarian interests, who had collaborated with Giolito in the publication of a series of popular historical works, the so-called historical jewels ('gioie historiche').[190] It was not so much his work for Giolito that made his reputation, as his collaboration with the engraver Porro in producing *L'isole più famose del mondo*, first published in 1572 and reissued on a number of occasions.[191] Porcacchi's choice of the dialogue form, with its obvious classical parentage, in his account of Henry's visit already suggests that the author's intention was to go beyond simple narrative, and at the beginning of the book he announces his intention to make historical parallels, above all with the visits of other princes who had been received in Venice, and to give some account of the life and achievements of the king. At the opening, Porcacchi begins by telling the story of Henry's birth and youth, stressing the formative role played by Catherine de Médicis in his education, and favourably comparing his youthful military successes against rebels and heretics to the victories of Caesar and the emperor Charles v.[192] This is typical of a style that, larded with references to classical literature and history, as well as to recent events and the Bible, assumes a broad knowledge on the part of the reader. It is only after the death of Charles ix and Henry's election to the throne of Poland have been treated at length (this section of the book includes a long digression on the character of the French monarchy) that the author begins his account of Henry's visit to Venice. Here too the discursive manner continues, inevitably encouraged by the dialogue form, to take in discussions of the nature of the Venetian constitution, the history of France and other contingent matters. It is entirely typical of Porcacchi's conception of his book as a compilation of historical analogies and narrative sources that a complete version of Cornelio Frangipane's *Tragedia*, as performed before Henry by the Gelosi, is embedded in the text.

To an extent that had not been experienced before, printed material of all kinds became a very important agent in the process in which the momentous years after the siege of Malta were not only described and commented on in the short term, but also memorialized and fitted into the constantly evolving Myth of Venice in the long one. Spanning the whole gamut of the order of books, from 'popular' prints to erudite histories in Latin, this extensive phenomenon provided one of the principal means by which Venetians of all social classes recorded and commemorated these events within their houses and palaces. And not only Venetians. Translations into French or Latin, and the printing of multiple editions of the same texts in different cities, indicate that the audience for these productions, as well as for other genres such as costume books, was international.[193] Certainly, it was a contemporary perception that written or printed accounts of ephemeral occasions were a form of permanent memorial. Writing of Henry's visit to northern Italy, Stefano Guazzo asked his readers to:

Give yourself the thought that this is not the work of a single man, and of a single day, and that as one our Italy gave its entire effort to rendering to such a King all the honours that can occur to the human mind. Each city through which he passed ordered a copious and rare history of the magnificences done for him.[194]

If, in many places, that 'copious and rare history' might take the form of traditional chronicle, copied into one of the local standard texts, for the majority of the citizens of the towns and cities that Henry passed through, it took the form of the printed book. This is most obviously true for the dozens of pamphlets describing Henry's progress that were produced. Some of these contained the simplest of narratives and the most basic of descriptions. Others, such as Dorron's rather longer text, or the book-length treatment of Porcacchi, have a clear memorializing function, something that is evident from their more learned style. In the case of Lepanto, Luigi Groto's *Trofeo della vittoria sacra* is a sort of *omnium gatherum*, a ready-made anthology of the most important historical and literary pieces through which the event could be recalled in later years. Even the single-sheet broadside and the crudely printed four-page pamphlet, often described as ephemera, could be used to create more substantial volumes whose function was essentially commemorative. Thirty, fifty or even a hundred small-print pieces relating to Henry's visit or to Lepanto are often found bound together in European libraries. Many are in eighteenth- or nineteenth-century bindings, but others are not, suggesting that this particular form of collectionism was a sixteenth-century phenomenon that responded to a taste for assembling personal commonplace books from broadsides and pamphlets, much as Sanudo incorporated printed material in his diaries.[195] A good many collections of this kind survive as testimony to the use of print to memorialize significant events,[196] and many more are probably disguised in later bindings. Of more limited circulation were the medals issued to commemorate the victory at Lepanto (pl. 122).[197] Exchanged as gifts, collected and preserved in cases or perhaps hung on walls, or even suspended from the neck as personal decoration, these too fixed the occasion for posterity.[198] These domestic repositories of memory and experience were in turn augmented by other cultural forms tied to other settings, including the expansion of public ritual and the embellishment

122   Anonymous, medal for the Victory of Lepanto, 1571. London, British Museum.

270

of sites and spaces, both public and private, with inscriptions, sculpture and paintings, which served to give physical form to the dying memories of transitory occasions. Together with a fresh spate of press activity in the 1590s, these were additional means of not only keeping these events vivid in the collective consciousness, even as their historical significance began to wane, but also of validating them for later generations.

CHAPTER TEN

Ritual Transformations

In terms of tradition and history, it was inevitable that the victory at Lepanto would be marked by a further expansion of the civic liturgy to accommodate an annual celebration. The main vehicle for this elaboration was a saint with strong local associations, St Justina, Virgin and Martyr, on whose feast-day the victory had taken place. A minor figure in the Roman calendar, Justina had always been more significant in a Venetian context, in part because her relics are preserved in Padua, in the church of the Benedictine monastery that bears her name.[1] According to legend, Justina was the daughter of Vitaliano, a Roman official in Padua, who arranged for her to be baptized. When a campaign to eliminate Christianity from the region was instigated under Emperor Claudius, both Justina and her father suffered martyrdom, she by the sword, having defended her faith under heavy questioning. Her body, buried outside Padua on the instructions of St Prosdocimus, who had originally been sent by St Peter to evangelize in the area, was moved to the church of Santa Giustina in the second century. Lost after an earthquake, her body was rediscovered and finally reinterred in the new church in 1562, just nine years before Lepanto. This, at least, was one seventeenth-century version of her life;[2] for the Paduans, Justina was an important local intercessor, whose relics had been authenticated by the usual hagiographical trajectory. Early images of her occur in the nave mosaics of the church of Sant'Apollinare Nuovo in Ravenna, as well as in the north transept of San Marco, clearly labelled in both cases. Since the early fifteenth century her feast-day had attracted some attention, since it coincided with a major victory over the Genoese at Modon in 1456, but the reburial of her remains together with her association with Lepanto now secured the promotion of Justina to a position of major importance within the official articulation of the Myth of Venice. A decree from the doge and Senate ordered that an annual procession, in the form of a full ducal *andata*, should be held from San Marco to the church and convent of Santa Giustina in the north of the city.[3] Founded in the seventh century and consecrated in the early thirteenth, this was one of the oldest churches in Venice and, since the middle of the fifteenth century, had been home to a congregation of Augustinian nuns from the monastery of the Angeli on Murano. In the early sixteenth century the convent of Santa Giustina took on a new lease of life; the church was reconsecrated, and a handsome bell-tower added to the modest complex of buildings.[4]

The *andata* to Santa Giustina was held for the first time in 1572. Since 7 October was now celebrated as one of the major feasts in the Venetian calendar, the Santa Giustina procession included not only the doge and Signoria with the ducal *trionfi*, but also the ambassadors and other foreign dignitaries.[5] On the *fondamenta* in front of the church the doge was received by the clergy dressed in ceremonial vestments. At the church itself a solemn mass was celebrated by one of the canons of San Marco; in this way the church was appropriated and ducal authority asserted through ceremony. The standard of Alvise Mocenigo, during whose dogeship the battle at Lepanto had been fought, was on display, and the vestments of the officiating clergy were trimmed with ermine from Mocenigo's ducal robes, as specified in his will.[6] There followed a brief ritual in which the hymn 'Salvum me fac' was sung and the doge presented specially minted coins, popularly known as *giustine*, to the nuns.[7] Both in Venice and Rome, medals and coins were an important way in which Lepanto was memorialized at an individual level (see pl. 122).[8] A form of symbolic reward that could be worn about the person, or exchanged as gifts, they functioned as portable propaganda that also fed into the construction of papal and ducal biographies.

Following this the celebrant intoned 'Exaudi nos', and the procession, chanting litanies as it went, returned to the Piazza San Marco, where there was a review of the *scuole* and of all the clergy of the city. This symbolic act emphasized the doge's authority over the ecclesiastical establishment; it was through such means that the Venetians were constantly reminded of the unity of church and state, placed under the patronage of St Mark and guided by his representative on earth. Through these ceremonial and liturgical acts, the Saint Giustina *andata* joined together a mass celebrating a great naval victory and a civic procession and parade in which officials of state, clergy and the *scuole* all participated in a public representation of a harmonious political order. As with other such events, the Santa Giustina *andata* provided the government of the Republic with the opportunity to honour a saint and commemorate the dead, while at the same time strengthening social cohesion through communal displays of piety and patriotism. In the case of the Turks, who remained uneasily and prominently lodged in the Venetian collective consciousness despite Lepanto, there was the added attraction of annually identifying a common enemy.

Official promulgation of the cult of St Justina did not stop with this weaving of yet another annual celebration into the rich fabric of the already crowded ceremonial life of Venice. Throughout the 1570s and beyond, Justina's newly acquired significance was frequently expressed in a wide range of plays, verse, paintings and sculpture that were employed to celebrate and recall the victory. Indeed, it was largely through her image that the Venetians were constantly reminded of the achievement of Lepanto in later years. One of the earliest literary examples is Celio Magno's play with music, the *Trionfo di Christo*, one of the better literary efforts thrown up by the celebrations. The published text of Magno's play is dedicated to the members of the League, and carries an exuberant preface that explicitly proclaims the victory as Christ's achievement.[9] The *Trionfo di Christo* was performed for the first time before the doge and Senate on the feast of St Stephen in 1572, a day with some local significance; since his body had been brought to Venice in 1109 and was buried in San Giorgio Maggiore, the saint occupied a prominent position in the Venetian calendar.[10] It was also on this day that the Carnival season, which lasted until the first day of Lent, began.[11] By convention, mass was said at San Giorgio in the presence of the doge, who then provided a banquet for the principal office-holders in the Doge's Palace, one of four such occasions held in the course of the year with the primary aim of reinforcing a sense of solidarity and common purpose among the leading patricians.[12]

The prototype for the performance of *rappresentazioni* on this occasion appears to have been another of Magno's works given in 1570, but the *Trionfo di Christo* inaugurated the practice of plays with music given at the end of the feast. None of the music has survived, but the *libretti* have, and from these it is clear that although traditional in conception they were quite elaborate in presentation, particularly under the dogeship of Marino Grimani (1595–1605).[13] The *Trionfo* itself is a short and simple drama cast in the mould of the traditional *sacra rappresentazione*, and presents the familiar theme of the Venetians as the Chosen People through whose courage the Infidel has been punished. It proceeds in an entirely emblematic fashion by first introducing David, then the patron saints of the three members of the Holy League, and finally St Justina and the Angel Gabriel, all of whom praise the League in general and the Venetians in particular as the agents of victory. In between these speeches there are choruses, perhaps the 'musiche straordinarie' that the Ferrarese ambassador Claudio Ariosti so admired.[14] In Magno's *Trionfo*, issues of history were neatly intertwined with the theme of Venetian sovereignty (by association with David), and the topic of the Venetians as the chosen race. Rescued from a position of comparative obscurity in the Venetian ritual calendar, St Justina was now indissolubly wedded to the crucial process of divine intervention that had secured the victory. In the ephemeral literature she was rapidly promoted. The title-page

of Paolo Paruta's funeral oration in honour of the
Venetian dead shows her supported by two lions
with, around the decorative frame, the affirmation
'In te Domine speravi' (pl. 124). Above the gateway
of the Arsenal, symbol and source of Venetian
naval power, her statue by Girolamo Campagna
was raised in 1578, together with an explanatory
inscription in Latin, VICTORIAE NAVALIS MONV-
MENTVM, and the date, M.D.L.XXI. Damaged in the
explosion of 1569, said to have been perpetrated by
Joseph Nasi's agents, the *Porta magna* of the
Arsenal was restored at about the same time to
incorporate flying *Victories* in the spandrels.[15] The
appearance of the entrance before further modifications, including the addition of a balustrade,
were made in the eighteenth century, can be seen
in an engraving by Giacomo Franco (pl. 125).

In the decades after Lepanto, Justina became
an increasingly familiar presence in works of art
of all kinds.[16] Among paintings the best known is
Paolo Veronese's *Allegory of the Battle of Lepanto*,
where the saint is

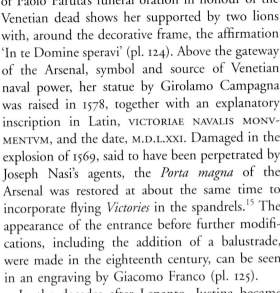

124   Paolo Paruta, *Oratione funebre*,
title page. Cambridge, University
Library.

shown, alongside the traditional figure of Venice
clothed in white rather than the traditional elaborate brocade (thus equating her with Faith),[17] in
the company of Sts Peter, James and Mark,
patrons of the members of the League, who offer
prayers to the Virgin while the battle rages below
(pl. 126).[18] Perhaps painted for Pietro Giustinian,
who as prior of the Knights of Malta and the
commander of their galley played a prominent
role in the action at Lepanto, it is recorded in
the mid-seventeenth century in the chapel of the
Confraternity of the Rosary in San Pietro
Martire in Murano; there it hung opposite the
Madonna of the Rosary by Veronese and his workshop, which had also been commissioned by the
confraternity (see pl. 130).[19] At a more general
level, Justina rapidly assumed the role of one of
the protectors of Venice and its government and
is shown as such, guiding a group of treasurers
and secretaries of the Republic, in Tintoretto's
canvas painted for the offices of the Camerlenghi

125   Giacomo Franco, *The Gateway of
the Arsenal*, engraving. Venice, Museo
Civico Correr.

126   Paolo Veronese, *Allegory of the Battle of Lepanto*, c.1571–3. Venice, Gallerie dell'
Accademia.

di Comun in the Palazzo dei Camerlenghi at the Rialto (pl. 127).[20] This is yet
a further variation of a standard scheme, in which specific state officials are
shown either in adoration or under the protection of the Virgin, Christ or St
Mark. Originally, the picture hung with other votive pictures in the same
iconographical format, including the *Madonna of the Treasurers* of 1566, also
by Tintoretto, which seems to be the prototype for the genre.[21] Perhaps the

127   Jacopo Tintoretto, *St. Justina with Three Treasurers of the Republic and their Secretaries*, 1580. Venice, Museo Civico Correr.

most striking of all the images of St Justina to be executed in these years is the large canvas painted for the Benedictine church of Santa Giustina in Padua. Although this completed the scheme for the reconstruction of the choir that had been in progress for some fifteen years, it may have been the victory itself that gave the authorities the extra impetus that prompted them to commission this altarpiece, begun in 1574 and completed the following year, from Veronese. Their choice of artist is not surprising; Veronese had been recently commissioned by the Benedictines to produce work for a number of their churches in north Italy: Santi Nazaro e Celso in Verona, Santa Maria di Praglia and San Benedetto Po, and San Giorgio in Venice. Against a background view of Padua, dominated by the distinctive domes of the church of Santa Giustina, it shows the saint, set back from the surface of the canvas, surrounded by a group of soldiers and priests, at the moment of her martyrdom (pl. 128).[22] The emphasis upon Christ, bathed in a brilliant heavenly light and framed by an angelic choir, represents an intermediate stage in the process in which, following Tridentine thinking, the titular saint was gradually replaced in altarpieces. Flanked by St John the Evangelist and the Virgin, Christ is here the

128   Paolo Veronese, *The Martyrdom of St. Justina*, 1574–5. Padua, Church of St. Justina.

object of intercession.[23] In 1582, during his first visit to Venice, Agostino Caracci made a two-plate engraving of Veronese's painting, making significant alterations to the composition in the process.[24]

It is clear that the celebrations for the feast-day of St Justina involved a good deal of music. The choir of San Marco walked in the *andata*, and according to the ceremony books simple double-choir litanies and psalms were sung along the route.[25] At the church itself polyphony was performed (one chronicler speaks of 'canti e suoni'). In 1610 Giovanni Stringa described the occasion as 'senza dubbio molto solenne',[26] and writing in the 1620s, Claudio Monteverdi, then *maestro di cappella* at San Marco, mentions the performance of 'solemn music' for the feast as something that required considerable preparation.[27] One piece that was evidently composed for performance on the day is Giovanni Bassano's five-voiced motet, 'Beata virgo et martyr Iustina', published in his *Motetti per concerti ecclesiastici* of 1598. Its non-liturgical text celebrates the circumstances of St Justina's martyrdom, much as the event is evoked in Veronese's painting:

> When the blessed virgin and martyr Justina
> was being dragged to punishment
> by the wicked tyrant,
> she called to the Lord:
> Lord, I give thanks to you,
> whom I have always loved,
> whom I have sought, whom I have desired,
> because you have thought fit
> to receive me into the company of martyrs.
> Alleluia.[28]

Best known as a virtuoso cornet player and author of an influential treatise on ornamentation, Bassano spent much of his career teaching singing at San Marco. As the dedication of the volume, to the procurators of San Marco, makes clear, Bassano was also in charge of the music at the Seminary, and the contents of the book were composed in connection with his official duties.

The final ceremonial act on the feast-day of St Justina occurred at second vespers in San Marco. As on all the major feasts in the Venetian calendar, of which this was now one, the choir was required to be present for this service, and polyphonic psalm settings for two choirs were sung while the Pala d'Oro was open to view. By this date Sansovino's tribunes were no longer in use for the performance of polyphony at Vespers, and the choir stood in the *pulpitum magnum* in front of the iconostasis. This may have deprived the liturgical choreography of a significant element of Doge Andrea Gritti's classicizing *renovatio*, but other historical resonances were strongly evoked as, above the tomb of St Mark and in the presence of the doge and Senate, in front of an altarpiece from Constantinople, the liturgy was enacted according to the unique requirements of the *patriarchino*. Throughout the following decades, as Venetian economic power declined and what was left of the *terra da mar* slowly disintegrated, this evocative combination continued to recall the events of 7 October 1571.

It was not uncommon for other churches, such as the parish church of Santa Marina, which was primarily associated with the recovery of Padua in 1509 and as such was also the object of an annual *andata* of its own,[29] to be acknowledged if not visited in the course of the Santa Giustina procession. In particular, the church of Santi Giovanni e Paolo was occasionally included on the route of the *andata* after 1575, when a separate chapel consecrated to the Madonna of the Rosary was established there.[30] This ritual detail made explicit the connections between Lepanto, St Justina and the rosary. At the same time, such amplifications of the Santa Giustina procession strengthened its prime function as a celebration, within a commonly understood civic and liturgical framework, of a great Venetian victory.

Devotion to the rosary, which involved the recitation of prayers in fifteen decades, each designed to encourage meditation on an important episode in the life of Christ and the Virgin, had been growing in strength since the middle of the fifteenth century, particularly among the increasing number of confraternities that were dedicated to the cult.[31] Although the rosary could be recited privately, either in church or at home, these groups of laymen normally maintained altars in parish churches so that the devotion could be carried out communally. Originally established in Cologne in 1475 by a Dominican, Jakob Sprenger, the idea of a rosary confraternity was introduced to Venice shortly afterwards, when the first example was established at San Domenico di Castello.[32] In 1506, during his second Italian journey, Albrecht Dürer executed a large panel painting, now in Prague and commonly known as the *Feast of the Rose Garlands*, for the German Confraternity of the Rosary, founded just eighteen months earlier and attached to the parish church of San Bartolomeo di Rialto, close to their *fondaco* at the foot of the Rialto bridge (pl. 129).[33] Although a group of merchants from Nuremberg had earlier founded a *scuola piccola*, also based in the church, this was the first time that there had been one for the whole German 'nation' in Venice, as there had been for some time for the Albanians, Greeks, Florentines and Milanese. Placed over their altar, where it was recorded by Sansovino,[34] Dürer's painting was visited by both the doge and the patriarch soon after its arrival, and gave fresh visibility and presence to the cult of the rosary in the city. The composition, based on the *Madonna of the Rosary* woodcut in the 1476 edition of the statutes of Sprenger's Cologne confraternity, is dominated by the central figure of the Virgin enthroned, with the Christ Child on her lap. St Dominic, who stands to her right, distributes rosaries (made up of roses) to a group of the faithful, including the pope and Emperor Maximilian I, who kneel in adoration.[35] As a proud label of his authorship, Dürer inserted a portrait of himself into the picture,

129   Albrecht Durer, *Feast of the Rosegarlands*, 1506. Prague, National Gallery.

holding a *cartolino* with the inscription 'Exegit quinque mestri spatio Albertus / Durer germanus / MDV' ('It took five months. Albrecht Dürer the German 1506'), accompanied by another figure, who, it has been suggested, is the founder of the Venetian confraternity, Leonhard Wild, a book publisher and merchant from Regensberg. Dürer's painting, which initially caused some local hostility, makes a number of gestures in the direction of Venetian traditions in both composition and altarpiece design.[36]

The increase in the popularity of the rosary that occurred in the last quarter of the sixteenth century was largely the result of changes to the Roman liturgy, which anchored it to the annual commemoration of Lepanto. This connection was initially established by Pius V, in the belief that the battle had been won through the intercession of the Virgin. According to his biographers, the pope recited the rosary daily, and as head of the universal church (and a Dominican), he used his position to promote and protect the cult. In his bull *Consueverunt*, issued in 1569, Pius emphasized the role of the rosary in combating heresy and promoting internal reform of the church. This had the effect of strengthening devotion by giving the rosary an increased doctrinal role, but the real impetus for a surge in its popularity came with Lepanto. Since the battle had taken place on the first Sunday of the month, a day when rosary confraternities usually met and processed, Pius proclaimed (in the bull *Salvator Domini* of 5 March 1572) that the victory was itself proof of the devotion's efficacy. Two weeks later the pope announced the establishment of the feast of Our Lady of Victory.[37] According to the Roman Breviary, it was also Pius who added the text and chants of 'Auxiliorum Christianorum' to the Litany of Loreto, which became standard during the second half of the sixteenth century. The historical reality is different, since 'Auxiliorum Christianorum' was already present in some versions of the litany published prior to Lepanto,[38] making this false claim part of the mythology that evolved around the figure of Pius himself. The connection between Lepanto and the rosary was further consolidated by his successor, Gregory XIII, who in 1573 designated the first Sunday in October as the feast of Our Lady of the Rosary.[39]

The fresh lease of life that its association with Lepanto brought to the devotion of the rosary was particularly strong in Venice and the Veneto, and is reflected in the activities of confraternities dedicated to the cult, and in particular to their patronage of buildings and the decorative arts. At Santi Giovanni e Paolo in Venice, the Scuola del Rosario, whose membership seems to have consisted largely of wealthy merchants, raised the considerable resources necessary to transform the Gothic chapel of San Domenico in the north transept of the church into a modern shrine dedicated to the rosary and in memory of the victory at Lepanto.[40] Alessandro Vittoria, placed in charge of the work, was also responsible for the statues of *St Dominic* and *St Justina*, as well as the stucco-work and two bronze candelabra placed in the chapel.[41] An ornate wooden ceiling was also installed,[42] adorned with canvases dealing with the origin of the devotion, and by the time that the high altar was consecrated in 1605, the effect was striking, so much so that Stringa considered it to be without parallel in the whole of Italy.[43] By this date the chapel was lined with more than thirty paintings executed by some of the most prominent Venetian artists of the day. Destroyed by fire in 1867, the decorative scheme is known to have included a strong Lepanto component. One large painting by Domenico Tintoretto, known from an engraving by Giacomo Franco, apparently showed a simple allegory of the victory as the achievement of the Holy League, secured through the intercession of the Virgin and St Justina, and sustained by Faith. In the foreground were to be seen the figures of Pius V, Philip II and Doge Mocenigo, and ranged behind them were Colonna, Don Juan of Austria and Sebastian Venier. Above, in the heavens, the images of the Virgin, Faith and St Justina looked down benevolently on those below, while the battle raged in the background.[44] Such group portraits are a common feature of Lepanto celebratory art. A particularly imposing example is Dario Varotari's *Celebrazione della Lega* of 1573, commissioned by Giacomo Emo for the Palazzo del Podestà in Padua. With its large cast of characters, which includes diplomats such as

130   Paolo Veronese and workshop, *Madonna of the Rosary*, *c*.1571. Murano, Museo Vetrario, on deposit in Venice, Gallerie dell'Accademia.

Marcantonio Barbaro and a contingent of Spanish and Genoese galley captains, it has been characterized as a 'group photograph' of the principal actors in the Lepanto drama.[45] Somewhat similar is the *Madonna of the Rosary* (pl. 130), normally attributed to Veronese and assistants, originally commissioned by another Confraternity of the Rosary for its chapel in the church of San Pietro Martire in Murano, where it was placed opposite Veronese's *Allegory of the Battle of Lepanto* (see pl. 126). This also shows the Virgin enthroned in glory being venerated by pope, doge and emperor surrounded by members of the confraternity, while St Dominic moves between them scattering handfuls of rose-petals.[46] While daylight is fading in the distant gulf, the luminescence of the upper register imparts an almost spiritual quality to the picture, which functions on both historical and allegorical levels.[47]

Members of the rosary confraternities must have formed a major component of the market for rosary manuals and prints,[48] as well as the small bronze plaquettes showing the *Madonna of the Rosary*, which were manufactured in some quantity in the last quarter of the sixteenth century. Two designs are known.[49] The first, which shows the *Coronation of the Virgin and Celebration of the Rosary*, is generally thought to have been produced in the circle around Girolamo Campagna and Alessandro Vittoria, both of whom were involved in the decoration of the rosary chapel in Santi Giovanni e Paolo. In its original state, this plaquette consists of an unmounted rectangle, but a good number of examples with elaborate Mannerist frames also survive.[50] A second style, showing the *Madonna of the Rosary* surrounded by Dominican saints and representatives of the Holy League (Pope Clement VIII, Emperor Rudolph II and Doge Marino Grimani), also exists in a number of variants.[51] Although there is little information about the commercial and social contexts in which plaquettes were manufactured and distributed, survivals suggest that they were often mounted on larger objects such as ink-wells, sword pommels and hat badges.[52] One specimen survives incorporated into a contemporary liturgical pax,[53] and a number of perforated examples suggest that plaquettes, like medals, could be hung on the wall as objects of devotion in the home. This intimate relationship to the materiality of everyday existence gave plaquettes an important role as one of the means through which Lepanto was commemorated and memorialized, a role that they shared with the single-sheet engravings and woodcuts of the *Madonna of the Rosary* that were produced in quantity in the last decades of the century.

The end of the plague in 1577 also gave the Venetians an annual opportunity to register their gratitude for this sign of divine benevolence, which, as with Lepanto, the Venetians took to be a confirmation of their favoured status. Even for Venice, a state that had resolutely opposed papal authority in local affairs for decades, and was to continue to do so in the years before the Interdict, when the entire Venetian population was excommunicated, the process of commissioning the church of the Redentore was novel. The procedures followed in choosing a site and determining a design show the Venetian state at work to realize its political, social and religious aims, not just through generalized support backed up by economic provision for a new building, but also by detailed control of the entire project. A committee of senators was charged with finding a site for the building, which was to be placed in the care of a monastic order. The final decision, made by the Senate, was to select an area on the Giudecca, and to elect the Capuchins as custodians of the new church. It seems that the ecclesiastical authorities were not consulted, and the Capuchins were later to complain strenuously that Palladio's design contravened their monastic principles.[54]

From the beginning of the project to build a votive church, in fulfilment of Doge Alvise Mocenigo's vow, it had been recognized that the Redentore had to meet rather particular ceremonial requirements. As part of its vote, the Senate had instituted an *andata* in thanksgiving for the city's liberation from the plague, and while the choice of the site was a Venetian adaptation of the common practice of constructing plague churches outside the city walls, it also produced a visually spectacular result, in which Palladio's imposing façade, reflected in the water, is primarily intended to be viewed from the Zattere, on the opposite side of the canal (pl. 131). It was from this perspective that the church was seen by the participants in the *andata* as they approached it on a temporary bridge slung across the water from the Zattere.

131   Church of the Redentore.

A temple in the classical style had been envisaged from the beginning, since long before any decision about either site or architect had been made, the Venetian Mint had issued five *oselle*, designed for public distribution, showing five different imaginary buildings of this type. In three of these the traditional iconography has been replaced by the image of the doge kneeling not in front of St Mark, but before Christ the Redeemer, while in another a façade that anticipates Palladio's design is shown (pl. 132).[55] It was also the Senate that determined the overall form of the scheme. On 9 February 1577 a debate was held in which it was agreed that the church should be 'quadrangular' rather than round.[56] An important element in the decision was the need to accommodate the doge, the Senate and a large number of officials on the occasion of the annual *andata*, which the Senate had already voted to institute. This required not only a sizeable processional area, but also a space where the doge and senators could be seated during the celebration of mass.[57] On this occasion, when mass was said by the prior of the Capuchins, and motets were sung, it must be assumed that the *cappella mar-*

ciana performed from the tribune, and that the monastic choir sat in the choirstalls housed to the east of the high altar, an arrangement that may also account for the generous acoustic of the building.[58] These considerations undoubtedly influenced Palladio's choice of a long nave and a spacious tribune leading directly to the chancel, so that those present were brought closer to the altar.

In some respects the design of the Redentore (pls 133, 134) recalls that of San Giorgio Maggiore, Palladio's other major Venetian church, also commissioned by the Cassinense branch of the Benedictines and, like the Redentore, based on the mother house of the order, Santa Giustina in Padua. The architect's work at the Redentore, particularly in relation to accommodating liturgy and music, was clearly shaped by his earlier experience at San Giorgio. Here too the needs of liturgy and ceremony were important, since San Giorgio was planned to provide a suitable theatre for the ceremonies that took place on the vigil and feast-day of St Stephen.[59] The saint's body had arrived at the monastery in the twelfth century; shortly afterwards the annual *andata* was instituted.[60] On Christmas Day, the doge and Senate, together with the ambassadors and other officials and a full complement of *trionfi* in the form of the ducal procession, crossed the lagoon and disembarked in the spacious foreground of San Giorgio. The arrangement of this prefatory area to the church itself was clearly designed to accommodate ceremonial practice. It was there that the ducal procession was met by the abbot and the community, before the entire company entered the church to begin the prescribed ceremonies, at the centre of which was the celebration of vespers.[61] In the old church the relic of St Stephen had been placed under the high altar, but in the new one it was situated in the transept. This change, made in accordance with Tridentine ideas, which held that the Sacrament should be placed on the high altar, may have provoked some of the more unusual aspects of Palladio's design relating to accessibility and visibility.

132   *Osella* for the foundation of the Church of the Redentore, 1577. Venice, Museo Civico Correr.

133   Church of the Redentore, ground plan.

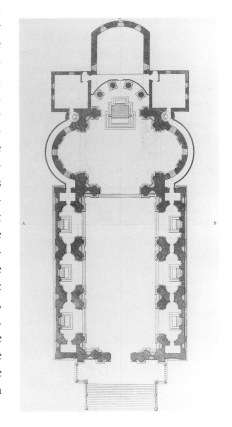

287

134 Interior of the Church of the Redentore.

The other novel aspects of the design of San Giorgio Maggiore are related to the liturgical and ceremonial needs of the interior spaces. In addition to the large number of officials who had to be accommodated in the area around the repositioned altar of St Stephen, some provision also had to be made for the performance of polyphony. In common with the other occasions in the calendar when the full *andata* was staged, the procession included not only the canons of San Marco, who were responsible for singing the chant, but also eight singers from the *cappella marciana* who were charged with performing double-choir vespers psalms according to the tradition practised on feast-days in San Marco itself. Although common to all ducal processions when the *trionfi* were carried, the transferral of ritual practices from the basilica to the point of arrival had a particularly strong political resonance in the case of San Giorgio, since the church was one of a number, including the two churches at Rialto, that were under the *ius patronatus* of the doge. In this way, as well as through others, including the ritualistic details of the initial meeting between doge and abbot, accompanied by their respective 'communities' before the celebration of vespers, the subservience of the chapter of San Giorgio to ducal authority was empha-sized.[62] It was presumably these ceremonial arrangements, as well as the dra-matic possibilities of the site, that encouraged Palladio to create a substantial square in front of the church, which functioned as a sort of apron stage on which the doge and abbot met together with their retinues. This moment is shown in Franco's engraving, which shows instrumentalists, in addition to the silver trumpets that were carried in procession as part of the *trionfi*. Their participation, at least in 1562 (at the very moment when a permanent nucleus of players was added to the basilica's musical forces), is confirmed by documents.[63] Similarly, the need to accommodate the singers from San Marco, who performed both at vespers on the vigil of St Stephen as well as at mass on the following day without unseemly crowding, explains the width of Palladio's transept, and his decision to extend both presbytery and apse.[64] Palladio's experiences at San Giorgio must have coloured his approach to the analogous situation at the Redentore. Certainly, the requirements of liturgy, ceremony and music were clearly uppermost in the architect's mind when he came to conceive both these churches, while other features of his plan, such as the elevation of the altar above the nave, which satisfied reformist demands for making the central mysteries of the liturgy more accessible, are indebted both to Counter-Reformation thought in general and to his previous church for the Benedictines.[65]

At an early stage in the deliberations, a site next to the convent of Santa Croce, which had been a place of popular pilgrimage since the plague of 1464, was considered as a suitable location for the Redentore.[66] As recorded in a manuscript known to have come from the convent,[67] at the height of the epidemic that took place in that year, when four of the nuns had already succumbed and a fifth was on her death-bed, an unknown man appeared at the entrance to the *parlatorio*. He claimed to be a knight of the king of France, and spoke with one of the sisters. After questioning her, he urged that the community pray to St Sebastian, one of the principal protectors against the disease, promising that if his advice was followed the convent would be freed from plague in perpetuity. Before taking his leave, he drank from the well. This story was revived during the plague of 1575–7, and the rumour spread that Santa Croce had indeed remained immune in keeping with the prophecy. From the summer of 1576, with the disease at its height, such large numbers arrived to drink the miraculous waters that a contingent of sailors from the Arsenal had to be brought in to keep order, and a conduit constructed to meet demand.[68] In the Venetian popular mentality this lent the area a mythical attraction, which intensified its appeal as the site of a plague church.

In the end, both the nunnery at Santa Croce, and an alternative site at San Vidal, were rejected, leaving the Capuchin friary on the Giudecca as the preferred option. The Capuchins were regarded as ideal custodians of the church, and the site itself was admired for its architectural possibilities. It was also the most suitable in terms of processional and theatrical requirements, since in addition to being visually spectacular when viewed from the opposite side of the Giudecca canal, the façade of the Redentore also functioned as a sort of *frons scenae* for the *andata* itself, which took place in July. On that day the doge and Signoria, accompanied by the *scuole grandi* and the religious orders and congregations of the city, processed to the church across two pontoon bridges constructed on top of flat-bottomed boats.[69] This, one of the more important and impressive *andate* in the Venetian festal calendar, involved large numbers of participants. Francesco Sansovino comments both on the large crowds that accompanied the procession and on the beauty of the scene, since, throughout the following three days, the Venetians crossed to the Giudecca in their thousands to visit the church and to give thanks.[70] This ceremonial function of the church, as the site of an annual public affirmation of gratitude for liberation from the plague, may have influenced the Senate's decision to opt for a cruciform plan for the church, a solution that was not only traditional in liturgical terms, but was also more spacious than the centrally planned design advocated by Marcantonio Barbaro and evidently preferred by the architect himself.[71] The need to accommodate the *andata*, together with the liturgical requirements of the Capuchins and the restrictions of a site that was both long and narrow, made a centralized project untenable.[72] In March 1577 the doge and Senate processed to the chosen site, and the foundation stone of Palladio's church was laid.[73]

On 13 July 1577 Venice was officially declared free of the plague, and one week later a procession to the site of the Redentore was held.[74] Descending from his apartments in the Doge's Palace, the new doge, Sebastian Venier, festally dressed and accompanied by the ambassadors and all the members of the Senate, heard mass in the basilica celebrated by the patriarch of Venice, followed by orations giving thanks for the lifting of the epidemic. In the Piazza San Marco and the Piazzetta some at least of the market stalls had been cleared away, and a ceremonial route had been marked out with banners suspended from flagpoles. Sansovino's Library had also been decorated with tapestries hung under the porticoes. At the offices of the health board, close to the Mint, a display of paintings, reminiscent of that put on during the Lepanto celebrations, had been mounted. One description noted in particular a painting showing Christ the Redeemer in heaven, while beneath there was a young woman in prayer and the figure of St Roch, on either side of a scene showing doctors tending the afflicted. In front of the building sat the three procurators of San Marco and the three *provveditori alla sanità*.

For this first *andata* a bridge had been built across the canal. Supported on more than eighty large craft of various kinds, it stretched from the Piazza San Marco to the church of San Giovanni on the Giudecca, and had been built in just four days. As was usual on major occasions, the *scuole grandi* carried displays of precious silver objects (the Scuola Grande di San Rocco is singled out for special mention), and the choir of San Marco took part in the procession as they were to do in successive years.[75] At the site itself an altar had been erected over the foundations of the church (which was not finally to be finished and consecrated until 1592), and the space around it had been arranged

135   Joseph Heintz the younger, *Procession to the Church of the Redentore*, c.1630. Venice, Museo Civico Correr.

'in the shape of a theatre', as a contemporary description puts it, with benches for the Senate.[76] These functional arrangements clearly anticipate the final design. Over the altar itself an oil painting of *Christ the Redeemer* had been set up. After mass had been celebrated, and the foundations blessed, the procession then returned to San Marco where another mass was celebrated and the traditional review of the *scuole* and the religious of the city took place in the presence of the doge. In successive years the *andata* took its place in the calendar as a splendid public spectacle, witnessed in admiration by foreign visitors to the city and depicted by artists (pl. 135). Following the procession, which for Venetians represented a symbolic annual reaffirmation of their special status as the recipients of divine favour, low mass was said by the prior of the Capuchins. Writing in the early seventeenth century, Giovanni Stringa noted that the *cappella marciana* performed motets at both the offertory and the elevation of the Host.[77] The feast of the Redentore, newly inserted into the festal calendar, had become yet a further expression, through musical and ceremonial strategies, of Venetian local identity.

CHAPTER ELEVEN

Gods and Heroes

On 7 October 1577, just a few months after this *andata* to the site of the Redentore, Sebastian Venier, accompanied by the Senate, the foreign ambassadors and
the rest of the Venetian ceremonial machine, made the *andata* to the church
of Santa Giustina for the first time after his election as doge. It must have been
a highly symbolic and triumphal moment, something of a high point in his
brief period at the pinnacle of the Venetian system. Since the victory at
Lepanto, Venier had become the focus of a fresh phase of Venetian auto-
celebration, and in this sense his election had more to do with *ragion di stato*
than with personal aptitude for the office. This had been evident as early as
November 1572, when Venier finally returned to Venice to be welcomed with
an official *entrata* that had been ordered by the Senate, a prerogative normally
reserved for distinguished visitors of high social rank. Having been met by the
nobility dressed in scarlet robes, his galley was escorted to the Piazzetta, where
he was greeted with applause by the waiting crowds. At the main door of San
Marco he was warmly received by the doge and Senate, and the celebration of
high mass followed.[1] Venier's election as doge in succession to Alvise Mocenigo
was regarded as a fitting conclusion to the glorious career of the hero of
Lepanto, who had served the state in a variety of roles before becoming captain-
general in 1570 at the age of 75. One writer described his election as a clear
sign of God's favour after the dark years in which many indignities had been
suffered by the Venetians, and made favourable comparisons between Venier
and some of the great figures from classical antiquity, including Alexander,
Caesar and Hannibal.[2] Such rhetoric is typical of the language, whether visual
or literary, that was deployed to celebrate the achievements of the heroes, saints

136   Alessandro Vittoria, bust of Francesco Duodo, late 1580s. Venice, Cà d'Oro.

137 Paolo Veronese, *Sebastiano Venier giving Thanks for the Victory at Lepanto*, c.1578.
Ducal Palace, Sala del Collegio.

and martyrs of the 1570s – whether Agostino Barbarigo, Marcantonio Bragadin
or Henry III of France, as seen through a Venetian optic.[3]

The twin themes of military prowess and divine protection make an appearance in a number of paintings, sculptures and engravings that celebrate Venier's
role, notably Veronese's votive canvas, prominently installed above the tribune in
the Sala del Collegio (recently refurbished to designs by Palladio) sometime
before 1581, when it was described by Francesco Sansovino (pl. 137). Veronese's
painting was executed as part of the wholesale refitting of the room, which had
been severely damaged in the fire of 1574. It shows Christ seated in the clouds,
his hand raised in benediction. Venier, clad in armour and wearing the ducal
mantle, kneels in adoration of Christ and St Justina, identified by the palm of
martyrdom that she is carrying. The elderly Venier is being assisted by St Mark,
while above him is the profile of his second-in-command at Lepanto, Agostino
Barbarigo, and galleys in the background make a clear reference to the battle
itself.[4] The finished version of the painting replaced an earlier scheme, for which
a sketch survives, in which Christ is replaced by St Mark and St Justina by the
figure of Venetia (pl. 138). It is clear that this preliminary version, in effect a personal coronation allegory, strongly evocative of the spirit of adulation that greeted
Venier's return to Venice and that continued throughout his dogeship, was
replaced *post mortem* (he died in March 1578) with an official state allegory, in
which the Republic's traditional aversion to personality cults intervened to secure
an interpretation of the victory that placed less emphasis on Venier's individual
contribution. Hence too, perhaps, the inclusion of Barbarigo as a counterweight.[5]

138 Paolo Veronese, *Sebastiano Venier giving Thanks for the Victory at Lepanto*, drawing, *c.*1578. London, British Museum.

The connection between Lepanto and Venier's election is made even more explicit in a full-length portrait, which shows him dressed in armour, with his helmet at his feet, holding the baton of command (pl. 139). Although the captain-general of the Venetian navy was elected by the Senate, the emblems of office (which in addition to the baton included one of the banners of St Mark from the Arsenal) were consigned by the doge in an elaborate ceremony in San Marco that contained ritual elements derived from the ducal investiture ceremony. This also included the performance of a polyphonic setting of the 'Oration di San Marco', of which survive a number of late sixteenth-century versions by composers connected with the basilica. Having turned over the banner to the admiral of the fleet, the captain-general was carried around the Piazza on a wooden platform by a contingent of sailors and threw coins to the crowd.[6] Described by Sansovino and illustrated in one of Franco's engravings, the ceremony was a public and familiar one.[7] In the

139 Jacopo Tintoretto, *Portrait of Sebastiano Venier with a Page*, 1577. Turin, private collection.

140 Alessandro Vittoria, *Bust of Sebastiano Venier*, late 1570s. Ducal Palace.

141 Giacomo Franco, *Sebastiano Venier as Captain General of the Fleet*, engraving. Venice, Museo Civico Correr.

background of Tintoretto's painting there is a clear allusion to Lepanto, and to the divine intervention that ensured the success of Venier's mission. While the battle rages, St Michael can be seen fighting on behalf of the confederates, and Christ appears in the heavens holding the banner of the League, while to Venier's right, at the front of the composition, a page hands him a letter announcing his election as doge.[8] The attribution to Tintoretto, followed by most writers, has recently been placed in doubt.[9] In functional terms the portrait forms part of a repertory of busts and portraits, including a marble sculpture by Alessandro Vittoria that was specifically left to the state by the artist in his will to be placed in the Sala del Consiglio di Dieci in the Doge's Palace.[10]

Through paintings such as these, as well as Vittoria's marble bust (pl. 140),[11] and above all through Franco's engraving (pl. 141), Venier was celebrated as one of the two Venetian architects of victory, an ideal model for male patricians, 'a mirror' as Pietro Contarini put it, 'for other Venetian nobles to hold up to themselves with respect to their Patria'.[12] The other critical actor was Mocenigo, whose role was endlessly memorialized in the many images that make use of the figures of doge, pope and emperor in marking the formation of the League, and during whose dogeship the victory was commemorated with a number of specially issued medals.[13] These post-Lepanto commemorations were the latest in a long process, in which the Venetians had celebrated the virtues and deeds of the heroes of the War of Cyprus. The fall of Nicosia, where the Turks had behaved with great brutality,[14] had already prompted Antonio Molino to publish, under his pseudonym Manoli Blessi, a long *barzalletta* written in *lingua stradiotesca* (Venetian dialect mixed with Greek, Istrian and Dalmatian elements), analysing the reasons why the

142   Paolo Veronese, *Allegory of the Holy League*, drawing, *c*.1470. Derbyshire, Chatsworth House, Devonshire Collection.

city had been taken by the Turks. On the one hand, according to Molino, the Venetians had not been adequately supported by the Cypriots, and on the other the failure of the Spanish fleet to arrive had been decisive. Following these general considerations Molino goes on to speak of the Turkish atrocities in Nicosia, and in particular of the execution of Nicolò Dandolo, whose head had been sent to Bragadin as a warning of the consequences of intransigence.[15] With his account of the loss of Nicosia, Molino was one of the first poets to be stirred to publication by the war. Following the fall of Famagusta he was followed by many others, inspired not only by the garrison's resolute defence of the city, but more particularly by the heroic deaths of Astorre Baglione and Marcantonio Bragadin. Together with the dozens of poems that were later printed in Venice to celebrate the military achievements of Marcantonio Colonna, Don Juan of Austria and Sebastian Venier, or the wisdom of Pius v, this corpus forms part of an extensive cultural phenomenon.

Paolo Veronese also makes a brief allusion to Bragadin's death in a spectacular *chiaroscuro* drawing for a project commemorating the formation of the Holy League (pl. 142). This would seem to be a *modello* for a major commission, perhaps for the Doge's Palace, that was never executed.[16] An autograph study shows the artist's earlier thoughts for the composition, many of which were later abandoned.[17] Conceived on a magisterial scale, this allegorical scene takes as its central action the public declamation of the articles of the Holy League, which historically took place in both Venice and Rome. In Veronese's composition these two occasions, conflated, are located in an imaginary architectural setting, dominated by monumental arches and buildings in the classical style that make allusions to both cities. In the foreground the figure of Faith, holding a chalice, encourages the members of the Holy League to action, while in the clouds above Sts James, Peter and Mark give their blessing to the military operations that are about to begin, tossing the laurel leaves of victory to a trio of *putti* below. On a raised dais are seated the pope, doge and emperor, protected by a balustrade. Watched by the Spanish entourage on the left, the cardinals in the centre and the Venetian councillors to the right, the doge encourages his colleagues to respond to Faith's appeal. In this left-hand area of the drawing the background architecture clearly quotes from both Sansovino's Library in the Piazzetta and, in the use of detached Corinthian columns in the lower storey and attic of the more distant building, from the Loggetta. The action on the right is framed by a building in a more rusticated style, together with a loggia supported by Corinthian columns. Under the colonnade is grouped a number of military commanders, presumably the immediate audience for the articles of the League that are being declaimed. One of them prominently supports an unbroken wheel, the symbol of both unity and good fortune, intended as a prediction of victory for the allies. The three allegorical female figures on the right are the Cardinal Virtues; one of them carries a yoke to be used for subjugating the Turks. On this side of the composition the background is filled out with an architectural fantasy whose details – a triumphal arch topped by the figure of *Justice*, a rotunda and an obelisk – evoke ancient Rome. In the background soldiers can be seen preparing for battle, and cannon are being discharged. The elderly naked and bearded man in the middle ground to the right may be Bragadin.

Veronese could not have begun work on this composition until the articles of the Holy League had finally been agreed, after months of tortuous negotiation, in July 1571. It must have been finished before news of the victory at Lepanto arrived in Venice. Paintings celebrating the victory invariably incorporate the figure of St Justina, absent from Veronese's drawing.[18] Since the composition also includes a possible reference to Bragadin, whose brutal execution took place on 17 August, it seems likely that the project for a monumental painting celebrating the formation of the League must have come to fruition between then and the middle of October, after which its message would have been outdated. The execution of Bragadin was then fresh in the Venetian collective consciousness, but before Veronese's project could be realized events had moved on, and news of the victory at Lepanto had altered both the priorities of memorialization and the iconographical language used to secure them.

Bragadin's memory, kept alive in both poetry and in standard historical accounts of the defence of Famagusta such as those by Contarini and Paruta,[19] was given additional prominence in 1596, when his remains, which had been removed from the Arsenal in Constantinople some years earlier and brought back to Venice, were installed in the church of Santi Giovanni e Paolo, one of the two great pantheons of Venetian *huomini illustri* and the burial place of many doges. Until the second half of the fourteenth century, areas within San Marco had been developed as a ducal mausoleum, but following the installation of Andrea Dandolo's tomb in about 1354,[20] the practice of burying doges in the basilica stopped, perhaps as a result of legislation designed to inhibit the development of personality cults. After this Santi Giovanni e Paolo, the main Dominican church in the city, became the principal site of ducal wall-tombs, which gradually came to occupy the place of honour close to the high altar, and then to fill up the nave.[21] The location of Bragadin's monument among this august company is an indication of his high status as both folk hero and Christian martyr. Standing against the southern wall of the nave, the white marble monument, once attributed to Vincenzo Scamozzi (this attribution is no longer accepted), is classical in style (pl. 143).[22] It is made up of three levels. The first, immediately above the floor of the church, incorporates an inscribed panel framed by columns and the Bragadin coat of arms, while the topmost section includes two symbolic figures surrounding a bas-relief showing the moment of his death. In between these two, in the middle area, the central bay houses a stone urn containing Bragadin's pathetic remains.[23]

143 The Bragadin Monument, 1596. Venice, Church of SS Giovanni e Paolo.

In terms of its general structure and composition, the monument is indebted to the tradition of Venetian ducal tombs that surround it, including the grandiose monument to Doge Alvise Mocenigo, which stands nearby. It functions as both memorial and reliquary, appropriately enough in the case of Bragadin, who is

144   Loggia del Capitaniato, Vicenza.

known to have expired reciting the *Miserere*, and whose death is often described by Venetian contemporaries as a martyrdom. Its location in the Dominican church of Santi Giovanni e Paolo, home of the Scuola del Rosario, strengthened the association of the church both with Marian devotion and the commemoration of Lepanto through the annual *andata* and its accompanying music and liturgy.

In general, Lepanto was commemorated through buildings and paintings in cities and towns throughout the Italian peninsula, even in places that did not have a particularly close connection with the League. The library of the Benedictine monastery of San Giovanni Evangelista in Parma, for example, was frescoed in 1573, following a complex iconographical programme that juxtaposed ancient and modern maps, chronological tables, allegories of Christian themes, scenes from the Bible and historical events. The most important source for most of these images was the *Biblia Sacra Hebraice, Chaldaice, Graece, et Latine*, edited by Benito Arias Montano for Philip II, and published in 1572 by Plantin in Antwerp, though Alciati was also drawn upon for emblems and Valeriano for hieroglyphs. The victory at Lepanto, shown as the most important historical event of modern times, occupies the central section of one of the long walls,[24] a reminder that, whatever the judgements of later historians, the significance of Lepanto for the contemporary inhabitants of the Italian peninsula was enormous.

This is not to claim that there was either a uniform approach or a common celebratory vocabulary for such schemes. While some themes are ubiquitous, it was also inevitable, given the different standpoints and concerns of the members of the League, that different modes and styles of celebration can be detected in the events that they organized. Even among the cities and provinces of the Venetian *terraferma* there was a tendency to emphasize the importance of local contributions. In Vicenza, for example, Andrea Palladio's design for the Loggia del Capitaniato, in the main square, was altered to take account of a victory that had been won with the help of two warships from the city, and a substantial financial assessment from its citizens (pl. 144). In its final form the lateral façade became a triumphal arch modelled on classical precedent, with statues of *Peace* (as Vicenza) and *Victory* (as Venice) on the lower storey, while above are displayed allegories of civic virtues and trophies. This decoration, executed by Lorenzo Rubini, is thematically linked to the main façade, whose windows and arches are surrounded by river gods, cartouches and military regalia *all'antica*, also in stucco. No reference is made to the existence of the League, or to the contributions of the Papacy and the Empire.[25] Such local accentuations, common enough at a provincial level, become extremely marked in the differing ways that the three principal members of the Holy League embarked upon memorializing Lepanto. One example, that of Rome, makes the point.

There the major celebration of the victory took place almost two months later, when Colonna made a formal entry into the city. His abilities as a naval strategist had been doubted from the first, but given the successful outcome of the engagement at Lepanto, it was perhaps inevitable that he should be accorded heroic status, at least by the Romans. For them the victory was the result of a potent combination of Pius v's initiatives, conceived as a divinely ordained Christian crusade along historical lines, and Colonna's courage and military prowess.[26] These intertwined themes are introduced in a wide range of post-Lepanto art, music and literature produced in Rome, from Giorgio

145   Funerary monument of Pius v, 1586–8. Rome, Basilica of S. Maria Maggiore.

Vasari's additions to the fresco cycle showing the triumphs of the Papacy in the Sala Regia in the Vatican, to madrigals by Palestrina.[27] The most eloquent statement of these paired topoi is to be seen in the Sistine chapel of the basilica of Santa Maria Maggiore in Rome. Sixtus v, who had been confessor to Pius, and like him was a Dominican, began the chapel that bears his name in 1585, and the matching tombs for himself and Pius were placed against the east and west walls between 1587 and 1591. Both follow a similar scheme, which incorporates five relief panels arranged around a central portrait statue, these elements in turn being embedded in a sequence of decorative frames, clearly resonant of classical triumphal arches, constructed of columns, caryatids and coloured marbles. These two wall-tombs are designed to address each other. The reliefs of Pius v's funerary monument are dedicated to the twin subjects of the defeat of the Huguenots and the victory at Lepanto (pl. 145).[28] Its clear if simple iconographical programme, informed by the theme of the Papacy at war, combating heresy and the Infidel on both land and sea, is a demonstration in the temporal sphere of the spiritual concept of papal authority. In this way, the suppression of the

Huguenots and the defeat of the Turks are presented as the two greatest achievements of Pius's pontificate.

The theme of papal achievement is given a more abstract, less personal formulation in the Galleria delle Carte Geografiche in the Vatican. Designed by the cartographer and cosmographer Egnazio Danti, who had been called to Rome by Gregory XIII to participate in discussions about the reform of the calendar, and executed by a team of artists beginning in 1583, the gallery presents Italy not as a geographical entity but as a new Holy Land, the home of the Church Militant.[29] This is achieved by juxtaposing the vault frescos, which show seventy-two episodes from the Old and New Testaments, church history and the lives of the saints, with those of the maps depicted on the walls,[30] while the relationship between the two is made explicit by an inscription. The vault shows pious deeds of holy men; the maps exhibit the places where they were done. As well as showing the cities and provinces of Italy, and the papal territory of Avignon, Danti's maps also include vignettes of important battles from both classical antiquity and the modern world. Most recent of all is Lepanto, depicted during the opening phase of the naval engagement, painted immediately beneath Danti's map of Corfu and identified with a cartouche bearing the legend CLASSIS TVRCARVM AD CROCYLEIVM

146 Ignazio Danti, *The Battle of Lepanto*, 1580–83. Vatican Palace, map gallery.

PROFLIGATA ('the Turkish fleet defeated near Crocyleium'), a learned reference to Lepanto's proximity to Pliny's Crocylé, located by Strabo on the island of Levkas (pl. 46). This, the most recent chapter in universal history, is presented as the culminating achievement of the church, which, under Italian leadership and with papal guidance, had secured the future of Christendom. The fresco, which occupies a prominent position on one of the short walls at one end of the long gallery, is counterbalanced by another showing a map of Malta in its upper half, and the siege of the island by the Ottoman fleet in 1565 in the lower one. Hovering above both is an angel carrying sword and book, dressed in the uniform of the Knights of Malta, whose heroic defence of the island eventually led to the Turkish withdrawal; the open pages of the book read MELITA OBSIDIONE LIBER-ATVR ('Malta freed from siege') (pl. 147). Taken together, these paired images, which flank the doorway leading into the gallery, resonate with the valiant actions of the Church Militant realized as the heroic achievements of the Church Triumphant.

The Venetian view of heroism was differently constructed, with a different cast of characters. Apart from Bragadin, who famously appears on the ceiling of the Consiglio, other prominent Venetian commanders were commemorated for the roles that they had played in the War of Cyprus. One, Agostino Barbarigo, defended his galley against an onslaught from six Turkish ships, but was wounded by an arrow that lodged in his left eye and died from his injuries two days later. Paolo Veronese's elegiac portrait presents the sitter in a reflective frame of mind, with the arrow held in the left hand as though it were an identifying attribute of saintly martyrdom (pl. 148).[31] Perhaps the most striking example of later memorialization of individual military heroes is that of Francesco Duodo, commander of the middle galleys at Lepanto. In some accounts of the battle, Duodo, who was responsible for dispatching an advance group of six ships, which, being equipped with a new type of cannon,

147 Ignazio Danti, *The Siege of Malta*, 1580–83. Vatican Palace, map gallery.

caused havoc among the enemy fleet, is credited with securing the victory. Spanish and papal commanders who worked alongside Duodo later testified to his courage and initiative during the battle.[32] Duodo's career in the service of the Republic followed a traditional *cursus honorem* for someone of his class and training. After four years studying naval design and construction in the Arsenal, he was posted to Corfu as *bailò* and *provveditore* (with responsibility for supplying the fleet in the Levant) and to Udine (where he spent two years as *luogotenente*). Later he was sent to Bergamo as *podestà*, Padua as *capitano*, and Brescia, where he reorganized the local garrison, in disarray after the plague. In

148   Paolo Veronese, *Portrait of Agostino Barbarigo*, 1571. Cleveland, Ohio,
The Cleveland Museum of Art.

the illuminated frontispiece to Doge Nicolò da Ponte's commission appointing
Duodo to this last post, he is shown kneeling in front of a female saint (most
probably Sant'Afra, one of the patrons of Brescia sometimes depicted, as here,
holding a pine cone), whose eyes are raised to the Holy Spirit hovering above.
In the background is Duodo's galley at sea. This scene takes place within a cartouche supporting the coats of arms of the five places where he held official
positions.[33] After his death, in November 1592, on service as *provveditore* in Friuli
in connection with the projected fortress at Palmanova, Duodo's body was
returned to Venice, where it was buried in the parish church of Santa Maria del
Giglio. The family, which had been prominent in the parish since the late fourteenth century, had embellished the chapel of San Francesco, which lies on the
north side of the church, and it was close to this spot that Duodo was interred.
As specified in his will, his standard was suspended from the ceiling, and flags
from his galley decorated the columns of the nave, where they were seen by
Stringa in the early seventeenth century.[34] The chapel itself contains an altarpiece by Domenico Tintoretto, painted during Duodo's lifetime, showing *Christ
the Redeemer with Sts Justina and Francis* (pl. 149). That the latter is a portrait

of Duodo himself becomes clear from comparison with Alessandro Vittoria's two portrait busts, one terracotta, the other marble (see pl. 136).[35] A single galley in the background of the painting alludes to his naval career. According to Duodo's will, Vittoria's marble bust, which had been sculpted from life as a private image, was also to be placed near the altar, though it seems that this was never done. Evidently the intention was to create a sort of shrine, as Duodo put it himself, 'in memoria delle mie fatiche fatte ad honor della maestà divina, et utile della nostra patria'. Service to the Republic, a duty expected of the patrician class, is invoked.

A further memorial to Duodo, at Monselice near Padua, is even more strongly Counter-Reformation in spirit and conception. At the end of the 1580s, Francesco and his brother Domenico began to consolidate their land holdings there, apparently with the intention of building a country villa and a private oratory.[36] A papal brief, issued by Clement VIII on 12 December 1592, authorized the demolition of the abandoned and derelict church of San Giorgio, which stood on Duodo land, to make way for the project. After Francesco's death it was probably his son Pietro, Venetian ambassador in Rome, who continued the work.[37] In addition to building the villa, which, beginning in 1593, was constructed to Scamozzi's designs,[38] Pietro, keen to smooth relations between the Papacy

149   Domenico Tintoretto, *Christ the Redeemer with Sts Justina and Francis de Paul*, c.1580. Venice, Santa Maria del Giglio.

and Venice during the troubled years of the Interdict, obtained a second brief from Paul V in 1605. This granted him the concession to duplicate the indulgences associated with the seven basilicas of Rome by constructing six chapels; together with the rebuilt church of San Giorgio, these would constitute a place of pilgrimage for the surrounding area. Although the result is not, strictly speaking, a *sacro monte* as such, the earliest example of which was built at Varallo in Piedmont at the end of the fifteenth century, the sanctuary at Monselice breathes a distinct atmosphere of Counter-Reformation ideology.[39] At Varallo, the long sequence of 'stations' is largely devoted to pictorial re-creations of scenes from the *Life of Christ*, with five episodes from the Via Crucis embedded in the scheme; this fulfilled one purpose of the *sacro monte*, as an alternative to the expensive and dangerous pilgrimage to the Holy Land itself.[40] This typology was not rigidly followed elsewhere. The example at Orta is dedicated to the *Life of St Francis*,[41] and that at Arona to *Carlo Borromeo* and the *Mysteries of the Rosary*, both strong Tridentine themes.[42] Monselice is evocative of the genre, being built upon a hill,

150 Monselice, the Via Sacra.

but it is more properly to be thought of as a sanctuary designed to transpose the experience of the 'Seven Churches', and the indulgences associated with it, from Rome to a local context. It has been suggested that the inspiration for the conception, inspired by the antique, was the Appian Way (pl. 150).[43] At Monselice each chapel was dedicated to the patron saints of the seven major Roman basilicas (Sts Peter and Paul being combined in a single shrine), and instead of the figural scenes characteristic of north Italian examples of the genre, a series of canvases showing these saints was commissioned from Palma il Giovane.[44] As originally planned and executed, the Duodo sanctuary was primarily intended to alleviate the effects of Venice's threatened excommunication during the Interdict crisis through displays of piety, and as such it had a clear political as well as devotional purpose. This may explain the seriousness with which it was evidently regarded by the pope, since the granting of indulgences to private chapels was itself a rarity.

Throughout the seventeenth and eighteenth centuries the battle of Lepanto continued to be commemorated and celebrated, particularly in the Veneto, and particularly through decorative cycles installed in churches. The examples of Santa Corona in Vicenza and the cathedral in Bassano recall to mind a phenomenon that was widespread. In this context, it is not surprising that Duodo's scheme was also further amplified, during the middle decades of the seventeenth century, by the addition of an entrance gate, alterations to the church of San Giorgio to accommodate its expanding collection of relics, and the construction of a memorial to three distinguished members of the family: Pietro (d. 1598), Domenico (d. 1597) and Francesco, the hero of Lepanto. The monument, erected by Pietro's nephew Alvise, a procurator, is built of stone, and contains three niches framed by pilasters supporting a cornice. Each niche originally contained a bust; those of Francesco and Domenico were sculpted by Alessandro Vittoria,[45] that of Pietro by an unknown seventeenth-century artist. The dated epigraphs under each show that the arrangement was begun in 1658 with the bust of Pietro, and completed in 1670 with that of Domenico.[46] The final arrangement is shown in an early eighteenth-century engraving by Francesco Guerra (pl. 151).[47] The juxtaposition of the Duodo memorial with Scamozzi's six chapels had the effect of incorporating it within the pilgrimage route of a reconstructed *via romana*. Although the establishment of the Via Sacra stood in stark polemical opposition to the increasingly anti-ecclesiastical stance of the *giovani*, who were now in the ascendant,

151 Francesco Guerra, *The Sanctuary of the Seven Churches, Monselice,*
engraving. Venice, Museo Civico Correr.

through this association the members of the family, and above all Francesco
Duodo, were mythologized as Counter-Reformation heroes.

Memorialization of the other great Venetian celebratory event of the 1570s,
Henry III's visit, was initially confined to inscriptions. At the Villa Contarini at
Mira, which the king visited after his departure from the city, a tablet was placed
on the outside of the building, where it was seen a few years later by Montaigne
on his trip through northern Italy in the autumn of 1580.[48] Mira had been deliberately selected as an appropriate stopping point for the king and his entourage
on their journey along the Brenta, since it could be represented to Henry as a
typical country villa of the Venetian patriciate; as such, it was the final demonstration of the elegant lifestyle of the prosperous ruling class, emblematic of the
well-being of the Republic.[49] For almost twenty years the only publicly visible
record in Venice itself of Henry's visit was an inscription, framed by Alessandro
Vittoria's elaborate sculptural surround, placed close to the Scala dei Giganti at
the Doge's Palace, where it was transcribed by Sansovino.[50] This had been done
in response to Henry's express wish, insistently transmitted through the French
ambassador.[51] The location of the inscription was one of considerable symbolic
significance, since it was here, framed by Sansovino's monumental statues of
Mars and *Neptune,* that newly elected doges completed the final phase of their
investiture ceremonies by making a public oath. Vittoria's stone tablet was in
turn commemorated in a single-sheet engraving (pl. 153).

It was only towards the end of the century that Henry's visit was finally commemorated in a number of paintings and engravings, all of which were pro-

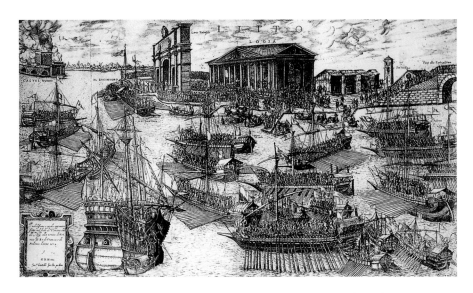

152   After Master G. D. M[oustier?], *The Reception of Henry III at the Lido*, engraving.
Venice, Museo Civico Correr.

153   Anonymous after Alessandro
Vittoria, *Inscription to Commemorate
the Visit of Henry III*, engraving.
Venice, Museo Civico Correr.

duced in the period following his assassination on
2 August 1589. The first of these to appear was a
print by the Master G. D. M., dated 1591, which
shows Henry's entry at the Lido; unlike Domenico
Zenoi's engraving of seventeen years earlier, which
places some emphasis on the temporary architecture, this later image, with its impressive collection
of galleys in the foreground, is more of a celebration of Venetian sea power (pl. 152).[52] Two years
later Andrea Vicentino's vast canvas was commissioned for the Doge's Palace. It shows Henry being
welcomed at the Lido by the doge and patriarch in
the midst of a crowd of patricians, while behind can
be seen the triumphal arch and loggia; on the far
left, Soranzo's galley is berthed in front of the
church of San Nicolò (pl. 154).[53] Except for the
façade of Palladio's arch, the inscriptions and elaborate iconographical scheme of pictures and statuary that decorated both the arch and the loggia at
the Lido are obscured. Deprived in this way of
detailed references to the specific context of 1574,
Vicentino's painting celebrates the more general
theme of Henry's welcome at the hands of the
Venetian patriciate headed by the doge and the

154   Andrea Vicentino, *The Arrival of Henry III at the Lido*, c.1593. Ducal Palace, Sala delle Quattro Porte.

patriarch; as such it is a group portrait designed to immortalize the participation of the principal actors.[54] Installed in the Sala delle Quattro Porte, more precisely between the two doors that lead to the Anticollegio and the Senate respectively, it occupies a strategic position directly opposite Titian's *Faith*. This, one of the few paintings executed by Titian in his capacity as official painter to the Republic, shows the personification of Faith wreathed in an aureole of golden light before the kneeling figure of Doge Antonio Grimani (1521–3), with the bacino of San Marco in the background. With its central message of Venice as Defender of the Faith,[55] a state ordained by God, with the doge as both *princeps in republica* and *princeps in ecclesia*, Titian's painting acts as the perfect pendant to Vicentino's record of the arrival, in Venice, of His Most Christian Majesty. It is also demonstrative of the image of Venice as the ultimate Christian republic that the patriciate was busily fashioning in the last decades of the sixteenth century.

Henry's entry into Venice at the Lido was not the only episode from his visit to be memorialized at a distance. The moment of the king's arrival at Ca' Foscari is shown in a painting by Palma il Giovane, executed some twenty years later, now in Dresden.[56] Clearly identifiable in the right foreground, having disembarked from the Bucintoro, are the king with the patriarch to the left and the doge to the right. On the left of the doge stands Pietro Foscari, and immediately to his left, wearing a black cloak, Henri d'Angoulême, the king's half-brother, who, with a rhetorical gesture, presents the monarch to the viewer. This detail of the composition is deliberately anti-historical, since Henri arrived in Venice only a few days after the king's entry. D'Angoulême's

155   Jacopo Palma Il Giovane, *The Arrival of Henry III at Ca' Foscari*, c.1593–5. Chateau of Azay-Le-Rideau.

gesture of identification is echoed by the prominent figure on the extreme left of the canvas, who points to a cartouche bearing the fleurs-de-lis. In order to show the accompanying entourage stretching back to the convent of the Carità, Palma realigned the perspective of the Grand Canal, a dramatic effect anticipated in the artist's preparatory drawing. The presence of Pietro Foscari, and the claim that Henry's features are copied from a portrait once in the Foscari collection,[57] reinforces the idea that the picture was originally a family commission. It may be significant that the Dresden painting exists in a second, unrecorded version, which hangs in the Château of Azay-le-Rideau, suggesting perhaps a commemorative function shared by different members of the family, or others close to the event (pl. 155).

   The reasons for this burst of commemoration so many years after the visit took place are not clear; it has been suggested that Vicentino's commission may have been prompted by the establishment of diplomatic relations between Venice and the Protestant king Henry IV, thus reversing an earlier policy.[58] In the context of the politics of the *giovani*, by the 1590s now increasingly powerful, who were keen to intensify relations with France, the decision to capitalize upon the dead king's connection with Venice may have been part of a deliberate policy, motivated as much by the age-old threat of Spanish dominion as much as by

156   Giovanni Battista Tiepolo, *The Visit of Henry III to the Villa Contarini at Mira*, c.1756. Paris, Musée Jacquemart.

worsening relations with Rome.[59] Certainly, it is noticeable that a number of memorials to Lepanto and the visit of Henry III, including Palma il Giovane's painting in the church of San Fantin, were commissioned during this period.[60] The symbolic importance of Henry's visit was sufficiently great for it to be recorded long afterwards, not only by the families that had been involved in organizing it, but even by those who had merely acquired buildings with Henrician associations. This is certainly the case with the Villa Contarini, which passed into the hands of the Pisani family, which, in 1745, to mark a family marriage, commissioned Giovanni Battista Tiepolo to decorate the atrium of the villa with frescos. The central narrative shows Fame announcing Henry's arrival at the villa, observed by spectators (including members of the Contarini family) arranged on balconies. Detached in 1893 and mounted on canvas, the frescos were bought by the French collector Edouard André and are now in the Museé Jacquemart-André in Paris (pl. 156).[61] For the art historian Henri de Chennevières, writing at a high point of French imperialism, this was their natural home: 'La dernière conquête de la collection ne paraît guère pouvoir être dépassée: c'est un magnifique Tiepolo . . . français . . . Le dernier grand vénitien . . . célébrant, en une fresque de toute lumière, un coin d'épisode de l'histoire de France.'[62] In this unexpected setting, the mutilated remains of Tiepolo's grandiose conception continued to fulfil a commemorative function, though one now transposed from a celebration of an important moment in the history of the Contarini family, to the rhetorical evocation of 'La gloire de la France'.[63]

CHAPTER TWELVE

Christ's Victory

The prime emphasis in the official Venetian celebrations of Lepanto was upon the confirmation of the victory as Christ's victory, and the same is true of many of the more permanent memorials that began to appear in the months following the battle. As early as the Consistory of May 1571, which had ratified the articles of the League, Pope Pius had attributed the successful conclusion of the discussions between Spain, Venice and the Papacy to divine protection, and in consequence had projected the League's military campaign as a divinely ordained Christian crusade on historical lines, pursued through the agency of papal guidance. This was common rhetoric. According to one Friulian writer, the military preparations that were undertaken on a grand scale in the area at the beginning of 1571 were 'not just to preserve our state, but for the health of all Christendom and particularly for the glory of God'.[1] Contemporary codes of chivalry required the nobility to fight crusades as and when they were required to do so. This, an important part of the pope's conception,[2] was taken up by writers and commentators everywhere.

In these circumstances it was inevitable that victory, when it came, was universally regarded as a manifestation of Divine Providence. Pietro Buccio's oration, one of a number that were delivered publicly, attributed even the mechanics of the battle to God's intervention. The ships of the League had triumphed, he wrote, because the wind changed in their favour at the crucial juncture, a sure sign of divine justice, while the fact that the Turks had clearly underestimated the size of the opposing fleet could be attributed only to divine goodness.[3] A sense of amazement at the unexpected reversal in Turkish military fortunes and of its significance was common; Cardinal Granvelle thought the

157   Detail of pl. 137.

158 Anonymous, *Parafrasi poetica sopra alcuni psalmi*, title page, Venice, 1571. Venice, Biblioteca Nazionale Marciana.

victory strange and miraculous since God, who had allowed the Turks to reign supreme at sea for so long, should now reduce them to ruin. Lepanto was surely the greatest victory in history, greater than anything that had been achieved by the Greeks or the Romans, declaimed Buccio. All this had happened because God had finally opened his ears to the prayers of the faithful.[4] The topos of Christ's victory, expressed in the title of Magno's play *Il Trionfo di Christo*, is a major component of Lepanto celebratory art in Venice and throughout the Veneto. When official representatives from Verona presented themselves to the doge to offer the congratulations of the city for the victory, and to confirm an annual subsidy for the continuation of the war, they referred explicitly to the idea that the hand of God had been responsible for defeating the enemy, destroying its fleet and flooding the sea with pagan blood.[5]

The general familiarity of this theme is neatly illustrated by the title-page of an anonymous pamphlet of poetic paraphrases of the psalms, 'accomodate', according to the title-page, 'per render gratie a Dio della vittoria donata al Christianesimo contra Turchi' (pl. 158).[6] Here, within a central decorative frame, the Lion of St Mark is shown being guided by the hand of God. Every conceivable ingenuity was deployed by Venetian poets and printers to exploit the Christian theme. In one commentary on the Pater Noster 'in lingua rustica' (dialect), the prayer itself is intertwined with celebratory observations on the victory, and paraphrases of the psalms and other well-known prayers are common in the Lepanto literature.[7] Similar resonances are present in the text of one of Andrea Gabrieli's eight-voiced polychoral pieces from the posthumous *Concerti* of 1587: 'Benedictus Dominus Deus Saboath', which may have been composed to celebrate the victory.[8]

In the literature that appeared in the bookshops and squares of Venice after Lepanto, comparison between the Israelites and the citizens of the Republic is commonplace.[9] This analogy was also taken up in Pietro Vinci's five-voiced motet 'Intret super eos formido et pavor', published in his *Secondo libro de mottetti* of 1572, which is headed in all the part-books 'In destructione Turcharum'. Vinci, a Sicilian by birth who had then been working as *maestro di cappella* at Santa Maria Maggiore in Bergamo for three years, gathered together a number of occasional pieces for this second motet collection, which is appropriately dedicated to the governors of the Misericordia in the city, and opens with a piece in their honour. It also includes a motet ('Calliope colles sibi legit Apollo') in honour of Bergamo, and two other pieces ('Urbs gladijs' and 'Plange urbs Bergomea'), lamenting the heroic death of Astorre Baglione at the siege of Famagusta.[10] Born in Perugia, Baglione had pursued an extremely successful military and administrative career, initially in the service of the Papacy and the Farnese, latterly in that of the Republic.[11] As a skilled military engineer he oversaw the fortifications at Udine, Padua and Bergamo; overseas, he served as governor of Corfu and Nicosia. At Bergamo his efforts were much admired by the authorities of the city, so much so that in 1560 he was given the honorary title of *capo dei priori*,[12] and in 1572 elaborate obsequies were organized for him in the church of Santa Maria Maggiore, where he had founded the Compagnia del Gonfalone di San Giuseppe.[13] In the centre of the church a sepulchre, mounted upon an obelisk, was draped with cloth of gold and surrounded by more than a hundred torches to create the traditional *cappella ardente*, familiar from imperial example. More than a hundred priests were present, half chanting the requiem, the rest incensing the sepulchre. At some point during the proceedings, Vinci's compositions were performed. It is as something of a consolatory pendant to these dark, funereal pieces that 'Intret super eos formido et pavor' celebrates the victory at Lepanto as if to emphasize that Baglione's sacrifice was not in vain. With its text, based on the account in Deuteronomy of the Israelites crossing the Red Sea, Vinci's motet is one of the clearest examples in the Venetian musical repertory of a specially composed text woven out of another common Lepanto theme, that of the Venetians as a chosen race:

'Let terror and dread descend upon them. In the greatness of your arm disband them and let them become motionless until your people, Lord, whom you have chosen, pass by.'[14]

The hand of God may have indeed destroyed the Turkish galleys in the faraway waters of the eastern Adriatic, but it was also active closer to home. As was only too evident, the plague of 1575–7 was just the latest in a series of disasters and misfortunes that had befallen the Venetians in a short space of time; these included the loss of Cyprus, the famine of 1569, the serious fire in the Arsenal that followed shortly afterwards, and the financially crippling Turkish war, which had finally been brought to an end with a much-criticized and somewhat disadvantageous treaty. One contemporary described these years as a dark period in which the Venetians had suffered hunger, wars, fires, floods and plague.[15] As another anonymous commentator put it, the fire in the Arsenal could be put down to Jews and traitors, but famine could be explained only as a clear sign of God's anger.[16] For all of the exultation that had greeted the news from Lepanto, and the pomp and splendour that accompanied Henry III's visit, Venetians were conscious that they were living in a time of uncertainty. There had been considerable public discontent with the peace treaty with the Turks, and much disquiet over the inadequate measures that had been taken to control the plague, some of which surfaced in the growing opposition of the aristocracy to the Council of Ten.[17] Francesco da Molin wrote in his chronicle that Lepanto came at a time of great affliction, so much so that it was not possible to fear worse.[18] Rocco Benedetti's graphic description of the horrors of the Lazzaretto Nuovo during the plague years contains a note of puzzlement:

> All these things represented a sad and sorrowful triumph of death. It seemed all the more horrible and cruel in that it appeared that Divine Justice had sent it deliberately as the other side of the coin to the splendid and sumptuous celebrations held previously . . . to welcome the Most Christian King of France.[19]

The characterization of these years as the apogee of the Venetian High Renaissance, with Titian, Tintoretto and Veronese all painting, and Palladio at work, does not engage fully with contemporary realities as experienced by the majority of Venetians. For them it was a dark decade.

For some, the explanation for this series of catastrophes was to be found at least partly in astrology, the plague itself being the product of particularly negative stellar conjunctions. As such it had also been predictable, having been preceded by clear and unambiguous 'signs'. Astrological pamphlets printed in Venice in these years are full of descriptions of natural and unnatural phenomena, from the fiery dragon that was sighted in the sky above the church of San Pietro in Montorio in Rome,[20] to the comet that appeared in November 1577.[21] Since their advent normally presaged major events, often disasters, the arrival of this one was inevitably associated with the fire in the Doge's Palace, which occurred on 20 December. One prominent and much-published astrologer, Antonio Raimondi, claimed that the causes of the plague could be traced to October 1574, when a combination of heavy rain and high seas had caused flooding, which in turn had contaminated the city's wells. The mixture of sea and fresh water, he wrote, had visited lethal long-term effects on those, mostly the poor, who could not afford wine, and who had continued to drink from the water supply.[22] This was a controversial view, much contested in print.[23]

Others pointed to the 'monstrous birth' that took place in the ghetto shortly before the epidemic began. From the anonymous *Discorso* that appeared a few days later, it emerges that a Jewish woman had given birth to Siamese twins, a phenomenon understood at the time only in terms of deformity and abnormality.[24] Since it was printed at least twice, by different printers, this pamphlet evidently generated a good deal of interest, and the new-born infants were added to the existing popular literature chronicling the appearance of malformed children and other curiosities. In contrast to the fantastic oriental creatures from the Indies that had haunted the late middle ages, the 'monsters' that peopled these popular booklets and prints were real and human, and often attracted sympathy, particularly when, as in this case, the victims died shortly after birth. Interest in them was not just the result of a fascination with the abnormal. Such births were part of a series of natural events – including floods, lightning attacks, earthquakes and planetary conjunctions – that were often taken as portents, 'signs' of momentous events to follow.[25] In the case of Lepanto it was taken not only as a good omen for the future, but also as a sign of divine favour, that roses, flowers and fruit had grown during the autumn and were still in flower in October 1571, and that it was still possible, on the day of the battle, to eat a whole range of fruits as if it were summer.[26]

Following a brief discussion of whether the Venetian Siamese twins had one soul or two, the *Discorso* continues with an astrological explanation of their condition illustrated by horoscopes cast at the times of their conception and birth, before concluding with the claim that this 'monstrous birth' was a prophecy of 'congiure ed occasioni'. Such predictions were common in the pamphlets and broadsheets that had reported such deformed births since the late fifteenth century, and which had appeared in particularly large numbers during the decades of the *calamità d'Italia*. The most celebrated example of the entire period, the birth of the monster of Ravenna (in March 1512), had been taken to foreshadow the battle of the following month, in which the pontifical forces had been squarely defeated by the French army.[27] In this way, vague predictions of catastrophe could be allied to a display of expertise that, by analysing the deformity, established the authority of a particular political viewpoint. In the case of the Venetian twins, the explanation offered in the *Discorso* gains credibility from its engagement with both theology and astrology, and subsequently from its knowledgeable catalogue of earlier instances of abnormal births with a divinatory significance. As a result, considerable propagandistic weight is lent to the concluding claim that disaster could be avoided only by the wholesale conversion of the Jews. This is an old theme, and the arrival of the plague in Venice within a matter of months would only have confirmed, in the mind of some, the wisdom and insight of the author, writing at the height of official intolerance towards the Jewish population of the city. Further admonitions to the inhabitants of the ghetto are embedded in the title of yet another pamphlet published after the death of the children, the *Nova et ridicolosa espositione del mostro nato in Ghetto*, which contains three dialect poems, one of which is advertised as the lament of the children's father, together with a full-page woodcut. While such episodes are indicative of common attitudes, not everyone interpreted them in the same way; at least one of the chroniclers reported the birth of the Jewish twins in a purely factual, neutral manner.[28]

As the plague grew in intensity, and as official medicine was increasingly shown to be incapable of offering solutions, the debate about the ultimate cause of the plague sharpened. In the literature that helped to fuel the controversy, every shade of opinion can be detected between those who elevated astrological considerations to a high level of importance within a more complex scheme of explanation, and others who, while taking account of many contingent factors, gave priority to divine judgement. In this rich skein of contemporary philosophical, astrological and theological ideas, suffused in the religious climate that followed the conclusion of the Council of Trent and the publication of its decrees, the notion that the plague was divinely authored in order to punish mankind for its wickedness is dominant. Again it is Benedetti who gives the most vivid impression of common Venetian mental attitudes during the horrifying summer of 1576; for him it was God, weary of the failings and weaknesses of the city and its citizens, who had dispatched the exterminating angel to express his anger.[29] This view runs like a thread, not only through the diaries and chronicles of the plague years,[30] but also through much of the medical writing as well. Typical is Gavardo's *Discorso sulla peste*, which, in the context of a medical analysis of the plague, at the end of which dietary advice is offered as a remedy, unambiguously states that the principal cause of the disease was the wrath of God, which could be appeased only through examination of conscience and prayers for forgiveness.[31] In also arguing in this way, Girolamo Donzellini was simply reflecting the general belief of the Venetian ruling class that when medicine had failed, and astrology could offer no explanation, the only recourse was to prayer. This too mirrored official attitudes and practices.[32]

At the beginning of the epidemic, disagreement over the dangers of public association had coloured official attitudes towards processions and religious services as appropriate vehicles for public expiation, with the health board on one side of the argument and the church on the other. But as the mortality rate began to climb, the impact of these differences began to dissolve as both the civil and religious authorities united behind the call for prayer, both public and private. Certainly domestic devotion had a role to play. Tommaso Contarini, a patrician translator of St Cyprian's reflections on the plague written in Africa, claimed that he had read the original with profit during the Venetian epidemic. The just, he concluded, need not fear death, since the Kingdom of God was close at hand.[33] In August 1576 the government called on all Venetians to continue to pray and fast, and a few days later the patriarch laid down a precise set of instructions for the faithful to follow. These included prayers at home, at work and in the street, together with acts of mortification. Naturally, it was ordinary Venetians, the *popolo minuto*, who responded best to these exhortations, but among patricians the call to religion was also taken seriously. As is clear from the careers of prominent patricians such as Federico Contarini, the dominant philosophy among the ruling Venetian elites in the post-Lepanto world was one that combined selfless devotion to the state with a strong sense of moral purpose, underpinned by the teachings of the church and supported by respect for its institutions.[34] If the Venetians were to be identified as the Chosen People as much Lepanto literature proclaimed, a role that had been delineated for them since the moment that the quadriga had been raised above the west door of San Marco, then Venice itself was to become the City of God.

For this it was in some ways well equipped. More than any other Italian city outside Rome, Venice attracted visitors because of its relics. In many cases politico-religious motivations seem to have been uppermost in selecting those to be acquired, often through the intervention of the doge. In other instances relics were evidently carried off specifically to adorn Venetian churches already erected in their honour, a process of accretion that often gave rise to increased ceremonial and new decorative schemes, and emphasized the importance of the city as a sacred repository. Pilgrims stopping there on their way to the Holy Land often followed a standard itinerary that took in the most important of them, and indulgences accumulated in the city's churches constituted the first phase of an ambitious spiritual undertaking that was to grow into a consider-able investment in salvation.[35] As the visitors walked from church to church in search of relics, Venice itself became the last and most imposing stop in a sequence of cult centres marking the route to the Holy Places, an introduction to redemption itself.[36]

The transferral of relics from one place to another through the process of *translatio*, what has been described as the movement of relics to people rather than that of people to relics, was a particular feature of the early medieval church,[37] and the practice was further encouraged by the crusades. By 1200 the body of St Stephen had been installed in San Giorgio Maggiore, and those of Sts Isidore and Donatus followed shortly afterwards. During the Fourth Crusade, which the Venetians had been instrumental in promoting and from which they greatly benefitted, the phenomenon reached epic proportions. Thereafter the process of acquisition continued. In 1462 the head of St George arrived from Aegina,[38] and later in the century other groups of relics were brought from the East, particularly from Constantinople, in the wake of the advancing Turks. As late as 1600 the head of St Titus was hastily transferred from Crete before the island was abandoned.[39] Each *translatio* was seen as prov-idential, increasing the city's resources as a spiritual centre, and was usually offi-cially sanctioned. The head of St George was retrieved by a captain in the Venetian navy on the instructions of the Senate, and the Republic's concern for the safety of relics, carefully locked up inside their respective churches, gave rise to a sizeable body of legislation.[40] By the sixteenth century, printed hagiographic manuals such as Pietro de Natali's *Catalogus sanctorum*, reprinted at least twice in accessible quarto editions after its initial appearance in a more formal folio format, advertised the enormous variety of relics to be found in Venetian churches, from the right hand of St Cyprian to the body of St Lucy. Giovanni Botero was convinced that in no other city could so many complete relics of important saints be venerated and, commenting on the same phenomenon, a Medici agent came to the conclusion that 'in matters of religion, the Venetians are not inferior to any other nation'.[41] The procurators were charged with car-rying out inspections to ensure that relics had not been lost or stolen, and in 1631 a fresh inventory, the earliest to survive, was made. By this time Venice had accumulated the most impressive hoard of relics outside Rome, including forty-nine complete bodies of saints.[42] For both residents and foreign visitors alike, this devotional patrimony was yet a further demonstration of the special character of a divinely protected city.

There was a particularly strong wave of relic veneration in the early seventeenth century, when five important reliquaries from San Marco, including samples of the Precious Blood and fragments of the True Cross, were rediscovered in the sanctuary of the basilica itself, together with a large number of less important relics. Giovanni Tiepolo, the *primicerio* of San Marco shortly to become the patriarch of Venice,[43] who was involved and wrote a short pamphlet describing the find and its importance, was a strong advocate of the display and veneration of relics; in this he was characteristic of the church after Trent. Relics were to be prized, coveted and made the objects of prayer and devotion precisely because of their potential in the process of intercession. In Counter-Reformation Venice the veneration of relics took on a heightened significance, not just because of its importance in the new spiritual order, but also because the uncertain circumstances of the time made appeals for divine assistance all the more urgent. Bouts of famine and epidemics had always been interpreted as punishments for human wickedness, and the severe outbreaks of bubonic plague that attacked Venice in the years 1575–7 and again in 1630–31 only intensified the tendency to conserve and embellish existing cults rather than create new ones. In a lengthy tract published shortly after the end of the second of these great Venetian plagues, in which a third of the population had perished, Tiepolo described how God had saved the city from the effects of war, famine and plague in response to the Venetians' recourse to the Virgin, as well as to St Sergius (whose body lay in the cathedral of San Pietro di Castello) and the recently beatified Lorenzo Giustiniani.[44]

In celebration of the find, the procurators organized a procession followed by mass in San Marco. The newly discovered relics were carried around the square in a procession in which members of the *scuole grandi* and representatives of a number of the city's parish churches participated, stopping at three places in the Piazza so that the relics could be displayed to the crowds. Four of the *scuole grandi* were each accompanied by two groups of musicians, one of singers, the other of instrumentalists, while later in the procession four singers, walking just in front of the relics, sang the Litany of the Saints. Some of the representatives of the Venetian churches carried portable platforms supporting statues and other images, and elsewhere the nine congregations of secular priests intoned the traditional Te Deum. As with all such public processions in Venice, the result was a kaleidoscopic sequence of colours, images and sounds. The onlookers were presented with different experiences by different elements of the procession as it passed before them, and responded in turn with prayers, devotional gestures and songs. On the three occasions that the procession stopped and the relics were presented to the crowds, the basil-

Detail of pl. 97.

ica's choir, under the direction of Claudio Monteverdi, performed a setting of 'Pretiosum sanguinem semper laudemus'. Once inside San Marco, the relics were displayed on a temporary altar that allowed them to be seen clearly and venerated, while the choir sang; a ceremonial high mass then followed.[45] In addition to the music sung by the *cappella marciana*, the procession was punctuated by hymns and simple liturgies in which all could participate.[46] In this way an event of importance in the spiritual life of the basilica, involving the rehabilitation of cult objects of the highest importance, was able to touch the lives of the Venetian population, who both participated in the procession and also observed it. Through this characteristic ritual of communal rehabilitation, relics that had a universal Christian significance were appropriated and given a local meaning. Those who were unable to be present in the Piazza were able to venerate them, displayed in an elaborate temporary construction in the basilica, or to read about them in the brief illustrated accounts that appeared in some number shortly after the event.[47]

It was at about the same time that the procurators drew up a scheme for the restoration of one of the most potent cult objects in the basilica's extensive treasury, the *Madonna Nicopeia*, which they now undertook to embellish with gold, silver and precious stones, and to place on the altar of St John the Baptist, which was to be specially reconstructed for the purpose. The work was carried out to a design by Tommaso Contin,[48] who also rebuilt the altar of the Holy Sacrament, on the south side of the nave, to the same design, at the same time. The rehousing of the *Madonna Nicopeia*, now displayed for the first time in its history on its own altar in the nave of the basilica, was part of a more general policy, designed to improve the visibility and accessibility of both the Sacrament and the icon. These changes in devotional practice, which Contin's scheme facilitated, were clearly in keeping with the teachings of Trent, where the popular devotion of the Forty Hours had been instituted.

The altar of the *Madonna Nicopeia*, protectress of Venice, symbolically placed in a chapel next to the high altar of San Marco, quickly became the focus of new rituals and practices, particularly during moments of crisis. Throughout the following centuries, as in previous ones, it was the *Madonna Nicopeia* that was publicly carried in procession to ask for deliverance from the plague and for success in war, and it was her image that graced the title-pages of the various reprints of the Litany of the Blessed Virgin Mary to be recited 'in time of war'.[49] During periods of drought or crop failure, the icon was removed from its altar and carried through the Piazza San Marco.[50] The *Nicopeia* had started life in the thirteenth century as a portent of Venetian victory in battle, and by the seventeenth the icon had been transformed into one of the most important cult objects in the basilica, along with the tomb of St Mark and the Pala d'Oro. In crises of all kinds, from famine and pestilence to drought and war, the Venetians had recourse to the *Nicopeia* as a major vehicle of divine intercession. In front of her altar prayers were said and litanies sung.

Building upon that strong attachment to the Virgin that had always been a component of Venetian civic and religious ritual, this rejuvenation of the *Nicopeia* was in turn merely one aspect of a more general increase in Marian devotion in the city during the late sixteenth century, which became even more pronounced after the plague of 1630–31. In musical terms these conditions are reflected in a wide range of Marian compositions written by composers working in Venice, from elaborate solo motets to simple litanies to be performed in processions.[51] It may well be that the role of the Council of Trent in this development has been exaggerated, and that for many Venetians the trauma of the plague of 1575–7 was a more important spur to increased religiosity than the dictates of the Papacy. For nineteenth-century Protestant historians the Interdict may have appeared as a heroic moment of rebellion against the power of an overbearing and autocratic Roman ecclesiastical hierarchy, but for ordinary citizens of the Republic it did rather less damage to traditional belief than has been claimed.

EPILOGUE

The further elaboration, in the post-Lepanto years, of the traditional concept of Venice as a Holy and Apostolic City marks yet a further phase in the developing Myth of Venice. There are various components to this familiar and potent political concept, but its central idea was eloquently expressed in 1364, when Petrarch wrote his famous description of the Venetian celebration of a victory in Crete in a letter to Pietro da Muglio:

> The august city of Venice rejoices, the one home today of liberty, peace and justice, the one refuge of honourable men, the one port to which can repair the storm-tossed, tyrant-hounded craft of men who seek the good life. Venice – city rich in gold but richer in renown, mighty in works but mightier in virtue, founded on solid marble but established on the more solid foundations of civic concord, surrounded by the salty waves but secure through her saltier councils.[1]

From its very beginnings, the myth was organic, an accumulation of inherited beliefs and meanings that accommodated different emphases and inflections according to changing historical and political circumstances. Its history has generated a good deal of discussion and debate, with modern historians emphasizing different stages of its development. For some, the earliest phase was decisive, so that by the fifteenth century the crucial concepts were firmly established, merely to be recycled with minor modifications in subsequent decades.[2] In this part of its history, the cult of Mark lay at the core of the myth. Although the Venetians were conscious of a number of different legends about their origins, it was the story of Mark that had initially defined a sense of identity,

159   Detail of pl. 162.

in which civic and religious elements were so inextricably intertwined that it is impossible to separate them. In this sense the true foundation stone of the state was the *translatio*, when Doge Giustiniano Partecipazio received Mark's body and welcomed it into the *commune veneciarum*.[3] When, during the fourteenth and early fifteenth centuries, Venice moved away from its conventional attachment to Byzantium in the direction of a closer orientation towards Italy and the West, the theme of Venice as a new or second Rome, a rhetorical construction that in the early middle ages had been applied to Milan and Pavia as well as to Constantinople itself, was further developed.[4] By the end of the fifteenth century a number of humanist writers had added a further gloss to the city's self-image. Starting from the inherited conception of Venice, Bernardo Giustiniani, the most distinguished of these commentators, incorporated an element of classical justification by adding to the existing cluster of foundation legends a new one in which Venice was settled by refugees from the disintegrating Roman empire.[5] Further, neo-classical dress was added by official historians such as Sabellico. Following the rout of the Venetians by the armies of the League of Cambrai at Agnadello in 1509, the parallel between Venice and Rome was yet further elaborated in encomiastic writings, such as Vergerio's *De republica veneta*,[6] where the concept is developed of Venice as a second but superior version of Rome itself.

The trauma induced by the dramatic defeat at Agnadello resulted in a further twist to the expanding myth. The effect was psychological as much as practical, particularly for the patrician class whose invincibility had been shattered. Although the Republic emerged relatively unscathed from seven years of war, and was able to recover most of its possessions on the mainland by 1515, it was now forced to operate in changed diplomatic and political circumstances. As a result of centuries of continual economic expansion, turn-of-the-century Venice had been the wealthiest and most powerful of all the Italian states, the centre of an extensive empire stretching from the islands of the Aegean to the cities of the *terraferma*. The defeat, unexpected by many Venetians, foreshadowed the loss of the entire mainland, an outcome so grave that some, including Doge Leonardo Loredan, regarded it as divine punishment for the indulgent habits of a city dedicated to luxurious living.[7] In the post-Agnadello world, self-confidence was gradually replaced with the growing realization that the Venetian role in international affairs was less than before, and that the foreign invasions of the 1490s had placed control of the peninsula in the hands of the Habsburgs and the French. Business was initially conducted much as it had always been, but the combined effects, in the years 1527–9, of the failing Venetian military campaigns in southern Italy, and both plague and famine at home, were severe. In the Treaty of Barcelona, concluded between Clement VII and Charles V, and the Peace of Cambrai that followed, Venetian interests were ignored and the Republic humiliated. The Peace of Bologna, which confirmed only that Venetian survival depended upon the delicate balancing and manipulation of French and Spanish interests, constitutes a watershed between the age of Venetian militant triumphalism and the new realities.[8] In this changed climate official discourse found a fresh voice, and began to speak in the rhetoric of peace. Venice, no longer belligerent, was now to be devoted to 'the political education of Europe'.[9] Critical to this process was the contribution of Gasparo Contarini, a member of the circle around Doge Andrea Gritti, and the author of *De magistratibus et republica venetorum*. Finished in the early 1530s but not published until a decade later, this treatise, which was frequently reprinted and also translated, presents a picture of the perfect state tied to a mixed constitution, providing the ideal conditions for the flowering of a culture that would instruct and fashion the world.[10] Contarini's contribution was the culmination of centuries of ritual that preceded the widespread dissemination of the myth, centuries in which both the cityscape and its soundscape were substantially moulded by the requirements of state ceremonial. Thereafter ritual and myth grew together in importance, as the Venetians evolved a post-Trent codicil to Petrarch's formulation.

Venetian moral power, the notion that the state was rich both materially and otherwise, 'mighty in her resources but mightier in virtue' as Petrarch had put it, had been present at least from the mid-fourteenth century, when the essential features of the myth included the connection between wealth and ethical behaviour, and the concern of the Republic's citizens had been with peace, justice, and the prosperity and security of the state.[11] In his encyclopaedic *Chronicon*, written about 1320, Benzo of Alexandria makes mention of precisely these elements.[12] As in Ambrogio Lorenzetti's magisterial fresco of *Good and Bad Government* in the Palazzo Pubblico in Siena, the association of the Cardinal Virtue of Justice with the medieval state was common enough, but in Venice it took the particular form of uniting the two in the figure of Venetia / Justice. Once this fusion had been established, these dual figures could function independently, while implicitly evoking each other, and the gentle evolution of such images over time facilitated the creation of an official visual language capable of communicating basic political concepts both to the citizens of the Republic and to the wider world.

Yet a further variation on this theme occurs in Paolo Veronese's *Apotheosis of Venice* painted for the Sala del Maggior Consiglio after the fire of 1577 (pl. 160). Repairs and redecoration, which included a new gilded ceiling to replace the old one, were put in hand almost immediately and were virtually complete within five years. The replacement paintings of the post-1577 cycle for the Ducal Palace were painted from beginning to end according to a single iconographical scheme, which reveals the major preoccupations of the Venetians at the end of the decade. Inevitably, both the visit of Henry III and the battle of Lepanto are included in two large canvasses by Andrea Vicentino, the first installed in the Sala delle Quattro Porte, the second in the Sala dello Scrutinio.[13] The design of the ceiling of the Sala del Maggior Consiglio called for

160   Paolo Veronese, *The Apotheosis of Venice (Pax Veneta)*,
*c.*1580. Ducal Palace, Sala del Maggior Consiglio.

three large central allegories flanked by twelve medium-sized canvases showing
scenes from Venetian history, and twenty smaller pictures.[14] This in turn forms
part of a cycle of paintings that decorate the walls and the ceiling of both the
Sala del Maggior Consiglio and the adjoining Sala dello Scrutinio, according
to a programme published in 1587 by the erudite Camaldolese monk Girolamo
Bardi, one of the committee appointed to devise it.[15] In Bardi's conception the
walls of both rooms were to illustrate Venice's relations to other rulers, including popes and emperors, while their ceilings were to show the Republic's victories over its enemies and the victorious deeds of individual citizens. On the
ceiling of the Sala dello Scrutinio were to be depicted the virtues that had supported these achievements and, as the climax of the scheme, the ceiling of the

161   Jacopo Palma il Giovane, *The Triumph of Venice*, c.1578–9. Ducal Palace, Sala del Maggior Consiglio.

Sala del Maggior Consiglio was to be designed to illustrate the glory that had accrued to Venice as a result of valorous action underpinned by the exercise of virtue.[16] The programme as executed rendered Bardi's scheme with considerable fidelity.

Together with two other large-scale allegories, Tintoretto's painting showing the Senate receiving the submission of the provinces and Palma il Giovane's *Triumph of Venice*, Veronese's *Apotheosis* brings the entire cycle to a heroic and triumphant conclusion.[17] Following traditional practice, Venice is represented in all three by a female figure of regal bearing. In Palma il Giovane's canvas she is shown, sceptre in hand, seated upon war trophies in the act of being crowned by a winged Victory (pl. 161).[18] Tintoretto's painting also shows the figure of

162 Jacopo Tintoretto, *The Senate receiving the Submission of the Provinces*, c.1580. Ducal Palace, Sala del Maggior Consiglio.

Venice crowned, though this time accompanied by the Lion of St Mark, present as the embodiment of the state, offering to the doge a palm branch, symbolic of victory, and an olive wreath, symbolic of peace (pl. 162).[19] In the overall context of this iconographically more complex construction, the message is that submission to Venice would bring the benefits of the *Pax Veneta*, an idea that is conveyed by other details of the painting.[20] In Veronese's *Apotheosis*, Venetia is surrounded by allegorical figures representing Peace, Abundance, Fame, Felicity, Security, Honour and Liberty, and is again in the act of being crowned by Victory.[21] The model here (and also in Palma's painting) is that of ancient Rome, where the image of Dea Roma, with a hovering Victory armed with a laurel wreath close to hand, was commonly found on classical intaglios, coins and medals. Its evocation by Palma and Veronese is designed to make an equivalence.[22]

Alongside the exercise of justice and the practice of moral rectitude, went the cultivation of piety.[23] Devotional life in Renaissance Venice had a particular character that distinguished it from other Italian cities. In part this was due to the extraordinary degree to which forms of social organization were connected to religious practice. Confraternities were common throughout the Catholic world, and had been since the middle ages, but nowhere else boasted the complementary *scuole grandi* and *scuole piccole*, both of which facilitated pious and charitable living among the majority of Venetian citizens. Their importance for everyday urban experience was largely achieved through public rituals, particularly the processions that criss-crossed the city and its major squares daily. On the most important feast-days the *scuole grandi* participated in the ducal *andata*, as sometimes did the representatives of a particular parish. The major activities of state were surrounded by religious observances, their activities framed by liturgical actions according to a specifically ducal rite in which the doge himself played a central, semi-sacral role. Music, present from the early middle ages in the chants of the *patriarchino*, came to be elaborated in more complex forms and styles as polyphony was introduced into the complex of civic and devotional ceremonial. Public acts of devotion and piety consolidated a socially cohesive belief system that defined and strengthened the body politic at all levels of Venetian society. Characteristic of the attitudes of a large sector of the patrician class in the last third of the sixteenth century were the views of Federico Contarini, who, having been ejected from the Council of Ten after the reforms of 1582–3, became a staunch supporter of the church.[24] In combination with a strictly hierarchical social order that had been in place since the early fifteenth century,[25] it was this more than any other single factor that accounted for Venetian stability in the decades after Trent. Once again, as so often in the history of the Republic, the Venetian elite carefully adjusted the rhetoric of the Myth of Venice so that it remained effective as both an expression of Venetian self-confidence as well as a means of social control, while still taking account of the lessons of recent history. For all of its shaky foundation,[26] the mythology continued as Venice slid into terminal decline.

NOTES

ABBREVIATIONS

Books

AS   *Acta sanctorum quotquot toto orbe coluntur, vel a catholicis scriptoribus celebrantur quae ex latinis et graecis, aliarum gentium antiquis monumentis*, 68 vols (Antwerp, 1643)

BS   *Bibliotheca sanctorum*, 15 vols (Rome, 1961–2000)

CE   *The Catholic Encyclopedia: An International Work of Reference on the Constitution, Doctrine, Discipline and History of the Catholic Church*, ed. C. G. Herbermann et al., 15 vols (London, 1907–12)

DA   *The Dictionary of Art*, ed. J. Shoaf Turner, 34 vols (London, 1996)

DBI   *Dizionario biografico degli italiani* (Rome, 1960–)

NG   *The New Grove Dictionary of Music and Musicians*, ed. S. Sadie, 29 vols (London, 2001)

RIS   *Rerum italicarum scriptores ab anno aerae christianae quingentesimo ad millesimumgentesimum quorum potissima pars nunc primum in lucem prodit ex Ambrosianae, Estensis, aliarumque insignium bibliothecarum codicibus Lodovicus Antonius Muratorius . . . collegit, ordinavit, & praefationibus auxit* (Milan, 1723–)

Institutions

ASF   Florence, Archivio di Stato
ASM   Mantua, Archivio di Stato
ASR   Rome, Archivio di Stato
ASV   Venice, Archivio di Stato
BAV   Vatican City, Biblioteca Apostolica Vaticana
BCV   Venice, Biblioteca Correr
BNM   Venice, Biblioteca Nazionale Marciana
MCV   Venice, Museo Correr

PROLOGUE

1 For a general account see A. M. Clark, *Pompeo Batoni: A Complete Catalogue of His Works with an Introductory Text* (Oxford, 1985).

2 On the commission, see A. M. Clark, 'Batoni's *Triumph of Venice*', *North Carolina Museum of Art Bulletin* IV (1963), pp. 5–11.

3 P. Fehl, 'A Literary Keynote for Pompeo Batoni's The Triumph of Venice', *North Carolina Museum of Art Bulletin* X/3 (1971), pp. 3–15.

4 David Rosand cited in B. Wilson, *The World in Venice: Print, the City and Early Modern Identity* (Toronto, 2005).

5 P. Fehl, 'Pictorial Precedents for the Representation of Doge Lionardo Loredan in Batoni's *Triumph of Venice*', *North Carolina Museum of Art Bulletin* XI/4 (1973), pp. 21–31.

6 Clark, *Pompeo Batoni*, p. 213, for the identifications.

7 F. Haskell, *Patrons and Painters: A Study in the Relations between Italian Art and Society in the Age of the Baroque* (London, 1963), p. 259.

CHAPTER ONE

1 *RIS,* XII/1, cols 9–523, at cols 14ff.

2 S. Tramontin, ed., 'Origini e sviluppi della legganda marciana', in *Le origini della chiesa di Venezia* (Venice, 1987), pp. 167–86.

3 G. Pavanello, 'San Marco nella leggenda e nella storia', *Rivista della città di Venezia* VI (1928), pp. 293–324; S. Tramontin, 'Realtà e leggenda nei racconti marciani veneti', *Studi veneziani* XII (1970), pp. 35–58; E. Muir, *Civic Ritual in Renaissance Venice* (Princeton, NJ, 1981), pp. 78–92; P. J. Geary, *Furta sacra: Thefts of Relics in the Central Middle Ages*, 2nd revd edn (Princeton, NJ, 1990), pp. 88–94.

4 From a large literature, see in particular H. C. Peyer, *Città e santi patroni nell'Italia medievale*, ed. A. Benvenuti (Florence, 1998), pp. 45–64; O. Demus, *The Church of San Marco in Venice: History, Architecture, Sculpture* (Washington, DC, 1960), particularly pp. 1–61; O. Demus, *The Mosaics of San Marco in Venice*, 2 vols in 4 (Chicago, IL, 1984), I/1; T. E. A. Dale, 'Inventing a Sacred Past: Pictorial Narratives of St Mark the Evangelist in Aquileia and Venice, ca. 1000–1300', *Dumbarton Oaks Papers* XLVIII (1994), pp. 53–104; T. E. A. Dale, *Relics, Prayer and Politics in Medieval Venetia: Romanesque Painting in the Crypt of Aquileia Cathedral* (Princeton, NJ, 1997).

5 Demus, *The Church of San Marco*, pp. 30–34; Dale, 'Inventing a Sacred Past', pp. 57–8; Dale, *Relics, Prayer and Politics*, p. 9.

6 Dale, 'Inventing a Sacred Past', pp. 59–61.

7 H. Buchwald, 'Eleventh Century Corinthian-Palmette Capitals in the Region of Aquileia', *Art Bulletin* XLVIII (1966), particularly pp. 155–8.

8 For Paul the Deacon and Paolino, patriarch of Aquileia, the only other eighth-century writer to refer to Mark's mission, see Tramontin, 'Realtà e leggenda', pp. 36–8.

9 Tramontin, 'Realtà e leggenda', p. 41.

10 Demus, *The Mosaics of San Marco*, I/1, pp. 58–62; H. R. Hahnloser, ed., *Il tesoro di San Marco*, 2 vols (Florence, 1971), I, p. 34 (no. 70).

11 See below, pp. 15–16.

12 Geary, *Furta sacra*, pp. 89–91.

13 Demus, *The Church of San Marco*, pp. 5–7; Geary, *Furta sacra*, pp. 110–11.

14 For the arguments on both sides, see Tramontin, 'Realtà e leggenda', pp. 49–54; A. Niero, 'Questioni ageografiche su San Marco', *Studi veneziani* XII (1970), particularly pp. 16–25.

15 Orléans, Bibliothèque Municipal, MS 197; see Tramontin, 'Realtà e leggenda', p. 50 n. 39, and, for a description of this, the earliest known source of the *translatio, Catalogue général des manuscrits des bibliothèques de France* (Paris, 1885–), XII, pp. 102–4.

16 Tramontin, 'Realtà e leggenda', pp. 44–5.

17 A. Pertusi, 'Venezia e Bisanzio, 1000–1204', *Dumbarton Oaks Papers* XXXIII (1979), pp. 1–22. On Theodore's early role, see A. Niero, 'I santi patroni', in S. Tramontin, ed., *Il culto dei santi a Venezia* (Venice, 1965), pp. 91–5; Tramontin, 'Realtà e leggenda', pp. 52–3; Muir, *Civic Ritual*, pp. 93–5; P. H. Labalme, 'Holy Patronage, Holy Promotion: The Cult of Saints in Fifteenth-century Venice', in S. Sticca, ed., *Saints: Studies in Hagiography* (Binghamton, NY, 1996), pp. 236–8.

18 *AS,* Feb. 11, pp. 23–37; *BS,* XII, cols 238–42; Niero, 'I santi padroni', pp. 91–2.

19 F. Corner, *Ecclesiae Venetae*, 13 vols (Venice, 1745), XIII, pp. 399–400; see Labalme, 'Holy Patronage, Holy Promotion', p. 245, n. 29.

20 L. Sartorio, 'San Teodoro: statua composita', *Arte veneta* I (1947), pp. 132–4.

21 Demus, *The Church of San Marco*, pp. 20–23; Geary, *Furta sacra*, pp. III–12; Niero, 'I santi patroni', pp. 91–3; Tramontin, 'Realtà e leggenda', pp. 52–3; Muir, *Civic Ritual*, pp. 93–5; Labalme, 'Holy Patronage, Holy Promotion', pp. 236–8.

22 J. B. Ward-Perkins, 'The Bronze Lion of St Mark at Venice', *Antiquity* XXI (1947), pp. 23–41.

23 Sanudo, *Le vite dei dogi*, ed. G. Monticolo (Città di Castello, 1900–01), p. 430.

24 M. Belozerskaya and K. Lapatin, 'Antiquity Consumed: Transformations at San Marco', in A. Payne, A. Kuttner and R. Smick, eds, *Antiquity and its Interpreters* (Cambridge, 2000), p. 86.

25 M. Sanudo, *De origine, situ et magistratibus urbis Venetae ovvero la città di Venetia, 1493–1530*, ed. A. Caracciolo Arico (Milan, 1980), p. 25; G. Ruggiero, *Violence in Early Renaissance Venice* (New Brunswick, NJ, 1980), pp. 47–9.

26 D. Pincus, 'Venice and the Two Romes: Byzantium and Rome as a Double Heritage in Venetian Cultural Politics', *Artibus et Historiae* XXVI (1992), pp. IOI–2.

27 The textual history of the *translatio* legend is treated in N. McCleary, 'Note storiche et archeologiche sul testo della "Translatio S. Marci"', *Memorie storiche forogiulesi* XXVII–XXIX (1931–3), pp. 223–4; for further discussion, see Geary, *Furta sacra*, pp. 88–94; G. R. Michiel, *Le origini delle feste veneziane*, 6 vols (Milan, 1817), I, pp. 63–83 and Muir, *Civic Ritual*, pp. 78–92.

28 Tramontin, 'Realtà e leggenda'.

29 Rome, Biblioteca Casanatense, MS 718, ff. 131v–34. For this and other sources, see McCleary, 'Note storiche', which also presents a critical edition of the text based on the Casanatense manuscript (pp. 235–64).

30 McCleary, 'Note storiche', p. 224; Geary, *Furta sacra*, p. 94.

31 Dale, *Relics, Prayer and Politics*, p. 7 and n. I

32 Florence, Biblioteca Riccardiana, MS 1919; see A. Limentani, ed., *Martin da Canal: les estoires de Venise. Cronaca veneziana in lingua francese dalle origini al 1275* (Florence, 1972), pp. XXVII–XXXII.

33 As in G. Stringa, *La chiesa di S. Marco, capella del serenissimo principe di Venetia, descritta brevemente* (Venice, 1610), pp. 26–44.

34 A. Manno, ed., *San Marco Evangelista: opere d'arte dalle chiese di Venezia* (Venice, 1995).

35 *RIS*, XII/I, p. 14.

36 Tramontin, 'Realtà e leggenda', pp. 45–6.

37 Florence, Biblioteca Riccardiana, MS 1919, ff. 123–4; see Limentani, ed., *Martin da Canal*, pp. CCXCIII–CCCIV.

38 Demus, *The Church of San Marco*, pp. 14–15.

39 Muir, *Civic Ritual*, pp. 119–20.

40 G. Fasoli, 'Nascità di un mito', *Studi storici in onore di Gioacchino Volpe* I (Florence, 1958), p. 451.

41 J. de Voragine, *The Golden Legend*, trans. W. G. Ryan, 2 vols (Princeton, NJ, 1995), I, p. 243.

42 Pertusi, 'Venezia e Bisanzio, 1000–1204', p. 6

43 F. Ongania, ed., *La basilica di S. Marco in Venezia illustrate nella storia e nell'arte da scrittori veneziani* (Venice, 1878–93), p. 3, no. 20.

44 M. Agazzi, *Platea Sancti Marci* (Venice, 1991), p. 13.

45 Demus, *The Church of San Marco*, pp. 64–9.

46 R. Krautheimer, *Early Christian and Byzantine Architecture* (Harmondsworth, 1965), p. 288

47 Demus, *The Church of San Marco*, pp. 5–7.

48 O. G. Von Simson, *Sacred Fortress: Byzantine Art and Statecraft in Ravenna* (Chicago, IL, 1948), pp. 15–18.

49 Procopius, *De aedificis*, I. iv. 9–24.

50 M. Harrison, *A Temple for Byzantium: The Discovery and Excavation of Anicia Juliana's Palace-Church in Istanbul* (London, 1989), pp. 20, 24.

51 Demus, *The Church of San Marco*, pp. 88–100; Demus, *The Mosaics of San Marco*, I/I, pp. 232–43; Krautheimer, *Early Christian and Byzantine Architecture*, p. 355.

52 Dale, 'Inventing a Sacred Past', pp. 58–62; Dale, *Relics, Prayer and Politics*, pp. 12–20.

53 Demus, *The Church of San Marco*, pp. 76–7.

54 Demus, *The Mosaics of San Marco*, I/I, pp. 1–17.

55 Demus, *The Church of San Marco*, pp. 89–90.

56 Demus, *The Church of San Marco*, pp. 90–100; Vickers, 'Wandering Stones', pp. 225–32.

57 D. Kinney, '*Spolia, Damnatio* and *Renovatio Memoriae*', *Memoirs of the American Academy in Rome* XLII (1997), p. 117. For what follows, see O. Demus et al., *Le sculture esterne di San Marco* (Milan, 1995), pp. 12–17.

58 M. Perry, 'Saint Mark's Trophies: Legend, Superstition and Archaeology in Renaissance Venice', *Journal of the Warburg and Courtauld Institutes* XL (1977), pp. 39–45. S. B. Butters, *The Triumph of Vulcan*, 2 vols (Florence, 1996), I, p. 67, n. 2.

59 M. Vickers, 'Wandering Stones: Venice, Constantinople and Athens', in K. L. Selig and E. Sears, eds, *The Verbal and the Visual: Essays in Honor of William Sebastian Heckscher* (New York, 1990), pp. 226–7.

60 F. Sansovino, *Venetia città nobilissima et singolare descritta in XIV libri* (Venice, 1581), ff. 118v–19.

61 Belozerskaya and Lapatin, 'Antiquity Consumed'.

62 M. Jacoff, *The Horses of San Marco and the Quadriga of the Lord* (Princeton, NJ, 1993), p. 44; Dale, 'Inventing a Sacred Past', p. 90.

63 Harrison, *A Temple for Byzantium*, pp. 137–44.

64 Harrison, *A Temple for Byzantium*, pp. 100–04; T. F. Mathews, *The Early Churches of Constantinople: Architecture and Liturgy* (University Park, PA, 1971), pp. 52–5; T. F. Mathews, *The Byzantine Churches of Istanbul: A Photographic Survey* (University Park, PA, and London, 1975), pp. 225–30; Vickers, 'Wandering Stones', pp. 231–32. For Constantinople as a 'Second Jerusalem', see P. Sherrard, *Constantinople: Iconography of a Sacred City* (Oxford, 1965), pp. 79–123.

65 Demus, *The Church of San Marco*, pp. 79–82; Demus, *The Mosaics of San Marco*, II/I, pp. 40–43, 185–91; Dale, 'Inventing a

Sacred Past', pp. 88–90; D. Howard, *Venice and the East: The Impact of the Islamic World on Venetian Architecture, 1100–1500* (New Haven, CT, and London, 2000), pp. 88–90.

66 Vickers, 'Wandering Stones', pp. 231–2.

67 Harrison, *A Temple for Byzantium*, p. 143.

68 R. Gnoli, *Marmora romana*, 2nd edn (Rome, 1988), pp. 122–44.

69 W. Dorigo, 'Una nuova lettura delle sculture del portale centrale di S. Marco', *Venezia arti* II (1988), pp. 8–23.

70 Demus, *Le sculture esterne*, pp. 14–16.

71 Berozerskaya and Lapatin, 'Antiquity Consumed', pp. 89–90.

72 A. Niero, 'Simbologia dotta e popolare nelle sculture esterne', in B. Bertoli, ed., *La basilica di San Marco: arte e simbologia* (Venice, 1993), pp. 125–48.

73 Perry, 'Saint Mark's Trophies', pp. 30–39.

74 Perry, 'Saint Mark's Trophies', pp. 28–9.

75 R. Polacco, 'San Marco e le sue sculture nel Duecento', in D. Rosand, ed., *Interpretazioni veneziane: studi di storia dell'arte in onore di Michelangelo Muraro* (Venice, 1984), pp. 59–75; Jacoff, *The Horses of San Marco*, pp. 12–41.

76 Jacoff, *The Horses of San Marco*, pp. 21–6.

77 Dale, 'Inventing a Sacred Past', pp. 96–9.

78 H. Buchthal, *Historia Troiana: Studies in the History of Mediaeval Secular Illustration* (London and Leiden, 1971), p. 55; Demus, *The Mosaics of San Marco*, I/I, p. 243.

79 According to some scholars, the Pala d'Oro was executed following a single programme in 1105, and this dating seems now to be generally accepted. For a number of other proposed dates and stages of development, see R. Gallo, *Il tesoro di San Marco e la sua storia* (Venice and Rome, 1967), pp. 89–93; Hahnloser, ed., *Il tesoro di San Marco*, I, pp. 89–93; M. E. Frazer, 'The Pala d'Oro and the Cult of St Mark in Venice', *Jahrbuch der österreichischen Byzantinistik* XXXII/5 (1982), pp. 273–9.

80 P. Lasko, *Ars sacra, 800–1200* (Harmondsworth, 1972), pp. 50–54; C. Hahn, 'Narrative on the Golden Altar of Sant'Ambrogio in Milan: Presentation and Reception', *Dumbarton Oaks Papers* LIII (1999), pp. 167–87, especially p. 185.

81 Frazer, 'The Pala d'Oro', p. 273.

82 Dale, 'Inventing a Sacred Past', pp. 63–7.

83 Dale, 'Inventing a Sacred Past', p. 64, citing earlier writers and presenting a reconstruction (plan 3); Dale, *Relics, Prayer and Politics,* pp. 48–9 and fig. 136.

84 Dale, 'Inventing a Sacred Past', pp. 66, 70–71, and for the relevant text of the *translatio,* McCleary, 'Note storiche et archeologiche', pp. 260–62. For further discussion of the appearance of the first church, see Demus, *The Church of San Marco,* pp. 64–9.

85 Demus, *The Church of San Marco,* p. 69; the inscription reads HIC SVSCIPIT VE[NE]TIA BEATVM MARCVM.

86 Frazer, 'The Pala d'Oro', pp. 274, 277.

87 For the dating of the cycle, see Demus, *The Mosaics of San Marco,* I/I, pp. 82–3; Dale, *Relics, Prayer and Politics,* p. 54.

88 Dale, 'Inventing a Sacred Past', p. 70.

89 Demus, *The Mosaics of San Marco,* I/I, pp. 68–9.

90 The accompanying inscription reads PONTIFICES CLERVS POPVLVS DVX MENTE SERENVS I LAVDIBVS ATQVE CHORIS EXCIPIVNT DVLCE CANORIS; see Demus, *The Church of San Marco,* p. 68.

91 C. Walter, 'Political Imagery in the Medieval Lateran Palace', *Cahiers archéologiques* XX (1970), pp. 155–76; XXI (1971), pp. 119–23.

92 Von Simson, *Sacred Fortress,* pp. 27–9.

93 M. Stroll, *Symbols as Power: The Papacy following the Investiture Contest* (Leiden, 1991), pp. 16–35, pls 8–10.

94 Demus, *The Mosaics of San Marco,* I/I, pp. 65–70; Dale, 'Inventing a Sacred Past', pp. 70–71; Dale, *Relics, Prayer and Politics,* pp. 54–5.

95 McCleary, 'Note storiche', p. 261.

96 Demus, *The Church of San Marco,* p. 47; Dale, 'Inventing a Sacred Past', p. 78; T. E. A. Dale, 'Stolen Property: St Mark's First Venetian Tomb and the Politics of Communal Memory', in E. Valdez del Alamo and C. Stamatis Pendergast, eds, *Memory and the Medieval Tomb* (Aldershot, 2000), p. 208.

97 For the most recent discussion, see P. F. Brown, *Venetian Narrative Painting in the Age of Carpaccio* (New Haven, CT, and London, 1988), pp. 144–50.

98 Demus, *The Mosaics of San Marco,* II/I, pp. 193–4.

99 Demus, *The Mosaics of San Marco,* II/I, pp. 199–206; Dale, 'Inventing a Sacred Past', pp. 88–93.

100 Dale, 'Inventing a Sacred Past', p. 91.

101 For the two interpretations, see Demus, *The Mosaics of San Marco,* I/I, pp. 201–6, and Dale, 'Inventing a Sacred Past', pp. 91–3.

102 Peyer, *Città e santi padroni,* p. 53.

103 McCleary, 'Note storiche', pp. 225–8.

104 Limentani, ed., *Martin da Canal,* pp. XXIV–XXV.

105 The text is given in Corner, *Ecclesiae Venetae,* IX, pp. 6–39.

106 Demus, *The Church of San Marco,* pp. 12–14.

107 R. A. Katzenstein, 'Three Liturgical Manuscripts from San Marco: Art and Patronage in Mid-Trecento Venice' (Ph.D. dissertation, Harvard University, 1987), pp. 220–21.

108 Demus, *The Church of San Marco,* pp. 70–75.

109 Tramontin, 'Realtà e leggenda', pp. 54–7. The earliest text to record the *apparitio,* which comes from the twelfth century, does not include the authenticating miracles and signs; see R. Cessi, 'L'apparitio Sancti Marci del 1094', *Archivio veneto* LXXXXV (1964), pp. 113–15, and, for the later sources, G. Monticolo, 'L'apparitio ed i suoi manoscritti', *Nuovo archivio veneto* V (1895), pp. 111–77.

110 G. Stringa, *Vita di S. Marco Protettore Invitissimo della Serenissima Republica di Venetia con la translatione, et apparitione del sacro suo corpo* (Venice, 1610), pp. 1–79.

111 Demus, *The Mosaics of San Marco,* II/I, pp. 27–44.

112 Dale, 'Stolen Property', pp. 209–12.

113 M. Muraro, 'Il pilastro del miracolo e il secondo programma dei mosaici marciani', *Arte veneta* XXXIX (1975), p. 60.

114 S. Sinding-Larsen, *Christ in the Council Hall: Studies in the Religious Iconography of the Venetian Republic* (Rome, 1974), pp. 199–203; S. Sinding-Larsen, 'Chiesa di

stato e iconografia musiva', in B. Bertoli, ed., *La basilica di San Marco: arte e simbologia* (Venice, 1993), pp. 38–42; Muraro, 'Il pilastro del miracolo', pp. 62–3; Dale, 'Stolen Property', p. 206.

115 Dale, 'Stolen Property', p. 212.

116 Dale, 'Inventing a Sacred Past', pl. 27.

117 Muraro, 'Il pilastro del miracolo', pp. 61–2.

118 P. G. Molmenti, *Studi e ricerche di storia e d'arte* (Turin and Rome, 1892), pp. 25–6; Tramontin, 'Realtà e leggenda', pp. 57–8; Muir, *Civic Ritual*, pp. 88–9.

119 Molmenti, *Studi e ricerche*, pp. 25–26; Tramontin, 'Realtà e leggenda', pp. 57–58.

120 Gallo, *Il Tesoro di S. Marco*, pp. 101–3; H. R. Hahnloser, ed., *Il tesoro di San Marco*, 2 vols (Florence, 1971), II, pp. 161–2 (cat. 158). The ring dates from before 1336, when it was listed in an inventory.

121 M. Sanudo, *I diarii*, ed. R. Fulin et al., 58 vols (Venice, 1879–1903), XVIII, col. 296 (1514); ibid., XXIV, cols 405–6 (1517), records two such occasions. For a discussion of both ring legends, see Gallo, *Il tesoro di San Marco*, pp. 101–3; Muir, *Civic Ritual*, pp. 88–90.

122 Sanudo, *I diarii*, LVIII, cols 372–3. Two folios of the manuscript, written in the fifth century and in Latin, not Greek, still survive; see Gallo, *Il tesoro di San Marco*, pp. 204–6; Hahnloser, *Il tesoro di San Marco*, II, pp. 151–2.

123 Hahnloser, *Il tesoro di San Marco*, II, pp. 162–3.

124 Hahnloser, *Il tesoro di San Marco*, II, pp. 183–4.

125 Brown, *Venetian Narrative Painting*, pp. 69–70, 287–90.

126 Geary, *Furta sacra*, pp. 94–103.

127 Labalme, 'Holy Patronage, Holy Promotion', p. 238.

128 Pertusi, 'Venezia e bisanzio, 1000–1204', pp. 6–7.

129 G. Musolino, 'Feste religiose popolari', in S. Tramontin, ed., *Il culto dei santi a Venezia* (Venice, 1965), p. 218; L. Fabbiani, *La fondazione monastica di San Nicolò di Lido*, 1053–1628 (Venice, 1988)

130 ASV Collegio, Ceremoniali I, f. VIIIv; B. Tamassia Mazzarotto, *Le feste veneziane, i giochi popolari, le ceremonie religiose e di*

governo (Florence, 1961), pp. 181ff.; Muir, *Civic Ritual*, pp. 119–34 and 97–8, where it is suggested that the *spozalizio* evolved from an earlier ceremony in which Nicholas's protection was invoked.

131 P. F. Brown, 'Measured Friendship, Calculated Pomp: The Ceremonial Welcomes of the Venetian Republic', in B. Wisch and S. Scott Munshower, eds, *'All the World's a Stage . . .': Art and Pageantry in the Renaissance and Baroque* (University Park, PA, 1990), pp. 137–86.

132 Muir, *Civic Ritual*, pp. 97–101, at p. 99.

133 Cessi, *Storia della repubblica di Venezia*, 2 vols (Venice, 1968), II, pp. 346–8.

134 Michiel, *Le origine delle feste veneziane*, II, pp. 139–91.

135 Brown, *Venetian Narrative Painting*, pp. 259–60.

136 D. Pincus, *The Arco Foscari: The Building of a Triumphal Gateway in Fifteenth-century Venice* (New York, 1976), pp. 21–2; W. Wolters, *Storia e politica nei dipinti di Palazzo Ducale: aspetti dell'autocelebrazione della Repubblica di Venezia nel Cinquecento* (Venice, 1987), p. 98.

137 BCV, MS Venier p.d. 517b.

138 J. H. Moore, *Vespers at St Mark's: Music of Alessandro Grandi, Giovanni Rovetta and Francesco Cavalli*, 2 vols (Ann Arbor, MI, 1981), p. 210.

139 ASV Collegio, Ceremoniali I, f. ix; Moore, *Vespers at St Mark's*, p. 228; L. Urban, *Processioni e feste dogali: 'Venetia est mundus'* (Vicenza, 1998), pp. 105–6.

140 ASV Collegio, Ceremoniali I, ff. ix–ix verso; ASV, San Marco Proc. de Supra, Reg. 99, ff. 409–13; Moore, *Vespers at St Mark's*, p. 300.

141 Moore, *Vespers at St Mark's*, pp. 210–13.

142 Moore, *Vespers at St Mark's*, pp. 211–12.

143 M. A. Sabellico, *Degl'istorici delle cose veneziane, i quali hanno scritto per pubblico decreto*, 10 vols (Venice, 1718–22), I, pp. 289–91; Sanudo, *Vite dei dogi*, p. 608.

144 For the building history of the Scuola, see P. L. Sohm, *The Scuola Grande di San Marco, 1437–1550: The Architecture of a Venetian Lay Confraternity* (New York, 1982), pp. 79–92, and T. Pignatti, ed., *Le scuole di Venezia* (Milan, 1981), pp. 132–5

and 145–9 (where the paintings are catalogued). For a more detailed account of the paintings and their documentation, see Brown, *Venetian Narrative Painting*, pp. 291–5, which includes a reconstruction of the *albergo*.

145 P. Humfrey, 'The Bellinesque *Life of St Mark Cycle* for the Scuola Grande di San Marco in Venice in its Original Arrangement', *Zeitschrift fur Kuntstgeschichte* XLVIII (1985), pp. 227–32.

146 Humfrey, 'The Bellinesque *Life of St Mark*', pp. 232, 236–7; P. Rylands, *Palma Vecchio* (Cambridge, 1992), pp. 242–4.

147 Humfrey, 'The Bellinesque *Life of St Mark*', pp. 239–41.

148 P. L. Sohm, 'Palma Vecchio's *Sea Storm*: A Political Allegory', *RACAR: Revue d'art canadienne/Canadian Art Review* VI (1979–80), pp. 85–96.

149 For reactions to the defeat, see F. Gilbert, 'Venice in the Crisis of the League of Cambrai', in J. Hale, ed., *Renaissance Venice* (London, 1973), pp. 274–92.

150 P. F. Brown, 'Honor and Necessity: The Dynamics of Patronage in the Confraternities of Renaissance Venice', *Studi veneziani* XIV (1987), pp. 198–9.

151 Brown, *Venetian Narrative Painting*, pp. 144–50, 233–4.

152 Brown, 'Honor and Necessity', particularly pp. 199–205.

153 Humfrey, 'The Bellinesque *Life of St Mark*', pp. 233–34.

154 R. C. Davis, *The War of the Fists: Popular Culture and Public Violence in Late Renaissance Venice* (Oxford, 1994).

155 Tramontiri, ed., *Il culto dei Santi*, pp. 241–74 (Musolino); Muir, *Civic Ritual*, p. 70.

156 Sinding-Larsen, *Christ in the Council Hall*, pp. 45, 234–5; D. Rosand, '*Venetia figurata*: The Iconography of a Myth', in Rosand, ed., *Interpretazioni veneziane*, pp. 177, 182–5; R. S. MacKenney, 'Public and Private in Renaissance Venice', *Renaissance Studies* XII (1998), pp. 122–8.

157 Petrarch, *Epistolae seniles*, IV, 3.

158 Sanudo, *I diarii*, XVII, p. 102.

159 Rosand, '*Venetia figurata*', pp. 179–80; D. Pincus, *The Tombs of the Doges of Venice* (Cambridge, 2000), pp. 121–3; D. Rosand,

Myths of Venice: The Figuration of a State (Chapel Hill, NC, and London, 2001), pp. 26–32.

160 Pincus, *The Tombs of the Doges of Venice*, pp. 105–20; D. Pincus, 'Hard Times and Ducal Radiance: Andrea Dandolo and the Construction of the Ruler in Fourteenth-century Venice', in J. Martin and D. Romano, eds, *Venice Reconsidered: The History and Civilization of an Italian City State, 1297–1797* (Baltimore, MD, and London, 2000), pp. 104–7.

161 F. Flores d'Arcais, *Guariento* (Venice, 1965), pp. 72–3; L. Sinding-Larsen, *Christ in the Council Hall: Studies in the Religious Iconography of the Venetian Republic* (Rome, 1974), pp. 45–7, 55–6; Rosand, 'Venetia figurata', pp. 181–2.

162 R. Pallucchini and P. Rossi, *Tintoretto: le opere sacre e profane*, 2 vols (Milan, 1982), I, cat. 465, and II, figs 589–90. For the most recent resumé of the literature relating to the *Paradize* commission see M. Falomir, ed., *Tintoretto* (Madrid, 2007), pp. 370–75.

163 Rosand, '*Venezia figurata*', p. 179; Rosand, *Myths of Venice*, pp. 20–33.

164 A. Kuhn; 'Venice, Queen of the Sea', in Sinding-Larsen, *Christ in the Council Hall*, pp. 263–8; Pallucchini and Rossi, *Tintoretto*, I, cat. 462, and II, fig. 591.

165 Kuhn, 'Venice Queen of the Sea', p. 267.

166 G. Gorini, 'Lepanto nelle medaglie', in G. Benzoni, ed., *Il mediterraneo nella seconda metà del '500 nella luce di Lepanto* (Florence, 1974), pp. 155–6.

167 P. Voltolina, *La storia di Venezia attraverso le medaglie*, 3 vols (Milan, 1998), I, pp. 248 (no. 204), and 360 (no. 313).

168 G. Parsons, *Siena, Civil Religion and the Sienese* (Aldershot, 2004), pp. 1–31.

169 Sherrard, *Constantinople*, pp. 79–84.

170 For an analysis, see Muir, *Civic Ritual*, pp. 119–34 and the literature cited there. On Marian cults in general in Venice, see S. Tramontin , ed., *Il culto dei santi a Venezia* (Venice, 1965), chapter 8.

171 G. R. Michiel, *Le origini delle feste veneziane*, 6 vols (Milan, 1817), I, pp. 169–79, II, pp. 139–91; L. Urban, *Processioni e feste dogali: 'Venetia est mundus'*

(Vicenza, 1998), pp. 89–96; Muir, *Civic Ritual*, pp. 97–8, 119–34.

172 ASV Collegio, Ceremoniali I, f. 8v; BNM, MS Lat. III 172 (2276), ff. 53–53v; F. Sansovino, *Venetia città nobilissima . . . descritta in XIIII libri . . . con aggiunta da D. Giustiniano Martinioni* (Venice, 1663), pp. 500–02.

173 Although no surviving music can be definitely associated with the ceremony, some possibilities are suggested in D. Bryant, 'Liturgy, Ceremonial and Sacred Music in Venice at the Time of the Counter-Reformation', 2 vols (Ph.D. dissertation, University of London, 1981), I, pp. 97–102 and Appendix I.

174 Muir, *Civic Ritual*, p. 132.

175 D. Calabi and P. Morachiello, *Rialto: le fabbriche e il ponte, 1514–1591* (Turin, 1987), p. 296; Rosand, *Myths of Venice*, pp. 16–18.

176 R. C. Davis, *Shipbuilders of the Venetian Arsenal: Workers and Workplace in the Preindustrial City* (Baltimore, MD, 1991), pp. 86–7.

177 S. Gramigna and A. Perissa, *Scuole di arti mestieri e devozione a Venezia* (Venice, 1981), cat. no.42/A; Rosand, *Myths of Venice*, pp. 71–2.

178 G. Bassano, *Motetti per concerti . . .* (Venice, 1598), where it opens the collection. See Bryant, 'Liturgy, Ceremonial and Sacred Music', I, pp. 24–5, 97–102, where a number of other non-liturgical motets that may have been performed at San Marco on Ascension Day are discussed. Bryant also suggests that Bassano's piece may have been written for the vespers of the Vigil of the Ascension in 1595, which coincided with the octave of the investiture of Doge Marino Grimani. Text and translation are taken from G. Bassano, *Opera omnia*, ed. R. Charteris (n.p., 1999–), I, p. XXXVIII.

179 Muir, *Civic Ritual*, pp. 66–8.

180 A. Pertusi, 'Gli inizi della storiografia umanistica nel Quattrocento', in Pertusi, ed., *La storiografia veneziana fino al secolo XVI: aspetti e problemi* (Florence, 1970), pp. 318–19.

181 P. H. Labalme, *Bernardo Giustiniani: A Venetian of the Quattrocento* (Rome, 1969), p. 262

182 Limentani, ed., *Martin da Canal*, p. 6.

183 Muir, *Civic Ritual*, pp. 70–72. For Dondi's chronicle, see V. Lazzarini, 'Il pretesto documento della fondazione di Venezia e la cronica del medico Jacopo Dondi', *Atti del Reale Istituto Veneto di Scienze, Lettere ed Arti* LXXV (1915–16), especially pp. 1264–5.

184 Labalme, *Bernardo Giustiniani*, pp. 305–6.

185 Labalme, *Bernardo Giustiniani*, pp. 306–9.

CHAPTER TWO

1 P. Brown, *The Cult of the Saints: Its Rise and Function in Latin Antiquity* (Chicago, IL, 1981), particularly pp. 86–127.

2 P. J. Geary, *Cult of the Saints: Thefts of Relics in the Central Middle Ages*, 2nd revd edn (Princeton, NJ, 1990), especially pp. 44–55.

3 T. E. A. Dale, 'Inventing a Sacred Past: Pictorial Narratives of St Mark the Evangelist in Aquileia and Venice, ca. 1000–1300', *Dumbarton Oaks Papers* XLVIII (1994), pp. 85–8. For the theme of the Chosen People as it is presented on the west façade of the basilica, see ibid., pp. 93–102; M. Jacoff, *The Horses of San Marco and the Quadriga of the Lord* (Princeton, NJ, 1993).

4 T. E. A. Dale, 'Stolen Property: St Mark's First Venetian Tomb and the Politics of Communal Memory', in E. Valdez del Alamo and C. Stamatis Pendergast, eds, *Memory and the Medieval Tomb* (Aldershot, 2000), p. 205.

5 B. Boucher, *The Sculpture of Jacopo Sansovino*, 2 vols (New Haven, CT, and London, 1991), I, p. 55; Dale, 'Stolen Property', p. 205.

6 A. Pertusi, 'Quaedam regalia insignia', *Studi veneziani* VII (1965), pp. 19–38; P. F. Brown, 'The Self-Definition of the Venetian Republic' in A. Molho, K. Rauflaub and J. Emlem, eds, *Athens and Rome, Florence and Venice: City-States in Classical Antiquity and Medieval Italy* (Stuttgart, 1991), p. 519; A. Stahl, *Zecca: The Mint of Venice in the Middle Ages* (Baltimore, MD, and London, 2000), p. 18.

7   N. Papadopoli, *Le monete di Venezia*, 4 vols (Venice, 1893–1919), I, p. 86, and table V, n. 6; Stahl, *Zecca*, pp. 18–19.

8   A. Stahl, 'The Coinage of Venice in the Age of Enrico Dandolo', in E. E. Kittell and T. F. Madden, eds, *Medieval and Renaissance Venice* (Urbana and Chicago, IL, 1999), p. 126.

9   S. Sinding-Larsen, *Christ in the Council Hall: Studies in the Religious Iconography of the Venetian Republic* (Rome, 1974), pp. 159–60; Stahl, *Zecca*, pp. 30–35.

10 D. Pincus, *The Tombs of the Doges of Venice* (Cambridge, 2000), pp. 78–9.

11 Papadopoli, *Le monete di Venezia*, I, p. 137, table VIII, n. 2 ; D. Pincus, 'Hard Times and Ducal Radiance: Andrea Dandolo and the Construction of the Ruler in Four-teenth-century Venice', in J. Martin and D. Romano, eds, *Venice Reconsidered: The History and Civilization of an Italian City State, 1297–1797* (Baltimore, MD, and London, 2000), pp. 97–8; Stahl, *Zecca*, pp. 28–33.

12 I am grateful to Warren Woodfin for this information.

13 O. Demus, *The Church of San Marco in Venice: History, Architecture, Sculpture* (Washington, DC, 1960), pp. 92–3.

14 Dale, 'Inventing a Sacred Past', pp. 61–3.

15 O. Demus, *The Mosaics of San Marco in Venice*, 2 vols in 4 (Chicago, IL, 1984), I/1, pp. 31–3.

16 H. Buchthal, 'The Carved Stone Orna-ment of the Middle Ages in San Marco, Venice', *Jahrbuch der Österreichischen byzantinischen Gesellschaft* XIII (1964), pp. 148–9 (giving a date in the thirteenth century); R. Polacco, 'Le colonne del ciborio di San Marco', *Venezia arti* I (1987), pp. 36–7.

17 Demus, *The Mosaics of San Marco*, I/1, pp. 54–83.

18 R. Gallo, *Il tesoro di San Marco e la sua storia* (Venice and Rome, 1967), pp. 175–7; H. R. Hahnloser and R. Polacco, eds, *La Pala d'oro*, 2nd edn (Venice, 1994), pp. 3–4; M. E. Frazer, 'The Pala d'Oro and the Cult of St Mark in Venice', *Jahrbuch der österreichischen Byzantinistik* XXXII/5 (1982), p. 273; D. Pincus, 'Andrea Dandolo,

1343–1354, and Visible History: The San Marco Project', in C. M. Rosenberg, ed., *Art and Politics in Late Medieval and Early Renaissance Italy, 1250–1550* (London, 1990), pp. 197–8.

19 R. Goffen, 'Paolo Veneziano e Andrea Dandolo: una nuova lettera della pala feriale', in H. R. Hahnloser and R. Polacco, eds, *La Pala d'oro*, 2nd edn (Venice, 1994), p. 175.

20 G. Fiocco, 'Le pale feriali', in H. R. Hahn-loser, ed., *Il tesoro di San Marco*, I: *La Pala d'Oro* (Florence, 1971), pp. 117–19.

21 Hahnloser and Polacco, eds, *Pala d'oro*, p. 87.

22 Petrarch, *Lettere familiare*, 8, 5a. For his further remarks about Dandolo, see *DBI*, the introduction to *RIS*, XII/1, pp. III–LXXVII, and G. Cracco, *Società e stato nel medioevo veneziano: secoli XII–XIV* (Florence, 1967), pp. 399–440.

23 *DBI, XXXII*, pp. 432–40; M. King, *Venet-ian Humanism in an Age of Patrician Dom-inance* (Princeton, NJ, 1986), pp. 214–15, 270.

24 A. Cutler, 'From Loot to Scholarship: Changing Modes in the Italian Response to Byzantine Artifacts', *Dumbarton Oaks Papers* XLIX (1995), pp. 337–8.

25 Gallo, *Il tesoro di San Marco*, pp. 9–13.

26 R. A. Katzenstein, 'Three Liturgical Manuscripts from San Marco: Art and Patronage in Mid-Trecento Venice' (Ph.D. dissertation, Harvard University, 1987), particularly pp. 218–32.

27 Katzenstein, *Three Liturgical Manuscripts*, pp. 236–41. For the three covers, which are now once more reunited with the manu-scripts following a restoration, see H. R. Hahnloser, ed., *Il tesoro di San Marco*, 2 vols (Florence, 1971), II, pp. 47–50, cat. nos 35–7.

28 I am grateful to Warren Woodfin for sug-gesting the analogy.

29 H. Kähler and C. Mango, *Hagia Sophia* (New York, 1967), p. 36; R. J. Mainstone, *Hagia Sophia: Architecture, Structure and Liturgy of Justinian's Great Church* (London, 1988), p. 226.

30 C. Hahn, 'Seeing and Believing: The Con-struction of Sanctity in Early-Medieval

Saints' Shrines', *Speculum* LXXII (1997), pp. 1083–4 for the general phenomenon.

31 For the text, see *RIS* XII/1, pp. 351–73, and for a discussion, G. Arnaldi, 'Andrea Dandolo-doge-cronista', in A. Pertusi, ed., *La storiografia veneziana fino al secolo xvi: aspetti e problemi* (Florence, 1970), pp. 138–47.

32 *RIS* XII/1, pp. 9–327; Arnaldi, 'Andrea Dandolo', pp. 172–233 in particular.

33 Pincus, 'Andrea Dandolo', pp. 191–2.

34 For the history of the relics, see Gallo, *Il tesoro di San Marco*, pp. 121–3.

35 Pincus, 'Andrea Dandolo', pp. 195–6.

36 Pincus, *The Tombs of the Doges*, pp. 135–7; Pincus, 'Hard Times', pp. 112–14.

37 Pincus, *The Tombs of the Doges*, pp. 90–92; Pincus, 'Hard Times', pp. 99–103.

38 Pincus, 'Hard Times', pp. 99–100.

39 Pincus, *The Tombs of the Doges*, p. 134; Pincus, 'Hard Times', pp. 111–12.

40 Hahnloser and Polacco, eds, *Pala d'oro*, p. 82; P. F. Brown, *Venice and Antiquity: The Venetian Sense of the Past* (New Haven, CT, and London, 1996), p. 38; Pincus, 'Hard Times', n. 69.

41 F. Sansovino, *Venetia città nobilissima et singolare descritta in XIV libri* (Venice, 1581), f. 36–36v; G. Stringa, *La chiesa di S. Marco, capella del serenissimo principe di Venetia, descritta brevemente* (Venice, 1610), ff. 23, 26.

42 W. Wolters, *La scultura veneziana gotica, 1300–1460*, 2 vols (Venice, 1976), i, cat. no. 27, p. 160.

43 See above, p. 46.

44 *RIS* XII/1, p. 53.

45 Pincus, *The Tombs of the Doges*, pp. 123–32; Pincus, 'Hard Times', pp. 107–11.

46 I am grateful to Warren Woodfin for this suggestion.

47 O. Demus, 'The Ciborium Mosaics of Parenzo', *Burlington Magazine* LXXXVII (1945), pp. 238–45.

48 E. Muir, *Civic Ritual in Renaissance Venice* (Princeton, NJ, 1981), p. 71; D. Rosand, '*Venetia figurata*: The Iconography of a Myth', in Rosand, ed., *Interpretazioni veneziane* (Venice, 1984), pp. 182–4.

49 A. Limentani, ed., *Martin da Canal: les estoires de Venise. Cronaca veneziana*

in lingua francese dalle origini al 1275 (Florence, 1972), p. 6.

50 Pincus, 'Hard Times', pp. 88–94, quote at p. 94.

51 B. Boucher, 'Jacopo Sansovino and the Choir of St Mark's', *Burlington Magazine* CXVIII (1976), pp. 552–66; B. Boucher 'Jacopo Sansovino and the Choir of St Mark's: The Evangelists, the Sacristy Door and the Altar of the Sacrament', *Burlington Magazine* CXXI (1979), pp. 155–68; B. Boucher, *The Sculpture of Jacopo Sansovino*, I, pp. 55–68.

52 Boucher, *The Sculpture of Jacopo Sansovino*, I, pp. 56–62

53 Boucher, *The Sculpture of Jacopo Sansovino*, I, pp. 63–5.

54 Boucher, *The Sculpture of Jacopo Sansovino*, I, pp. 66–8 (quote on p. 66).

55 Boucher, 'Jacopo Sansovino and the Choir of St Mark's', p. 554.

56 F. Sansovino (ed. G. Stringa), *Venetia città nobilissima et singolare descritta in XIIII libri hora con molta diligenza corretta, emendata, e più d'un terzo di cose nuove ampliata dal M. R. D. Giovanni Stringa* (Venice, 1604), ff. 32v–36; see Boucher, *The Sculpture of Jacopo Sansovino*, I, p. 56; L. Moretti, 'Architectural Spaces for Music: Jacopo Sansovino and Adrian Willaert at St Mark's', *Early Music History* XXIII (2004), pp. 165–8.

57 C. Innocenti, 'Gli arazzi di manifattura medicea con storie di San Marco', in R. Polacco, ed., *Storia dell'arte marciana* (Venice, 1997), pp. 324–32; Da Villa Urbani, 'Gli arazzi marciani del XVI secolo', in I. Favaretto and M. Da Villa Urbani, eds, *Arazzi e tappeti dei dogi nella basilica di San Marco* (Venice, 1999), pp. 44–51.

58 F. Kieslinger, 'Le trasenne della basilica di San Marco del secolo XIII', *Ateneo Veneto* 131 (1944), pp. 57–61; R. Polacco, 'I plutei della cattedrale di Torcello e l'iconostasi contariniana della Basilica di San Marco', *Arte veneta* XXIX (1975), especially p. 38.

59 MCV, inv. 1330.

60 S. Tramontin, 'Il "kalendarium" veneziano', in Tramontin, ed., *Il culto dei santi a Venezia* (Venice, 1965), pp. 278–9.

61 G. Cappelletti, *Storia della chiesa di Venezia dalla sua fondazione sino ai nostri giorni*, 8 vols (Venice, 1849–60), I, pp. 411–14; for the early phase in detail, see P. H. Labalme, 'No Man but an Angel: Early Efforts to Canonize Lorenzo Giustiniani, 1381–1456', in P. Pecorari and G. Silvano, eds, *Continuità e discontinuità nella storia politica, economica e religiosa: studi in onore di Aldo Stella* (Vicenza, 1993), pp. 15–43.

62 G. Cozzi, *Il doge Nicolò Contarini: ricerche sul patriziato veneziano agli inizi del Seicento* (Venice and Rome, 1958), p. 218; A. Niero, 'Culto dei santi militari nel Veneto', in *Armi e cultura nel Bresciano, 1420–1870* (Brescia, 1981), pp. 225–72; A. Niero, 'Pietà popolare e interessi politici nel culto di S. Lorenzo Giustiniani', *Archivio veneto* CXVII (1981), pp. 198–212.

63 Niero, 'Pietà popolare', pp. 200–01; G. Cozzi, 'Note su Giovanni Tiepolo, primicerio di San Marco e patriarca di Venezia: l'unità ideale della chiesa veneta', in B. Bertoli, ed., *Chiesa, società, stato a Venezia: miscellanea di studi in onore di Silvio Tramontin* (Venice, 1994), pp. 121–50.

64 A. Pasini, 'Rito antico e ceremoniale della basilica', in *La basilica di San Marco* (Venice, 1888), pp. 65–71, provides a brief general introduction to the operations of the *patriarchino*. See also G. Fasoli, 'Liturgia e ceremoniale ducale', in A. Pertusi, ed., *Venezia e il Levante fino al secolo XV*, 3 vols (Florence, 1983), I, pp. 261–95; M. Dal Tin, 'Note di liturgia patriarchina e canti tradizionali della basilica di San Marco a Venezia', *Jucunda Laudatio* I–IV (1973), pp. 90–130. The sources of the *patriarchino* have recently been exhaustively described and analysed in G. Cattin, *Musica e liturgia a San Marco: testi e melodie per la liturgia delle ore dal XII al XVII secolo. Dal graduale tropato del duecento ai graduali cinquecenteschi*, 4 vols (Venice, 1990–92), which contains a selection of texts and melodies for the mass and office (vol. III), and introit tropes (vol. IV).

65 G. Mariani Canova and G. Cattin, 'Un prezioso antifonario veneziano del Duecento: miniature, liturgia e musica', *Arte veneta* XXXV (1981), pp. 9–26, especially pp. 18–26.

66 Berlin, Staatsbibliothek Preussischer Kulturbesitz, Mus. MS. 40608; see Catlin, *Musica e liturgia a San Marco*, I, pp. 70–73.

67 See above, pp. 15–16; 30–32.

68 Now Venice, Museo di San Marco, MSS without shelfmark; see M. Gemmani, 'Libri corali del Museo di San Marco', in I. Favaretto and M. Da Villa Urbani, eds, *Il Museo di San Marco* (Venice, 2003), pp. 160–62.

69 For the historical origins of the sacral role of the doge, see P. Prodi, 'The Structure and Organisation of the Church in Renaissance Venice: Suggestions for Research', in J. Hale, ed., *Renaissance Venice* (London, 1973), pp. 379–408, especially pp. 413–15.

70 Fasoli, 'Liturgia e ceremoniale ducale', p. 283; G. Musolino, 'Feste religiose popolari', in S. Tramontin, ed., *Il culto dei santi a Venezia* (Venice, 1965), pp. 214–15.

71 D. Bryant, 'The *cori spezzati* of St Mark's: Myth and Reality', *Early Music History* I (1981), pp. 165–86; J. H. Moore, 'The *Vespero delli Cinque Laudate* and the Role of Salmi spezzati at St Mark's', *Journal of the American Musicological Society* XXXIV (1981), pp. 249–78.

72 This process is usefully outlined in A. Baumstark, *Liturgia romana e liturgia dell'esarcato: il rito detto in seguito patriarchino e le origini del canon missae romano* (Rome, 1904), pp. 17–73.

73 J. H. Moore, *Vespers at St Mark's: Music of Alessandro Grandi, Giovanni Rovetta and Francesco Cavalli*, 2 vols (Ann Arbor, MI, 1981), I, p. 113.

74 G. Fedalto, 'Le minoranze straniere a Venezia tra politica e legislazione', in H. G. Beck, M. Manoussacas and A. Pertusi, eds, *Venezia centro di mediazione tra oriente e occidente (secoli XV–XVI): aspetti e problemi*, 2 vols (Florence, 1977), I, p. 149; Politis, 'Venezia come centro della stampa e della diffusione della prima letteratura neoellenica', in ibid. pp. 443–82; E. Follieri, 'Il libro Greco per i greci nelle imprese editoriali romane e veneziane della

75 D. Conomos, 'Experimental Polyphony, "According to the . . . Latins", in late Byzantine Psalmody', *Early Music History* II (1982), pp. 1–16. For music in Venetian parish churches see E. Quaranta, *Oltre San Marco: organizzazione e prassi della musica nelle chiese di Venezia nel Rinascimento* (Florence, 1998).

76 M. Adamis, 'An Example of Polyphony in Byzantine Music of the Late Middle Ages', in *Report of the Eleventh International Musicological Society Congress, Copenhagen 1971*, 2 vols (Copenhagen, 1972), II, pp. 737–47.

77 O. Strunk, 'A Cypriot in Venice', in *Essays on Music in the Western World* (New York, 1974), pp. 79–93.

78 For the history of the *cappella marciana* at San Marco during the sixteenth century, see R. B. M. Lenaerts, 'La chapelle de Saint-Marc à Venise sous Adrien Willaert', *Bulletin de l'institut historique belge de Rom* XIX (1938), pp. 205–55, and G. Ongaro, 'Sixteenth-century Patronage at St Mark's, Venice', *Early Music History* VIII (1988), pp. 81–115.

79 *CE* XII, pp. 426–7.

80 G. Cozzi, 'Giuspatronato del doge e prerogative del primicerio sulla cappella ducale di San Marco: controversie con i procuratori di San Marco "de supra" e i patriarchi di Venezia', *Atti dell'Istituto Veneto di Scienza, Lettere ed Arti* CLI (1992–3), pp. 8–17; this and other privileges are recorded in ASV, Consultatori in iure, Reg. 550.

81 Cozzi, 'Giuspatronato del doge'; Cozzi, 'Note su Giovanni Tiepolo'; Cozzi, 'I rapporti fra stato e chiesa', in G. Gullino, ed., *La chiesa di venezia tra riforma protestante e riforma cattolica* (Venice, 1990), pp. 11–16.

82 For the Alexandrine Donation, see Pertusi, 'Quaedam regalia insignia'; Muir, *Civic Ritual*, pp. 103–19; see below, pp. 120–21.

83 For the duties of the master ceremonies, see S. Sinding-Larsen, *The Burden of the Ceremony Master: Image and Action in San Marco, Venice, and in an Islamic Mosque:*

84 *The* Rituum ceremoniale *of 1564* (Rome, 2000), pp. 43–51.

84 BNM, Cod. Lat. III, 172 (= 2276); now partly transcribed in Sinding-Larsen, *The Burden*, pp. 265–323. For an early four-teenth-century manuscript of the statutes of the chapter see B. Betto, *Il capitolo della Basilica di S. Marco in Venezia: Statuti e consuetudini dei primi decenni del sec. XIV* (Padua, 1984).

85 F. Caffi, *Storia della musica sacra nella già cappella ducale di S. Marco dal 1318 al 1797*, 2 vols (Venice, 1854–5), I, pp. 35–6.

86 ASV, PSM, Giornali Cassier Reg. I; see F. A. D'Accone, The Performance of Sacred Music in Josquin's Time', in E. E. Lowinsky and B. J. Blackburn, eds, *Josquin des Prez* (London and New York, 1976), p. 606; Ongaro, 'Sixteenth-century Patronage at St Mark's', pp. 85–6.

87 G. Ongaro, 'Willaert, Gritti e Luppato: miti e realtà', *Studi musicali* XVII (1988), pp. 64–5; Ongaro, 'Sixteenth-century Patronage at St Mark's', pp. 88–9; Ongaro, 'All Work and No Play', The Organisation of Work among Musicians in Late Renaissance Venice', *Journal of Medieval and Renaissance Studies* XXV (1995), pp. 57–8.

88 Ongaro, 'Sixteenth-century Patronage at St Mark's', pp. 114–15.

89 Glixon, 'The Musicians of the *Cappella*'; G. Ongaro, 'All Work and No Play?, pp. 55–72.

90 J. Glixon, 'A Musicians' Union in Six-teenth-century Venice', *Journal of the American Musicological Society* (1983), pp. 395–413.

91 G. Pollard, *Medaglie italiane del Rinascimento nel Museo Nazionale del Bargello*, 3 vols (Florence, 1984–5), III, no. 822; P. Voltolina, *La storia di Venezia attraverso le medaglie*, 3 vols (Milan, 1998), I, no. 349; I. Fenlon, *Music, Print and Culture in Early Sixteenth-century Italy* (London, 1995), pp. 83–4.

92 G. Cattin, 'Church Patronage of Music in Fifteenth-century Italy', in I. Fenlon, ed., *Music in Medieval and Early Modern Europe: Patronage, Sources and Texts* (Cambridge, 1981), p. 23; Ongaro, 'Sixteenth-century Patronage at St Mark's', pp. 84–6.

93 A. Romano, *Antonii Romani opera*, ed. F. A. Gallo (Bologna, 1965), pp. v–viii; Cumming, 'Music for the Doge', pp. 362–3.

94 D'Accone, 'The Performance of Sacred Music', p. 606.

95 ASV, PSM Reg.131, f. 65v; see, *inter alia*, D. Arnold, *Giovanni Gabrieli and the Music of the Venetian High Renaissance* (Oxford, 1986), pp. 129–30, E. Selfridge–Field, *Venetian Instrumental Music from Gabrieli to Vivaldi* (Venice, 1975), pp. 14–15; G. Ongaro, 'Gli inizi della musica strumentale a San Marco', in F. Passadore and F. Rossi, eds, *Giovanni Legrenzi e la cappella ducale di San Marco* (Florence, 1994), pp. 215–26.

96 Ongaro, 'All Work and No Play', pp. 57–62.

97 M. Bent, 'The Fourteenth-century Italian Motet', in *L'ars nova italiana del trecento* (Certaldo, 1992), pp. 96–7; for a modern edition, see J. Ciconia, *The Works*, Polyphonic Music of the Fourteenth Century XXIV, ed. M. Bent and A. Hallmark (Monaco, 1985), pp. 77–80.

98 See A. Simioni, *Storia di Padova dale origini alla fine del secolo XVIII* (Padua, 1968), p. 566.

99 King, *Venetian Humanism*, pp. 285–6; J. E. Cumming, 'Music for the Doge in Early Renaissance Venice', *Speculum* LXVII (1992), pp. 333–5.

100 R. Casimiri, 'Musica e musicisti nella cattedrale di Padova nei secoli XIV, XV, XVI: contributi per una storia', *Note d'archivio per la storia musicale* XVIII (1941), pp. 1–31, 101–80, 180–214; XIX (1942), pp. 49–92; P. Petrobelli, 'La musica nelle cattedrale e nelle città ed i suoi rapporti con la cultura letteraria', in G. Arnaldi and M. Stocchi, eds, *Storia della cultura veneta*, 6 vols in 10 parts (Vicenza, 1976–87), II, pp. 440–68; G. Cattin, 'Formazione e attività della cappelle polifoniche nelle cattedrali: la musica nelle città', in G. Arnaldi and M. Stocchi, eds, *Storia della cultura veneta*, 6 vols in 10 parts (Vicenza, 1976–87), III/3, pp. 270–77; and for a general picture of Padua as an intellectual centre, see Simioni, *Storia*, pp. 573–639.

101 G. Cattin, 'Ricerche sulla musica a Santa Giustina di Padua all'inizio del quattrocento: il copista Rolando da Casale – nuovi frammenti musicali nell'Archivio di Stato', *Annales musicologiques* VII (1964–77); D. Plamenac, 'Another Paduan Fragment of Trecento Music', *Journal of the American Musicological Society* VIII (1955), pp. 165–81; Bent, 'The Fourteenth–Century Italian Motet', table 1.

102 L. Lutteken, ' "Musicus et cantor diu in ecclesia Sancti Marci de Veneciis": note biografiche su Johannes de Quadris', *Rassegna veneta di studi musicali* V–VI (1989–90), pp. 43–62.

103 F. A. Gallo, 'Musiche veneziane nel MS 2216 della Biblioteca Universitaria di Bologna', *Quadrivium* VI (1964), pp. 107–16, and the same author's introduction to *Antonii Romani Opera*, pp. V–VIII; D. Stevens, 'Ceremonial Music in Medieval Venice', *Musical Times* CXIX (1978), pp. 321–7.

104 For the tradition, see Bent, 'The Fourteenth-century Italian Motet'; Cumming, 'Music for the Doge'.

105 Oxford, Bodleian Library, MS Canonici Misc. 213, f. 13v: '1436 mensis maij Venec[iis]'. See G. Cattin, *Johannes de Quadris, musico del sec. XV* (Bologna, 1971), pp. 5–8; modern edition in J. de Quadris, *Opera*, ed. G. Cattin (Bologna, 1972), p. 1. For a facsimile edition with introduction see *Oxford, Bodleian Library MS. Canon. Misc. 213 with an Introduction and Inventory by David Fallows* (Chicago and London, 1995).

106 R. Strohm, *The Rise of European Music, 1380–1500* (Cambridge, 1993), p. 588.

107 Modern edition: Quadris, *Opera*, pp. 9, 64.

108 Vicenza, Seminario Vescovile, MS U. VIII. 11; see G. Cattin, 'Uno sconosciuto codice quattrocentesco dell'Archivio Capitolare di Vicenza e le lamentazioni di Johannes de Quadris', *L'ars nova italiana del trecento* III (Certaldo, 1970), pp. 281–304. Modern edition: Quadris, *Opera*, p. 10.

109 M. Bent, 'Pietro Emiliani's Chaplain Bartolomeo Rossi da Carpi and the Lamentations of De Quadris in Vicenza', *Il saggiatore musicale* II (1995), pp. 7–15.

110 Bologna, Civico Museo Bibliografico Musicale, MS Q15; G. de Van, 'An Inventory of the Manuscript Bologna, Liceo Musicale, Q15 (*olim* 37)', in *Musica Disciplina* II (1948), pp. 231–57; M. Bent, 'A Contemporary Perception of Early Fifteenth-century Style: Bologna Q15 as a Document of Scribal Editorial Initiative', *Musica Disciplina* XLI (1987), pp. 183–201.

111 M. Bent, 'Music and the Early Veneto Humanists', *Proceedings of the British Academy* CI (1999), pp. 111–24.

112 *Lamentationum Jeremie prophete*, f. 30; see C. Sartori, *Bibliografia delle opere musicali stampate da Ottaviano Petrucci* (Florence, 1948), no. 26; S. Boorman, *Ottaviano Petrucci: catalogue raisonné* (New York, 2006).

113 G. Croce, *Devotissime lamentationi et improperii per la settimana santa con le lettioni della natività di Nostro Signore a quatro voci* (Venice, 1604); see J. Bettley, 'The Office of Holy Week at St Mark's, Venice, in the Late Sixteenth Century and the Musical Contributions of Giovanni Croce', *Early Music* XXII (1994), p. 53.

114 S. Curi Nicolardi, *Una società tipografico-editoriale a Venezia nel secolo XVI: Melchiorre Sessa e Pietro di Ravani (1516–1525)* (Florence, 1984), pp. 70–71, no. 45.

115 B. J. Blackburn, 'Petrucci's Venetian Editor: Petrus Castellanus and his Musical Garden', *Musica Disciplina* XLIX (1995), pp. 22–3.

116 See below, p. 146.

117 F. A. Gallo, 'The Practice of Cantus Planus Binatim in Italy from the Beginning of the 14th to the Beginning of the 16th Century', in C. Corsi and P. Petrobelli, eds, *Le polifonie primitive in Friuli e in Europa* (Rome, 1989), pp. 14–23.

118 P. Petrobelli, *Le polifonie primitive di Cividale* (Udine, 1980); Gallo, 'The Practice of Cantus Planus Binatim', pp. 17–18; R. Camilot-Oswald, *Die liturgischen Musikhandschriften aus dem mittelalterlichen Patriarchat Aquileia* (Kassel, 1997); C. Scalon and L. Pani, eds, *I codici della Biblioteca Capitolare di Cividale del Friuli* (Florence, 1998).

119 M. Bent, 'The Definition of Simple Polyphony: Some Questions', in C. Corsi and P. Petrobelli, eds, *Le polifonie primitive in Friuli e in Europa* (Rome, 1989), pp. 33, 40–41.

120 M. Bradshaw, *Falsobordone: A Study in Renaissance and Baroque Music* (Neuhausen and Stuttgart, 1978); I. Macchiarella, *Il falsobordone fra tradizione orale e tradizione scritta* (Lucca, 1995).

121 Bradshaw, *Falsobordone*, pp. 19–20.

122 Amsterdam, University Library, Collection Begijnhof MS XXV C 76. For an edition see C. J. Gonnet, ed., 'Bedevaart nach Jerusalem', *Bijdragen voor geschiednis van het bisdom Haarlem* XI (1882); and for a discussion, I. Fenlon, 'Strangers in Paradise: Dutchmen in Venice in 1525', in Fenlon, *Music and Culture in Late Renaissance Italy* (Oxford, 2002), pp. 24–43.

123 Göttingen, Universitäts-Bibliothek, MS Histor. 823i (*olim* 830).

124 See Hahnloser, ed., *Il tesoro di San Marco*, II, p. 171, cat. no. 168, pl. CLXII, describes a processional cross that originally incorporated a relic of the True Cross.

125 Gonnet, ed., 'Bedevaart nach Jerusalem', p. 35.

126 Gonnet, ed., 'Bedevaart nach Jerusalem', p. 36.

127 *Di Adriano et di Jachet*. For a modern edition, see A. Willaert, *Opera omnia*, ed. H. Zenck et al. (Rome, 1950–), VIII, with an introduction establishing the three typologies.

128 R. J. Mainstone, *Hagia Sophia: Architecture, Structure and Liturgy of Justinian's Great Church* (London, 1988), pp. 222–3.

129 This was the practice in the early seventeenth century; see G. Stringa, *Vita di S. Marco Protettore Invitissimo della Serenissima Republica di Venetia con la translatione, et apparitione del sacro suo corpo* (Venice, 1610) f. 24–24v.

130 A. Hopkins, 'Architecture and *Infirmitas*: Doge Andrea Gritti and the Chancel of San Marco', *Journal of the Society of Architectural Historians* LVII (1998), pp. 183–5.

131 See Boucher, 'Jacopo Sansovino and the Choir of St Mark's', p. 565; Hopkins, 'Architecture and *Infirmitas*', pp. 189–90; Moretti, 'Architectural Spaces for Music', pp. 168–71.

132 Moretti, 'Architectural Spaces for Music', p. 172.

133 I. Cacciavillani, *Andrea Gritti nella vita di Nicolo Barbarigo* (Venice, 1995); A. Da Mosto, *I dogi di Venezia con particolare riguardo alle loro tombe* (Venice, 1939), p. 242; for the argument, see Hopkins, 'Architecture and *Infirmitas*', p. 194.

134 *I salmi appertinenti alli vesperi per tutte le feste dell'anno, parte a versi, e parte spezzadi accomodati da cantare a uno et a duoi chori* (Venice, 1550).

135 G. Zarlino, *Le istituzioni harmoniche* (Venice, 1558), p. 268.

136 F. Sansovino, *Delle cose notabili che sono in Venetia* (Venice, 1561), f. 26

137 For an explanation of this term, derived from the practice of the canons of San Giorgio in Alga, see Fenlon, 'Strangers in Paradise', pp. 24–43.

138 Venice, Biblioteca Nazionale Marciana, MS III 172, f. 47.

139 Sansovino, *Venetia città nobilissima* (Venice, 1604), Cap. LXXIII, f. 44v: 'All'-incontro de i soprascritti pulpiti, ne i quali, come s'è detto, il Vangelo & l'Epistola si cantano, è posto, & collocato il pergolo de i Musici, il quale è in forma ottangola, & da sette colonne di finissima pietra sostenuto; e due altre mediocre vi si veggono vicino al muro poste, che ancor esse qualche parte sua sostengono, sopra questo quasi per l'ordinario, e special-mente nelle feste solenni, e quando dis-cende la Signoria in Chiesa, cantano i Musici alla Messa maggiore, & al vespro gli ufficij divini.'

140 T. Coryate, *Coryat's crudities hastily gobled up in five moneths travells in France, Savoy, Italy, Rhetia* (London, 1611), p. 213; Stringa, *Vita di San Marco*, f. 24v.

141 See J. G. Links, *Canaletto* (Oxford, 1982), pp. 215–16.

142 A. Carver, *Cori spezzati: The Development of Sacred Polychoral Music to the Time of Schutz*, 2 vols (Cambridge, 1988), I, p. 33. Willaert's 'invention' is based on a misun-derstanding of a passage in Zarlino's *Isti-tutioni harmoniche*; see G. D'Alessi, 'Precursors of Adriano Willaert in the Practice of Coro Spezzato', *Journal of the American Musicological Society* V (1952), pp. 188–90.

143 Treviso, Biblioteca Capitolare, MS 11b (dated 1556–60); see D'Alessi, 'Precursors of Adriano Willaert', pp. 203–9; Carver, *Cori spezzati*, I, p. 14; D. Princivalli, 'Francesco Santacroce', *Musica e storia* IX (2001), pp. 307–74, especially pp. 322–3; D. Bryant and M. Pozzobon, *Musica devozione città: la scuola di Santa Maria Battuti (e un suo manoscritto musicale) nella Treviso del Rinascimento* (Treviso, 1995), pp. 22–28.

144 Carver, *Cori spezzati*, I, p. 22.

145 See D'Alessi, 'Precursors of Adriano Willaert', p. 192; B. J. Blackburn, E. E. Lowinsky and C. A. Miller, eds, *A Corre-spondence of Renaissance Musicians* (Oxford, 1991), pp. 709–11.

146 Now Bergamo, Biblioteca Civica, MSS 1207D, 1208D and 1209D.

147 *Di Adriano et di Jachet, I salmi apperti-nenti alli vesperi*, which contains eight *salmi spezzati* by Willaert; see H. Zenck, 'Adrian Willaerts "Salmi spezzati"', *Die Musikforschung* II (1949), pp. 97–107.

148 D'Alessi, 'Precursors of Adriano Willaert', pp. 190–92.

149 J. R. Hale and M. E. Mallett, *The Mili-tary Organization of a Renaissance State: Venice, c. 1400 to 1617* (Cambridge, 1984), pp. 268, 410.

150 Da Mosto, *I dogi di Venezia*, p. 160; E. Finlay, *Politics in Renaissance Venice* (London, 1980), p. 155; M. Tafuri, *Venice and the Renaissance* (Cambridge, MA, and London, 1989), p. 108; *DBI* LIX, pp. 727–34.

151 J. R. Hale, 'Industria del libro e cultura militare a Venezia nel Rinascimento', in G. Arnaldi and M. Pastore Stocchi, eds, *Storia della cultura Veneta* 3/II, pp. 245–89.

152 It was disbanded in 1562 and reinstated, though only briefly, in 1565; see Ongaro, 'Willaert, Gritti e Luppato', p. 57, n. 7.

153 For a discussion of the term, see Fenlon, 'Strangers in Paradise', pp. 40–41.

154 Ongaro, 'Willaert, Gritti e Luppato', p. 68.

155 Ongaro, 'Sixteenth-century Patronage at St Mark's', p. 82.

156   *I salmi appertinenti.*

157   Moretti, 'Architectural Spaces for Music', n. 24.

158   G. Zarlino, *Quinque vocum moduli, motecta vulgo nuncupata, opus nunquam alias typis excussum, ac nupor accuratissime in lucem aeditum, liber primus* (Venice, 1549), C. Merulo, *Liber primus sacrarum cantiorum quinque vocibus* (Venice, 1578).

159   See below, pp. 138–46.

160   See below, pp. 248–9.

161   See below, pp. 211–13.

CHAPTER THREE

1   F. C. Lane, *Venice: A Maritime Republic* (London, 1973), pp. 1–21; W. Dorigo, *Venezia origini*, 3 vols (Milan, 1983), II, pp. 531–91; A. Bellavitis and G. Romanelli, *Venezia* (Rome and Bari, 1985), pp. 31–41; J. Schulz, 'Urbanism in Medieval Venice', in A. Molho, ed., *City States in Classical Antiquity and Medieval Italy* (Stuttgart, 1991), pp. 419–20; E. Crouzet-Pavan, *'Sopra le acque salse': Espaces, pouvoir et societe à Venise à la fin du moyen âge*, 2 vols (Rome, 1992), I, pp. 165–73.

2   Schulz, 'Urbanism in Medieval Venice', pp. 432–41; M. Agazzi, *Platea Sancti Marci* (Venice, 1991), pp. 16–20.

3   Schulz, 'Urbanism in Medieval Venice'. For the Rialto, see also E. Crouzet-Pavan, 'Sviluppo e articolazione della città', in G. Arnaldi, G. Cracco and A. Tenenti, eds, *Storia di Venezia dalle origini alla caduta della serenissima* III (Rome, 1997), pp. 743–6, and, for the Arsenal, E. Concina, *L'Arsenale della Repubblica di Venezia: techniche e istituzioni dal medioevo all'età moderna* (Milan, 1984), pp. 9–25.

4   S. B. Butters, *The Triumph of Vulcan*, 2 vols (Florence, 1996), I, pp. 67–70.

5   M. Harrison, *A Temple for Byzantium: The Discovery and Excavation of Anicia Juliana's Palace-Church in Istanbul* (London, 1989), pp. 100, 143.

6   M. Vickers, 'Wandering Stones: Venice, Constantinople and Athens', in K. L. Selig and E. Sears, eds, *The Verbal and the Visual: Essays in Honor of William Sebastian Heckscher* (New York, 1990), pp. 231–2; S. Sinding-Larsen, *Christ in the Council Hall: Studies in the Religious Iconography of the Venetian Republic* (Rome, 1974), pp. 170–71; W. Wolters, *La scultura veneziana gotica, 1300–1460*, 2 vols (Venice, 1976), cat. 245.

7   D. Rosand, ed., *Myths of Venice: The Figuration of a State* (Chapel Hill, NC, and London, 2001), pp. 97–100.

8   P. Sherrard, *Constantinople: Iconography of a Sacred City* (Oxford, 1965), pp. 79–100.

9   S. Rankin, 'From Liturgical Ceremony to Public Ritual: "Quem Queritis" and St Mark's Venice', in G. Cattin, ed., *Da Bisanzio a San Marco: musica e liturgia* (Venice, 1997), pp. 150–75.

10   G. R. Michiel, *Le origini delle feste veneziane*, 6 vols (Milan, 1817), IV, pp. 129–43; B. Tamassia Mazzarotto, *Le feste veneziane, i giochi popolari, le ceremonie religiose e di governo* (Florence, 1961), p. 165. For later versions of the procession, see BCV, MS Cicogna 1295.

11   P. Casola, *Viaggio a Gerusalemme* (Milan, 1899), pp. 15–19; H. Ellis, ed., *The Pylgrymage of Sir Richard Gwylforde to the Holy Land, AD 1506* (London, 1851), pp. 8–9.

12   U. Tucci, 'I servizi marittimi veneziani per il pellegrinaggio in Terrasanta nel medioevo', *Studi veneziani* IX (1985), pp. 64–5.

13   Tamassia Mazzarotto, *Le feste veneziane*, p. 165, also reproducing (on p. 168) a sixteenth-century engraving by Donato Rasciotto showing pilgrims in the procession.

14   M. Rubin, *Corpus Christi: The Eucharist in Late Medieval Culture* (Cambridge, 1991), pp. 243–71; E. Muir, *Civic Ritual in Renaissance Venice* (Princeton, NJ, 1981), pp. 223–30; I. Fenlon, 'Music, Ceremony and Self-Identity in Renaissance Venice', in F. Passadore and F. Rossi, eds, *La cappella musicale di S. Marco nell'età moderna* (Venice, 1998), pp. 8–9.

15   A. Zorzi, *Venezia scomparsa*, 2 vols (Milan, 1977), II, pp. 382–5; F. Sansovino, *Venetia città nobilissima . . . descritta in XIIII libri . . . con aggiunta da D. Giustiniano Martinioni* (Venice, 1663), pp. 76–9.

16   Agazzi, *Platea Sancti Marci*, p. 79.

17   Schulz, 'Urbanism in Medieval Venice', p. 437.

18 Schulz, 'Urbanism in Medieval Venice', pp. 438–9.

19 M. Belozerskaya and K. Lapatin, 'Antiquity Consumed: Transformations at San Marco', in A. Payne, A. Kuttner and R. Smick, eds, *Antiquity and its Interpreters* (Cambridge, 2000), pp. 85–6.

20 Sansovino, *Venetia città nobilissima* (1663), pp. 496–7; ASV Collegio, Ceremoniali I, f. 8; BCV, MS Venier PD 517b; BNM, MS Latin III, 172 (2276), ff. 52v–53; Michiel, *Le origini delle feste veneziane*, I, pp. 43–52; Muir, *Civic Ritual*, pp. 109–10.

21 BNM, MS It VII 121, ff. 57–57v.

22 P. F. Brown, *Venetian Narrative Painting in the Age of Carpaccio* (New Haven, CT, and London, 1988), pp. 282–6. For an analysis of the buildings shown in Bellini's painting and in de' Barbari's woodcut, see Agazzi, *Platea Sancti Marci*, pp. 96–7.

23 For descriptions, see G. Cassini, *Piante e vedute prospettiche di Venezia (1479–1855) con una interpretazione urbanistica di E. Trincanato* (Venice, 1971), pp. 40–45; J. Schulz, *The Printed Plans and Panoramic Views of Venice, 1486–1797* (Venice, 1970), pp. 41–2 and figs 14–15.

24 J. Schulz, 'Jacopo de' Barbari's View of Venice: Map Making, City Views and Moralized Geography before the Year 1500', *Art Bulletin* LX (1978), pp. 425–31; B. Wilson, *The World in Venice: Print, the City and Early Modern Identity* (Toronto, 2005), pp. 23–69. For earlier views, see Schulz, *The Printed Plans*, cat. 154–9.

25 Schulz, 'Jacopo de' Barbari's View of Venice', p. 468.

26 Schulz, 'Jacopo de' Barbari's View of Venice', p. 439.

27 M. Tafuri, *Venezia e il Rinascimento: religione, scienza, architettura* (Turin, 1985), pp. 246–71; F. Barbieri and G. Beltramini, *Vincenzo Scamozzi, 1548–1616* (Venice, 2003), pp. 211–20 (Hopkins).

28 W. Lotz, 'La trasformazione sansoviniana di Piazza San Marco e l'urbanistica del Cinquecento', *Bolletino del Centro Internazionale di Studi di Architettura 'Andrea Palladio'* VIII/2 (1966), pp. 114–16.

29 *DA* V, p. 177. For Bon's work, see J. McAndrew, *Venetian Architecture of the Early Renaissance* (Boston, MA, 1980), pp. 507–27. The traditional attribution of the Procuratie Vecchie to Bartolomeo Bon is derived from F. Sansovino, *Venetia città nobilissima et singolare descritta in XIV libri* (Venice, 1581), f. 105.

30 M. Tafuri, *Venice and the Renaissance* (Cambridge, MA, and London, 1989), pp. 103–38.

31 See the introduction to M. Tafuri, ed., *'Renovatio urbis': Venetia nell'età di Andrea Gritti, 1523–1538* (Rome, 1984), particularly pp. 28–38.

32 Tafuri, *Venice and the Renaissance*, especially pp. 104–12.

33 D. Howard, 'Rome and Venetian Art and Architecture', *Edinburgh Architecture Research* XVIII (1991), pp. 44–70.

34 R. C. Mueller, 'The Procuratori di San Marco and the Venetian Credit Market' (Ph.D. dissertation, Johns Hopkins University, 1969), pp. 3–4.

35 O. Demus, *The Church of San Marco in Venice: History, Architecture, Sculpture* (Washington, DC, 1960), p. 54; Mueller, 'The Procuratori di San Marco', p. 5.

36 Mueller, 'The Procuratori di San Marco', pp. 6–7.

37 Mueller, 'The Procuratori di San Marco', pp. 8–9.

38 R. Finlay, 'The Venetian Republic as a Gerontocracy: Age and Politics in the Renaissance', *Journal of Medieval and Renaissance Studies* VIII (1978), pp. 157–78.

39 S. Chojnacki, *Women and Men in Renaissance Venice: Twelve Essays on Patrician Society* (Baltimore, MD, and London, 2000), pp. 227–8.

40 D. E. Queller, *The Venetian Patriarcate: Reality versus Myth* (Chicago, 1986), p. 62.

41 Queller, *The Venetian Patriarcate*, especially the conclusion on pp. 247–53.

42 Mueller, 'The Procuratori di San Marco', p. 11.

43 M. Sanudo, *I diarii*, ed. R. Fulin et al., 58 vols (Venice, 1879–1903), XXII, cols 230–31, 258–9 and 261–2.

44 G. Rosenthal, ed., *Italian Paintings XIV–XVIII Centuries from the Collection of the Baltimore Museum of Art* (Baltimore, MD, 1981), pp. 131–4.

45 P. Rossi, 'I ritratti di Jacopo Tintoretto', in *Jacopo Tintoretto: ritratti* (Milan, 1994), p. 34; Finlay, 'The Venetian Republic as a Gerontocracy'. See also the recent remarks in M. Falomir, ed., *Tintoretto* (Madrid, 2007), pp. 95–114.

46 Rosenthal, ed., *Italian Paintings*, pp. 136–7.

47 B. Boucher, *The Sculpture of Jacopo Sansovino*, 2 vols (New Haven, CT, and London, 1991), I, pp. 40–42.

48 See M. Tafuri, *Jacopo Sansovino e l'architettura del '500 a Venezia*, 2nd edn (Padua, 1972), pp. 42–82; D. Howard, *Jacopo Sansovino: Architecture and Patronage in Renaissance Venice* (New Haven, CT, and London, 1975), pp. 8–61; M. Morresi, *Jacopo Sansovino* (Milan, 2000), pp. 443–51.

49 Howard, *Jacopo Sansovino*, pp. 10–16; J. Onians, *Bearers of Meaning: The Classical Orders in Antiquity, the Middle Ages and the Renaissance* (Princeton, NJ, 1988), pp. 287–99.

50 J. Ackerman, 'Observations on Renaissance Church Planning in Venice and Florence, 1470–1570', in *Florence and Venice: Comparisons and Relations*, 2 vols (Florence, 1980), II, pp. 291–2; Tafuri, 'Pietas repubblicana, neobizantismo e umanesimo', pp. 24–78.

51 M. D'Evelyn, 'Venice as Vitruvius's City in Daniele Barbaro's Commentaries', *Studi veneziani* XXXII (1996), pp. 87–91.

52 F. C. Lane and R. Mueller, *Money and Banking in Medieval and Renaissance Venice*, 2 vols (Baltimore, MD, and London, 1985), I, pp. 205–6.

53 A. Stahl, *Zecca: The Mint of Venice in the Middle Ages* (Baltimore, MD, and London, 2000), pp. 281–6.

54 Lane and Mueller, *Money and Banking in Renaissance Venice*, I, pp. 235–8.

55 Tafuri, *Jacopo Sansovino*, pp. 72–82; Howard, *Jacopo Sansovino*, pp. 38–47; Morresi, *Jacopo Sansovino*, pp. 182–91.

56 E. Gleason, 'Confronting New Realities: Venice and the Peace of Bologna, 1530', in J. Martin and D. Romano, eds, *Venice Reconsidered: The History and Civilization of an Italian City State, 1297–1797* (Baltimore, MD, and London, 2000), pp. 168–78.

57 For a translation, see D. Chambers and B. Pullan, eds, *Venice: A Documentary History, 1450–1630* (Oxford, 1992), pp. 390–91.

58 G. Vasari, *Le vite de' piu eccellenti architetti, pittori, et scultori italiani*, ed. G. Milanesi, 9 vols (Milan, 1878–85), VII, p. 505. For a discussion of Vasari's contacts with Sansovino, see Onians, *Bearers of Meaning*, pp. 304–9.

59 S. Serlio, *Tutte l'opere d'architettura et prospettiva diviso in sette libri* (Venice, 1619), IV, f. 133v: 'è molto grata all'occio, & rappresenta in se gran fortezza. Per tanto io giudicherei convenirsi più questa ad una fortezza che alcun'altra'.

60 F. Sansovino, *Delle cose notabili che sono in Venetia* (Venice, 1561), ff. 25v–26. See also F. Sansovino, *Venetia città nobilissima* (1581), f. 115–115v.

61 Howard, *Jacopo Sansovino*, p. 40; Onians, *Bearers of Meaning*, pp. 288–90.

62 Chambers and Pullan, eds, *Venice: A Documentary History*, p. 391.

63 L. Labowsky, *Bessarion's Library and the Biblioteca Marciana: Six Early Inventories* (Rome, 1979), pp. 57–73.

64 For the building history of the Library, see Tafuri, *Jacopo Sansovino*, pp. 54–64; Howard, *Jacopo Sansovino*, pp. 17–28; Morresi, *Jacopo Sansovino*, pp. 191–213.

65 Cited in Howard, *Jacopo Sansovino*, from ASV, PS, Atti, reg. 126, ff. 165v–67.

66 Labowsky, *Bessarion's Library*, p. 92. For a general account of the ceiling decoration, see O. Ruggieri, 'La decorazione pittorica della Libreria Marciana', in V. Branca and C. Ossola, eds, *Cultura e società nel Rinascimento tra riforme e manierismi* (Florence, 1984), pp. 313–33.

67 Tafuri, *Venezia e il Rinascimento*, pp. 252–71; M. Morresi, *Piazza San Marco: istituzioni, poteri e architettura a Venezia nel primo Cinquecento* (Milan, 1999), pp. 55–7; Barbieri and Beltramini, *Vincenzo Scamozzi*, pp. 202–9 (Hopkins).

68 The number of bays in Sansovino's original design is disputed; see Tafuri, *Jacopo Sansovino*, pp. 54–64; Howard, *Jacopo*

Sansovino, pp. 25–6; M. Morresi, *Piazza San Marco*, pp. 92–104; Morresi, *Jacopo Sansovino*, pp. 182–91,

69 D. M. Breiner, 'Vincenzo Scamozzi, 1548–1616: A Catalogue Raisonné', 2 vols (Ph.D. dissertation, Cornell University, 1994), I, pp. 117–27.

70 Breiner, 'Vincenzo Scamozzi', I, pp. 133–43.

71 On the Accademia Venetiana, see P. L. Rose, 'The Accademia Venetiana: Science and Culture in Renaissance Venice', *Studi veneziani* XI (1969), pp. 191–242; P. Pagan, 'Sulla Accademia "Venetiana" o della Fama', *Atti dell'Istituto Veneto di Scienze, Lettere ed Arti* CXXXII (1973–4), pp. 359–92; L. Bolzoni, 'L'Accademia veneziana: splendore e decadenza di una utopia enciclopedica', in L. Boehm and E. Raimondi, eds, *Università, accademie e società scientifiche in Italia e in Germania* (Bologna, 1981), pp. 117–67; L. Bolzoni, 'Rendere visibile il sapere: L'Accademia Veneziana fra modernità e utopia', in D. S. Chambers and F. Quiviger, eds, *Italian Academies of the Sixteenth Century* (London, 1995), pp. 61–75; Tafuri, *Venice and the Renaissance*, pp. 114–22; I. Fenlon, 'Gioseffo Zarlino and the Accademia Venetiana della Fama', in Fenlon, *Music and Culture in Late Renaissance Italy* (Oxford, 2002), pp. 118–38. The full text of Badoer's petition to the procurators of San Marco, setting out the Academy's ambitions and intentions, is translated in Chambers and Pullan, eds, *Venice: A Documentary History*, pp. 364–6. For Contile's remarks, see his *Delle lettere di Luca Contile: primo (-secondo) volume diviso in due libri* (Pavia, 1564), II, p. 173.

72 S. Bargagli, *Delle lodi delle accademie*, reprinted in his *Dell'imprese* (Venice, 1589), pp. 511–45. Similar sentiments are expressed in T. Garzoni, *La piazza universale di tutte le professioni del mondo* (Venice, 1585), p. 144, where academies are praised for bringing distinction to their cities.

73 Tafuri, *Venice and the Renaissance*, pp. 114–15.

74 Rose, 'The Accademia Venetiana', p. 209.

75 On Scamozzi's intervention, see Breiner, 'Vincenzo Scamozzi', I, pp. 127–30; Barbieri and Beltramini, *Vincenzo Scamozzi*, pp. 339–41 (Gasparotto).

76 G. Cozzi, 'Federico Contarini: un antiquario veneziano tra Rinascimento e Controriforma', *Bolletino dell'Istituto di Storia della Societa e dello Stato Veneziano* III (1961), pp. 211–16.

77 M. Perry, 'The *Statuario Pubblico* of the Venetian Republic', *Saggi e memorie di storia dell'arte* VIII (1972), pp. 75–150, 221–53; M. Perry, 'Cardinal Grimani's Legacy of Ancient Art to Venice', *Journal of the Warburg and Courtauld Institutes* XLI (1978), pp. 215–44; I. Favaretto and G. L. Ravagnan, eds, *Lo statuario pubblico della Serenissima: due secoli di collezionismo di antichità, 1596–1797* (Padua, 1997). For the general theme, see P. F. Brown, *Venice and Antiquity: The Venetian Sense of the Past* (New Haven, CT, and London, 1996), p. 248.

78 Tafuri, *Jacopo Sansovino*, pp. 65–71; Howard, *Jacopo Sansovino*, pp. 28–35; Boucher, *The Sculpture of Jacopo Sansovino*, I, pp. 73–88; Morresi, *Jacopo Sansovino*, pp. 213–27; Rosand, ed., *Myths of Venice*, pp. 127–36.

79 W. Lotz, 'The Roman Legacy in Sansovino's Venetian Buildings', *Journal of the Society of Architectural Historians* XXII (1963), p. 6.

80 C. Davis, 'Jacopo Sansovino's "Loggetta di San Marco" and Two Problems in Iconography', *Mitteilungen des Kunsthistorisches Institut in Florenz* XXIX (1985), pp. 397–9.

81 Boucher, *The Sculpture of Jacopo Sansovino*, I, p. 84.

82 J. Pope-Hennessy, *Italian High Renaissance and Baroque Sculpture*, 4th edn (London, 1996), pp. 236–8; D. Rosand, 'Venezia e gli dei', in M. Tafuri, ed., *'Renovatio urbis': Venetia nell'età di Andrea Gritti, 1523–1538* (Rome, 1984), pp. 202–3; Boucher, *The Sculpture of Jacopo Sansovino*, I, pp. 84–6.

83 Boucher, *The Sculpture of Jacopo Sansovino*, I, pp. 86–8.

84 Rosand, ed., *Myths of Venice*, pp. 121–8. F. Sansovino, *Venetia città nobilissima* (1663), p. 293.

85 Rosand, ed., *Myths of Venice*, pp. 121–8.

86 Howard, *Jacopo Sansovino*, p. 34.

87 L. Bolzoni, *The Gallery of Memory: Literary and Iconographic Models in the Age of the Printing Press* (Toronto, London and Buffalo, NY, 2001), pp. 227–32.

88 J. B. Bury, 'The Loggetta in 1540', *Burlington Magazine* CXXII (1980), p. 632. For the later history of the Loggetta, see Boucher, *The Sculpture of Jacopo Sansovino*, I, p. 74.

89 Onians, *Bearers of Meaning*, pp. 294–5.

90 Serlio, *Tutte l'opere*, II, f. 46–46v; see Onians, *Bearers of Meaning*, p. 295.

91 E. J. Johnson, 'Jacopo Sansovino, Giacomo Torelli and the Theatricality of the Piazzetta', *Journal of the Society of Architectural Historians* LIX (2000), particularly pp. 436, 448–9.

92 Sansovino, *Venezia città nobilissima* (1663), p. 406; Michiel, *Le origini delle feste veneziane*, II, pp. 37–41; G. Tassini, *Feste, spettacoli, divertimenti e piaceri degli antichi veneziani*, 2nd edn (Venice, 1961), pp. 23–4; Tamassia Mazzarotto, *Le feste veneziane*, pp. 31–2; Muir, *Civic Ritual*, pp. 160–64; E. Muir, 'Manifestazioni e cerimonie nella Venezia di Andrea Gritti', in M. Tafuri, ed., *'Renovatio urbis': Venetia nell'età di Andrea Gritti, 1523–1538* (Rome, 1984), pp. 61–8; A. Giurea, 'Theatre of the Flesh: The Carnival of Venice and the Theatre of the World' (Ph.D. dissertation, University of California, Los Angeles, 1987), pp. 44–52.

93 Sanudo, *I diarii*, XL, col. 791.

94 Johnson, 'Jacopo Sansovino', pp. 443–4.

95 Muir, *Civic Ritual*, p. 162.

96 Sanudo, *I diarii*, LVII, cols 531–2; see Muir, 'Manifestazioni e ceremonie', p. 68.

97 E. Muir, 'Images of Power: Art and Pageantry in Renaissance Venice', *American Historical Review* LXXXIV (1979), pp. 16–52, particularly pp. 36–50.

98 Cassini, *Piante e vedute*, p. 37.

99 D. Howard, 'Two Notes on Jacopo Sansovino', *Architettura* IV (1974), pp. 132–3. The idea that the shops were designed by Sansovino has been disproved; see Morresi, *Jacopo Sansovino*, pp. 351–3, and the literature cited there.

100 Stahl, *Zecca*, p. 282, and fig. 14.

101 Lane and Mueller, *Money and Banking in Renaissance Venice*, I, p. 209.

102 M. Agazzi, 'I granai della Repubblica', *Venezia arti* VII (1993), pp. 52–3.

103 D. Calabi, 'Città e spazi di mercato nella Repubblica veneta', *Eidos. Rivista di cultura* I (1987), p. 83.

104 Lane and Mueller, *Money and Banking in Renaissance Venice*, II, p. 29.

105 Howard, 'Two Notes', p. 134

106 ASV, Maggior Consiglio, Diana, f. 64; for further documents, see Howard, *Jacopo Sansovino*, pp. 10–16.

107 Howard, *Jacopo Sansovino*, pp. 11–14.

108 See, for example, K. Baetjer and J. G. Links, eds, *Canaletto* (New York, 1989), no. 55 (*Piazza S. Marco: The Northeast Corner*) and no. 116 (*Piazza S. Marco, Looking East*).

109 Johnson, 'Jacopo Sansovino', pp. 445–6.

110 G. Ruggiero, *Violence in Early Renaissance Venice* (New Brunswick, NJ, 1980), pp. 180–82.

111 Butters, *The Triumph of Vulcan*, I, pp. 94–5.

112 For which see Tafuri, *Venice and the Renaissance*, p. 33.

113 Lane and Mueller, *Money and Banking in Renaissance Venice*, II, pp. 83–4.

114 Lane and Mueller, *Money and Banking in Renaissance Venice*, I, pp. 152–3.

115 U. Tucci, 'Mercanti, viaggiatori, pellegrini nel quattrocento', in G. Arnaldi and M. Stocchi, eds, *Storia della cultura veneta*, 6 vols in 10 parts (Vicenza, 1976–87), III/2, pp. 317–53.

116 Tucci, 'I servizi marittimi veneziani'; see also the introduction to M. Newett, ed., *Canon Pietro Casola's Pilgrimage to Jerusalem in the Year 1494* (Manchester, 1907).

117 Lane and Mueller, *Money and Banking in Renaissance Venice*, I, pp. 152–3.

118 T. Coryate, *Coryat's crudities hastily gobled up in five moneths travells in France, Savoy, Italy, Rhetia* (London, 1611), pp. 272–5.

119 Sanudo, *I diarii*, LVIII, col. 542.

120 Niccoli, 'Profezie in piazza: note sul profetismo popolare nell'Italia del primo Cinquecento', *Quaderni storici* XLI (1979), pp. 508–11.

121 K. Park, 'Country Medicine in the City Marketplace: Snakehandlers as Itinerant Healers', *Renaissance Studies* XV (2001), pp. 104–6.

122 Coryate, *Coryat's Crudities*, p. 274; M. A. Katritzky, 'Marketing Medicine: The Image of the Early Modern Mountebank', *Renaissance Studies* XV (2001), p. 122.

123 P. Burke, *Popular Culture in Early Modern Europe* (London, 1978), p. 95.

124 D. Gentilcore, '"Tutti i modi che adoperano i ceretani per far bezzi": Towards a Database of Italian Charlatans', *Ludica* V–VI (2000), p. 213, n. 31.

125 D. Calabi, 'Il rinnovamento urbano del primo Cinquecento', in A. Tenenti and U. Tucci, eds, *Storia di Venezia dalle origini alla caduta della serenissima* V (Rome, 1996), pp. 102–10; D. Calabi, *Il mercato e la città: piazze, strade, architetture d'Europa in età moderna* (Venice, 1993), pp. 63–6, 81–5.

126 Calabi, 'Città e spazi', p. 84.

127 Lane and Mueller, *Money and Banking in Renaissance Venice*, I, pp. 146–9, 153–60.

128 Lane and Mueller, *Money and Banking in Renaissance Venice*, II, pp. 3–32, and chapter 3.

129 Sanudo, *I diarii*, XVII, p. 485.

130 For its building history, see P. C. Hamilton, 'The Palazzo dei Camerlenghi in Venice', *Journal of the Society of Architectural Historians* XLII (1983), pp. 258–71; D. Calabi and P. Morachiello, *Rialto: le fabbriche e il ponte, 1514–1591* (Turin, 1987), pp. 79–90.

131 P. Cottrell, 'Corporate Colors: Bonifacio and Tintoretto at the Palazzo dei Camerlenghi in Venice', *Art Bulletin* LXXXII (2000), pp. 658–78, which lists all surviving paintings and reconstructs the original positioning of some of them within the building.

132 For the rebuilding, see D. Calabi and P. Morachiello, 'Rialto, 1514–1538: gli anni della ricostruzione', in M. Tafuri, ed., *'Renovatio urbis': Venetia nell'età di Andrea Gritti, 1523–1538* (Rome, 1984), pp. 313–17. The *andata* to San Giovanni Elemosinario is described in Sansovino, *Venetia città nobilissima* (1663), p. 519; the church itself is described on pp. 186–7.

133 A description of the church and its history is given in Sansovino, *Venetia città nobilissima* (1663), pp. 196–9; the *andata* is described on pp. 519–20.

134 For the sixteenth-century form of the ceremonial *andata*, which is clearly derived from that described by Canal in the thirteenth century, see below, pp. 122–5.

135 A. Limentani, ed., *Martin da Canal: les estoires de Venise. Cronaca veneziana in lingua francese dalle origini al 1275* (Florence, 1972), pp. 246–7.

136 Limentani, ed., *Martin da Canal*, pp. 6–8.

137 A. Pertusi, 'Venezia e Bisanzio, 1000–1204', in *Dumbarton Oaks Papers* XXXIII (1979), p. 21.

138 F. Sansovino, *Venetia città nobilissima* (1663), p. 479.

139 A. Pertusi, 'Quaedam regalia insignia', *Studi veneziani* VII (1965), pp. 3–123; Muir, *Civic Ritual*, pp. 103–19, 204–11.

140 Muir, *Civic Ritual*, pp. 110–11; W. Wolters, *Storia e politica nei dipinti di Palazzo Ducale: aspetti dell'autocelebrazione della Repubblica di Venezia nel Cinquecento* (Venice, 1987), pp. 162–78, particularly pp. 173–8.

141 Limentani, ed., *Martin da Canal*, pp. 248–9.

142 E. H. Kantorowicz, *Laudes Regiae: A Study in Liturgical Acclamations and Medieval Ruler Worship* (Berkeley, CA, 1946), pp. 153–6.

143 I. Cavallini, 'Antiche acclamazioni con musica in Dalmazia e Istria', in Cavallini, ed., *Studi in onore di Giuseppe Vecchi* (Modena, 1989), pp. 39–52.

144 The entire series is reproduced in Muir, *Civic Ritual*, pp. 193–7.

145 F. Sansovino, *Venetia città nobilissima* (1581), ff. 183–4v, 193v–94; see M. Bury, *The Print in Italy, 1550–1620* (London, 2001), pp. 183–4.

146 Wilson, *The World in Venice*, pp. 66–67; for an authoritative listing of the participants in the *andata*, see ASV Collegio, Ceremoniali I, ff. VII–VIII.

147 Muir, *Civic Ritual*, pp. 189–211.

148 G. Fasoli, 'Liturgia e ceremoniale ducale', in A. Pertusi, ed., *Venezia e il Levante fino al secolo XV*, 3 vols (Florence, 1983), I, pp. 261–95.

149 For a discussion, arguably too schematic, see Muir, 'Images of Power'; Muir, *Civic Ritual*, pp. 189–204.

150 J. Wheeler, 'Neighbourhoods and Local Loyalties', in A. Cowan, ed., *Mediterranean Urban Culture, 1400–1700* (Exeter, 2000), pp. 32–3. For music in parish churches see E. Quaranta, *Oltre San Marco*.

151 Tafuri, *Venice and the Renaissance*, pp. 1–3.

152 J. H. Moore, *Vespers at St Mark's: Music of Alessandro Grandi, Giovanni Rovetta and Francesco Cavalli*, 2 vols (Ann Arbor, MI, 1981), I, p. 184; for the *scuole*, see J. Glixon, '"Far una bella processione": Music and Public Ceremony at the Venetian Scuole Grandi', in R. Charteris, ed., *Altro Polo. Essays on Italian Music in the Cinquecento* (Sydney, 1990), pp. 190–220.

153 Brown, *Venetian Narrative Painting*, pp. 144–50; H. M. Brown, 'On Gentile Bellini's *Processione in San Marco (1496)*', in *International Musicological Society Congress Report XII: Berkeley, 1977* (Kassel and London, 1981), pp. 649–58.

154 For the general phenomenon, see Rubin, *Corpus Christi*, pp. 243–71.

155 BCV, MS Cicogna 2043, pp. 17–18.

156 Ellis, ed., *The Pylgrymage*, pp. 8–9; G. Nori, ed., *Antonio da Crema: itinerario al Santo Sepolcro 1486* (Pisa, 1996), pp. 33–4.

157 I. Fenlon, 'Strangers in Paradise: Dutchmen in Venice in 1525', in Fenlon, *Music and Culture in Late Renaissance Italy* (Oxford, 2002), pp. 32–4.

158 J. Glixon, 'The Polyphonic Laude of Innocentius Dammonis', *Journal of Musicology* VIII (1990), pp. 19–53.

159 BCV, MS Cicogna 1295, p. 138.

160 Newett, *Canon Pietro Casola's Pilgrimage*, p. 146; J. Glixon, 'Music at the Venetian Scuole Grandi, 1440–1540', in I. Fenlon, ed., *Music in Medieval and Early Modern Europe: Patronage, Sources and Texts* (Cambridge, 1981), pp. 193–208, and now the relevant setions of J. Glixon, *Honoring God and the City. Music at the Venetian Confraternities 1260–1807* (New York, 2003).

CHAPTER FOUR

1 R. Cessi, ed., *I diarii di Girolamo Priuli* (Bologna, 1938), II, p. 394.

2 M. Sanudo, *I diarii*, ed. R. Fulin et al., 58 vols (Venice, 1879–1903), VI, pp. 258–60.

3 Cessi, ed., *I diarii di Girolamo Priuli*, II, p. 394.

4 For a discussion, see M. Brunetti, 'Il doge non è "segno di taverna"', *Nuovo archivio veneto* XXXIII (1917), pp. 351–5.

5 D. Giannotti, *Libro de la republica de Vinitiani* (Rome, 1540), f. 72.

6 G. Contarini, *The Common-wealth and Government of Venice* (London, 1599), p. 42.

7 E. H. Kantorowicz, *Laudes Regiae: A Study in Liturgical Acclamations and Medieval Ruler Worship* (Berkeley, CA, 1946), p. 153; G. Fasoli, 'Liturgia e ceremoniale ducale', in A. Pertusi, ed., *Venezia e il Levante fino al secolo XV*, 3 vols (Florence, 1983), I, pp. 276–8.

8 Montpellier, Bibliothèque de l'Ecole de Médecine, MS 409, ff. 343v–344.

9 Kantorowicz, *Laudes Regiae*, pp. 1–12.

10 H. E. J. Cowdrey, 'The Anglo-Norman Laudes Regiae', *Viator* XII (1981), pp. 43–7.

11 Kantorowicz, *Laudes Regiae*, pp. 76–84; A. Pertusi, 'Quaedam regalia insignia', *Studi veneziani* VII (1965), pp. 92–5.

12 E. Wellesz, *A History of Byzantine Music and Hymnography* (Oxford, 1949), pp. 87–106.

13 A. Limentani, ed., *Martin da Canal: les estoires de Venise. Cronaca veneziana in lingua francese dalle origini al 1275* (Florence, 1972), p. 280.

14 V. Lazzarini, 'I titoli dei dogi', *Nuovo archivio veneto* V (1903), p. 294; *RIS* XII, col. 330.

15 Kantorowicz, *Laudes Regiae*, pp. 153, 213.

16 Kantorowicz, *Laudes Regiae*, pp. 153–56.

17 I. Cavallini, 'Antiche acclamazioni con musica in Dalmazia e Istria', in Cavallini, ed., *Studi in onore di Giuseppe Vecchi* (Modena, 1989), pp. 39–52.

18 J. E. Cumming, 'Music for the Doge in Early Renaissance Venice', *Speculum* LXVII (1992), pp. 346–52.

19 Kantorowicz, *Laudes Regiae*, p. 182.

20 Bologna, Biblioteca universitaria, MS 2216, ff. 30v–31. For its Bergamasque origins, see Gallo, 'Musiche veneziane', pp. 107–8.

21 F. A. Gallo, 'Musiche veneziane nel MS 2216 della Biblioteca Universitaria di Bologna', *Quadrivium* VI (1964), p. 110; Fasoli, 'Liturgia e ceremoniale ducale', p. 277.

22 M. Bent, 'The Fourteenth-century Italian Motet', in *L'ars nova italiana del trecento* (Certaldo, 1992), table 1; Cumming, 'Music for the Doge', pp. 329–61.

23 D. Pincus, *The Arco Foscari: The Building of a Triumphal Gateway in Fifteenth-century Venice* (New York, 1976), pp. 384–401.

24 R. Goy, *The House of Gold: Building a Palace in Medieval Venice* (Cambridge, 1992), pp. 263–5.

25 E. Muir, *Civic Ritual in Renaissance Venice* (Princeton, NJ, 1981), p. 253.

26 H. J. Trevor-Roper, 'Doge Francesco Foscari', in J. H. Plumb, ed., *Renaissance Profiles* (New York, 1965), p. 121.

27 P. F. Grendler, 'The Leaders of the Venetian State, 1540–1609: A Prosopographical Analysis', *Studi veneziani* XIX (1990), pp. 51–7.

28 R. Finlay, 'The Venetian Republic as a Gerontocracy: Age and Politics in the Renaissance', *Journal of Medieval and Renaissance Studies* VIII (1978), p. 178.

29 Muir, *Civic Ritual*, pp. 263–8.

30 O. Demus, *The Mosaics of San Marco in Venice*, 2 vols in 4 (Chicago, IL, 1984), II/1, pp. 192–8.

31 ASV Collegio, Ceremoniali I, ff. 1–6; BNM, MS Latin III, 172 (2276), ff. 67–77; BNM, MS It. VII 1219 (9598); BNM, MS It. VII 708 (7899); Sanudo, *I diarii*, cols 387–402. F. Sansovino (ed. G. Stringa), *Venetia città nobilissima et singolare descritta in XIIII libri hora con molta diligenza corretta, emendata, e più d'un terzo di cose nuove ampliata dal M R.D. Giovanni Stringa* (Venice, 1604), ff. 270–73. A. Da Mosto, *I dogi di Venezia con particolare riguardo alle loro tombe* (Venice, 1939), pp. xxiii–xxxi; Muir, *Civic Ritual*, pp. 268–79; E. Muir, 'The Doge as *Primus Inter Pares*: Interregnum Rites in Early Six-

teenth-century Venice', in S. Bertelli and G. Ramakus, eds, *Essays Presented to Myron P. Gilmore*, 2 vols (Florence, 1978), I, pp. 145–60.

32 BNM, MS Ital. VII. 1219; Sanudo, *I diarii*, XXX, col. 388.

33 B. Betto, *Le nove congregazioni del clero di Venezia, secoli XI–XV: ricerche storiche, matricole e documenti vari* (Padua, 1984).

34 BNM, MS Ital. VII. 1219.

35 Da Mosto, *I dogi*, p. 368; Muir, *Civic Ritual*, pp. 269–70.

36 BCV, MS. Cicogna 2479, 'Alvise Mocenigo'.

37 BNM, MS Ital. VII. 1219.

38 E. Finlay, *Politics in Renaissance Venice* (London, 1980), pp. 141–4, citing Wootton on p. 141. The two most important contemporary accounts of the election process are those in M. Sanudo, *Cronachetta*, ed. R. Fulin (Venice, 1880), pp. 70–74, and F. Sansovino, *Venetia città nobilissima . . . descritta in XIIII libri . . . con aggiunta da D. Giustiniano Martinioni* (Venice, 1663), pp. 475–6. See also Mosto, *I dogi*, pp. xvi–xvii, and two annotated pamphlets: *La elettione del principe di Venetia* (Venice, 1556), and *Modo dell'elettione del principe di Venetia* (Venice, 1595).

39 BNM, MS Ital. VII. 1219.

40 BNM, MS Ital. VII. 1219; ASV Collegio, Ceremoniali I, f. IV.

41 Sanudo, *I diarii*, XXX, col. 389. For the significance of scarlet see J. H. Munro, 'The Medieval Scarlet and the Economics of Sartorial Splendour', in N. B. Harte and K. G. Ponting, eds, *Cloth and Clothing in Medieval Europe: Essays in Memory of Professor E. M. Caru-Wilson* (London, 1983), pp. 13–70.

42 ASV Collegio, Ceremoniali I, f. LIII.

43 Sanudo, *I diarii*, XXX, cols 398–9.

44 The most important contemporary accounts of ducal coronations and funerals are those recorded at the end of the sixteenth century in ASV Collegio, Ceremoniali I and II, and that drawn up for the *maestro del ceremoniale* in BNM, MS Lat. III. 172 (2276), ff. 67v–71r. See also Sanudo, *I diarii*, XXX, cols 479–90; XXXI, cols 7–11. For modern accounts, see Da

Mosto, *I dogi*, pp. xxiii–xxxi; Muir, 'The Doge as Primus Inter Pares'.

45 Sanudo, *I diarii*, xxx, col. 388.

46 BNM, MS Ital. VII. 1219.

47 BNM, MS Ital. VII. 1219.

48 Sanudo, *I diarii*, xxx, cols 398–9.

49 O. Demus, *The Church of San Marco in Venice: History, Architecture, Sculpture* (Washington, DC, 1960), pp. 45–6.

50 D. Pincus, *The Tombs of the Doges of Venice* (Cambridge, 2000), pp. 132–47, especially pp. 146–7.

51 Pincus, *The Tombs of the Doges*, pp. 148–65.

52 Pincus, *The Tombs of the Doges*, pp. 105–47.

53 D. Pincus, 'The Tomb of Doge Nicolò Tron and Venetian Renaissance Ruler Imagery', in L. F. Sandler and M. Barasch, eds, *Art the Ape of Nature: Essays in Honor of H. W. Janson* (New York, 1981), pp. 127–50, particularly pp. 144–5.

54 Pincus, *The Arco Foscari*, pp. 402–38.

55 ASV Collegio, Ceremoniali I, f. LVIV.

56 Muir, *Civic Ritual*, p. 279.

57 ASV Collegio, Ceremoniali I, f. LVIV; BCV, MS Cicogna 2479 (unfoliated), 'Sebastiano Venier'.

58 S. Sinding-Larsen, *Christ in the Council Hall: Studies in the Religious Iconography of the Venetian Republic* (Rome, 1974), pp. 159–66.

59 ASV, Collegio ceremoniale I, f. IV; BCV, MS Cicogna PD 381b (unfoliated), 'Pietro Lando', reports a different version.

60 J. Verpeaux, ed., *Pseudo-Kodinos, traité des offices* (Paris, 1906), pp. 267–8. I am grateful to Warren Woodfin for pointing out this parallel.

61 ASV Collegio, Ceremoniali I, f. IV.

62 ASV Collegio, Ceremoniali I, f. IV, 'Staum e honorem ecclesiam Sancti Marci bona fide et sine fraude conservare'.

63 See pp. 50–51; pls 30–31.

64 'Evangelicae praedicationis gratia sublimasti; / tribue quaesumus, eius nos semper / et eruditione proficere et oratione defendi. Alleluia.

65 G. Bassano, *Concerti ecclesiastici a cinque, sei, sette, otto e dodeci voci . . . libro secondo* (Venice, 1599), p. 13; modern edition in

G. Bassano *Opera omnia*, ed. R. Charteris (n.p., 1999–), I, p. 94. A. Gabrieli and G. Gabrieli, *Concerti . . . continenti musica di chiesa, madrigali, & altro, per voci e stromenti musicali . . .* (Venice, 1587); G. Gabrieli, *Sacrae symphoniae . . .* (Venice, 1597).

66 D. Bryant, 'Liturgy, Ceremonial and Sacred Music in Venice at the Time of the Counter-Reformation', 2 vols (Ph.D. dissertation, University of London, 1981), pp. 20, 24–5, 73, 157.

67 Bryant, 'Liturgy, Ceremonial and Sacred Music', pp. 99–100. For a setting of this text, see G. Bassano, *Motetti per concerti ecclesiastici . . .* (Venice, 1598).

68 Cited in S. Tramontin, 'San Marco', in Tramontin, ed., *Il culto dei santi a Venezia* (Venice, 1965), p. 64.

69 M. Muraro, 'La scala senza giganti', in M. Meiss, ed., *De artibus opuscula XL: Essays in Honor of Erwin Panofsky* (New York, 1961), pp. 351–5.

70 B. Boucher, *The Sculpture of Jacopo Sansovino*, 2 vols (New Haven, CT, and London, 1991), I, pp. 128–41.

71 ASV Collegio, Ceremoniali I, f. IVV, 'Accipe coronam Ducatus Venetiarum'.

72 Sansovino, *Venetia città nobilissima* (1663), p. 470.

73 ASV Collegio, Ceremoniali I, f. LVII.

74 G. B. Gallicciolli, *Storie e memorie venete profane ed ecclesiastiche*, 8 vols (Venice, 1795), VI, p. 124.

75 G. Fasoli, 'Liturgia e ceremoniale ducale', in A. Pertusi, ed., *Venezia e il Levante fino al secolo XV*, 3 vols (Florence, 1983), I, p. 264.

76 Fasoli, 'Liturgia', pp. 267–8.

77 According to the account of Antonio de Faustiniis, a Venetian parish priest, first published in G. B. Gallicciolli, *Delle memorie Venete antiche, profane ed ecclesiastiche*, 8 vols (Venice, 1795), IV, p. 193, and confirmed by the later 'Statuti antichi dei canonici di San Marco', from the time of Primicerio Mattea Venerio (*c.* 1303–29), in Gallicciolli, *Delle memorie*, VI, p. 101. See Pertusi, 'Quedam regalia insignia', p. 72.

78 Both the investiture 'per vexillum' and the *promissione ducale* were evidently in use,

perhaps for the first time, at the investiture of Pietro Polani; see Pertusi, 'Quaedam regalia insignia', pp. 73–4.

79 See the account of Lorenzo Tiepolo's coronation in 1268 in Limentani, ed., *Martin da Canal*, p. 278.

80 Details from Sinding-Larsen, *Christ in the Council Hall*, pp. 213–14; A. Cameron, 'The Construction of Court Ritual: The Byzantine *Book of Ceremonies*', in D. Cannadine and S. Price, eds, *Rituals of Royalty: Power and Ceremonial in Traditional Societies* (Cambridge, 1987), pp. 106–36; A. Hopkins, 'Architecture and *Infirmitas*: Doge Andrea Gritti and the Chancel of San Marco', *Journal of the Society of Architectural Historians* LVII (1998), pp. 182–97.

81 Sansovino, *Venetia città nobilissima* (1663), pp. 518–22; J. Bettley, 'The Office of Holy Week at St Mark's, Venice, in the Late Sixteenth Century and the Musical Contributions of Giovanni Croce', *Early Music* XXII (1994), pp. 45–50; L. Urban, *Processioni e feste dogali: 'Venetia est mundus'* (Vicenza, 1998), pp. 76–85.

82 Verpeaux, ed., *Pseudo-Kodinos*, pp. 228–9. I am grateful to Warren Woodfin for remarking on the parallel.

83 The thirteenth-century sources are: Venice, Biblioteca Correr, MS 1006, edited in G. Cattin, *Musica e liturgia a San Marco: testi e melodie per la liturgia delle ore dal XII al XVII secolo. Dal graduale tropato del duecento ai graduali cinquecenteschi*, 4 vols (Venice, 1990–92), II, pp. 499–502, and Berlin, Staatsbibliothek Preussischer Kulturbesitz Mus., MS 40608, for which see S. Marcon, 'I codici della liturgia di San Marco', in Cattin, ed., *Musica e liturgia a San Marco*, I, p. 229, and S. Marcon, *I libri di San Marco: i manoscritti liturgici della basilica marciana* (Venice, 1995), pp. 110–111. For a discussion, see S. Rankin, 'From Liturgical Ceremony to Public Ritual: "Quem Queritis" and St Mark's Venice', in G. Cattin, ed., *Da Bisanzio a San Marco: musica e liturgia* (Venice, 1997), pp. 141–56. The sixteenth-century sources are: Venice, Biblioteca Nazionale Marciana, MS Lat. III.

172 (= 2276); A. da Castello, *Liber sacerdotalis* (Venice, 1523); G. Stringa, ed., *Officium Maioris Hebdomadae...* (Venice, [1597]); and Stringa's edition (with his additions) of Sansovino, *Venetia città nobilissima* (1604). For discussion, see Bettley, 'The Office of Holy Week', and Rankin, 'From Liturgical Ceremony to Public Ritual', pp. 160–74.

84 D. Rosand and M. Muraro, *Titian and the Venetian Woodcut* (Washington, DC, 1976), pp. 282–8.

85 BCV, MS 1295, p. 60.

86 Stringa, *Officium Maioris Hebdomadae*, ff. 4–64; Sansovino, *Venetia città nobilissima* (1604), ff. 347v–48; Cattin, *Musica e liturgia a San Marco*, II, p. 212; III, pp. 40–42; Bettley, 'The Office of Holy Week', pp. 46–8.

87 Stringa, *Officium Maoris Hebdomadae*, ff. 83–99 (Wednesday); ff. 99v–195 (Thursday); ff. 195–242 (Friday); ff. 242v–280 (Saturday); Sansovino, *Venetia città nobilissima* (1604), ff. 348–48v (Wednesday); f. 348v (Thursday); f. 348v (Friday); ff. 349v–50 (Saturday); Cattin, *Musica e liturgia a San Marco*, II, p. 213; III, pp. 42–3 (Wednesday); II, pp. 213–15; III, pp. 43–4 (Thursday); II, p. 215; III, pp. 45–7 (Friday); II, pp. 215–16; III, pp. 47–9 (Saturday); Bettley, 'The Office of Holy Week', pp. 48–9.

88 See G. Cattin, *Johannes de Quadris, musico del sec. XV* (Bologna, 1971), and above pp. 72–3.

89 See above, pp. 30–32.

90 Sanudo, *I diarii*, XLIV, col. 520; XXVII, col. 194; for the tapestries, see R. Gallo, *Il tesoro di San Marco e la sua storia* (Venice and Rome, 1967), pp. 8, 17–19.

91 Rankin, 'From Liturgical Ceremony to Public Ritual', pp. 175–9, discussing a number of related paintings and drawings; K. Baetjer and J. G. Links, eds, *Canaletto* (New York, 1989), p. 154, argue that the these show the reception of the relics of a Venetian doge, Blessed Pietro Orseolo, on 7 January 1732.

92 Castello, *Liber sacerdotalis*, ff. 267v–269v, prints de Quadris's two-voice settings of the *invitatorium* and *responsorium* sung

during the procession. See also above, p. 73.

93 Sanudo, *I diarii*, XXXVIII, col. 183.

94 BCV, MS 1006, ff. 23–53; Stringa, *Officium Maioris Hebdomadae*, ff. 280–96; Sansovino, *Venetia città nobilissima* (1604), ff. 350–350v; Cattin, *Musica e liturgia*, II, pp. 216–17; III, pp. 49–51; Bettley, 'The Office of Holy Week', pp. 49–50; Rankin, 'From Liturgical Ceremony to Public Ritual', pp. 160–74.

95 Rankin, 'From Liturgical Ceremony to Public Ritual', pp. 169–74.

CHAPTER FIVE

1 *Il gran lamento & pianto che fa il populo Surrentino, & di Massa* (n.p. [1557]): 'Piangi Massa e Surrento la tua sorte, / Piangete o Christiani i nostri affani, / Meglio per noi seria stata la morte . . . Tutti i Christiani signor in una schiera / Aiutateme fuor di tal errore / Ogni Città, Castel per ogni fiera'.

2 G. Maldacca, *Storia di Sorrento*, 2 vols (Naples, 1841), II, p. 17.

3 K. M. Setton, *The Papacy and the Levant, 1204–1571*, 4 vols (Philadelphia, PA, 1976–84), II, pp. 365–75.

4 R. Filangieri di Candida Gonzaga, *Storia di Massa Lubrense* (Naples, 1910), pp. 168–74.

5 F. Braudel, *The Mediterranean and the Mediterranean World in the Age of Philip II*, trans. S. Reynolds, 2 vols (London, 1975), II, pp. 973–87.

6 J. F. Guilmartin, 'Ideology and Conflict: The Wars of the Ottoman Empire, 1453–1606', *Journal of Interdisciplinary History* XVIII (1988), pp. 721–47, especially pp. 727–37.

7 Braudel, *The Mediterranean*, II, pp. 1014–20.

8 P. Attwood, *Italian Medals, c. 1530–1600, in British Public Collections*, 2 vols (London, 2003), I, pp. 396–8, nos 967–71. See also below, pp. 302–3.

9 C. Weiss, ed., *Papiers d'état du Cardinal Granvelle*, 9 vols (Paris, 1841–1852), IX, p. 88 (28 March 1565).

10 *Calendar of State Papers, Foreign, Elizabeth I, Preserved in the State Paper Department of Her Majesty's Public Record Office*, 23 vols (London, 1863–1950), VIII, p. 8.

11 Braudel, *The Mediterranean*, II, p. 1022.

12 F. Gaeta et al., eds, *Nunziature di Venezia* (Rome, 1958–), VIII, p. 74 (Venice, 13 July 1566).

13 Braudel, *The Mediterranean*, II, pp. 1033–4.

14 Gaeta et al., eds, *Nunziature di Venezia*, VIII, p. 77 (Venice, 20 July 1566); p. 88 (Venice, 3 August 1566).

15 C. Douais, ed., *Dépêches de M Fourquevaux, ambassadeur du roi Charles IX en Espagne, 1565–1572*, 3 vols (Paris, 1896–1904), I, p. 123 (3 September 1566).

16 Setton, *The Papacy and the Levant*, III, p. 433.

17 Bessarion, *Ad illustrissimos Italiae principes contra Turcas exhortatio* (Rome, 1537).

18 L. von Pastor, *The History of the Popes from the Close of the Middle Ages*, ed. F. I. Antrobus et al., 40 vols (London and St Louis, MO, 1898–1953), XVII, p. 53, n. 1.

19 Pastor, *The History of the Popes*, XVII, p. 62.

20 Braudel, *The Mediterranean*, II, p. 1043.

21 Douais, ed., *Dépêches de M Fourquevaux*, I, p. 89 (8 May 1566); pp. 91–2 (12 June 1566).

22 Braudel, *The Mediterranean*, II, pp. 1038, 1044.

23 Braudel, *The Mediterranean*, II, p. 1047.

24 Savorgnan, *Descrittione delle cose di Cipro*; MSS. consulted: Paris, Bibliothèque nationale, Fonds ital. 1500; BNM, MSS Lat. XIV. 52, It. VI. 178; It. VI. 310; It. VII. 530.

25 J. R. Hale, 'From Peacetime Establishment to Fighting Machine: The Venetian Army and the War of Cyprus and Lepanto', in G. Benzoni, ed., *Il mediterraneo nella seconda metà del '500 nella luce di Lepanto* (Florence, 1974), p. 175.

26 Setton, *The Papacy and the Levant*, IV, p. 923.

27 Douais, ed., *Dépêches de M Fourquevaux*, I, p. 243 (2 August 1567); p. 311 (26 December 1567).

28 Braudel, *The Mediterranean*, II, p. 1047.

29 Gaeta et al., eds, *Nunziature di Venezia*, VIII, pp. 424–5 (Venice, 7 August 1568); p. 439 (Venice, 22 September 1568).

30 Braudel, *The Mediterranean*, II, pp. 1055–60.

31 P. Paruta, *Della guerra di Cipro* (Venice, 1605), pp. 5–6.

32 Gaeta et al., eds, *Nunziature di Venezia*, IX, p. 109 (Venice, 10 August 1569).

33 BNM, MS It. VII. 519, ff. 324v–25; Paruta, *Della guerra di Cipro*, pp. 21–3.

34 B. Arbel, 'Venezia, gli ebrei e l'attività di Salamone Ashkenasi nella guerra di Cipro', in G. Cozzi, ed., *Gli ebrei a Venezia, secoli XIV–XVIII* (Milan, 1987), p. 171.

35 BNM, MS It. VII. 18, f. 239v.

36 Gaeta et al., eds, *Nunziature di Venezia*, IX, pp. 175–6 (Venice, 21 December 1569); see also pp. 188–9 (Venice, 25 January 1570).

37 C. Coco and F. Manzonetto, *Baili veneziani alla sublime porta: storia e caratteristiche dell'ambasciata veneta a Costantinopoli* (Venice, [1985]), pp. 45–51.

38 Gaeta et al., eds, *Nunziature di Venezia*, IX, p. 190 (Venice, 27 January 1570).

39 Paruta, *Della guerra di Cipro*, p. 23.

40 E. Gleason, 'Confronting New Realities: Venice and the Peace of Bologna, 1530', in J. Martin and D. Romano, eds, *Venice Reconsidered: The History and Civilization of an Italian City State, 1297–1797* (Baltimore, MD, and London, 2000), p. 178.

41 Hale, 'From Peacetime Establishment to Fighting Machine', particularly pp. 173–84.

42 *DBI*, 'Baglione, Astorre'.

43 A. Tenenti, *Cristoforo da Canal: la marine vénitienne avant Lépante* (Paris, 1962), pp. 175–87.

44 Paruta, *Della guerra di Cipro*, p. 26; Gaeta et al., eds, *Nunziature di Venezia*, IX, pp. 191–4 (Venice, 31 January 1570); F. C. Lane, 'Wages and Recruitment of Venetian Galeotti, 1470–1580', *Studi veneziani* VI (1982), pp. 40–41.

45 J. R. Hale and M. E. Mallett, *The Military Organization of a Renaissance State: Venice, c. 1400 to 1617* (Cambridge, 1984), p. 233.

46 BNM, MS It. VII. 519, f. 325.

47 BNM, MS It. VII. 553, pp. 13–14.

48 Gaeta et al., eds, *Nunziature di Venezia*, IX, p. 200 (Venice, 4 February 1570).

49 BNM, MS It. VII. 519, f. 325.

50 Setton, *The Papacy and the Levant*, IV, pp. 953–4.

51 Paruta, *Della guerra di Cipro*, p. 63; A. Da Mosto, *I dogi di Venezia con particolare riguardo alle loro tombe* (Venice, 1939), pp. 178–81.

52 Da Mosto, *I dogi*, p. 180; see also the extracts from the *Cronaca Agostini* and the commentary to it in D. Chambers and B. Pullan, *Venice: A Documentary History, 1450–1630* (Oxford, 1992), pp. 108–13.

53 BNM, MS It. VII. 519, f. 327.

54 G. Mantese, 'Nel quarto centenario della battaglia di Lepanto', *Archivio veneto* XCIV (1971), pp. 6–8; F. Barbieri, *La basilica palladiana*, Corpus Palladianum II (Vicenza, 1968), pp. 80–81.

55 BNM, MS It. VII. 224 (8309), p. 16.

56 A. Avena, 'Memorie veronesi della guerra di Cipro e della battaglia di Lepanto', *Nuovo archivio veneto*, n.s. XXIV (1912), pp. 97–9.

57 Paruta, *Della guerra di Cipro*, p. 42.

58 A. Dragonetti de Torres, *La lega di Lepanto nel carteggio diplomatico inedito di Don Luys de Torres, nunzio straordinario di S. Pio V a Filippo II* (Turin, 1931), pp. 97–161.

59 Braudel, *The Mediterranean*, II, pp. 1084–7.

60 Gaeta et al., eds, *Nunziature di Venezia*, IX, p. 287 (Rome, 10 June 1570).

61 Hale and Mallett, *The Military Organization of a Renaissance State*, pp. 234–5.

62 Gaeta et al., eds, *Nunziature di Venezia*, IX, p. 375 (Rome, 25 October 1570).

63 Setton, *The Papacy and the Levant*, IV, pp. 1027–44.

64 C. S. Brenzone, *Vita et fatti del valorissimo capitan Astorre Baglione da Perugia* (Verona, 1591), p. 91.

65 G. P. Contarini, *Historia delle cose successe dal principio della guerra mossa da Selim ottomano a Venetiani fino al di della gran giornata vittoriosa contra Turchi* (Venice, 1572), ff. 23v–31; Paruta, *Della guerra di Cipro*, pp. 183, 194–7; Brenzone, *Vita et fatti*; BNM, MS It. VII. 519, ff. 331v–32; BNM, MS It. VII. 553, pp. 26–9; BAV, MS Patetta 969, ff. 105v–108. Modern accounts in *DBI*, XIII, pp. 686–9 (Ventura); Setton, *The Papacy and the Levant*, IV, pp. 1039–42.

66 N. Martinengo, *Relatione di tutto il successo di Famagosta . . .* (Venice, 1572).

67 BNM, MS It. VII. 364 (= 7934), ff. 22–24v, at f. 23v.

68 Gaeta et al., eds, *Nunziature di Venezia*, IX, p. 456 (Venice, 7 March 1571).

69 U. Tucci, 'Il processo a Girolamo Zane mancato difensore di Cipro', in G. Benzoni, ed., *Il mediterraneo nella seconda metà del '500 nella luce di Lepanto* (Florence, 1974), pp. 418–33.

70 E. Poullet and C. Piot, eds, *Correspondance du Cardinal Granvelle, 1566–1586*, 12 vols (Brussels, 1877–96), IV, p. 51: letter of 14 December 1570.

71 Braudel, *The Mediterranean*, II, pp. 1088–92.

72 Gaeta et al., eds, *Nunziature di Venezia*, IX, p. 311 (Rome, 22 July 1570); p. 316 (Rome, 29 July 1570). For the treaty of 1538, negotiations for which had begun the previous year, see Setton, *The Papacy and the Levant*, III, pp. 428–9.

73 Gaeta et al., eds, *Nunziature di Venezia*, IX, p. 414 (Venice, 23 December 1570).

74 AS Mod. Cancelleria ducale. Estero, Ambasciatori, agenti e correspondenti esteri. Italia, Venezia, b. 54 fasc. 96 ix: letters of Claudio Ariosti, 31 March 1571; 6 March 1571; 16 March 1571.

75 Gaeta et al., eds, *Nunziature di Venezia*, IX, pp. 486–7 (Venice, 14 April 1571).

76 Gaeta et al., eds, *Nunziature di Venezia*, IX, p. 495 (Venice, 2 May 1571).

77 Gaeta et al., eds, *Nunziature di Venezia*, IX, p. 498 (Venice, 9 May 1571).

78 Letter of Frances de Álava to Philip II, Poissy, 5 August 1570; cited in Braudel, *The Mediterranean*, II, p. 1091.

79 Gaeta et al., eds, *Nunziature di Venezia*, IX, p. 499 (Venice, 9 May 1570).

80 ASM, b.1504 (letter of Cavaliere Capilupi, 31 March 1571).

81 ASR, Arch. Santacroce 124, ff. 301–303v; Gaeta et al., eds, *Nunziature di Venezia*, IX, p. 505 (Rome, 21 May 1571).

82 *Relatione fatta alla maestà cattolica* and the *Capitoli della lega* (various editions). The full text of the articles of the Holy League are given, in their original Latin, in L. Serrano, *La liga de Lepanto*, 2 vols (Madrid, 1918–19), IV, p. 299ff., and in Italian in BNM, It. VII. 519, f. 330–330v. See also BNM, MS It. VII. 364 (7934), ff. 33–34v.

83 Braudel, *The Mediterranean*, II, p. 1091.

84 Gaeta et al., eds, *Nunziature di Venezia*, I, pp. 30–31 (Venice, 26 May 1571).

85 M. Sanudo, *I diarii*, ed. R. Fulin et al., 58 vols (Venice, 1879–1903), LII, col. 435.

86 BNM, MS It. VII. 142, pp. 298–9.

87 The principal printed account is *Il bellissimo et suntuoso trionfo fatto nella magnifica citta di Venetia nella publicatione della Lega* (Brescia, 1571); see also the shorter but still useful *Ceremonie fatte nella publicatione della lega fatta in Venetia con la dechiaratione di solari & altre cose come legendo inendereti* (n.p., n.d.). Among manuscript accounts the most useful are those in ASV Collegio, Ceremoniali I, pp. XXXVIII–XXXIX; BNM, MS It. VII. 142 (7147), ff. 298ff.; BNM, MS It. VII. 519 (8438), f. 330vff.; BNM, MS It. VII. 321 (8838), ff. 250–250v; ASV, Proc. de Supra 98, ff. 140v–141; and the long and detailed report of the Mantuan ambassador in ASM, 1504, and of the imperial ambassador, Vito di Dornberg, in Vienna, Haus-, Hof und Staatsarchiv, Venedig, Berichte II (1571). I am grateful to Robert Lindell for transcribing this for me. For further on the writer, see S. Cavazza, '"Così buono et savio cavalliere": Vito di Dornberg, Patrizio Goriziano del Cinquecento', *Annali di storia isontina* III (1990), pp. 7–36, especially pp. 11–19. The occasion is discussed in E. H. Gombrich, 'Celebrations in Venice of the Holy League and of the Victory of Lepanto', in *Studies in Renaissance and Baroque Art Presented to Anthony Blunt on his Sixtieth Birthday* (London, 1967), pp. 62–8; and I. Fenlon, 'Lepanto: The Arts of Celebration in Renaissance Venice,' *Proceedings of the British Academy* LXIII (1987), pp. 201–36, at pp. 203–7.

88 Gombrich, 'Celebrations in Venice', p. 62.

89 *Ceremonie fatte nella publicatione della lega.*

90 B. Wilson, *The World in Venice: Print, the City and Early Modern Identity* (Toronto, 2005), pp. 147–9.

91 M. L. King, 'Personal, Domestic and Republican Values in the Moral Philosophy of Giovanni Caldiera', *Renaissance Quarterly* XXVII (1975), pp. 559–65; E. Muir, *Civic Ritual in Renaissance Venice* (Princeton, NJ, 1981), pp. 16, 186; M. King, *Venetian Humanism in an Age of Patrician*

Dominance (Princeton, NJ, 1986), pp. 98–117, particularly pp. 105–12.

92 Sanudo, *I diarii*, XLII, cols 62–79; *Calendar of State Papers and Manuscripts Existing in the Archives and Collections of Venice and in Other Libraries of Northern Italy*, 42 vols (London, 1864–1947), III [1520–26], p. 579, no. 1343.

93 As described in Collini, *Esplicatione*.

94 BAV, Urb. Lat. 1042, f. 67v, report of 26 May 1571; ASR, Arch. Santacroce 124, ff. 301–2.

95 BAV, Urb. Lat. 1042, f. 68v, report of 30 May 1571; ASR, Arch. Santacroce 124, ff. 302v–305v.

96 G. Pollard, *Medaglie italiane del Rinascimento nel Museo Nazionale del Bargello*, 3 vols (Florence, 1984–5), II, pp. 1071–2.

97 Setton, *The Papacy and the Levant*, III, pp. 448–9.

98 MacKenney, '"A Plot Discover'd"', p. 188.

99 BNM, MS It. VII. 364 (7934), ff. 25v, 30v.

100 Hale and Mallett, *The Military Organization of a Renaissance State*, pp. 236–7.

101 Attwood, *Italian Medals*, I, p. 402.

102 Poullet and Piot, eds, *Correspondance du Cardinal Granvelle*, p. 71

103 Braudel, *The Mediterranean*, II, pp. 1102–3. Some contemporary accounts give different figures; see Setton, *The Papacy and the Levant*, IV, pp. 1052–3.

104 Hale and Mallett, *The Military Organization of a Renaissance State*, p. 238.

105 G. Diedo, *Lettera all'illustrissimo Sig. Marc'Antonio Barbaro Eccellentissimo Bailo in Constantinopli . . .* (Venice, 1573), f. 17.

106 Contarini, *Historia delle cose successe*, ff. 52v–53v. As a counterbalance to such official views see Aurelio Scetti's eyewitness account of the battle in L. Monga, ed. and trans., *The Journal of Aurelio Scetti. A Florentine Galley Slave at Lepanto (1565–1577)* (Tempe, Arizona, 2004), particularly pp. 116–23.

CHAPTER SIX

1 For a revisionist assessment, see F. Braudel, *The Mediterranean and the Mediterranean World in the Age of Philip II*, trans. S. Reynolds, 2 vols (London, 1975), II, pp. 661–9.

2 W. J. Bouwsma, *Venice and the Defense of Republican Liberty: Renaissance Values in the Age of the Counter Reformation* (Berkeley, CA, 1968), p. 192.

3 Details of the reactions in Brussels are revealed in a letter of 30 October 1571 from Paolo Moro, a Mantuan, to the *castellano* of his native city in ASM 1503. News from Madrid is found in a letter from Luigi Rogna (Rome, 1 December 1571) to Aurelio Zibramonte in Mantua, in ASM 906, and in the direct report to the duke of Mantua from Giulio Riva (Madrid, 7 November 1571) in ASM 596.

4 For general discussions of the immediate literary reactions to the victory, see A. Medin, *La storia della Repubblica di Venezia nella poesia* (Milan, 1904), pp. 244–89; G. A. Quarti, *La battaglia di Lepanto nei canti popolari dell'epoca* (Milan, 1930); C. Dionisotti, 'Lepanto nella cultura italiana del tempo', in G. Benzoni, ed., *Il mediterraneo nella seconda metà del '500 nella luce di Lepanto* (Florence, 1974), pp. 127–51.

5 L. Groto, *Oratione fatta in Vinegia, per l'allegrezza della vittoria ottenuta contra Turchi dalla Santissima Lega* (Venice, 1571), f. Aii.

6 R. Benedetti, *Ragguaglio delle allegrezze, solennita, e feste, fatte in Venetia per la felice vittoria* (Venice, 1571), ff. A2–A3.

7 The following details of the immediate reactions to the news in Venice are mostly taken from ASV Collegio, Ceremoniali I, ff. 40v–41; BNM, MS It. VII. 553, p. 29; BNM, MS It. VII. 142 (7147), p. 308; BNM, MS It. VII. 73 (8265), f. 393v, and the letters of Paolo Moro in ASM 1503. See also Benedetti, *Ragguaglio*; G. Diedo, *Lettera all'illustrissimo Sig. Marc'Antonio Barbaro Eccellentissimo Bailo in Constantinopli . . .* (Venice, 1573), ff. 28v–29; G. P. Contarini, *Historia delle cose successe dal principio della guerra mossa da Selim ottomano a Venetiani fino al di della gran giornata vittoriosa contra Turchi* (Venice, 1572), ff. 54–6; K. M. Setton, *The Papacy and the Levant, 1204–1571*, 4 vols (Philadelphia, PA, 1976–84), IV, pp. 1059–61.

8   B. Wilson, *The World in Venice: Print, the City and Early Modern Identity* (Toronto, 2005), p. 123.

9   Benedetti, *Ragguaglio*, f. B1.

10 G. Dolcetti, *Il 'Libro d'argento' dei cittadini di Venezia e del Veneto*, 5 vols (Venice, 1922–8), I, pp. 23–4; A. Da Mosto, *I dogi di Venezia con particolare riguardo alle loro tombe* (Venice, 1939), p. 74.

11 For more on Benedetti, see below, pp. 223–4.

12 For Rome, see I. Fenlon, *Music and Culture in Late Renaissance Italy* (Oxford, 2002), pp. 139–61.

13 BNM, MS It. VII. 553, p. 30; Benedetti, *Ragguaglio*, f. [A3]v.

14 BNM, MS It. VII. 553, p. 30.

15 BNM, MS It. VII. 519 (8438), p. 308; BNM, MS It. VII. 73 (8265), f.3 94v.

16 BNM, MS It. VII. 142 (7147), p. 308; BNM, MS It. VII. 73 (8265), f. 394.

17 F. Sansovino (ed. G. Stringa), *Venetia città nobilissima et singolare descritta in XIIII libri hora con molta diligenza corretta, emendata, e più d'un terzo di cose nuove ampliata dal M. R. D. Giovanni Stringa* (Venice, 1604), f. 91v.

18 S. M. Mason Rinaldi, *Palma il Giovane: l'opera completa* (Milan, 1984), p. 119; *Venezia e la difesa del Levante da Lepanto a Candia, 1570–1670* (Venice, 1986), p. 44.

19 S. M. Mason Rinaldi, 'Jacopo Palma il Giovane e la decorazione dell'Oratorio dei Crociferi', in S. Lunardon, ed., *Hospitale S. Mariae Cruciferorum* (Venice, 1985), pp. 19–84; Mason Rinaldi, *Palma il Giovane: l'opera completa*, pp. 30–31.

20 See, for example, the official notification to Elizabeth I in *Calendar of State Papers, Foreign, Elizabeth I, Preserved in the State Paper Department of Her Majesty's Public Record Office*, 23 vols (London, 1863–1950), IX, p. 551, dated 7 October 1571; F. Gaeta et al., eds, *Nunziature di Venezia* (Rome, 1958–), X, p. 117.

21 ASV, Sen. Secreta Reg. 78, ff. 21v–22; see Setton, *The Papacy and the Levant*, IV, pp. 1061–2.

22 Groto, *Oratione fatta in Vinegia, per l'allegrezza della vittoria*, f. B.

23 Benedetti, *Ragguaglio*, f. [A3]v; BNM, MS It. VII. 73 (8265), f. 394–394v.

24 BNM, MS It. VII. 73 (8265), f. 394.

25 BNM, MS It. VII. 142 (7147), f. 308; Benedetti, *Ragguaglio*, f. A4.

26 BNM MS It. VII. 73 (8265), f. 394v; Benedetti, *Ragguaglio*, f. A4.

27 Benedetti, *Ragguaglio*, f. A4: 'si fecero concerti divinissimi, perché sonandosi quando l'uno, e quando l'altro organo con ogni sorte di stromenti, e di voci, conspiranno ambi a un tempo in un tuono, che veramente pareva, che s'aprissero le cattaratte dell' harmonia celeste, & ella diluviasse da i chori angelici'. See also the report of the papal nuncio given in Gaeta et al., eds, *Nunziature di Venezia*, X, pp. 118–20. Benedetti's account is confirmed by the description of the Mantuan Paolo Moro, who notes the 'voci rissonanti' accompanied by 'varii et molti instrumenti di mano et da fiato' (Moro's letter, Venice, 22 October 1571, is in ASM 1503).

28 Original texts in A. Gabrieli and G. Gabrieli, *Concerti . . .* (Venice, 1587). For the arguments, see D. Bryant, 'Liturgy, Ceremonial and Sacred Music in Venice at the Time of the Counter-Reformation', 2 vols (Ph.D. dissertation, University of London, 1981), I, pp. 44–54, summarized in the same author's 'Andrea Gabrieli e la "musica di stato veneziana"', in *Andrea Gabrieli, 1585–1985*, pp. 29–45.

29 Original text in Gabrieli and Gabrieli, *Concerti*. See Bryant, 'Liturgy, Ceremonial and Sacred Music in Venice', I, p. 49: 'Benedictus Deus Deus Saboath. Benedicti qui pugnant in nomine Domini. Manus enim fortis et terribilis pugnat pro eis. Manus Domini protegit illos. Pugnavit Sanson, pugnavit Gedeon, vicit Sanson, vicit Gedeon. Pugnaverunt nostri in nomine Domini. Pugnavit Dominus pro nobis et vicit Dominus inimicos eius. Laetamini et exultate et psallite.'

30 See Giulano Scarpa in F. Sansovino, *Delle oratori recitate a principi di Venetia nella loro creatione da gli ambasciadori di diverse citta libro primo* (Venice, 1562), p. 66v; L. Groto, *Le orationi volgari* (Venice, 1598), pp. 37, 108, 111; F. Sansovino, *Venetia città nobilissima et singolare descritta in XIV libri* (Venice, 1581), p. 137.

31 G. Croce, *Motetti a otto voci* . . . (Venice, 1599): 'Percussit Saul mille & David decem millia quia manus Domini erat cum. illo. Percussit Philistaeum & abstulit opprobrium. Nonno iste David de quo canebat in choro dicentes Percussit Saul mille & David decem millia quia manus Domini erat cum illo.' For the Old Testament text, see I Samuel 18:7, repeated by the servant of Achish, 21:11. See also Deuteronomy 32:30.

32 See above, pp. 154–5.

33 P. Attwood, *Italian Medals, c. 1530–1600, in British Public Collections*, 2 vols (London, 2003), I, pp. 397–8, no. 970.

34 G. Croce, *Messe a otto voci* (Venice, 1596). For the Venetian repertory of battle-pieces, see below, pp. 262–3.

35 *DBI* XXXI, p. 210; *NG* VI, pp. 700–11.

36 See above, p. 154.

37 Benedetti, *Ragguaglio*, f. A4v.

38 Benedetti, *Ragguaglio*, f. B1. The official requiem for the Venetian dead is mentioned in the account in ASV Collegio, Ceremoniali I, ff. XLV–XLI. For the text of the oration, which praises the fallen as heroes who had fought for both Venice and the faith, see G. B. Rasario, *De victoria Christianorum ad Echinadas oratio* (Venice, 1571). See also BNM, MS It. VII. 73 (8265), f. 394v. For a list of patricians, headed by Agostino Barbaraigo and his nephew, killed in the battle, see BNM, MS It. VII. 364 (7934), ff. 41v–42.

39 Benedetti, *Ragguaglio*, f. B2–B2v ('sopra i pergoli diversi bei concerti'); further details are given in BNM. MS It. VII. 519 (8438), f. 333v, and BNM, MS It. VII. 553, p. 31, both of which mention the 'solenne musica', and BNM, MS It. VII. 73 (8265), f. 395v, which specifically refers to the 'tamburi, trombe squarciate, piffari e altri istromenti' that accompanied the firework displays.

40 BNM, MS It. VII. 73 (8265), f. 396–396v.

41 M. Sanudo, *I diarii*, ed. R. Fulin et al., 58 vols (Venice, 1879–1903), XVI, col. 38; XXIII, cols 488–9.

42 BNM, MS It. VII. 73 (8265), f. 396.

43 Benedetti, *Ragguaglio*, f. B2v.

44 E. H. Gombrich, 'Celebrations in Venice of the Holy League and of the Victory of Lepanto', in *Studies in Renaissance and Baroque Art Presented to Anthony Blunt on his Sixtieth Birthday* (London, 1967), p. 64.

45 J. Fletcher, 'Fine Art and Festivity in Renaissance Venice: The Artist's Part', in J. Onians, ed., *Essays on Art and Culture in Honour of E. H. Gombrich at 85* (London, 1994), pp. 133–5.

46 *Il vero e mirabilissimo apparato over conciero con il glorioso trionfo nell'inclita citta di Venetia* . . . (Venice, 1571); Gombrich, 'Celebrations in Venice', pp. 64–5.

47 D. Rosand, *Myths of Venice: The Figuration of a State* (Chapel Hill, NC, and London, 2001), pp. 41–6.

48 R. Pallucchini and P. Rossi, *Tintoretto: le opere sacre e profane*, 2 vols (Milan, 1982), cat A 29 and fig. 656.

49 F. Sansovino, *Venetia città nobilissima* . . . *descritta in XIIII libri* . . . *con aggiunta da D. Giustiniano Martinioni* (Venice, 1663), pp. 186–7, 362–4. See above pp. 116–20.

50 BNM, MS It. VII. 73 (8265), f. 396–396v; Benedetti, *Ragguaglio*, f. B3; BAV, MS Patetta 969, ff. 100v–101v.

51 Benedetti, *Ragguaglio*, f. B3v.

52 Benedetti, *Ragguaglio*, f. B4; also BCV, 1897 (unfoliated).

53 BNM, MS It. VII. 553, pp. 31–2.

54 Benedetti, *Ragguaglio*, f. B4; BCV, 1897 (unfoliated); R. Benedetti, *Le feste et trionfi fatti dalla serenissima signoria di Venetia nella felice venuta di Henrico III Christianissimo Re di Francia et III di Polonia* . . . (Venice, 1574); R. Toscano, Le feste et trionfi de li mercanti della seta per l'allegrezza della vittoria ottenuta contra turchi ([Venice, 1571]); Gombrich, 'Celebrations in Venice', pp. 66–7.

55 *Ordine et dechiaratione di tutta la mascherata fatta nella citta di Venetia la domenica di carnevale MDLXXI per la gloriosa vittoria contra turchi* (Venice, 1572), f. A2; Gombrich, 'Celebrations in Venice', pp. 67–8; A. Giurgea, 'Theatre of the Flesh: The Carnival of Venice and the Theatre of the World' (Ph.D. dissertation, University of California, Los Angeles, 1987), pp. 72–4. Since the *mascherata* was not organized by the state, there are no surviving accounts in official sources.

56 BCV, MS 1897 (unfoliated).

57 L. Puppi, *Andrea Palladio*, 2 vols (Milan, 1973), I, no. 115, pp. 397–8. For Palladio's dispute with the Scuola, see D. Chambers and B. Pullan, eds, *Venice: A Documentary History, 1450–1630* (Oxford, 1992), pp. 432–3.

58 D. Howard, *Jacopo Sansovino: Architecture and Patronage in Renaissance Venice* (New Haven, CT, and London, 1975), p. 110.

59 M. Tafuri, *Jacopo Sansovino e l'architettura del '500 a Venezia*, 2nd edn (Padua, 1972), pp. 12–19; Howard, *Jacopo Sansovino*, pp. 99–112; M. Morresi, *Jacopo Sansovino* (Milan, 2000), pp. 95–114.

60 R. S. MacKenney and P. Humfrey, 'The Venetian Trade Guilds as Patrons of Art in the Renaissance', *Burlington Magazine* CXXVIII (1986), p. 318; D. Howard, 'La Scuola Grande della Misericordia di Venezia', in G. Fabbri, ed., *La Scuola Grande della Misericordia di Venezia: storia e progetto* (Milan, 1999), pp. 33–5, and, for a different view, Morresi, *Jacopo Sansovino*, p. 113.

61 Patrizi in *De regno et regis institutione*, as quoted in Q. Skinner, *The Foundations of Modern Political Thought*, 2 vols (Cambridge, 1978), I, pp. 125–8.

62 Wilson, *The World in Venice*, pp. 65–9.

63 *Ordine et dechiaratione*, f. [A4]v; 'Let us sing, therefore let us sing; and from every heavenly quarter may thanks be given to the highest King of Heaven. And let praise and glory be given only to Him with sincere zeal, for the good that He has imparted to us.'

64 A. Gabrieli, *Madrigali et ricercari a quattro voci* (Venice, 1589). The identification of Gabrieli's music with the *mascherata* is made in A. Einstein, *The Italian Madrigal*, 3 vols (Princeton, NJ, 1949), II, pp. 523–5.

65 P. G. Molmenti, *La storia di Venezia nella vita privata dalle origini alla caduta della Repubblica*, 3 vols, 7th edn (Trieste, 1973), pp. 55–84, 287–328; G. Tassini, *Feste, spettacoli, divertimenti e piaceri degli antichi veneziani*, 2nd edn (Venice, 1961), pp. 23–8, 35–40, 64–9, 122–7; B. Tamassia Mazzarotto, *Le feste veneziane, i giochi popolari, le ceremonie religiose e di governo*

(Florence, 1961), pp. 31–6, 103–25; E. Muir, *Civic Ritual in Renaissance Venice* (Princeton, NJ, 1981), pp. 156–81.

66 G. R. Michiel, *Le origini delle feste veneziane*, 6 vols (Milan, 1817), II, pp. 37–41; Tassini, *Feste, spettacoli*, p. 23; Tamassia Mazzarotto, *Le feste veneziane*, pp. 31–2; Muir, *Civic Ritual*, pp. 160–64; E. Muir, 'Manifestazioni e ceremonie nella Venezia di Andrea Gritti', in M. Tafuri, ed., *'Renovatio urbis': Venetia nell'età di Andrea Gritti, 1523–1538* (Rome, 1984), pp. 61–8.

67 *Canzon de San Martin, con la laude de i fortarioli da cantar per i putti* (Venice, 1579); see Quarti, *La battaglia di Lepanto*, p. 270. The text in the *Ordine et dechiaratione* reads: 'Putti siamo ò Gentildonne che con gnachere sonando se n'andiamo, e ancor cantando del turchesco stuolo infranto cari putti accorde il canto ne fe piu tanto romore!'

68 E. Lovarini, *Studi sul Ruzzante e la letteratura pavana*, ed. G. Folena (Padua, 1965), pp. 237–70.

69 Gombrich, 'Celebrations in Venice', p. 68; G. J. Van der Sman, 'Print Publishing in Venice in the Second Half of the Sixteenth Century', *Print Quarterly* XVII (2000), p. 246.

70 O. Toscanella, *Essortatione ai Cristiani contra il Turco* (Venice, 1572).

71 M. Brunetti, 'La crisi finale della Sacra Lega (1573)', in *Miscellanea in onore di Roberto Cessi* (Rome, 1958), II, pp. 147–9. Letter of Donà and Priuli, Madrid, 17 April 1573; see M. Brunetti and E. Vitale, eds, *La corrispondenza da Madrid dell'ambasciatore Leonardo Donà (1570–73)*, 2 vols (Venice and Rome, 1963), II, no. 262, at p. 680.

72 As in, for example, BNM, MS It. VII. 519, f. 335v. The separate peace is passed over in a few lines in most of the chronicles; cf. BNM, MS It. VII. 73 (8265), f. 400.

73 Wilson, *The World in Venice*, p. 143.

74 A. C. Hess, 'The Battle of Lepanto and its Place in Mediterranean History', *Past and Present* 57 (1972), pp. 62–5.

75 BNM, MS It. VII. 364 (7934), f. 60v.

76 Brunetti, 'La crisi finale della Sacra Lega (1573)', pp. 150–51. Letter from Donà and

Priuli, Madrid, 19 April 1573, in Brunetti and Vitale, eds, *La corrispondenza da Madrid*, no. 263.

77 ASF, Arch. Med. del Principato, f. 2982; letter of Orazio Urbani, 2 May 1573, to the grand duke of Tuscany.

78 G. Turba, *Venetianische Depeschen vom Kaiserhof*, 3 vols (Vienna, 1889–96), III, p. 524; letter of 13 April 1573.

CHAPTER SEVEN

1 T. Porcacchi, *Le attioni d'Arrigo terzo re di Francia et quarto di Polonia descritte in dialogo . . .* (Venice, 1574), f. 22v; BNM, MS It. VII. 553, pp. 56–7; BNM, MS It. VII. 2585 (*olim* Philipps 2514), p. 254.

2 The major studies are P. De Nolhac and A. Solerti, *Il viaggio in Italia di Enrico III re di Francia e le feste a Venezia, Ferrara, Mantova e Torino* (Turin, 1890); M. M. McGowan et al., 'The Festivals for Henry III in Cracow, Venice, Orléans and Rouen', in R. Mulryne, H. Watanabe-O'Kelly and M. Shewring, eds, *Europa Triumphans: Court and Civic Festivals in Early Modern Europe*, 2 vols (Aldershot, 2004), I, pp. 103–215; and A. L. Bellina, 'A suon di musica da Cracovia a Lione: i trionfi del cristianissimo Enrico III', in U. Artioli and C. Grazioli, eds, *I Gonzaga e l'Impero: itinerari dello spettacolo* (Florence, 2005), pp. 81–106.

3 *La entrata che fece in Vinegia l'Illustrissimo et Eccellentissimo S. Duca Alfonso II Estense, Duca V. di Ferrara* (Venice, 1562), ff. 3v–4; C. Zio, *La solennissima entrata dell'illustrissimo & eccellentissimo signor Duca di Ferrara, nella citta di Venetia, cominciando dalla partita di sua eccellenza da Ferrara, per infino al suo ritorno* (Bologna, 1562), f. A3.

4 M. Casini, *I gesti del principe: la festa politica a Firenze e Venezia in età rinascimentale* (Venice, 1996), pp. 207–8.

5 BNM, MS It. VII. 393 (8647), unfoliated.

6 De Nolhac and Solerti, *Il viaggio in Italia di Enrico III*, pp. 228–9, after BCV 2043 (già Cicogna 1209), p. 87. J. Fletcher, 'Fine Art and Festivity in Renaissance Venice:

The Artist's Part', in J. Onians, ed., *Essays on Art and Culture in Honour of E. H. Gombrich at 85* (London, 1994), p. 136.

7 N. Ivanoff, 'Henri III a Venise', *Gazette des Beaux-Arts* LXXX (1972), p. 316.

8 ASF, Arch. Med. del Principato, 2983. Letter of Urbani to the grand duke of Tuscany, 7 July 1574.

9 De Nolhac and Solerti, *Il viaggio in Italia di Enrico III*, pp. 230–31; Porcacchi, *Le attioni*, f. 27v. For the Gelosi, see (the still valuable account) in K. M. Lea, *Italian Popular Comedy: A Study in the Commedia dell'arte, 1560–1620, with Special Reference to the English Stage*, 2 vols (Oxford, 1934), I, pp. 261–9.

10 *Le allegrezze et solennita fatta in Cracovia citta principale del regno di Polonia . . .* ([Venice, 1574]), f. A4.

11 E. Muir, *Mad Blood Stirring: Vendetta and Factions in Friuli during the Renaissance* (Baltimore, MD, and London, 1993).

12 For Henry's trip through Friuli and the Veneto, see in particular Porcacchi, *Le attioni d'Arrigo terzo*; N. Lucangeli da Bevagna, *Successi del viaggio d'Henrico III christianiss[i]mo re di Francia, e di Polonia, dalla sua partita di Cracovia fino all'arrivo in Turino* (Venice, 1574); BNM, MS It. VII. 393 (8647); BNM, MS It. VII. 73 (8265), ff. 403–8.

13 *DBI*, 'Alfonso d'Este'.

14 Porcacchi, *Le attioni d'Arrigo terzo*, f. 19.

15 *I gran trionfi fatti nella nobil città di Treviso nella venuta del Christianissimo Re di Francia & di Polonia Henrico Terzo* (Venice, 1574); Lucangeli da Bevagna, *Successi del viaggio*, pp. 27–9; G. Manzini, *Il gloriosissimo apparato fatto dalla serenissima republica venetiana per la venuta, per la dimora, & per la partenza del christianissimo Enrico III re di Francia et di Polonia* (Venice, 1574), ff. A3v–A4; Porcacchi, *Le attioni d'Arrigo terzo*, f. 20.

16 M. M. McGowan, 'Festivals and the Arts in Henry III's Journey from Poland to France', in Mulryne, Watanabe-O'Kelly and Shewring, eds, *Europa Triumphans*, pp. 125–6.

17 De Nolhac and Solerti, *Il viaggio in Italia di Henrico III*, after AS Mod., Avviso e

notizie dall'estero, which includes a long description of the entry; cf. also BNM, MS It. VII. 73, f. 404–404v.

18 BNM, MS It. VII. 73, f. 404.

19 They are listed by name in BNM, MS It. VII. 393 (8647), unfoliated.

20 BNM, MS It. VII. 73, f. 404, specifies trumpets and drums.

21 BNM, MS It. VII. 142, p. 313.

22 Porcacchi, Le attioni d'Arrigo terzo, f. 21v: 'una dolcissima & rara musica, tanto di voci humane quanto di variati instrumenti'. According to BNM. MS It. VII. 393 (8647), unfoliated, Antonio Moro and Vincenzo Erizzo had been placed in charge of 'suoni e strepiti'.

23 M. Della Croce, L'historia della publica et famosa entrata in Venegia del serenissimo Henrico III di Francia et Polonia… (Venice, 1574), p. 12; for a discussion of its authorship, see W. Wolters, 'Le architetture erette al lido per l'ingresso di Enrico III a Venezia nel 1574', Bolletino del centro internazionale di studi di architettura Andrea Palladio XXI (1979), pp. 280–88. I follow the most recent discussion, in T. E. Cooper, Palladio's Venice (New Haven and London, 2005), pp. 218–27, in accepting the two structures as Palladio's work.

24 E. Verheyen, 'The Triumphal Arch on the Lido: On the Reliability of Eyewitness Accounts', in K. L. Selig and E. Sears, eds, The Verbal and the Visual: Essays in Honor of William Sebastian Heckscher (New York, 1990), pp. 214–20.

25 'Henrico III. Franciae atque Poloniae Regi Christianis. & invictiss. Christianae religionis acerrimo propugnatori advenienti, Venetorum Resp. ad veteris benevolentiae, atquae observantiae declarationem', reported in most accounts; cf. Della Croce, L'historia della publica et famosa entrata, p. 13; Manzini, Il gloriosissimo apparato, f. A4; Porcacchi, Le attioni d'Arrigo terzo, f. 24.

26 Verheyen, 'The Triumphal Arch on the Lido', pp. 220–21, for a caution.

27 Della Croce, L'historia della publica et famosa entrata, pp. 13–14. For the arch, see Ivanoff, 'Henri III a Venise', pp. 314–15.

28 F. Yates, The Valois Tapestries, 2nd edn (London, 1975), pp. 67–72.

29 R. Benedetti, Le feste et trionfi fatti dalla serenissima signoria di Venetia nella felice venuta di Henrico III Christianissimo Re di Francia et III di Polonia… (Venice, 1574), f. 6; Della Croce, L'historia della publica et famosa entrata, pp. 14–15.

30 Zio, La solenissima entrata, f. A2v; La entrata che fece in Vinegia, ff. 2v–3.

31 Fletcher, 'Fine Art and Festivity', pp. 136–7.

32 Porcacchi, Le attioni d'Arrigo terzo, f. 23v.

33 Lucangeli da Bevagna, Successi del viaggio, p. 31: 'da eccellentissimi musici il Te Deum laudamus & altre lodi'; BCV, Mariegola 102 (già Cicogna 384), f. 31v: 'li musici cantorno il Te Deum laudamus'.

34 R. Benedetti, I trionfi e le gran feste fatte dalla Serenissima Signoria di Venetia nella venuta del Christianissimo, et invitissimo Henrico III di Francia et di Polonia (Venice, 1574), f. 31v.

35 Benedetti, Le feste et trionfi fatti (1574), f. 6.

36 'Henrico III. Franciae & Poloniae Regi Optimo atque fortissimo, hospiti incomparabili, Venetorum Respub. ob eius adventum foelicissimum'; Della Croce, L'historia della publica et famosa entrata, p. 13. The inscription is clearly legible in Domenico Zenoi's engraving. See also Benedetti, Le feste et trionfi fatti (1574), f. 4v.

37 Della Croce, L'historia della publica et famosa entrata, p. 14.

38 Benedetti, I trionfi, f. 32; Benedetti, Le feste e fatti (1574), f. 6v.

39 The text is reported in Lucangeli da Bevagna, Successi del viaggio, p. 31; the music does not survive.

40 BCV, MS Mariegola 102 (già Cicogna 384), f. 31–31v.

41 H. T. van Veen, 'Republicanism in the Visual Propaganda of Cosimo I de' Medici', Journal of the Warburg and Courtauld Institutes LV (1992), pp. 200–02; R. Scorza, 'Vincenzo Borghini and Invenzione: The Florentine Apparato of 1565', Journal of the Warburg and Courtauld Institutes XLIV (1981), pp. 57–75; R. Scorza, 'A Florentine Sketchbook: Architecture, Apparati and the Accademia del Disegno',

Journal of the Warburg and Courtauld Institutes LIV (1991), pp. 172–85, and the literature cited there.

42 *La entrata che fece in Vinegia*, ff. 2v–3.

43 M. Savorgnano, *La venuta della serenissima Bona Sforza et d'Aragona reina di Polonia et duchessa di Bari nella magnifica citta di Padova a ventisette di marzo . . .* (Venice, 1556), f. A4. See also A. Bassano, *Dichiaratione dell'arco fatto in Padova nella venuta della serenissima reina Bona di Polonia* (Padua, 1556), and the discussion in L. Cini, 'Passaggio della regina Bona Sforza per Padova nell'anno 1556', in *Relazioni tra Padova e la Polonia: studi in onore dell'Università di Cracovia nel VI centenario della sua fondazione* (Padua, 1964), pp. 27–65.

44 *DA* XXVII, pp. 757–63 (Davies and Hemsoll); P. Davies and D. Hemsoll, *Michele Sanmicheli* (Milan, 2004), pp. 261–9, at pp. 265–6.

45 M. L. S. Todro, 'The First Temporary Triumphal Arch in Venice (1557)', in R. Mulryne and E. Goldring, eds, *Court Festivals of the European Renaissance: Art, Politics and Performance* (Aldershot, 2002), pp. 335–62.

46 Wolters, 'Le architetture', p. 279; B. Wilson, ' "Il bel sesso, e l'austero Senato": The Coronation of Dogaressa Morosina Morosini Grimani', *Renaissance Quarterly* LII (1999), pp. 73–139.

47 Wolters, 'Le architetture', p. 287.

48 B. Boucher, *Andrea Palladio: The Architect in his Time* (New York, 1994), pp. 216–29, especially p. 224.

49 D. Howard, *Jacopo Sansovino: Architecture and Patronage in Renaissance Venice* (New Haven, CT, and London, 1975), p. 34.

50 Della Croce, *L'historia della publica et famosa entrata*, p. 12.

51 Porcacchi, *Le attioni d'Arrigo terzo*, f. 28v.

52 Lucangeli da Bevagna, *Successi del viaggio*, p. 32.

53 BCV, 1897 (unfoliated).

54 De Nolhac and Solerti, *Il viaggio in Italia di Enrico III*, p. 102.

55 R. S. MacKenney, *Tradesmen and Traders: The World of the Guilds in Venice and Europe, c.1250–c.1650* (London and Sydney, 1987), p. 144.

56 Porcacchi, *Le attioni d'Arrigo terzo*, f. 24v.

57 Della Croce, *L'historia della publica et famosa entrata*, pp. 7–11.

58 Porcacchi, *Le attioni d'Arrigo terzo*, ff. 25–25v.

59 *Le entrata che fece in Vinegia*, f. 3v; Zio, *La solenissima entrata*, f. A3.

60 BCV, MS Mariegola 102 (già Cicogna 384), ff. 29v–32.

61 De Nolhac and Solerti, *Il viaggio in Italia di Enrico III*, pp. 34–6.

62 Benedetti, *Le feste et trionfi fatti* (1574), f. 5v.

63 Anonymous chronicle in BCV, MS 1897 (unfoliated) (già Cicogna 283), cited in De Nolhac and Solerti, *Il viaggio in Italia di Enrico III*, p. 106, n. 2.

64 Fletcher, 'Fine Art and Festivity', p. 136.

65 C. Dorron, *Discours des choses mémorables faittes à l'entrée du Roy de France et de Pologne en la ville de Venize* (Lyons, 1574); BNM, MS It. VII. 553, p. 59. See also De Nolhac and Solerti, *Il viaggio in Italia di Enrico III*, p. 108, n. 2

66 Benedetti, *Le feste et trionfi fatti* (1574), f. 7; Porcacchi, *Le attioni d'Arrigo terzo*, f. 33–33v.

67 Porcacchi, *Le attioni d'Arrigo terzo*, f. 26v: 'la vaghezza dei Vinitiani quella d'ogni altro in sentir la dolcezza delle musiche, fatte la state in gondola per lo fresco'.

68 I. Palombo-Fossati, 'L'interno della casa dell'artigiano e dell'artista nella Venezia del Cinquecento', *Studi veneziani* VIII (1984), pp. 109–53, particularly pp. 126–7; W. Brulez, *Marchands flamands a Venise I (1568–1605)* (Brussels and Rome, 1965), pp. 579–82, 630–43; P. F. Brown, *Private Lives in Renaissance Venice* (New Haven and London, 2004), pp. 123–25 and now Flora Dennis's essay about music and instruments in M. Ajmar-Wallheim and F. Dennis, eds, *At Home in Renaissance Italy* (London, 2006), pp. 228–43.

69 C. Vecellio, *De gli habiti antichi e moderni di tutto il mondo* (Venice, 1590), ff. 122–123v. For a discussion of Vecellio and other primary sources see D. Romano, 'The Gondola as a Marker of Station in Venetian Society', *Renaissance Studies* VIII (1994), pp. 359–74.

70 BNM, MS It. VII. 73, f. 406.

71 Henry and his retainers occupied both Ca'
Foscari and the two adjoining Giustiniani
palaces, which made it easy to pass from
one to the other; BNM, MS It. VII. 2585
(*olim* Philipps 2514), p. 254. Apparently, all
three had been prepared at public expense
(see BNM, MS It. VII. 73 (8265), f. 405v).

72 Benedetti, *Le feste et trionfi fatti* (1574),
p. 5; Porcacchi, *Le attioni d'Arrigo terzo*,
p. 27.

73 A. Gabrieli and G. Gabrieli, *Concerti
concinenti musica di chiesa*. See D. Rosand,
'Music in the Myth of Venice', *Renaissance
Quarterly* XXX (1977), pp. 530–31;
D. Nutter, 'The Italian Polyphonic Dia-
logue of the Sixteenth Century', 2 vols
(Ph.D. dissertation, University of Not-
tingham, 1978), I, pp. 225–7, 530–31;
Bryant, 'Andrea Gabrieli e la musica di
stato', p. 38; D. Nutter, 'A Tragedy for
Henry III of France, Venice, 1574', in A.
Morragh et al., eds, *Renaissance Studies in
Honor of Craig Hugh Smyth*, 2 vols (Flo-
rence, 1985), I, p. 596; L. Stras, '"Onde
havrà'l mond'esempio et vera historia":
Musical Echoes of Henri III's Progress
through Italy', *Acta musicologica* LXXII
(2000), pp. 19–21.

74 First noted in F. Caffi, *Storia della musica
sacra nella già cappella ducale di S. Marco
dal 1318 al 1797*, 2 vols (Venice, 1854–5),
I, p. 171.

75 BNM, MS It. VII. 73, f. 406; Benedetti,
Le feste et trionfi fatti (1574), f. 6.

76 BNM MS It. VII. 73, f. 406v; Benedetti,
Le feste et trionfi fatti (1574), ff. 6v–7.

77 As in 1562; cf. *La entrata che fece in
Vinegia*, ff. 5v–6, and Zio, *La solenissima
entrata*, f. A3v.

78 Benedetti, *Le feste et trionfi fatti* (1574),
p. 8: 'fu cantato musicalmente sonandosi
i due organi il Te Deum'; BNM, MS It. VII.
73, f. 406v: 'fu cantato il Te Deum musicalmente'. Della Croce, *L'historia della
publica et famosa entrata*, p. 20: 'si canto
musicalmente suonando i due organi il Te
Deum'; Lucangeli da Bevagna, *Successi del
viaggio*, pp. 35–6: 'et cantosi il Te Deum
laudamus, & altre catholiche lodi, co'l
suono dell'uno, e l'altro organo'. Cf. BNM,

MS It. VII. 553, p. 60: 'da eccellentissimi
musici fu cantato con tutti dui li organi il
Te Deum'.

79 Lucangeli da Bevagna, *Successi del viaggio*,
pp. 35–6. Porcacchi, *Le attioni d'Arrigo
terzo*, ff. 27v–32, mentions that the two
organists were Andrea Gabrieli and
Claudio Merulo, and that the choir was
under the direction of Zarlino.

80 Details in BNM, MS It. VII. 73, f. 406–
406v.

81 The complete text, issued as a libretto presumably for those present to have in their
hands, is also reported in full in Porcacchi,
Le attioni d'Arrigo terzo, ff. 29–32.

82 Benedetti, *I trionfi*, f. 33v.

83 C. Dorron, *Narratio rerum memorabilium
. . .* (Venice, 1574), pp. 21–2.

84 Porcacchi, *Le attioni d'Arrigo terzo*, f. 28v:
'Partito son da l'onde di Nettuno, / Dove
ho lasciato li marini armenti; / E per veder
si gloriose pompe / Era salito sopra questi
liti . . .'.

85 See J. Haar, 'Arie per cantar stanze ariotesche', in M. A. Balsano, ed., *L'Ariosto
la musica, i musicisti: quattro studi e sette
madrigali ariosteschi* (Florence, 1981),
pp. 31–46.

86 R. A. Edwards, 'Claudio Merulo: Servant
of the State and Musical Entrepreneur in
Later Sixteenth-century Venice' (Ph.D.
dissertation, Princeton University, 1990),
pp. 220–23; R. Edwards, 'Claudio Metulo,
l'altro gioiello nella contona di Correggio',
in M. Capra, ed., *A Messor Claudio,
musico, ne arti molteplici di Claudio Menilo
da Correggio (1533–1604) tra Venezia e
Parma* (Venice, 2006), pp. 15–29.

87 For the text, see C. Frangipane, *Tragedia
. . . al christianissimo et invitissimo Henrico
III Re di Francia e di Polonia recitata nella
sala del gran consiglio di Venetia* (Venice,
1574), and Porcacchi, *Le attioni d'Arrigo
terzo*, ff. 28v–32. For further discussion of
the music (now lost), see Nutter, 'A
Tragedy for Henry III of France, Venice',
pp. 591–611, at p. 603, and Edwards,
'Claudio Merulo', pp. 223–8.

88 The significance of Frangipane's *Tragedia*
and Merulo's music was first recognized by
Alfred Einstein: see *The Italian Madrigal*,

3 vols (Princeton, NJ, 1949), II, pp. 549–50. See also Nutter, 'A Tragedy for Henry III of France, Venice', pp. 603, 605.

89 For an overview, see N. Pirrotta and E. Povoledo, *Music and Theatre from Poliziano to Monteverdi*, trans. K. Eales (Cambridge, 1982), pp. 173–236.

90 Frangipane, *Tragedia*, f. B3v; Nutter, 'A Tragedy for Henry III of France, Venice', p. 603.

91 Lucangeli da Bevagna, *Successi del viaggio,* p. 36.

92 R. C. Davis, *Shipbuilders of the Venetian Arsenal: Workers and Workplace in the Preindustrial City* (Baltimore, MD, 1991), pp. 4, 80; De Nolhac and Solerti, *Il viaggio in Italia di Enrico III*, p. 143,

93 Porcacchi, *Le attioni d'Arrigo terzo*, f. 34: 'soave concerti di musica'.

94 L. Venturi, 'Le compagnie della calza (sec. XV–XVI)', *Nuovo archivio veneto* XVI (1908), pp. 161–221; XVII (1909), pp. 140–233; E. Muir, *Civic Ritual in Renaissance Venice* (Princeton, NJ, 1981), pp. 167–73.

95 Mometto, '"Vizi privati, pubbliche virtù"', and, for an earlier period, M. Newett, 'The Sumptuary Laws of Venice in the Fourteenth and Fifteenth Centuries', in F. Tout and J. Tait, eds, *Historical Essays by Members of the Owens College, Manchester* (London, 1902), pp. 245–78.

96 As in, for example, BNM, MS It. VII. 142, p. 313.

97 Benedetti, *Le feste et trionfi fatti* (1574), p. 8. For a discussion, see M. Padoan, 'I balli per Enrico III re di Francia durante il suo viaggio in Italia nel 1574', *Quaderni di Palazzo Te* I (1994), pp. 71–7.

98 McGowan, 'Festivals and the Arts', pp. 122–3.

99 Benedetti, *Le feste et trionfi fatti* (1574), p. 9; Porcacchi, *Le attioni d'Arrigo terzo*, ff. 37v–38.

100 Davis, *Shipbuilders*, pp. 135–49; R. C. Davis, *The War of the Fists: Popular Culture and Public Violence in Late Renaissance Venice* (Oxford, 1994), particularly pp. 19–46; R. C. Davis, 'The Spectacle Almost Fit for a King: Venice's Guerra de' canne of 26 July 1574', in E. E. Kittell and T. F. Madden, eds, *Medieval and Renaissance*

Venice (Urbana and Chicago, IL, 1999), pp. 181–212.

101 Davis, *The War of the Fists*, pp. 44–5; for Giovedì Grasso, see G. Tassini, *Feste, spettacoli, divertimenti e piaceri degli antichi veneziani*, 2nd edn (Venice, 1961), pp. 23–8, 35–40, 64–9, 122–7; G. Tamassia Mazzarotto, *Le feste veneziane, i giochi popolari, le ceremonie religiose e di governo* (Florence, 1961), pp. 31–6, 103–25; Muir, *Civic Ritual*, pp. 156–81, and above, pp. 110–12.

102 *La entrata che fece in Vinegia*, f. 7v.

103 De Nolhac and Solerti, *Il viaggio in Italia di Enrico III*, p. 151.

104 BNM, MS It. VII. 142, p. 314.

105 BCV, MS Cicogna 3161, ff. 2–4.

106 For a detailed account, see Davis, 'The Spectacle', pp. 201–5.

107 Lucangeli da Bevagna, *Successi del viaggio,* p. 33.

108 BCV 3161/45; De Nolhac and Solerti, *Il viaggio in Italia di Enrico III*, p. 153; Davis, *The War of the Fists*, p. 47.

109 Porcacchi, *Le attioni d'Arrigo terzo*, ff. 32–3; Benedetti, *Le feste et trionfi fatti*, f. 6v.

110 The purchases are recorded in Paris, Bibliothèque nationale, MS Fr. 3321, f. 20v; see De Nolhac and Solerti, *Il viaggio in Italia di Enrico III*, pp. 250–51

111 BNM, MS It. VII. 142, p. 314.

112 G. Soranzo, 'Come fu data e come fu accolta a Venezia la notizia della "S.te Barthélemy"', in *Miscellanea in onore di Roberto Cessi* (Rome, 1958), II, pp. 129–35.

113 Soranzo, 'Come fu data', p. 136.

114 Porcacchi, *Le attioni d'Arrigo terzo*, ff. 3v–4.

115 Benedetti, *Le feste et trionfi fatti*, f. A3v.

116 Porcacchi, *Le attioni d'Arrigo terzo*, ff. 3v–4.

117 Savorgnano, La *venuta della serenissima Bona Sforza*, f. Biiiv.

CHAPTER EIGHT

1 Details from ASV, Secreta, Materie miste notabili, reg. 95, f. 151, and F. Stabile, *Brevis quaedam defensio contra nonnullos*

asserentes pudendorum inflammationem non esse pestis signum (Venice, 1576); see R. Palmer, 'The Control of Plague in Venice and Northern Italy' (Ph.D. dissertation, University of Kent at Canterbury, 1978), p. 211.

2 Benedetti, 'Successo della peste l'anno 1576' in BCV, MS Cicogna 3682, f. [1]v (the manuscript is unfoliated); R. Benedetti and M. Lumina, *Raguaglio minutissimo del successo della peste di Venetia...* (Tivoli, 1577), f. A2; F. Gaeta et al., eds, *Nunziature di Venezia* (Rome, 1958–), XI, p. 315.

3 BNM, MS It. VII. 553, p. 66.

4 A. Canobbio, *Il successo della peste occorsa in Padova l'anno MDLXXVI* (Venice, 1577), ff. 1v–3v; BNM, MS It. VII. 73, f. 411.

5 A. Raimondo, *Discorso quale chiaramente si conosce la viva et vera cagione, che ha generato le fiere infermità, che tanto hanno molestato l'anno 1575, e tanto il 1576 acerbamente molestano il popolo de l'invittissima città di Venetia...* (Padua, 1586), f. [B3].

6 ASF (Archiv. Med. del Principato), f. 2983; letter of Orazio Urbani, 15 November 1575, to the grand duke of Tuscany.

7 BCV, MS 3682, f. [8]; Palmer, 'The Control of Plague in Venice and Northern Italy', p. 195.

8 Benedetti and Lumina, *Raguaglio*, f. A2v; BNM, MS Ital. VII. 194 (8493), ff. 164ff.

9 Palmer, 'The Control of Plague in Venice and Northern Italy', pp. 74–5; R. Palmer, 'L'azione della Repubblica di Venezia nel controllo della peste: lo sviluppo della politica governativa', in *Venezia e la peste, 1348–1797* (Venice, 1980), pp. 108–9; for the *capitolare* of 1541, which summarizes the history, legislation and powers of the *sanità*, see ASV, Provveditori alla Sanità, Reg. 2, ff. 1–45, 101–11.

10 P. Preto, 'Le grandi pesti dell'età moderna, 1575–77 e 1630–31', in *Venezia e la peste*, p. 123.

11 Palmer, 'The Control of Plague in Venice and Northern Italy', pp. 238–9.

12 Gaeta et al., eds., *Nunziature*, XI, p. 443 (October 1575); XI, p. 465 (November 1575).

13 Canobbio, *Il successo della peste*, f. 4.

14 BNM, MS It. VII. 73, f. 412.

15 P. Preto, 'La società veneta e le grandi epidemie di peste', in G. Arnaldi and M. Stocchi, eds, *Storia della cultura veneta*, 6 vols in 10 parts (Vicenza, 1976–87), IV/2, pp. 378–9. For the view that the epidemic could not be the plague because only the lower orders had been affected, see also the written opinion of the Paduan doctors Gerolamo Mercuriale and Girolamo Capodivacca in BNM, MS Ital. VII. 806 (9557).

16 Palmer, 'The Control of Plague in Venice and Northern Italy', pp. 238–44.

17 A. Morosini, *Historiae venetae* in *Istorici delle cose veneziane* VI (Venice, 1719), p. 624.

18 ASF (Archiv. Med. del Principato), letter of Orazio Urbani, 2 June 1575, to the grand duke of Tuscany.

19 See, for example, BNM, MS It. VII. 364 (7934), ff. 68v–69.

20 P. Preto, *Peste e società a Venezia, 1576*, 2nd edn (Vicenza, 1984), p. 112, and the literature cited there. The figures on which all arguments about the mortality rate are based are those given by Cornelio Morello, *scrivan* of the *Sanità* (copies of his original text, which is in ASV, Secreta, Materie miste notabili, reg. 95, f. 164, are in BNM, MS It. VII 194 [8493], and BCV, MS. Cicogna 1547). The statistic for the plague of 1630–31 is taken from D. Beltrami, *Storia della popolazione di Venezia dalla fine del secolo XVI alla caduta della repubblica* (Padua, 1954), p. 62. See also Palmer, 'The Control of Plague in Venice and Northern Italy', pp. 277–8.

21 The episode of the Paduan doctors and the debate over whether or not the epidemic was the true plague is described in BCV, MS Cicogna 3682, ff. [3]v–[4]v; Benedetti and Lumina, *Raguaglio*, f. A3v; BNM, MS It. VII. 194 (8493); and BNM, MS It. VII. 553, pp. 66–7, among other places; see also Preto, *Peste e società a Venezia*, p. 49, and Palmer, 'The Control of Plague in Venice and Northern Italy', pp. 243–71.

22 BCV, MS Donà delle Rose 181/14, together with other broadsheets relating to the plague; Preto, *Peste e società a Venezia*, pp. 90–97.

23 BCV, MS Cicogna 3682, f. [12]v; Benedetti and Lumina, *Raguaglio*, f. A8–A8v.

24 Benedetti and Lumina, *Raguaglio*, f. 5v.

25 *Venezia e la peste*, p. 145.

26 BNM, MS It. VII. 142, p. 318; BNM, MS It. VII. 73, f. 413–413v

27 BCV, MS 3682, f. [8]; F. Sansovino, *Venetia città nobilissima et singolare descritta in XIV libri* (Venice, 1581), f. 85. For the arrangements, see ASV, Secreta, Materie miste notabili, reg. 95, ff. 56v, 153v–155.

28 Palmer, 'The Control of Plague in Venice and Northern Italy', p. 195.

29 A copy is preserved in BCV, MS Donà Delle Rose 181/21. See also BCV, MS Cicogna 3682, ff. [4]v–[5].

30 Canobbio, *Il successo della peste*, f. 4.

31 BCV, MS Cicogna 3682, f. [9]v.

32 Benedetti and Lumina, *Raguaglio*, f. A4v.

33 BNM, MS It. VII. 2585 (*olim* Philipps 2514), p. [256].

34 BCV, MS Cicogna 3682, f. [14].

35 BNM, MS It. VII. 142, pp. 318–19.

36 Benedetti and Lumina, *Raguaglio*, f. B–Bv; for a printed copy of the Senate's decree see BCV, MS Donà Delle Rose 181/29. The figures are taken from Doge Leonardo Donà's notes of his experiences during the plague in BCV, MS Donà delle rose 465, fasc. 5, f. [1].

37 ASV, Senato Terra, Reg. 51, f. 125; *Venezia e la peste*, p. 136.

38 Palmer, 'The Control of Plague in Venice and Northern Italy', pp. 202–3.

39 P. Allerston, 'The Market in Second-Hand Clothes and Furnishings in Venice, c. 1500–c. 1650' (Ph.D. dissertation, European University Institute, 1996), chapter 6; S. K. Cohn, *The Black Death Transformed: Disease and Culture in Early Renaissance Europe* (London, 2002), p. 113.

40 For a copy of the printed regulations, see BCV, MS Donà Delle Rose 181/22.

41 BCV, MS Cicogna 3682, ff. [17]v–[18].

42 BCV, MS Cicogna 3682, ff. [5]v–[7]v. The English translation (by Richard Palmer) is from D. Chambers and B. Pullan, eds, *Venice: A Documentary History, 1450–1630* (Oxford, 1992), pp. 117–19.

43 Palmer, 'The Control of Plague in Venice and Northern Italy', pp. 280–84.

44 ASV, Sant'Uffizio, Processi b. 39; *Venezia e la peste*, p. 137.

45 Sansovino, *Venetia città nobilissima* (1581), f. 85; BNM, MS It. VII. 73, f. 413v.

46 BNM, MS It. VII. 2585 (*olim* Phillips 2514), p. [256].

47 Cohn, *The Black Death Transformed*, pp. 48–9, 114–19.

48 BCV, MS Donà delle Rose 181.

49 A. da Castello, *Liber sacerdotalis* (Venice, 1523), ff. 295–6; *Officium Hebdomadae Sanctae . . .* (Venice, 1722), ff. 225v–228.

50 *Missale praedicatorum nuper impressum ac emendatum cum multis missis orationibus* (Venice, 1504), ff. 282v–283v.

51 BNM, MS It, VII. 8636, f. 437v: 'Almighty God, King of Glory, [we pray you] deliver us from this plague, in the name of your Son who died for us, have mercy upon us.'

52 For the general phenomenon, see S. Tramontin, 'Influsso orientale nel culto dei santi a Venezia fino al secolo XV', in A. Pertusi, ed., *Venezia e il Levante fino al secolo XV*, 3 vols (Florence, 1983), I, pp. 817–20.

53 Tiepolo, *Trattato dell'imagine della Gloriosa Vergine dipinta da San Luca. Conservata gia molti secoli nella Ducal Chiesa di San Marco della Citta di Venetia* (Venice, 1618) provides a history of the icon.

54 M. Sanudo, *I diarii*, ed. R. Fulin et al., 58 vols (Venice, 1879–1903), XXI, col. 130.

55 See *Supplicationes. Ad Sanctissimam Verginem Mariam. Tempore belli. Secondum consuetudinem Ducalis Basilicae S; Marci Venetiarum* (Venice, 1695); for the early seventeenth-century rehabilitation of the *Madonna Nicopeia*, see below, pp. 322–3.

56 *Officium Hebdomadae Sanctae secundum consuetudem Ducalis Ecclesiae S. Marci Venetiarum, a Dominica Palmarum usque ad Diem Paschae inclusive . . .* (Venice, 1722), pp. 383–8.

57 The three days of processions and the Senate vote of 4 September are reported in ASV Collegio, Ceremoniali I, ff. XLVIIV–XLVIIIV. Excerpts are given in W. Timofiewitsch, *La chiesa del Redentore* (Vicenza, 1969), app. III, nos 1–2 ,and also in G. Zorzi, *Le chiese e i ponti di Andrea Palladio* (Vicenza, 1967), pp. 130–31, nos 1–2.

58 BNM, MS It. VII. 142, p. 319; BNM, MS It. VII. 553, p. 80.

59 ASV Collegio, Ceremoniali I, ff. XLVIII–XLVIIIv.

60 'Nativitas tua, dei genetrix virgo, gaudium annunciavit universo mundo: Ex te enim ortus est sol iustitiae, Christus, Deus noster: Qui solvens maledictionem dedit benedictionem, et confundens mortem donavit nobis sempiternam.' For the liturgy, see G. Cattin, *Musica e liturgia a San Marco: testi e melodie per la liturgia delle ore dal XII al XVII secolo*, 4 vols (Venice, 1990–92), pp. 114–15. As noted there, the same text occurs as a responsory in the second nocturn at matins on the same day, when it would have been chanted. The music is in A. Gabrieli and G. Gabrieli, *Concerti . . .* (Venice, 1587).

61 The general appropriateness of the text for the plague years is noted in D. Bryant, 'Liturgy, Ceremonial and Sacred Music in Venice at the Time of the Counter-Reformation', 2 vols (Ph.D. dissertation, University of London, 1981), I, p. 56.

62 BNM, MS It. VII. 365 (7934), f. 60.

63 L. Sinding-Larsen, *Christ in the Council Hall: Studies in the Religious Iconography of the Venetian Republic* (Rome, 1974), p. 1.

64 See the detailed accounts in ASV Collegio, Ceremoniali I, f. LII–LIIv; BNM, MS It. VII. 393 (8647), unfoliated; BNM, MS It. VII. 519, f. 336; BNM, MS It. VII. 553, pp. 51–4; ASF, Arch. Med. del Principato 2983, letters of Urbani to the grand duke of Tuscany, 12 May and 26 May 1574.

65 G. Zorzi, 'Nuove rivelazioni sulla ricostruzione delle salle del piano nobile del Palazzo Ducale di Venezia dopo l'incendio dell'11 maggio 1574, *Arte veneta* VII (1953), pp. 123–51, particularly pp. 124–41.

66 ASV Collegio, Ceremoniali I, ff. LXIVv–lxvv.

67 BNM, MS It VII. 142, p. 321.

68 BNM, MS It. VII. 364 (7934), ff. 71v–72.

69 G. Zorzi, 'Il contributo di Andrea Palladio e di Francesco Zamberlan al restauro del Palazzo Ducale di Venezia dopo l'incendio del 20 dicembre 1577', *Atti dell'Istituto Veneto di Scienze, Lettere ed Arti* CXV (1956–7), pp. 15–18; BNM, MS It. VII. 519, f. 337–337v.

CHAPTER NINE

1 V. Scholderer, 'Printing at Venice to the End of 1481', in Scholderer, *Fifty Essays in Fifteenth- and Sixteenth-century Bibliography* (Amsterdam, 1966), pp. 74–89; N. Pozza, 'L'editoria veneziana da Giovanni da Spira ad Aldo Manuzio: i centri editoriali di terraferma', in G. Arnaldi and M. Stocchi, eds, *Storia della cultura veneta*, 6 vols in 10 parts (Vicenza, 1976–87), III/2, pp. 215–32.

2 P. Needham, 'Venetian Printers and Publishers in the Fifteenth Century', *La bibliofilia* C (1998), pp. 158–61.

3 V. Gerulaitis, *Printing and Publishing in Fifteenth-century Venice* (Chicago, IL, and London, 1976), especially pp. 1–11; H. F. Brown, *The Venetian Printing Press, 1469–1800: An Historical Study Based upon Documents for the Most Part Hitherto Unpublished* (London, 1891); R. Hirsch, *Printing, Selling and Reading, 1450–1550*, 2nd revd edn (Wiesbaden, 1974), pp. 58–60; T. Pesenti, 'Stampatori e letterati nell'industria editoriale a Venezia e in terraferma', in Arnaldi and Stocchi, eds, *Storia della cultura veneta*, IV/1, pp. 93–106; C. Di Filippo Bareggi, 'L'editoria veneziana fra '500 e '600', in G. Cozzi and P. Prodi, eds, *Storia di Venezia dalle origini alla caduta della serenissima* VI (Rome, 1994), pp. 615–48.

4 M. Lowry, *The World of Aldus Manutius: Business and Scholarship in Renaissance Venice* (Oxford, 1979), pp. 137–67.

5 M. Manoussakas and C. Staikos, eds, *L'attività editoriale dei Greci durante il Rinascimento italiano, 1469–1523* (Athens, OH, 1986), pp. 127–42.

6 P. F. Grendler, *The Roman Inquisition and the Venetian Press, 1540–1605* (Princeton, NJ, 1977), pp. 6–8, for the overall figure for the century as well as a profile of sixteenth-century Venetian book production.

7 B. Pullan, *Rich and Poor in Renaissance Venice: The Social Institutions of a Catholic State to 1620* (Oxford, 1971), chapter 3, especially pp. 239–55.

8 E. Gleason, 'Confronting New Realities: Venice and the Peace of Bologna, 1530', in

J. Martin and D. Romano, eds, *Venice Reconsidered: The History and Civilization of an Italian City State, 1297–1797* (Baltimore, MD, and London, 2000), pp. 168–78.

9 Grendler, *The Roman Inquisition*, pp. 16–17; Filippo Bareggi, 'L'editoria veneziana', pp. 622–4.

10 P. F. Grendler, *Critics of the Italian World, 1530–1620: Anton Francesco Doni, Nicolò Franco and Ortensio Lando* (Madison, WI, and London, 1969), p. 6.

11 See S. Bongi, *Annali di Gabriel Giolito de' Ferrari da Trino di Monferrato, stampatore in Venezia*, 2 vols (Rome, 1890–97), I, pp. XXVIII–XXIX.

12 B. Richardson, *Print Culture in Renaissance Italy: The Editor and the Vernacular Text, 1470–1600* (Cambridge, 1994), pp. 90–108; *DBI*, LV, pp. 160–65.

13 M. A. Lewis, *Antonio Gardano, Venetian Music Printer, 1538–1569: A Descriptive Bibliography and Historical Study*, 3 vols to date (New York and London, 1988–), I, pp. 17–25; I. Fenlon, *Music, Print and Culture in Early Sixteenth-century Italy* (London, 1995), chapter III; J. Bernstein, *Music Printing in Renaissance Venice: The Scotto Press, 1539–1572* (New York and London, 1998), pp. 42–7.

14 M. Bury, *The Print in Italy, 1550–1620* (London, 2001), p. 170; G. J. Van der Sman, 'Print Publishing in Venice in the Second Half of the Sixteenth Century', *Print Quarterly* XVII (2000), pp. 235–47, at p. 235.

15 S. Curi Nicolardi, *Una società tipografico-editoriale a Venezia nel secolo XVI: Melchiorre Sessa e Pietro di Ravani (1516–1525)* (Florence, 1984), pp. 13–19.

16 Grendler, *The Roman Inquisition*, pp. 4–5.

17 I. Matozzi, '"Mondo del libro" e decadenza a Venezia, 1570–1730', *Quaderni storici* LXXII (1989), p. 749.

18 Pesenti, 'Stampatori e letterati', pp. 93–4.

19 Richardson, *Print Culture in Renaissance Italy*, pp. 39, 140.

20 [F. Sansovino], *Delle cose notabili che sono in Venetia libri due* (Venice, 1561), dedication [this book, published under the pseudonym A. Guisconi, appeared for the first time in 1561 as Sansovino's]; see B. Wilson, *The World in Venice: Print, the City and Early Modern Identity* (Toronto, 2005), pp. 3–5.

21 A. J. Schutte, 'Printing, Piety and the People in Italy: The First Thirty Years', *Archiv für Reformationsgeschichte* LXXI (1980), pp. 5–19, and, for a bibliography, A. J. Schutte, *Printed Italian Vernacular Religious Books, 1465–1550: A Finding List* (Geneva, 1983).

22 Barbieri, 'Tradition and Change', particularly pp. 113–15.

23 Grendler, *The Roman Inquisition*, p. 133. On the firm see A. Nuovo and C. Coppens, *I Giolito e la stampa nell' Italia del XVI secolo* (Geneva, 2005).

24 Barbieri, 'Tradition and Change', p. 115.

25 G. Zappella, *Le marche dei tipografi e degli editori italiani del Cinquecento*, 2 vols (Milan, 1986), I, no. LXX; II, figs 392–3, 395–6. On the connections between shop signs and printers' marks, see G. Moro, 'Insegne librarie e marche tipografiche in un registro veneziano del '500', *La bibliofilia* XCI (1989), pp. 51–80.

26 For the most recent overview, see E. Bonora, *Ricerche su Francesco Sansovino imprenditore librario e letterato* (Venice, 1994).

27 P. F. Grendler, 'Francesco Sansovino and Italian Popular History, 1560–1600', *Studies in the Renaissance* XVI (1969), pp. 139–80.

28 Bonora, *Ricerche su Francesco Sansovino*, pp. 97–137; for portrait books containing images of the Ottomans. see Wilson, *The World in Venice*, pp. 221–47.

29 A. A. Renouard, *Annales de l'imprimerie des Alde; ou, histoire des trois Manuce et de leurs editions*, 3rd edn (Paris, 1834), pp. 107–215 (Paolo Manuzio); pp. 215–55 (Aldo).

30 P. Camerini, *Annali dei Giunti*, 2 vols (Florence, 1962–3).

31 D. Javitch, *Proclaiming a Classic: The Canonization of Orlando Furioso* (Princeton, NJ, 1991), p. 10.

32 A. Tinto, *Annali tipografici dei Tramezzino* (Venice, 1968), p. 103.

33 S. Casali, *Annali della tipografia veneziana di Francesco Marcolini da Forlì* (Forlì, 1861), p. 86.

34 Casali, *Annali della tipografia veneziana*, nos 12 and 13.

35 Lewis, *Antonio Gardano*, I, pp. 246–9.

36 Fenlon, *Music, Print and Culture*, pp. 87–91; Bernstein, *Music Printing in Renaissance Venice*, pp. 125–38

37 P. F. Grendler, 'Form and Function in Italian Renaissance Popular Books', *Renaissance Quarterly* XLVI (1993), pp. 451–3.

38 E. Carrara and S. Gregory, 'Borghini's Print Purchases from Giunti', *Print Quarterly* XVII (2000), pp. 3–17.

39 S. Reed Welsh and R. Wallace, *Italian Etchers of the Renaissance and Baroque* (Boston, MA, 1989), p. 145.

40 D. Landau and P. Parshall, *The Renaissance Print, 1470–1550* (New Haven, CT, and London, 1994), p. 359.

41 Javitch, *Proclaiming a Classic*, p. 14.

42 C. Pasero, 'Giacomo Franco, editore, incisore e calcografo nei secoli XVI e XVII', *La bibliofilia* XXXVII (1935), pp. 335–6.

43 Van der Sman, 'Print Publishing in Venice', pp. 237–8.

44 Van der Sman, 'Print Publishing in Venice', p. 237.

45 Reed Welsh and Wallace, *Italian Etchers of the Renaissance and Baroque*, p. 58.

46 N. Nelli, *Libro de marchi de cavalli* (Venice, 1569).

47 Reed Welsh and Wallace, *Italian Etchers of the Renaissance and Baroque*, pp. 47–52; Van der Sman, 'Print Publishing in Venice', pp. 246–7.

48 N. Nelli, *Sommario et alboro delli principi ottomani con li loro veri ritratti* (Venice, 1567); for the trend, see Wilson, *The World in Venice*, pp. 224–31.

49 A. Omodeo, *Mostra di stampe popolari venete del '500* (Florence, 1965), pp. 3–4.

50 P. Bellini, 'Printmakers and Dealers in Italy during the 16th and 17th Centuries', *Print Collector* XIII (1975), p. 33; Reed Welsh and Wallace, *Italian Etchers of the Renaissance and Baroque*, pp. 47–52, for a short biography and reproductions of two of his prints; for illustrations of more of his work, see Omodeo, *Mostra di stampe popolari venete*, plates 7–10, 15, 17, 21 and 34. Bellini, 'Printmakers and Dealers in Italy, p. 33.

51 A. Caravia, *Naspo bizaro* (Venice, 1565); for a detailed description of the two known editions, see R. Mortimer, *Harvard College Library, Department of Printing and Graphic Arts, Catalogue of Books and Manuscripts. Part II: Italian 16th Century Books*, 2 vols (Cambridge, MA, 1974), I, pp. 151–3. For Caravia, see R. S. MacKenney, *Tradesmen and Traders: The World of the Guilds in Venice and Europe, c.1250–c.1650* (London and Sydney, 1987), pp. 176–8; J. Martin, *Venice's Hidden Enemies: Italian Heretics in a Renaissance City* (Berkeley, CA, 1993), pp. 156–8.

52 M. A. Katritsky, 'Italian Comedians in Renaissance Prints', *Print Quarterly* IV (1987), pp. 237–9.

53 P. G. Molmenti, *La storia di Venezia nella vita privata dalle origini alla caduta della Repubblica*, 3 vols, 7th edn (Trieste, 1973), II, pp. 334–5. For the wedding episode, see P. Allerston, 'Wedding Finery in Sixteenth-century Venice', in T. Dean and K. Lowe, eds, *Marriage in Italy, 1300–1650* (Cambridge, 1998), pp. 25–7.

54 E. Borea, 'Stampa figurativa e pubblico dalle origini all'affermazione nel Cinquecento', in G. Previtali, ed., *Storia dell'arte italiana* I/2 (Turin, 1979), pp. 399–401.

55 D. Woodward, *Maps as Prints in the Italian Renaissance: Makers, Distributors and Consumers* (London, 1996), pp. 1–5.

56 Woodward, *Maps as Prints in the Italian Renaissance*, pp. 99–100.

57 A. M. Petrioli Tofani, 'Stampe popolari venete del Cinquecento agli Uffizi', *Antichità viva* IV (1965), p. 66.

58 P. F. Brown, *Venetian Narrative Painting in the Age of Carpaccio* (New Haven, CT, and London, 1988), p. 234.

59 Borea, 'Stampa figurativa e pubblico', p. 398.

60 Woodward, *Maps as Prints in the Italian Renaissance*, pp. 94–9.

61 O. Niccoli, 'Un aspetto della propaganda religiosa nell'Italia del Cinquecento: opuscioli e fogli volanti', *Libri, idee e sentimenti religiosi nel Cinquecento italiano, 3–5 aprile 1986* (Modena, 1987), p. 31.

62 There is a particularly useful series of inventories in ASV, Cancell. inferiore,

misc. notai diversi buste 34–45; see I. Palombo-Fossati 'Livres et lecteurs a Venise du xvie siècle', *Revue française d'histoire du livre* LIV (1985), pp. 481–513.

63 A. M. Hind, *An Introduction to the Woodcut with a Detailed Survey of Work Done in the Fifteenth Century*, 2 vols (London, 1935), I, pp. 76–8; M. Bury, 'The Taste for Prints in Italy to *c.* 1600', *Print Quarterly* II (1985), p. 12; Borea, 'Stampa figurativa e pubblico', pp. 325–6.

64 I. Palombo-Fossati, 'L'interno della casa dell'artigiano e dell'artista nella Venezia del Cinquecento', *Studi veneziani* VIII (1984), p. 151; Woodward, *Maps as Prints in the Italian Renaissance*, pp. 79–84.

65 Grendler, 'Form and Function in Italian Renaissance Popular Books', pp. 453–4.

66 ASV, SU, b. 15, Scudieri; MacKenney, *Tradesmen and Traders*, p. 183; G. Ongaro, 'The Library of a Sixteenth Century Music Teacher', *Journal of Music* XII (1994), pp. 357–75; Fenlon, *Music, Print and Culture*, pp. 88–9.

67 ASV, SU, b. 48.

68 ASV, SU, b. 48, Zonca; MacKenney, *Tradesmen and Traders*, pp. 193–5.

69 F. Ambrosini, ' "Descrittioni del mondo" nelle case venete dei secoli XVI e XVII', *Archivio veneto* CXVI (1981), pp. 67–79.

70 MacKenney, *Tradesmen and Traders*, pp. 182–3.

71 Martin, *Venice's Hidden Enemies*, pp. 89–95, 150–52, 242–7.

72 MacKenney, *Tradesmen and Traders*, p. 184.

73 For the tradition, see F. Novati, 'Contributo alla storia della lirica musicale italiana popolare e popolareggiante nei secoli XV, XVI, XVII', in *Scritti varii di erudizione e di critica in onore di R. Renier* (Turin, 1912), pp. 900–80; E. Levi, *I cantari leggendari del popolo italiano nei secoli XIV e XV* (Turin, 1914); J. Haar, 'Arie per cantar stanze ariotesche', in M. A. Balsano, ed., *L'Ariosto la musica, i musicisti: quattro studi e sette madrigali ariosteschi* (Florence, 1981), pp. 31–46; J. Haar, *Essays on Italian Poetry and Music in the Renaissance, 1350–1600* (Berkeley, Los Angeles and London, 1986), particularly pp. 82–99; I. Cavallini, 'Sugli improvvisatori del Cinque–Seicento: persistenze, nuovi reper-

tori e qualche riconoscimento', *Recercare* I (1989), pp. 23–39.

74 P. Burke, *Popular Culture in Early Modern Europe* (London, 1978), p. 95; K. Park, 'Country Medicine in the City Marketplace: Snakehandlers as Itinerant Healers', *Renaissance Studies* XV (2001), pp. 104–20.

75 M. A. Katritsky, 'Marketing Medicine: The Image of the Early Modern Mountebank', *Renaissance Studies* XV (2001), pp. 121, 124–5.

76 G. Pesenti, 'Libri censurati a Venezia nei secoli XVI–XVII', *La bibliofilia* LVIII (1956), p. 17.

77 O. Niccoli, *Prophecy and People in Renaissance Italy* (Princeton, NJ, 1990), p. 12.

78 'To give delight and infinite pleasure to all those who are waiting. But first I need to perform my duty, before I begin.'

79 Caravia, *Naspo bizaro*, f. 4; 'To relieve my melancholy, which is breaking my heart and tearing up my soul, [and] to soothe my spleen, I will sing different things from those who sing in the square, who are always telling lies . . . I am neither a charlatan who would tell lies, nor a grocer who want to sell you carrots, O Zan Polo, give me a hand, so that I can assemble some love poetry in my heart, accompanying myself on the lute.'

80 J. E. Everson, *The Italian Romance Epic in the Age of Humanism: The Matter of Italy and the World of Rome* (Oxford, 2001), p. 113.

81 *La cronica della guerra successa tra Christiani e'l Turco . . .* (Venice, 1609); 'Gentle, benevolent people, I want to ask that you all listen to me, as I have come to tell you of an heroic battle, the most famous that ever happened at sea.'.

82 For the tradition, see *Guerre in ottava rime*, 4 vols (Modena, 1989).

83 A. Medin and L. Frati, *Lamenti storici dei secoli XIV, XV e XVI*, 4 vols (Bologna, 1887–94), IV, p. 210.

84 Manoli Blessi [Antonio Molino], *Dialogo de Selin con Giosuf Hebreo* (Venice, [1572]).

85 Grendler, *The Roman Inquisition*, pp. 9–12.

86 B. Richardson, *Printing, Writers and Readers in Renaissance Italy* (Cambridge, 1999), pp. 86–7.

87 For Ruscelli, see Grendler, *The Roman Inquisition*, p. 10, and for Castiglione, Richardson, *Printing, Writers and Readers*, p. 90.

88 Richardson, *Printing, Writers and Readers*, p. 43; Grendler, *The Roman Inquisition*, p. 9.

89 R. Agee, 'A Venetian Music Printing Contract and Edition Size in the Sixteenth Century', *Studi musicali* XV (1986), pp. 59–65, especially pp. 64–5.

90 Grendler, *The Roman Inquisition*, pp. 12–14 and table 1.

91 Allerston, 'Wedding Finery in Sixteenth-century Venice', pp. 35–7.

92 P. Allerston, 'The Market in Second-Hand Clothes and Furnishings in Venice, *c.* 1500–*c.* 1650' (Ph.D. dissertation, European University Institute, Florence, 1996), pp. 234–50. See also the articles by Evelyn Welch, Patricia Allerston, and Jacqueline Marie Musacchio in M. Fantoni, L. C. Mathew and S. F. Mathews-Grieco, eds, *The Art Market in Italy, 15th–17th Centuries* (Ferrara, 2003), section 5, pp. 283–323.

93 Fenlon, *Music, Print and Culture*, pp. 85–6.

94 R. Agee, 'The Venetian Privilege and Music: Printing in the Sixteenth Century', *Early Music History* III (1983), p. 8.

95 B. Pullan, 'Wage-earners and the Venetian Economy', *Economic History Review* XVI (1964), pp. 157–8.

96 F. C. Lane, *Venice: A Maritime Republic* (London, 1973), pp. 333–4.

97 F. C. Lane, 'Wages and Recruitment of Venetian Galeotti, 1470–1580', *Studi veneziani* VI (1982), p. 24.

98 B. Richardson, 'The Debates on Printing in Renaissance Italy', *La bibliofilia* C (1998), pp. 138–41.

99 Filippo Bareggi, 'L'editoria veneziana', pp. 630–32.

100 The general economic effects of the plague are discussed in Pullan, *Rich and Poor in Renaissance Venice*, pp. 315–19, 325. For the impact on the press, see Brown, *The Venetian Printing Press*, pp. 238–9, and Grendler, *The Roman Inquisition*, pp. 225–33.

101 Bongi, *Annali*, 2.

102 Woodward, *Maps as Prints*, p. 5 and fig. 1.

103 Bury, *The Print in Italy*, pp. 174–5.

104 Grendler, *The Roman Inquisition*, p. 229 and table 5.

105 For an alternative view, see Di Filippo Bareggi, 'L'editoria veneziana', pp. 614–17.

106 Grendler, *The Roman Inquisition*; S. Cavazza, 'Libri in volgare e propaganda eterodossa: Venezia, 1543–47', in *Libri, idee e sentimenti religiosi nel Cinquecento italiano* (Modena, 1987), pp. 9–28; M. Jacoviello, 'Proteste di editori e librai veneziani contro l'introduzione della censura sulla stampa a Venezia, 1543–1555', *Archivio storico italiano* CLI (1993), pp. 27–56.

107 G. Cozzi, 'Federico Contarini: un antiquario veneziano tra Rinascimento e Contrariforma', *Bolletino dell'Istituto di Storia della Società e dello Stato Veneziano* III (1961), pp. 190–220, especially pp. 195–205.

108 P. F. Grendler, 'The *Tre Savii sopra Eresia*, 1547–1605: A Prosopographical Study', *Studi veneziani* III (1979), pp. 283–340, particularly pp. 283–95.

109 G. Spini, *Tra rinascimento e riforma: Antonio Brucioli* (Florence, 1940), pp. 92–9; C. De Frede, 'Tipografi, editori, librai italiani del Cinquecento coinvolti in processi d'eresia', *Rivista di Storia della Chiesa in Italia* XXIII (1969), pp. 24–5, G. Fragnito, *La bibbia al rogo. La censura ecclesiastica e i volgarizzamenti della Scrittura (1471–1605)* (Bologna, 1997), pp. 29–32, 34–9, 63–5. For Brucioli, see also *DBI*, XIV, pp. 480–84.

110 Translation from MacKenney, *Tradesmen and Traders*, pp. 175–8.

111 See R. C. Davis, *The War of the Fists: Popular Culture and Public Violence in Late Renaissance Venice* (Oxford, 1994), particularly pp. 100–01, and, for the contest organized for the visit of Henry III to Venice, above, pp. 211–13.

112 E. B. Clementi, *Riforma religiosa e poesia popolare a Venezia nel Cinquecento: Alessandro Caravia* (Florence, 2000), pp. 88–9.

113 Clementi, *Riforma religiosa*, pp. 115–18, 300–03.

114 Da Frede, 'Tipografi, editori, librai italiani', pp. 29–30.

115 Grendler, *The Roman Inquisition*, p. 226, table 4.

116 De Frede, 'Tipografi, editori, librai italiani', pp. 39–48.

117 G. Cozzi, *Il doge Nicolò Contarini: ricerche sul patriziato veneziano agli inizi del Seicento* (Venice and Rome, 1958); G. Cozzi, *Paolo Sarpi tra Venezia e l'Europa* (Turin, 1979), chapter 3; F. Seneca, *Il doge Leonardo Donà: la sua vita e la sua preparazione politica prima del dogado* (Padua, 1959); P. Ulvioni, 'Cultura politica e cultura religiosa a Venezia nel secondo Cinquecento: un bilancio', *Archivio storico italiano* CXLI (1983), pp. 591–651.

118 C. L. C. E. Witcombe, *Copyright in the Renaissance: Prints and the Privilegio in Sixteenth-century Venice and Rome* (Leiden, 2004), pp. 65–9.

119 For its foundation and character, see a number of the chapters in R. C. Davis and B. Ravid, eds, *The Jews of Early Modern Venice* (Baltimore, MD, and London, 2001), in particular Ravid, 'The Venetian Government and the Jews', pp. 3–26, and Calabi, 'The "City of the Jews"'.

120 R. C. Head, 'Religious Boundaries and the Inquisition in Venice: Trials of Jews and Judaizers, 1548–1580', *Journal of Medieval and Renaissance Studies* XX (1990), pp. 175–204.

121 B. Ravid, 'Christian Travelers in the Ghetto of Venice: Some Preliminary Observations', in S. Nash, ed., *Between History and Literature: Studies in Honor of Isaac Barzilay* (B'nei B'rak, 1997), pp. 111–50.

122 Ravid, 'The Venetian Government and the Jews', p. 22.

123 Grendler, *The Roman Inquisition*, pp. 91–3; Jacoviello, 'Proteste di editori e librai'; P. F. Grendler, 'The Destruction of Hebrew Books in Venice, 1568', *Proceedings of the American Academy for Jewish Research* XLV (1978), 105–7.

124 For Venetian stereotypical views of the Turks, see Wilson, *The World in Venice*, pp. 143, 243.

125 Lane, *Venice: A Maritime Republic*, pp. 301–3; B. Arbel, 'Venezia, gli ebrei e l'attività di Salamone Ashkenasi nella guerra di Cipro', in G. Cozzi, ed., *Gli ebrei a Venezia, secoli XIV–XVIII* (Milan, 1987), pp. 168–72; B. Arbel, *Trading Nations: Jews and Venetians in the Early-Modern Eastern Mediterranean* (Leiden, 1995), pp. 56–61.

126 Grendler, *The Roman Inquisition*, p. 141.

127 Blessi, *Dialogo de Selin*; Arbel, *Trading Nations*, p. 57

128 Grendler, 'The Destruction of Hebrew Books', pp. 120–29.

129 Jacoviello, 'Proteste di editori e librai', pp. 40–44.

130 Grendler, *The Roman Inquisition*, pp. 301–3; Pesenti, 'Stampatori e letterati', p. 102.

131 For a detailed discussion of the text, see L. Pierozzi, 'La vittoria di Lepanto nell'escatologia e nella profezia', *Rinascimento* XXXIV (1994), pp. 317–63, particularly pp. 326–45; see also B. Paul, 'Identità e alterità nella pittura veneziana al tempo della battaglia di Lepanto', *Venezia Cinquecento: studi di storia dell'arte e della cultura* XV (2005), pp. 155–87, at pp. 162–8.

132 Nazari's *Della trasmutatione metallica* (various editions) includes a formidable bibliographical listing of alchemical sources; see L. Thorndike, *A History of Magic and Experimental Science*, 8 vols (New York, 1923–58), V, pp. 625, 679–95.

133 G. B. Nazari, *Discorso della futura et sperata vittoria contro il Turco, estratto dai sacri profeti e da altre profetie, prodigij et prognostici* (Venice, 1570). There were at least three other editions: see Pierozzi, 'La vittoria di Lepanto', p. 327, n. 42.

134 Pierozzi, 'La vittoria di Lepanto', pp. 330–32.

135 Niccoli, *Prophecy and People in Renaissance Italy*, pp. 185–8.

136 G. Garenzio, *La vera et famosa indovinatione della sibilla eritrea fatta a istanza de' prencipi di Greci, quando gli dimandaron consiglio intorno l'impresa di Troia* (Venice, 1570), f. CI. For the Latin text of this prophecy, see Pierozzi, 'La vittoria di Lepanto, pp. 345–7.

137 B. Meduna, *Dialogo sopra la miracolosa vittoria ottenuta dall'armata della Santissima Lega Christiana . . .* (Venice, 1572).

138 Bongi, *Annali*, II, pp. 337, 374.

139 'O Holy Shepherd, those unusual sounds and sorrowful voices, which are filling the air with misery and grief, come from that impious and cruel man, traitor to his King, and to God and his people, and from his followers, most wicked men, who have been annihilated and defeated with him. By means of your faithful chosen people the holy Michael was moved to pity [responding] to your compelling laments. Now Rome, like the golden lilies, ought to show signs of sincere joy, and her most illustrious sons [should] sing cheerfully about how it was delivered from a great peril not by the force of human nature, but by the infallible power of the heavenly kingdom.' P. Vinci, *Il terzo libro de madrigali a cinque voci* (Venice, 1571). The dedication, to Londonio, is dated 15 April 1571, which rules out the possibility, suggested in C. MacClintock, *Giaches de Wert, 1535–1596: Life and Works* (n.p., 1966), p. 100, that the text is a *madrigale spirituale* written after the battle of Lepanto.

140 *Canzone sopra la vittora*; 'After seeing that the Cross was being defiled, and His law violated, and after hearing the lament of His people, [God] sent his Angel Michael to earth, as Peter, to make war on them . . .'.

141 D. Harran, 'The Concept of Battle in Music of the Renaissance', *Journal of Medieval and Renaissance Studies* XVII (1987), pp. 175–94.

142 A. Gabrieli and G. Gabrieli, *Concerti . . .* (Venice, 1587); for a modern edition, see A. Gabrieli, *Complete Madrigals*, ed. A. Tillman Merritt, 12 vols (Madison, WI, 1981–4), XI, pp. 65–80.

143 *Dialoghi musicali de diversi eccellentissimi . . . con due battaglie a otto voci, per sonar de istrumenti da fiato, di Annibale Padoano et de Andrea Gabrieli* (Venice, 1590).

144 See D. Nutter, ed., *Orazio Vecchi: Battaglia d'Amor e Dispetto and Mascherata detta Malinconia et Allegrezza* (Madison, WI, 1987), p. xix.

145 E. Selfridge-Field, *Venetian Instrumental Music from Gabrieli to Vivaldi* (Venice, 1975), p. 67.

146 A. Medin, *La storia della Repubblica di Venezia nella poesia* (Milan, 1904); G. A. Quarti, *La battaglia di Lepanto nei canti popolari dell'epoca* (Milan, 1930); C. Dionisotti, 'Lepanto nella cultura italiana del tempo', in G. Benzoni, ed., *Il mediterraneo nella seconda metà del '500 nella luce di Lepanto* (Florence, 1974), pp. 127–51.

147 Wilson, *The World in Venice*, pp. 153–6

148 Medin, *La storia della Repubblica*, p. 245.

149 R. Benedetti, *Ragguaglio delle allegrezze, solennità, e feste, fatte in Venetia per la felice vittoria* (Venice, 1571), f. BIV.

150 U. Rozzo, 'La battaglia di Lepanto nell'editoria dell'epoca e una miscellanea fontiniana', *Rara volumina* I–II (2000), p. 52.

151 C. Dionisotti, 'La guerra d'Oriente nella letteratura veneziana del Cinquecento', *Lettere italiane* XVI (1964), pp. 233–50; reprinted in *Geografia e storia della letteratura italiana* (Turin, 1967), pp. 164, 179. For the Sack of Rome, see M. Miglio et al., *Il sacco di Roma del 1527 e l'immaginario collettivo* (Rome, 1986); M. Firpo, 'Il Sacco di Roma del 1527 tra profezie, propaganda e riforma religiosa', in Firpo, *Dal Sacco di Roma allo Inquisizione* (Alessandria, 1998), pp. 7–60; A. Chastel, *The Sack of Rome, 1527*, trans. B. Archer (Princeton, NJ, 1983), especially pp. 123–29; I. Fenlon, 'Music and Crisis in Florence and Rome, 1527–30', in C. Shaw, ed., *Italy and the European Powers: The Impact of War, 1500–1530* (Leiden, 2006), pp. 279–98.

152 L. Groto, *Le orationi volgari* (Venice, 1598).

153 L. Groto, *Oratione fatta in Vinegia, per l'allegrezza della vittoria ottenuta contra Turchi dalla Santissima Lega* (Venice, 1571).

154 L. Groto, *Canzone nella morte del Clarissimo M. Agostin Barbarigo* (Venice, 1572).

155 L. Groto, *Trofeo della vittoria sacra, ottenuta dalla christianissima Lega contra Turchi nell'anno MDLXXI* (Venice, 1572).

156 BNM, MS It. VII. 73 (8265), f. 396v.

157 Dionisotti, 'La guerra d'Oriente', p. 180.

158 M. Cortelazzo, 'Plurilinguismo celebrativo', in G. Benzoni, ed., *Il mediterraneo nella seconda metà del '500 nella luce di Lepanto* (Florence, 1974), pp. 121–6, especially pp. 123–6.

159 P. Gherardi, *In foedus et victoriam contra Turcas . . . poemata varii* (Venice, 1572).

160 Cardinal Bessarion, *Lettere et orationi tradotte in lingua italiana . . .* (Venice, 1573).

161 O. Toscanella, *Essortatione ai Cristiani contra il Turco* (Venice, 1572).

162 Molino's 'Lamento de Selin' appears in Manola Blessi, *Sopra la presa de Margaritin. Con un dialogo piacevole di un greco, & di un fachino* (Venice, 1571), f. [A3].

163 *L'acerbo pianto della moglie di Caracossa* (n.p., n.d.).

164 'My song, please reach Selim, and beg him not to drink so much wine, but to recognize Christ as his God, just, merciful, and holy, because He is the only one who can rescue him from destruction on land and at sea.' This characteristic piece of advice is taken from the *Canzon a Selim imperator de Turchi . . .* (n.p., n.d.).

165 Wilson, *The World in Venice*, p. 143.

166 'What advantage is there / O Selim salamelech, / In the union of Hic, & Hec, and Hoc? / Sixty-thousand of your crazy men / Already got stuck with three hundred galleys // And the souls of Alì, Pialì, Caracossa and Siroc, / Are expecting you over there in Mecca, / Since neither in Byzantium, Alger nor Morocco, / Will you be safe from the Grand Scanderbech // Did you think that you have to deal with brainless people / Like you, and who, like you, are used to getting drunk, / Despising the Holy Sabbath? // The Eagle, with her beak and claws, together with the Lion, / Will tear your heart out of your breast, / Just wait to hear il tof, il taf, il tif!' The text alone appears, among other places, in Groto, *Trofeo della vittoria sacra*, f. 114; for the music, see G. Ferretti, *Il primo libro delle canzoni alla napolitana a sei voci* (Venice, 1573).

167 *Selim*: Sultan Selim II (1524–74).

168 *Hic, Hec, Hoc* signify 'Rex, Ecclesia, Dominus'.

169 *Ali*: Mehemed Ali Pascia, commander of the Ottoman fleet at Lepanto.

170 *Piali*: Piali Murad, the renegade Ucchiali.

171 *Caracossa*: Kara Hodja or Caracoz, Turkish corsair active in the upper Adriatic.

172 *Siroc*: Muhammad Saulac, Turkish captain killed at Lepanto.

173 *Scanderbech*: Jorge Castriota, Albanian patriot who defended his country against the Turks.

174 *Usag al bif*: Ironic comment on Muslim abstention from alcohol.

175 *Santo Sabaot*: Holy Saturday.

176 *L'Aquila*: Habsburg emblem.

177 *Lio*: The lion of St Mark.

178 *Tof, taf, tif*: sounds of battle.

179 The text alone appears in Groto, *Trofeo della vittoria sacra*, ff. 17–19v. In the part-books of Baccusi's *Il secondo libro de madrigali a sei voci* (Venice, 1572), which unfortunately do not survive complete, 'Fuor fuori o Muse' is headed 'Canzone nella vittoria contra l'Armata Turchesca'.

180 For the text 'Ai piu gravi accenti' by Vincenzo Giusto of Udine, see Groto, *Trofeo della vittoria sacra*, ff. 37–38v. The music survives in Baccusi, *Il secondo libro de madrigali a cinque voci* (Venice, 1572).

181 See, for example, 'Al dolce suon dei tuoi leggiadri accenti', directed to Magno and published in Groto, *Trofeo della vittoria sacra*, f. 87v.

182 P. De Nolhac and A. Solerti, *Il viaggio in Italia di Enrico III re di Francia e le feste a Venezia, Ferrara, Mantova e Torino* (Turin, 1890), pp. 8–21 (referred to by number).

183 De Nolhac and Solerti, *Il viaggio in Italia di Enrico III*, no. 5.

184 De Nolhac and Solerti, *Il viaggio in Italia di Enrico III*, no. 4. Viani can be identified as the printer through his mark, which appears on the title-page together with the motto 'Virtus est firma possessio'; cf. Zappella, *Le marche dei tipografi*, I, p. 455, no. 435. Viani's shortened text is also used in the Veronese edition printed by Bastian and Giovanni Dalle Donne; cf. De Nolhac and Solerti, no. 6.

185 This second unidentified printer, recognizable by his mark of three fleurs-de-lis and the word FRANZA, specialized in literature generated by Henry's visit.

186 De Nolhac and Solerti, *Il viaggio in Italia di Enrico III*, no. 15 (in French); no. 31 (in Latin).

187 C. Dorron, *Narratio rerum memorabilium* (Venice, 1574), was printed anonymously but carries one of Valgrisi's marks on its

title-page; cf. Zappella, *Le marche dei tipografi*, II, fig. 1036.

188   De Nolhac and Solerti, *Il viaggio in Italia di Enrico III*, no. 8; Bongi, *Annali*, II, p. 340.

189   De Nolhac and Solerti, *Il viaggio in Italia di Enrico III*, no. 7.

190   Grendler, 'Francesco Sansovino and Italian Popular History', pp. 158-61; A. Nuovo and C. Coppens, *I Giolito e la Stampa nell' Italia del XVI secolo* (Geneva, 2005) pp. 460-62 and appendix.

191   R. V. Tooley, *Maps and Map-makers*, 6th edn (London, 1978), p. 19.

192   T. Porcacchi *Le attioni d'Arrigo terzo re di Francia et quarto di Polonia descritte in dialogo* . . . (Venice, 1574), ff. 3v-4.

193   For the latter, see Wilson, *The World in Venice*, pp. 72-4.

194   Guazzo, *Dialoghi piacevoli*, cited and translated in L. Stras, '"Onde havrà'l mond'esempio et vera historia": Musical Echoes of Henri III's Progress through Italy', *Acta musicologica* LXXII (2000), p. 7.

195   For one example, in the Biblioteca Guarneriana in San Daniele del Friuli (shelfmark VII D 6), put together before 1590, see Rozzo, 'La battaglia di Lepanto', pp. 59-69.

196   Including Cambridge, Emmanuel College, Bancroft Collection S15.1.32; Florence, Biblioteca Nazionale Centrale, Pal. 12.2.4.14, and Pal. 12.3.4.38; Treviso, Biblioteca Civica, Misc. 269; BNM, Misc. 168 and Misc 2573.

197   G. Gorini, 'Lepanto nelle medaglie', in G. Benzoni, ed., *Il mediterraneo nella seconda metà del '500 nella luce di Lepanto* (Florence, 1974), pp. 153-60.

198   On the functions of medals, see P. Attwood, *Italian Medals, c. 1530–1600, in British Public Collections*, 2 vols (London, 2003), I, pp. 53-61.

CHAPTER TEN

1   *AS*, Oct. III, pp. 790-826; *BS*, VI, cols 1345-9; S. Tramontin, ed., *Il culto dei santi a Venezia* (Venice, 1965), pp. 223-4.

2   G. B. Martini, *Vita di S. Giustina vergine e martire, protettrice della citta di Padova* . . . (Padua, 1627), ff. 1-4.

3   ASV Collegio, Ceremoniali I, f. XL.

4   A. Da Mosto, *L'Archivio di Stato di Venezia*, 2 vols (Rome, 1940), II, p. 136; U. Franzoi and D. Di Stefano, *Le chiese di Venezia* (Venice, 1976), pp. 450-52; G. Tassini, *Curiosità veneziane ovvero origini delle denominazioni stradali di Venezia*, 5th edn (Venice, 1915), pp. 344-5; MCV, MS Gradenigo 37: *Cronica della chiesa e monastero e contrada di S. Giustina in Venezia*.

5   For the *andata* to Santa Giustina, see Tramontin, ed., *Il culto dei santi a Venezia*, pp. 223-4; L. Urban, *Processioni e feste dogali: 'Venetia est mundus'* (Vicenza, 1998), pp. 129-32. Additional details are taken from ASV, Proc. de Supra Reg. 99, f. 317-317v, with *aggiunte* for subsequent years; BCV, MS Cicogna 2770, p. 134, and BCV, MS Venier P.D. 517b (Ottobre). The occasion is also briefly noted by the Ferrarese ambassador in Venice in a letter of 8 October to the duke of Ferrara: AS Mod. Ambasciatori (Venezia) 96.

6   A. Da Mosto, *I dogi di Venezia con particolare riguardo alle loro tombe* (Venice, 1939), pp. 277-8.

7   L. Rizzoli, 'La figurazione di Santa Giustina su monete di Venezia', *Atti dell'Istituto Veneto di Scienze, Lettere ed Arti* XCIX (1939-40), pp. 251-3; N. Papadopoli, *Le monete di Venezia*, 4 vols (Venice, 1893-1919), II, pp. 311, 318-22, tables 1-2.

8   For an overview of the repertory of Lepanto medals, see G. Gorini, 'Lepanto nelle medaglie', in G. Benzoni, ed., *Il mediterraneo nella seconda metà del '500 nella luce di Lepanto* (Florence, 1974), pp. 153-62.

9   C. Magno, *Trionfo di Christo per la vittoria contra Turchi, rappresentato al serenissimo prencipe di Venetia, il di di San Stefano* (Venice, 1571), also reprinted in L. Groto, *Trofeo della vittoria sacra, ottenuta dalla christianissima Lega contra Turchi nell'anno MDLXXI* (Venice, 1572). Magno's contribution to the Lepanto literature is assessed in R. Scrivano, *Il manierismo nella letteratura del Cinquecento* (Padua, 1959), pp. 99-108.

10   ASV Collegio, Ceremoniali I, f. ix-ixv.

11   From 1609 the feast of St Stephen was added to the calendar of days on which

the ducal *andata* was held; cf. BCV, MS Venier P.D. 517b (Dicembre).

12 F. Sansovino (ed. G. Stringa), *Venetia città nobilissima et singolare descritta in XIIII libri hora con molta diligenza corretta, emendata, e più d'un terzo di cose nuove ampliata dal M. R. D. Giovanni Stringa* (Venice, 1604), ff. 326v–327; E. Muir, *Civic Ritual in Renaissance Venice* (Princeton, NJ, 1981), p. 256.

13 J. Schiff, *Venetian State Theater and the Games of Siena, 1595–1605: The Grimani Banquet Plays* (Lewiston, NY, 1993).

14 The letter, which originally but no longer included a copy of Magno's text, from Claudio Ariosti to the duke of Ferrara, 26 December 1571, is in AS Mod. Ambasciatori (Venezia) 96, and records that 'habbiamo havuto al sudetto Banchetto di musiche straordinarie et rapresentatione delle persone'.

15 E. Concina, *L'Arsenale della Repubblica di Venezia: technice e istituzioni dal medioevo all'età moderna* (Milan, 1984), pp. 51–73, 156.

16 For an overview, see S. M. Mason Rinaldi, 'Le virtù della Repubblica e la gesta dei capitani: dipinti votivi, ritratti, pietà', in *Venezia e la difesa del Levante da Lepanto a Candia, 1570–1670* (Venice, 1986), pp. 13–18.

17 For the traditional iconography, see D. Rosand, '*Venetia figurata*: The Iconography of a Myth', in Rosand, ed., *Interpretazioni veneziane: studi di storia d'arte in onore di Michelangelo Muraro* (Venice, 1984), pp. 177–96.

18 A. Palluchini, 'Echi della battaglia di Lepanto nella pittura veneziana del '500', in G. Benzoni, ed., *Il mediterraneo nella seconda metà del '500 nella luce di Lepanto* (Florence, 1974), p. 282; *Venezia e la difesa del Levante*, pp. 29–30; T. Pignatti and F. Pedrocco, *Veronese*, 2 vols (Milan, 1995), I, pp. 277–9, cat. 181; E. Camara, 'Pictures and Prayers: Madonna of the Rosary Imagery in Post-Tridentine Italy' (Ph.D. dissertation, Johns Hopkins University, 2002), pp. 247–9.

19 T. Pignatti, *Veronese*, 2 vols (Milan, 1976), I, p. 197, no. A214; Camara, 'Pictures and Prayers', pp. 249–52.

20 R. Pallucchini and P. Rossi, *Tintoretto: le opere sacre e profane*, 2 vols (Milan, 1982), cat. 406 and fig. 520; *Venezia e la difesa del Levante*, pp. 30–31.

21 P. Cottrell, 'Corporate Colors: Bonifacio and Tintoretto at the Palazzo dei Camerlenghi in Venice', *Art Bulletin* LXXXII (2000), pp. 671–2.

22 Pignatti and Pedrocco, *Veronese*, II, cat. 202.

23 P. Humfrey, 'Altarpieces and Altar Dedications in Counter-Reformation Venice and the Veneto', *Renaissance Studies* X (1996), pp. 374–9; R. Cocke, 'Exemplary Lives: Veronese's Representations of Martyrdom and the Council of Trent', *Renaissance Studies* X (1996), pp. 388–95. R. Cocke, *Paolo Veronese: Piety and Display in an Age of Religious Reform* (Aldershot, 2001), pp. 41–5

24 M. Bury, *The Print in Italy, 1550–1620* (London, 2001), p. 109.

25 BCV, MS Cicogna 2770.

26 G. Stringa, *La chiesa di S. Marco, capella del serenissimo principe di Venetia, descritta brevemente* (Venice, 1610), p. 75.

27 See Monteverdi's letters of 10 September and 25 September 1627 in D. Stevens, ed., *The Letters of Claudio Monteverdi*, revd edn (Oxford, 1995), letters 107 and 111.

28 'Beata virgo et martyr Iustina raperetur ad supplitium cum ab impiisimo tiranno clamabat ad Dominum gratias tibi ago Domine quem semper amavi quem quaesivi quem optavi quia me in numerum martyrum accipere dignatus fuisti. Alleluia.' G. Bassano *Motetti per concerti ecclesiastici . . .* (Venice, 1598); modern edition in G. Bassano, *Opera omnia*, ed. R. Charteris (n.p., 1999–), I, pp. 9–17, from which the translation is taken.

29 BCV, MS Cicogna 2770, p. 134. For the ceremonies at Santa Marina to mark the recovery of Padua, see F. Sansovino, *Venetia città nobilissima . . . descritta in XIIII libri . . . con aggiunta da D. Giustiniano Martinioni* (Venice, 1663), pp. 503–4, and G. R. Michiel, *Le origini delle feste veneziane*, 6 vols (Milan, 1817), V, pp. 24–132. Descriptions of the procession occur in all the major ceremony books: see

ASV Collegio, Ceremoniali I, f. 9; BMV, MS Lat. III 172 (2276), f. 53v; and MCV, MS Venier P.D. 517b (Luglio).

30 As in 1577 and 1578; see the *aggiunte posteriori* to the copy of the *ceremoniali* in ASV, Proc. di Supra 98, f. 144; BCV, MS Cicogna 1295, p. 172; BCV, MS Cicogna 2769, f. 73–73v; BCV, MS Cicogna 2770, f. 134.

31 A. Winston, 'Tracing the Origins of the Rosary: German Vernacular Texts', *Speculum* LXVIII (1993), pp. 619–36; A. Winston-Allen, *Stories of the Rose: The Making of the Rosary in the Middle Ages* (University Park, PA, 1997), pp. 13–30.

32 A. Niero, 'La mariegola della più antica scuola del rosario di Venezia', *Rivista di storia della chiesa in Italia* XV (1961), pp. 324–36. See also A. Niero, 'Ancora sull'origine del rosario a Venezia e sulla sua iconografia', *Rivista di storia della chiesa in Italia* XXVIII (1974), pp. 465–78.

33 G. G. Meersseman, 'L'inizio della confraternita del Rosario e della sua iconografia in Italia: a proposito di un quadro veneziano del Dürer (1506)', *Atti e Memorie dell'Accademia Patavina di Scienze, Lettere ed Arti* LXXVI (1963–4), pp. 223–56; P. Humfrey, 'Dürer's Feast of the Rosegarlands: A Venetian Altarpiece', *Bulletin of the Society for Renaissance Studies* IV/I (1986), pp. 29–39; P. Humfrey, 'La festa del Rosario di Albrecht Dürer', *Eidos. Rivista di cultura* II (1988), pp. 4–15; P. Humfrey, *The Altarpiece in Renaissance Venice* (New Haven, CT, and London, 1993), pp. 265–6; Camara, 'Pictures and Prayers', pp. 238–40.

34 Sansovino, *Venetia città nobilissima* (1581), f. 48v.

35 Camara, 'Pictures and Prayers', pp. 233–8.

36 Humfrey, 'Dürer's Feast of the Rosegarlands'; Humfrey, 'La festa del Rosario'.

37 Camara, 'Pictures and Prayers', pp. 104–9.

38 CE, IX, p. 289.s.

39 P. G. Molmenti, *Sebastiano Veniero dopo la battaglia di Lepanto* (Venice, 1915), pp. 131–2; Camara, 'Pictures and Prayers', p. 109.

40 For a detailed account of the progress of the project, see Camara, 'Pictures and Prayers', pp. 252–85.

41 V. Avery, 'Nuove fonti archivistiche per il rinnovo cinquecentesco della Cappella del Rosario ai Santi Giovanni e Paolo', in L. Finocchi Gersi, ed., *Alessandro Vittoria e l'arte veneta della maniera. Atti del Convegno Internazionale di Studi: Università di Udine, 26–27 ottobre 2000* (Udine, 2001), pp. 175–97.

42 J. Schulz, *Venetian Painted Ceilings of the Renaissance* (Berkeley, CA, 1968), p. 132.

43 Sansovino, ed. Stringa, *Venetia città nobilissima* (1604), ff. 125–6.

44 The original appearance of the chapel is described in G. A. Moschini, *Guida per la città di Venezia all'amico delle belle arti*, 2 vols (Venice, 1815), I, p. 153; see also C. A. Levi, *Notizie storiche di alcune antiche scuole di arti e mestieri scomparse a esistente ancora in Venezia* (Venice, 1895), p. 82.

45 Padua, Museo Civico, inv. no. 681; see *Venezia e la difesa del Levante*, p. 21, cat. 5.

46 Pignatti, Veronese, I, p. 197, no. A214; *Venezia e la difesa del Levante*, pp. 30–31, cat. 16; Camara, 'Pictures and Prayers', pp. 249–52.

47 B. Wilson, *The World in Venice: Print, the City and Early Modern Identity* (Toronto, 2005), p. 150.

48 For which see Camara, 'Pictures and Prayers', pp. 124–43.

49 I am grateful to Douglas Lewis for his advice, and for providing references to his forthcoming *Systematic Catalogue* of plaquettes in the National Gallery of Art, Washington, DC.

50 U. Middeldorf and O. Goetz, *Medals and Plaquettes from the Sigmund Morgenroth Collection* (Chicago, IL, 1944), no. 85 and plate XXI, D. Lewis, *Systematic Catalogue* (forthcoming), II, no. 506.

51 See, *inter alia*, F. Rossi, *Accademia Carrara: sculture, bronzi, porcellane e ceramiche* (Bergamo, 1992), p. 108; P. Voltolina, *La storia di Venezia attraverso le medaglie*, 3 vols (Milan, 1998), no. 707; Lewis, *Systematic Catalogue*, II, nos 503–4.

52 C. B. Fullerton, 'The Master IO. F. F. and the Function of Plaquettes', in A. Luchs, ed., *Italian Plaquettes* (Hanover, NH, and London, 1989), p. 143.

53 Washington, DC, National Gallery of Art 2002.102.2; see Lewis, *Systematic Catalogue*, II, no. 504.

54 J. Ackerman, 'The Geopolitics of Venetian Architecture in the Time of Titian', in D. Rosand, ed., *Titian: His World and his Legacy* (New York, 1982), p. 62.

55 W. Timofiewitsch, *La chiesa del Redentore* (Vicenza, 1969), app. II, figs XVII–XXII.

56 G. Zorzi, *Le chiese e i ponti di Andrea Palladio* (Vicenza, 1967), p. 133; Timofiewitsch, *La chiesa del Redentore*, p. 67.

57 Ackerman, 'Geopolitics', pp. 63–5.

58 P. Murray, 'Palladio's Churches', in *Arte in Europa: scritti di storia dell'arte in onore di Edoardo Arslan*, 2 vols (Milan, 1966), I, p. 606.

59 T. E. Cooper, '"Locus meditandi et orandi": Architecture, Liturgy and Identity at San Giorgio Maggiore', in F. Passadore and F. Rossi, eds, *Musica, scienza e idee nella Serenissima durante il Seicento* (Venice, 1996), pp. 79–105 and now T. E. Cooper, *Palladio's Venice. Architecture and Society in a Renassance Republic* (New Haven and London, 2005), pp. 229–57.

60 Sansovino, *Venetia città nobilissima* (1581), f. 201–201v; Sansovino, ed. Stringa, *Venetia città nobilissima* (1604), ff. 346v–347; Sansovino, *Venetia città nobilissima* (1663), pp. 504–5.

61 See ASV, San Giorgio Maggiore, b. 44, proc .50. This ceremony book of 1562 is transcribed in Cooper, '"Locus meditandi et orandi"', pp. 93–105.

62 Cooper, '"Locus meditandi et orandi"', p. 89.

63 ASV, San Giorgio Maggiore b. 44, fasc. III; see Cooper, "Locus meditandi et orandi"', p. 95.

64 Cooper, '"Locus meditandi et orandi"', pp. 86–8.

65 Ackerman, 'Geopolitics', p. 63.

66 See Zorzi, *Le chiese e i ponti di Andrea Palladio*, p. 123.

67 London, Wellcome Institute for the History of Medicine, MS 808a; see W. Schupbach, 'A Venetian "Plague Miracle" in 1464 and 1576', *Medical History* (1976), pp. 312–16.

68 Schupbach, 'A Venetian "Plague Miracle"', p. 315.

69 ASV Collegio, Ceremoniali I, f. lx–lx v.

70 Sansovino, *Venetia città nobilissima* (1581), f. 205.

71 Timofiewitsch, *La chiesa del Redentore*, pp. 15–18.

72 S. Sinding-Larsen, 'Palladio's Redentore: A Compromise in Composition', *Art Bulletin* XLVII (1965), pp. 430–31.

73 ASV Collegio, Ceremoniali I, f. li–liv; see Timofiewitsch, *La chiesa del Redentore*, p. 68.

74 ASV Collegio, Ceremoniali I, f. lix v; BNM, MS It. VII. 364 (7934), f. 71.

75 ASV Collegio, Ceremoniali I, f. lix v, together with Mutio Lumina's eyewitness account (published as *La liberatione di Vinegia*) on f. lx; see Timofiewitsch, *La chiesa del Redentore*, app. III, nos 9–10, and Zorzi, *Le chiese e i ponti di Andrea Palladio*, pp. 135–6, nos 15–16, where Lumina's letter is given at greater length.

76 Zorzi, *Le chiese e i ponti di Andrea Palladio*, p. 135.

77 Sansovino, ed. Stringa, *Venetia città nobilissima* (1604), f. 336v.

CHAPTER ELEVEN

1 BNM, MS It. VII. 73 (8265), f. 396v.

2 G. B. Bellavere, *Oratione nella creatione del serenissimo prencipe di Venetia Sebastiano Veniero* (n.p., n.d.), ff. A4v–A6.

3 For painting, see W. Wolters, *Storia e politica nei dipinti di Palazzo Ducale: aspetti dell'autocelebrazione della Repubblica di Venezia nel Cinquecento* (Venice, 1987), and G. Tagliaferro, 'Martiri, eroi, principi e beati: i patrizi veneziani e la pittura celebrativa nell'età di Lepanto', in M. Chiabò and F. Doglio, eds, *Guerre di religione sulle scene del Cinque–Seicento* (Rome, 2006), pp. 337–90.

4 S. Sinding-Larsen, *Christ in the Council Hall: Studies in the Religious Iconography of the Venetian Republic* (Rome, 1974), pp. 95–8; T. Pignatti and F. Pedrocco, *Veronese*, 2 vols (Milan, 1995), I, pp. 373–4 and cat. 261.

5 S. Sinding-Larsen, 'The Changes in the Iconography and Composition of Veronese's

Allegory of the Battle of Lepanto in the Doge's Palace', *Journal of the Warburg and Courtauld Institutes* XIX (1956), pp. 298–302.

6 E. Muir, *Civic Ritual in Renaissance Venice* (Princeton, NJ, 1981), pp. 258–9. For musical settings of the 'Oration di San Marco' see above, pp. 140–41.

7 F. Sansovino (ed. G. Stringa), *Venetia città nobilissima et singolare descritta in XIIII libri hora con molta diligenza corretta, emendata, e più d'un terzo di cose nuove ampliata dal M. R. D. Giovanni Stringa* (Venice, 1604), f. 353v.

8 *Venezia e la difesa del Levante da Lepanto a Candia, 1570–1670* (Venice, 1986), p. 27, cat. 12.

9 A. Bacchi, L. Camerengo and M. Leithe-Jasper, eds, 'La bellissima maniera', in *Alessandro Vittoria e la scultura veneta del Cinquecento* (Trent, 1999), pp. 292–3.

10 For the decoration of these rooms, see Wolters, *Storia e politica nei dipinti di Palazzo Ducale*, pp. 239–46.

11 T. Martin, *Remodelling Antiquity: Alessandro Vittoria and the Portrait Bust in Renaissance Venice* (Oxford, 1998), pp. 125–6; Bacchi, Camerlengo and Leithe-Jasper, eds, 'La bellissima maniera', pp. 290–91.

12 B. Wilson, *The World in Venice: Print, the City and Early Modern Identity* (Toronto, 2005), p. 186.

13 G. Gorini, 'Lepanto nelle medaglie', in G. Benzoni, ed., *Il mediterraneo nella seconda metà del '500 nella luce di Lepanto* (Florence, 1974), pp. 154–60.

14 F. Gaeta et al., eds, *Nunziature di Venezia* (Rome, 1958–), IX, p. 403 (Venice, 6 December 1570).

15 Manoli Blessi [Antonio Molino], *Il vero successo della presa di Nicosia* (Venice, 1572). For further on his poetry for the War of Cyprus, see A. Medin, *La storia della Repubblica di Venezia nella poesia* (Milan, 1904), pp. 233–40.

16 The identification of this drawing with the conclusion of the Holy League was first suggested in H. Burns et al., eds, *Andrea Palladio, 1508–1580: The Portico and the Farmyard* ([London], 1975), pp. 161–2 (no. 283). See also R. Cocke, *Veronese's Drawings: A Catalogue Raisonné* (London, 1984), p. 150 (no. 62); *Venezia e la difesa del Levante*, pp. 20–21 (no. 4); M. Jaffé, *The Devonshire Collection of Italian Drawings: Venetian and North Italian Schools* (London, 1994), pp. 138–9 (no. 846); W. R. Rearick, *The Art of Paolo Veronese, 1528–1588* (Cambridge, 1988), pp. 106–8.

17 Rearick, *The Art of Paolo Veronese*, p. 106.

18 *Venezia e la difesa del Levante*, pp. 20–21; Rearick, *The Art of Paolo Veronese*, p. 108.

19 G. P. Contarini, *Historia delle cose successe dal principio della guerra mossa da Selim ottomano a Venetiani fino al di della gran giornata vittoriosa contra Turchi* (Venice, 1572), ff. 23v–31; P. Paruta, *Della guerra di Cipro* (Venice, 1605), pp. 194–7.

20 D. Pincus, *The Tombs of the Doges of Venice* (Cambridge, 2000), pp. 121–47.

21 Pincus, *The Tombs of the Doges*, pp. 148–65.

22 F. Barbieri and G. Beltramini, *Vincenzo Scamozzi, 1548–1616* (Venice, 2003), p. 541.

23 For further details, see D. M. Breiner, 'Vincenzo Scamozzi, 1548–1616: A Catalogue Raisonné', 2 vols (Ph.D. dissertation, Cornell University, 1994), II, pp. 691–3.

24 M. L. Madonna, 'La biblioteca', in B. Adorni, ed., *L'abbazia benedettina di San Giovanni Evangelista a Parma* (Milan, 1979), p. 178; J. Schultz, 'Maps as Metaphors: Mural Map Cycles of the Italian Renaissance', in D. Woodward, ed., *Art and Cartography* (Chicago, IL, and London, 1987), pp. 119–20.

25 R. Wittkower, *Architectural Principles in the Age of Humanism*, 4th edn (London, 1973), pp. 86–9; J. Ackerman, *Palladio* (Harmondsworth, 1966), pp. 120–23; A. Venditti, *La loggia del capitaniato* (Vicenza, 1969), pp. 25–7; B. Boucher, *Andrea Palladio: The Architect in his Time* (New York, 1994), pp. 273–6.

26 I. Fenlon, *Music and Culture in Late Renaissance Italy* (Oxford, 2002), pp. 139–61.

27 L. Partridge and R. Starn, 'Triumphalism in the Sala Regia', in B. Wisch and S. Scott Munshower, eds, *'All the World's a Stage . . .': Art and Pageantry in the Renaissance and Baroque* (University Park, PA,

1990), pp. 23–82, with a chronology of the Lepanto frescos on p. 59; Fenlon, *Music and Culture in Late Renaissance Italy*, with a discussion of music by Palestrina and Gasparo Fiorino on pp. 144–5 and 149–52.

28 A. Herz, 'The Sistine and Pauline Tombs: Documents of the Counter-Reformation', *Storia dell'arte* XLIII (1981), pp. 241–62; C. Pietrangeli, ed., *La basilica romana di Santa Maria Maggiore* (Florence, 1987), pp. 221–2.

29 Schulz, 'Maps as Metaphors', pp. 107–8.

30 The complete cycle is reproduced in L. Gambi and A. Pinelli, eds, *La Galleria delle Carte Geografiche in Vaticano*, 3 vols (Modena, 1994).

31 Rearick, *The Art of Paolo Veronese*, pp. 108–9. See also *Venezia e la difesa del Levante*, p. 28. Pignatti and Pedrocco, *Veronese*, pp. 284–5.

32 For Duodo's biography, see E. A. Cicogna, *Delle iscrizioni veneziane*, 6 vols (Venice, 1827), III, pp. 177–8; *DBI*, XLII, pp. 30–33; BCV, MS P.D. II c.

33 Huntington Library, San Marino (California), MS EL 9 H 13. This is kept with other fragments of illuminated documents, mostly Venetian, including the frontispiece to Duodo's commission as *podestà* of Bergamo, and that appointing him as procurator (dated 28 March 1587).

34 Sansovino, ed. Stringa, *Venetia città nobilissima* (1604), f. 89v.

35 R. Pallucchini and P. Rossi, *Tintoretto: le opere sacre e profane*, 2 vols (Milan, 1982), I, p. 254, A 113; the authors cite the description of the altar in the records of the 1581 visitation as 'Altare sancta Justina nob. Francisci Duodo'. See also Martin, *Remodelling Antiquity*, pp. 102–5; Bacchi, Camerlengo and Leithe-Jasper, eds, 'La bellissima maniera', pp. 298–301.

36 Puppi and Puppi Olivato, 'Scamozziana', pp. 56, 58, 70, n. 37.

37 For the project, see Puppi and Puppi Olivato, 'Scamozziana', pp. 55–8, 62–6; Breiner, 'Vincenzo Scamozzi', I, pp. 384–93 (villa), II, pp. 579–91 (church of San Giorgio and six chapels).

38 BCV, Classe III, nos 1315, 1321, 1323 and 1324; these four autograph drawings are illustrated in Barbieri and Beltramini, *Vincenzo Scamozzi*, cat. 34.1a, 34.1b, 34.3a, 34.3b.

39 Kubler, 'Sacred Mountains', pp. 414–18.

40 W. Hood, 'The *Sacro Monte* of Varallo: Renaissance Art and Popular Religion', in T. Verdon, ed., *Monasticism and the Arts* (Syracuse, NY, 1984), pp. 293–300.

41 E. De Filippis, 'Il vescovo Carlo Bascapè e il Sacro Monte di Orta', in L. Vaccaro and F. Riccardi, eds, *Sacri monti: devozione, arte e cultura della controriforma* (Milan, 1992), pp. 385–95.

42 A. Buratti Mazzotta, 'L'apoteosi di Carlo Borromeo disegnata in due secoli di progetti per il sacro monte di Arona', in Vaccaro and Riccardi, eds, *Sacri monti*, pp. 231–9.

43 Barbieri and Beltramini, *Vincenzo Scamozzi*, p. 371.

44 S. M. Mason Rinaldi, *Palma il Giovane: l'opera completa* (Milan, 1984), pp. 95, nos 164–9 and figs 460, 462, 464, 466, 467, 468.

45 Martin, *Remodelling Antiquity*, pp. 102–4, 136–7.

46 The inscriptions are reported in Cicogna, *Delle iscrizioni veneziane*, III, p. 177.

47 Barbieri and Beltramini, *Vincenzo Scamozzi*, cat. 34.3d.

48 P. De Nolhac and A. Solerti, *Il viaggio in Italia di Enrico III re di Francia e le feste a Venezia, Ferrara, Mantova e Torino* (Turin, 1890), pp. 159–60.

49 G. Cozzi, 'Federico Contarini: un antiquario veneziano tra Rinascimento e Controriforma', *Bolletino dell'Istituto di Storia della Societa e dello Stato Veneziano* III (1961), p. 193.

50 F. Sansovino, *Venetia città nobilissima et singolare descritta in XIV libri* (Venice, 1581), ff. 119v–120.

51 W. Wolters, *Storia e politica nei dipinti di Palazzo Ducale: aspetti dell'autocelebrazione della Repubblica di Venezia nel Cinquecento* (Venice, 1987), pp. 218–19; J. Fletcher, 'Fine Art and Festivity in Renaissance Venice: The Artist's Part', in J. Onians, ed., *Essays on Art and Culture in Honour of E. H. Gombrich at 85* (London, 1994), pp. 136–7.

52 M. Bury, *The Print in Italy, 1550–1620* (London, 2001), pp. 182–3.

53 Fantelli, 'L'ingresso di Enrico III'; Wolters, *Storia e politica nei dipinti di Palazzo Ducale*, pp. 216–20.

54 N. Ivanoff, 'Henri III à Venise', *Gazette des Beaux-Arts* LXXX (1972), pp. 313–30; Wolters, *Storia e politica nei dipinti di Palazzo Ducale*, p. 216.

55 M. Bergstein, '"La Fede": Titian's Votive Painting for Antonio Grimani', *Arte veneta* XL (1986), pp. 29–37.

56 Dresden, Gemäldegalerie Alte Meister. See Ivanoff, 'Henri III à Venise', pp. 316–17; Mason Rinaldi, *Palma il Giovane: l'opera completa*, cat. 88, D196, figs 150–51.

57 Mason Rinaldi, *Palma il Giovane: l'opera completa*, p. 80.

58 Wolters, *Storia e politica nei dipinti di Palazzo Ducale*, pp. 216–22

59 F. Seneca, *Il doge Leonardo Donà: la sua vita e la sua preparazione politica prima del dogado* (Padua, 1959), pp. 172ff.; G. Cozzi, *Il doge Nicolò Contarini: ricerche sul patriziato veneziano agli inizi del Seicento* (Venice and Rome, 1958), pp. 21ff.

60 See above, pp. 177–8.

61 N. Sainte-Fare Garnot, 'Les Tiepolo du Musée Jacquemart-André', in L. Puppi, ed., *Giambattista Tiepolo*, 2 vols (Padua, 1998), pp. 51–61.

62 H. de Chennevières, 'Les Tiepolo de L'hotel Eduoard André', *Gazette des Beaux-Arts* XV (1896), p. 121.

63 Tiepolo's frescos have recently been restored; see J.-P. Babelon and N. Sainte-Fare Garnot, *Les fresques de Tiepolo* (Paris, 1998), pp. 1–29.

CHAPTER TWELVE

1 Udine, Biblioteca civica, MS 58 (Annales 1571–4), f. 15; M. G. Alta Merello and D. Frangipane, 'Giovanni di Strassoldo, la patria del Friuli e la "guerra turchesca" sul mare (1571)', in P. C. Ioly Zorattini and A. M. Caproni, eds, *Memor fui dierum antiquorum: studi in memoria di Luigi di Biasio* (Udine, 1995), p. 16.

2 Alta Merello and Frangipane, 'Giovanni di Strassoldo', p. 17.

3 P. Buccio, *Oratione sopra la vittoria christiana contra Turchi ottenuta l'anno felicissimo MDLXXI* (Venice, 1571), ff. 4v–5.

4 Buccio, *Oratione*, ff. 4v–5.

5 A. Avena, 'Memorie veronesi della guerra di Cipro e della battaglia di Lepanto', *Nuovo archivio veneto*, n.s. XXIV (1912), p. 110.

6 [G. Fiamma], *Parafrasi poetica sopra alcuni salmi di David molto accomodati per render grazie a Dio della vittoria donata al christianesimo e contra a' Turchi* (Venice, 1571), title-page.

7 *Discorso sopra il Pater Noster in lingua rustica, per la vittoria de Christiani contra Turchi* (n.p., n.d.).

8 See above, pp. 179–80.

9 Among many examples, B. Meduna della Motta, *Dialogo sopra la miracolosa vittoria ottenuta dall'armata della Santissima Lega Christiana . . .* (Venice, 1572), f. [A2]v.

10 For a description, see J. Bernstein, *Music Printing in Renaissance Venice: The Scotto Press, 1539–1572* (New York and London, 1998), pp. 893–5, no. 396.

11 *DBI*, V, pp. 197–9 (De Capo).

12 *DBI*, V, pp. 197–9 (De Capo).

13 *Le suntuosissime esequie celebrata nella magnifica città di Bergamo . . .* (Perugia, 1572), dedication (to Ginevra Salviati de Baglioni).

14 'Intret super eos formido et pavor. In magnitudine Brachij tui Domine disperde illos et fiant immobiles donec transeat populus tuus quem possedisti.' P. Vinci, *Il secondo libro de' motetti a cinque voci* (Venice, 1572).

15 G. B. Bellavere, *Oratione nella creatione del serenissimo prencipe di Venetia Sebastiano Veniero* (n.p., n.d.), f. A2v.

16 BNM, MS It. VII. 519, f. 325.

17 A. Stella, 'La regolazione delle pubbliche entrate e la crisi politica veneziana del 1582', in *Miscellanea in onore di Roberto Cessi* (Rome, 1958), II, p. 170.

18 BNM, MS It. VII. 553, p. 29

19 BCV, MS Cicogna 3682, ff. [6]v–[7].

20 B. Pisanelli, *Discorso sopra il dragone di fuoco apparso in Roma l'anno 1575* (Bologna: 1575).

21 Saravezza, *Il breve discorso*; Marzari, *Discorso*.

22 BCV, MS Cicogna 3682, f. [12]; A. Raimondi, *Discorso quale chiaramente si conosce la viva et vera cagione, che ha generato le fiere infermita, che tanto hanno molestato l'anno 1575 . . .* (Padua, 1586).

23 As in A. Glisente, *Risposta fatta per il sumario delle cause pestilenti alla apologia dell'eccellente M. Annibal Raimondo Veronese* (n.p., [1576]).

24 *Discorso sopra gli accidenti del parto mostruoso nato in una Hebrea in Venetia nell'anno 1575 a di XXVI di Maggio . . .* ([Venice, 1575]) [both editions are relevant].

25 O. Niccoli, *Prophecy and People in Renaissance Italy* (Princeton, NJ, 1990), pp. 30–60.

26 G. Diedo, *Lettera all'illustrissimo Sig. Marc'Antonio Barbaro Eccellentissimo Bailo in Constantinopli . . .* (Venice, 1573), f. 29; R. Benedetti, *Ragguaglio delle allegrezze, solennita, e feste, fatte in Venetia per la felice vittoria* (Venice, 1571), f. [Aiii].

27 Niccoli, *Prophecy and People*, p. 35.

28 BNM, MS It. VII. 73 (8265), f. 410v.

29 BCV, MS Cicogna 3682, f. [12]v; P. Preto, *Peste e società a Venezia, 1576*, 2nd edn (Vicenza, 1984), p. 73.

30 BNM, MS It. VII. 553, p. 66.

31 The *Discorso*, which is unpublished, is in BNM, MS It. VII. 806 (9557).

32 G. Donzellini, *Discorso nobilissimo e dottissimo preservativo et curativo della peste* (Venice, 1577); Preto, *Peste e società*, pp. 62–3.

33 G. Contarini, *Oratione della pestilenza tradotta . . . del Sig. Conte Del Zaffo* (Padua, 1577).

34 G. Cozzi, 'Federico Contarini: un antiquario veneziano tra Rinascimento e Contrariforma', *Bolletino dell'Istituto di Storia della Societa e dello Stato Veneziano* III (1961), pp. 190–220.

35 See, in general, R. Gallo, 'Reliquie e reliquiari veneziani', *Rivista di Venezia* XIII (1934), pp. 187–214, and S. Tramontin, ed., *Il culto dei santi a Venezia* (Venice, 1965).

36 D. Howard, *Venice and the East: The Impact of the Islamic World on Venetian Architecture, 1100–1500* (New Haven, CT, and London, 2000), p. 216.

37 P. Brown, *The Cult of the Saints: Its Rise and Function in Latin Antiquity* (Chicago, IL, 1981), pp. 88–9.

38 K. M. Setton, 'St George's Head', *Speculum* XLVIII (1973), pp. 1–12.

39 S. Tramontin, 'Influsso orientale nel culto dei santi a Venezia fino al secolo XV', in A. Pertusi, ed., *Venezia e il Levante fino al secolo XV*, 3 vols (Florence, 1983), I, pp. 803–9.

40 Gallo, 'Reliquie e reliquiari veneziani', p. 187.

41 G. Botero, *Relatione della republica venetiana con un discorso intorno allo stato della chiesa* (Venice, 1605), p. 105; A. Segarizzi, ed., *Relazioni degli ambasciatori veneti al senato*, 2 vols (Bari, 1912–13), p. 141.

42 Gallo, 'Reliquie e reliquiari veneziani', pp. 189–92.

43 On Tiepolo, see G. Cozzi, 'Note su Giovanni Tiepolo, primicerio di San Marco e patriarca di Venezia: l'unità ideale della chiesa veneta', in B. Bertoli, ed., *Chiesa, società, stato a Venezia: miscellanea di studi in onore di Silvio Tramontin* (Venice, 1994), pp. 121–50.

44 G. Tiepolo, *Dell'ira di Dio e de' flagella e calamità che per essa vengona al mondo* (Venice, 1632), pp. 283, 812–926, 1025–30.

45 G. C. Vergaro, *Racconto dell'apparato et solennita fatta nella ducal chiesa di San Marco di Venetia . . .* (Venice, 1617), pp. 6–12.

46 The *Officium de inventione sanguinis D. N. Iesu Christi, quod Mantuae in festo eius celebratur, in eademquae civitate hactenus pluries impressum* (Venice, 1617), printed in response to the rediscovery of the relics and in particular to that of the Precious Blood, sets out the liturgy on that feast-day in the basilica of Sant'Andrea in Mantua, where one of the most prestigious relics of the Precious Blood was kept. According to this, the five psalms performed at vespers were 'Dixit Dominus', 'Confitebor Domine', 'Beatus Vir', 'Laudate pueri' and 'Laudate Dominum'.

47 The principal printed descriptions of the rediscovery of the relics, of the procession and of their exposition in the basilica are G. Tiepolo, *Trattato delle santissime reliquie, ultimamente ritrovate nel suantuario della chiesa di San Marco* (Venice, 1617); A. Suriano, *Breve descrittione del*

sacro thesoro delle reliquie, ritrovate nel santuario della Chiesa Ducale di San Marco, & honorate con solenne processione a 28 di Maggio del 1617 (Venice, 1617); and Vergaro, *Racconto dell'apparato et solennita fatta nella ducal chiesa di San Marco di Venetia*. For a discussion of one of the relics discovered in 1617, see D. Pincus, 'Christian Relics and the Body Politic: A Thirteenth-century Relief Plaque in the Church of San Marco', in D. Rosand, ed., *Interpretazioni veneziane: studi di storia d'arte in onore di Michelangelo Muraro* (Venice, 1984), pp. 39–57.

48 Contin had previously been involved in a number of public works, and had also been employed at San Fantin; see F. Ongania, ed., *La basilica di S. Marco in Venezia illustrate nella storia e nell'arte da scrittori veneziani* (Venice, 1878–93), p. 220; ASV, San Fantin, b. 2, compendio, f. 2.

49 *Supplicationes. Ad Sanctissimam Verginem Mariam. Tempore belli. Secondum consuetudinem Ducalis Basilicae S; Marci Venetiarum* (Venice, 1695).

50 As in Tiepolo, *Dell'ira di Dio*, p. 1025.

51 See J. H. Moore, 'Music for the Madonna Nicopeia and Santa Maria della Salute', *Journal of the American Musicological Society* XXXVII (1984), pp. 299–355.

EPILOGUE

1 Petrarch, *Epistolae seniles*, IV, 3.

2 G. Fasoli, 'Nascità di un mito', *Studi storici in onore di Gioacchino Volpe*, I (Florence, 1958), pp. 445–79.

3 G. Fasoli, 'Commune Veneciarum', in *Venezia dalla Prima Crociata alla conquista di Costantinopoli del 1204* (Florence, 1965), p. 486.

4 W. Hammer, 'The Concept of the New or Second Rome in the Middle Ages', *Speculum* XIX (1944), pp. 51–5, 60–62, and, for fourteenth-century Venice, E. Muir, *Civic Ritual in Renaissance Venice* (Princeton, NJ, 1981), pp. 24–5.

5 P. H. Labalme, *Bernardo Giustiniani: A Venetian of the Quattrocento* (Rome, 1969), pp. 247–304.

6 B. Marx, *Venezia – altera Roma? ipotesi sull'umanesimo veneziano* (Venice, 1978), pp. 9–10.

7 F. Gaeta, 'Alcune considerazioni sul mito di Venezia', *Bibliothèque d'humanisme et Renaissance* XXIII (1961), pp. 58–75.

8 F. Gilbert, 'Venice in the Crisis of the League of Cambrai', in J. Hale, ed., *Renaissance Venice* (London, 1973), p. 277.

9 E. Gleason, 'Confronting New Realities: Venice and the Peace of Bologna, 1530', in J. Martin and D. Romano, eds, *Venice Reconsidered: The History and Civilization of an Italian City State, 1297–1797* (Baltimore, MD, and London, 2000), pp. 171–8.

10 W. J. Bouwsma, 'Venice and the Political Education of Europe', in J. Hale, ed., *Renaissance Venice* (London, 1973), p. 445.

11 E. Gleason, *Gasparo Contarini: Venice, Rome and Reform* (Berkeley, CA, 1993), especially chapters 1–2; Gleason, 'Confronting New Realities', pp. 178–80.

12 Fasoli, 'Nascità di un mito'.

13 D. Robey and J. Law, 'The Venetian Myth and the *De Republica Veneta* of Pier Paolo Vergerio', *Rinascimento* XV (1975), p. 9, and, for Benzo's text, pp. 56–7.

14 P. L. Fantelli, 'L'ingresso di Enrico III a Venezia di Andrea Vicentino', *Quaderni della Soprintendenza ai Beni Artistici e Storia di Venezia* VII (1979), pp. 95–99; W. Wolters, *Storia e politica nei dipinti di Palazzo Ducale; aspetti dell' autocerestrazione della Repubblica di Venezia nel Cinquecento* (Venice, 1987), pp. 213–18.

15 J. Schulz, *Venetian Painted Ceilings of the Renaissance* (Berkeley, CA, 1968), pp. 107–11.

16 G. Bardi, *Dichiaratione di tutte le istorie che si contengono ne i quadri posti nelle salle dello Scrutinio & del Gran Consiglio, del Palagio Ducale della serenissima republica di Vinegia* (Venice, 1587), f. 2v. For a manuscript version, see Wolters, *Storia e politica nei dipinti di Palazzo Ducale*, pp. 343–54.

17 Bardi, *Dichiaratione*, ff. 3–3v, 5v.

18 For the complete programme, see Bardi, *Dichiaratione*, ff. 62v–63v, and for discussions, Schulz, *Venetian Painted Ceilings of the Renaissance*, p. 110; S. Sinding-Larsen,

Christ in the Council Hall: Studies in the Religious Iconography of the Venetian Republic (Rome, 1974), pp. 220–40; D. Rosand, *Myths of Venice: The Figuration of a State* (Chapel Hill, NC, and London, 2001), pp. 39–46.

19 S. M. Mason Rinaldi, *Palma il Giovane: l'opera completa* (Milan, 1984), p. 140, cat. 528. See Sinding-Larsen, *Christ in the Council Hall*, pp. 224–5.

20 R. Pallucchini and P. Rossi, *Tintoretto: le opere sacre e profane*, 2 vols (Milan, 1982), I, pp. 95–8 II, pp. 216–17, cat. 401. Some commentators have seen the wreath as being of laurel as is specified in Bardi's programme; see Sinding-Larsen, *Christ in the Council Hall*, p. 229.

21 Sinding-Larsen, *Christ in the Council Hall*, p. 228.

22 T. Pignatti and F. Pedrocco, *Veronese*, 2 vols (Milan, 1995), II, pp. 407–8, cat. 295.

23 Sinding-Larsen, *Christ in the Council Hall*, pp. 230–32.

24 C. Kallendorf, *Virgil and the Myth of Venice: Books and Readers in the Italian Renaissance* (Oxford, 1999), p. 13.

25 G. Cozzi, 'Federico Contarini: un antiquario veneziano tra Rinascimento e Contrariforma', *Bolletino dell'Istituto di Storia della Societa e dello Stato Veneziano* III (1961), pp. 195–8.

26 D. Romano, *Patricians and Popolani: The Social Foundations of the Venetian Renaissance State* (Baltimore, MD, and London, 1987), pp. II, 152–8.

BIBLIOGRAPHY

BOOKS PRINTED BEFORE 1700

A. F., *Sonetto a M. Celio Magno, sopra la sua canzone, nella vittoria dell'armata Christiana, contra la Turchesca* (Venice, 1572)

L'acerbo pianto della moglie di Caracossa (n. p., n. d.)

Adrario, A., *Per la vittoria dell'armata christiana* (Venice: [D. Farri], [1571])

Di Adriano et di Jachet: i salmi appertinenti alli vesperi per tutte le feste dell'anno, parte a versi, et parte spezzadi accomodati da cantare a uno et a duoi chori (Venice: A. Gardano, 1550)

Albertonio, F., *L'entrate che fece l'ecllentissimo [sic] Marcantonio Colonna in Roma alli 4 di dicembre 1571. Dove minutamente si narra il viaggio, il numero della gente, l'ordine et le livree, et altre cose . . . Con l'avviso della solennita che fu poi fatta in Santa Maria d'Aracoeli il giorno di Santa Lucia* (Viterbo, 1572)

Alcune compositioni volgari et latine nelle quali si ricordano le misere conditioni della mortal pestilenza successa in Vinegia l'anno MDLXXVI (Vicenza: G. Angelieri, 1576)

Alfabeto sententioso sopra la vittoria dell armata christiana contra infideli (n. p., [1571])

Alla Santità di Papa Pio Quinto. Al serenissimo signor Don Giovanni d'Austria, et a tutti gli altri vivi, & morti in battaglia; A Sultan Seli. Mastro Gottardo da Sech ([Bologna], stampato in San Mammolo, [1571])

Le allegrezze et solennita fatta in Cracovia citta principale del regno di Polonia. Nella coronatione del Serenissimo Re Enrico di Valois fratello di Carlo IX Christianissimo Re di Francia ([Venice, 1574])

Le allegrezze fatte in Venetia per la miracolosa vittoria ottenuta dalla Santissima Liga il di de Santa Iustina adi 7 Ottobrio 1571 (n. p., n. d.)

Altomira, F., *Narratione della guerra di Nicosia, fatta nel regno di Cipro da' Turchi l'anno MDLXX* (Bologna: B. Bignami, 1571)

Amalteo, G. B., *Canzone . . . sopra la vittoria seguita contra l'armata turchesca* (Venice: O. Farri, 1572)

Antiphonae, psalmi, preces et orationes, ad usum supplicationum tempore pestis (Milan: P. Pontio, 1577)

Aretino, P., *Le lettere* (Venice: F. Marcolini, 1538)

—, *Cortigiana. Comedia* (Venice: F. Marcolini, 1538)

Avanzo, M., *Aviso della solennissima et trionfante entrata nella inclita citta di Venezia, del val-*

orosissimo, e prudentissimo capitano generale dell'armata della serenissima republica venetiana, l'illustrissimo S. Sebastiano Veniero, benemeritissimo procurator della chiesa di San Marco (Venice: [D. & G. Guerra], 1574)

—, ed., *Bella dotta e giuditiosa canzone venuta da Verona fatta in lode dell'eccellentissimo general Veniero* (Venice: D. Farri, 1573)

Aviso a Sultan Selim de la rotta de la sua armada & la morte de i suoi capitani, composta il lingua vinitiana, con un sonetto, il qual lo esorta a venir a la fede di Christo (n. p., n. d.)

Avvisi particolari della felice, et gloriosa incoronatione di Henrico III re di Francia et IIII di Polonia (Venice: B. de' Valenti, 1575)

Baccusi, I., *Il secondo libro de madrigali a cinque voci, con una canzone nella gran vittoria contra i turchi* (Venice: G. Scotto, 1572)

—, *Il secondo libro de madrigali a sei voci, con una canzone nella gran vittoria contra i turchi* (Venice: G. Scotto, 1572)

Ballino, G., *Tre canzoni sopra la guerra turchesca, et sopra la vittoria, nuovamente contra quella natione ottenuta* (Venice: D. & G. B. Guerra, 1571)

Barbante, A., *Canzona in allegrezza della felicissima vittoria ricevuta dall'armata christiana contro l'armata turchesca* ([Venice: O. Farri, 1571])

Bardi, G., *Dichiaratione di tutte le istorie che si contengono ne i quadri posti nelle salle dello Scrutinio & del Gran Consiglio, del Palagio Ducale della serenissima republica di Vinegia* (Venice: F. Valgrisio, 1587)

—, *Vittoria navale ottenuta dalla republica venetiana contra Othone, figliuolo di Federico, primo imperadore, per la restitutione di Alessandro terzo, pontefice massimo* (Venice: F. Ziletti, 1584)

Bargagli, S., *Dell'imprese* (Venice: F. de' Franceschi, 1589)

Bassano, A., *Dichiaratione dell'arco fatto in Padova nella venuta della serenissima reina Bona di Polonia* (Padua: G. Percacino, 1556)

Bassano, G., *Concerti ecclesiastici a cinque, sei, sette, otto e dodeci voci . . . libro secondo* (Venice: G. Vincenti, 1599)

—, *Motetti per concerti ecclesiastici a 5, 6, 7, 8, & 12 voci di Giovanni Bassano Musico della Serenissima Signoria di Venetia, Et Maestro di Musica del Seminario di San Marco* (Venice: G. Vincenti, 1598)

Bellavere, G. B., *Oratione nella creatione del serenissimo prencipe di Venetia Sebastiano Veniero* (n. p., n. d.)

Il bellissimo et suntuoso trionfo fatto nella magnifica citta di Venetia nella publicatione della Lega (Brescia, 1571)

Il bellissimo ordine dell'armata della Santa Lega, contra gl'infedeli (Milan: G. B. Ponte, 1571)

Bembo, P., *Della historia vinitiana* (Venice: G. Scotto, 1552)

Benedetti, R., *Ad urbem Venetiarum tempore belli adversus Turcas psalmus* ([Venice: D. de' Franceschi], 1570)

—, *Al serenissimo sig. don Giovanni d'Austria . . . salmo tradotto in rime sciolte* (Bologna: A. Benaccio, 1571)

—, *Le feste et trionfi fatti dalla serenissima signoria di Venetia nella felice venuta di Henrico III Christianissimo Re di Francia et di Polonia* (Venice: alla libraria della stella 1574)

—, *Le feste et trionfi fatti dalla serenissima signoria di Venetia nella felice venuta di Henrico III Christianissimo Re di Francia et III di Polonia et in questa seconda editione sono aggiunti molti diversi & degni particolari, che nella prima non erano* (Venice: alla libraria della stella, 1574) [references are to this edition]

—, *Le feste et trionfi fatti dalla serenissima signoria di Venetia nella felice venuta di Henrico III Christianissimo Re di Francia et di Polonia* (Venice: [V. & B. Viani], 1574)

—, *Le feste et trionfi fatti dalla serenissima signoria di Venetia nella felice venuta di Henrico III Christianissimo Re di Francia et di Polonia insieme l'allegrezze fatte in Treviso, & nella città di Ferrara, fino a la sua partita per la città di Mantova* (Verona: B. & G. dalle Donne, 1574)

—, *Pio, e catholico ragionamento del sommo pontefice et della verita* (Venice: G. Perchacino, 1571)

—, *Ragguaglio delle allegrezze, solennita, e feste, fatte in Venetia per la felice vittoria* (Venice: G. Perchacino, 1571)

—, *Relatione d'alcuni casi occorsi in Venetia al tempo della peste l'anno 1576 e 1577* (Bologna: 1630)

—, *I trionfi et le gran feste fatte dalla Serenissima Signoria di Venetia nella venuta del Christianissimo, et invitissimo Henrico III di Francia et di Polonia* (Venice: D. Farri, 1574)

—, and M. Lumina, *Raguaglio minutissimo del successo della peste di Venetia, con gli casi occorsi, provisioni fatte, & altri particolari, infino alla liberatione di essa. Et la relatione particolare della publicata liberatione, con le solenne e devote pompe* (Tivoli: D. Piolato, 1577)

Bessarion, Cardinal, *Ad illustrissimos Italiae principes contra Turcas exhortatio* (Rome: A. Blado, 1537)

—, *Lettere et orationi tradotte in lingua italiana. Nelle quali esorta i prencipe d'Italia alla lega I à prendere la guerra contra il turco* (Venice: Comin da Trino, 1573)

Besta, G. F., *Vera narratione del successo della peste, che afflisse l'inclita città di Milano, l'anno 1576 & di tutte le provisioni fatte a salute di essa città* (Milan: P. G. & P. Ponte, 1578)

Bidelli, G., *Centoni del Petrarca* ([Venice]: ad instantia di Leonardo detto il Furlano, 1544)

Bisciola, P., *Relatione verissima del progresso della peste di Milano* (Bologna: A. Benacci, 1577)

Blessi, Manoli [Antonio Molino], *Dialogo de Selin con Giosuf Hebreo* (Venice, [1572])

—, *Il primo libro delle greghesche con la musicha disopra, composta da diversi autori, a quatro, a cinque, a sei, a sette, & a otto voci* (Venice: A. Gardano, 1564)

—, *Pianto et lamento de Selin drian imperador de Turchi: ella rotta, & destruttion della so armada. Con un' esortation fatta a Occhiali* (Venice, 1571)

—, *Sopra la presa de Margaritin. Con un dialogo piacevole di un greco, & di un fachino* (Venice: A. Muschio, 1571)

—, *Il vero successo della presa di Nicosia* (Venice: [D. Farri], 1572)

Boccarini, G., *Dui libri del veneto senato dove si tratta in ottava rima della edificatione di Venetia, & delli fatti heroi della serenis. republica.* (Venice: D. Farri, 1583)

Bolognetti, F., *La christiana vittoria maritima* (Bologna: A. Benaccio, 1572)

Borgarucci, B., *L'afflition di Venetia. Nella quale si ragiona di tutti gli accidenti occorsi in Vinetia, l'anno 1576 per cagion di peste* (Florence: A. Padovani, 1578)

Boschini, M., *Le minere della pittura* (Venice: F. Nicolini, 1664)

Botero, G., *Della ragion di stato libri dieci, con tre libri delle cause della grandezza della citta* (Venice: Gioliti, 1589)

—, *Relatione della republica venetiana con un discorso intorno allo stato della chiesa* (Venice: G. Varisco, 1605)

Brenzone, C. S., *Vita et fatti del valorissimo capitano Astorre Baglione da Perugia* (Verona: S. dalle Donne, 1591)

Buccio, P., *Le coronationi di Polonia, et di Francia del christianissimo Re Henrico III. Con le attioni, et successi de' suoi viaggi descritte in dieci giornate* (Padua, L. Pasquati, 1576)

—, *Oratione sopra la vittoria christiana contra Turchi ottenuta l'anno felicissimo MDLXXI* (Venice: D. de' Franceschi, 1571)

Bugati, G., *I fatti di Milano, al contrario della peste, over pestifero contagio. Dal primo agosto 1576 fino a l'ultimo dell'anno 1577* (Milan: P. G. and P. Ponte, 1578)

Camocio, G. F., *L'ordine delle galere et le insegne loro, con li fano, nomi, & cognomi delli magnifici, & generosi patroni di esse, che si ritrovorno nella armata della santissima Lega, al tempo della vittoriosa, & miracolosa impresa ottenuta, & fatta con lo aiuto divino, contra la orgogliosa, & superba armata turchesca* (Venice: G. F. Camocio, 1571)

Canato, B., *Capitolo in laude di Venezia* (Venice: D. Farri, 1560)

Canobbio, A., *Il successo della peste occorsa in Padova l'anno MDLXXVI* (Venice: P. Megietti, 1577)

Cantico reprehensible de sier alessio i disconzi a Selin imperator de Turchi (n. p., n. d.)

Canzon de San Martin, con la laude de i fortarioli da cantar per i putti (Venice, 1579)

Canzon a Selim imperator de turchi. In desperation della sua armata, e gente persa. Composta nuovamente & data in luce. Con due sonetti bellissimi e sentiosi (n. p., n. d.)

Canzone sopra la vittoria dell'armata christiana contra la turchesca (Venice, G. Perchacino, 1571)

Canzon sora l'armà d'i cofani de Selin turcho sbatezo . . . de reoto d'i bertiviegi (n. p., [1571])

Canzone al Signor Dio sopra la felicissima vittoria dell'armata della santissima lega, contra la turchesca (Venice: s. n. [D. Farri], 1572)

Canzone fatta intorno allo stato calamitoso dell'inclitta città di Venetia, nel colmo de' maggiori suoi passati travagli per la peste (Padua, 1577)

Canzone per la gloriosa vittoria contra il turco, con due sonetti et una epigramma latina (Venice, [1571])

Canzone sopra la citta di Venetia liberata da la peste (Verona: S. & G; dalle Donne, 1577)

Capitolo della Academia de Altin, ditta la Sgionfa, corretto per el Zenzega dottor e legislator povieiotto, sora la vittoria christiana (n. p., [1571])

Capitoli della lega tra la santita del nostro signor Papa Pio V et il serenissimo re catolico, et la illustrissima signoria di Venetia (n. p., [1570])

Capitolo di Venetia ove trattasi di tutte e principi loro, con loro vittorie, honori, & dignitati, edification di chiese, palagi, guerre, ribillioni ufficii, e molte altre bellissime cose (Venice: F. di A. Bindoni & M. Pasini, 1532)

Caracciolo, F., *I commentari delle guerre fatte coi Turchi da Don Giovanni d'Austria* (Florence: G. Marescotti, 1581)

Caravia, A., *Naspo bizaro* (Venice: D. Nicolino, 1565)

—, *Il sogno dil Caravia* (Venice: G. A. da Sabbio, 1541)

—, *La verra antiga dei Castellani, Canaruoli e Gnatti, con la morte de Giurco e Gnagni in lengua brava* (Venice, 1550)

Castello, A. da, *Liber sacerdotalis* (Venice: M. Sessa and P. de Ravanis, 1523)

—, *Rosario della gloriosa Vergine Maria* (Venice: M. Sessa and P. de [Ravanis] da le Serena, 1524)

Catena, G., *Vita del gloriosissimo Papa Pio Quinto* (Rome: V. Accolti, 1586)

Cavagnini, G., *Compilatione delli veri et fedeli rimedi da preservarsi, et curarsi dalla peste, con la cura degli antraci, carboni et giandusse* (Brescia: V. Sabbio, 1576)

Cavalcanti, B., *Trattati overo discorsi sopra gli ottimi reggimenti delle repubbliche antiche e moderne. Con un discorso di M. Sebastiano Erizo gentil'huomo vinitiano de' governi civili* (Venice: J. Sansovino, 1570)

Ceremonie fatte nella publicatione della lega fatta in Venetia con la dechiaratione di solari & altre cose come legendo inendereti (n. p., n. d.)

Ceremonie osservate per l'alleanza de' Veneziani con Paolo III e con l'Imperatore contro il Turco (Venice, 1537)

Collini, G. L., *Esplicatione de i carri trionfali fatti nella processione per la pace tra Franza e Spagna* (Venice: M. A. Zaltieri, 1598)

Contarini, G., *The Common-wealth and Government of Venice* (London: J. Windet, 1599)

—, *La Republica e i magistrati di Vinegia* (Venice: G. Scotto, 1544)

—, *Oratione della pestilenza tradotta . . . del Sig. Conte Del Zaffo* (Padua: L. Pasquati, 1577)

Contarini, G. P., *Historia delle cose successe dal principio della guerra mossa da Selim ottomano a Venetiani fino al di della gran giornata vittoriosa contra Turchi* (Venice: F. Rampazetto, 1572)

Contile, L., *Delle lettere di Luca Contile: primo (-secondo) volume diviso in due libri* (Pavia: G. B. Turlini, 1564)

Cortesi, C., *Giustina reina di Padova* (Vicenza: P. Greco and G. Cescato, 1607)

Coryate, T., *Coryat's crudities hastily gobled up in five moneths travells in France, Savoy, Italy, Rhetia* (London: William Stansby, 1611)

Croce, G., *Devotissime lamentationi et improperii per la settimana santa con le lettioni della natività di Nostro Signore a quatro voci* (Venice: G. Vincenti, 1604)

—, *Mascarate piacevole et ridicolese per il carnevale, a 4.5.6.7. & otto voci* (Venice: G. Vincenti, 1590)

—, *Motetti a otto voci di Giovanni Croce Chiozzotto Vice Maestro di Capella della Serenissima Signoria di Venetia, in San Marco. Commodi per le voci, e per cantar con ogni stromento. Novamente ristampati, & corretti* (Venice: G. Vincenti, 1599)

—, *Triaca musicale nella quale vi sono diversi caprici* (Venice: G. Vincenti, 1595)

—, *Messe a otto voci* (Venice: G. Vincenti, 1596)

La cronica della guerra successa tra Christiani e'l Turco . . . (Venice: G. B. Bonfadino, 1609)

D'Angeli, B., *Oratione nella creatione del Serenissimo Prencipe di Vinegia Sebastiano Veniero* (n. p., n. d.)

Della Croce, M., *L'historia della publica et famosa entrata in Venegia del serenissimo Henrico III di Francia et Polonia con la descrittione particolare della pompa, e del numero, et varieta delli bregantini, paleschermi et altri vascelli, con la dechiaratione dell'edificio, et arco fatto al Lido* (Venice: [Comin da Trino], 1574)

Dialoghi musicali de diversi eccellentissimi autori, a sette, otto, nove, dieci, undeci, et dodeci voci . . . con due battaglie a otto voci, per sonar de istrumenti da fiato, di Annibale Padoano et de Andrea Gabrieli, già organisti della Serenissima Signoria di Venetia in San Marco (Venice: A. Gardano, 1590)

Diedo, G., *Lettera all'illustrissimo Sig. Marc'Antonio Barbaro Eccellentissimo Bailo in Constantinopli, nella quale cosi fedelmente, come partitamente, et appieno si descrive la gran battaglia navale seguito l'anno MDLXX a Curzolari* (Venice: Heirs of F. Ziletti, 1573)

Discorso sopra due grandi e memorabili battaglie navali fatte nel mondo l'una di Cesare Augusto con M. Antonio l'altra delli Sig. Venetiani e della santissima Lega con Sultan Selim Signor di Turchi (Bologna: A. Benaccio, 1572)

Discorso sopra gli accidenti del parto mostruoso nato in una Hebrea in Venetia nell'anno 1575 a di XXVI di Maggio. Dove si ragiona altamente del futuro destino de gli Hebrei ([Venice, 1575])

Discorso sopra gli accidenti del parto mostruoso nato in una Hebrea in Venetia nell'anno 1575 a di XXVI di Maggio . . . Di novo ristampato, e con le annotationi di Giovanni Gioseppe Gregorio Cremonese ampliato (Venice: D. Farri, 1575)

Discorso sopra il Pater Noster in lingua rustica, per la vittoria de Christiani contra Turchi (n. p., n. d.)

Discorso sopra il significato mostruoso (Venice, 1575)

Doglioni, G. N., *La citta di Venezia, con l'origine e governo di quella et i Dogi che vi sono stati, et tutte le cose notabili, che da tempo in tempo vi sono avvenate* (Venice, 1594)

Donzellini, G., *Discorso nobilissimo e dottissimo preservativo et curativo della peste* (Venice: H. de i Gobi da Salo, 1577)

Dorron, C., *Discours des choses mémorables faittes à l'entrée du Roy de France et de Pologne en la ville de Venize* (Lyons: B. Rigaud, 1574)

—, *Narratio rerum memorabilium, quae propter adventum Christianissimi Invictissimique Henrici III Franciae & Poloniae Regis, a totius orbis florentissima Venetorum Republica factae sunt* (Venice, 1574)

Due canzoni in barzelletta, per i putti di cantar per S. Martino ([Venice], n. d.)

La elettione del principe di Venetia (Venice: M. Pagan, 1556)

La entrata che fece in Vinegia l'Illustrissimo et Eccellentissimo S. Duca Alfonso II Estense, Duca V. di Ferrara (Venice, 1562)

Episcopale bononiensis civitatis et diocesis. Raccolta di varie cose che in diversi tempi sono state ordinate da Monsig. Illustriss. & Reverendiss. Cardinale Paleotti Vescovo di Bologna (Bologna, 1580)

Exhortation fatta a Occhiali (n. p., n. d.)

Fabri, A., *Diversarum nationum ornatus* (Padua, 1593)

Fantasia composta in laude di Veniesia (Venice: F. Rampazetto, 1582)

Faroldo, G., *Annali veneti* (Venice: G. Varisco, 1577)

Ferretti, G., *Il primo libro delle canzoni alla napolitana a sei voci* (Venice: G. Scotto, 1573)

Ferro, S., *Trattato della peste et sua preservatione et cura* (Foligno: V. Cantagallo, 1575)

Le feste et trionfi fatti nella nobilissima città di Padoa nella felicissima venuta, et passagio di Henrico III, Christianissimo Re di Francia & Pollonia (Padua and Venice: [V. and B. Viani], 1574)

[Fiamma, G]., *Parafrasi poetica sopra alcuni salmi di David molto accomodati per render grazie a Dio della vittoria donata al christianesimo e contra a' Turchi* (Venice: N. Bevilacqua, 1571)

Ficino, M., *Contro alla peste* (Florence: Giunti, 1576)

Filiarchi, C., *Trattato della guerra, et dell'unione de' principi christiani contra i Turchi, & gli altri infedeli* (Venice: G. Gioliti, 1572)

—, *Trattato della Lega e del seguitar la guerra contra il Turco* (Rome: V. Eliano, 1573)

Fioravanti, L., *Del regimento della peste* (Venice: A. Ravenoldo, 1565)

Franco, G., *Habiti delle donne venetiane intagliate in rame* (Venice, n. d.)

—, *Habiti d'huomeni et donne venetiane con la processione della serenissima signoria et altri particolari cioe trionfi feste cerimonie publiche della nobilissima citta di Venetia* (Venice: G. B. Franco, 1610)

Frangipane, C., *Tragedia . . . al christianissimo et invitissimo Henrico III Re di Francia e di Polonia recitata nella sala del gran consiglio di Venetia* (Venice: D. Farri, 1574)

—, *Oratione recitata al prencipe S. Veniero* (Venice: G. B. Guerra, 1577)

Gabrieli, A., *Libellus hospitalis munificentiae venetorum in excipienda Anna regina Hungariae* (Venice, 1502)

Gabrieli, A., *Gregesche et iustiniane . . . a tre voci . . . libro primo* (Venice: A. Gardano, 1571)

—, *Madrigali et ricercari a quattro voci* (Venice: A. Gardano, 1589)

—, and G. Gabrieli, *Concerti . . . continenti musica di chiesa, madrigali, & altro, per voci e stromenti musicali, a 6. 7. 8. 10. 12. & 16 . . . libro primo e secondo* (Venice: A. Gardano, 1587)

Gabrieli, G., *Sacrae symphoniae . . . senis 7, 8, 10, 12, 14, 15, and 16 tam vocibus, quam instrumentus* (Venice: A. Gardano, 1597)

Gabutio, G. A., *De vita et rebus gestis Pii V Pont. Max. Libri sex* (Rome, 1605)

Gambara, L., *Rerum sacrarum liber* (Antwerp: C. Plantin, 1577)

Garenzio, G., *La vera et famosa indovinatione della sibilla eritrea fatta a istanza de' prencipi di Greci, quando gli dimandaron consiglio intorno l'impresa di Troia* (Venice, 1570)

Garnet, H., *The Societie of the Rosary* (London, at Father Garnet's press, 1593)

Garzoni, T., *La piazza universale di tutte le professioni del mondo* (Venice: G. B. Somasco, 1585)

Gentile, P., *Della historia di Malta e successo della guerra* (n. p., n. d.)

Gherardi, P., ed., *In foedus et victoriam contra Turcas . . . poemata varii* (Venice: Guerra, 1572)

Giannotti, D., *Libro de la republica de Vinitiani* (Rome: A. Blado, 1540)

Giustiniani, B., *De origine urbis Venetiarum* (Venice: per B. Benalio, 1493)

—, *Historia dell'origine di Vinegia et delle cose fatte da Vinitiani . . . tradotta da M. Lodovico Domenichi* (Venice: B. Bindoni, 1545)

Giustiniani, L., *Doctrina . . . della vita monastica* (Venice: B. Bernalio, 1494)

Giustiniani, P., *Le historie venetiane di nuovo rivedute et ampliate . . . pur hora in lingua volgare tradotte* (Venice: 1576)

Giusti, V., *Boscherezza canzone nella foelicissima vittoria christiana contra infideli* (Venice: D. and G. B. Guerra, 1571)

Glisente, A., *Risposta fatta per il sumario delle cause pestilenti alla apologia dell'eccellente M. Annibal Raimondo Veronese* (n. p., [1576])

—, *Il summario delle cause che dispongono i corpi de gli huomini a patire la corrottione pestilente del presente anno MDLXXVI* (n. p., [1576])

—, *Trattato del regimento del vivere, et delle altre cose che devono usare gli huomini per preservarsi sani nelli tempi pestilenti* (n. p., n. d.)

Gradenigo, F., *Sopra le imprese della Republica dipinte nella Sala di Scrutinio* (Venice, 1594)

Il gran lamento & pianto che fa il populo Surrentino, & di Massa, per esser presi, sacchegiati, & morti dalla armata Turchesca. L'anno mdlvii. Alli xiii del mese di Luglio (n. p. [1557])

I gran trionfi fatti nella nobil città di Treviso nella venuta del Christianissimo Re di Francia & di Polonia Henrico Terzo (Venice, 1574)

Grassi, L., *Canzone sopra la peste, nuovamente posta in luce* (Vicenza: G. Angelieri, 1576)

Gratiolo, A., *Discorso di peste* (Venice: G. Polo, 1576)

Groto, L., *Canzone nella morte del Clarissimo M. Agostin Barbarigo* (Venice: O. Farri, 1572)

—, *Oratione fatta in Vinegia, per l'allegrezza della vittoria ottenuta contra Turchi dalla Santissima Lega* (Venice: F. Rocca and B. de Ventura, 1571)

—, *Oratione . . . nella creatione del Serenissimo Prencipe di Vinegia, Luigi Mocenigo nella qual is rallegra della sua dignita, et esshorta tutti i Prencipi Christiani all'impresa contra Turchi* (Venice: A. Arrivabene, 1570)

—, *Oratione nella creatione del Serenissimo Prencipe di Vinegia Sebastian Veniero* (Venice: F. and A. Zoppini, 1577)

—, *Le orationi volgari* (Venice: li Zoppini, 1598)

—, *Trofeo della vittoria sacra, ottenuta dalla christianissima Lega contra Turchi nell'anno MDLXXI* (Venice: S. Bordogna and F. Patriani, 1572)

Gualtieri, G., *Canzone sopra la vittoria ottenuta dall'armata de' prencipi christiani contra la turchesca* (Venice: A. Muschio, 1571)

—, *Relationi della venuta de gli ambasciatori Giaponesi a Roma, fino alla partita di Lisbona. Con una descrittione del lor paese, e costumi, e con le accoglienze fatte loro da tutti i prencipe Christiani, per dove sono passati* (Venice: F. Zanetti, 1586)

Guisconi, A. [F. Sansovino], *Dialogo di tutte le cose notabili che sono in Venetia* (Venice, [1556])

Howell, J., *A Survey of the Signorie of Venice* (London, 1651)

Index librorum prohibitorum, cum regulis confectis per Patres a Tridentina Synodo delectos, auctoritate Sanctiss. D. N. Pii IIII, Pont. Max. comprobatus (Venice: [P. Manuzio], 1564)

Indice copioso, e particolare, di tutti li libri stampati dalli Gioliti in Venetia, fino all'anno 1592 ([Venice: G. P. Giolito de Ferrari, 1592])

Infantas, F. de las, *Sacrarum varii styli cantionum tituii spiritus santi. Liber primus cum quatuor vocibus* (Venice: A. Gardano, 1578)

Lamentationum Jeremie prophete liber primus (Venice: O. Petrucci, 1506)

Leoni, B., *Canzone fatta intorno allo stato calamitoso dell'inclita citta di Vinetia, nel colmo de' maggiori suoi passati travagli per la peste. Et nuovamente data in luce* (Florence: G. Marescotti, 1577)

Lettera nella quale si descrive l'ingresso nel palazzo ducale della Serenissima Morosina Morosini Grimani Principessa di Venetia con la ceremonia della rosa benedetta mandatale a donare dalla Santita di Nostro Signore (Venice, 1597)

Lucangeli da Bevagna, N., *Successi del viaggio d'Henrico III christianiss[i]mo re di Francia, e di Polonia, dalla sua partita di Cracovia fino all'arrivo in Turino* (Venice, 1574)

Luis, de Granada, *Rosario della Sacratissima Vergine Maria* (Rome: G. degl' Angeli, 1573)

Lumina, M., *La liberatione di Vinegia dalla peste* (Venice: E. di Alaris 1577)

Magno, C., *Trionfo di Christo per la vittoria contra Turchi, rappresentato al serenissimo prencipe di Venetia, il di di San Stefano* (Venice: D. and G. B. Guerra, 1571)

—, and O. Giustiniano, *Rime* (Venice: A. Muschio, 1600)

Malombra, B., *Al magno Henrico III di Francia* (Venice, 1574)

—, *Canzone a Cristiani essorandoli alla santissima unione contra gli infideli* (Venice: n. p., 1573)

—, *Nuova canzone nella felicissima vittoria contra fideli* (Venice: A. Muschio, 1571)

—, *Poesia rappresentata inanzi la sublimita del P. Alvise Mocenigo, et la serenissima signoria di Venetia a XXVI Decembre MDLXXIII* (Venice, 1574)

—, *Stanze sopra l'incendio della polvere, & in lode di Venetia* (Venice, 1569)

Manolesso, E. M., *La fausta et felice elettione in Re di Polonia, del Serenissimo et valorissimo Henrico di Valois, Duca d'Angio, fratello di Carlo IX christianissimo Re di Francia* (Venice: P. Dehuchino, 1573)

—, *Historia nova nella quale si contengono tutti i successi della guerra turchesca dal anno MDLXX fino al presente hora* (Padua: L. Pasquati, 1572)

Manzini, G., *Il gloriosissimo apparato fatto dalla serenissima republica venetiana per la venuta, per la dimora, & per la partenza del christianissimo Enrico III re di Francia et di Polonia* (Venice: G. Perchacino, 1574)

Marostica, V., *Venetia trionfante* (Venice: D. Farri, 1572)

Martinengo, N., *Relatione di tutto il successo di Famagosta. Dove s'intende minutissimamente tutte le scaramuccie, batterie, mine, & assalti dati ad essa fortezza. Et ancora i nomi dei capitani, & numero delle genti morte, cosi de Christiani, come de Turchi. Et medesimamente di quelli che sono restati pregioni* (Venice: G. Angelieri, 1572)

Martini, G. B., *Vita di S. Giustina vergine e martire, protettrice della citta di Padova. Cavata dall'archivio del monastero a detta santa consecrato* (Padua, 1627)

Martinioni, G.; see Sansovino

Mascherate di Andrea Gabrieli et altri autori eccellentissimi a tre, quattro, cinque, sei, et otto voci (Venice: A. Gardano, 1601)

Masi, A., *Essequie del Serenissimo D. Ferdinando Medici Gran Duca di Toscana III. Celebrate in Venezia dalla Nazione Fiorentina* (Venice, 1609)

Meduna della Motta, B., *Dialogo sopra la miracolosa vittoria ottenuta dall'armata della Santissima Lega Christiana, contra la Turchesca nel quale si dimostra essa vittoria esser venuta dalla sola mano di Dio. Et si discorre a pieno l'ordine del conflitto* (Venice, 1572)

—, *Vita della gloriosa Vergine Maria* (Venice: G. Giolito, 1574)

Menichini, A., *Capitolo nel qual la santissima religion catholica e introdotta a favellar co'l christianissimo potentissimo & invitissimo Henrico III gloriosissimo re di Francia, et di Polonia* (Venice: B. Zaltieri, 1574)

Merulo, C., *Liber primus sacrarum cantionum quinque vocibus* (Venice: A. Gardano, 1578)

Michele, A., *Oratione a Dio per ottenere vittoria contra Turchi* (n. p., [1572])

Miracoli della Croce Santissima della Scuola di San Giovanni Evangelista (Venice, 1590)

Missale praedicatorum nuper impressum ac emendatum cum multis missis orationibus (Venice: Giunta, 1504)

Modo dell'elettione del principe di Venetia (Venice: Rampazetto, 1595)

Molino; see Blessi

Moravio, G., *Panegirico nella traslazion dell'imagine di Nostra Signora nella capella nuova della Chiesa di S. Marco* (Venice: A. Pinelli, 1618)

Morlopino, Abbate., *Le illustri attioni de Serenissimi Principi della famiglia Moceniga* (Venice, 1572)

Moschetta, V., *Vita e trionfo di Giustina vergine et martire santissima. Nell'allegrezza della vittoria ottenuta contra Turchi il giorno della sua passione. Con alcune annotationi, ove si dichiarano molte historie, et anco si ragiona di tutti li corpi santi che sono nella chiesa di S. Giustina di Padova* (Venice: G. Perchacino, 1572)

Musica da diversi auttori illustri per sette, otto, nove, dieci, undeci, et duodeci voci . . . libro primo (Venice: G. Vincenti and R. Amadino, 1584)

Nazari, G. B., *Discorso della futura et sperata vittoria contro il Turco, estratto dai sacri profeti e da altre profetie, prodigij et prognostici* (Venice: S. Bordogna, 1570)

Nelli, N., *Libro de marchi de cavalli* (Venice: N. Nelli, 1569)

—, *Sommario et alboro delli principi ottomani con li loro veri ritratti* (Venice: F. Sansovino, 1567)

Neri, G., *Giudicio overo presagio sopra l'anno 1576 nel quale oltra al giudicio delle quattro parti de l'anno si vede il guidicio sopra l'eclissi della luna* (Verona, n. d.)

Nores, G. de., *Panegirico di Iason de Nores in laude della Serenissima Republica di Venetia, al clarissimo Signor Benedetto Georgio dell'Illustrissimo Signor Alvise patron. et protettor sempre oss.mo* (Padua: P. Meitti, 1590)

Nova et ridicolosa espositione del mostro nato in Ghetto. Con il lamento di suo padre per la morte di quello et quello vogli pronosticare a gli Hebrei non lo havendo potuto circoncidere (Venice, 1575)

Officium Hebdomadae Sanctae secundum consuetudem Ducalis Ecclesiae S. Marci Venetiarum, a Dominica Palmarum usque ad Diem Paschae inclusive. Ad antiquum ritum & integritatem restitutum (Venice: A. Bortoli and B. Maldura, 1722)

Officia propria festi Sancti Marci (Venice, 1602)

Officia proprium Beatae Justinae (Venice, 1584)

Officium de inventione sanguinis D. N. Iesu Christi, quod Mantuae in festo eius celebratur, in eademquae civitate hactenus pluries impressum (Venice: A. Pinelli, 1617)

Opera nova sopra l'allegrezza de' buoni christiani nel sperar mediante il buon provedimento de' signori christiani, la felice vittoria contra infideli, composta in aere di barcelletta (n. p., 1570)

Ordine et dechiaratione di tutta la mascherata fatta nella citta di Venetia la domenica di carnevale MDLXXI per la gloriosa vittoria contra turchi (Venice: G. Angelieri, 1572)

L'ordine tenuto dal clarissimo M. Alvise Grimani. In consignare lo standaro del generalato all'illustrissimo et eccellentissimo S. Giacomo Foscarini, dignissimo capitanio generale dell'armata venetiana nella citta di Zara. Con li trionfi, feste et ceremonie seguite in tal consignatione (Venice, 1572)

Panvinio, O., *Comentario dell'uso et ordine de' trionfi antichi* (Venice: M. Tramezzino, 1571)

Papadopulo, N., *Risposta de Sultan Selim Imperator di Turchi a tutti i sonetti a lui fatti da diversi auttori, & in varie lingue. Medesimamente lui risponde per questi versi, in lingua sua Turchesca, Latina & Italiano. Et con il suo comento dichiarando il tutto* (n. p., n. d.)

Parafrasi poetica sopra alcuni salmi di David molto accomodati per render grazie a Dio della vittoria donata al christianesimo e contra a' Turchi (Venice: N. Bevilacqua, 1571)

Il particulare annotamento del assedio di Malta (n. p., n. d.)

Paruta, P., *Della guerra di Cipro* (Venice, 1605)

—, *Della perfettione della vita politica . . . libri tre* (Venice: D. Nicolini, 1579)

—, *Discorsi politici . . . ne i quali si considerano diversi fatti illustri, e memorabili di principi, e di republiche antiche, e moderne* (Venice: D. Nicolini, 1599)

—, *Historia vinetiana* (Venice: D. Nicolini, 1605)

—, *Oratione funebre . . . in laude de' morti nella vittoriosa battaglia contra Turchi sequita a Curzolari l'anno 1571 alli 7 d'ottobre* (Venice: B. Zaltiero, 1572)

Piccha, G., *Oratione per la guerra contra Turchi a Sisto Quinto Pont. Massimo, et a gl' altri prencipi christiani* (Rome: G. Ferrario, 1589)

Pigafetta, F., *Lettere et oratione del Reverendissimo Cardinale Bessarione tradotte in lingua italiana. Nelle quali esorta il prencipi d'Italia alla Lega et a prendere la guerra contra il Turco* (Venice: Comin da Trino, 1573)

Pino, G., *La vita di S. Rocco* (Venice: 1576)

Pisanelli, B., *Discorso sopra il dragone di fuoco apparso in Roma l'anno 1575* (Bologna: 1575)

—, *Discorso sopra la peste* (Rome: A. Blado, 1577)

Porcacchi, T., *Le attioni d'Arrigo terzo re di Francia et quarto di Polonia descritte in dialogo . . .* (Venice: G. Angelieri, 1574)

Le suntuosissime esequie celebrata nella magnifica città di Bergamo in morte dello illustrissimo signore A. B. con alcuni leggiadri componimenti latini e volgari (Perugia: per V. Panizza, 1572)

Psalterium Davidicum per hebdomadam dispostum (Venice, 1609)

Il quarto libro delle muse a cinque voci composto da diversi eccellentissimi musici, insieme dui mad. à sei, novamente stampati et dati in luce, intitolati benigni spirti (Venice: A. Gardano, 1574)

Raimondo, A., *Discorso quale chiaramente si conosce la viva et vera cagione, che ha generato le fiere infermita, che tanto hanno molestato l'anno 1575, e tanto il 1576 acerbamente molestano il popolo de l'invittissima citta di Venetia indirizzato a tutti quelli che non sono idioti delle cose naturali, de gli accidenti, e che molto intendono la prattica della citta di Vinetia* (Padua, 1586)

Rapicius, J., *De aristocratiae venetae et serenissimi in ea principis Andrea Griti laudibus oratio* (Venice, 1534)

Rappresentatione al Serenissimo Prencipe di Venetia Nicolo da Ponte, il giorno di S. Stefano l'anno 1579 (Venice, 1579)

Rasario, G. B., *De victoria Christianorum ad Echinadas oratio* (Venice: V. Valgrisi, 1571)

Relatione fatta alla maesta Cattolica in Madrid, alli XV di Luglio 1571 di tutta la spesa ordinaria che correra per la lega in 200 galere, 100 navi et 50 mila fanti ogn' anno (Rome, 1571)

Ridolfi Sforza, B., *Vita di Giacopo Foscarini, Cavaliere e Procuratore di S. Marco* ([Venice], 1624)

Sabellico, M. A., *Le historie vinitiane . . . divise in tre deche con tre libri della quarta deca* (Venice: C. T. di Navo, 1544)

Saetti, G., *Sogno sopra la vittoria ottenuta de la Santa Lega contra il Turco* (Venice: [D. Farri], 1572)

Sansovino, F., *Delle cose notabili che sono in Venetia libri due* (Venice: Comin da Trino, 1561); see also Guisconi, A.

—, *Gl'annali turcheschi, ovvero vite de principi della casa othomana* (Venice: F. Sansovino, 1571)

—, *Delle cose notabili della citta di Venetia, libri II . . . nuovamente riformati, accresciuti & abbelliti con l'aggionta della istorie che sono state dipinte ne i quadri delle sale dello Scrutinio, & del gran Consiglio del Palagio Ducale* (Venice: F. Valgrisio, 1587)

—, *Delle orationi recitate a principi di Venetia nella loro creatione da gli ambasciadori di*

diverse citta libro primo (Venice: F. Sansovino, 1562)

—, Dell'istoria universale dell'origine et imperio
de' Turchi (Venice: F. Sansovino, 1568)

—, Lettera o vero discorso sopra le preditioni le
quali pronosticano la nostra futura felicità
(Venice, 1570)

—, Sommario et alboro delli Principi Othomani,
con li loro veri ritratti al naturale di N. Nelli
((Venice, 1567)

—, Venetia città nobilissima et singolare descritta
in XIV libri (Venice: D. Farri, 1581)

— (ed. G. Stringa), Venetia città nobilissima et
singolare descritta in XIIII libri hora con molta
diligenza corretta, emendata, e più d'un terzo
di cose nuove ampliata dal M. R. D. Giovanni
Stringa (Venice: A. Salicato, 1604)

— (ed. G. Martinioni), Venetia città nobilissima
. . . descritta in XIIII libri . . . con aggiunta da
D. Giustiniano Martinioni (Venice: S. Curti,
1663)

Saravezza, B. da, Il breve discorso sopra la cometa
detta la Scarpigliata (Piacenza: G.
Bazzacho and A. Conti, 1577)

Savorgnano, M., La venuta della serenissima
Bona Sforza et d'Aragona reina di Polonia et
duchessa di Bari nella magnifica citta di
Padova a ventisette di marzo. Con l'entrata
nella inclita citta di Vinegia, il di 26 Aprile
1556, et la sua partita per Bari (Venice, 1556)

Scalvo, B., Le meditationi del rosario della Maria
Vergine (Milan: P. Pontio, 1569)

Serlio, S., Tutte l'opere d'architettura et prospettiva diviso in sette libri (Venice: G. de
Franceschi, 1619)

La solenissima entrata dell'illustrissimo et eccellentissimo signor Duca di Ferrara ne la citta
di Venetia cominciando dalla partita di sua
eccellenza da Ferrara per insino al suo ritorno
(Bologna: P. Bonardo, 1562)

Sommario et alboro delli principi othomani con
li loro ritratti (Venice: F. Sansovino, 1567)

Stabile, F., Brevis quaedam defensio contra nonnullos asserentes pudendorum inflammationem
non esse pestis signum (Venice: G.Petchacimo,
1576)

Stringa, G., La chiesa di S. Marco, capella del
serenissimo principe di Venetia, descritta brevemente (Venice: F. Rampazetto, 1610)

—, ed., Officia propria festi Sancti Marci apos-
toli et evangelistae cum octava nec non
Translaionis et Apparitionis corporis eiusdem
(Venice, 1602)

—, ed., Officium Maioris Hebdomadae, iuxta
consuedtudinem Ecclesiae S. Marci Venetiarum; a Dominica Palmarum, usque ad
diem Resurrectionis Domini inclusive (Venice:
F. Rampazetto, [1597])

—, Vita di S. Marco Protettore Invitissimo della
Serenissima Republica di Venetia con la trans-
latione, et apparitione del sacro suo corpo
(Venice: F. Rampazetto, 1610)

—; see also Sansovino

Summario delli capitoli della lega fatta tra Sua
Santita il Sereniss. Re Catholico, & la illustrissima signoria di Venetia (n. p., n. d.)

Le suntuosissime esequie celebrata nella magnifica
città di Bergamo in morte dello illustrissimo
signore A. B. con alcuni leggiadri componimenti latini e volgari (Perugia: per V. Panizza,
1572)

Supplicationes. Ad Sanctissimam Verginem
Mariam. Tempore belli. Secondum consuetudinem Ducalis Basilicae S; Marci Venetiarum (Venice, 1695)

Suriano, A., Breve descrittione del sacro thesoro
delle reliquie, ritrovate nel santuario della
Chiesa Ducale di San Marco, & honorate con
solenne processione a 28 di Maggio del 1617
(Venice, 1617)

Suriano, M., Negoziato et conclusione di Lega
contra il Turco fra Pio V sommo Pontefice, Re
Cattolico et sua signoria di Venetia (Venice,
1571)

Tassolo, D., and B. Mariotti, I trionfi feste, et
livree fatte dalli Signori Conservatori
& Popolo Romano, & da tutte le arti di Roma,
nella felicissima & honorata entrata
dell'Illustrissimo Signor Marcantonio Colonna
(Venice: S. Dalle Donne, 1571)

Tiepolo, G., Dell'ira di Dio e de' flagella e
calamità che per essa vengona al mondo
(Venice: G. Sarzina, 1632)

—, Trattato delle santissime reliquie, ultimamente ritrovate nel santuario della chiesa di
San Marco (Venice, 1617)

—, Trattato dell'imagine della Gloriosa Vergine
dipinta da San Luca. Conservata gia molti

secoli nella Ducal Chiesa di San Marco della Citta di Venetia (Venice: A. Polo, 1618)

Toscanella, O., *Essortatione ai Cristiani contra il Turco* (Venice: S. Bordogna & F. Patriani, 1572)

—, *Oratio nella creatione del Serenissimo Prencipe di Venetia Sebastiano Veniero* (Venice, 1577)

Toscano, R., *Le feste et trionfi de li mercanti della seta per l'allegrezza della vittoria ottenuta contra turchi* ([Venice, 1571])

—, *Il vero e superbo apparato fatto da li integerimi merchanti toschani in Rivoalto novo per la grande allegrezze havuta per la vittoria de' Christiani in honor de la Santissima Lega* ([Venice], 1571)

Varii componimenti di diversi auttori sopra la vittoria dell'armata della santissima lega (n. p., n. d.)

Vecellio, C., *De gli habiti antichi e moderni di tutto il mondo* (Venice: D. Zenaro, 1590)

—, *Habiti antichi et moderni. Vestibus antiquorum recentiorumque* (Venice: G. B. Sessa, 1598)

La venuta della serenissima Bona Sforza et d'Aragona Reina di Polonia et Duchessa di Bari nella magnifica città di Padova a ventisette di Marzo, con l'entrata nella inclita città di Vinegia, il dì 26 Aprile 1556 (Venice, 1556)

La venuta della serenissima Bona Sforza et d'Aragona Reina di Polonia et Duchessa di Bari nella magnifica città di Vinegia il di 26 Aprile et la sua partita per Bari. Tratta da una lettera scritta all'illustre S. Mario Savorgnano (Venice, 1556)

Vergaro, G. C., *Breve descritione del sacro thesoro . . . figura della retra dietro la quale si e ritrovato con le altre reliquie, il Preciosissimo Sangue che nel giorno della Santiss. Croce si espone* (Venice: A. Pinelli, 1617)

—, *Breve descritione del sacro thesoro delle reliquie ritrovate nel santuario della Chiesa Ducale di San Marco, & honorate con solenne processione a 28 di Maggio del 1617* (Venice: A. Pinelli, 1617)

—, *Racconto dell'apparato et solennita fatta nella ducal chiesa di San Marco di Venetia con l'occasione dell'inventione & espositione del Sangue Pretiosissimo del costato di Christo, del latte della Beata Vergine, con altre santissime reliquie li 28 Maggio 1617* (Venice: A. Pinelli, 1617)

Vergerio, P. P., *De republica veneta liber primus* (Tuscolano: Paganinis, 1526)

Il vero e mirabilissimo apparato over conciero con il glorioso trionfo nell'inclita città di Venetia, in rivoalto celebrato, per i dignissimi e integerrimi merchanti drappieri, in essaltatione de la Santa Fede con cerimonie sante per la gloriosa vitoria avuta contra lo inhumanissimo Selim imperator de' Turchi (Venice, 1571)

Vinci, P., *Il secondo libro de' motetti a cinque voci* (Venice: G. Scotto, 1572)

—, *Il terzo libro de madrigali a cinque voci* (Venice: G. Scotto, 1571)

Willaert, A.; see *Di Adriano e di Jachet: i salmi appertinenti*

Zarlino, G., *Le istituzioni harmoniche* (Venice: [P. da Fino], 1558)

—, *Quinque vocum moduli, motecta vulgo nuncupata, opus nunquam alias typis excussum, ac nupor accuratissime in lucem aeditum, liber primus* (Venice: A. Gardano, 1549)

Zio, C., *La solennissima entrata dell'illustrissimo & eccellentissimo signor Duca di Ferrara, nella citta di Venetia, cominciando dalla partita di sua eccellenza da Ferrara, per infino al suo ritorno* (Bologna: P. Bonardo, 1562)

MODERN WORKS

Ackerman. J., 'The Geopolitics of Venetian Architecture in the Time of Titian', in D. Rosand, ed., *Titian: His World and his Legacy* (New York, 1982), pp. 41–71

—, 'Observations on Renaissance Church Planning in Venice and Florence, 1470–1570', in *Florence and Venice: Comparisons and Relations*, 2 vols (Florence, 1980), II, pp. 440–65

—, *Palladio* (Harmondsworth, 1966)

Adamis, M., 'An Example of Polyphony in Byzantine Music of the Late Middle Ages', in *Report of the Eleventh International Musicological Society Congress, Copenhagen 1971*, 2 vols (Copenhagen, 1972), II, pp. 737–47

Adams, H. M., *Catalogue of Books printed on the Continent of Europe, 1501–1600, in Cambridge Libraries*, 2 vols (Cambridge, 1967)

Adorni, B., ed., *L'abbazia benedettina di San Giovanni Evangelista a Parma* (Milan, 1979)

Agazzi, M., 'I granai della Repubblica', *Venezia arti* VII (1993), pp. 51–62

—, *Platea Sancti Marci* (Venice, 1991)

Agee, R., *The Gardano Music Printing Firms, 1569–1611* (Rochester, NY, 1998)

—, 'A Venetian Music Printing Contract and Edition Size in the Sixteenth Century', *Studi musicali* XV (1986), pp. 59–65

—, 'The Venetian Privilege and Music: Printing in the Sixteenth Century', *Early Music History* III (1983), pp. 1–42

Agnew, J. A., and J. S. Duncan, eds, *The Power of Place: Bringing Together Geographical and Sociological Imaginations* (Boston, MA, 1989)

Aikema, B., *Jacopo Bassano and his Public: Moralizing Pictures in an Age of Reform, ca. 1535–1600* (Princeton, NJ, 1996)

—, and D. Meijers, *Nel regno dei poveri: arte e storia dei grandi ospedali veneziani in età moderna* (Venice, 1989)

Ajmor-Wollheim, M., and F. Dennis eds, *At Home in Renaissance Italy* (London, 2006) [Exhibition catalogue]

Albèri, E., ed., *Relazioni degli ambasciatori veneti al Senato*, 15 vols (Florence, 1839–63)

Allerston, P., 'The Market in Second-Hand Clothes and Furnishings in Venice, *c.* 1500–*c.* 1650' (Ph.D dissertation, European University Institute, Florence, 1996)

—, 'Wedding Finery in Sixteenth-Century Venice', in T. Dean and K. Lowe, eds, *Marriage in Italy, 1300–1650* (Cambridge, 1998), pp. 25–40

Alta Merello, M. G., and D. Frangipane, 'Giovanni di Strassoldo, la patria del Friuli e la "guerra turchesca" sul mare (1571)', in P. C. Ioly Zorattini and A. M. Caproni, eds, *Memor fui dierum antiquorum: studi in memoria di Luigi di Biasio* (Udine, 1995), pp. 15–25

Ambrosini, F., ' "Descrittioni del mondo" nelle case venete dei secoli XVI e XVII', *Archivio veneto* CXVI (1981), pp. 67–79

Andrea Gabrieli, 1585–1985 (Venice, 1985) [XLII Festival Internazionale di Musica Contemporanea]

Angeleri, C., *Bibliografia delle stampe popolari a carattere profano dei secoli XVI e XVII conservate alla Biblioteca Nazionale di Firenze* (Florence, 1953)

Arbel, B., *Trading Nations: Jews and Venetians in the Early-Modern Eastern Mediterranean* (Leiden, 1995)

—, 'Venezia, gli ebrei e l'attività di Salamone Ashkenasi nella guerra di Cipro', in G. Cozzi, ed., *Gli ebrei a Venezia, secoli XIV–XVIII* (Milan, 1987), pp. 163–90

Architettura e utopia nella Venezia del Cinquecento (Milan, 1980) [exhibition catalogue]

Arnaldi, G., 'Andrea Dandolo-doge-cronista', in A. Pertusi, ed., *La storiografia veneziana fino al secolo XVI: aspetti e problemi* (Florence, 1970), pp. 127–268

—, and M. Stocchi, eds, *Storia della cultura veneta*, 6 vols in 10 parts (Vicenza, 1976–87)

Arnold, D., 'Ceremonial Music in Venice at the Time of the Gabrielis', *Proceedings of the Royal Musical Association* LXXXII (1955–6), pp. 47–59

—, *Giovanni Gabrieli and the Music of the Venetian High Renaissance* (Oxford, 1986)

—, 'Music at the Scuola di S. Rocco', *Music and Letters* XL (1959), pp. 229–41

—, 'Music at a Venetian Confraternity in the Renaissance', *Acta musicologica* XXXVII (1965), pp. 62–72

Artioli, U., and C. Grazioli, eds, *I Gonzaga e l'Impero: itinerari dello spettacolo* (Florence, 2005)

Ascarelli, F., and M. Menato, *La tipografia del '500 in Italia* (Florence, 1989)

Attwood, P., *Italian Medals, c. 1530–1600, in British Public Collections*, 2 vols (London, 2003)

Avena, A., 'Memorie veronesi della guerra di Cipro e della battaglia di Lepanto', *Nuovo archivio veneto*, n. s. XXIV (1912), pp. 96–128

Avery, V., 'Nuove fonti archivistiche per il rinnovo cinquecentesco della Cappella del Rosario ai Santi Giovanni e Paolo', in L. Finocchi Gersi, ed., *Alessandro Vittoria e l'arte veneta della maniera. Atti del Convegno Internazionale di Studi: Università di Udine, 26–27 ottobre 2000* (Udine, 2001), pp. 175–97

Azzi Visentini, M., 'Ancora un'inedita pianto prospettica di Venezia in un dipinto di Odoardo Fialetti per Sir Henry Wootton', *Civici musei veneziani d'arte e di storia: bolletino* XXV (1980), pp. 19–25

Babelon, J.-P., and N. Sainte-Fare Garnot, *Les fresques de Tiepolo* (Paris, 1998)

Bacchi, A., L. Camerengo and M. Leithe-Jasper, eds, 'La bellissima maniera', in *Alessandro Vittoria e la scultura veneta del Cinquecento* (Trent, 1999)

Baetjer, K., and J. G. Links, eds, *Canaletto* (New York, 1989) [exhibition catalogue]

Baiocchi, A., 'Paolo Paruta: ideologia e politica nel cinquecento veneziano', *Studi veneziani* XVII–XVIII (1975–6), pp. 157–233

—, 'Venezia nella storiografia fiorentina del Cinquecento', *Studi veneziani,* n. s. III (1980), pp. 203–82

Baldacchini, L., *Bibliografia delle stampe popolari religiose del XVI–XVII secolo. Biblioteche Vaticana, Alessandrina, Estense* (Florence, 1980)

Balsano, M. A., ed., *L'Ariosto la musica, i musicisti: quattro studi e sette madrigali ariosteschi* (Florence, 1981)

Barbieri, F., *La basilica palladiana*, Corpus Palladianum II (Vicenza, 1968)

—, and G. Beltramini, *Vincenzo Scamozzi, 1548–1616* (Venice, 2003) [exhibition catalogue]

Barcham, W. L., *The Religious Paintings of Giambattista Tiepolo: Piety and Tradition in Eighteenth-Century Venice* (Oxford, 1989)

Bassano, G., *Opera omnia*, ed. R. Charteris (n. p., 1999–)

Battistella, A., 'Il dominio del golfo', *Nuovo archivio veneto* XXXV (1918), pp. 5–102

—, 'La politica ecclesiastica della Repubblica Veneta', *Archivio veneto* XVI (1898), pp. 386–420

Battiston, O., ed., *Chiese e monasteri distrutti a Castello dopo il 1807* (Venice, 1992)

Baumstark, A., *Liturgia romana e liturgia dell'esarcato: il rito detto in seguito patriarchino e le origini del canon missae romano* (Rome, 1904)

Beeching, J., *The Galleys at Lepanto* (London, 1982)

Beck, H. G., M. Manoussacas and A. Pertusi, eds, *Venezia centro di mediazione tra oriente e occidente (secoli XV–XVI): aspetti e problemi,* 2 vols (Florence, 1977)

Beloch, G., 'La popolazione di Venezia nei secoli XVI e XVII', *Nuovo archivio veneto* III (1902), pp. 5–49

Bellavitis, A., 'La famiglia "cittadina" veneziana nel sedecisimo secolo, dote e successioni: le leggi e le fonti', *Studi veneziani,* n. s. XXX (1995), pp. 55–68

—, and G. Romanelli, *Venezia* (Rome, 1985)

Bellina, A. L., 'A suon di musica da Cracovia a Lione: i trionfi del cristianissimo Enrico III', in U. Artioli and C. Grazioli, eds, *I Gonzaga e l'Impero: itinerari dello spettacolo* (Florence, 2005), pp. 81–106

Bellini, P., 'Printmakers and Dealers in Italy during the 16th and 17th Centuries', *Print Collector* XIII (1975), pp. 17–45

Belozerskaya, M., and K. Lapatin, 'Antiquity Consumed: Transformations at San Marco', in A. Payne, A. Kuttner and R. Smick, eds, *Antiquity and its Interpreters* (Cambridge, 2000), pp. 83–95

Beltrami, D., *La penetrazione economica dei veneziani in terraferma: forze di lavoro e proprietà fondiaria nelle campagne venete dei secoli XVII e XVIII* (Venice, 1961)

—, *Storia della popolazione di Venezia dalla fine del secolo XVI alla caduta della repubblica* (Padua, 1954)

Bent, M., 'A Contemporary Perception of Early Fifteenth-Century Style: Bologna Q15 as a Document of Scribal Editorial Initiative', *Musica Disciplina* XLI (1987), pp. 183–201

—, 'The Definition of Simple Polyphony: Some Questions', in C. Corsi and P. Petrobelli, eds, *Le polifonie primitive in Friuli e in Europa* (Rome, 1989), pp. 33–42

—, 'The Fourteenth-Century Italian Motet', in *L'ars nova italiana del trecento* (Certaldo, 1992), pp. 85–125

—, 'Music and the Early Veneto Humanists', *Proceedings of the British Academy* CI (1999), pp. 101–30

—, 'Pietro Emiliani's Chaplain Bartolomeo Rossi da Carpi and the Lamentations of De Quadris in Vicenza', *Il saggiatore musicale* II (1995), pp. 5–16

Benvenuti, G., *Andrea e Giovanni Gabrieli e la musica strumentale in S. Marco,* 2 vols (Milan, 1931–2)

Benzoni, G., 'Aspetti della cultura urbana nella società veneta, del '5–600: le accademie', *Archivio veneto* CXLIII (1977), pp. 87–159

—, 'Enrico III a Venezia, Venezia ed Enrico III , in *Venezia e Parigi* (Milan, 1989), pp. 79–112

—, *Gli affanni della cultura: intellettuali e potere nell'Italia della controriforma e barocca* (Milan, 1978)

—, ed., *Il mediterraneo nella seconda metà del '500 nella luce di Lepanto* (Florence, 1974)

—, ed., *Venezia e la terraferma: la cultura* (Bergamo, 1990)

—, *Venezia nell'età della controriforma* (Milan, 1973)

Berchet, G., 'La antiche ambasciate giapponesi in Italia', *Archivio veneto* XIII (1877), pp. 245–85; 14 (1877), pp. 150–203

Bergstein, M., ' "La Fede": Titian's Votive Painting for Antonio Grimani', *Arte veneta* XL (1986), pp. 29–37

Berlinguer, L., and F. Colao, eds, *Crimine, giustizia e società veneta in età moderna* (Milan, 1989)

Bernasconi, J. G., 'The Dating of the Cycle of the Miracles of the Cross from the Scuola di San Giovanni Evangelista', *Arte veneta* XXXV (1981), pp. 198–202

Bernoni, G., *Leggende fantastiche popolari veneziane* (Venice, 1875)

Bernstein, J., *Music Printing in Renaissance Venice: The Scotto Press, 1539–1572* (New York and London, 1998)

Bertelli, S., and G. Ramakus, eds, *Essays Presented to Myron P. Gilmore*, 2 vols (Florence, 1978)

Bertoli, B., ed., *La basilica di San Marco: arte e simbologia* (Venice, 1993)

—, ed., *La chiesa di Venezia nel seicento* (Venice, 1992)

—, ed., *Chiesa, società, stato a Venezia: miscellanea di studi in onore di Silvio Tramontin* (Venice, 1994)

Bettley, J., 'The Office of Holy Week at St Mark's, Venice, in the Late Sixteenth Century and the Musical Contributions of Giovanni Croce', *Early Music* XXII (1994), pp. 45–60

—, 'Psalm-Texts and the Polyphonic Vespers Repertory of St Mark's, Venice', in F. Passadore and F. Rossi, eds, *La cappella musicale di S. Marco nell'età moderna* (Venice, 1998), pp. 103–17

Betto, B., 'I capitoli di San Pietro e di San Marco: l'arcidiacono e il primicerio', *Archivi e chiesa locale: studi e contributi*, ed. Francesca Cavazzana Romanelli and Isabella Ruol (Venice, 1993), pp. 107–120

—, *Il capitolo della basilica di S. Marco in Venezia: statuti e consuetudini dei primi decenni del secolo XIV* (Padua, 1984)

—, 'La chiesa ducale', in B. Bertoli, ed., *La chiesa di Venezia nel seicento* (Venice, 1992), pp. 125–71

—, *Le nove congregazioni del clero di Venezia, secoli XI–XV: ricerche storiche, matricole e documenti vari* (Padua, 1984)

Biadone, S., ed., *Venezia: piante e vedute* (Venice, 1982)

Biblioteca Columbina: catalogo de sus impresos, 7 vols (Seville and Madrid, 1888–1948)

Biliński, B., 'Venezia nelle peregrinazioni polacche del '500 e lo "sposalizio del mare" di Giovanni Siemuszowski (1565)', in M. Brahmer, ed., *Italia, Venezia e Polonia tra umanesimo e Rinascimento* (Wroclaw, Warsaw and Cracow, 1967), pp. 233–90

Blackburn, B. J., 'Petrucci's Venetian Editor: Petrus Castellanus and his Musical Garden', *Musica Disciplina* XLIX (1995), pp. 15–45

—, E. E. Lowinsky and C. A. Miller, eds, *A Correspondence of Renaissance Musicians* (Oxford, 1991)

Blunt, A., 'El Greco's "Dream of Philip II": An Allegory of the Holy League', *Journal of the Warburg and Courtauld Institutes* III (1939–40), pp. 58–69

Boccato, C., 'La mortalità nel Ghetto di Venezia durante la peste del 1630', *Archivio Veneto* CXL (1993), pp. 111–46

Boerio, G., *Dizionario di dialetto veneziano*, 2nd edn (Venice, 1856)

Boholm, Å., *The Doge of Venice: The Symbolism of State Power in the Renaissance* (Gothenburg, 1990)

Boito, C., ed., *The Basilica of S. Mark in Venice Illustrated from the Point of View of Art and History by Venetian Writers*, trans. William Scott (London, 1888)

Bolzoni, L., 'L'Accademia veneziana: splendore e decadenza di una utopia enciclopedica', in L. Boehm and E. Raimondi, eds, *Università, accademie e società scientifiche in Italia e in Germania* (Bologna, 1981), pp. 117–67

—, *The Gallery of Memory: Literary and Iconographic Models in the Age of the Printing Press* (Toronto, London and Buffalo, NY, 2001)

—, 'Rendere visibile il sapere: L'Accademia Veneziana fra modernità e utopia', in D. S. Chambers and F. Quiviger, eds, *Italian Academies of the Sixteenth Century* (London, 1995), pp. 61–75

Bongi, S., *Annali di Gabriel Giolito de' Ferrari da Trino di Monferrato, stampatore in Venezia*, 2 vols (Rome, 1890–97)

Bonora, E., *Ricerche su Francesco Sansovino imprenditore librario e letterato* (Venice, 1994)

Bonser, W., 'Medical Folklore of Venice and Rome', *Folklore* LXVII (1956), pp. 1–15

Boone, M., and P. Stabel, eds, *Shaping Urban Identity in Late Medieval Europe* (Leuven and Apeldoorn, 2000)

Boorman, S., *Ottaviano Petrucci: catalogue raisonné* (New York, 2006)

Borea, E., 'Stampa figurativa e pubblico dalle origini all'affermazione nel Cinquecento', in G. Previtali, ed., *Storia dell'arte italiana* I/2 (Turin, 1979), pp. 319–413

Bordignon Favero, E., 'La "Santa Lega" contro il Turco e il rinnovamento del duomo di Bassano: Volpato, Meyring e la "Madonna del Rosario"', *Studi veneziani*, n. s. XI (1986), pp. 20–31

Bortolan, D., *S. Corona: chiesa e convento dei domenicani in Vicenza. Memorie storiche* (Vicenza, 1889)

Boselli, P., *Dizionario di toponomastica bergamasca e cremonese* (Florence, 1990)

Boucher, B., *Andrea Palladio: The Architect in his Time* (New York, 1994)

—, 'Il Sansovino e i Procuratori di San Marco', *Archivio veneto* CLXXIII (1986), pp. 59–74

—, 'Jacopo Sansovino and the Choir of St Mark's', *Burlington Magazine* CXVIII (1976), pp. 552–66

—, 'Jacopo Sansovino and the Choir of St Mark's: The Evangelists, the Sacristy Door and the Altar of the Sacrament', *Burlington Magazine* CXXI (1979), pp. 155–68

—, *The Sculpture of Jacopo Sansovino*, 2 vols (New Haven, CT, and London, 1991)

Bouwsma, W. J., *The Waning of the Renaissance, 1550–1640* (New Haven, CT, and London, 2000)

—, *Venice and the Defense of Republican Liberty: Renaissance Values in the Age of the Counter Reformation* (Berkeley, CA, 1968)

—, 'Venice and the Political Education of Europe', in J. Hale, ed., *Renaissance Venice* (London, 1973), pp. 431–44

Bozza, T., *Scrittori politici italiani dal 1550 al 1650: saggio di bibliografia* (Rome, 1949)

Bradshaw, M., *Falsobordone: A Study in Renaissance and Baroque Music* (Neuhausen and Stuttgart, 1978)

Branca, V., and C. Ossola, eds, *Crisi e rinnovamento nell'autunno del Rinascimento a Venezia* (Florence 1991)

—, eds, *Cultura e società nel Rinascimento tra riforme e manierismi* (Florence, 1984)

Braudel, F., *The Mediterranean and the Mediterranean World in the Age of Philip II*, trans. S. Reynolds, 2 vols (London, 1975)

—, 'La vita economica di Venezia nel secolo XVI', in *La civiltà veneziana del Rinascimento* (Florence, 1958), pp. 81–102

Braunstein, P., 'Remarques sur la population allemande a Venise à la fin du moyen âge', in H. G. Beck, M. Manoussacas and A. Pertusi, eds, *Venezia centro di mediazione tra oriente e occidente (secoli XV–XVI): aspetti e problemi*, 2 vols (Florence, 1977), I, pp. 233–43

—, and C. Klapisch-Zuber, 'Note critique. Florence et Venise: les rituels publics a l'époque de la Renaissance', *Annales ESC* XXXVIII/5 (1983), pp. 1110–23

Breiner, D. M., 'Vincenzo Scamozzi, 1548–1616: A Catalogue Raisonné', 2 vols (Ph.D dissertation, Cornell University, 1994)

Brevi cenni sopra la prodigiosa immagine di Maria Vergine che si venera nella basilica di San Marco in Venezia (Venice, 1883)

Brown, H. F., *Studies in the History of Venice*, 2 vols (New York, 1907)

—, *The Venetian Printing Press, 1469–1800: An Historical Study Based upon Documents for the Most Part Hitherto Unpublished* (London, 1891)

Brown, H. M., 'On Gentile Bellini's *Processione in San Marco* (1496)', in *International Musi-*

cological Society Congress Report XII: Berkeley, 1977 (Kassel and London, 1981), pp. 649–58

Brown, J. C., and R. C. Davis, eds, *Gender and Society in Renaissance Italy* (London, 1998)

Brown, P., *The Cult of the Saints: Its Rise and Function in Latin Antiquity* (Chicago, IL, 1981)

Brown, P. F., 'Acquiring a Classical Past: Historical Appropriation in Renaissance Venice', in A. Payne, A. Kuttner and R. Smick, eds, *Antiquity and its Interpreters* (Cambridge, 2000), pp. 27–39

—, 'Behind the Walls., The Material Culture of Venetian Elites', in J. Martin and D. Romano, eds, *Venice Reconsidered: The History and Civilization of an Italian City State, 1297–1797* (Baltimore, MD, and London, 2000), pp. 295–38

—, 'Honor and Necessity: The Dynamics of Patronage in the Confraternities of Renaissance Venice', *Studi veneziani*, n. s. XIV (1987), pp. 179–210

—, 'Measured Friendship, Calculated Pomp: The Ceremonial Welcomes of the Venetian Republic', in B. Wisch and S. Scott Munshower, eds, *'All the World's a Stage...': Art and Pageantry in the Renaissance and Baroque* (University Park, PA, 1990), pp. 137–86

—, 'Painting and History in Renaissance Venice', *Art History* VII (1984), pp. 263–94

—, *Private Lives in Renaissance Venice: Art, Architecture and the Family* (New Haven, CT, and London, 2004)

—, '*Renovatio* or *Conciliatio*? How Renaissances Happened in Venice', in A. Brown, ed., *Language and Images of Renaissance Italy* (Oxford, 1995), pp. 127–54

—, 'The Self-Definition of the Venetian Republic', in A. Molho, K. Rauflaub and J. Emlem, eds, *Athens and Rome, Florence and Venice: City-States in Classical Antiquity and Medieval Italy* (Stuttgart, 1991), pp. 511–48

—, *Venetian Narrative Painting in the Age of Carpaccio* (New Haven, CT, and London, 1988)

—, *Venice and Antiquity: The Venetian Sense of the Past* (New Haven, CT, and London, 1996)

Brulez, W., *Marchands flamands à Venise, I: 1568–1605* (Brussels and Rome, 1965); see also Devos and Brulez

Brugnera, M., 'Disinfezioni e disposizioni durante una pestilenza', *Atti e memorie della Accademia italiana di storia della farmacia* IX (1992), pp. 55–9

Brunetti, M., 'La crisi finale della Sacra Lega (1573)', in *Miscellanea in onore di Roberto Cessi* (Rome, 1958), II, pp. 145–55

—, 'Il doge non è "segno di taverna"', *Nuovo archivio veneto* XXXIII (1917), pp. 351–5

—, and E. Vitale, eds, *La corrispondenza da Madrid dell'ambasciatore Leonardo Donà (1570–73)*, 2 vols (Venice and Rome, 1963)

Bruni, A., 'Mobiltà sociale e mobiltà geografica nella Venezia di fine '500: la parrochia di S. Salvador', *Annali veneti* II (1985), pp. 75–83

Bryant, D., 'Andrea Gabrieli e la "musica di stato: veneziana', in *Andrea Gabrieli, 1585–1985* (Venice, 1985), pp. 29–45

—, 'The *cori spezzati* of St Mark's: Myth and Reality', *Early Music History* I (1981), pp. 165–86

—, 'Liturgy, Ceremonial and Sacred Music in Venice at the Time of the Counter-Reformation', 2 vols (Ph.D dissertation, University of London, 1981)

—, 'La musica nelle istituzioni religiose e profane di Venezia', in G. Arnaldi and M. Stocchi, eds, *Storia della cultura veneta*, 6 vols in 10 parts (Vicenza, 1976–87), IV/I, pp. 433–47

—, and M. Pozzobon, *Musica devozione città: la scuola di Santa Maria Battuti (e un suo manoscritto musicale) nella Treviso del Rinascimento* (Treviso, 1995)

Bryce, J., *Cosimo Bartoli (1503–1572): The Career of a Florentine Polymath* (Geneva, 1983)

Buchthal, H., 'The Carved Stone Ornament of the Middle Ages in San Marco, Venice', *Jahrbuch der Österreichischen byzantinischen Gesellschaft* XI–XII (1962–3), pp. 162–209; XIII (1964), pp. 137–70

—, *Historia Troiana: Studies in the History of Mediaeval Secular Illustration* (London and Leiden, 1971)

Buchwald, H., 'Eleventh Century Corinthian-Palmette Capitals in the Region of Aquileia', *Art Bulletin* XLVIII (1966), pp. 147–58

Burke, P., 'Early Modern Venice as a Centre of Information and Communication', in J.

Martin and D. Romano, eds, *Venice Reconsidered: The History and Civilization of an Italian City State, 1297–1797* (Baltimore, MD, and London, 2000), pp. 389–419

—, *Popular Culture in Early Modern Europe* (London, 1978)

—, *Venice and Amsterdam: A Study of Seventeenth-Century Elites* (London, 1974)

Burns, H., et al., eds, *Andrea Palladio, 1508–1580: The Portico and the Farmyard* ([London], 1975) [exhibition catalogue]

Burratti Mazzotta, 'L'apoteosi di Carlo Borromeo disegnata in due secoli di progetti per il sacro monte di Arona', in L. Vaccaro and F. Riccardi, eds, *Sacri monti: devozione, arte e cultura della controriforma* (Milan, 1992), pp. 231–9

Bury, J. B., 'The Loggetta in 1540', *Burlington Magazine* CXXII (1980), pp. 631–5

Bury, M., *The Print in Italy, 1550–1620* (London, 2001) [exhibition catalogue]

—, 'The Taste for Prints in Italy to *c.* 1600', *Print Quarterly* II (1985), pp. 12–26

Busbecq, Baron O. G. de, *The Life and Letters of Ogier Ghiselin de Busbecq, by Charles Thornton Foster and F. H. Blackburne Daniell* (London, 1881)

Butters, S. B., *The Triumph of Vulcan*, 2 vols (Florence, 1996)

Cacciavillani, I., *Andrea Gritti nella vita di Nicolo Barbarigo* (Venice, 1995)

Cadel, A. M., 'La pietà popolare nelle piccole scuole veneziane: appunti', *Archivio veneto* CLXXII (1985), pp. 175–7

—, 'Il sentimento della morte nelle scuole piccole veneziane', *Ateneo veneto* XXXIV (1996), pp. 113–28

Caffi, F., *Storia della musica sacra nella già cappella ducale di S. Marco dal 1318 al 1797*, 2 vols (Venice, 1854–5)

Calabi, D., 'Città e spazi di mercato nella Repubblica veneta', *Eidos. Rivista di cultura* I (1987), pp. 76–87

—, *Il mercato e la città: piazze, strade, architture d'Europa in età moderna* (Venice, 1993)

—, 'Il rinnovamento urbano del primo Cinquecento', in A. Tenenti and U. Tucci, eds, *Storia di Venezia dalle origini alla caduta della serenissima* V (Rome, 1996), pp. 101–63

—, and P. Morachiello, *Rialto: le fabbriche e il ponte, 1514–1591* (Turin, 1987)

—, and —, 'Rialto, 1514–1538: gli anni della ricostruzione', in M. Tafuri, ed., *'Renovatio urbis': Venetia nell'età di Andrea Gritti, 1523–1538* (Rome, 1984), pp. 291–334

Calendar of State Papers, Foreign, Elizabeth I, Preserved in the State Paper Department of Her Majesty's Public Record Office, 23 vols (London, 1863–1950)

Calendar of State Papers and Manuscripts Existing in the Archives and Collections of Venice and in Other Libraries of Northern Italy, 42 vols (London, 1864–1947)

Camara, E., 'Pictures and Prayers: Madonna of the Rosary Imagery in Post-Tridentine Italy' (Ph.D dissertation, Johns Hopkins University, 2002)

Camerini, P., *Annali dei Giunti*, 2 vols (Florence, 1962–3)

—, 'Notizia sugli Annali Giolitini di Salvatore Bongi', in *Atti e memorie della R. Accademia di scienze, lettere ed arte in Padova. Memorie della classe di scienze morali* LI (1934–5), pp. 103–238

Cameron, A., 'The Construction of Court Ritual: The Byzantine *Book of Ceremonies*', in D. Cannadine and S. Price, eds, *Rituals of Royalty: Power and Ceremonial in Traditional Societies* (Cambridge, 1978), pp. 106–36

Camilot-Oswald, R., *Die liturgischen Musikhandschriften aus dem mittelalterlichen Patriarchat Aquileia* (Kassel, 1997)

Canal, Martino da: see Limentani, A.

Candela, G., *Manierismo e condizioni della scrittura in Anton Francesco Doni* (New York, 1993)

Cannadine, D., and S. Price, eds, *Rituals of Royalty: Power and Ceremonial in Traditional Societies* (Cambridge, 1978)

Cappelletti, G., *Storia della chiesa di Venezia dalla sua fondazione sino ai nostri giorni*, 8 vols (Venice, 1849–60)

Carile, A., *La cronachista veneziana (secoli XIII–XVI) di fronte alla spartizione della Romania nel 1204* (Florence, 1969)

—, 'Le origini di Venezia nelle più antiche cronache veneziane', in *Mnemosynon Sophias Antoniade* (Venice, 1974), pp. 27–40

Caroll, L., 'Carnival Rites as Vehicles of Protest in Renaissance Venice', *Sixteenth Century Journal* XVI (1985), pp. 487–502

Carrara, E., and S. Gregory, 'Borghini's Print Purchases from Giunti', *Print Quarterly* XVII (2000), pp. 3–17

Carver, A., *Cori spezzati: The Development of Sacred Polychoral Music to the Time of Schutz*, 2 vols (Cambridge, 1988)

Casali, S., *Annali della tipografia veneziana di Francesco Marcolini da Forli* (Forli, 1861); see also Servolini

Casimiri, R., 'Musica e musicisti nella cattedrale di Padova nei secoli XIV, XV, XVI: contributi per una storia', *Note d'archivio per la storia musicale* XVIII (1941), pp. 1–31, 101–80, 180–214; XIX (1942), pp. 49–92

Casini, M., 'La cittadinanza originaria a Venezia tra i secoli XV e XVI: una linea interpretiva', in *Studi veneti offerti a Gaetano Cozzi* (Venice, 1992), pp. 133–50

—, *I gesti del principe: la festa politica a Firenze e Venezia in età rinascimentale* (Venice, 1996)

—, 'Realtà e simboli del cancellier grande veneziano in età moderna (sec. XVI–XVII)', *Studi veneziani* n. s. XXII (1991), pp. 195–251

Casola, P., *Viaggio a Gerusalemme* (Milan, 1899)

Cassini, G., *Piante e vedute prospettiche di Venezia (1479–1855) con una interpretazione urbanistica di E. Trincanato* (Venice, 1971)

Cattin, G., 'Church Patronage of Music in Fifteenth-Century Italy', in I. Fenlon, ed., *Music in Medieval and Early Modern Europe: Patronage, Sources and Texts* (Cambridge, 1981), pp. 21–36

—, ed., *Da Bisanzio a San Marco: musica e liturgia* (Venice, 1997)

—, 'La cultura e la vita musicale a Venezia nel periodo padovano di Galilei', in *Galileo Galilei e la cultura veneziana* (Venice, 1995)

—, 'Formazione e attività della cappelle polifoniche nelle cattedrali: la musica nelle città', in G. Arnaldi and M. Stocchi, eds, *Storia della cultura veneta*, 6 vols in 10 parts (Vicenza, 1976–87), III/3, pp. 270–77

—, *Johannes de Quadris, musico del sec. XV* (Bologna, 1971)

—, *Musica e liturgia a San Marco: testi e melodie per la liturgia delle ore dal XII al XVII secolo.*

Dal graduale tropato del duecento ai graduali cinquecenteschi, 4 vols (Venice, 1990–92)

—, 'Ricerche sulla musica a Santa Giustina di Padua all'inizio del quattrocento: il copista Rolando da Casale – nuovi frammenti musicali nell'Archivio di Stato', *Annales musicologiques* VII (1964–77)

—, 'Uno sconosciuto codice quattrocentesco dell'Archivio Capitolare di Vicenza e le lamentazioni di Johannes de Quadris', *L'ars nova italiana del trecento* III (Certaldo, 1970), pp. 281–304

—, and A. Lovato, eds, *Contributi per la storia della musica sacra a Padova* (Padua, 1993)

Cavallini, I., 'Antiche acclamazioni con musica in Dalmazia e Istria', in Cavallini, ed., *Studi in onore di Giuseppe Vecchi*, pp. 39–52

—, 'Sugli improvvisatori del Cinque–Seicento: persistenze, nuovi repertori e qualche riconoscimento', *Recercare* I (1989), pp. 23–39

—, ed., *Studi in onore di Giuseppe Vecchi* (Modena, 1989)

Cavallo, G., and R. Chartier, eds, *A History of Reading in the West* (Amherst, MA, 1999)

Cavazza, S., '"Così buono et savio cavalliere": Vito di Dornberg, Patrizio Goriziano del Cinquecento', *Annali di storia isontina* III (1990), pp. 7–36

—, 'Libri in volgare e propaganda eterodossa: Venezia, 1543–47', in *Libri, idee e sentimenti religiosi nel Cinquecento italiano* (Modena, 1987), pp. 9–28

Cecchetti, B., *La Republica di Venezia e la corte di Roma nei rapporti della religione,* 2 vols (Venice, 1874)

Census Catalogue of Manuscript Sources of Polyphonic Music, 1400–1550, 5 vols (Neuhausen and Stuttgart, 1979–88)

Cervelli, I., *Machiavelli e la crisi dello stato veneziano* (Naples, 1974)

—, 'Storiografia e problemi intorno alla vita religiosa e spirituale a Venezia nella prima metà del 1500', *Studi veneziani* VIII (1966), pp. 447–76

Cessi, R., 'L'apparitio Sancti Marci del 1094', *Archivio veneto* LXXXXV (1964), pp. 113–15

—, 'Bartolomeo e Camillo Zanetti, tipografi e calligrafi del '500', *Archivio veneto–tridentino* VIII (1925), pp. 174–82

—, 'L'investitura ducale', *Atti dell'Instituto Veneto di Scienze, Lettere ed Arti* CXXVI (1967–8), pp. 251–94

—, *Storia della repubblica di Venezia*, 2 vols (Venice, 1968)

Chabod, F., 'Venezia nella politica italiana ed europea del cinquecento', in *La civiltà veneziana del Rinascimento* (Florence, 1958), pp. 27–55

Chambers, D., *The Imperial Age of Venice, 1380–1580* (London, 1970)

—, and B. Pullan, eds, *Venice: A Documentary History, 1450–1630* (Oxford, 1992)

Charrière, E., *Negotiations de la France dans le Levant*, 4 vols (Paris, 1840–60)

Chartier, R., *The Order of Books*, trans. L. Cochrane (Oxford, 1994)

—, 'Reading Matter and 'Popular' Reading: From the Renaissance to the Seventeenth Century', in G. Cavallo and R. Chartier, eds, *A History of Reading in the West* (Amherst, MA, 1999), pp. 269–83

Chastel, A., 'Palladio et l'art des fêtes', *Bollettino del Centro Internazionale degli Studi sull'Architettura 'Andrea Palladio'*, II (1960), pp. 29–33

—, *The Sack of Rome, 1527*, trans. B. Archer (Princeton, NJ, 1983)

Chennevières, H. de, 'Les Tiepolo de L'hotel Eduoard André', *Gazette des Beaux-Arts* XV (1896), pp. 121–30

Chojnacki, S., *Women and Men in Renaissance Venice: Twelve Essays on Patrician Society* (Baltimore, MD, and London, 2000)

Cicogna, E. A., *Delle iscrizioni veneziane*, 6 vols (Venice, 1827)

—, *Saggio di bibliografia veneziana* (Venice, 1847)

—, 'Saggio del catalogo dei codici di Emmanuele A. Cicogna', *Archivio veneto* IV (1872), pp. 59–132, 337–98

Ciconia, J., *The Works, Polyphonic Music of the Fourteenth Century* XXIV, ed. M. Bent and A. Hallmark (Monaco, 1985)

Cinagli, A., *Le monete de' Papi descritte in tavole sinottiche* (Fermo, 1848)

Cini, L., 'Passaggio della regina Bona Sforza per Padova nell'anno 1556', in *Relazioni tra Padova e la Polonia: studi in onore dell'Uni-versità di Cracovia nel VI centenario della sua fondazione* (Padua, 1964), pp. 27–65

Ciriacono, S., 'Mass Consumption Goods and Luxury Goods: The De-Industrialization of the Republic of Venice from the Sixteenth to the Eighteenth Century', in H. van der Wee, ed., *The Rise and Decline of Urban Industries in Italy and the Low Countries: Late Middle Ages – Early Modern Times* (Louvain, 1988), pp. 41–61

La civiltà veneziana del Rinascimento (Florence, 1958)

Clark, A. M., 'Batoni's *Triumph of Venice*', *North Carolina Museum of Art Bulletin* IV (1963), pp. 5–11

—, *Pompeo Batoni: A Complete Catalogue of His Works with an Introductory Text* (Oxford, 1985).

Clementi, E. B., *Riforma religiosa e poesia popolare a Venezia nel Cinquecento: Alessandro Caravia* (Florence, 2000)

Cocke, R., 'Exemplary Lives: Veronese's Representations of Martyrdom and the Council of Trent', *Renaissance Studies* 10 (1996), pp. 388–404

—, *Paolo Veronese: Piety and Display in an Age of Religious Reform* (Aldershot, 2001)

—, *Veronese's Drawings: A Catalogue Raisonné* (London, 1984)

Coco, C., and F. Manzonetto, *Baili veneziani alla sublime porta: storia e caratteristiche dell'ambasciata veneta a Costantinopoli* (Venice, [1985])

Cohn, S. K., Jr, *The Black Death Transformed: Disease and Culture in Early Renaissance Europe* (London, 2002)

Colas, R., *Bibliographie generale du costume et de la mode* (Paris, 1933)

Concina, E., 'Ampliar la città: spazio urbano, "res publica" e architettura', in G. Cozzi and P. Prodi, eds, *Storia di Venezia dalle origini alla caduta della serenissima* VI (Rome, 1994), pp. 253–73

—, *L'Arsenale della Repubblica di Venezia: techniche e istituzioni dal medioevo all'età moderna* (Milan, 1984)

—, *Storia dell'architettura di Venezia dal VII al XX secolo* (Milan, 1995)

Conomos, D., 'Experimental Polyphony, "According to the . . . Latins", in late Byzantine

Psalmody', *Early Music History* II (1982), pp. 1–16

Cooper, T. E., 'The History and Decoration of the Church of San Giorgio Maggiore in Venice' (Ph.D dissertation, Princeton University, 1990)

—, '"Locus meditandi et orandi": Architecture, Liturgy and Identity at San Giorgio Maggiore', in F. Passadore and F. Rossi, eds, *Musica, scienza e idee nella Serenissima durante il Seicento* (Venice, 1996), pp. 79–105

—, *Palladio's Venice. Architecture and Society in a Renaissance Republic* (New Haven and London, 2005)

Cope, M. E., *The Venetian Chapel of the Sacrament in the Sixteenth Century* (New York and London, 1979)

Corboz, A., *Canaletto: una Venezia immaginaria*, 2 vols (Milan, 1985)

Corner, F., *Ecclesiae Venetae*, 13 vols (Venice, 1745)

—, *Notizie storiche delle chiese e monasteri di Venezia e di Torcello* (Padua, 1758)

Corsi, C., and P. Petrobelli, eds, *Le polifonie primitive in Friuli e in Europa* (Rome, 1989)

Cortelazzo. M., 'I fatti e le prodezze di Manilio Blessi: titolo e nome imitati o parodiati?', *Quaderni veneti* XXIX (1999), pp. 177–80

—, 'Plurilinguismo celebrativo', in G. Benzoni, ed., *Il mediterraneo nella seconda metà del '500 nella luce di Lepanto* (Florence, 1974), pp. 121–6

Corti, U., 'La francazione del debito pubblico della Repubblica di Venezia proposta da Gian Francesco Priuli', *Nuovo archivio veneto* IV (1894), pp. 331–64

Cosgrove, D., 'Mapping New Worlds: Culture and Cartography in Sixteenth-Century Venice', *Imago Mundi* 44 (1992), pp. 1–25

—, *The Palladian Landscape: Geographical Change and its Cultural Representations in Sixteenth-Century Italy* (Leicester, 1993)

Cottrell, P., 'Corporate Colors: Bonifacio and Tintoretto at the Palazzo dei Camerlenghi in Venice', *Art Bulletin* LXXXII (2000), pp. 658–78

Cowan, A., ed., *Mediterranean Urban Culture, 1400–1700* (Exeter, 2000)

—, *The Urban Patriciate: Lübeck and Venice, 1580–1700* (Cologne and Vienna, 1986)

Cowdrey, H. E. J., 'The Anglo-Norman Laudes Regiae', *Viator* XII (1981), pp. 37–78

Cozzi, G., *Ambiente veneziano, ambiente veneto: saggi su politica, società cultura nella Repubblica di Venezia in età moderna* (Venice, 1997)

—, 'Authority and the Law in Renaissance Venice', in J. Hale, ed., *Renaissance Venice* (London, 1973), pp. 293–345

—, 'Cultura, politica e religione nella "pubblica storiografia: veneziana del '500', *Bollettino dell'Istituto di Storia della Società e dello Stato Veneziano* V–VI (1963–4), pp. 215–94

—, 'Un documento sulla crisi della "sacra lega": le confidenze del padre Francisco Toledo all'Avogadore di Comun, Nicolo Barbarigo (ottobre 1572)', *Archivio veneto* LXVII (1960), pp. 76–96

—, *Il doge Nicolò Contarini: ricerche sul patriziato veneziano agli inizi del Seicento* (Venice and Rome, 1958)

—, ed., *Gli ebrei a Venezia, secoli XIV–XVIII* (Milan, 1987)

—, 'Federico Contarini: un antiquario veneziano tra Rinascimento e Contrariforma', *Bolletino dell'Istituto di Storia della Società e dello Stato Veneziano* III (1961), pp. 190–220

—, 'Giuspatronato del doge e prerogative del primicerio sulla cappella ducale di San Marco: controversie con i procuratori di San Marco "de supra" e i patriarchi di Venezia', *Atti dell'Istituto Veneto di Scienza, Lettere ed Arti* CLI (1992–3), pp. 1–69

—, 'Note su Giovanni Tiepolo, primicerio di San Marco e patriarca di Venezia: l'unità ideale della chiesa veneta', in B. Bertoli, ed., *Chiesa, società, stato a Venezia: miscellanea di studi in onore di Silvio Tramontin* (Venice, 1994), pp. 121–50

—, *Paolo Sarpi tra Venezia e l'Europa* (Turin, 1979)

—, 'Politica, cultura e religione', in V. Branca and C. Ossola, eds, *Cultura e società nel Rinascimento tra riforme e manierismi* (Florence, 1984), pp. 21–42

—, 'I rapporti fra stato e chiesa', in G. Gullino, ed., *La chiesa di venezia tra riforma protestante e riforma cattolica* (Venice, 1990), pp. 11–16

—, 'Risvolti politico-religiosi di una controversia architettonica e monumentale tra doge e procuratori di San Marco nella seconda metà del Cinquecento', in P. Pecorari and G. Silvano, eds, *Continuità e discontinuità nella storia politica, economica e religiuosa: studi in onore di Aldo Stella* (Vicenza, 1993), pp. 127–38

—, ed., *Stato, società e giustizia nella Repubblica Veneta (sec. XV–XVIII)*, 2 vols (Rome, 1980)

Cracco, G., 'Esperienze di vita canonicale e Lorenzo Giustiniani', in G. Vian, ed., *La chiesa di Venezia tra medioevo ed età moderna* (Venice, 1989), pp. 91–112

—, *Società e stato nel medioevo veneziano: secoli XII–XIV* (Florence, 1967)

—, and M. Knapton, eds, *Dentro lo 'stado italico': Venezia e la terraferma fra Quattro e Seicento* (Trent, 1984)

Crouzet-Pavan, E., 'La maturazione dello spazio urbano', in A. Tenenti and U. Tucci, eds, *Storia di Venezia dalle origini alla caduta della serenissima* V (Rome, 1996), pp. 3–100

—, *'Sopra le acque salse': Espaces, pouvoir et societe à Venise à la fin du moyen âge*, 2 vols (Rome, 1992)

—, 'Sviluppo e articolazione della città', in G. Arnaldi, G. Cracco and A. Tenenti, eds, *Storia di Venezia dalle origini alla caduta della serenissima* III (Rome, 1997), pp. 729–81

—, *Venice Triumphant: Horizons of a Myth* (Baltimore, 2002)

Cumming, J. E., 'Music for the Doge in Early Renaissance Venice', *Speculum* LXVII (1992), pp. 324–64

Cummings, A. M., 'Towards an Interpretation of the Sixteenth-Century Motet', *Journal of the American Musicological Society* XXIV (1981), pp. 43–59

Curi Nicolardi, S., *Una società tipografico-editoriale a Venezia nel secolo XVI: Melchiorre Sessa e Pietro di Ravani (1516–1525)* (Florence, 1984)

Cutler, A., 'From Loot to Scholarship: Changing Modes in the Italian Response to Byzantine Artifacts', *Dumbarton Oaks Papers* XLIX (1995), pp. 237–67

D'Accone, F. A., 'The Performance of Sacred Music in Josquin's Time', in E. E. Lowinsky and B. J. Blackburn, eds, *Josquin des Prez* (London and New York, 1976), pp. 601–18

D'Alessi, G., 'Precursors of Adriano Willaert in the Practice of Coro Spezzato', *Journal of the American Musicological Society* V (1952), pp. 187–210

Dal Fiume, A., 'Medici, medicine e peste nel Veneto durante il sec. XVI', *Archivio veneto* CXVI (1981), pp. 33–58

Dal Tin, M., 'Note di liturgia patriarchina e canti tradizionali della basilica di San Marco a Venezia', *Jucunda Laudatio* I–IV (1973), pp. 90–130

Dale, T. E. A., 'Easter, Saint Mark and the Doge: The *Deposition* Mosaic in the Choir of San Marco in Venice', *Thesaurismata* XXV (1995), pp. 21–33

—, 'Inventing a Sacred Past: Pictorial Narratives of St Mark the Evangelist in Aquileia and Venice, ca. 1000–1300', *Dumbarton Oaks Papers* XLVIII (1994), pp. 53–104

—, *Relics, Prayer and Politics in Medieval Venetia: Romanesque Painting in the Crypt of Aquileia Cathedral* (Princeton, NJ, 1997)

—, 'Stolen Property: St Mark's First Venetian Tomb and the Politics of Communal Memory', in E. Valdez del Alamo and C. Stamatis Pendergast, eds, *Memory and the Medieval Tomb* (Aldershot, 2000), pp. 205–25

Damerini, G., *L'isola e il cenobio di San Giorgio Maggiore* (Venice, [1956])

Da Mosto, A., *L'Archivio di Stato di Venezia*, 2 vols (Rome, 1940)

—, *I dogi di Venezia con particolare riguardo alle loro tombe* (Venice, 1939)

Da Portogruaro, D. M., *Il tempio del Redentore e il convento dei Cappucini di Venezia* (Venice, 1930)

Davidson, N., ' "As Much for its Culture as for its Arms": The Cultural Relations of Venice and its Dependent Cities, 1400–1700', in A. Cowan, ed., *Mediterranean Urban Culture, 1400–1700* (Exeter, 2000), pp. 197–214

—, 'The Clergy of Venice in the Sixteenth Century', *Bulletin of the Society for Renaissance Studies* II/2 (1984), pp. 19–31

Davies, M., *Aldus Manutius: Printer and Publisher of Renaissance Venice* (London, 1995)

Davies, P., and D. Hemsoll, *Michele Sanmicheli* (Milan, 2004)

Da Villa Urbani, 'Gli arazzi marciani del XVI secolo', in I. Favaretto and M. Da Villa

Urbani, eds, *Arazzi e tappeti dei dogi nella basilica di San Marco* (Venice, 1999), pp. 44–51

Davis, C., 'Jacopo Sansovino's "Loggetta di San Marco" and Two Problems in Iconography', *Mitteilungen des Kunsthistorisches Institut in Florenz* XXIX (1985), pp. 396–400

Davis, J. C., *The Decline of the Venetian Nobility as a Ruling Class* (Baltimore, MD, 1962)

—, *A Venetian Family and its Fortune, 1500–1900: The Donà and the Conservation of their Wealth* (Philadelphia, PA, 1975)

—, *A Venetian Family and its Fortunes, 1500–1900* (Padua, 1975)

Davis, R. C., 'The Geography of Gender in the Renaissance', in J. C. Brown and R. C. Davis, eds, *Gender and Society in Renaissance Italy* (London, 1998), pp. 19–38

—, *Shipbuilders of the Venetian Arsenal: Workers and Workplace in the Preindustrial City* (Baltimore, MD, 1991)

—, 'The Spectacle Almost Fit for a King: Venice's Guerra de' canne of 26 July 1574', in E. E. Kittell and T. F. Madden, eds, *Medieval and Renaissance Venice* (Urbana and Chicago, IL, 1999), pp. 181–212

—, *The War of the Fists: Popular Culture and Public Violence in Late Renaissance Venice* (Oxford, 1994)

—, and B. Ravid, eds, *The Jews of Early Modern Venice* (Baltimore, MD, and London, 2001)

Dean, T., and K. Lowe, eds, *Crime, Society and the Law in Renaissance Italy* (Cambridge, 1994)

—, eds, *Marriage in Italy, 1300–1650* (Cambridge, 1998)

De Filippis, E., 'Il vescovo Carlo Bascapè e il Sacro Monte di Orta', in L. Vaccaro and F. Riccardi, eds, *Sacri monti: devozione, arte e cultura della controriforma* (Milan, 1992), pp. 385–95

De Frede, C., 'Tipografi, editori, librai italiani del Cinquecento coinvolti in processi d'eresia', *Rivista di Storia della Chiesa in Italia* XXIII (1969), pp. 21–53

Degrada, F., ed., *Andrea Gabrieli e il suo tempo. Atti del convegno internazionale: Venezia, 16–18 settembre 1985* (Florence, 1987)

Del Col, A., 'Il controllo della stampa a Venezia e i processi di Antonio Brucioli (1548–1559)', *Critica storica* XVII (1980), pp. 457–510

Demus, O., *The Church of San Marco in Venice: History, Architecture, Sculpture* (Washington, DC, 1960)

—, 'The Ciborium Mosaics of Parenzo', *Burlington Magazine* LXXXVII (1945), pp. 238–45

—, *The Mosaics of San Marco in Venice*, 2 vols in 4 (Chicago, IL, 1984)

—, et al., *Le sculture esterne di San Marco* (Milan, 1995)

Denton, J., ed., *Orders and Hierarchies in Late Medieval and Renaissance Europe* (Basingstoke, 1999)

De Nolhac, P., and A. Solerti, *Il viaggio in Italia di Enrico III re di Francia e le feste a Venezia, Ferrara, Mantova e Torino* (Turin, 1890)

D'Evelyn, M., 'Venice as Vitruvius's City in Daniele Barbaro's Commentaries', *Studi veneziani,* n.s. XXXII (1996), pp. 83–104

Devos, G., and W. Brulez, *Marchands flamands à Venise II, 1606–1621* (Brussels and Rome, 1986)

Diclich, G., *Rito veneto antico detto patriarchino* (Venice, 1823)

Di Filippo Bareggi, C., 'L'editoria veneziana fra '500 e '600', in G. Cozzi and P. Prodi, eds, *Storia di Venezia dalle origini alla caduta della serenissima* VI (Rome, 1994), pp. 615–48

—, *Il mestiere di scrivere: lavoro intellettuale e mercato librario a Venezia nel Cinquecento* (Rome, 1988)

Di Mauro, A., *Bibliografia delle stampe popolari profane dal fondo Capponi della Biblioteca Vaticana* (Florence, 1981)

Dionisotti, C., 'La guerra da'Oriente nella letteratura veneziana del Cinquecento', *Lettere italiane* XVI (1964), pp. 233–50; reprinted in *Geografia e storia della letteratura italiana* (Turin, 1967), pp. 163–82

—, 'Lepanto nella cultura italiana del tempo', in G. Benzoni, ed., *Il mediterraneo nella seconda metà del '500 nella luce di Lepanto* (Florence, 1974), pp. 127–51

Dolcetti, G., *Il 'Libro d'argento' dei cittadini di Venezia e del Veneto*, 5 vols (Venice, 1922–8)

Dorigo, W., 'Una nuova lettura delle sculture del portale centrale di S. Marco', *Venezia arti* II (1988), pp. 5–23

—, *Venezia origini*, 3 vols (Milan, 1983)

Douais, C., ed., *Dépêches de M Fourquevaux, ambassadeur du roi Charles IX en Espagne, 1565–1572*, 3 vols (Paris, 1896–1904)

Dragonetti de Torres, A., *La lega di Lepanto nel carteggio diplomatico inedito di Don Luys de Torres, nunzio straordinario di S. Pio v a Filippo II* (Turin, 1931)

Edwards, R. A., 'Claudio Merulo: Servant of the State and Musical Entrepreneur in Later Sixteenth-Century Venice' (Ph.D dissertation, Princeton University, 1990)

Edwards, R., 'Claudio Menilo, l'altro gioiello nella corona di Correggio', in M. Capra, ed., *A Messer Claudio, musico. Le arti molteplici di Claudio Menilo da Correggio (1533–1604) tra Nenezia e Parma* (Venice, 2006), pp. 15–29

Einstein, A., *The Italian Madrigal*, 3 vols (Princeton, NJ, 1949)

Eisenstein, E., *The Printing Press as an Agent of Change: Communications and Cultural Transformations in Early Modern Europe*, 2 vols (Cambridge, 1979)

Ellis, H., ed., *The Pylgrymage of Sir Richard Gwylforde to the Holy Land, AD 1506* (London, 1851)

Ethos e cultura: studi in onore Ezio Riondato (Padua, 1991)

Everson, J. E., *The Italian Romance Epic in the Age of Humanism: The Matter of Italy and the World of Rome* (Oxford, 2001)

Fabbiani, L., *La fondazione monastica di San Nicolò di Lido, 1053–1628* (Venice, [1988])

Fabbri, G., ed., *La Scuola Grande della Misericordia di Venezia: storia e progetto* (Milan, 1999)

Fabbri, P., 'Fatti e prodezze di Manoli Blessi', *Rivista italiana di musicologia* XI (1976), pp. 182–96

Falomir, M., ed., *Tintoretto* (Madrid, 2007) [Exhibition catalogue]

Fantelli, P. L., 'L'ingresso di Enrico III a Venezia di Andrea Vicentino', *Quaderni della Soprintendenza ai Beni Artistici e Storici di Venezia* VIII (1979), pp. 95–99

Fantoni, M., L. C. Mathew and S. F. Mathews-Grieco, eds, *The Art Market in Italy, 15th–17th Centuries* (Ferrara, 2003)

Fasoli, G., 'Commune Veneciarum', in *Venezia dalla Prima Crociata alla conquista di Costantinopoli del 1204* (Florence, 1965), pp. 73–103

—, 'Liturgia e ceremoniale ducale', in A. Pertusi, ed., *Venezia e il Levante fino al secolo XV*, 3 vols (Florence, 1983), I, pp. 261–95

—, 'Nascità di un mito', *Studi storici in onore di Gioacchino Volpe* I (Florence, 1958), pp. 445–79

Favaretto, I., and M. Da Villa Urbani, eds, *Arazzi e tappeti dei dogi nella basilica di San Marco* (Venice, 1999)

—, eds, *Il Museo di San Marco* (Venice, 2003)

—, and G. L. Ravagnan, eds, *Lo statuario pubblico della Serenissima: due secoli di collezionismo di antichità, 1596–1797* (Padua, 1997)

Febvre, L., and H. J. Martin, *The Coming of the Book: The Impact of Printing, 1450–1800*, trans. D. Gerard (London, 1976)

Fedalto, G., 'Le minoranze straniere a Venezia tra politica e legislazione', in H. G. Beck, M. Manoussacas and A. Pertusi, eds, *Venezia centro di mediazione tra oriente e occidente (secoli XV–XVI): aspetti e problemi*, 2 vols (Florence, 1977), I, pp. 143–62

—, *Ricerche storiche sulla posizione giuridica ed ecclesiastica dei Greci a Venezia nei secoli XV e XVI* (Florence, 1967)

Fehl, P., *Decorum and Wit: The Poetry of Venetian Painting. Essays in the History of the Classical Tradition* (Vienna, 1992)

—, 'A Literary Keynote for Pompeo Batoni's The Triumph of Venice', *North Carolina Museum of Art Bulletin* X/3 (1971), pp. 3–15

—, 'Pictorial Precedents for the Representation of Doge Lionardo Loredan in Batoni's *Triumph of Venice*', *North Carolina Museum of Art Bulletin* XI/4 (1973), pp. 21–31

Feldman, M., *City Culture and the Madrigal in Venice* (Berkeley, CA, 1995)

Fenlon, I., 'Gioseffo Zarlino and the Accademia Venetiana della Fama', in Fenlon, *Music and Culture in Late Renaissance Italy* (Oxford, 2002), pp. 118–38

—, '*In destructione Turcharum*: The Victory of Lepanto in Sixteenth-Century Music and Letters', in F. Degrada, ed., *Andrea Gabrieli e il suo tempo. Atti del convegno internzionale: Venezia, 16–18 settembre 1985* (Florence, 1987), pp. 293–317

—, 'Lepanto: The Arts of Celebration in Renaissance Venice,' *Proceedings of the British Academy* LXIII (1987), pp. 201–36

411

—, 'Magnificence as Civic Image: Music and Ceremonial Space in Early Modern Venice', in Fenlon, *Music and Culture in Late Renaissance Italy* (Oxford, 2002), pp. 1–23

—, 'Music and Crisis in Florence and Rome, 1527–30', in C. Shaw, ed., *Italy and the European Powers: The Impact of War, 1500–1530* (Leiden, 2006), pp. 279–98

—, 'Music, Ceremony and Self-Identity in Renaissance Venice', in F. Passadore and F. Rossi, eds, *La cappella musicale di S. Marco nell'età moderna* (Venice, 1998), pp. 7–21

—, *Music and Culture in Late Renaissance Italy* (Oxford, 2002)

—, ed., *Music in Medieval and Early Modern Europe: Patronage, Sources and Texts* (Cambridge, 1981)

—, *Music, Print and Culture in Early Sixteenth-Century Italy* (London, 1995)

—, 'Strangers in Paradise: Dutchmen in Venice in 1525', in Fenlon, *Music and Culture in Late Renaissance Italy* (Oxford, 2002), pp. 24–43

Ferraro, J. M., *Family and Public Life in Brescia, 1580–1650: The Foundations of Power in the Venetian State* (Cambridge, 1993)

—, *Marriage Wars in Late Renaissance Venice* (Oxford, 2001)

Filangieri di Candida Gonzaga, R., *Storia di Massa Lubrense* (Naples, 1910)

Finlay, R., *Politics in Renaissance Venice* (London, 1980)

—, 'The Venetian Republic as a Gerontocracy: Age and Politics in the Renaissance', *Journal of Medieval and Renaissance Studies* VIII (1978), pp. 157–78

Finocchi Gersi, L., ed., *Alessandro Vittoria e l'arte veneta della maniera. Atti del Convegno Internazionale di Studi: Università di Udine, 26–27 ottobre 2000* (Udine, 2001)

Fiocco, G., 'Le pale feriali', in H. R. Hahnloser, ed., *Il tesoro di San Marco*, I: *La Pala d'Oro* (Florence, 1971), pp. 115–23

Firpo, M., *Dal Sacco di Roma allo Inquisizione* (Alessandria, 1998)

—, 'Il Sacco di Roma del 1527 tra profezie, propaganda e riforma religiosa', in Firpo, *Dal Sacco di Roma allo Inquisizione* (Alessandria, 1998), pp. 7–60

Fletcher, J., 'Fine Art and Festivity in Renaissance Venice: The Artist's Part', in J. Onians, ed., *Essays on Art and Culture in Honour of E. H. Gombrich at 85* (London, 1994), pp. 129–51

Flores d'Arcais, F., *Guariento* (Venice, 1965)

Fogolari, G., 'Processionii veneziane', *Dedalo* V (1924–5), pp. 775–80

Follieri, E., 'Il libro Greco per i greci nelle imprese editoriali romane e veneziane della prima metà del Cinquecento', in H. G. Beck, M. Manoussacas and A. Pertusi, eds, *Venezia centro di mediazione tra oriente e occidente (secoli XV–XVI): aspetti e problemi*, 2 vols (Florence, 1977), I, pp. 483–508

Fragnito, G., *La Bibbia al rogo. La censura ecclesiastica e i volgarizzamenti della scrittura (1471–1606)* (Bologna, 1997)

Franzoi, U., *Storia e leggenda del palazzo ducale di Venezia* (Venice, 1982)

—, and D. Di Stefano, *Le chiese di Venezia* (Venice, 1976)

—, T. Pignatti and W. Wolters, *Il Palazzo Ducale di Venezia* (Treviso, 1990)

Frazer, M. E., 'The Pala d'Oro and the Cult of St Mark in Venice', *Jahrbuch der österreichischen Byzantinistik* XXXII/5 (1982), pp. 273–9

Frémy, E., *Un ambassadeur libéral sous Charles IX et Henry III: ambassades à Venise d'Arnaud Du Ferrier d'après sa correspondance inédite (1563–1567, 1570–1582)* (Paris, 1880)

Fullerton, C. B., 'The Master IO. F. F. and the Function of Plaquettes', in A. Luchs, ed., *Italian Plaquettes* (Hanover, NH, and London, 1989), pp. 143–62

Gabrieli, A., *Complete Madrigals*, ed. A. Tillman Merritt, 12 vols (Madison, WI, 1981–4)

—, *Edizione nazionale delle opere* (Milan, 1988–)

Gabrieli, G., *Opera omnia*, ed. D. Arnold and R. Charteris (Rome, 1956–)

Gaeta, F., 'Alcune considerazioni sul mito di Venezia', *Bibliothèque d'humanisme et Renaissance* XXIII (1961), pp. 58–75

—, *Un nunzio pontificio a venezia nel Cinquecento: Girolamo Aleandro* (Venice and Rome, 1960)

—, et al., eds, *Nunziature di Venezia* (Rome, 1958–)

Galante, A., 'Per la storia giuridica della basilica di San Marco', *Zeitschrift der Savigny-*

Stiftung fur Rechtsgeschichte XXXIII (1912), pp. 283–98

Galliccioli, G. B., *Delle memorie Venete antiche, profane ed ecclesiastiche*, 8 vols (Venice, 1795)

—, *Storie e memorie venete, profane ed ecclesiastiche*, 8 vols (Venice, 1795)

Gallo, F. A., 'Musiche veneziane nel MS. 2216 della Biblioteca Universitaria di Bologna', *Quadrivium* VI (1964), pp. 107–16

—, 'The Practice of *Cantus Planus Binatim* in Italy from the Beginning of the 14th to the Beginning of the 16th Century', in C. Corsi and P. Petrobelli, eds, *Le polifonie primitive in Friuli e in Europa* (Rome, 1989), pp. 13–30

Gallo, R., 'Reliquie e reliquiari veneziani', *Rivista di Venezia* XIII (1934), pp. 187–214

—, *Il tesoro di San Marco e la sua storia* (Venice and Rome, 1967)

Gambi, L., and A. Pinelli, eds, *La Galleria delle Carte Geografiche in Vaticano*, 3 vols (Modena, 1994)

Ganado, A., and M. Agius-Adalà, *A Study in Depth of 143 Maps Representing the Great Siege of Malta of 1565*, 2 vols (Valletta, 1994–6)

Geary, P. J., *Furta sacra: Thefts of Relics in the Central Middle Ages*, 2nd revd edn (Princeton, NJ, 1990)

Gemmani, M., 'Libri corali del Museo di San Marco', in I. Favaretto and M. Da Villa Urbani, eds, *Il Museo di San Marco* (Venice, 2003), pp. 160–62

Gentilcore, D., *Healers and Healing in Early Modern Italy* (Manchester, 1998)

—, ' "Tutti i modi che adoperano i ceretani per far bezzi": Towards a Database of Italian Charlatans', *Ludica* V–VI (2000), pp. 201–15

Georgopoulou, M., *Architecture and Urbanism in Venice's Mediterranean Colonies* (Cambridge, 2001)

Gerola, G., 'Candia, Palmanova e Lepanto in un dipinto allegorico di Valpolicella', *Pro Verona* (October 1910), pp. 3–4

Gerulaitis, V., *Printing and Publishing in Fifteenth-Century Venice* (Chicago, IL, and London, 1976)

Gilbert, F., 'Biondo, Sabellico and the Beginnings of Venetian Official Historiography', in J. G. Rowe and W. H. Stockdale, eds, *Essays Presented to Wallace K. Ferguson* (Toronto, 1971), pp. 275–83

—, 'The Date of the Composition of Contarini's and Giannotti's Books on Venice', *Studies in the Renaissance* XIV (1967), pp. 172–84

—, 'The Last Will of a Venetian Grand Chancellor', in E. P. Mahoney, ed., *Philosophy and Humanism: Renaissance Essays in Honor of Paul Oscar Kristeller* (Leiden, 1976), pp. 502–17

—, 'The Venetian Constitution in Florentine Political Thought', in N. Rubenstein, ed., *Florentine Studies: Politics and Society in Renaissance Florence* (London, 1968), pp. 463–500

—, 'Venice in the Crisis of the League of Cambrai', in J. Hale, ed., *Renaissance Venice* (London, 1973), pp. 274–92

Gilmore, M., 'Myth and Reality in Venetian Political Theory', in J. Hale, ed., *Renaissance Venice* (London, 1973), pp. 431–44

Ginsburg, C., *The Cheese and the Worms: The Cosmos of a Sixteenth-Century Miller* (London, 1980)

Giomo, G., 'Le spese del nobil uomo Marco Grimani nella sua elezione a doge di Venezia', *Archivio veneto* XXXIII (1887), pp. 443–54

Giurgea, A., 'Theatre of the Flesh: The Carnival of Venice and the Theatre of the World' (Ph.D dissertation, University of California, Los Angeles, 1987)

Gleason, E., 'Confronting New Realities: Venice and the Peace of Bologna, 1530', in J. Martin and D. Romano, eds, *Venice Reconsidered: The History and Civilization of an Italian City State, 1297–1797* (Baltimore, MD, and London, 2000), pp. 168–84

—, *Gasparo Contarini: Venice, Rome and Reform* (Berkeley, CA, 1993)

Glixon, J., 'Ad honor de misser San Rocho: La musica nella Scuola Grande, 1478–1806', in *La scuola Grande di San Rocco nella musica e nelle feste veneziane* (Venice, 1996), pp. 7–32

—, ' "Con canti et organo": Music at the Venetian Scuole Piccole in the Renaissance', in J. A. Owens and Anthony Cummings, eds, *Music in Renaissance Cities and Courts:*

Studies in Honor of Lewis Lockwood (Warren, MI, 1997), pp. 123–40

—, '"Far una bella processione": Music and Public Ceremony at the Venetian Scuole Grandi', in R. Charteris, ed., *Altro Polo: Essays on Italian Music in the Cinquecento* (Sydney, 1990), pp. 190–220

—, *Honoring God and the City. Music at the Venetian Confraternities 1260–1807* (New York, 2003)

—, 'Music and Ceremony at the Scuole Grande di San Giovanni Evangelista: A New Document from the Venetian State Archives', in K. Eisenbichler, ed., *Crossing the Boundaries: Christian Piety and the Arts in Italian Medieval and Renaissance Confraternities* (Kalamazoo, MI, 1991), pp. 56–89

—, 'Music at the Scuole in the Age of Andrea Gabrieli', in F. Degrada, ed., *Andrea Gabrieli e il suo tempo. Atti del convegno internzionale: Venezia, 16–18 settembre 1985* (Florence, 1987), pp. 59–74

—, 'Music at the Venetian Scuole Grandi, 1440–1540', in I. Fenlon, ed., *Music in Medieval and Early Modern Europe: Patronage, Sources and Texts* (Cambridge, 1981), pp. 193–208

—, 'The Musicians of the *Cappella* and the *Scuole*: Collaboration or Competition', in F. Passadore and F. Rossi, eds, *La cappella musicale di San Marco nell'età moderna* (Venice, 1998), pp. 301–12

—, 'A Musicians' Union in Sixteenth-Century Venice', *Journal of the American Musicological Society* (1983), pp. 392–421

—, 'The Polyphonic Laude of Innocentius Dammonis', *Journal of Musicology* VIII (1990), pp. 19–53

Gnoli, R., *Marmora romana*, 2nd edn (Rome, 1988)

Goffen, R., *Giovanni Bellini* (New Haven, CT, and London, 1989)

—, 'Paolo Veneziano e Andrea Dandolo: una nuova lettera della pala feriale', in H. R. Hahnloser and R. Polacco, eds, *La Pala d'oro*, 2nd edn (Venice, 1994), pp. 173–84

—, *Piety and Patronage in Renaissance Venice: Bellini, Titian and the Franciscans* (New Haven, CT, and London, 1986)

Goldthwaite, R., *Wealth and the Demand for Art in Italy, 1300–1600* (Baltimore, MD, 1993)

Göllner, C., *Turcica: Die europäischen Türkendrucke des XVI Jahrhunderts*, 2 vols (Budapest and Baden-Baden, 1961–8)

Goltz, 'The Role of Music on the Stages of Quacks', *Ludica* V–VI (2000), pp. 103–15

Gombrich, E. H., 'Celebrations in Venice of the Holy League and of the Victory of Lepanto', in *Studies in Renaissance and Baroque Art Presented to Anthony Blunt on his Sixtieth Birthday* (London, 1967), pp. 62–8

Gonnet, C. J., ed., 'Bedevaart nach Jerusalem', *Bijdragen voor geschiednis van het bisdom Haarlem* XI (1882)

Gorini, G., 'Lepanto nelle medaglie', in G. Benzoni, ed., *Il mediterraneo nella seconda metà del '500 nella luce di Lepanto* (Florence, 1974), pp. 153–62

Goy, R., *The House of Gold: Building a Palace in Medieval Venice* (Cambridge, 1992)

Gramigna, S., and A. Perissa, *Scuole di arti mestieri e devozione a Venezia* (Venice, 1981)

Grendler, P. F., *Critics of the Italian World, 1530–1620: Anton Francesco Doni, Nicolò Franco and Ortensio Lando* (Madison, WI, and London, 1969)

—, 'The Destruction of Hebrew Books in Venice, 1568', *Proceedings of the American Academy for Jewish Research* XLV (1978), pp. 103–30

—, 'Form and Function in Italian Renaissance Popular Books', *Renaissance Quarterly* XLVI (1993), pp. 451–85

—, 'Francesco Sansovino and Italian Popular History, 1560–1600', *Studies in the Renaissance* XVI (1969), pp. 139–80

—, 'The Leaders of the Venetian State, 1540–1609: A Prosopographical Analysis', *Studi veneziani*, n.s. XIX (1990), pp. 35–85

—, *The Roman Inquisition and the Venetian Press, 1540–1605* (Princeton, NJ, 1977)

—, *Schooling in Renaissance Italy: Literacy and Learning, 1300–1600* (Baltimore, MD, 1989)

—, 'The *Tre Savii sopra Eresia*, 1547–1605: A Prosopographical Study', *Studi veneziani* III (1979), pp. 283–340

Grubb, J., 'Elite Citizens', in J. Martin and D. Romano, eds, *Venice Reconsidered: The*

History and Civilization of an Italian City State, 1297–1797 (Baltimore, MD, and London, 2000), pp. 339–64

—, *Firstborn of Venice: Vicenza in the Early Renaissance State* (Baltimore, MD, and London, 1988)

—, 'Memory and Identity: Why Venetians Didn't Keep *ricordanze*', *Renaissance Studies* VIII (1994), pp. 375–87

—, 'When Myths Lose Power: Four Decades of Venetian Historiography', *Journal of Modern History* LVIII (1986), pp. 43–94

Guerre in ottava rime, 4 vols (Modena, 1989)

Guilmartin, J. F., *Gunpowder and Galleys: Changing Technology and Mediterranean Warfare at Sea in the Sixteenth Century* (Cambridge, 1974)

—, 'Ideology and Conflict: The Wars of the Ottoman Empire, 1453–1606', *Journal of Interdisciplinary History* XVIII (1988), pp. 721–47

Gullino, G., ed., *La chiesa di venezia tra riforma protestante e riforma cattolica* (Venice, 1990)

Haar, J., 'Arie per cantar stanze ariostesche', in M. A. Balsano, ed., *L'Ariosto la musica, i musicisti: quattro studi e sette madrigali ariosteschi* (Florence, 1981), pp. 31–46

—, *Essays on Italian Poetry and Music in the Renaissance, 1350–1600* (Berkeley, Los Angeles and London, 1986)

Hahn, C., 'Narrative on the Golden Altar of Sant'Ambrogio in Milan: Presentation and Reception', *Dumbarton Oaks Papers* LIII (1999), pp. 167–87

—, 'Seeing and Believing: The Construction of Sanctity in Early-Medieval Saints' Shrines', *Speculum* LXXII (1997), pp. 1079–1106

Hahnloser, H. R., ed., *Il tesoro di San Marco*, 2 vols (Florence, 1971)

—, and R. Polacco, eds, *La Pala d'Oro*, 2nd edn (Venice, 1994)

Hale, J. R., 'From Peacetime Establishment to Fighting Machine: The Venetian Army and the War of Cyprus and Lepanto', in G. Benzoni, ed., *Il mediterraneo nella seconda metà del '500 nella luce di Lepanto* (Florence, 1974), pp. 163–84

—, 'Industria del libro e cultura militare a Venezia nel Rinascimento', in G. Arnaldi

and M. Pastore Stocchi, eds, *Storia della cultura Veneta* 3/II, pp. 245–89

—, ed., *Renaissance Venice* (London, 1973)

—, and M. E. Mallett, *The Military Organization of a Renaissance State: Venice, c. 1400 to 1617* (Cambridge, 1984)

Haliczar, S., ed., *Inquisition and Society in Early Modern Europe* (London and Sydney, 1987)

Hamilton, P. C., 'The Palazzo dei Camerlenghi in Venice', *Journal of the Society of Architectural Historians* XLII (1983), pp. 258–71

Hammer, W., 'The Concept of the New or Second Rome in the Middle Ages', *Speculum* XIX (1944), pp. 50–62

Harran, D., 'The Concept of Battle in Music of the Renaissance', *Journal of Medieval and Renaissance Studies* XVII (1987), pp. 175–94

Harrison, M., *A Temple for Byzantium: The Discovery and Excavation of Anicia Juliana's Palace-Church in Istanbul* (London, 1989)

Harrisse, H., *Excerpta Columbiniana* (Paris, 1887)

—, *Fernand Columb: sa vie, ses oeuvres* (Paris, 1872)

Harte, N. B., and K. G. Ponting, eds, *Cloth and Clothing in Medieval Europe: Essays in Memory of Professor E. M. Caru-Wilson* (London, 1983)

Haskell, F., *Patrons and Painters: A Study in the Relations between Italian Art and Society in the Age of the Baroque* (London, 1963)

Head, R. C., 'Religious Boundaries and the Inquisition in Venice: Trials of Jews and Judaizers, 1548–1580', *Journal of Medieval and Renaissance Studies* XX (1990), pp. 175–204

Herz, A., 'The Sistine and Pauline Tombs: Documents of the Counter-Reformation', *Storia dell'arte* XLIII (1981), pp. 241–62

Hess, A. C., 'The Battle of Lepanto and its Place in Mediterranean History', *Past and Present* 57 (1972), pp. 53–73

Hills, P., 'Piety and Patronage in Cinquecento Venice: Tintoretto and the Scuole del Sacramento', *Art History* VI (1983), pp. 30–43

—, *Venetian Colour: Marble, Mosaic, Painting and Glass* (New Haven and London, 1999)

Hind, A. M., *A History of Engraving and Etching from the Fifteenth Century to the Year 1914* (London, 1963)

—, *An Introduction to the Woodcut with a Detailed Survey of Work Done in the Fifteenth Century*, 2 vols (London, 1935)

Hirsch, R., *Printing, Selling and Reading, 1450–1550*, 2nd revd edn (Wiesbaden, 1974)

Hirte, T., *Il foro all'antica di Venezia: la trasformazione di Piazza S. Marco nel Cinquecento* (Venice, 1986)

Hood, W., 'The *Sacro Monte* of Varallo: Renaissance Art and Popular Religion', in T. Verdon, ed., *Monasticism and the Arts* (Syracuse, NY, 1984), pp. 291–311

Hopkins, A., 'Architecture and *Infirmitas*: Doge Andrea Gritti and the Chancel of San Marco', *Journal of the Society of Architectural Historians* LVII (1998), pp. 182–97

—, 'Longhena's Second Sanctuary Design for Santa Maria Salute', *Burlington Magazine* CXXXVI (1994), pp. 498–501

—, 'Plans and Planning for S. Maria della Salute, Venice', *Art Bulletin* LXXIX (1997), pp. 440–65

—, *Santa Maria della Salute: Architecture and Ceremony in Baroque Venice* (Cambridge, 2000)

Howard, D., *Jacopo Sansovino: Architecture and Patronage in Renaissance Venice* (New Haven, CT, and London, 1975)

—, 'Ritual Space in Renaissance Venice', *Scroope* V (1993–4), pp. 4–11

—, 'Rome and Venetian Art and Architecture', *Edinburgh Architecture Research* XVIII (1991), pp. 44–70

—, 'La Scuola Grande della Misericordia di Venezia', in G. Fabbri, ed., *La Scuola Grande della Misericordia di Venezia: storia e progetto* (Milan, 1999), pp. 13–70

—, 'Two Notes on Jacopo Sansovino', *Architettura* IV (1974), pp. 132–46

—, *Venice and the East: The Impact of the Islamic World on Venetian Architecture, 1100–1500* (New Haven, CT, and London, 2000)

Humfrey, P., *The Altarpiece in Renaissance Venice* (New Haven, CT, and London, 1993)

—, 'Altarpieces and Altar Dedications in Counter-Reformation Venice and the Veneto', *Renaissance Studies* X (1996), pp. 371–87

—, 'The Bellinesque Life of St Mark Cycle for the Scuola Grande di San Marco in Venice

in its Original Arrangement', *Zeitschrift fur Kuntsgeschichte* XLVIII (1985), pp. 225–42

—, 'Competitive Devotions: The Venetian "Scuole Piccole" as Donors of Altarpieces in the Years around 1500', *Art Bulletin* LXX (1988), pp. 401–23

—, 'Co-ordinated Altarpieces in Renaissance Venice: The Progress of an Idea', in Humfrey and Kemp, eds, *The Altarpiece in the Renaissance*, pp. 190–211

—, 'Dürer's Feast of the Rosegarlands: A Venetian Altarpiece', *Bulletin of the Society for Renaissance Studies* IV/1 (1986), pp. 29–39

—, 'La festa del Rosario di Albrecht Dürer', *Eidos. Rivista di cultura* II (1988), pp. 4–15

—, and M. Kemp, eds, *The Altarpiece in the Renaissance* (Cambridge, 2000)

Huse, N., and W. Wolters, *The Art of Renaissance Venice: Architecture, Sculpture and Painting, 1460–1590* (Chicago, IL, 1990)

Innocenti, C., 'Gli arazzi di manifattura medicea con storie di San Marco', in R. Polacco, ed., *Storia dell'arte marciana: sculture, tesoro, arazzi. Atti del convegno internazionale di studi: Venezia, 11–14 ottobre 1994* (Venice, 1997), pp. 324–32

Ioly Zorattini, P. C., and A. M. Caproni, eds, *Memor fui dierum antiquorum: studi in memoria di Luigi di Biasio* (Udine, 1995)

Italian Sacred and Ceremonial Music, Polyphonic Music of the Fourteenth Century XIII, ed. K. von Fischer and F. Alberto Gallo (Monaco, 1987)

Ivanoff, N., 'Henri III à Venise', *Gazette des Beaux-Arts* LXXX (1972), pp. 313–30

—, 'La Libreria Marciana: arte e iconologia', *Saggi e memorie di storia dell'arte* VI (1968), pp. 33–78

Jacoff, M., *The Horses of San Marco and the Quadriga of the Lord* (Princeton, NJ, 1993)

Jacopo Tintoretto: ritratti (Milan, 1994) [exhibition catalogue]

Jacoviello, M., 'Proteste di editori e librai veneziani contro l'introduzione della censura sulla stampa a Venezia, 1543–1555', *Archivio storico italiano* CLI (1993), pp. 27–56

Jacquot, J., ed., *Le lieu théâtral à la Renaissance* (Paris, 1964)

Jaffé, M., *The Devonshire Collection of Italian Drawings: Venetian and North Italian Schools* (London, 1994)

Jardine, L., *Worldly Goods: A New History of the Renaissance* (London, 1996)

—, and J. Brotton, *Global Interests: Renaissance Art between East and West* (Ithaca, NY, and London, 2000)

Javitch, D., *Proclaiming a Classic: The Canonization of Orlando Furioso* (Princeton, NJ, 1991)

Johns, Adrian, *The Nature of the Book: Print and Knowledge in the Making* (London, 1998)

Johnson, E. J., 'Jacopo Sansovino, Giacomo Torelli and the Theatricality of the Piazzetta', *Journal of the Society of Architectural Historians* LIX (2000), pp. 436–53

Johannes de Quadris; see Quadris

Kähler, H., and C. Mango, *Hagia Sophia* (New York, 1967)

Kallendorf, C., *Virgil and the Myth of Venice: Books and Readers in the Italian Renaissance* (Oxford, 1999)

Kantorowicz, E. H., *Laudes Regiae: A Study in Liturgical Acclamations and Medieval Ruler Worship* (Berkeley, CA, 1946)

Katritzky, M. A., 'Italian Comedians in Renaissance Prints', *Print Quarterly* IV (1987), pp. 236–54

—, 'Marketing Medicine: The Image of the Early Modern Mountebank', *Renaissance Studies* XV (2001), pp. 121–53

Katzenstein, R. A., 'Three Liturgical Manuscripts from San Marco: Art and Patronage in Mid-Trecento Venice' (Ph.D dissertation, Harvard University, 1987)

Kieslinger, F., 'Le trasenne della basilica di San Marco del secolo XIII', *Ateneo Veneto* 131 (1944), pp. 57–61

King, M. L., 'Personal, Domestic and Republican Values in the Moral Philosophy of Giovanni Caldiera', *Renaissance Quarterly* XXVII (1975), pp. 559–65

—, *Venetian Humanism in an Age of Patrician Dominance* (Princeton, NJ, 1986)

Kingdon, R. M., 'Patronage, Piety and Printing in Sixteenth-Century Europe', in D. H. Pinkney and T. Ropp, eds, *A Festschrift for Frederick B. Artz* (Durham, NC, 1964), pp. 19–36

Kinney, D., '*Spolia, Damnatio* and *Renovatio Memoriae*', *Memoirs of the American Academy in Rome* XLII (1997), pp. 117–48

Kittell, E. E., and T. F. Madden, eds, *Medieval and Renaissance Venice* (Urbana and Chicago, IL, 1999)

Klarwill, V. von, *The Fugger Newsletters: Being a Selection of Unpublished Letters from the Correspondents of the House of Fugger During the Years 1568–1605*, 2 vols (London, 1925–6)

Krautheimer, R., *Early Christian and Byzantine Architecture* (Harmondsworth, 1965)

Kubler, G., 'Sacred Mountains in Europe and America', in T. Verdon and J. Henderson, eds, *Christianity and the Renaissance: Image and Religious Imagination in the Quattrocento* (Syracuse, NY, 1990), pp. 413–41

Kuhn, A., 'Venice, Queen of the Sea', in S. Sinding-Larsen, *Christ in the Council Hall: Studies in the Religious Iconography of the Venetian Republic* (Rome, 1974), pp. 263–8

Kuntz, M. L., 'Profezia e politica nella Venezia del sedicesimo secolo: il caso di Dionisio Gallo', in P. Pecorari and G. Silvano, eds, *Continuità e discontinuità nella storia politica, economica e religiosa: studi in onore di Aldo Stella* (Vicenza, 1993), pp. 153–77

Labalme, P. H., *Bernardo Giustiniani: A Venetian of the Quattrocento* (Rome, 1969)

—, 'Holy Patronage, Holy Promotion: The Cult of Saints in Fifteenth-Century Venice', in S. Sticca, ed., *Saints: Studies in Hagiography* (Binghamton, NY, 1996), pp. 233–49

—, 'No Man but an Angel: Early Efforts to Canonize Lorenzo Giustiniani, 1381–1456', in P. Pecorari and G. Silvano, eds, *Continuità e discontinuità nella storia politica, economica e religiuosa: studi in onore di Aldo Stella* (Vicenza, 1993), pp. 15–43

Labowsky, L., *Bessarion's Library and the Biblioteca Marciana: Six Early Inventories* (Rome, 1979)

Landau, D., 'Printmaking in Venice and the Veneto', in J. Martineau and C. Hope, eds, *The Genius of Venice, 1500–1600* (London, 1984), pp. 303–54

—, and Parshall, P., *The Renaissance Print, 1470–1550* (New Haven, CT, and London, 1994)

Lane, F. C., 'Public Debt and Private Health, Particularly in Sixteenth-Century Venice', in *Mélanges en l'honneur de Fernand Braudel* (Toulouse, 1973), pp. 317–25

—, *Venice and History: The Collected Papers of Frederick C. Lane, Edited by a Committee of Colleagues and Former Students* (Baltimore, MD, [1966])

—, *Venice: A Maritime Republic* (London, 1973)

—, 'Wages and Recruitment of Venetian Galeotti, 1470–1580', *Studi veneziani,* n.s. VI (1982), pp. 15–43

—, and R. Mueller, *Money and Banking in Medieval and Renaissance Venice*, 2 vols (Baltimore, MD, and London, 1985–97)

La Rocca, P., and A. Pontremoli, *La danza a Venezia nel Rinascimento* (Vicenza, 1993)

Lasko, P., *Ars sacra, 800–1200* (Harmondsworth, 1972)

Laven, M., *Virgins of Venice: Broken Vows and Cloistered Lives in the Renaissance Convent* (New York, 2003)

Laven, P., 'Banditry and Lawlessness on the Venetian Terraferma in the Later Cinquecento', in T. Dean and K. P. Lowe, eds, *Crime, Society and the Law in Renaissance Italy* (Cambridge, 1994), pp. 221–48

Lax, E., ed., *Claudio Monteverdi, 1567–1643: lettere* (Florence, 1994)

Lazzarini, V., 'Il preteso documento della fondazione di Venezia e la cronica del medico Jacopo Dondi', *Atti del Reale Istituto Veneto di Scienze, Lettere ed Arti* LXXV (1915–16), pp. 1263–77

—, 'Il testamento del Doge Andrea Dandolo', *Nuovo archivio veneto* VII (1904), pp. 139–48

—, 'I titoli dei dogi', *Nuovo archivio veneto* V (1903), pp. 271–311

Lea, K. M., *Italian Popular Comedy: A Study in the Commedia dell'arte, 1560–1620, with Special Reference to the English Stage*, 2 vols (Oxford, 1934)

Lebe, R., *Quando San Marco approdo a Venezia: il culto dell'evangelista e il miracolo politico della Repubblica di Venezia* (Rome, 1981)

Lenaerts, R.B.M., 'La chapelle de Saint-Marc à Venise sous Adrien Willaert', *Bulletin de l'institut historique belge de Rom* XIX (1938), pp. 205–55

Levi, C. A., *Notizie storiche di alcune antiche scuole di arti e mestieri scomparse a esistente ancora in Venezia* (Venice, 1895)

Levi, E., *I cantari leggendari del popolo italiano nei secoli XIV e XV* (Turin, 1914)

Lewis, M. A., 'Antonio Gardane's Early Connections with the Willaert Circle', in I. Fenlon, ed., *Music in Medieval and Early Modern Europe: Patronage, Sources and Texts* (Cambridge, 1981), pp. 209–26

—, *Antonio Gardano, Venetian Music Printer, 1538–1569: A Descriptive Bibliography and Historical Study*, 3 vols to date (New York and London, 1988–)

Libby, L. J., 'Venetian History and Political Thought after 1509', *Studies in the Renaissance* 20 (1973), pp. 7–45

Il libro italiano del Cinquecento: produzione e commercio (Rome, 1989)

Limentani, A., ed., *Martin da Canal: les estoires de Venise. Cronaca veneziana in lingua francese dalle origini al 1275* (Florence, 1972)

Links, J. G., *Canaletto* (Oxford, 1982)

Litaniae secundum consuetudinem ducalis ecclesiae Sancti Marci (Venice, 1719)

Logan, O. M. T., 'Studies in the Religious Life of Venice in the Sixteenth and Early Seventeenth Centuries: The Venetian Clergy and Religious Orders, 1520–1630' (Ph.D. dissertation, University of Cambridge, 1967)

—, *Culture and Society in Venice, 1470–1790: The Renaissance and its Heritage* (London, 1972)

Lorenzi, G. B., *Monumenti per servire alla storia del palazzo ducale di Venezia* (Venice, 1868)

Lotz, W., 'The Roman Legacy in Sansovino's Venetian Buildings', *Journal of the Society of Architectural Historians* XXII (1963), pp. 3–12

—, *Studies in Italian Renaissance Architecture* (Cambridge, MA, and London, 1977)

—, 'La trasformazione sansoviniana di Piazza San Marco e l'urbanistica del Cinquecento', *Bolletino del Centro Internazionale di Studi di Architettura 'Andrea Palladio'* VIII/2 (1966), pp. 114–22

Lovarini, E., *Studi sul Ruzzante e la letteratura pavana*, ed. G. Folena (Padua, 1965)

Lowry, M., *Nicholas Jensen and the Rise of Venetian Publishing* (Oxford, 1991)

—, *The World of Aldus Manutius: Business and Scholarship in Renaissance Venice* (Oxford, 1979)

Luchs, A., ed., *Italian Plaquettes* (Hanover, NH, and London, 1989)

Lunardon, S., 'Interventi di Palladio sui luoghi pii: Le Zitelle', in L. Puppi, ed., *Palladio e Venezia* (Florence, 1982), pp. 103–20

—, ed., *Hospitale S. Mariae Cruciferorum: l'ospizio dei Crociferi a Venezia* (Venice, 1984)

—, 'L'ospedale dei Crociferi', in Lunardon, ed., *Hospitale S. Mariae Cruciferorum*, pp. 19–84

Lutteken, L., '"Musicus et cantor diu in ecclesia Sancti Marci de Veneciis": note biografiche su Johannes de Quadris', *Rassegna veneta di studi musicali* V–VI (1989–90), pp. 43–62

McAndrew, J., *Venetian Architecture of the Early Renaissance* (Boston, MA, 1980)

MacClintock, C., *Giaches de Wert, 1535–1596: Life and Works* (n. p., 1966)

McCleary, N., 'Note storiche et archeologiche sul testo della "Translatio S. Marci"', *Memorie storiche forogiulesi* XXVII–XXIX (1931–3), pp. 223–64

McCormick, M., 'Analyzing Imperial Ceremonies', *Jahrbuch der Österreichischen byzantinischen Gesellschaft* XXXV (1985), pp. 1–20

McDonald, M. P., *Ferdinand Columbus: Renaissance Collector (1488–1539)* (London, 2005) [Exhibition catalogue]

—, 'The Print Collection of Ferdinand Columbus', *Print Quarterly* XVII (2000), pp. 43–6

—, 'The Print Collection of Philip II at the Escorial', *Print Quarterly* XV (1998), pp. 15–35

McGowan, M. M., 'Festivals and the Arts in Henry III's Journey from Poland to France', in R. Mulryne, H. Watanabe-O'Kelly and M. Shewring, eds, *Europa Triumphans: Court and Civic Festivals in Early Modern Europe*, 2 vols (Aldershot, 2004), pp. 122–9

McGowan, R. A., 'The Venetian Printer Giuseppe Sala: New Information based upon Archival Documents', *Fontes artis musicae* 36 (1989), pp. 102–7

MacKenney, R. S., 'Arti e stato a Venezia tra tardo medioevo e '600', *Studi veneziani*, n.s. V (1981), pp. 127–43

—, *The City-State, 1500–1700: Republican Liberty in an Age of Princely Power* (London, 1989)

—, 'Continuity and Change in the *scuole piccole* of Venice, c.1250–c.1600', *Renaissance Studies* VIII (1994), pp. 388–403

—, 'Devotional Confraternities in Renaissance Venice', in W. J. Sheils and D. Wood, eds, *Voluntary Religion* (Oxford, 1986), pp. 85–96

—, 'Guilds and Craftsmen in Sixteenth-Century Venice', *Bulletin of the Society for Renaissance Studies* II (1984), pp. 7–18

—, 'The Guilds of Venice: State and Society in the Long Durée', *Studi veneziani*, n.s. XXXIV (1997), pp. 15–43

—, '"A Plot Discover'd?": Myth, Legend and the "Spanish Conspiracy against Venice in 1618"', in J. Martin and D. Romano, eds, *Venice Reconsidered: The History and Civilization of an Italian City State, 1297–1797* (Baltimore, MD, and London, 2000), pp. 185–216

—, 'Public and Private in Renaissance Venice', *Renaissance Studies* XII (1998), pp. 109–30

—, 'The *scuole piccole* of Venice: Formations and Transformations', in N. Terpstra, ed., *The Politics of Ritual Kinship: Confraternities and Social Order in Early Modern Italy* (Cambridge, 2000), pp. 172–89

—, 'Trade Guilds and Devotional Confraternities in the State and Society of Venice to 1620' (Ph.D dissertation, University of Cambridge, 1982)

—, *Tradesmen and Traders: The World of the Guilds in Venice and Europe, c.1250–c.1650* (London and Sydney, 1987)

—, 'Venice', in R. S. Porter and M. Teich, eds, *The Renaissance in National Context* (Cambridge, 1992), pp. 53–67

—, and P. Humfrey, 'The Venetian Trade Guilds as Patrons of Art in the Renaissance', *Burlington Magazine* CXXVIII (1986), pp. 317–30

Macchiarella, I., *Il falsobordone fra tradizione orale e tradizione scritta* (Lucca, 1995)

Madonna, M. L., 'La biblioteca', in B. Adorni, ed., *L'abbazia benedettina di San Giovanni Evangelista a Parma* (Milan, 1979), pp. 177–94

Mainstone, R. J., *Hagia Sophia: Architecture, Structure and Liturgy of Justinian's Great Church* (London, 1988)

Maldacca, G., *Storia di Sorrento*, 2 vols (Naples, 1841)

Mann, N., 'Petrarca e la cancelleria veneziana', in G. Arnaldi and M. Stocchi, eds, *Storia* della cultura veneta, 6 vols in 10 parts (Vicenza, 1976–87), II, pp. 517–35

Manno, A., ed., San Marco Evangelista: opere d'arte dalle chiese di Venezia (Venice, 1995)

Manoussakas, M., and C. Staikos, eds, L'attività editoriale dei Greci durante il Rinascimento italiano, 1469–1523 (Athens, OH, 1986)

Mantese, G., 'Nel quarto centenario della battaglia di Lepanto', Archivio veneto XCIV (1971), pp. 5–34

Marchesan, A., ed., Vita e prose scelte di Francesco Benaglio (Treviso, 1894)

Marciani, C., 'Editori tipografi librai veneti nel regno di Napoli nel Cinquecento', Studi veneziani X (1968), pp. 457–554

Marcon, S., 'I codici della liturgia di San Marco', in G. Cattin, ed., Musica e liturgia a San Marco: testi e melodie per la liturgia delle ore dal XII al XVII secolo. Dal graduale tropato del duecento ai graduali cinquecenteschi, 4 vols (Venice, 1990–92), I, pp. 191–267

—, I libri di San Marco: i manoscritti liturgici della basilica marciana (Venice, 1995) [exhibition catalogue]

Mariacher, G., Il palazzo ducale di Venezia (Florence, 1950)

Mariani Canova, G., and G. Cattin, 'Un prezioso antifonario veneziano del Duecento: miniature, liturgia e musica', Arte veneta, XXXV (1981), pp. 9–26

Martin, J., 'L'Inquizione romana e la criminalizzazione del dissenso religioso a Venezia all'inizio dell'età moderna', Quaderni storici LXVI (1987), pp. 777–802

—, 'Out of the Shadow: Heretical and Catholic Women in Renaissance Venice', Journal of Family History X (1985), pp. 21–33

—, 'Popular Culture and the Shaping of Popular Heresy in Renaissance Venice', in S. Haliczar, ed., Inquisition and Society in Early Modern Europe (London and Sydney, 1987), pp. 115–28

—, 'Salvation and Society in Sixteenth-Century Venice: Popular Evangelism in a Renaissance City', Journal of Modern History LX (1988), pp. 205–33

—, Venice's Hidden Enemies: Italian Heretics in a Renaissance City (Berkeley, CA, 1993)

Martin, J., and D. Romano, eds, Venice Reconsidered: The History and Civilization of an Italian City State, 1297–1797 (Baltimore, MD, and London, 2000)

Martin, R., Witchcraft and the Inquisition in Venice, 1550–1650 (Oxford, 1989)

Martin, T., Remodelling Antiquity: Alessandro Vittoria and the Portrait Bust in Renaissance Venice (Oxford, 1998)

Martineau, J., and C. Hope, eds, The Genius of Venice, 1500–1600 (London, 1984) [exhibition catalogue]

Marx, B., 'Il mito di Venezia nel primo Cinquecento', in A. Buck and B. Guthmuller, eds, La città italiana del Rinascimento fra utopia e realtà (Venice, 1984), pp. 137–63

—, Venezia – altera Roma? ipotesi sull'umanesimo veneziano (Venice, 1978)

Maschio, R., 'Le Scuole Grandi a Venezia', in G. Arnaldi and M. Stocchi, eds, Storia della cultura veneta, 6 vols in 10 parts (Vicenza, 1976–87), III/3, pp. 193–206

Mason, W., 'The Architecture of St. Mark's Cathedral and the Venetian Polychoral Style: A Clarification', in J. W. Pruett, ed., Studies in Musicology, Essays in the History, Style, and Bibliography of Music in Memory of Glen Haydon (Chapel Hill, 1969), pp. 163–78

Mason Rinaldi, S. M., 'Le immagini della peste nella cultura figurativa veneziana', in Venezia e la peste, 1348–1797 (Venice, 1980), pp. 209–86

—, 'Jacopo Palma il Giovane e la decorazione dell'Oratorio dei Crociferi', in S. Lunardon, ed., Hospitale S. Mariae Cruciferorum (Venice, 1985), pp. 19–84

—, Palma il Giovane, 1548–1628: disegni e dipinti (Milan, 1990) [exhibition catalogue]

—, Palma il Giovane: l'opera completa (Milan, 1984)

—, 'Le virtù della Repubblica e la gesta dei capitani: dipinti votivi, ritratti, pietà', in Venezia e la difesa del Levante da Lepanto a Candia, 1570–1670 (Venice, 1986), pp. 13–18

Mathews, T. F., The Byzantine Churches of Istanbul: A Photographic Survey (University Park, PA, and London, 1975)

—, The Early Churches of Constantinople: Architecture and Liturgy (University Park, PA, 1971)

Matozzi, I., 'Il politico e il pane a Venezia, 1570–1650', *Studi veneziani*, n.s. VII (1983), pp. 197–222

—, '"Mondo del libro" e decadenza a Venezia, 1570–1730', *Quaderni storici* LXXII (1989), pp. 743–86

Mavrodi, F., *Aspetti della società veneziana del '500: la confraternità di S. Nicolo dei Greci* (Ravenna, 1989)

Maylender, M., *Storie delle accademie d'Italia*, 5 vols (Bologna, 1926–30)

Mazzatinti, G., *Inventari dei manoscritti delle biblioteche d'Italia, LXVIII: Venezia, Civico Museo Correr, Manoscritti Morosini-Grimani* (Florence, 1939)

Mazzi, G., 'La cartografia per il mito: le immagini di Venezia nel Cinquecento', in *Architettura e utopia nella Venezia del Cinquecento* (Milan, 1980), pp. 50–57

Medin, A., *La storia della Repubblica di Venezia nella poesia* (Milan, 1904)

—, and L. Frati, *Lamenti storici dei secoli XIV, XV e XVI*, 4 vols (Bologna, 1887–94)

Meersseman, G. G., 'L'inizio della confraternita del Rosario e della sua iconografia in Italia: a proposito di un quadro veneziano del Dürer (1506)', *Atti e Memorie dell'Accademia Patavina di Scienze, Lettere ed Arti* LXXVI (1963–4), pp. 223–56

Meschinello, G., *La chiesa ducale di S. Marco, colle notizie del suo inalzamento spiegazione delli mosaici e delle iscrizioni*, 3 vols (Venice, 1753–74)

Michiel, G. R., *Le origini delle feste veneziane*, 6 vols (Milan, 1817)

Middeldorf, U., and O. Goetz, *Medals and Plaquettes from the Sigmund Morgenroth Collection* (Chicago, IL, 1944)

Miglio, M., et al., *Il sacco di Roma del 1527 e l'immaginario collettivo* (Rome, 1986)

Miscellanea in onore di Roberto Cessi, 3 vols (Rome, 1958)

Molà, L., *The Silk Industry of Renaissance Venice* (Baltimore, MD, and London, 2000)

Molho, A., ed., *City States in Classical Antiquity and Medieval Italy* (Stuttgart, 1991)

Molmenti, P. G., 'Il bucintoro', *Nuova archeologia* LXXXVI (1900), pp. 442–51

—, *Sebastiano Veniero dopo la battaglia di Lepanto* (Venice, 1915)

—, *Sebastiano Veniero e la battaglia di Lepanto* (Florence, 1899)

—, *La storia di Venezia nella vita privata dalle origini alla caduta della Repubblica*, 3 vols, 7th edn (Trieste, 1973)

—, *Studi e ricerche di storia e d'arte* (Turin and Rome, 1892)

—, 'Venezia nell'arte e nella letterature francese', *Archivio veneto* XXXVII (1889), pp. 5–33

Mometto, P., '"Vizi privati, pubbliche virtù": Aspetti e problemi della questione del lusso nella repubblica di Venezia (secolo XVI)' in L. Berlinguer and F. Colao, eds, *Crimine, giustizia e società veneta in eta moderna* (Milan, 1989)

Monga, L., ed. and trans., *The Journal of Aurelio Scetti, A Florentine Galley Slave at Lepanto (1565–1577)* (Tempe, Arizona, 2004)

Monticolo, G., 'L'apparitio ed i suoi manoscritti', *Nuovo archivio veneto* V (1895), pp. 111–77

Moore, J. H., 'Music for the Madonna Nicopeia and Santa Maria della Salute', *Journal of the American Musicological Society* XXXVII (1984), pp. 299–355

—, 'The *Vespero delli Cinque Laudate* and the Role of Salmi spezzati at St Mark's, *Journal of the American Musicological Society* XXXIV (1981), pp. 249–78

—, *Vespers at St Mark's: Music of Alessandro Grandi, Giovanni Rovetta and Francesco Cavalli*, 2 vols (Ann Arbor, MI, 1981)

Morando, E., *Libro d'arme di Venezia* (Verona, 1979)

Morell, M., 'New Evidence for the Biographies of Andrea and Giovanni Gabrieli', *Early Music History* III (1983), pp. 101–22

Moretti, L., 'Architectural Spaces for Music: Jacopo Sansovino and Adrian Willaert at St Mark's, *Early Music History* XXIII (2004), pp. 153–84

Moro, G., 'Insegne librarie e marche tipografiche in un registro veneziano del '500', *La bibliofilia* XCI (1989), pp. 51–80

Moro, L., and G. Cattin, 'Il codice 359 del seminario di Padova (anno 1505): canti liturgici a due voci e laude dei canonici di San Giorgio in Alga', in G. Cattin and A. Lovato, eds, *Contributi per la storia della musica sacra a Padova* (Padua, 1993), pp. 141–89

Morosini, A., *Historiae venetae* in *Istorici delle cose veneziane* VI (Venice, 1719)

Morpurgo, E., *Marco Foscarini e Venezia nel secolo XVIII* (Florence, 1880)

Morragh, A., et al., eds, *Renaissance Studies in Honor of Craig Hugh Smyth*, 2 vols (Florence, 1985)

Morresi, M., *Jacopo Sansovino* (Milan, 2000)

—, *Piazza San Marco: istituzioni, poteri e architettura a Venezia nel primo Cinquecento* (Milan, 1999)

Mortimer, R., *Harvard College Library, Department of Printing and Graphic Arts, Catalogue of Books and Manuscripts. Part II: Italian 16th Century Books*, 2 vols (Cambridge, MA, 1974)

Moschini, G. A., *Guida per la città di Venezia all'amico delle belle arti*, 2 vols (Venice, 1815)

Mueller, R. C., 'The Procuratori di San Marco and the Venetian Credit Market' (Ph.D dissertation, Johns Hopkins University, 1969)

—, 'The Procurators of San Marco in the Thirteenth and Fourteenth Centuries: A Study of the Office as a Financial Trust', *Studi veneziani* XIII (1971), pp. 105–220

Muir, E., *Civic Ritual in Renaissance Venice* (Princeton, NJ, 1981)

—, 'The Doge as *Primus Inter Pares*: Interregnum Rites in Early Sixteenth-Century Venice', in S. Bertelli and G. Ramakus, eds, *Essays Presented to Myron P. Gilmore*, 2 vols (Florence, 1978), I, pp. 145–60

—, 'Images of Power: Art and Pageantry in Renaissance Venice', *American Historical Review* LXXXIV (1979), pp. 16–52

—, *Mad Blood Stirring: Vendetta and Factions in Friuli during the Renaissance* (Baltimore, MD, and London, 1993)

—, 'Manifestazioni e ceremonie nella Venezia di Andrea Gritti', in M. Tafuri, ed., '*Renovatio urbis': Venetia nell'età di Andrea Gritti, 1523–1538* (Rome, 1984), pp. 59–77

—, 'The Virgin on the Street Corner: The Place of the Sacred in Italian Cities', in S. Ozment, ed., *Religion and Culture in the Renaissance and Reformation* (Kirksville, MO, 1989), pp. 25–40

—, and R. Weissman, 'Social and Symbolic Places in Renaissance Venice and Florence', in J. A. Agnew and J. S. Duncan, eds, *The Power of Place: Bringing Together Geographical and Sociological Imaginations* (Boston, MA, 1989), pp. 81–103

Mulryne, R., and E. Goldring, eds, *Court Festivals of the European Renaissance: Art, Politics and Performance* (Aldershot, 2002)

—, H. Watanabe-O'Kelly and M. Shewring, eds, *Europa Triumphans: Court and Civic Festivals in Early Modern Europe*, 2 vols (Aldershot, 2004)

Munro, J. H., 'The Medieval Scarlet and the Economics of Sartorial Splendour', in N. B. Harte and K. G. Ponting, eds, *Cloth and Clothing in Medieval Europe: Essays in Memory of Professor E. M. Caru-Wilson* (London, 1983), pp. 13–70

Muraro, M. T., 'Le lieu des spectacles (publics ou prives) à Venise au XVe et au XVIe siècles', in J. Jacquot, ed., *Le lieu théâtral à la Renaissance* (Paris, 1964), pp. 85–93

Muraro, M., 'Il pilastro del miracolo e il secondo programma dei mosaici marciani', *Arte veneta* XXXIX (1975), pp. 60–65

—, 'La scala senza giganti', in M. Meiss, ed., *De artibus opuscula XL: Essays in Honor of Erwin Panofsky* (New York, 1961), pp. 350–70

Murray, P., 'Palladio's Churches', in *Arte in Europa: scritti di storia dell'arte in onore di Edoardo Arslan*, 2 vols (Milan, 1966), I, pp. 597–608

Musatti, E., *Storia della promissione ducale* (Padua, 1888)

Musolino, G., 'Feste religiose popolari', in S. Tramontin, ed., *Il culto dei santi a Venezia* (Venice, 1965), pp. 209–37

Nappo, T., and P. Noto, *Indice biografico italiano*, 4 vols (Munich, London and New York, 1993)

Needham, P., 'Venetian Printers and Publishers in the Fifteenth Century', *La bibliofilia* C (1998), pp. 157–200

Newett, M., ed., *Canon Pietro Casola's Pilgrimage to Jerusalem in the Year 1494* (Manchester, 1907)

—, 'The Sumptuary Laws of Venice in the Fourteenth and Fifteenth Centuries', in F. Tout and J. Tait, eds, *Historical Essays by Members of the Owens College, Manchester* (London, 1902), pp. 245–78

Newton, S. M., *The Dress of the Venetians, 1495–1525* (Aldershot, 1988)

Niccoli, O., 'Un aspetto della propaganda religiosa nell'Italia del Cinquecento: opuscioli e fogli volanti', *Libri, idee e sentimenti religiosi nel Cinquecento italiano: [Ferrara], 3–5 aprile 1986* (Modena, 1987), pp. 29–37

—, 'Profezie in piazza: note sul profetismo popolare nell'Italia del primo Cinquecento', *Quaderni storici* XLI (1979), pp. 500–39

—, *Prophecy and People in Renaissance Italy* (Princeton, NJ, 1990)

Nicol, D. M., *Byzantium and Venice: A Study in Diplomatic Relations* (Cambridge, 1988)

Nicoletti, G., 'Dei banchetti pubblici al tempo della Repubblica Veneta', *Archivio veneto* XXXIII (1887), pp. 165–9

Niero, A., 'Ancora sull'origine del rosario a Venezia e sulla sua iconografia', *Rivista di storia della chiesa in Italia* XXVIII (1974), pp. 465–78

—, 'Culto dei santi militari nel Veneto', in *Armi e cultura nel Bresciano, 1420–1870* (Brescia, 1981), pp. 225–72

—, 'La mariegola della più antica scuola del rosario di Venezia', *Rivista di storia della chiesa in Italia* XV (1961), pp. 324–36

—, 'I mosaici della basilica di S. Marco: celebrazione della fede cristiana e della storia politica di Venezia', in F. Tonon, ed., *La chiesa di Venezia nei secoli XI–XIII* (Venice, 1988), pp. 179–206

—, *I patriarchi di Venezia da Lorenzo Giustinian ai nostri giorni* (Venice, 1961)

—, 'La pietà popolare: feste civiche religiose', in S. Tramontin, ed., *Patriarcato di Venezia* (Venice and Padua, 1991), pp. 279–302, 323–31

—, 'Pietà popolare e interessi politici nel culto di S. Lorenzo Giustiniani', *Archivio veneto* CXVII (1981), pp. 197–224

—, 'Questioni ageografiche su San Marco', *Studi veneziani* XII (1970), pp. 18–27

—, ed., *San Marco: aspetti storici e agiografici* (Venice, 1996)

—, 'I santi patroni', in S. Tramontin, ed., *Il culto dei santi a Venezia* (Venice, 1965), pp. 75–98

—, 'Simbologia dotta e popolare nelle sculture esterne', in B. Bertoli, ed., *La basilica di San Marco: arte e simbologia* (Venice, 1993), pp. 125–48

—, et al., *Culto dei santi nella terraferma veneziana* (Venice, 1967)

Nori, G., ed., *Antonio da Crema: itinerario al Santo Sepolcro 1486* (Pisa, 1996)

Novati, F., 'Contributo alla storia della lirica musicale italiana popolare e popolareggiante nei secoli XV, XVI, XVII', in *Scritti varii di erudizione e di critica in onore di R. Renier* (Turin, 1912), pp. 900–80

—, *La storia e la stampa nella produzione popolare italiana* (Bergamo, 1907)

Nunziature di Venezia; see Gaeta et al.

Nuovo, A., and C. Coppens, *I Giolito e la stampa nell' Italia del XVI secolo* (Geneva, 2005)

Nutter, D., 'The Italian Polyphonic Dialogue of the Sixteenth Century', 2 vols (Ph.D dissertation, University of Nottingham, 1978)

—, ed., *Orazio Vecchi: Battaglia d'Amor e Dispetto and Mascherata detta Malinconia et Allegrezza* (Madison, WI, 1987)

—, 'A Tragedy for Henry III of France, Venice, 1574', in A. Morragh et al., eds, *Renaissance Studies in Honor of Craig Hugh Smyth*, 2 vols (Florence, 1985), I, pp. 591–611

Officium hebdomadae sanctae secundum consuetudinem Ducalis Ecclesiae Sancti Marci Venetiarium (Venice, 1722)

Officium in nocte Navitatis Domini ad matutinum, secundum conduetudinem Ducalis Ecclesiae Sancti Marci Venetiarum (Venice, 1754)

Olivieri, A., 'L'intellettuale e le accademie fra '500 e '600: Verona e Venezia', *Archivio veneto* CXIX (1988), pp. 31–56

—, 'Il principe e lo spazio urbano a Venezia: il dogado di Andrea Gritti ed Erasmo', *Studi veneziani*, n.s. XXXII (1996), pp. 15–27

—, 'Il significato escatologico di Lepanto nella storia religiosa del Mediterraneo del Cinquecento', in G. Benzoni, ed., *Il mediterraneo nella seconda metà del '500 nella luce di Lepanto* (Florence, 1974), pp. 257–77

Omodeo, A., *Mostra di stampe popolari venete del '500* (Florence, 1965) [exhibition catalogue]

Ongania, F., ed., *La basilica di S. Marco in Venezia illustrate nella storia e nell'arte da scrittori veneziani* (Venice, 1878–93)

—, ed., *Documenti per la storia dell'augusta ducale Basilica di San Marco in Venezia: dal nono secolo sino alla fine del decimo ottavo dall'Archivio di Stato e dall Biblioteca marciana in Venezia* ([Venice], 1886)

Ongaro, G., 'All Work and No Play? The Organisation of Work among Musicians in Late Renaissance Venice', *Journal of Medieval and Renaissance Studies* XXV (1995), pp. 55–72

—, 'Gli inizi della musica strumentale a San Marco', in F. Passadore and F. Rossi, eds, *Giovanni Legrenzi e la cappella ducale di San Marco* (Florence, 1994), pp. 215–26

—, 'The Library of a Sixteenth Century Music Teacher', *Journal of Music* XII (1994), pp. 357–75

—, 'Sixteenth-Century Patronage at St Mark's, Venice', *Early Music History* VIII (1988), pp. 81–115

—, 'The Tieffenbruckers and the Business of Lute-Making in Sixteenth-Century Venice', *Galpin Society Journal* XLI (1991), pp. 46–54

—, 'Willaert, Gritti e Luppato: miti e realtà', *Studi musicali* XVII (1988), pp. 55–70

Onians, J., *Bearers of Meaning: The Classical Orders in Antiquity, the Middle Ages and the Renaissance* (Princeton, NJ, 1988)

—, ed., *Essays on Art and Culture in Honour of E. H. Gombrich at 85* (London, 1994)

Ostrow, S. F., *Art and Spirituality in Counter-Reformation Rome: The Sistine and Pauline Chapels in S. Maria Maggiore* (Cambridge, 1996)

Ozment, S., ed., *Religion and Culture in the Renaissance and Reformation* (Kirksville, MO, 1989)

Padoan, G., *La commedia rinascimentale veneta, 1433–1565* (Vicenza, 1973)

Padoan, M., 'I balli per Enrico III re di Francia durante il suo viaggio in Italia nel 1574', *Quaderni di Palazzo Te* I (1994), pp. 71–7

Padoan Urban, L., 'Apparati scenografici nelle feste veneziane cinquecentesche', *Arte veneta* XXIII (1969), pp. 145–55

—, 'La festa della Sensa nelle arti e nell'iconografia', *Studi veneziani* X (1968), pp. 291–353

—, 'Le feste sull'acqua a Venezia nel secolo XVI e il potere politico', in M. de Panizza Lorch, ed., *Il teatro italiano del Rinascimento* (Milan, 1980), pp. 483–505

—, 'Gli spettacoli urbani e l'utopia', in *Architettura e utopia nella Venezia del Cinquecento* (Milan, 1980), pp. 144–66

—, 'Teatri e "teatri del mondo" nella Venezia del Cinquecento', *Arte veneta* XX (1966), pp. 137–46

Padoan Urban; see also Urban

Pagan, P., 'Sulla Accademia "Venetiana" o della Fama', *Atti dell'Istituto Veneto di Scienze, Lettere ed Arti* CXXXII (1973–4), pp. 359–92

Pallucchini, A., 'Echi della battaglia di Lepanto nella pittura veneziana del '500', in G. Benzoni, ed., *Il mediterraneo nella seconda metà del '500 nella luce di Lepanto* (Florence, 1974), pp. 279–87

Pallucchini, R., and P. Rossi, *Tintoretto: le opere sacre e profane*, 2 vols (Milan, 1982)

Palmer, R., 'L'azione della Repubblica di Venezia nel controllo della peste: lo sviluppo della politica governativa', in *Venezia e la peste, 1348–1797* (Venice, 1980), pp. 103–10

—, 'The Control of Plague in Venice and Northern Italy' (Ph.D dissertation, University of Kent at Canterbury, 1978)

Palombo-Fossati, I., 'La casa veneziana di Gioseffo Zarlino nel testamento e nell'inventario dei beni del grande teorico musicale', *Nuova rivista musicale italiana* IV (1986), pp. 633–49

—, 'Il collezionista Sebastiano Erizzo e l'inventario dei suoi beni', *Ateneo veneto* CLXXIV (1984), pp. 201–18

—, 'L'interno della casa dell'artigiano e dell'artista nella Venezia del Cinquecento', *Studi veneziani* n.s. VIII (1984), pp. 109–53

—, 'Livres et lecteurs a Venise du XVIe siècle', *Revue francaise d'histoire du livre* LIV (1985), pp. 481–513

Panizza, L., ed., *Women in Italian Renaissance Culture and Society* (Oxford, 2000)

Pantani, I, ed., *Libri di poesia* (Milan, 1996)

Papadopoli, N., *Le monete di Venezia*, 4 vols (Venice, 1893–1919)

Park, K., 'Country Medicine in the City Marketplace: Snakehandlers as Itinerant Healers', *Renaissance Studies* XV (2001), pp. 104–20

Parshall, P. W., 'The Print Collection of Ferdinand, Archduke of Tyrol', *Jahrbuch der Kunsthistorischen Sammlungen in Wien* LXXVIII (1982), pp. 139–84

Parsons, G., *Siena, Civil Religion and the Sienese* (Aldershot, 2004)

Partridge, L., and R. Starn, 'Triumphalism in the Sala Regia', in B. Wisch and S. Scott Munshower, eds, *'All the World's a Stage . . .': Art and Pageantry in the Renaissance and Baroque* (University Park, PA, 1990), pp. 23–82

Pasero, C., 'Giacomo Franco, editore, incisore e calcografo nei secoli XVI e XVII', *La bibliofilia* XXXVII (1935), pp. 332–56

Pasini, A., 'Rito antico e ceremoniale della basilica', in *La basilica di San Marco* (Venice, 1888), pp. 65–71

Passadore, F., and F. Rossi, eds, *La cappella musicale di San Marco nell'età moderna* (Venice, 1998)

—, eds, *Giovanni Legrenzi e la cappella ducale di San Marco* (Florence, 1994)

—, eds, *Musica, scienza e idée nella serenissima durante il seicento* (Venice, 1996)

Pastor, L. von, *The History of the Popes from the Close of the Middle Ages*, ed. F. I. Antrobus et al., 40 vols (London and St Louis, MO, 1898–1953)

Pastorello, E., *Tipografi, editori, librai a Venezia nel secolo XVI* (Florence, 1924)

Paul, B., 'Identità e alterità nella pittura veneziana al tempo della battaglia di Lepanto', *Venezia Cinquecento: studi di storia dell'arte e della cultura* XV (2005), pp. 155–87

Pavanello, G., 'San Marco nella leggenda e nella storia', *Rivista della città di Venezia* VI (1928), pp. 293–324

Pavanini, P., 'Abitazioni popolari e borghesi nella Venezia Cinquecentesca', *Studi veneziani*, n.s. V (1981), pp. 63–126

Payne, A., A. Kuttner and R. Smick, eds, *Antiquity and its Interpreters* (Cambridge, 2000)

Pecorari, P., and G. Silvano, eds, *Continuità e discontinuità nella storia politica, economica e religiosa: studi in onore di Aldo Stella* (Vicenza, 1993)

Pedani, M. P., 'Monasteri di agostiniane a Venezia', *Archivio veneto* CXXV (1985), pp. 35–78

Perry, M., 'Cardinal Grimani's Legacy of Ancient Art to Venice', *Journal of the Warburg and Courtauld Institutes* XLI (1978), pp. 215–44

—, 'Saint Mark's Trophies: Legend, Superstition and Archaeology in Renaissance Venice', *Journal of the Warburg and Courtauld Institutes* XL (1977), pp. 27–49

—, 'The *Statuario Pubblico* of the Venetian Republic', *Saggi e memorie di storia dell'arte* VIII (1972), pp. 75–150, 221–53

Pertusi, A., 'Bisanzio e le insegne regali dei dogi di Venezia', *Rivista di studi bizantini e neoellenici* II–III (XII–XIII) (1965–6), pp. 277–84

—, 'Gli inizi della storiografia umanistica nel Quattrocento', in Pertusi, ed., *La storiografia veneziana*, pp. 269–332

—, 'Quaedam regalia insignia', *Studi veneziani* VII (1965), pp. 3–123

—, ed., *La storiografia veneziana fino al secolo XVI: aspetti e problemi* (Florence, 1970)

—, 'Venezia e Bisanzio, 1000–1204', *Dumbarton Oaks Papers* XXXIII (1979), pp. 1–22

Pesenti, G., 'Libri censurati a Venezia nei secoli XVI–XVII', *La bibliofilia* LVIII (1956), pp. 15–30

Pesenti, T., 'Stampatori e letterati nell'industria editoriale a Venezia e in terraferma', in G. Arnaldi and M. Stocchi, eds, *Storia della cultura veneta*, 6 vols in 10 parts (Vicenza, 1976–87), IV/1, pp. 93–129

Petrioli Tofani, A. M., 'Stampe popolari venete del Cinquecento agli Uffizi', *Antichità viva* IV (1965), pp. 62–7

Petrobelli, P., 'La musica nelle cattedrale e nelle città ed i suoi rapporti con la cultura letteraria', in G. Arnaldi and M. Stocchi, eds, *Storia della cultura veneta*, 6 vols in 10 parts (Vicenza, 1976–87), II, pp. 440–68

—, *Le polifonie primitive di Cividale* (Udine, 1980)

Petrucci, A., ed., *Libri, editori e pubblico nell'Europa moderna: guida storica e critica* (Bari, 1989)

Peyer, H. C., *Città e santi patroni nell'Italia medievale*, ed. A. Benvenuti (Florence, 1998) [2nd edn, with a new introduction of *Stadt und Stadtpatron im Mittelalterlichen Italien* (Zurich, 1955)]

Piazza S. Marco: l'architettura, la storia, le funzioni (Padua, 1970)

Piegadi, A., *Archivio capitolare de' monsignori canonici della patriarcale metropolitana basilica di S. Marco in Venezia* (Venice, 1866)

Pierozzi, L., 'La vittoria di Lepanto nell'escatologia e nella profezia', *Rinascimento* XXXIV (1994), pp. 317–63

Pietrangeli, C., ed., *La basilica romana di Santa Maria Maggiore* (Florence, 1987)

Pignatti, T., ed., *Le scuole di Venezia* (Milan, 1981)

—, *Veronese*, 2 vols (Milan, 1976)

—, and F. Pedrocco, *Veronese*, 2 vols (Milan, 1995)

Pilo, G. M., 'Il procuratore di San Marco Jacopo Soranzo jr e il ritratto recuperato di Jacopo Tintoretto già in Procuratia de Supra', in R. Polacco, ed., *Storia dell'arte marciana: i mosaici* (Venice, 1997), pp. 209–21

Pilot, A., 'Del protestantesimo a Venezia e delle poesie religiose di Celio Magno (1536–1602)', *L'Ateneo veneto* XXXII (1909), pp. 199–233

—, 'Di alcuni versi inediti sulla peste del 1575', *L'Ateneo veneto* XXVI (1903), pp. 350–58

Pincus, D., 'Andrea Dandolo, 1343–1354, and Visible History: The San Marco Project', in C. M. Rosenberg, ed., *Art and Politics in Late Medieval and Early Renaissance Italy, 1250–1550* (London, 1990), pp. 191–206

—, *The Arco Foscari: The Building of a Triumphal Gateway in Fifteenth-Century Venice* (New York, 1976)

—, 'Christian Relics and the Body Politic: A Thirteenth-Century Relief Plaque in the Church of San Marco', in D. Rosand, ed., *Interpretazioni veneziane: studi di storia dell'arte in onore di Michelangelo Muraro* (Venice, 1984), pp. 39–57

—, 'Hard Times and Ducal Radiance: Andrea Dandolo and the Construction of the Ruler in Fourteenth-Century Venice', in J. Martin and D. Romano, eds, *Venice Reconsidered: The History and Civilization of an Italian City State, 1297–1797* (Baltimore, MD, and London, 2000), pp. 89–136

—, 'The Tomb of Doge Nicolò Tron and Venetian Renaissance Ruler Imagery', in L. F. Sandler and M. Barasch, eds, *Art the Ape of Nature: Essays in Honor of H. W. Janson* (New York, 1981), pp. 127–50

—, *The Tombs of the Doges of Venice* (Cambridge, 2000)

—, 'Venice and the Two Romes: Byzantium and Rome as a Double Heritage in Venetian Cultural Politics', *Artibus et Historiae* XXVI (1992), pp. 101–14

Pirrotta, N., 'Music and Cultural Tendencies in Fifteenth-Century Italy', *Journal of the American Musicological Society* XIX (1966), pp. 127–61

—, and E. Povoledo, *Music and Theatre from Poliziano to Monteverdi*, trans. K. Eales (Cambridge, 1982)

Piva, V., *Il Patriarcato di Venezia e le sue origini*, 2 vols (Venice, 1938–60)

Plamenac, D., 'Another Paduan Fragment of Trecento Music', *Journal of the American Musicological Society* VIII (1955), pp. 165–81

Plumb, J. H., ed., *Renaissance Profiles* (New York, 1965)

Polacco, R., 'San Marco e le sue sculture nel Duecento', in D. Rosand, ed., *Interpretazioni veneziane: studi di storia dell'arte in onore di Michelangelo Muraro* (Venice, 1984), pp. 59–75

—, 'Le colonne del ciborio di San Marco', *Venezia arti* I (1987), pp. 32–8

—, 'I plutei della cattedrale di Torcello e l'iconostasi contariniana della Basilica di San Marco', *Arte veneta* XXIX (1975), pp. 38–42

—, *San Marco: La basilica d'oro* (Milan, 1991)

—, ed., *Storia dell'arte marciana: l'architettura* (Venice, 1997)

—, ed., *Storia dell'arte marciana: sculture, tesoro, arazzi. Atti del convegno internazionale di studi: Venezia, 11–14 ottobre 1994* (Venice, 1997)

Politis, L., 'Venezia come centro della stampa e della diffusione della prima letteratura neoellenica', in H. G. Beck, M. Manoussacas and A. Pertusi, eds, *Venezia centro di mediazione tra oriente e occidente (secoli XV–XVI): aspetti e problemi*, 2 vols (Florence, 1977), I, pp. 443–82

Pollard, G., *Medaglie italiane del Rinascimento nel Museo Nazionale del Bargello*, 3 vols (Florence, 1984–5)

—, and A. Ehrman, *The Distribution of Books by Catalogue from the Invention of Printing to AD 1800 Based on Material in the Broxbourne Library* (Cambridge, 1965)

Pomian, K., *Collectors and Curiosities: Paris and Venice, 1500–1800* (Cambridge, 1990)

Pope-Hennessy, J., *Italian High Renaissance and Baroque Sculpture*, 4th edn (London, 1996)

Porter, R. S., and M. Teich, eds, *The Renaissance in National Context* (Cambridge, 1992)

Posocco, F., *Scuola grande di San Rocco: la vicenda urbanistica e lo spazio scenico* (Cittadella, 1997)

Poullet, E., and C. Piot, eds, *Correspondance du Cardinal Granvelle, 1566–1586*, 12 vols (Brussels, 1877–96)

Povolo, C., 'The Creation of Venetian Historiography', in J. Martin and D. Romano, eds, *Venice Reconsidered: The History and Civilization of an Italian City State, 1297–1797* (Baltimore, MD, and London, 2000), pp. 491–519

Pozza, N., 'L'editoria veneziana da Giovanni da Spira ad Aldo Manuzio: i centri editoriali di terraferma', in G. Arnaldi and M. Stocchi, eds, *Storia della cultura veneta*, 6 vols in 10 parts (Vicenza, 1976–87), III/2, pp. 215–44

Preto, P., *Epidemia, paura e politica nell'Italia moderna* (Bari, 1987)

—, 'Le grandi pesti dell'età moderna, 1575–77 e 1630–31', in *Venezia e la peste, 1348–1797* (Venice, 1980), pp. 123–26

—, *Peste e società a Venezia, 1576*, 2nd edn (Vicenza, 1984)

—, 'La società veneta e le grandi epidemie di peste', in G. Arnaldi and M. Stocchi, eds, *Storia della cultura veneta*, 6 vols in 10 parts (Vicenza, 1976–87), IV/2, pp. 377–406

—, *Venezia e i Turchi* (Florence, 1975)

Primhak, V., 'Benedictine Communities in Venetian Society: The Convent of S. Zaccaria', in L. Panizza, ed., *Women in Italian Renaissance Culture and Society* (Oxford, 2000), pp. 92–104

Princivalli, D., 'Francesco Santacroce', *Musica e storia* IX (2001), pp. 307–74

Priuli; see Cessi

Le procuratie vecchie in Piazza San Marco (Rome, 1994)

Prodi, P., 'The Structure and Organisation of the Church in Renaissance Venice: Suggestions for Research', in J. Hale, ed., *Renaissance Venice* (London, 1973), pp. 379–408

Pryor, J. H., *Geography, Technology and War: Studies in the Maritime History of the Mediterranean, 649–1571* (Cambridge, 1988)

Pullan, B., ed., *Crisis and Change in the Venetian Economy in the 16th and 17th Centuries* (London, 1968)

—, *The Jews of Europe and the Inquisition of Venice, 1550–1670* (Oxford, 1983)

—, 'Natura e carattere delle Scuole', in T. Pignatti, ed., *Le scuole di Venezia* (Milan, 1981), pp. 9–26

—, 'The Occupations and Investments of the Venetian Nobility in the Middle and Late Sixteenth Century', in J. Hale, ed., *Renaissance Venice* (London, 1973), pp. 379–408

—, 'Poverty, Charity and the Reason of State: Some Venetian Examples', *Bolletino dell'Istituto di Storia della Società e dello Stato Veneziano* II (1960), pp. 17–60

—, *Rich and Poor in Renaissance Venice: The Social Institutions of a Catholic State to 1620* (Oxford, 1971)

—, 'Le scuole grandi e la loro opera nel quadro della Controriforma', *Studi veneziani* XIV (1972), pp. 83–109

—, 'The Scuole Grandi of Venice: Some Further Thoughts', in T. Verdon and J. Henderson, eds, *Christianity and the Renaissance: Image and Religious Imagination in the Quattrocento* (Syracuse, NY, 1990), pp. 272–301

—, 'Service to the Venetian State: Aspects of Myth and Reality in the Early Seventeenth Century', *Studi secenteschi* V (1964), pp. 95–148

—, '"Three Orders of Inhabitants": Social Hierarchies in the Republic of Venice', in J. Denton, ed., *Orders and Hierarchies in Late Medieval and Renaissance Europe* (Basingstoke, 1999), pp. 147–68

—, 'Wage-earners and the Venetian Economy', *Economic History Review* XVI (1964), pp. 407–26

Puppi, L., *Andrea Palladio*, 2 vols (Milan, 1973)

—, 'Iconografia di Andrea Gritti', in M. Tafuri, ed., *'Renovatio urbis': Venetia nell'età di Andrea Gritti, 1523–1538* (Rome, 1984), pp. 216–35

—, ed., *Giambattista Tiepolo*, 2 vols (Padua, 1998)

Puppi, L., and Puppi Olivato, L., "Scamozziana: progetti per la "via romana" di Monselice e alucune altre novità grafiche con qualche quesito', *Antichità viva* XIII (1974), pp. 54–80

Quadris, J. de., *Opera*, ed. G. Cattin (Bologna, 1972)

Quaranta, E., *Oltre San Marco: organizzazione e prassi della musica nelle chiese a Venezia nel Rinascimento* (Florence, 1998)

Quarti, G. A., *La battaglia di Lepanto nei canti popolari dell'epoca* (Milan, 1930)

Queller, D. E., *The Fourth Crusade* (Philadelphia, PA, 1977)

—, *The Venetian Patriarcate: Reality versus Myth* (Chicago, 1986)

Quondam, A., '"Mercanzia d'onore/mercanzia d'utile"', in A. Petrucci, ed., *Libri, editori e pubblico nell'Europa moderna: guida storica e critica* (Bari, 1989), pp. 51–104

Radke, G. M., 'Nuns and their Art: The Case of San Zaccaria in Venice', *Renaissance Quarterly* XLVI (1993), pp. 430–59

Ranke, L. von, *The History of the Popes during the Last Four Centuries*, trans. E. Forster, revised G. R. Dennis, 3 vols (London, 1908)

Rankin, S., 'From Liturgical Ceremony to Public Ritual: "Quem Queritis" and St Mark's Venice', in G. Cattin, ed., *Da Bisanzio a San Marco: musica e liturgia* (Venice, 1997), pp. 137–91

Rapp, R. T., *Industry and Economic Decline in Seventeenth-Century Venice* (Cambridge, MA, 1976)

Rava, C. E., *Supplement à Max Sander: Le livre à figures italien de la Renaissance* (Milan, 1969)

Ravid, B., 'Christian Travelers in the Ghetto of Venice: Some Preliminary Observations', in S. Nash, ed., *Between History and Literature: Studies in Honor of Isaac Barzilay* (B'nei B'rak, 1997), pp. 111–50

—, 'Curfew Time in the Ghetto of Venice', in E. E. Kittell and T. F. Madden, eds, *Medieval and Renaissance Venice* (Urbana and Chicago, IL, 1999), pp. 237–75

—, 'The Venetian Government and the Jews', in R. C. Davis and B. Ravid, eds, *The Jews of Early Modern Venice* (Baltimore, MD, and London, 2001), pp. 3–30

Rearick, W. R., *The Art of Paolo Veronese, 1528–1588* (Cambridge, 1988)

—, 'Circle of Palma il Giovane, Portrait of a Venetian Procurator', in G. Rosenthal, ed., *Italian Paintings XIV–XVIII Centuries from the Collection of the Baltimore Museum of Art* (Baltimore, MD, 1981), pp. 131–46

Reed Welsh, S., and R. Wallace, *Italian Etchers of the Renaissance and Baroque* (Boston, MA, 1989)

Relazioni tra Padova e la Polonia: studi in onore dell'Università di Cracovia nel VI centenario della sua fondazione (Padua, 1964)

Renouard, A. A., *Annales de l'imprimerie des Alde; ou, histoire des trois Manuce et de leurs editions*, 3rd edn (Paris, 1834)

Rhodes, D. E., 'La battaglia di Lepanto e la stampa popolare a Venezia: studio bibliografico', in A Scarsella, ed., *Metodologia bibliografica e storia del libro*, Miscellanea marciana X–XI (1995–6), pp. 9–63

—, *Silent Printers: Anonymous Printing at Venice in the Sixteenth Century* (London, 1995)

Richardson, B., 'The Debates on Printing in Renaissance Italy', *La bibliofilia* C (1998), pp. 135–55

—, *Print Culture in Renaissance Italy: The Editor and the Vernacular Text, 1470–1600* (Cambridge, 1994)

—, *Printing, Writers and Readers in Renaissance Italy* (Cambridge, 1999)

Ringbom, S., '*Maria in Sole* and the Virgin of the Rosary', *Journal of the Warburg and Courtauld Institutes* XXV (1962), pp. 326–30

Rivoli, Duc de, *Les missels imprimes à Venise de 1481 à 1600* (Paris, 1896)

Rizzi, A., 'La Madonna Nicopeia', *Quaderni della Soprintendenza ai beni culturali e storici di Venezia* VIII (1979), pp. 13–19

—, 'Il San Marco a San Marco: l'emblema lapideo della Repubblica Veneta nel suo cuore politico', *Archivio Veneto* CLXXVII (1990), pp. 7–46

Rizzoli, L., 'La figurazione di Santa Giustina su monete di Venezia', *Atti dell'Istituto Veneto di Scienze, Lettere ed Arti* XCIX (1939–40), pp. 249–72

Robey, D., and J. Law, 'The Venetian Myth and the *De Republica Veneta* of Pier Paolo Vergerio', *Rinascimento* XV (1975), pp. 3–59

Roche, J., 'Liturgical Aspects of the Motets of Andrea Gabrieli published in 1565 and 1576', in F. Degrada, ed., *Andrea Gabrieli e il suo tempo. Atti del convegno internzionale: Venezia, 16–18 settembre 1985* (Florence, 1987), pp. 215–29

Rodini, E., 'Describing Narrative in Gentile Bellini's *Procession in Piazza San Marco*', *Art History* XXI (1988), pp. 26–44

Romanin, S., *Storia documentata di Venezia*, 10 vols, 2nd edn (Venice, 1853–61)

Romano, A., *Antonii Romani opera*, ed. F. A. Gallo (Bologna, 1965)

Romano, D., 'Aspects of Patronage in Fifteenth- and Sixteenth-Century Venice', *Renaissance Quarterly* XLVI (1993), pp. 712–33

—, 'Charity and Community in Early Renaissance Venice', *Journal of Urban History* XI (1984), pp. 63–81

—, 'Gender and the Urban Geography of Renaissance Venice', *Journal of Social History* XXIII (1989), pp. 339–53

—, 'The Gondola as a Marker of Station in Venetian Society', *Renaissance Studies* VIII (1994), pp. 359–74

—, *Housecraft and Statecraft: Domestic Service in Renaissance Venice* (Baltimore, MD, and London, 1996)

—, *Patricians and Popolani: The Social Foundations of the Venetian Renaissance State* (Baltimore, MD, and London, 1987)

Rosand, D., ed., *Interpretazioni veneziane: studi di storia dell'arte in onore di Michelangelo Muraro* (Venice, 1984)

—, *Myths of Venice: The Figuration of a State* (Chapel Hill, NC, and London, 2001)

—, *Painting in Cinquecento Venice: Titian, Veronese, Tintoretto* (Cambridge, 1997)

—, '*Venetia figurata*: The Iconography of a Myth', in Rosand, ed., *Interpretazioni veneziane*, pp. 177–96

—, 'Venezia e gli dei', in M. Tafuri, ed., '*Renovatio urbis': Venetia nell'età di Andrea Gritti, 1523–1538* (Rome, 1984), pp. 201–15

—, and M. Muraro, *Titian and the Venetian Woodcut* (Washington, DC, 1976)

Rosand, E., 'Music in the Myth of Venice', *Renaissance Quarterly* XXX (1977), pp. 511–37

Rose, C. J., 'The Evolution of the Image of Venice, 1500–1630' (Ph.D dissertation, Columbia University, 1971)

Rose, P. L., 'The Accademia Venetiana: Science and Culture in Renaissance Venice', *Studi veneziani* XI (1969), pp. 191–242

—, *The Italian Renaissance of Mathematics: Studies on Humanists and Mathematicians from Petrarch to Galileo* (Geneva, 1975)

Rosenberg, C. M., ed., *Art and Politics in Late Medieval and Early Renaissance Italy, 1250–1550* (London, 1990)

Rosenthal, G., ed., *Italian Paintings XIV–XVIII Centuries from the Collection of the Baltimore Museum of Art* (Baltimore, MD, 1981)

Rossi, F., *Accademia Carrara: sculture, bronzi, porcellane e ceramiche* (Bergamo, 1992)

Rossi, P., 'I ritratti di Jacopo Tintoretto', in *Jacopo Tintoretto: ritratti* (Milan, 1994), pp. 13–37

Roth, C., *The History of the Jews of Venice* (Philadelphia, PA, 1930)

Rozzo, U., 'La battaglia di Lepanto nell'editoria dell'epoca e una miscellanea fontiniana', *Rara volumina* I–II (2000), pp. 41–69

Rubin, M., *Corpus Christi: The Eucharist in Late Medieval Culture* (Cambridge, 1991)

Rubinstein, N., ed., *Florentine Studies: Politics and Society in Renaissance Florence* (London, 1968)

—, 'Italian Reactions to Terraferma Expansion in the Fifteenth Century', in J. Hale, ed., *Renaissance Venice* (London, 1973), pp. 197–217

Rudmann, V., 'Lettera della canzone per la peste di Venezia di Maffeo Venier', *Atti dell'Istituto Veneto di Scienze, Lettere ed Arti* CXXI (1962–3), pp. 599–641

Rudt de Collenberg, W. H., 'Il leone di San Marco: aspetti storici e formali nell'emblema statale della serenissima', *Archivio veneto* CLXXVI (1989), pp. 57–84

Ruggieri, O., 'La decorazione pittorica della Libreria Marciana', in V. Branca and C. Ossola, eds, *Cultura e società nel Rinascimento tra riforme e manierismi* (Florence, 1984), pp. 313–33

Ruggiero, G., *Binding Passions: Tales of Magic, Marriage and Power at the End of the Renaissance* (Oxford, 1993)

—, *The Boundaries of Eros: Sex, Crime and Sexuality in Renaissance Venice* (Oxford, 1985)

—, 'The Cooperation of Physicians and the State in the Control of Violence in Renaissance Venice', *Journal of the History of Medicine and Allied Science* XXIII (1978), pp. 156–66

—, *Violence in Early Renaissance Venice* (New Brunswick, NJ, 1980)

Runciman, S., *The Fall of Constantinople* (Cambridge, 1965)

Rylands, P., *Palma Vecchio* (Cambridge, 1992)

Saba, A., *Storia dei Papi*, 2 vols (Turin, 1936)

Sabellico, M. A., *Degl'istorici delle cose veneziane, i quali hanno scritto per pubblico decreto*, 10 vols (Venice, 1718–22)

Saccardi, G., 'I pilastri acritani', *Archivio veneto* XXXIV (1887), pp. 285–309

Sacconi, A., 'I leoni dell'Arsenale di Venezia', *Venezia e l'archeologia* (Rome, 1990), pp. 231–6

Sainte-Fare Garnot, N., 'Les Tiepolo du Musée Jacquemart-André', in L. Puppi, ed., *Giambattista Tiepolo*, 2 vols (Padua, 1998), pp. 51–61

Sandal, E., 'Stampatori bergamaschi a Venezia tra Quattro e Cinquecento', in G. Benzoni, ed., *Venezia e la terraferma: la cultura* (Bergamo, 1990), pp. 39–52

Sander, M., *Les livres à figures italien depuis 1467 jusqu'à 1530: essai de la bibliographie et de son histoire*, 6 vols (Milan, 1943)

Sandler, L. F., and M. Barasch, eds, *Art the Ape of Nature: Essays in Honor of H. W. Janson* (New York, 1981)

Santoro, C., ed., *La stampa in Italia nel Cinquecento* (Rome, 1992)

—, ed., *Stampe popolari della Biblioteca Trivulziana* (Milan, 1964)

Santosuosso, A., 'Religious Orthodoxy, Dissent and Suppression in Venice in the 1540s', *Church History* XLII (1973), pp. 476–85

Sanudo, M., *Cronachetta*, ed. R. Fulin (Venice, 1880)

—, *I diarii*, ed. R. Fulin et al., 58 vols (Venice, 1879–1903)

—, *De origine, situ et magistratibus urbis Venetae ovvero la città di Venetia, 1493–1530*, ed. A. Caracciolo Arico (Milan, 1980)

—, *Le vite dei dogi*, ed. G. Monticolo (Città da Castello, 1900–01)

—, *Le vite dei dogi, 1474–1494*, ed. A. Caracciolo Aricò, 2 vols (Padua, 1989–2001)

Sartori, C., *Bibliografia delle opere musicali stampate da Ottaviano Petrucci* (Florence, 1948)

Sartorio, L., 'San Teodoro: statua composita', *Arte veneta* I (1947), pp. 132–4

Scalon, C., and Pani, L., *I codici della Biblioteca Capitolane di Cividale del Friuli* (Florence, 1998)

Schiff, J., *Venetian State Theater and the Games of Siena, 1595–1605: The Grimani Banquet Plays* (Lewiston, NY, 1993)

Scholderer, V., 'Printing at Venice to the End of 1481', in Scholderer, *Fifty Essays in Fifteenth- and Sixteenth-Century Bibliography* (Amsterdam, 1966), pp. 74–89

Schulz, J., 'Jacopo de' Barbari's View of Venice: Map Making, City Views and Moralized Geography before the Year 1500', *Art Bulletin* LX (1978), pp. 425–74

—, 'Maps as Metaphors: Mural Map Cycles of the Italian Renaissance', in D. Woodward, ed., *Art and Cartography* (Chicago, IL, and London, 1987), pp. 97–122

—, 'La piazza medievale di San Marco', *Annali di Architettura* IV–V (1992–3), pp. 134–56

—, *The Printed Plans and Panoramic Views of Venice, 1486–1797* (Venice, 1970)

—, 'Urbanism in Medieval Venice', in A. Molho, ed., *City States in Classical Antiquity and Medieval Italy* (Stuttgart, 1991), pp. 419–46

—, *Venetian Painted Ceilings of the Renaissance* (Berkeley, CA, 1968)

Schupbach, W., 'A Venetian "Plague Miracle" in 1464 and 1576', *Medical History* (1976), pp. 312–16

Schutte, A. J., *Printed Italian Vernacular Religious Books, 1465–1550: A Finding List* (Geneva, 1983)

—, 'Printing, Piety and the People in Italy: The First Thirty Years', *Archiv für Reformationsgeschichte* LXXI (1980), pp. 5–19

Scorza, R., 'A Florentine Sketchbook: Architecture, *Apparati* and the Accademia del Disegno', *Journal of the Warburg and Courtauld Institutes* LIV (1991), pp. 172–85

—, 'Vincenzo Borghini and Invenzione: The Florentine *Apparato* of 1565', *Journal of the Warburg and Courtauld Institutes* XLIV (1981), pp. 57–75

Scrivano, R., *Il manierismo nella letteratura del Cinquecento* (Padua, 1959)

—, *Cultura e letteratura nel Cinquecento* (Rome, 1966)

Segarizzi, A., *Bibliografia delle stampe popolari italiane della R. Biblioteca Nazionale di S. Marco di Venezia* (Bergamo, 1913)

—, ed., *Relazioni degli ambasciatori veneti al senato*, 2 vols (Bari, 1912–13)

Selfridge-Field, E., *Venetian Instrumental Music from Gabrieli to Vivaldi* (Venice, 1975)

Selig, K. L., and E. Sears, eds, *The Verbal and the Visual: Essays in Honor of William Sebastian Heckscher* (New York, 1990)

Seneca, F., *Il doge Leonardo Donà: la sua vita e la sua preparazione politica prima del dogado* (Padua, 1959)

—, 'Il mancato soccorso di Nicolo Donà a Famagosta', in *Romische historische Mitteilungen* XXXI (1989), pp. 211–26

—, 'La spedizione navale cristiana dell'agosto 1572 in una lettera di Nicolo Donà', in *Ethos e cultura: studi in onore Ezio Riondato* (Padua, 1991), pp. 1115–32

Serrano, L., *La liga de Lepanto*, 2 vols (Madrid, 1918–19)

Servolini, L., *Supplemento agli annali della tipografia veneziana di Francesco Marcolini compilati da Scipione Casali* (Bologna, 1958)

Setton, K. M., *The Papacy and the Levant, 1204–1571*, 4 vols (Philadelphia, PA, 1976–84)

—, 'St George's Head', *Speculum* XLVIII (1973), pp. 1–12

Sherrard, P., *Constantinople: Iconography of a Sacred City* (Oxford, 1965)

Sforza, G., 'Riflessi della Controriforma nella Repubblica di Venezia', *Archivio storico italiano* XCIII/1 (1935), pp. 5–34, 189–216; XCIII/2 (1935), pp. 25–52, 173–86

Shaw, C., ed., *Italy and the European Powers: The Impact of War, 1500–1530* (Leiden, 2006)

Sheard, W., 'Sanudo's List of Notable Things in Venetian Churches', *Yale Italian Studies* I (1977), pp. 219–68

Short-title Catalogue of Books printed in Italy and of Italian Books printed in other Countries from 1465 to 1600 now in the British Museum (London, 1958)

Simioni, A., *Storia di Padova dale origini alla fine del secolo XVIII* (Padua, 1968)

Simoncelli, P., 'Su Jacopo Nardi, i Giunti e la "Nazione fiorentina" di Venezia', in L. Borgia, et al., eds, *Studi in onore di Arnaldo d'Addario*, 4 vols in 5 (Lecce, 1995), III, pp. 937–49

Sinding-Larsen, S., *The Burden of the Ceremony Master: Image and Action in San Marco, Venice, and in an Islamic Mosque: The Rituum ceremoniale of 1564* (Rome, 2000)

—, 'The Changes in the Iconography and Composition of Veronese's *Allegory of the Battle of Lepanto* in the Doge's Palace', *Journal of the Warburg and Courtauld Institutes* XIX (1956), pp. 298–302

—, 'Chiesa di stato e iconografia musiva', in B. Bertoli, ed., *La basilica di San Marco: arte e simbologia* (Venice, 1993), pp. 25–45

—, *Christ in the Council Hall: Studies in the Religious Iconography of the Venetian Republic* (Rome, 1974)

—, 'Palladio's Redentore: A Compromise in Composition', *Art Bulletin* XLVII (1965), pp. 431–7

Skinner, Q., *The Foundations of Modern Political Thought*, 2 vols (Cambridge, 1978)

Smith, A. A., 'Gender, Ownership and Domestic Space: Inventories and Family Archives in Renaissance Verona', *Renaissance Studies* XII (1998), pp. 375–91

Smith, L. P., *Life and Letters of Sir Henry Wooton*, 2 vols (Oxford, 1907)

Sohm, P. L., 'Palma Vecchio's *Sea Storm*: A Political Allegory', *RACAR: Revue d'art canadienne/Canadian Art Review* VI (1979–80), pp. 85–96

—, *The Scuola Grande di San Marco, 1437–1550: The Architecture of a Venetian Lay Confraternity* (New York, 1982)

Solerti, A., 'Le rappresentazioni musicali di Venezia dal 1571–1605 per la prima volta descritte', *Rivista musicale italiana* IX (1902), pp. 503–53

—, 'I signori di Correggio alle feste veneziane per Enrico III di Valois: la corte di Ferrara e Torquato Tasso a Venezia nel luglio 1574', *Rassegna emiliana di Storia, Lettere ed Arti* II (1889), pp. 99–111

Soranzo, G., *Bibliografia veneziana compilata da Girolamo Soranzo in aggiunta e continuazione del 'Saggio' di E. A. Cicogna* (Venice, 1885)

—, 'Come fu data e come fu accolta a Venezia la notizia della "S.te Barthélemy"', in *Miscellanea in onore di Roberto Cessi* (Rome, 1958), II, pp. 129–55

Spini, G., *Tra rinascimento e riforma: Antonio Brucioli* (Florence, 1940)

Stahl, A., 'The Coinage of Venice in the Age of Enrico Dandolo', in E. E. Kittell and T. F. Madden, eds, *Medieval and Renaissance Venice* (Urbana and Chicago, IL, 1999), pp. 124–40

—, *Zecca: The Mint of Venice in the Middle Ages* (Baltimore, MD, and London, 2000)

Stella, A., *Chiesa e stato nelle relazioni dei nunzi pontifici as Venezia sul giurisdizionalismo dal XVI al XVIII secolo* (Vatican City, 1964)

—, 'La crisi economica veneziana della seconda metà del secolo XVI', *Archivio veneto* LVIII–LIX (1956), pp. 17–69

—, 'La regolazione delle pubbliche entrate e la crisi politica veneziana del 1582', in *Miscellanea in onore di Roberto Cessi* (Rome, 1958), II, pp. 157–71

—, 'La società veneziana al tempo di Tiziano', in *Tiziano nel quarto centenario della sua morte, 1576–1976* (Venice, 1977), pp. 103–21

Stevens, D., 'Ceremonial Music in Medieval Venice', *Musical Times* CXIX (1978), pp. 321–7

—, ed., *The Letters of Claudio Monteverdi*, revd edn (Oxford, 1995)

Stevens, K. M., and P. F. Gehl, '*The Eye of Commerce*: Visual Literacy Among the Makers of Books in Italy', in M. Fantoni, L. C. Mathew and S. F. Mathews-Grieco, eds, *The Art Market in Italy, 15th–17th Centuries* (Ferrara, 2003), pp. 273–81

Sticca, S., *Saints: Studies in Hagiography* (Binghamton, NY, 1996)

Storia di Venezia dalle origini alla caduta della Repubblica, 11 vols (Milan, 1991–8)

Stras, L., '"Onde havrà'l mond'esempio et vera historia": Musical Echoes of Henri III's Progress through Italy', *Acta musicologica* LXXII (2000), pp. 7–41

Strohm, R., *The Rise of European Music, 1380–1500* (Cambridge, 1993)

Stroll, M., *Symbols as Power: The Papacy following the Investiture Contest* (Leiden, 1991)

Strunk, O., 'A Cypriot in Venice', in *Essays on Music in the Western World* (New York, 1974), pp. 79–93

Tafuri, M., *Jacopo Sansovino e l'architettura del '500 a Venezia*, 2nd edn (Padua, 1972)

—, '"La nuova Costantinopoli": La rappresentazione della "renovatio" nella Venetia dell'umanesimo, 1450–1509', *Rassegna Rappresentazioni. Problemi di architettura degli ambienti* IV (1982), pp. 25–38

—, ed., *'Renovatio urbis': Venetia nell'età di Andrea Gritti, 1523–1538* (Rome, 1984)

—, *Venezia e il Rinascimento: religione, scienza, architettura* (Turin, 1985)

—, *Venice and the Renaissance* (Cambridge, MA, and London, 1989)

Tagliaferri, A., ed., *Relazioni dei rettori veneti in Terraferma*, 14 vols (Milan, 1973–9)

Tagliaferro, G., 'Martiri, eroi, principi e beati: i patrizi veneziani e la pittura celebrativa nell'età di Lepanto', in M. Chiabò and F. Doglio, eds, *Guerre di religione sulle scene del Cinque–Seicento* (Rome, 2006), pp. 337–90

Tamassia Mazzarotto, B., *Le feste veneziane, i giochi popolari, le ceremonie religiose e di governo* (Florence, 1961)

Tassini, G., *Curiosità veneziane ovvero origini delle denominazioni stradali di Venezia*, 5th edn (Venice, 1915)

—, *Feste, spettacoli, divertimenti e piaceri degli antichi veneziani*, 2nd edn (Venice, 1961)

Tenenti, A., *Cristoforo da Canal: la marine vénitienne avant Lépante* (Paris, 1962)

—, 'Luc'Antonio Giunti il giovane, stampatore e mercante', in *Studi in onore di Armando Sapori*, 2 vols (Milan, 1957), II, pp. 1021–60

—, *Piracy and the Decline of Venice, 1580–1615* (Berkeley, CA, 1967)

—, 'Il potere dogale come rappresentazione', in *Stato: un'idea, una logica. Dal comune italiano all'assolutismo francese* (Bologna, 1987), pp. 193–216

—, 'The Sense of Space and Time in the Venetian World of the Fifteenth and Sixteenth Centuries', in J. Hale, ed., *Renaissance Venice* (London, 1973), pp. 17–46

Theuws, F., and J. L. Nelson, eds, *Rituals of Power: From Late Antiquity to the Early Middle Ages* (Leiden, 2000)

Thiriet, F., 'Les chroniques venetiennes de la Marcienne', *Mélanges d'archéologie et d'histoire* LXV (1954), pp. 241–92

Thorndike, L., *A History of Magic and Experimental Science*, 8 vols (New York, 1923–58)

Thornton, D., *The Scholar in his Study: Ownership and Experience in Renaissance Italy* (New Haven, CT, and London, 1997)

Thornton, P., *The Italian Renaissance Interior, 1400–1600* (London, 1991)

Timofiewitsch, W., *La chiesa del Redentore* (Vicenza, 1969)

Tinto, A., *Annali tipografici dei Tramezzino* (Venice, 1968)

Todro, M. L. S., 'The First Temporary Triumphal Arch in Venice (1557)', in R. Mulryne and E. Goldring, eds, *Court Festivals of the European Renaissance: Art, Politics and Performance* (Aldershot, 2002), pp. 335–62

Tolnay, C. de, 'Il "Paradiso" del Tintoretto, note sull'interpretazione della tela in Palazzo Ducale', *Arte veneta* XXIV (1970), pp. 103–10

—, 'The Music of the Universe', *Journal of the Walters Art Gallery* VI (1943), pp. 83–104

Tonon, F., ed., *La chiesa di Venezia nei secoli XI–XIII* (Venice, 1988)

Tooley, R. V., *Maps and Map-makers*, 6th edn (London, 1978)

Tout, F., and J. Tait, eds, *Historical Essays by Members of the Owens College, Manchester* (London, 1902)

Tramontin, S., ed., *Il culto dei santi a Venezia* (Venice, 1965)

—, 'La figura del vescovo secondo il Concilio di Trento e i suoi reflessi veneziani', *Studi veneziani* X (1968), pp. 423–56

—, 'Influsso orientale nel culto dei santi a Venezia fino al secolo XV', in A. Pertusi, ed., *Venezia e il Levante fino al secolo XV*, 3 vols (Florence, 1983), I, pp. 801–20

—, 'Gli inizi dei due seminari di Venezia', *Studi veneziani* VII (1965), pp. 363–77

—, 'Il "kalendarium" veneziano', in Tramontin, ed., *Il culto dei santi a Venezia*, pp. 277–327

—, 'Origini e sviluppi della leggenda marciana', in *Le origini della chiesa di Venezia* (Venice, 1987), pp. 167–86

—, 'Realtà e leggenda nei racconti marciani veneti', *Studi veneziani* XII (1970), pp. 35–58

—, 'Il Redentore: il voto, il tempio, la festa', *Archivio veneto* CLXXX (1993), pp. 65–76

—, ed., *Venezia e Lorenzo Giustiniani* (Venice, 1984)

—, 'La visita apostolica del 1581 a Venezia', *Studi veneziani* IX (1967), pp. 453–533

Trebbi, G., 'Il segretario veneziano: una descrizione cinquecentesca della cancelleria ducale', *Archivio storico italiano* CXLIV (1986), pp. 35–73

Trevor-Roper, H. J., 'Doge Francesco Foscari', in J. H. Plumb, ed., *Renaissance Profiles* (New York, 1965), pp. 107–21

Tristano, C., 'Economia del libro in Italia tra la fine del XV e l'inizio del XVI secolo: il prezzo del libro "vecchio"', *Scrittura e civiltà* XIV (1990), pp. 199–241

Tucci, U., 'Mercanti, viaggiatori, pellegrini nel quattrocento', in G. Arnaldi and M. Stocchi, eds, *Storia della cultura veneta*, 6 vols in 10 parts (Vicenza, 1976–87), III/2, pp. 317–53

—, 'Il processo a Girolamo Zane mancato difensore di Cipro', in G. Benzoni, ed., *Il mediterraneo nella seconda metà del '500 nella luce di Lepanto* (Florence, 1974), pp. 409–34

—, 'The Psychology of the Venetian Merchant in the Sixteenth Century', in J. Hale, ed., *Renaissance Venice* (London, 1973), pp. 348–78

—, 'I servizi marittimi veneziani per il pellegrinaggio in Terrasanta nel medioevo', *Studi veneziani*, n.s. IX (1985), pp. 43–66

—, 'Venezia nel Cinquecento: una città industriale?', in V. Branca, and C. Ossola, eds, *Crisi e rinnovamento nell'autunno del Rinascimento a Venezia* (Florence 1991), pp. 61–83

Turba, G., *Venetianische Depeschen vom Kaiserhof*, 3 vols (Vienna, 1889–96)

Turrini, G., *L'Accademia filarmonica di Verona dalla fondazione (maggio 1543) al 1600 e il suo patrimonio musicale antico* (Verona, 1941)

Ulvioni, P., 'Cultura politica e cultura religiosa a Venezia nel secondo Cinquecento: un bilancio', *Archivio storico italiano* CXLI (1983), pp. 591–651

Urban, L., *Processioni e feste dogali: 'Venetia est mundus'* (Vicenza, 1998)

Vaccaro, L., and F. Riccardi, eds, *Sacri monti: devozione, arte e cultura della controriforma* (Milan, 1992)

Van, G. de, 'An Inventory of the Manuscript Bologna, Liceo Musicale, Q15 (*olim* 37)', *Musica Disciplina* II (1948), pp. 231–57

Van der Sman, G. J., 'Print Publishing in Venice in the Second Half of the Sixteenth Century', *Print Quarterly* XVII (2000), pp. 235–47

Van Veen, H. T., 'Republicanism in the Visual Propaganda of Cosimo I de' Medici', *Journal of the Warburg and Courtauld Institutes* LV (1992), pp. 200–09

van der Wee, H., ed., *The Rise and Decline of Urban Industries in Italy and the Low Countries: Late Middle Ages–Early Modern Times* (Louvain, 1988)

Vasari, G., *Le vite de' piu eccellenti architetti, pittori, et scultori italiani,* ed. G. Milanesi, 9 vols (Milan, 1878–85)

Venditti, A., *La loggia del capitaniato* (Vicenza, 1969)

Venezia dalla prima crociata alla conquista di Costantinopoli del 1204 (Florence, 1966)

Venezia e la difesa del Levante da Lepanto a Candia, 1570–1670 (Venice, 1986) [exhibition catalogue]

Venezia e la peste, 1348–1797 (Venice, 1980) [exhibition catalogue]

Venezia e i Turchi (Milan, 1985)

Ventura, A., *Nobilità e popolo nella società veneta del '400 e '500* (Bari, 1964)

Venturi, L., 'Le compagnie della calza (sec. XV–XVI)', *Nuovo archivio veneto* XVI (1908), pp. 161–221; XVII (1909), pp. 140–233

Vercellin, G., 'Mercanti turchi e sensali a Venezia', *Studi veneziani,* n.s. IV (1980), pp. 45–78

Verdon, T., ed., *Monasticism and the Arts* (Syracuse, NY, 1984)

—, and J. Henderson, eds, *Christianity and the Renaissance: Image and Religious Imagination in the Quattrocento* (Syracuse, NY, 1990)

Verheyen, E., 'The Triumphal Arch on the Lido: On the Reliability of Eyewitness Accounts', in K. L. Selig and E. Sears, eds, *The Verbal and the Visual: Essays in Honor of William Sebastian Heckscher* (New York, 1990), pp. 213–23

Verpeaux, J., ed., *Pseudo-Kodinos, traité des offices* (Paris, 1966)

Vickers, M., '"New" Parthenon Fragments in Venice', *Antiquity* LXII (1988), pp. 718–23

—, 'Wandering Stones: Venice, Constantinople and Athens', in K. L. Selig and E. Sears, eds, *The Verbal and the Visual: Essays in Honor of William Sebastian Heckscher* (New York, 1990), pp. 225–47

Vivo, F. de, 'Historical Justifications of Venetian Power in the Adriatic', *Journal of the History of Ideas* LXIV (2003), pp. 159–76

Voinovitch, L., *Depeschen des Francesco Gondola gesandten der Republik Ragusa bei Pius V und Gregor XIII, 1570–1573* (Vienna, 1909)

Voltolina, P., *La storia di Venezia attraverso le medaglie,* 3 vols (Milan, 1998)

Von Simson, O. G., *Sacred Fortress: Byzantine Art and Statecraft in Ravenna* (Chicago, IL, 1948)

Voragine, J. de, *The Golden Legend,* trans. W. G. Ryan, 2 vols (Princeton, NJ, 1995)

Wagner, K., and M. Carrera, *Catalogo dei libri a stampa in lingua italiana della Biblioteca Colombina di Siviglia* (Modena, 1991)

Walter, C., 'Political Imagery in the Medieval Lateran Palace', *Cahiers archéologiques* XX (1970), pp. 155–76; XXI (1971), pp. 109–36

Ward-Perkins, J. B., 'The Bronze Lion of St Mark at Venice', *Antiquity* XXI (1947), pp. 23–41

Weiner, G., 'The Demographic Effects of the Venetian Plague of 1576–77 and 1630–31', *Genus* XXVI (1970), pp. 41–57

Weiss, C., ed., *Papiers d'état du Cardinal Granvelle,* 9 vols (Paris, 1841–52)

Wellesz, E., *A History of Byzantine Music and Hymnography* (Oxford, 1949)

Wethey, H., *The Paintings of Titian* (London, 1975)

Wheeler, J., 'Neighbourhoods and Local Loyalties', in A. Cowan, ed., *Mediterranean Urban Culture, 1400–1700* (Exeter, 2000), pp. 31–42

Willaert, A., *Opera omnia,* ed. H. Zenck et al. (Rome, 1950–)

Wilson, B., '"Il bel sesso, e l'austero Senato": The Coronation of Dogaressa Morosina Morosini Grimani', *Renaissance Quarterly* LII (1999), pp. 73–139

—, *The World in Venice: Print, the City and Early Modern Identity* (Toronto, 2005)

Wilson, C. C., *Renaissance Small Bronze Sculpture and Associated Decorative Arts at the National Gallery of Art* (Washington, DC, 1983)

Winston, A., 'Tracing the Origins of the Rosary: German Vernacular Texts', *Speculum* LXVIII (1993), pp. 619–36

Winston-Allen, A., *Stories of the Rose: The Making of the Rosary in the Middle Ages* (University Park, PA, 1997)

Wish, B., and S. S. Munshower, eds, *'All the World's a Stage . . .': Art and Pageantry in the Renaissance and Baroque*, 2 vols (University Park, PA, 1990)

Witcombe, C. L. C. E., *Copyright in the Renaissance: Prints and the Privilegio in Sixteenth-Century Venice and Rome* (Leiden, 2004)

Wittkower, R., *Architectural Principles in the Age of Humanism*, 4th edn (London, 1973)

—, 'Titian's Allegory of "Religion Succoured by Spain"', *Journal of the Warburg and Courtauld Institutes* III (1939–40), pp. 138–40

Wolters, W., 'Le architetture erette al lido per l'ingresso di Enrico III a Venezia nel 1574', *Bolletino del centro internazionale di studi di architettura Andrea Palladio* XXI (1979), pp. 273–89

—, *La scultura veneziana gotica, 1300–1460*, 2 vols (Venice, 1976)

—, *Storia e politica nei dipinti di Palazzo Ducale: aspetti dell'autocelebrazione della Repubblica di Venezia nel Cinquecento* (Venice, 1987)

Wood, D., ed., *The Church and Sovereignty, c. 590–1918: Essays in Honour of Michael Wilks* (Oxford, 1991)

Woodward, D., *Maps as Prints in the Italian Renaissance: Makers, Distributors and Consumers* (London, 1996)

Wooton, D., *Paolo Sarpi: Between Renaissance and Enlightenment* (Cambridge, 1983)

Wright, A. D., 'Republican Tradition and the Maintenance of "National" Religious Traditions in Venice', *Renaissance Studies* X (1996), pp. 405–16

—, 'Venetian Law and Order: A Myth?', *London University Institute of Historical Research Bulletin* LIII (1982), pp. 192–202

—, 'The Venetian Mediterranean Empire after the Council of Trent', in D. Wood, ed., *The Church and Sovereignty, c. 590–1918: Essays in Honour of Michael Wilks* (Oxford, 1991), pp. 467–77

Yates, F., *The Valois Tapestries*, 2nd edn (London, 1975)

Zanaredi, M., ed., *I gesuiti a Venezia: momenti e problemi di storia veneziana della compagnia di Gesù* (Venice, 1994)

Zappella, G., *Le marche dei tipografi e degli editori italiani del Cinquecento*, 2 vols (Milan, 1986)

Zenck, H., 'Adrian Willaerts "Salmi spezzati"', *Die Musikforschung* II (1949), pp. 97–107

Zorzi, A., *Venezia scomparsa*, 2 vols (Milan, 1977)

Zorzi, G., 'Altre due perizie per il restauro del Palazzo Ducale dopo l'incendio del 20 dicembre 1577', *Atti dell'Istituto Veneto di Scienze, Lettere ed Arti* CXV (1956–57), pp. 133–74

—, *Le chiese e i ponti di Andrea Palladio* (Vicenza, 1967)

—, 'Il contributo di Andrea Palladio e di Francesco Zamberlan al restauro del Palazzo Ducale di Venezia dopo l'incendio del 20 dicembre 1577', *Atti dell'Istituto Veneto di Scienze, Lettere ed Arti* CXV (1956–7), pp. 11–68

—, 'Nuove rivelazioni sulla ricostruzione delle salle del piano nobile del Palazzo Ducale di Venezia dopo l'incendio dell'11 maggio 1574', *Arte veneta* VII (1953), pp. 123–51

—, *Le opere pubbliche e i palazzi privati di Andrea Palladio* (Venice, 1965)

Zorzi, M., 'La circolazione del libro a Venezia nel Cinquecento: biblioteche private e pubbliche', *Archivio veneto* CLXXVII (1990), pp. 117–89

—, *La libreria di San Marco: libri, lettori, società nella Venezia dei dogi* (Milan, 1987)

Zucconi, G., 'Architettura e topografia delle istituzioni nei centri minori della terraferma XV e XVI secolo', *Studi veneziani, n.s.* XVII (1989), pp. 27–49

PHOTOGRAPH CREDITS

INDEX